D0391140

THE ROUGH GUIDE TO THE
DORDOGNE
& THE LOT

written and researched by
Jan Dodd

with additional contributions by
Stuart Butler and Zoe Smith

**ROUGH
GUIDES**

Contents

INTRODUCTION   4

Where to go   5   Things not to miss   12
When to go   10   Itineraries   18

BASICS   20

Getting there   21   Sports and outdoor activities   32
Getting around   24   Shopping and markets   34
Accommodation   27   Travelling with children   34
Food and drink   29   Travel essentials   35
Festivals   32

THE GUIDE   42

1 Périgueux and the north   42   4 The Upper Dordogne valley and
2 Bergerac and around   84   Rocamadour   166
3 Sarlat and the Périgord Noir   116   5 The Lot valley and around   196
                                                  6 South of the River Lot   248

CONTEXTS   286

History   287   French   305
Books   303   Glossary   314

SMALL PRINT & INDEX   316

Introduction to
The Dordogne & the Lot

The green, secluded valleys of the Dordogne and the Lot have long attracted artists and lovers of the good life. In the many caves that tunnel into the honey-coloured limestone cliffs, prehistoric peoples painted some of the world's earliest masterpieces, depicting the pot-bellied ponies, mammoths and muscular bison that once lived in the region's woodlands. Later occupants expressed their faith by building the delicate Romanesque churches found on many a hilltop, as well as an array of abbeys and towering cathedrals, while the legacy of a less refined and more bellicose era lies in the medieval fortresses perched on craggy pinnacles of rock.

In addition to this richly layered history, the Dordogne and Lot are endowed with a tremendous variety of scenery, from the dry limestone plateaux of the *causses*, sliced through with narrow gorges, to densely wooded valleys and the serried ranks of gnarled grape vines which yield the region's fabulous wines. Through these landscapes slide the great rivers that unify and define southwest France: running swiftly through its deeply cloven valley, the **Vézère** hurtles into the **Dordogne**, which in turn flows placidly out to the Atlantic coast. Further south the serpentine **Lot** writhes its way across the country to join the mighty **Garonne**, which along with its tributaries, the **Tarn** and **Aveyron**, mark this region's southern border.

This peaceful corner of France is best savoured at its own unhurried pace. There is always some forgotten corner to stumble upon, a market or a village *fête* to enjoy, or something to catch the eye, from the postcard-perfect villages of blue-shuttered stone houses to fields of luminous sunflowers and gurgling willow-lined rivers. The Dordogne and the Lot are certainly not undiscovered – indeed, some sights are numbered among the most visited in the country – but the region's heartland is still steeped in what the French call the *douceur de vivre*, the gentle way of life, where there's plenty of time for a long, lazy lunch, be it a picnic of market-fresh produce under the shade of a riverbank tree or a restaurant spread of the region's classic dishes.

ABOVE A GABARE NAVIGATING THE DORDOGNE; MONSIEUR GUICHARD AND HIS GOATS **RIGHT** CARENNAC AT SUNSET

FOOD AND DRINK IN THE DORDOGNE AND THE LOT

The Dordogne and the Lot are blessed with some of the most sought-after delicacies in the culinary world, including the celebrated **black truffle** and rich **foie gras** (fattened duck- or goose-liver pâté). Deep in the oak forests, *cèpes* cluster in generous numbers and hordes of wild *sangliers* (boars) roam. On the high limestone *causses* lie secluded dairy farms, where **goat's cheese** reaches its apogee in the creamy *Cabécou*, while swathes of delicate violet flowers – the **saffron crocus** – thrive in the harsh conditions. Between the neatly combed vineyards (*Cabécou*), **walnut** plantations provide barrels of precious walnut oil and the region's famous dessert, *tarte aux noix*. Accompanying this copious feast are the rich, dark **wines** of Cahors and the fragrant, golden Monbazillac of Bergerac. South of the Lot valley the landscape changes to the baking fields of the Quercy Blanc and temperatures shift up a gear to ripen acres of yellow sunflowers, heaps of **melons** and orchards dripping with **peaches**, **plums** and **apricots**.

Where to go

The principal northern gateway to the Dordogne and the Lot is the charming city of **Brive-la-Gaillarde** (usually shortened to Brive), whose cosy café culture exudes the spirit of the south, a hint of pleasures to come. West lies **Périgueux**, where an extraordinary Byzantine-style cathedral stands above a tangle of medieval lanes. The city is the capital of a broad sweep of rolling pasture and woodland known as **Périgord Vert** (Green Périgord). This region's loveliest river is the Dronne and its most appealing town water-bound **Brantôme**, known for its rock-cut sanctuaries and plethora of restaurants. East of here is castle-country: **Château de Puyguilhem** stands out for its elegant Renaissance architecture,

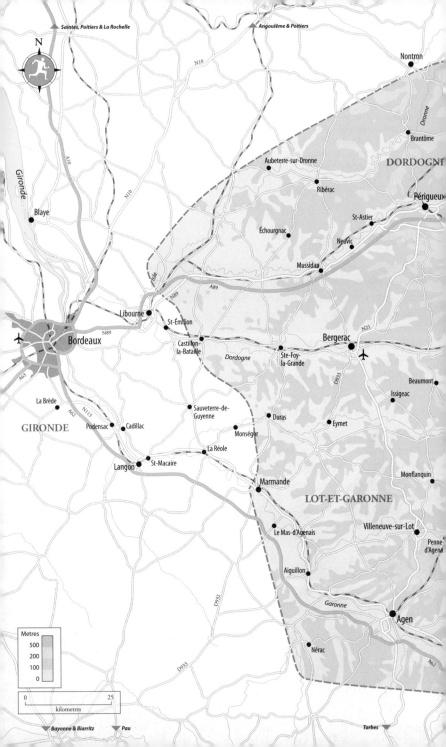

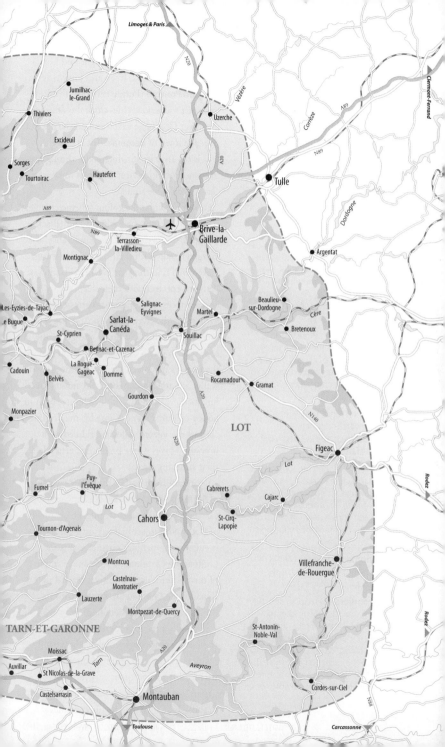

FACT FILE

- The area covered by this Guide amounts to some 22,000 square kilometres, about the size of Wales, but has a population of under a million, one of the lowest population densities in metropolitan France.

- The French Air Force has special permission to perform occasional low-level flying practice in the Lot valley, on the premise that there is less chance of tragedy should an accident occur.

- The economy is based on tourism and agriculture, primarily **wine** production. Bergerac has 120 square kilometres of vines while the Cahors' vineyards amount to about 43 square kilometres. Originally planted by the Romans in 50 BC they are said to be the oldest in France.

- The region boasts three **World Heritage Sites** – the Vézère valley, with its prehistoric cave art, the entire Causses du Quercy and a dozen or so sites listed under the pilgrims' route to Santiago de Compostela.

- The iconic French **jam**, Bonne Maman, with its distinctive red-checked lid, is made in Biars, in the northern Lot.

- During a *fête*, when the soup course comes to a close, it is *de rigueur* for gentlemen to tip a glass of Cahors wine into the empty bowl, swill it round and drink it down in one, to the boisterous cheers of their companions.

- The Causses du Quercy is known to **astronomers** the world over as the "black triangle" because it has the lowest light pollution in France.

- **Pigeonniers** – vernacular structures originally built as pigeon lofts and often highly ornamental – encapsulate the Quercy landscape. The oldest were constructed on stilts in order to facilitate the collection of manure. They are still built as architectural features today and nearly every sizeable house has one.

while the **Château de Hautefort** is one of the grandest castles in the Dordogne and Lot.

South of Périgueux, in an area known as **Périgord Pourpre** (Purple Périgord) thanks to its wine production, vines cloak the slopes of the lower Dordogne valley around the pleasant riverside town of **Bergerac**. The star of this area is the river itself, which loops through two immense meanders near **Trémolat** to create a classic Dordogne scene.

East of Trémolat the colour scheme changes again as you enter the **Périgord Noir** (Black Périgord), named for the preponderance of evergreen oaks with their dark, dense foliage. Here you'll find the greatest concentration of Périgord cottages with their steep, stone-covered roofs, and dramatic fortresses perched high above the river. Here, too, are the walnut orchards and flocks of ducks and geese, the source of so much of the produce featured in the region's markets. Of these the most vivid is that at **Sarlat-la-Canéda**, held among the fine medieval and Renaissance houses built in honey-coloured stone. Close by, the beetling cliffs of the **Vézère valley** are riddled with limestone caves where prehistoric artists left their stunning legacy.

Upstream from Sarlat, the abbey-church of **Souillac** offers remarkable Romanesque carvings, while the nearby pilgrimage town of **Rocamadour**, set halfway up a cliff face, is equally compelling. Further east is the **Château de Castelnau**, a supreme example of medieval military architecture, and the Renaissance **Château de Montal**, with its exquisite ornamental detailing.

Shadowing the Dordogne to the south, the Lot flows through comparatively wild country where, even in high summer, it's possible to find quiet corners. The departmental capital, **Cahors**, is home to France's best surviving fortified medieval

bridge, **Pont Valentré**, while upstream the perched village of **St-Cirq-Lapopie** provides the valley's most dramatic sight. From near here the pretty Célé valley cuts northeast to **Figeac**, which boasts a highly rewarding museum, dedicated to Champollion, the man who unravelled the mystery of hieroglyphics. West of Cahors, atmospheric **Monflanquin** and **Monpazier** represent outstanding examples of *bastide* villages (see box, p.244), poignant echoes of a violent past. South of the river both landscape and colour change yet again, while temperatures (see box below) ramp up a gear to ripen the sunflowers, vineyards and orchards of the **Quercy Blanc**. You have only to glance at an empty field, bleached by the sun, lavishly dusted with white stone and perhaps decorated with a vernacular *borie* (dry-stone hut), to understand the reason for its sobriquet.

The highlights of the Garonne valley to the south are the Romanesque carvings of the abbey-church at **Moissac** and the river's dramatic gorges around the attractive old town of **St-Antonin-Noble-Val** and the evocative ruined fortress of **Najac**.

When to go

Winters are variable in this diverse region. In the north they are generally wet, while in the southern regions they can be short and very dry indeed – on sunny days it's possible to sit outside even in December. January and February, however, can see temperatures plummeting to well below zero. **Spring** is usually the wettest period, although some years see glorious weather. Temperatures begin to pick up around April and can reach the mid-30s in high **summer**, though usually hover in the high 20s. **Autumn** is longer and drier than spring, bringing sunny weather until the end of October.

The most important factor in deciding when to visit is the **holiday seasons**. By far the busiest period is July and August, peaking in the first two weeks of August, when hotels and campsites are bursting at the seams and top-rank sights are absolutely heaving. Conversely, from November to Easter many places close down completely. Overall, the **best time to visit** is September and early October, with May and June coming a close second.

AVERAGE MONTHLY TEMPERATURES AND RAINFALL

	Jan	Feb	Mar	Apr	May	Jun	Jul	Aug	Sep	Oct	Nov	Dec
CAHORS												
Max/min (°C)	9/1	12/2	15/5	18/7	22/12	24/13	28/14	29/15	25/12	20/9	13/4	10/2
Rainfall (mm)	66	71	73	69	66	71	47	44	59	68	71	76
SARLAT												
Max/min (°C)	8/1	11/2	14/4	16/6	20/10	23/11	26/14	27/13	2312	18/9	12/4	9/3
Rainfall (mm)	73	78	79	80	85	78	59	64	65	79	78	77

Author picks

Our authors have admired prehistoric caves and charming villages, consumed far more cheese and wine than is strictly necessary and developed excellent canoeing skills – it's a hard job, but someone's got to do it. Here are their favourite things to do, see and eat:

Truffle markets Between December and March, the area's countless wonderful town and village markets are given an exotic foodie twist with the arrival of the delicious, and expensive, fungi (p.72).

River trips The Dordogne and Lot's many rivers offer superb water-bound activities, though it's hard to beat a gentle canoe paddle along the Vézère river, and in particular the stretch between Montignac and Les Eyzies (p.133).

Must-see medieval With its solid, soaring towers and graceful arches, the all-powerful Pont Valentré (p.206) in Cahors is a masterpiece of medieval architecture.

Underground church The Dordogne's most unique ecclesiastical treasure, the Église St-Jean (p.64) in Aubeterre-sur-Dronne is a stupendous 20m-high chamber carved into the rock face.

Black tipple So-named because of its dark colour and strong taste, the black wine of Cahors (p.209) is harvested from what are reputedly some of the oldest vineyards in the country, and is worth sampling any time of the year.

Cool cave Glittering stalactites, prehistoric cave paintings and child-friendly activities are three good reasons to make a beeline for the Grotte de Villars (p.68), hidden away amid the lush Périgord Vert.

Giddy up The racetrack at Arnac-Pompadour (p.80) is one of France's most spectacular, and a great place to watch magnificent thoroughbreds in action.

Cracking castles The fairytale Château de Beynac (p.156) lords it over the Dordogne river, while Hautefort (p.73) is a superb example of French Renaissance architecture at its best.

> Our author recommendations don't end here. We've flagged up our favourite places – a perfectly sited hotel, an atmospheric café, a special restaurant – throughout the Guide, highlighted with the ★ symbol.

FROM TOP TRUFFLES; ARNAC-POMPADOUR; CAHORS WINE

17

things not to miss

It's not possible to see everything that the Dordogne and Lot has to offer in one trip – and we don't suggest you try. What follows is a selective and subjective taste of the region's highlights: spectacular castles, quaint villages and eye-catching architecture. All highlights are colour-coded by chapter and have a page reference to take you straight into the Guide, where you can find out more.

1 ST-CIRQ LAPOPIE
Page 212

Tumbling down a sheer cliff towards the River Lot, this higgledy-piggledy village of half-timbered old houses is one of the most picturesque in the region.

2 THE GARDENS OF MANOIR D'EYRIGNAC
Page 128

Explore these ornate gardens dating back to the eighteenth century.

3 ABBAYE DE CADOUIN
Page 114

The astonishing abbey at Cadouin was once a major pilgrimage site, with a richly decorated cloister and a fine Romanesque church.

4 CANOEING
Page 33

A gentle paddle along the region's serpentine rivers gives a unique perspective on the changing scenery.

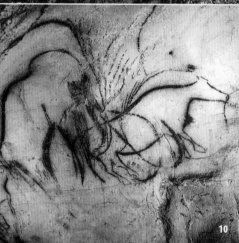

5 CHÂTEAU DE NAJAC
Page 283
The crumbled ruins of Najac's château afford a startling panorama over the Aveyron valley.

6 MARCHÉS AUX TRUFFES
Page 269
Of the many winter truffle markets held in southwest France, Lalbenque's is one of the best, with the village streets suffused with the unique scent of this precious fungi.

7 PARC NATUREL RÉGIONAL DES CAUSSES DU QUERCY
Page 198
Explore swathes of wild limestone plateau, carved by imposing rivers and dotted with grazing sheep.

8 MONPAZIER
Page 246
One of the region's best-preserved *bastide* towns, in the typical grid-style, with many buildings dating from the thirteenth century.

9 ROCAMADOUR
Page 175
Cliff-side pilgrimage town which will take your breath away – if you avoid the peak-season crowds.

10 PREHISTORIC CAVES
Page 132
The caves and rock shelters around Les Eyzies contain stunning examples of prehistoric art.

11 SARLAT-LA-CANÉDA
Page 121
Lose yourself in Sarlat's intriguing maze of narrow medieval lanes, and try to make your visit coincide with the fantastic Saturday market.

16

 LOCAL PRODUCE
Page 29
Famous gastronomic treats
from the region include foie
gras, walnut oil, goat's cheese
and truffles.

 GOUFFRE DE PADIRAC
Page 186
Take a boat ride through this
expansive cave system, which
houses stalagmites taller than the
average house.

 VINEYARD VISITS
Page 209
From grand châteaux such as
Lagrezette to tiny, family-run
concerns, a visit and tasting at
a wine château provides a
memorable experience.

 CORDES-SUR-CIEL
Page 280
Pearl of the *bastides*, this picturesque
hill-town was named France's
favourite village in 2014.

 ST-ANTONIN-NOBLE-VAL
Page 278
This handsome town, sheltering
under towering limestone cliffs,
boasts a hoard of medieval houses
from its glorious heyday.

 CAHORS
Page 200
Trapped in a tight meander of
the Lot river, glorious Cahors is
steeped in history, from the richly
decorated double-domed
cathedral to the fortified
Pont Valentré.

13

14

15

16

17

Itineraries

The following itineraries are designed to lead you up, down and round about the enduringly beautiful Dordogne and Lot – picking out the area's prettiest towns and villages, most impressive medieval architecture and the tastiest food and drink.

LE GRAND TOUR

❶ Aubeterre-sur-Dronne Two marvellous churches – one a remarkable subterranean cavern – are the highlights of this gorgeous little hillside town on the Charente border. **See p.64**

❷ Périgueux A rich confection of Roman remains, old-town Renaissance buildings and grand ecclesiastical architecture makes a visit to Périgueux imperative. **See p.47**

❸ Bergerac Hop aboard a traditional *gabare* for a scenic river cruise before heading to one of the town's many excellent bars to indulge in a glass or two of Bergerac wine. **See p.89**

❹ Trémolat and Limeuil Defined by the two dramatic bends at Trémolat and Limeuil, this is the prettiest stretch of the Dordogne river. **See p.109**

❺ Les Eyzies Prepare to be dazzled by some of the world's finest prehistoric cave art, most impressively at the Font-de-Gaume and Abri du Cap Blanc caves. **See p.130**

❻ Sarlat-la-Canéda Run through with handsome medieval houses and honey-coloured Renaissance stone buildings, Sarlat is perhaps the Dordogne's most alluring town. **See p.121**

❼ Rocamadour Not only is Rocamadour possessed of a breathtaking cliff-top location, but it's one of the country's most important pilgrimage sites. **See p.175**

❽ Figeac Straddling the River Célé, this town boasts a raft of splendid medieval architecture and a quite superb museum of writing. **See p.220**

❾ Moissac The Romanesque carvings of the abbey-church of St Pierre rate among the most impressive in the country, not least those on its magnificent tympanum. **See p.261**

GASTRONOMIC ODYSSEY

❶ Foie gras, Thiviers Undoubtedly the region's culinary star, the fattened liver of duck or goose is best eaten on its own in succulent slabs, though it's also delicious pan-fried with a fruit compôte; learn more at the Maison du Foie Gras museum. **See p.68**

❷ Truffles, Sorges Evocatively known as the "black diamonds of the Périgord", these expensive black fungi crop up in all sorts of dishes, from rich Périgourdin sauces to the humble omelette – head to the museum in Sorges to get the lowdown. **See p.72**

❸ Monbazillac Sample a drop of this sumptuously sweet white wine at the eponymous château, just outside Bergerac, or in any number of the surrounding wineries. **See p.96**

❹ Cèpes, Monpazier These plump, brown mushrooms can be sampled just about anywhere in the Dordogne, but you'll find an abundance of them around Monpazier and Villefranche-du-Périgord. **See p.246**

ABOVE SAFFRON AND APRICOT JAM; TAKING A BREAK NEAR LIMEUIL

❺ Le Bugue market Most towns and villages in the Dordogne and Lot put on terrific markets once or twice a week, but the extravaganza at pretty Le Bugue is one of the best. **See p.139**

❻ Walnuts, Beynac Though traditionally used to make oil, the humble but wonderfully versatile walnut can also be found in breads, cakes and desserts. For more nutty kicks, follow the Route de la Noix between Argentat and Beynac. **See p.160**

❼ Cabécou cheese, Rocamadour The region boasts few speciality cheeses, but this is a beauty; a little flat medallion of goat's cheese, typically served on toast or a bed of lettuce with walnut oil. **See p.181**

❽ Saffron, Cajarc Numerous farms in the region produce this age-old spice, but your best bet is to make a beeline for the marvellous saffron fair in Cajarc at the end of October. **See p.216**

MEDIEVAL DORDOGNE

❶ Château de Jumilhac Nestled amid thick woodland in the lush Périgord Vert region, Jumilhac is a classic fairy-tale castle, complete with requisite towers, turrets and ramparts. **See p.70**

❷ Châteaux Beynac and Castelnaud Situated on opposing sides of the Dordogne river, these two magnificent, semi-ruined castles are pre-eminent among the region's many châteaux. **See p.156 & p.158**

❸ Cadouin Attractive village known for its twelfth-century Cistercian abbey, though it's the adjoining cloister, with stunningly carved capitals, that is the real show-stealer. **See p.114**

❹ Monpazier The most complete of the *bastide* towns, with intact medieval gates, a fine church and a perfect central square. **See p.246**

❺ Eymet Laid out on a classic *bastide* chequerboard plan, Eymet is centred on a handsome, arcaded main square lined with half-timbered houses. **See p.100**

❻ Pont Valentré A formidable construction straddling the Lot river in Cahors, this is perhaps the finest example of a fortified medieval bridge in the entire country. **See p.206**

❼ St-Antonin-Noble-Val Set against a stunning backdrop of white limestone cliffs, St-Antonin's medieval heritage is writ large throughout the village. **See p.278**

❽ Cordes-sur-Ciel Heavily fortified in its heyday, this charming, mist-clad hilltop village is now home to artisans and craftspeople of many persuasions. **See p.280**

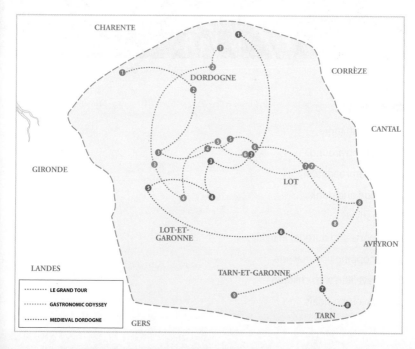

CHARENTE

CORRÈZE

DORDOGNE

CANTAL

GIRONDE

LOT

LOT-ET-GARONNE

AVEYRON

LANDES

TARN-ET-GARONNE

LE GRAND TOUR

GASTRONOMIC ODYSSEY

MEDIEVAL DORDOGNE

GERS

TARN

GEESE IN THE DORDOGNE

Basics

21 Getting there

24 Getting around

27 Accommodation

29 Food and drink

32 Festivals

32 Sports and outdoor activities

34 Shopping and markets

34 Travelling with children

35 Travel essentials

Getting there

The Dordogne and Lot is easy to reach by plane, with several airlines flying to the region from numerous UK airports. Travelling overland is another, possibly more attractive option, with the Eurostar making the journey from London to Paris, from where you can connect to fast and efficient TGV services. Alternatively, both the Channel Tunnel and cross-Channel ferries allow you to make the journey by car. From the US, Canada, Australia, New Zealand and South Africa, you'll have to fly to Paris, and take an onward connection from there, be it by plane or train.

Fares often depend on how far in advance you can book: earlier is often, but not always, cheaper. Much depends on the **season**, with the highest prices generally from June to August, and around Christmas and the New Year; fares drop during the "shoulder" seasons – roughly September to October and April to May – and you'll get the best prices during the low season, November to March.

It's invariably cheaper to **book tickets online**, though bear in mind that most of the budget airlines charge extra for checked baggage and for ticketing changes, and may not refund cancelled flights. It's always best to book via the company's own website; using a third-party site usually makes ticket changes more complicated and expensive.

Flights from the UK and Ireland

Flying time to the Dordogne and the Lot from the UK or Ireland is between one and a half and two hours, depending on your departure airport. There are currently four **airlines** flying directly to the region from the UK, almost all of which fly **to Bergerac**: Ryanair (Ⓦryanair.com) from London Stansted, Bristol, East Midlands and Liverpool; Jet2 (Ⓦjet2.com) from Leeds Bradford; British Airways (Ⓦba.com) from London City; and Flybe (Ⓦflybe .com), which flies from nearly half a dozen regional

airports across the UK. **Tickets** with all these airlines can cost as little as £50–60 return, including tax, but double that is more usual.

Flying **to Bordeaux** is another option, being just a short train or car journey from the Dordogne: easyJet (Ⓦeasyjet.com) links Belfast, London Gatwick, Glasgow, Luton, Liverpool and Bristol with the city, Flybe flies from Birmingham and Southampton, while Ryanair offers services from Cork, Edinburgh and Stansted; British Airways (Ⓦba.com) offers daily direct flights from London Gatwick. **From Dublin**, Aer Lingus (Ⓦaerlingus.com) also has direct flights to Bordeaux.

Flights from the US and Canada

The only **direct flights from the US or Canada** to the region is the summer-only, twice-weekly Montréal–Bordeaux service offered by Air Transat (Ⓦairtransat.com). However, most major airlines operate scheduled flights to Paris, from where you can take a domestic flight (check there's no inconvenient transfer between Charles de Gaulle and Orly airports) or transfer to the rail network. Air France (Ⓦairfrance.com) has the most frequent and convenient service, with daily flights from more than half a dozen US cities, but their fares tend to be pricey. Other airlines offering services **to Paris from US cities** include American Airlines (Ⓦaa .com) from New York, Chicago, Dallas and Miami; Delta (Ⓦdelta.com) from Atlanta, Chicago, Cincinnati, Houston and New York; and United (Ⓦunited .com) from Chicago and New York. Air Canada (Ⓦaircanada.ca) offers direct services to Paris **from Montréal and Toronto**.

Thanks to such intense competition, transatlantic **fares** to France are fairly reasonable. A typical return fare to Paris, flying midweek outside peak season, costs around US$700 from Houston or Los Angeles and US$550 from New York. From Canada, prices to Paris start from Can$850 from Montréal and Toronto or Can$950 from Vancouver. Air Transat's return fares on the non-stop Montréal–Bordeaux route start at around Can$900.

A BETTER KIND OF TRAVEL

At Rough Guides we are passionately committed to travel. We believe it helps us understand the world we live in and the people we share it with – and of course tourism is vital to many developing economies. But the scale of modern tourism has also damaged some places irreparably, and climate change is accelerated by most forms of transport, especially flying. All Rough Guides' flights are carbon-offset, and every year we donate money to a variety of environmental charities.

Flights from Australia, New Zealand and South Africa

Travelling **from Australia or New Zealand**, there are scheduled flights to Paris from Sydney, Melbourne, Brisbane, Perth and Auckland, all of which involve at least one stop en route. Alternatively, you can fly via another European hub and get a connecting flight to Bordeaux from there. Flights via Asia or the Gulf States with a transfer or overnight stop in the airline's home port are generally the cheapest option. The cheapest return **fares** start at around Aus$1700 from Sydney, Perth and Darwin and NZ$2300 from Auckland.

From South Africa, Air France operates direct flights from Johannesburg and Cape Town to Paris, from where you can pick up a connecting flight to Bordeaux. With other airlines you'll be routed through another European hub such as London, Amsterdam, Madrid or Frankfurt, and again pick up a connecting flight. In terms of **fares** to Paris, you're looking at anything upwards of R7500 from Johannesburg and R9000 from Cape Town.

By train

Eurostar (Ⓦeurostar.com) operates high-speed passenger trains daily from St Pancras International to the Continent via the **Channel Tunnel**; most but not all services stop at either Ebbsfleet or Ashford in Kent (30min from London). Services depart roughly every hour (from around 5.30am to 8pm) for Paris Gare du Nord (2hr 20min), most of which stop at Lille (1hr 30min). You can connect with TGV trains to the southwest at either station.

Standard **fares** from London to Paris average at about £100 for a non-refundable, non-exchangeable return. Otherwise, you're looking at around £245 for a fully refundable "Business Premier" class ticket with no restrictions. Ticket prices are often significantly lower for those under 26.

Note that Inter-Rail and Eurail **rail passes** (see below) entitle you to discounts on Eurostar trains. It's possible to take your **bike** on Eurostar (see p.26).

Rail passes

Rail Europe (Ⓦraileurope.com) issues a number of **rail passes** for travel within France and for trips combining France with other European countries. Note that these passes must be purchased in your home country.

If you plan to visit several countries and are a European resident, the best bet is an **Inter-Rail Pass** (Ⓦinterrailnet.com), which entitles you to unlimited travel within the specified period and geographical area. The passes (Global and One Country Passes) come in over-26 and (cheaper) under-26 versions, and cover thirty European countries. The France Rail Pass version allows between three and eight days of unlimited travel within a month (€203 for three days, €313 for eight days); first-class passes and cheaper passes for children, those under 26 and seniors are also available. For non-European residents there are various **Eurail passes** (Ⓦeurail.com), covering either several countries or just France.

By car from the UK

If you have the time and inclination, then travelling to the Dordogne **by car** – a distance of some 850km from London – is certainly an attractive proposition. Given the distance, it's well worth going slow and turning the drive into a part of the holiday, with lots of breaks and perhaps an overnight stop en-route.

Ferries from the UK and Ireland

The ferries plying the waters **between Dover and Calais** offer the cheapest means of getting to the other side of the Channel, and are particularly convenient if you live in southeast England, from where the quickest crossings take 1hr 30min. Operators on this route include P&O Ferries (Ⓦpo ferries.com) and DFDS Seaways (Ⓦdfdsseaways.com). If your starting point is west of London, it may be worth heading to one of the south-coast ports and catching a **ferry to Brittany or Normandy**; the quickest crossing from Portsmouth is around three hours. Brittany Ferries (Ⓦbrittany-ferries.co.uk) operates plentiful services from Portsmouth to Caen, Cherbourg, Le Havre and St Malo, from Poole to Cherbourg, and from Plymouth to Roscoff. Condor Ferries (Ⓦcondorferries.co.uk) also goes from Portsmouth to Cherbourg, and to several ports in northern France via the Channel Islands. If you're coming from the north of England or Scotland, you could consider the overnight crossing **from Hull to Zeebrugge** (Belgium) operated by P&O Ferries, though it'd be quicker just to drive down to the south coast and take a ferry there.

Another option is to take a ferry from Portsmouth **to Santander or Bilbao** (Brittany Ferries) in northern Spain. Crossing times are long (24–32hr), and once you touch dry land in Santander you've still got a six-hour drive north into the Dordogne or five hours from Bilbao.

From Ireland, Irish Ferries (W irishferries.com) go from Dublin to Cherbourg or Rosslare (near Wexford) to Roscoff or Cherbourg.

Return fares for a car and four passengers start at around £50 on the Dover–Calais route, £184 for Potsmouth–Caen, £158 for Portsmouth–Cherbourg, £168 for Portsmouth–Le Havre, £183 for Portsmouth–St Malo and £234 for Plymouth–Roscoff. The voyage from the UK's south coast to northern Spain costs around £520 return for a car and four people. From Ireland, return fares for a car and two adults start at around €350 on the Rosslare–Cherbourg route. Most ferry companies also offer **fares for foot passengers**, typically around £20 return on cross-Channel routes; accompanying bicycles can usually be carried free in the low season, though there may be a small charge during peak periods.

An easy way to compare prices and get an overview of possible routes is via Ferry Savers (W ferrysavers.com) and EuroDrive (W eurodrive.co.uk), both of which offer cut-price fares; the latter caters only for people taking their cars across the Channel.

Eurotunnel

Drive-on drive-off shuttle trains operated by **Eurotunnel** (W eurotunnel.com) run continuously between Folkestone and Coquelles, near Calais, with up to four departures per hour at peak times (one every two hours from midnight to 6am) and take 35min (slightly longer at night), though you must arrive at least 30min before departure. It is possible to turn up and buy your ticket at the check-in booths, but you'll pay the highest rate on the day. Standard **fares** start at £58 one-way if you book far enough ahead and/or travel off peak, rising to £178 on the day. Fully refundable and changeable FlexiPlus fares cost £214 return.

AutoTrain

If you don't want to drive too far when you've reached France, you can take advantage of SNCF's **AutoTrain** (W uk.voyages-sncf.com). This entails putting your car on a train at Paris Bercy station, which then travels overnight for the journey south to Brive; meanwhile, you make your own way down – preferably by train too – whereupon you meet your car at the destination. You do have two days to collect your vehicle, however, useful if you want to hang around in Paris for a day, or wish to make a detour. The service operates most days between early June and early September, and is reduced to two or three services per week during

the rest of the year. The cheapest non-flexible tickets start at around £100 one-way, just for the car.

Agents and tour operators

There are a vast number of **travel agents** and **tour operators** offering holidays in the Dordogne and Lot, the majority of which are geared to providing trips centred around outdoor activities such as cycling and canoeing, or food and wine.

AGENTS AND OPERATORS

Backroads US ☎ 800 462 2848, W backroads.com. Luxury cycling and walking tours of the Bordeaux vineyards and the Dordogne and Vézère valleys. Family trips, too.

Cycling for Softies UK ☎ 020 7471 7760, W cycling-for-softies.co.uk. An easy-going cycle-holiday operator offering a seven-day Dordogne and Garonne trip. Accommodation and restaurants tend to be top-end, including the occasional Michelin-starred restaurant.

Cyclomundo France ☎ 33 450 872109, W cyclomundo.com. Defining itself as the "bike rider's travel agency", and specializing in custom-made "biking à la carte" trips for serious cyclists. Guided and self-guided trips including six different Dordogne and Lot tours.

Equestrian Escapes UK ☎ 01829 781123, W equestrian-escapes.com. Five-day horseback holidays in the northern part of the Dordogne, catering to all levels, from beginners to advanced.

Eurocamp UK ☎ 01606 787125, W eurocamp.co.uk. Self-drive, go-as-you-please holidays with tent or mobile home.

Exodus UK ☎ 020 3131 2008, W exodus.co.uk. Eight-day Family Adventure trips, involving canoeing on the Dordogne and Vézère rivers. There's also an eight-day Dordogne cycling holiday, with a bit of culture thrown in too.

France Afloat UK ☎ 0870 011 0538, W franceafloat.com. UK-based French canal- and river-cruising specialist leading trips on the Garonne Canal around Moissac and Agen, and the Canal du Midi.

French Travel Connection Australia ☎ 1300 858 304, W french travel.com.au. Australia-based online agent offering everything to do with travel to and around France, including accommodation, canal boats, walking tours, train travel, cookery classes, car rental and more.

The International Kitchen US ☎ 1 800 945 8606 or ☎ 312 467 0560, W theinternationalkitchen.com. "Cooking school vacations" in a Bordeaux wine château, or in the Dordogne and the Quercy.

Lot Cycling Holidays France 05 65 32 70 02, W lotcyclingholidays.com. Seven-day cycling tours of the Lot and Dordogne are available with this French-based agency.

North South Travel UK ☎ 01245 608 291, W northsouthtravel.co.uk. Friendly, competitive travel agency, offering discounted fares worldwide – profits are used to support projects in the developing world, especially the promotion of sustainable tourism.

STA Travel US ☎ 1 800 781 4040, UK ☎ 0333 321 0099, Australia ☎ 134 782, New Zealand ☎ 0800 474 400, South Africa ☎ 0861 781 781; W statravel.com. Worldwide specialists in low-cost flights and tours for students and under-26s, though other customers are welcome.

Getting around

France has the most extensive train network in Western Europe. The nationally owned French train company, the SNCF (Société Nationale des Chemins de Fer), runs fast, modern trains between all the main towns in the Dordogne and Lot, and even between some of the minor ones. In rural areas where branch lines have been closed, certain routes (such as Agen to Villeneuve-sur-Lot) are covered by buses operated by the SNCF or in partnership with independent lines. It's an integrated service, with buses timed to meet trains and the same ticket covering both. However, as so many of the region's highlights are out in the countryside and in little villages, you'll need your own transport to fully explore the Dordogne and Lot.

By rail

SNCF has pioneered one of the most efficient, comfortable and user-friendly railway systems in the world. Pride and joy of the French rail system is the high-speed **TGV** (*train à grande vitesse*; W tgv .com). The quickest way to reach the Dordogne by train is to take a TGV from Paris Montparnasse to Bordeaux (3hr); some of these services continue on along the main line to Agen and Montauban, or you can take an Intercité train across to Périgueux. Alternatively, take a TGV from Paris to Libourne, with an onward connection to Périgueux. Brive, meanwhile, is served by a handful of direct Intercité trains each day from Paris Austerlitz. Elsewhere, the majority of trains you will use here are designated TER (*Train Express Régional*) which cover shorter distances and stop at more and smaller stations. A scenic branch traces much of the Dordogne valley linking Bordeaux with Bergerac and Sarlat, while three north–south axes cross the Dordogne and Lot valleys (Périgueux–Agen, Brive–Cahors–Montauban and Brive–Figeac–Toulouse). In all these cases, schedules are thin, with often big gaps between trains, so it's imperative to check timetables in advance. Paper copies of **timetables** are available free at most stations, or check W voyages-sncf.com. *Autocar* (often abbreviated to *car*) at the top of a column means it's an SNCF bus service, on which rail tickets and passes are valid.

Tickets

Tickets for all SNCF trains can be bought online with a credit card through W sncf.com, which has an English-language option, or by phone and at any train station (*gare SNCF*). Here you can buy tickets at the ticket office, or one of the yellow touch-screen machines (in English). If boarding at a very small station, which has neither machines nor a ticket office, you can buy your ticket from the guard on the train. All tickets – but not passes or internet tickets printed out at home – must be **validated** in the orange machines located at the entrance to the platforms; it is an offence not to follow the instruction *Compostez votre billet* (Validate your ticket).

Fares

Fares are cheaper if you travel off peak (*période bleue*; blue period) rather than during peak hours (*période normale* or *période blanche*; normal or white period) – in general, peak period means Monday mornings and Friday and Sunday evenings. A leaflet (*le calendrier voyageurs*) showing the blue and white periods is available at train stations. For longer journeys it's worth checking the advance special discount offers, known as *tarifs Prem's*, on the SNCF website. A limited number of these are available on some main lines and can be bought online between two months and two weeks in advance. Even cheaper internet-only TGV fares can be purchased through W idtgv.com on services from Paris to Bordeaux and Toulouse; tickets go on sale four months before departure. Try to book in advance for all TGV trains, as **seat reservations** are obligatory, and are included in the ticket price, though note that you will have to pay extra for them if you are travelling on an Inter-Rail pass. Anybody under 26 is entitled to a discount of 25 percent off all blue-period trains in France.

By bus

Travelling around the Dordogne and Lot region by bus is not particularly recommended. A very limited timetable serves a few routes, and those services that do exist are usually governed by the needs of schoolchildren rather than tourists, running once or twice a day in term-time only – and hence hardly a practical option for most visitors.

The most convenient **bus services** are those operated as an extension of rail links by SNCF, which run between train stations and serve areas not accessible by rail. In addition to SNCF buses, private, municipal and departmental buses can be useful for local and some cross-country journeys, though be prepared for early starts and careful planning if you want to see much outside the main towns.

Timetables for SNCF services are available at Ⓦ sncf-voyages.fr, but times for services run by private companies can be frustrating to track down. If you can read French then a trawl through the website Ⓦ dordogne.fr will reveal a downloadable PDF of main timetables, but frankly it's easiest just to ask at local tourist offices.

Larger towns usually have a *gare routière* (**bus station**), often next to the *gare SNCF*, though this is often little more than just a couple of bus stands. However, the private bus companies don't always work together and you'll frequently find them leaving from an array of different points (here, too, the local tourist office should be able to help).

One final thing to note is that many rural bus services only operate *sur réservation* or "on demand". This means that you need to phone the operating company by 6pm the day before you wish to travel (or by 6pm on Friday for travel on Monday). Such services are usually indicated by a telephone icon in the bus timetable.

By car

Driving in the Dordogne and Lot can be a real pleasure, and is often the only practical means of reaching the more remote sights. There are three **autoroutes** in the area: the A20 cuts south from Limoges to Toulouse via Cahors; the A62 runs along the Garonne from Bordeaux to Toulouse; and the A89 links Bordeaux with Périgueux and Brive. Motorway **tolls** are payable in cash or by credit card (get in the lane marked CB) at the frequent tollgates (*péages*). The Michelin website (Ⓦ viamichelin.fr) details the cost of tolls on any particular journey. Slower and more congested are the toll-free **national roads** (marked, for example, N21 or RN21 on signs and maps). The smaller **routes départementales** (marked with a D) are generally uncongested and make for an even more scenic drive; as with N or R roads, they offer easier access to lunch stops in the small towns en route.

For up-to-the-minute **information** regarding traffic jams and roadworks on *autoroutes*, consult Ⓦ vinci-autoroutes.com; for other roads, visit Ⓦ www.bison-fute.equipement.gouv.fr. You can also tune into the radio on 107.7FM to listen to live traffic updates for main routes.

At the time of writing, petrol prices were hovering around €1.40 a litre for unleaded (*sans plomb*) and €1.12 a litre for diesel (*gazole* or *gasoil*); you'll find prices lowest at out-of-town hypermarkets. Note that in rural areas most petrol stations close at night, on Sundays and on bank holidays, and some may also close on Mondays. The majority of fuel stations have card machines on the pump meaning they can be used even when the station is unstaffed.

If you run into **mechanical difficulties** you'll find garages and service stations in the Yellow Pages of the phone book under *"Garages d'automobiles"*; for **breakdowns**, look under *"Dépannages"*. If you have an accident or theft, you should contact the local police – and keep a copy of their report in order to file an insurance claim. Within Europe, most vehicle **insurance** policies cover taking your car to France; check with your insurer. However, you're advised to take out extra cover for motoring assistance in case your vehicle breaks down; contact your insurer or motoring organizations such as the AA or RAC for a quote.

Rules of the road

US, Canadian, Australian, New Zealand and all EU **driving licences** are valid in France, though an International Driver's Licence makes life easier. The minimum driving age is 18 and you must hold a full (not a provisional) licence. Drivers are required to carry their licence, insurance papers and vehicle registration document (*carte grise*) with them in the car.

Since the French drive on the right, drivers of right-hand-drive cars must adjust their **headlights** to dip to the right. This is most easily done by sticking on black glare deflectors, which can be bought at motor accessory shops and at the Channel ferry ports or the Eurostar terminal. Motorcyclists must drive with their headlights on, and must also wear a **helmet**.

All non-French vehicles must display their **national identification letters** (GB, etc), either on the number plate or by means of a sticker, and all vehicles must carry a red warning triangle, two fluorescent jackets and a single-use breathalyser. **Seat belts** are compulsory front and back, and children under 10 years are not allowed to sit in the front of the car. It is illegal to use a hand-held **mobile phone** while driving.

The law of *priorité à droite* – **giving way** to traffic coming from your right, even when it is coming from a minor road – was mostly phased out years ago. However, it still applies on a very few roads in built-up areas, so it pays to be vigilant at junctions. A sign showing a yellow diamond on a white background gives you right of way, while the same sign with a diagonal black slash across it warns you that vehicles emerging from the right have priority. *Stop* signs mean you must stop completely; *Cédez le passage* means "Give way".

Unless otherwise indicated, **speed limits** are: 130kph (80mph) on *autoroutes*; 110kph (68mph) on dual carriageways; 90kph (55mph) on other roads;

and 50kph (31mph) in towns. In wet weather, and for drivers with less than two years' experience, these limits are 110kph (68mph), 100kph (62mph) and 80kph (50mph) respectively, while the town limit remains constant. **Speed cameras** have become much more common in the past few years: if you speed you will almost certainly get caught and fined – and don't think that having foreign plates will mean you can get away without paying a fine, as nowadays you will be chased up. The legal blood **alcohol limit** is 0.05 percent alcohol (0.5 grams per litre), and police frequently make random breath tests, as well as saliva tests for drugs. There are stiff **penalties** for driving violations, ranging from on-the-spot fines for minor infringements, to the immediate confiscation of your licence and/or car for more serious offences.

Car rental

To rent a car in France you must be over 21 and have driven for at least one year. **Car rental** in France costs upwards of €50 for a day and €200 for a week for the smallest car, but is usually cheaper if arranged online before you leave home. You'll find the big firms represented in most of the bigger towns, while a few of these also have desks at Bergerac and Brive airports. Local firms can be cheaper but most don't offer one-way rentals. Unless you specify otherwise, you'll get a car with manual transmission.

The **cost** of car rental includes the minimum car insurance required by law. Under the standard contract you are liable for an excess (*franchise*) for any damage to the vehicle. This starts at around €500 for the smallest car and can be covered by credit card.

By bicycle

Bicycles (*vélos*) have high status in France, where cyclists are given respect both on the roads and as customers at restaurants and hotels. In addition, local authorities are actively promoting cycling, not only with urban cycle lanes but also with comprehensive networks in rural areas (frequently using disused railways). Tourist offices can usually provide maps of local routes. Note that all cyclists are required by law to wear a **reflective safety jacket** at night outside urban areas and in the daytime during periods of poor visibility, or risk being fined up to €35.

Most towns have well-stocked retail and **repair shops**, where parts are normally cheaper than in Britain or the US. However, if you're using a foreign-made bike with nonstandard metric wheels, it's a good idea to carry spare tyres.

The **train** network runs various schemes for cyclists, all of them covered online at ⓦvelo.sncf.com. It's possible to take your bike for free on all trains – make sure you arrive in good time to get a slot in the bike rack. To take bikes for free on TGV and Intercité services, they must be dismantled or folded and placed in a cycle bag; if not, you'll pay an €10 fee. You'll also need to make a bike reservation on TGV/Intercité services, or you may incur a €45 fine and will be asked to leave the train at the next station.

Eurostar will carry all folding bicycles for free, as long as they're smaller than 85cm when folded. Otherwise, you have to send unfolded bikes via their registered baggage service, Eurodespatch; if you book this in advance (£30), the bike will travel on the same train as you; if you don't book, you pay £25 on the day of travel and the bike will go on the next available train. **Ferries** usually carry bikes free (though you may need to register them), as do some **airlines** such as British Airways, while others charge – check when making your booking.

Bikes – either mountain bikes (*vélos tout-terrain* or VTT) or hybrid bikes (*vélos tout-chemin* or VTC) – are widely available to **rent** from campsites and hostels, as well as from specialist cycle shops and some tourist offices; rental costs are usually €15–20 per day. As for **maps**, a minimum requirement is the IGN 1:100,000 series (see p.38) – the smallest scale that carries contours. The UK's national cyclists' organization, the CTC (ⓦctc.org.uk), can suggest routes. Companies offering specialist bike touring **holidays** are listed on p.23.

By boat

Boating is a leisurely way to explore the Lot and Garonne valleys. From April to September the **River Lot** is navigable for motorboats from St-Cirq Lapopie downstream to Luzech (65km), and from Fumel down to its confluence with the Garonne (78km). From October through to March the current is too swift and the river too high to be safe. But the Lot is a capricious river at any time, so it pays to follow the guidelines provided by rental companies carefully.

The other option is to potter along the **Garonne Canal**, which tracks the Garonne eastwards from Castets-en-Dorthe, near Langon, to Toulouse (190km), where it joins the Canal du Midi. You can also combine the Garonne Canal with the River Lot and the **River Baïse** south to Nérac.

Boats are usually rented by the week, though shorter periods are also available outside the July and August peak. **Rates** range from €800 to €2500 per week for a four- to ten-person boat, depending on the season and level of comfort. No licence is required, but you'll receive instruction before taking the controls. You should also be given a **carte de plaisance**, guaranteeing that the boat is insured and in good working order.

BOAT RENTAL COMPANIES IN THE LOT

Babou Marine ☎ 05 65 30 08 99, **⊛** baboumarine.com.
Locaboat Plaisance ☎ 03 86 91 72 72, **⊛** locaboat.com.
Lot Navigation ☎ 05 65 24 32 20, **⊛** lot-navigation.com.
Nautic ☎ 03 85 53 76 74, **⊛** nautic.fr.
Nicols ☎ 02 41 56 46 56, **⊛** nicols.com.

Accommodation

Throughout the Dordogne and Lot, there's an excellent spread of hotels and chambres d'hôtes, which are complemented by some smart campsites and a smattering of hostels. In general you'll be able to get a simple double for around €45, though sometimes with shared facilities, while €60 should secure a reasonable level of comfort. At most times of the year you can turn up in any town and find a room or a place in a campsite, but it's best to book in advance, especially if you have your heart set on a particular place.

Problems may arise between mid-July and the end of August, when the French (and Germans, Spanish, Dutch and others) take their own vacations en masse. During this period, hotel and hostel accommodation can be hard to come by – particularly in the most popular towns, such as Sarlat – and you may find yourself falling back on local tourist offices for help. Some offer a **booking service**, though they can't guarantee rooms at a particular price, and all provide lists of hotels, hostels, campsites and bed-and-breakfast possibilities. With **campsites**, you can be more relaxed about finding an empty pitch somewhere for a tent, though it may be more difficult with a caravan or camper van.

Hotels

Most French hotels are **graded** from zero to five stars. The price more or less corresponds to the number of stars, though the system is rather simplistic, having more to do with ratios of bathrooms-per-guest and so forth than genuine quality.

What you get for your money varies enormously between establishments. Paying under €50, you take your chances somewhat: there won't be soundproofing and the showers (*douches*) and toilets (WC or *toilettes*) may well be communal (*dans le palier*). However, you should have your own bidet and washbasin (*lavabo*), often partitioned off from the rest of the room in an area referred to as a *cabinet de toilette*. Over €50 should get you a room with its own bath or shower though not necessarily toilet and, though the decor may not be anything to write home about, comfortable furniture. For around €60 you can expect a decent en-suite room with smart furnishings, while anything over €80 should give you something approaching luxury. **Single rooms** – if the hotel has any – are only marginally cheaper than doubles, so sharing always slashes costs, especially since most hotels willingly provide rooms with **extra beds** for three or more people at good discounts.

Breakfast, which is not normally included, will add between €7 and €16 per person to a bill, sometimes more – though there is no obligation to take it. Unless otherwise stated, all hotels listed in this guide offer free **wi-fi**, although it doesn't always reach every room.

Note that many family-run hotels close down for two or three weeks a year. In smaller towns and villages they may also close for one or two nights a week, usually Sunday or Monday. Details are given where possible in the Guide, but dates change from year to year and some places will close for a few days in low season if they have no bookings. The best precaution is to phone ahead to be sure.

A useful option, especially if you're driving and looking for somewhere late at night, are the modern **chain hotels** located at motorway exits and on the

---

ACCOMMODATION PRICES

The prices quoted in this book are for the **cheapest double room in high season**. For much of the year, however, you can expect to pay ten percent or so less, especially as online booking becomes the norm (with prices based on availability rather than season). Our quoted prices include **breakfast** except where noted.

For **campsites**, high-season prices are included for a pitch, two adults, a car and electricity; where available, we've also given prices for mobile homes or chalets that can be rented directly from the campsite.

outskirts of major towns. Among the cheapest (from around €35 for a three-person room with communal toilets and showers) are the one-star Formule 1 chain (Ⓦ www.hotelformule1.com) and the slightly more comfortable Ibis Budget (formerly Etap; Ⓦ ibisbudget hotel.ibis.com).

There are also a number of well-regarded **hotel federations** in France, the biggest and most useful of which is **Logis** (Ⓦ logishotels.fr), an association of over three thousand hotels nationwide; standards are generally good, though they can sometimes come across as a bit dated. Two other, more upmarket federations worth mentioning are the Châteaux & Hôtels Collection (Ⓦ chateauxhotels.com) and Relais du Silence (Ⓦ relaisdusilence.com), both of which offer very high-class accommodation in beautiful older properties, often in rural locations.

Chambres d'hôtes, Airbnb and self-catering

Predominantly in country areas, but increasingly found in towns, **chambres d'hôtes** offer bed-and-breakfast accommodation in someone's house, château or farm. Though the quality can vary, on the whole the standards are very high, and in many cases, the properties are blessed with an abundance of charm and character. Moreover, the owners may also provide traditional home cooking and a great insight into French life. In general, prices range between €50 and €100 for two people including breakfast; payment is almost always expected in cash. Some offer meals on request (tables d'hôtes), usually evenings only, while others are attached to fermes auberges, farm-restaurants serving local produce. All things considered, a well-run chambre d'hôte is very often a vastly more enticing place to stay than a hotel.

The Dordogne and Lot are a long way behind Paris, which has more available rooms than any other city in the world, but **Airbnb** (Ⓦ airbnb.com) is still a viable alternative to the region's chambres d'hôtes, with some three hundred options listed in the Dordogne region.

If you're planning to stay a week or more in any one place it might be worth considering renting **self-catering accommodation**. This will generally consist of self-contained country cottages known as gîtes or gîtes ruraux, many in converted barns or farm outbuildings. While some can be quite grand, quite a few gîtes can be a bit dowdy.

You can get lists of both gîtes and chambres d'hôtes from **Gîtes de France** (Ⓦ gites-de-france .com). They also publish annual guides such as Nouveaux Gîtes Ruraux, Chambres et Tables d'Hôtes and Chambres d'Hôtes de Charme, and more comprehensive regional or departmental guides that include photos. All these guides are available online or from departmental offices of Gîtes de France, as well as from local bookshops and tourist offices. Tourist offices will also have lists of places in their area that are not affiliated to Gîtes de France.

You'll also find self-catering accommodation, much of it foreign-owned, on Ⓦ frenchconnections.co.uk and Ⓦ cheznous.co.uk; or try one of the agents listed in the Travel Shop section of the official French tourist office website, Ⓦ www.franceguide.com.

Hostels, foyers and gîtes d'étape

At around €14–20 per night for a dormitory bed, usually with breakfast thrown in and the opportunity to prepare your own meals in a shared kitchen, **youth hostels** – auberges de jeunesse – are invaluable for single travellers on a budget; per-person prices of dorm beds are given throughout the Guide.

Most hostels are run either by the municipality or by the French **hostelling association**, the Fédération Unie des Auberges de Jeunesse (FUAJ). Many can be reserved online through the FUAJ website, Ⓦ fuaj.org. To stay at FUAJ hostels you normally have to show a current HI (Hostelling International) **membership card**, which you can buy at Ⓦ hihostels.com. It's usually cheaper and easier to join before you leave home, provided your national Youth Hostel association is a full member of HI.

Unfortunately, there aren't that many youth hostels in the Dordogne and Lot region. Sometimes, as is the case in Villefranche-de-Rouergue and Périgueux, hostel accommodation is provided in workers' hostels (**Foyers de Jeunes Travailleurs**). These tend to be functional and centrally located, with good canteens. Other hostels, most notably that at Cadouin, are more beautifully sited, though you might have to factor in the cost of a taxi in order to get there.

In the countryside, hostel-style **gîtes d'étape** are aimed primarily at hikers and long-distance bikers. Often run by the local village or municipality, they are less formal than hostels and provide bunk beds, primitive kitchen and washing facilities from around €15. They are marked on the large-scale IGN walkers' maps and listed in the individual Topo-guides (see p.304). For more information check out the Gîtes de France booklet Gîtes d'Étapes et de Séjours (€10), and Gîtes d'Étape et Refuges, published by Rando Éditions, downloadable at Ⓦ gites-refuges .com (€5 for the southwest region).

Camping

The French are great campers and practically every village and town in France has at least one **campsite** to cater for the thousands of people who spend their holiday under canvas. Most sites open from around Easter to September or October. The vast majority are graded into four **categories**, from one to four stars, by the local authority. One- and two-star sites are very basic, with toilets and showers (not necessarily with hot water), but little else, and standards of cleanliness are not always brilliant. At the other extreme, four-star sites are far more spacious, have hot-water showers and electrical hook-ups, swimming pools – sometimes several and sometimes heated – as well as washing machines, a shop, sports facilities and children's activities, and will provide refreshments or meals in high season. At three-star sites you can expect a selection of these facilities and less spacious plots. A further designation, **Camping Qualité** (Ⓦ campingqualite.com), indicates those campsites with particularly high standards of hygiene, service and privacy, while the Clef Verte (Ⓦ laclefverte.org) label is awarded to sites (and hotels and hostels) run along environmentally friendly lines. For those who really like to get away from it all, **camping à la ferme** – on somebody's farm – is a good, simple option. Facilities will be minimal but the setting is often blissfully rural, with lots of space plus peace and quiet – things often missing from the fancier campsites. Lists of farm sites are available at local tourist offices.

Though **charging systems** vary, most places charge per pitch and per person, usually including a car, while others apply a global figure. As a rough guide, two people with a tent and car might pay as little as €12 at a simple municipal site to as much as €42 at a four-star in a prime location. In peak season and if you plan to spend a week or more at one site, it's wise to book ahead, and note that many of the big sites have caravans and chalet bungalows for rent, though there's often a one-week minimum stay for these in high season.

The **Fédération Française de Camping et de Caravaning** (Ⓦ ffcc.fr) has some 1200 affiliated sites and publishes an annual guide covering ten thousand campsites, details of which can also be found on the excellent Ⓦ campingfrance.com. If you'd rather have everything organized for you, a number of companies specialize in **camping holidays**, including Eurocamp (see p.23).

Lastly, a word of **caution**: never camp rough (*camping sauvage*, as the French call it) on anyone's land without first asking permission. If the dogs don't get you, the guns might – farmers have been known to shoot first and ask later. On the other hand, a politely phrased request for permission will as often as not get positive results. Camping on public land is not officially permitted, but is widely practised by the French, and if you are discreet and pack up first thing in the morning (and leave no litter) you're not likely to have problems.

Food and drink

The cuisine of the Dordogne and Lot region is predominantly simple, country cooking (cuisine de terroir), revolving around duck and goose, garlic, a host of mushrooms, walnuts and whatever else the land has to offer. It's the sort of cuisine best sampled in little family-run places, where it's still possible to eat well for €15 or less. That said, every restaurant worth its salt offers a menu du terroir, featuring local specialities. Expensive gastronomique restaurants throughout the region, and most mid-priced establishments, also offer a smattering of fish dishes. The food glossary is on p.309.

Breakfast and light meals

For most locals, **breakfast** is a quick no-frills affair consisting of a bit of baguette with jam or a croissant and coffee. In hotels, though, it's often a different story and the standard hotel breakfast comprises cereals, yoghurt, bread and/or pastries, jam, orange juice and a jug of coffee or tea, and usually costs €6–12. More expensive hotels typically offer fresh fruit, cheeses and hot and cold meats in addition to the above. If you're not staying in a hotel (or don't want to fork out that much), head to a café-bar and grab a croissant or *pain au chocolat* with coffee or hot chocolate, which will cost around €4.

Traditionally, the big meal of the day for the French is **lunch**, still long, leisurely and the cornerstone service in rural areas. Most restaurants offer a weekday lunchtime **plat du jour** (daily special) and/ or a **menu du jour** (menu of the day), a three-course meal with wine for €13–20. *Menus* are great value – the multiple courses mean you may only need a light snack in the evening. At the lower end of the price scale the offerings are often very traditional but good, while at the upper end you're likely to be served much more inventive and unusual food.

More popular for lunch with foreign tourists than most French are snacks such as *croques-monsieur* and *croques-madame* (variations on the toasted-cheese sandwich), along with *frites*, *gaufres* (waffles) and fresh-filled baguettes. You could also try a **crêpe** (pancake with a filling): the savoury buckwheat variety (*galettes*) are the main course; sweet, white-flour crêpes are dessert. **Pizzerias**, usually *au feu de bois* (wood-fired), are also very common, though more popular with the French in the evening.

For **picnics**, local markets or supermarkets will provide you with almost everything you need. Cooked meat, prepared snacks, ready-made dishes and assorted salads are also available at charcuteries (delicatessens), which you'll find in some villages, and in most supermarkets. You'll find boulangeries (bakeries) just about everywhere – often several in one village – and it's here you can pick up some delicious breads and, usually, a mouthwatering array of cakes and pastries too, though a pâtisserie is more of a specialist cake shop. Look for the word *artisanal* after the name of a boulangerie or pâtisserie – this means its bread or cakes are home-made.

Restaurant meals

There's no difference between restaurants (or *auberges* or *relais* as they sometimes call themselves) and brasseries in terms of quality or price range. The distinction is that **brasseries**, which resemble cafés, serve quicker meals at most hours of the day, while **restaurants** tend to stick to the traditional meal times of noon to 2pm, and 7pm to 9pm or 9.30pm. In touristy areas in high season, and for all the more upmarket places, it's wise to make reservations – easily done on the same day in most cases.

When hunting for places to eat, don't forget that **hotel restaurants** are open to non-residents, and can be very good value (we've given opening hours for recommended places within accommodation reviews in this Guide). In country areas keep an eye out for **fermes auberges**, farm-restaurants where the majority of ingredients are produced on the farm itself. These are often the best places to sample really traditional local cuisine at very reasonable

TOP 5 RESTAURANTS
Déjeuner sur l'Herbe, St-Léon-sur-Vézère p.145
Le Gindreau, St Médard p.231
Jehan de Valon, Rocamadour p.181
La Table d'Oliver, Brive-la-Gaillarde p.80
Vieux Logis, Trémolat p.109

prices; a four-course meal for between €18 and €35 is the norm, including an apéritif and wine, but reservations are a must.

Prices, and what you get for them, must be posted outside. Normally there's a choice between one or more **menus fixes** – with a set number of courses and a limited choice – and choosing individually from the *carte* (menu). *Menus fixes*, often referred to simply as *menus*, are normally the cheapest option, especially at lunch (see p.29) but going **à la carte** offers greater choice and, in the better restaurants, unlimited access to the chef's inventiveness – though you'll pay much more for the privilege. **Wine** (*vin*) or a drink (*boisson*) is sometimes included in the cost of a *menu fixe*. Otherwise, the cheapest option will be the house wine, usually served in a jug (*pichet*) or carafe; you'll be asked if you want *un quart* (0.25 litre), *un demi* (0.5 litre) or *un litre* (1 litre).

One final note is that you should always call the waiter or waitress *Monsieur* or *Madame* (*Mademoiselle* if a young woman), never *Garçon*.

Vegetarian food

On the whole, **vegetarians** can expect a fairly lean time in the Dordogne and Lot region. That said, in the very best restaurants you'll often find one or two fantastically creative vegetarian dishes on the menu, typically featuring *cèpes* (mushrooms) as the star ingredient. Otherwise your best bet is to head for a crêperie or pizzeria, while Chinese or North African restaurants (though these are normally only found in the bigger towns) can be good standbys. Occasionally they'll be willing to replace a meat dish on the fixed-price menu (*menu fixe*); at other times you'll have to pick your way through the *carte*. Remember

SERVICE CHARGES AND TIPPING
The vast majority of restaurants and hotels include a **service charge** of fifteen percent in their prices, denoted on menus as *service compris* (*s.c.*) or *prix nets*. Very occasionally you'll see *service non compris* (*s.n.c.*) or *servis en sus*, which means that it's up to you whether you leave a **tip** or not. Most French leave just a couple of euros in loose change, though something more substantial is expected in upmarket places; in general, though, tipping is not deemed as important here as in the US. It's also customary to tip porters, tour guides and taxi drivers one or two euros.

to ask "*Je suis végétarien(ne); est-ce qu'il y a quelques plats sans viande?*" (I'm a vegetarian; are there any non-meat dishes?). **Vegans**, however, should probably forget about eating in restaurants and stick to self-catering: expect blank looks if you try to ask if restaurant dishes are gluten- or dairy-free.

Drinks

In France **drinking** is done at a leisurely pace whether it's a prelude to food (*apéritif/apéro*) or a sequel (*digestif*), and cafés are the standard places to do it. Every bar or café has to display its full price list, including service charges. You normally pay when you leave, and it's usually perfectly acceptable to sit for hours over just one cup of coffee. Note that the minimum age for buying alcohol is 18, though younger teenagers may drink wine in a restaurant if with their parents. Public displays of drunkenness are very much frowned upon.

Wine

French wine (*vin*), drunk at just about every meal or social occasion, is unrivalled in the world for its range, sophistication, diversity and status. The house wine served in restaurants can be very good value in this wine-producing region, or opt for a bottle of AOP (*appellation d'origine protégée*) wine if you want a more sophisticated taste. You can buy a very decent bottle of wine for €6 in a shop or from the producer, while €10 and over will get you something worth savouring. A glass of wine in a bar will typically cost €3 to €5.

The best way of **buying wine** is directly from the producers (*vignerons*) at their vineyards, or at Maisons or Syndicats du Vin (representing a group of wine-producers) and Coopératifs Vinicoles (producers' co-ops). At all of these you can usually sample the wines first. The most interesting option is to visit the vineyard itself, where the owner will often include a tour of the *chais* in which the wine is produced and aged. The most economical method is to buy *en vrac*, which you can do at some wine shops (*caves*), filling a plastic five- or ten-litre container (generally sold on the premises) straight from the barrel. Supermarkets often have good bargains, too.

There are strict limitations on the extent to which wine-growers can interfere in the natural process – it's illegal even to water vines. The result is that, far more than in other countries, French wines are the product of a very specific bit of land or *terroir*, and there will often be significant differences in taste between the wines of two neighbouring producers. This makes tasting wines a real joy, and even if you're

not an expert, it's well worth trying to establish which grape types you particularly like or dislike, and whether you like your wine fruity or dry, light or heavy. Waiters and wine producers are usually delighted to give you advice in making a choice.

For basic wine vocabulary, see p.313.

Beer

Light Belgian and German **beers**, plus various French brands from Alsace, account for most of the beer you'll find. Draught beer (*à la pression*) – very often Kronenbourg – is the cheapest drink you can have next to coffee and wine; *une pression* (usually 0.33 litre) will cost around €3. For a wider choice of draught and bottled beer you need to go to special beer-drinking establishments such as the English- and Irish-style pubs found in larger towns and cities. A small bottle at one of these places can cost up to twice as much as a *demi* in an ordinary café-bar. Buying bottled or canned beer in supermarkets is much cheaper.

Spirits and liqueurs

Strong alcohol, including **spirits** (*eaux-de-vie*), such as cognac and armagnac, and **liqueurs** such as locally made walnut liqueurs (*vins de noix*), are always available. Refreshing *pastis* – the generic name for aniseed drinks such as Pernod or Ricard – is served diluted with water and ice (*glace* or *glaçons*). Among less familiar names, try Poire William (pear brandy), or Marc (a spirit distilled from grape pulp). Measures are generous, but they don't come cheap: the same applies for imported spirits such as whisky (usually called Scotch). Two drinks designed to stimulate the appetite – *un apéritif* – are Pineau (cognac and grape juice) and Kir (white wine with a dash of cassis – blackcurrant liqueur – or with champagne instead of wine for a Kir Royal). For a post-meal *digestif*, don't miss out on armagnac, oak-aged brandy from the south of the Garonne but available in bars and restaurants throughout the region.

Soft drinks

On the **soft drink** front, you can buy cartons of unsweetened fruit juice in supermarkets, although in cafés, the bottled (sweetened) nectars such as apricot (*jus d'abricot*) and blackcurrant (*cassis*) still

---

TOP 5 FOODIE TREATS

Foie gras p.69
Monbazillac wine p.96
Rocamadour cheese p.181
Truffles p.72
Walnuts p.160

hold sway. Fresh orange or lemon juice (*orange/citron pressé*) is a much more refreshing choice on a hot day. Other soft drinks to try are syrups (*sirops*) of mint, grenadine and other flavours mixed with water. The standard fizzy drinks of lemonade (*limonade*), Coke (*coca*) and so forth are all available. Bottles of **mineral water** (*eau minérale*) and spring water (*eau de source*) – either sparkling (*gazeuse*) or still (*plate*) – abound. But there's not much wrong with the tap water (*l'eau de robinet*), which will always be brought free to your table if you ask for it.

Coffee, tea and hot chocolate

Coffee served after a meal is always espresso: small, black and very strong. You can also get it with a dash of milk (*noisette*). *Un café* or *un express* is the regular vesion. The French only drink milky coffee in the morning with breakfast, when you could ask for *un café au lait* – espresso in a large cup or bowl filled up with hot milk; at other times of the day ask for *un crème* (*grand crème* for a large cup). *Un déca* is decaffeinated, and is available everywhere. Ordinary **tea** (*thé*) – Lipton's nine times out of ten – is normally served black (*nature*) or with a slice of lemon (*au citron*); the French never add milk to tea but if you prefer it like that then ask for *un peu de lait frais* (some fresh milk), but expect the result to be a dishwater-weak brew. *Chocolat chaud* – **hot chocolate** – lives up to the high standards of French food and drink and is available at any café and at some specialist chocolate shops, where it's invariably superb. After meals, **herb teas** (*infusions* or *tisanes*), are offered by most restaurants: most commonly *verveine* (verbena), *tilleul* (lime blossom), *menthe* (mint) and *camomille* (camomile).

Festivals

It's hard to beat the experience of arriving in a small French village, expecting no more than a bed for the night, to discover the streets decked out with flags and streamers, a band playing in the square and the entire population out celebrating the feast of their patron saint. As well as the country-wide Fête de la Musique (June 21) and Bastille Day (July 14), there are any number of festivals – both traditional and of more recent origin – throughout the Dordogne and Lot.

The region's cathedrals, churches and châteaux make superb venues for festivals of **music** and **theatre**. All the major towns, and many of the smaller ones, put on at least one such festival a year, usually in summer, when you can often catch free performances in the streets. Anyone interested in contemporary theatre should make a beeline for Périgueux in early August, when international mime artists gather for Mimos, one of France's most exciting and innovative festivals.

Popular local culture is celebrated in the Félibrée, a festival established in 1903 to promote and safeguard the local *Occitan* (or *Oc*) language and culture. The **Félibrée** takes place on the first Sunday in July, when there is a procession, an *Occitan* Mass and – of course – a blow-out Périgordin meal. Nowadays the celebrations also continue for around ten days either side of the Félibrée itself in the form of folk concerts, crafts demonstrations, theatre and so forth. It takes place in a different town in the Dordogne *département* each year; contact the tourist office in Périgueux (see p.55) for the latest information.

More recent introductions are the **historical spectaculars** held at places such as Castillon-la-Bataille, where the final battle of the Hundred Years War is re-enacted by hundreds of local thespians. Such events may be touristy, but the atmosphere – most are held at night – and general enthusiasm more than compensate.

In such dedicated **wine** country, there are inevitably festivals coinciding with the grape harvest, when each village stages its own celebrations.

For details of the region's most important and interesting festivals, see the boxes at the beginning of each chapter of the Guide.

Sports and outdoor activities

The Dordogne and Lot region offers a terrific range of sports and outdoor activities, including hiking, cycling, trekking and waterborne diversions such as canoeing and kayaking. By far the most popular spectator sport in the region is rugby, particularly in Brive, but you'll find a team of some description in just about every town.

Walking

Walking is undoubtedly the best way to enjoy this region of France. Well-maintained long-distance paths known as *sentiers de grande randonnée*, or simply **GRs**, cut across country, signed with red and white waymarkers and punctuated with campsites and *gîtes d'étapes* at convenient distances. Some of the main routes in the region are the GR6, linking Ste-Foy-la-Grande in the west to Figeac; the GR36, which wanders southeast from Périgueux via Les Eyzies and Cahors to the Gorges de l'Aveyron; and the GR65, the great pilgrimage route passing through Figeac, Cahors and Moissac on the way to Santiago de Compostela in Spain.

The entire GR65 and parts of the GR36 and GR6 are described in a **Topo-guide** (available outside France in good travel bookshops), which gives a detailed account of the route, including maps, campsites, refuges, sources of provisions, etc. In France, the guides are available from bookshops and some tourist offices, or direct from the principal French walkers' organization, the Fédération Française de la Randonnée Pédestre (W ffrandonnee.fr).

In addition, many tourist offices produce guides to their local footpaths; where there is no tourist office, try asking at the *mairie*. For recommendations on walking **maps**, see p.38.

Cycling

The region's minor roads and demarcated **cycling** routes provide plenty of opportunities for cyclists; it's best to avoid main roads if you want to enjoy yourself, particularly in the high season. Among the long-distance routes, there's the "Grand Traversée du Périgord" running 180km from Mareuil in the far northwest via Brantôme, Périgueux and Les Eyzies to Monpazier. In the Lot-et-Garonne, the "Véloroute" follows the River Lot 80km from Aiguillon northeast to Fumel and Bonaguil. Many tourist offices can provide details of cycle paths in their area, while the French Federation of Cycling has lots of useful information on their website (W ffct.org). For recommendations on cycling **maps**, see p.38.

Canoeing and kayaking

Canoeing is hugely popular in the Dordogne and Lot region, and in the summer months every navigable river has outfits renting canoes and organizing excursions, which we've listed throughout the Guide. Those along Dordogne itself are the busiest, particularly

TOP 5 BEAUTIFUL VILLAGES
St-Cirq Lapopie p.212
Cordes-sur-Ciel p.280
Limeuil p.109
St-Jean-de-Côle p.66
St-Léon-sur-Vézère p.145

the stretch between La Roque-Gageac and Beynac, where you pass beneath some of the region's most dramatic castles; and the Vézère, where you can stop off at various points to visit the valley's prehistoric sights. Other, quieter options include the River Lot, through the Aveyron gorges and the smaller Dronne, Dropt and Célé rivers.

You can **rent** two- to three-person canoes and single-seater kayaks on all these rivers; every tourist office also stocks lists of local operators. Although it's possible to rent by the hour, it's best to take at least a half-day and simply cruise downstream. The company you book through will provide transport as required. Prices vary according to what's on offer, but you can expect to pay anywhere between €15 and €30 per person for a day's canoe rental, and around €4 more for a kayak.

On the Dordogne and Lot rivers you can make **longer excursions** of up to two weeks, either accompanied or on your own, sometimes in combination with cycling or walking. Various tour operators (see p.23) offer canoeing packages or you can book direct with the local company. Two of the biggest along the Dordogne valley are Canoës Loisirs (T 05 53 28 23 43, W canoes-loisirs.com) and Copeyre Canoë (T 05 65 32 72 61, W canoes-dordogne.fr).

The length of the canoeing **season** depends on the weather and the water levels. Most operators function daily in July and August, on demand in May, June and September, and close between October and April when the rivers are too high for inexperienced canoeists. One or two, however, stay open throughout the year. All companies are obliged to equip you with lifejackets (*gilets*) and teach you basic safety procedures. You must be able to swim, and children under 5 years old are not allowed aboard.

Horseriding

Horseriding is an excellent way of enjoying the countryside. Practically every town in the Dordogne and Lot, and many farms, have equestrian centres (*centres équestres*) where you can ride with a guide or unaccompanied – depending on your level of experience – on the marked riding trails that span the region. Local and departmental tourist offices can provide details, or you can contact the Comité National du Tourisme Équestre (W ffe.com).

Rock climbing and caving

In the limestone regions of the Dordogne and the Lot **rock climbing** (*escalade*) and **caving** (*spéléologie*) are popular activities. Several local canoe-rental outfits, such as Couleurs Périgord (☎05 53 30 37 61, 🌐ladordogneencanoe.com) and Kalapca (☎05 65 24 21 01, 🌐kalapca.com) offer beginners' courses and half-day or full-day outings in the region. Further information is available from tourist offices or the national federations: Fédération Française de la Montagne et de l'Escalade (🌐ffme.fr) for rock climbing, and Fédération Française de Spéléologie (🌐ffspeleo.fr) for caving.

Swimming

There are several pebbly beaches which give access to the water along the Dordogne and Lot rivers, but it's often too shallow or fast-flowing to be ideal for **swimming**. An alternative is to head for one of the natural or man-made lakes which pepper the region. Many have leisure centres (*bases de plein airs*) at which you can rent pedaloes, windsurfing equipment and dinghies, as well as larger boats and jet-skis (on the bigger reservoirs). It's worth noting, however, that in high summer, when the water is at its lowest, pollution warnings have been issued on rivers and lakes in the region. Check with local tourist authorities for the current situation. Many hotels and campsites also have their own swimming pools for guests to make use of. One thing to be aware of is that some impose strict rules on what sort of swimming costumes can and can't be worn: for men, long or baggy swimming shorts are often outlawed.

Rugby

Despite the influence of France's footballing prowess, **rugby** remains the most important and closely followed field game throughout this region. In season (mid-September to mid-May) virtually every town worth its salt boasts a team and if you go along to a match you'll soon get swept up in the camaraderie; unless it's a final, tickets are easy to buy at the gate and are reasonably priced (€10–15). The top two teams to look out for are Sporting Union Agen and Brive, which both play in the First Division (Top 14).

Boules

Once the preserve of elderly men in berets, **boules**, and its variant *pétanque* (in which contestants must keep both feet on the ground when throwing), has been growing in popularity in recent years and broadening its appeal to include more young people and women. There is even a world championship and talk – not all of it in jest – of getting *boules* recognized as an Olympic sport.

Shopping and markets

The quickest and most convenient places to shop are the hypermarkets and supermarkets you'll find in and around every major town; even some villages have a "superette". But more interesting by far are the specialist food shops and, of course, the markets which are still held at least once a week in towns throughout the region.

Many of these **markets** have been held on the same day for centuries. One of the region's biggest and best is that at Sarlat, but the competition is fierce and it's worth including several market days in your itinerary. Other terrific markets are held in Brantôme, Brive, Cahors, Le Bugue, Périgueux and Ribérac, among many other towns and villages. In recent years the hordes of visitors in summer have meant an inevitable increase in the volume of generic tack sold at the biggest markets, but they still boast more than enough enticing local produce and genuine craftsmanship to be unmissable.

In winter time, you'll also find most towns in the Dordogne and Lot hold *marchés aux gras* when whole fattened livers of duck and goose are put up for sale alongside the other edible bits of the fowl. Often these events double up as truffle markets and are one of the few places in France where **bargaining** is acceptable. For a list of the region's most important and interesting markets, see the boxes at the beginning of each chapter of the Guide.

Travelling with children

The Dordogne and Lot region is one of the most appealing parts of France for family holidays. There are lots of child-friendly activities and sights that will appeal to kids, from visiting castles to exploring some of the caves

In the summer season, almost every tourist town and sight of note puts on special **children's activities**, which can range from kid-oriented guided tours to pottery and art classes, face-painting and more. Ask at tourist offices for details of what's on.

In terms of **accommodation**, most hotels have one or two family rooms and can provide cots. *Chambres d'hôtes* are less predictable and it's best to

THE DORDOGNE AND LOT FOR KIDS

Caves The Grotte de Villars (see p.68) boasts rock formations, wall paintings, a garden of cavemen and lots of children's activities. At the Grotte de Rouffignac (see p.138) you can ride a miniature train underground and admire ancient wall art, while the Gouffre de Padirac (see p.186) offers a boat ride along a subterranean river and spectacular stalagmites.

Castles The region's châteaux are often a delight for kids, with child-friendly activities in the holidays: at Château de Castelnaud (see p.158), kids can even have a go at firing a trebuchet siege engine.

Boating Keep a lookout for kingfishers and damsel flies while riding a silent electric boat down the Dronne from Montagrier (see p.60).

Gardens Check out the giant maze, fountains, playground and craft activities for children at the Jardins Suspendus de Marqueyssac (see p.157).

ask in advance; we've highlighted family-friendly places throughout the Guide. Camping is very popular with French families, and for good reason: most of the better sites offer swimming pools, activity centres and sometimes even kids' clubs.

With the exception of some gourmet places (where you probably wouldn't want to eat with kids in tow anyway), most **restaurants** have children's menus and highchairs, and in general, the French take a laidback approach to eating out with children.

Baby-changing facilities can be found at all the bigger tourist sights, while at smaller, less frequented places, space will be made available for you to change a baby if you ask. Most restaurants, however, don't have dedicated changing facilities.

Formula milk, **baby food**, nappies and other necessities are available in all supermarkets, chemists and most small shops.

Travel essentials

Costs

Although **prices** have been rising steadily in recent years, the Dordogne and Lot is not an outrageously expensive place to visit, especially compared to the regions further south towards the coast, and east towards the Alps. When and where you go, however, will make a difference: in prime tourist spots, hotel rates can go up by a third during July and August.

For a reasonably comfortable existence, including a double room in a mid-range hotel, lunch and dinner in a restaurant, plus moving around, café stops and museum visits, you need to allow a **daily budget** of around €120/£100/US$130 per person based on two people sharing a room. But by counting the pennies, staying at youth hostels or camping, and being strong-willed about extra cups

of coffee and doses of culture, you could manage on around €70/£60/US$80 a day each, to include a cheap restaurant meal.

Youth and student discounts

Once obtained, various official and quasi-official youth/student ID cards soon pay for themselves in savings. Full-time students are eligible for the **International Student ID Card** (ISIC; Ⓦ isic.org or Ⓦ statravel.co.uk in the UK), which entitles you to special air, rail and bus fares, and discounts at museums, theatres and other attractions. It also gives you access to a free 24-hour helpline to call in the event of a medical or legal emergency. You have to be 25 or under to qualify for the **International Youth Travel Card**, while teachers are eligible for the **International Teacher Card**, offering similar discounts. Both are available through universities and student travel specialists such as STA Travel, USIT and Travel CUTS.

Taxes

The majority of goods and services in France are subject to **value-added tax** (*taxe sur la valeur ajoutée* or *TVA*), usually at a rate of 19.6 percent, which is included in the price. Most local authorities also levy a **tourism tax** on hotel and *chambre d'hôte* accommodation – called a *taxe de séjour* – generally not more than €1 per person per night depending on the category; in some areas this tax only applies in peak season. While the tax is not included in room rates, it must be clearly indicated as a separate item.

Crime and personal safety

In the more rural parts of the Dordogne and Lot region, crime is extremely rare. However, it obviously makes sense to take the normal **precautions**: don't flash wads of notes around; carry your bag or wallet securely; never leave cameras, mobile phones or other valuables lying around; and park your car overnight in a monitored parking garage or, at the very least, on a busy and well-lit street. It's wise to keep a separate record of bank card numbers, and the phone numbers for cancelling them. Finally, make sure you have a good travel insurance policy (see opposite).

There are two main types of **police** in France: the Police Nationale and the Gendarmerie Nationale. The former deals with all crime, parking and traffic affairs within large and mid-sized towns, where you will find them in the Commissariat de Police. The Gendarmerie Nationale covers the rural areas.

If you need to **report a theft**, go to the local Gendarmerie or Commissariat de Police (addresses of commissariats are given in the Guide for the major towns), where they will fill out a *constat de vol*. The first thing they'll ask for is your passport, and vehicle documents if relevant. Although the police are not always as cooperative as they might be, it is their duty to assist you if you've lost your passport or all your money. As in most European countries, the police generally won't do more than a cursory investigation into car break-ins.

If you have an **accident** while driving, you must fill in and sign a *constat d'accident* (declaration form) or, if another car is also involved, a *constat aimable* (jointly agreed declaration); these forms should be provided with the car's insurance documents. The police can impose on-the-spot fines for minor **driving offences** and take away your licence for anything more serious.

Drugs

Drug use is just as prevalent in France as anywhere else in Europe – and just as risky. People caught smuggling or possessing drugs, even just a few grams of marijuana, are liable to find themselves in jail. Should you be **arrested** on any charge, you have the right to contact your consulate, though don't expect much sympathy.

Racism

Unfortunately, **racist attitudes** are not uncommon in France, particularly towards the country's Arab and black communities. Visitors to the Dordogne and Lot are unlikely to experience aggression or open hostility, but may encounter an unwelcome degree of curiosity or suspicion from shopkeepers, hoteliers, bar and club owners and the like. Equally, given the current political climate and the pervasiveness of racial profiling, especially in the light of recent terrorist activity in France, it may be a good idea for non-white visitors to comply with French law and carry passport ID at all times. Note also that whilst wearing a **niqab** – the full-face veil – is illegal in France (police will issue on-the-spot fines), the so-called **burkini ban**, which prohibits the wearing of full-body swimsuits in public – does not apply in the Dordogne and Lot.

Electricity

The **electricity** supply in France is almost always 220V, using plugs with two round pins. If you need a transformer, it's a good idea to buy one before leaving home, though you can find them in big department stores.

Entry requirements

Citizens of the European Union (EU), and most of those from European countries not in the EU, can travel freely in France, while those from Australia, Canada, New Zealand and the United States, among other countries, do not need a visa for a stay of up to ninety days. However, the situation can change and it's advisable to check with your nearest French embassy or consulate before departure.

All non-EU citizens who plan to remain longer than ninety days should apply for a **long-stay visa**, for which you have to show proof of – among other things – a regular income or sufficient funds to support yourself and medical insurance. For further information about visa regulations consult the Ministry of Foreign Affairs website: ⓦdiplomatie .gouv.fr.

Health

Visitors to the Dordogne and Lot region have little to worry about as far as **health** is concerned. No vaccinations are required, there are no nasty diseases to be wary of and tap water is safe to drink. The worst that's likely to happen is a case of sunburn or an upset stomach from eating too much rich food – or a hangover from all that wonderful wine. If you do need treatment, however, you should be in good hands: the French healthcare system is rated one of the best in the world.

Under the French health system, all services, including doctor's consultations, prescribed medicines, hospital stays and ambulance call-outs, incur a charge which you have to pay upfront. **EU citizens** are entitled to a refund (usually between 70 and 80 percent), providing the doctor is government registered (*un médecin conventionné*), on presentation of a **European Health Insurance Card** (EHIC; *Carte Européenne d'Assurance Maladie*; Ⓦehic.org.uk). Note that everyone in the family, including children, must have their own cards, which are free. At the time of writing, British citizens were still covered by the EHIC scheme, but given the 2016 Brexit vote, checking the situation online is advisable before you travel.

While the EHIC guarantees free or reduced-cost medical care in the event of minor injuries and emergencies, it won't cover every eventuality – you'll have to pay for X-rays, lab tests and the like, as well as hospital stays, so travel insurance (see below) is also essential. If you don't have an EHIC card, you'll be charged for everything and will have to claim it back from your insurance, so get receipts. All **non-EU visitors** should also ensure they have adequate medical insurance cover.

For minor complaints go to a **pharmacie**, signalled by an illuminated green cross. You'll find at least one in every small town and even some villages. They keep normal shop hours (roughly Mon–Sat 9am–noon & 3–6/7pm), though some stay open late and, in larger towns, at least one (known as the *pharmacie de garde*) is open 24 hours according to a rota; details are displayed in all pharmacy windows (although you might actually have to phone the pharmacy to get someone to come and open up).

For anything more serious you can get the name of a **doctor** from a pharmacy, local police station, tourist office or your hotel. Alternatively, look under "Médecins" in the Yellow Pages (*Pages Jaunes*) phone directory. A consultation fee is in the region of €23–25. You'll be given a statement of treatment (*Feuille de Soins*) for later insurance claims. Any prescriptions will be fulfilled by a pharmacy and must be paid for; little price stickers (*vignettes*) from each medicine will be stuck on the *Feuille de Soins*.

In serious **emergencies** you will always be admitted to the nearest general hospital (*centre hospitalier*). Phone numbers and addresses are given in the Guide for all the main cities. The national number for calling an ambulance is ☎15.

Insurance

Even though EU citizens are entitled to some health-care privileges in France, it's advisable to take out a **travel insurance** policy to cover against theft, loss and illness or injury. Before paying for a new policy, however, it's worth checking whether you are already covered: some all-risks home insurance may cover your possessions when overseas, and many private medical schemes include cover when abroad. In Canada, provincial health plans usually provide partial cover for medical mishaps overseas. Students will often find that their student health coverage extends during the vacations and for one term beyond the date of last enrolment.

A typical travel insurance **policy** will provide cover for the loss of baggage, tickets and – up to a certain limit – cash or cheques, as well as cancellation or curtailment of your journey. Most policies exclude so-called dangerous sports unless an extra premium is paid: in the Dordogne and Lot this would include rock climbing and pot-holing and sometimes such apparently benign activities as canoeing, so it's best to check the small print carefully. Many policies can be chopped and changed to exclude coverage you don't need.

If you need to **make a claim**, you should keep receipts for medicines and medical treatment, and in the event you have anything stolen, you must obtain an official statement from the police (called *un constat de vol*).

ROUGH GUIDES TRAVEL INSURANCE

Rough Guides has teamed up with WorldNomads.com to offer great travel insurance deals. Policies are available to residents of over 150 countries, with cover for a wide range of adventure sports, 24hr emergency assistance, high levels of medical and evacuation cover and a stream of travel safety information. Roughguides.com users can take advantage of their policies online 24/7, from anywhere in the world – even if you're already travelling. And since plans often change when you're on the road, you can extend your policy and even claim online. Roughguides.com users who buy travel insurance with WorldNomads.com can also leave a positive footprint and donate to a community development project. For more information, go to Ⓦroughguides.com /travel-insurance.

Internet

Wi-fi is available in even the cheapest French hotels and *chambres d'hôtes* as well as the majority of campsites (bar basic farm sites), and is almost always free; all accommodation listed in this Guide has wi-fi unless otherwise stated. Most cafés also have wi-fi available free to customers.

Laundry

Laundries are still reasonably common in French towns – just ask in your hotel, or the tourist office, or look in the phone book under "*Laveries automatiques*" or "*Laveries en libre-service*". They are usually unattended, and while some have machines for changing notes, it's prudent to come armed with small change. Washing powder (*la lessive*) is always available on site. Machines are graded in different wash sizes, costing in the region of €4 to €5 for 7kg. Most hotels forbid doing any laundry in your room, though you should get away with just one or two small items.

LGBT travellers

In general, France has a more liberal attitude to homosexuality than many other European countries. The legal age of consent is 15 and civil unions between same-sex couples were made legal in 1999; gay marriage and adoptions by same-sex couples were legalized in 2013.

On a day-to-day level, the French mostly consider sexuality to be a private matter, and homophobic assaults are extremely rare. Nevertheless, **gays** tend to be discreet outside specific gay venues, **lesbians** even more so. You can expect to be received with tolerance, but not necessarily a warm welcome.

USEFUL CONTACTS

Spartacus International Gay Guide Ⓦ spartacusworld.com.
An extensive section on France, with some info for lesbians.
Têtu Ⓦ tetu.com. France's best-selling gay/lesbian magazine, with events listings and contact addresses; you can buy it in bookshops, newsagents or through their website, which is also an excellent source of information.

Mail

French **post offices**, known as La Poste and identified by bright yellow-and-blue signs, are generally open from around 9am to 5pm or 6pm Monday to Friday, and 9am to noon on Saturday. Those in smaller towns and villages usually also close from noon to 2pm.

Stamps (*timbres*) are sold at *tabacs* and newsagents as well as post offices. Visit Ⓦ laposte.fr for information on postal rates. **Postboxes** are bright yellow; make sure, where necessary, to put your letter in the box marked *étranger* (abroad).

Maps

In addition to the **maps** in this guide and the various free town plans you'll be offered along the way, the one extra map you might want is a good, up-to-date road map of the region. The best are the regional maps produced by Michelin (Ⓦ michelinonline.co.uk) and IGN (Ⓦ ign.fr). To cover the area encompassed by this guide, IGN's Dordogne map (1:200,000), and Michelin's Aquitaine and Midi-Pyrénées maps (1:200,000) are all worth seeking out. Alternatively, both companies issue large spiral-bound road atlases covering the whole of France at around the same scale.

If you're planning to walk or cycle, it's well worth investing in the more detailed IGN maps. The Carte de Randonnée (1:25,000) series is specifically designed for walkers, while the Carte de Promenade (1:100,000) is ideal for cyclists.

Money

France's currency is the **euro** (€), which is divided into 100 cents (also called *centimes*). There are seven notes – in denominations of 5, 10, 20, 50, 100, 200 and 500 euros – and eight different coins: 1, 2, 5, 10, 20 and 50 cents, and 1 and 2 euros. It's very rare to see anything larger than a €50 note; staff in shops and restaurants may refuse to accept larger denominations. Consult Ⓦ xe.com for up-to-date **exchange rates** with the euro.

The best way to access money in France is to use your **credit** or **debit card** to withdraw cash from an **ATM** (known as *un distributeur de billets* or *un point argent*); most machines give instructions in several European languages. Note that there is often a transaction fee, so it's more efficient to take out a sizeable sum each time rather than making lots of small withdrawals.

Credit and debit cards are widely accepted in shops, hotels and restaurants, though some smaller establishments don't accept cards, or only for sums above a certain threshold. Visa – called Carte Bleue in France – is almost universally recognized, followed by MasterCard (also known as EuroCard). American Express ranks a lot lower.

You can **change cash** at most banks and main post offices. There are money-exchange counters (*bureaux de change*) at French airports, major train stations and usually one or two in city centres as well, though they don't always offer the best exchange rates.

Newspapers and radio

The large number of Brits living in France has led to an active English-language press in the country. The main monthly **newspaper** in English is *The Connexion* (Ⓦ connexionfrance.com), available from newsagents (*maisons de la presse*) and, in larger towns, from streetside kiosks.

As for **radio**, Radio Liberté (Ⓦ radioliberte.fr) broadcasts an English-language show with news during the week.

Opening hours and public holidays

Basic **hours of business** are 9am to noon and 2 to 6pm. Small food shops often don't reopen till halfway through the afternoon, closing around 7.30 or 8pm, just before the evening meal. Supermarkets also tend to stay open to at least 7.30pm.

The standard **closing day** is Sunday, though some food shops, particularly bakeries (boulangeries) and newsagents are open in the morning. Many independent shops and businesses, particularly in the rural areas, also close on one other day a week.; it's often a Monday but this varies from town to town.

Core **banking hours** are Monday to Friday 9am to noon and 2 to 6pm. Some branches close on Monday, while others stay open at midday and may also open on Saturday morning. All are closed on Sundays and public holidays.

Most **tourist offices** are open all day every day throughout July and August, but hours outside these months vary considerably. **Museums** tend to open around 9.30 or 10am, close for lunch from noon until 1 or 2pm, and then run through to 5 or 6pm. In summer some stay open all day and close later, while in winter, many open only in the afternoon. Museum closing days are usually Monday or Tuesday, sometimes both. Many state-owned museums have one day of the week or month when they're free or half price.

Churches are generally open from around 8am to dusk, but may close at lunchtime and are

PUBLIC HOLIDAYS
January 1 New Year's Day
March/April Easter Monday
Ascension Day (forty days after Easter)
Pentecost or Whitsun (seventh Sunday after Easter)
May 1 Labour Day
May 8 Victory in Europe (VE) Day 1945
July 14 Bastille Day
August 15 Assumption of the Virgin Mary
November 1 All Saints' Day
November 11 Armistice Day 1918
December 25 Christmas Day

reserved for worshippers during services (times of which will usually be posted on the door). Country churches are increasingly kept locked; there may be a note on the door saying where to get the key, usually from the priest's house (*le presbytère*) or someone else living nearby, or from the *mairie*.

France celebrates eleven **public holidays** (*jours fériés*), when banks and most shops and businesses (though not necessarily restaurants), and some museums, are closed.

Phones

French **telephone numbers** have ten digits. Those beginning ☏ 0800 or 0805 are free-dial numbers; ☏ 081 and ☏ 086 are charged as a local call; and anything else beginning ☏ 08 is premium-rated. Numbers starting ☏ 06 and 07 are for mobiles.

Payphones (*cabines*) are increasingly rare, but where you do find one, you can make and receive domestic and international **calls** – look for the number in the top right-hand corner of the information panel. The vast majority of public phones require a **phone card** (*télécarte*); they're available (in 50 and 120 units; €7.50 and €15 respectively) from *tabacs* and newsagents, but these days you may have to hunt around for a shop that still sells them. You can also use **credit cards** in many call boxes.

CALLING HOME FROM ABROAD

Note that the initial zero is omitted from the area code when dialling the UK, Ireland, Australia and New Zealand from abroad.

Australia international access code + 61
New Zealand international access code + 64
UK international access code + 44
US and Canada international access code + 1
Republic of Ireland international access code + 353
South Africa international access code + 27

Mobile phones

If you have a non-European mobile phone and want to use it in France, contact your phone provider before leaving home to check whether it will work locally, and what the call charges are.

French mobile phones operate on the European GSM standard, so many **US cellphones** won't work in France unless they are "tri-band". The quickest and cheapest option is probably to change your phone and/or service provider.

In June 2016, **roaming charges** were drastically reduced for mobile phone tariffs that originate in an EU country, and will be abolished completely in 2017. The situation with British mobile phones might change following the 2016 Brexit vote; check with your service provider.

Smoking

Smoking is banned in all enclosed public spaces, including museums, hotels, restaurants, bars and nightclubs.

Time

France lies in the **Central European Time Zone** (GMT+1): one hour ahead of the UK, six hours ahead of Eastern Standard Time, and nine hours ahead of Pacific Standard Time. Between April and October France is eight hours behind eastern Australia and ten hours behind New Zealand; from November to March it is ten hours behind south-eastern Australia and twelve hours behind New Zealand. Daylight Saving Time (GMT+2) in France lasts from the last Sunday of March to the last Sunday of October.

Tourist information

The **French Government Tourist Office** (Maison de la France, Ⓦ france.fr) increasingly refers you to their website for information, though they still produce a number of useful brochures. For information specific to the Dordogne and Lot region, contact the regional or departmental tourist offices before you leave home.

Tourist offices

In the Dordogne and Lot region you'll find a tourist office – usually an **Office du Tourisme** (OT) but sometimes a **Syndicat d'Initiative** (SI) – in practically every town and many villages (addresses, contact details and opening hours are detailed in the Guide). For the practical purposes of visitors, there is little difference between them; sometimes they share premises and call themselves an OTSI. In small villages where there is no OT or SI, the *mairie* (town hall) will offer a similar service.

All these offices are well stocked with information, both locally and regionally, including hotels and restaurants, leisure activities, bike rental, markets and festivals, while those in the wine regions will provide information on local vineyards, and in peak season may also conduct vineyard tours; many can also book accommodation for you.

Most offices can provide a town/village plan and/ or walking leaflets, while an increasing number now provide audioguides (with English language) for self-guided town or village walks, though there will be a charge for this. Most, too, have maps and local walking guides on sale.

REGIONAL AND DEPARTMENTAL TOURIST OFFICES

Aquitaine Ⓦ tourisme-aquitaine.fr.
Corrèze Ⓦ tourismecorreze.com.
Dordogne Ⓦ dordogne-perigord-tourisme.fr.
Lot Ⓦ tourisme-lot.com.
Lot-et-Garonne Ⓦ tourisme-lotetgaronne.com.

Travellers with disabilities

The French authorities have been making a concerted effort to improve facilities for **disabled travellers**. Though haphazard parking habits and stepped village streets remain serious obstacles for anyone with mobility problems, ramps and other forms of access are gradually being added to hotels, museums and other public buildings. All but the oldest hotels are required to adapt at least one room to be **wheelchair accessible**, and a growing number of *chambres d'hôtes* are doing likewise. Accessible hotels, sights and other facilities are gradually being inspected and, if they fulfil certain criteria, issued with a "Tourisme & Handicap" certificate. Listings produced by Logis (see p.28) and Gîtes de France (see p.28) indicate places with specially adapted rooms. It's essential to double-check when booking that the facilities meet your needs.

Most **train stations** now make provision for travellers with reduced mobility. Spaces for wheelchairs are available in first-class carriages of all **TGVs** for the price of the regular, second-class fare; note that these must be booked in advance. For other trains, a wheelchair symbol in the timetable indicates services offering special on-board facilities, though it's best to double-check when booking. SNCF also runs a scheme called Accès Plus, through which they assist travellers with disabilities, including ticket reservations, baggage assistance and a full reception service. You must, though, get in contact with them 48 hours in advance. Full details are on the website ⓦ accessibilite.sncf.com, which also includes a downloadable guide.

Drivers of **taxis** are legally obliged to help passengers in and out of the vehicle and to carry guide dogs. Ask at the local tourist office or *mairie* for further information on specially adapted taxis. All the big **car rental** agencies can provide automatic cars if you reserve sufficiently far in advance, while most agencies should also be able to able to offer cars with hand controls on request – again, make sure you give them plenty of notice.

If you can read French, there are some other excellent guides to make use of. The association Vacances Accessibles, (ⓦ www.vacances-accessibles .apf.asso.fr) produces the *Handi-plus Aquitaine* (ⓦ handiplusaquitaine.fr) booklet, which outlines suitable itineraries across the whole region. *Handi-tourisme*, published annually by Petit Futé (ⓦ petit fute.com) covers the whole of France.

For general **information** about accessibility, special programmes and discounts contact one of the organizations listed below before you leave home.

CONTACTS FOR TRAVELLERS WITH DISABILITIES

Access Tourisme Service ⓦ access-tourisme.com. Organized and customized holidays for people with special needs, including adapted vehicle rental, accessible hotels and even travel companions if required.

Access Travel ⓦ access-travel.co.uk. Tour operator that can arrange flights, transfer and accommodation, including *gîtes* in Aquitaine. This is a small business, personally checking out places before recommendation.

Accessible Journeys ⓦ disabilitytravel.com. Well-established travel agent offering both group tours and advice on independent travel for disabled travellers.

APF (Association des Paralysés de France) ⓦ apf.asso.fr. National association that can answer general enquiries and put you in touch with their departmental offices.

Work and study in the Dordogne and Lot

EU citizens are free to work in France on the same basis as a French citizen, so don't have to apply for a residence or work permit. Most **non-EU citizens**, however, will need a work permit (*autorisation de travail*) and a residence permit along with a whole host of other papers; contact your nearest French consulate or, if already in France, your local *mairie* or *préfecture* to check what rules apply in your particular situation. Whatever your nationality, once you have a work permit, you are entitled to exactly the same conditions as French workers, including the national **minimum wage** (SMIC), currently set at €9.67 per hour.

When **looking for a job**, a good starting point is to read one of the books on working abroad published by Vacation Work (ⓦ vacationwork.co.uk). You could also try the websites ⓦ monster.fr and ⓦ jobs-ete.com; the latter focuses on summer jobs for students. Once in France, you'll find "Offres d'Emploi" (Job Offers) in the national and regional papers, or there's the national employment agency, *pôle emploi* (ⓦ pole-emploi.fr), with offices all over France and which advertises temporary jobs in all fields. Non-EU citizens will have to show a work permit to apply for any of their jobs.

A degree and a TEFL (Teaching English as a Foreign Language) or similar qualifications are normally required for **English-language teaching** posts. The online *EL Gazette* newsletter (ⓦ elgazette .com) is a useful source of information, as is the annual *Teaching English Abroad* (available from online retailers). The TEFL website (ⓦ tefl.com) has a good database of English-teaching vacancies.

Foreign students pay the same as French nationals to enrol for a course and you'll be eligible for subsidized accommodation, meals and all the student reductions. French **universities** are fairly informal, but there are strict entry requirements, including an exam in French for undergraduate degrees, but not for postgraduate courses. For full details and prospectuses, contact the Cultural Service of any French embassy or consulate.

FURTHER CONTACTS

AFS Intercultural Programs ⓦ afs.org. Opportunities for high-school students to study in France for a term or full academic year, living with host families.

Campus France ⓦ campusfrance.org. Government-run agency set up to promote French higher education abroad.

Erasmus ⓦ britishcouncil.org. EU-run student exchange programme enabling students at participating universities in Britain and Ireland to study in one of 31 European countries.

Language Courses Abroad ⓦ languagesabroad.co.uk. Long- or short-term language courses throughout France, some combined with other activities such as cookery and skiing.

World Wide Opportunities on Organic Farms (WWOOF) ⓦ wwoof.fr. Volunteer to work on an organic farm in return for board and lodging.

Périgueux and the north

47 Périgueux

57 Brantôme

59 The lower Dronne valley

65 La Double

66 The Northern Périgord Vert

70 Jumilhac-le-Grand

71 Excideuil

73 Hautefort and around

76 Brive-la-Gaillarde

80 Arnac-Pompadour

82 Turenne

83 Collonges-la-Rouge

CATHÉDRALE ST-FRONT, PÉRIGUEUX

1

Périgueux and the north

The north of the Dordogne *département* is its least known and most rural corner, a land with few people and large tracts of pasture and woodland, its intimate green valleys lending it the name of the Périgord Vert. It's a region that will appeal to those who love peace and quiet, picnics in flower meadows, somnolent villages and gentle countryside ambles. But there is some urban excitement to be found here. With its searing-white old town, pineapple-capped cathedral and superb Roman remains, Périgueux – capital of both Périgord Blanc and of the whole *département* – is an easy city to fall for, but really it's the countryside around that holds the region's best attractions.

One of the loveliest parts of the entire Dordogne is the **Dronne valley**, which shadows the River Isle to the north of Périgueux. At **Brantôme** the Dronne's still, water-lilied surface mirrors the limes and weeping willows along its banks, before flowing on past the twin fortresses of **Bourdeilles** to **Ribérac**, a market town beloved by the British, and **Aubeterre-sur-Dronne** just over the border in the Charente region. As at Brantôme, the river-carved cliffs at Aubeterre were hollowed out into primitive churches by twelfth-century monks. Others built dozens of little Romanesque churches on the sunny hills around, while south of the Dronne their successors helped tame the marshy, insalubrious plateau of **La Double**. In doing so they created the pine and chestnut forests that blanket the area today.

Upstream from Brantôme, two tributaries of the Dronne lead northeast through woodlands and butterfly-speckled pastures to the tiny village of **St-Jean-de-Côle** and the decorative, Renaissance pile of **Château de Puyguilhem**. Further northeast, there's no mistaking the warlike nature of the hulking granite castle at **Jumilhac-le-Grand**. As a break from the châteaux trail, connoisseurs of foie gras should head south to the little museum in **Thiviers**, while truffle-lovers might like to press on to **Sorges**, where there's a marked path through truffle country and another small museum to explain it all. These two towns are close to the southeast border of the Périgord Vert, where the scenery becomes softer towards the lovely Auvézère valley. Here, in a spectacular spot high over the river, the **Château de Hautefort** reveals the elegance of past lives.

East of Hautefort, across the border in the Corrèze *département*, **Brive-la-Gaillarde** lies on an important crossroads and provides an alternative to Périgueux as a gateway to the region. For such a large city, Brive has a surprisingly compact and enjoyable old centre with more than enough to detain you for a day or two. The countryside around also holds a few surprises, from the National Stud at **Arnac-Pompadour** to the appropriately named **Collonges-la-Rouge**, a village built with rich red sandstone, and neighbouring **Turenne**, another absurdly pretty village capped by the substantial remains of its eponymous fortress.

Festivals, events and markets p.49
Daumesnil: the peg-leg general p.52
Follow the river p.54
Markets in Périgueux p.57
Activities in Brantôme p.59
Boating with damselflies p.60

La Voie Verte p.66
Foie gras p.69
The black diamonds of Périgord p.72
Rugby in Brive p.76
Brive's markets and fairs p.79
Visiting the National Stud p.81

BRANTÔME

Highlights

❶ Périgueux From prehistoric and Gallo-Roman remains via Renaissance-era mansions to the cathedral's Byzantine extravagance, Périgueux has something for everyone. **See p.47**

❷ Brantôme Stroll the tree-shaded waterways, bridges and parks of this handsome town, then paddle a kayak along the lily-strewn Dronne. **See p.57**

❸ Bourdeilles Perched precariously over the River Dronne, the château of Bourdeilles guards one of the prettiest villages in the Dordogne. **See p.60**

❹ Église Souterraine Saint-Jean Explore the cool, dark cavern of Aubeterre's mysterious subterranean church. **See p.64**

❺ Grotte de Villars A rare opportunity to see displays of stalagmites and stalactites alongside prehistoric wall paintings in these wonderful caves. **See p.68**

❻ Château de Hautefort Built to rival the châteaux of the Loire, Hautefort stands out for its elegance and architectural harmony. **See p.73**

❼ Brive-la-Gaillarde Vibrant, energetic and with a beautifully restored city centre, rugby-loving Brive is worth a day's exploration. **See p.76**

HIGHLIGHTS ARE MARKED ON THE MAP ON P.46

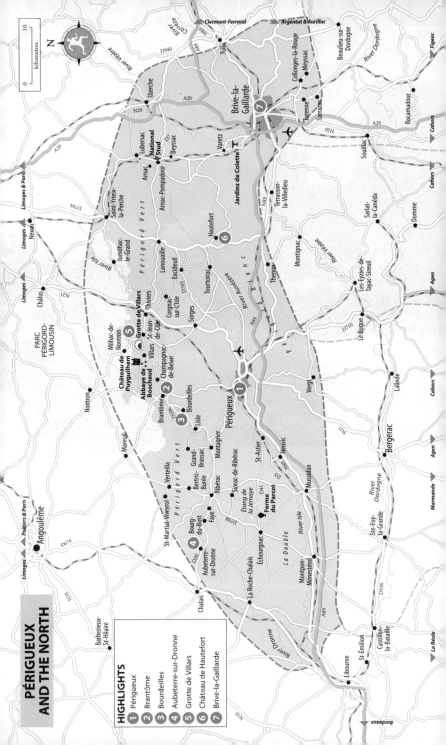

PÉRIGUEUX AND THE NORTH

HIGHLIGHTS

1 Périgueux
2 Brantôme
3 Bourdeilles
4 Aubeterre-sur-Dronne
5 Grotte de Villars
6 Château de Hautefort
7 Brive-la-Gaillarde

Both Périgueux and Brive are major transport hubs, the latter especially so now that there are **flights** to the UK to and from Brive-Vallée de la Dordogne airport. In addition both cities have frequent flights to Paris. Périgueux and Brive also have reasonable **train** connections, both to other towns in the region (such as Les Eyzies, Thiviers, Bergerac and Sarlat-la-Canéda) and to destinations beyond the Dordogne. Local **bus** services throughout the region, however, are very sporadic – we've detailed those that do exist at the relevant points in the text, but as many of these are geared towards schoolchildren to tie in with drop-off and pick-up times, they're not much of an option for visitors – a car is pretty much essential if you wish to explore the more remote areas.

Périgueux

PÉRIGUEUX, capital of the Dordogne, might be the biggest urban centre in the Dordogne, but at heart it's just an attractive market town for a province made rich by tourism and specialized farming. Its name derives from the Petrocorii, the local Gaulish tribe, but it was the Romans who transformed it into an important settlement. While a few **Roman remains** survive, it is the city's **medieval and Renaissance core** that gives Périgueux its particular appeal. Pretty, sun-bleached stone-flagged squares and a maze of narrow alleys harbour richly ornamented merchants' houses, while above it all rises the startlingly white spire of St-Front cathedral, flanked by its cluster of pinnacled, Byzantine domes. It looks best at night – particularly from across the river – when floodlights soften the sharper edges and accentuate its exotic silhouette.

Périgueux's compact **historic centre** – much of it pedestrianized – sits on the west bank of the River Isle, occupying a rough square formed by the river, the tree-shaded cours Tourny to the north, boulevard Michel Montaigne to the west and cours Fénelon to the south. Though the hilltop **Cathédrale St-Front** provides a natural magnet, the surrounding streets hide some particularly fine Renaissance architecture as well as the **Musée d'Art et d'Archéologie du Périgord**, with its collection of Paleolithic tools, and a remnant of **medieval wall**. The main commercial hub is concentrated around rue Taillefer, running from the cathedral west to place Bugeaud, and along pedestrianized rue Limogeanne to the north. At the southwest corner of the old town lies the wide place Francheville, from where rue de la Cité leads westwards towards Périgueux's other principal area of interest, **La Cité**, centred around a rather mutilated church. This is where you'll find the smart Gallo-Roman Museum, **Vesunna**, featuring the foundations of a Roman villa. Everything is within easy walking distance, making it possible to explore the city comfortably in a day or two.

Brief history

Périgueux began life some time after the fourth century BC as a fortified settlement inhabited by the **Petrocorii** ("Four Tribes"), whose craftsmen were noted for their ironwork. After 51 BC, however, the area came under Roman rule and a thriving town known as **Vesunna** (Vésone in French) began to develop, complete with amphitheatre, temples and luxurious villas. By the first century AD its population had reached an estimated twenty thousand, but the glory was shortlived. Vesunna, like many other towns, had neglected its defences under the *pax romana* and was caught unprepared by a succession of **barbarian invasions** in the third century. When Germanic tribes swept through the area in 275 AD, the population used stone from the surrounding civic monuments to construct defensive walls that helped the town survive, but in a much reduced state. As it faded it became known as La Cité des Pétrocores, then simply **La Cité**.

La Cité and Le Puy-St-Front

St Front arrived on the Périgueux scene some time in the fourth century to convert the local population to Christianity. After giving La Cité a new breath of life by founding what eventually became St-Étienne de la Cité cathedral, the saint was later buried on a neighbouring hilltop, or *puy*, where his tomb became a pilgrimage centre. By the

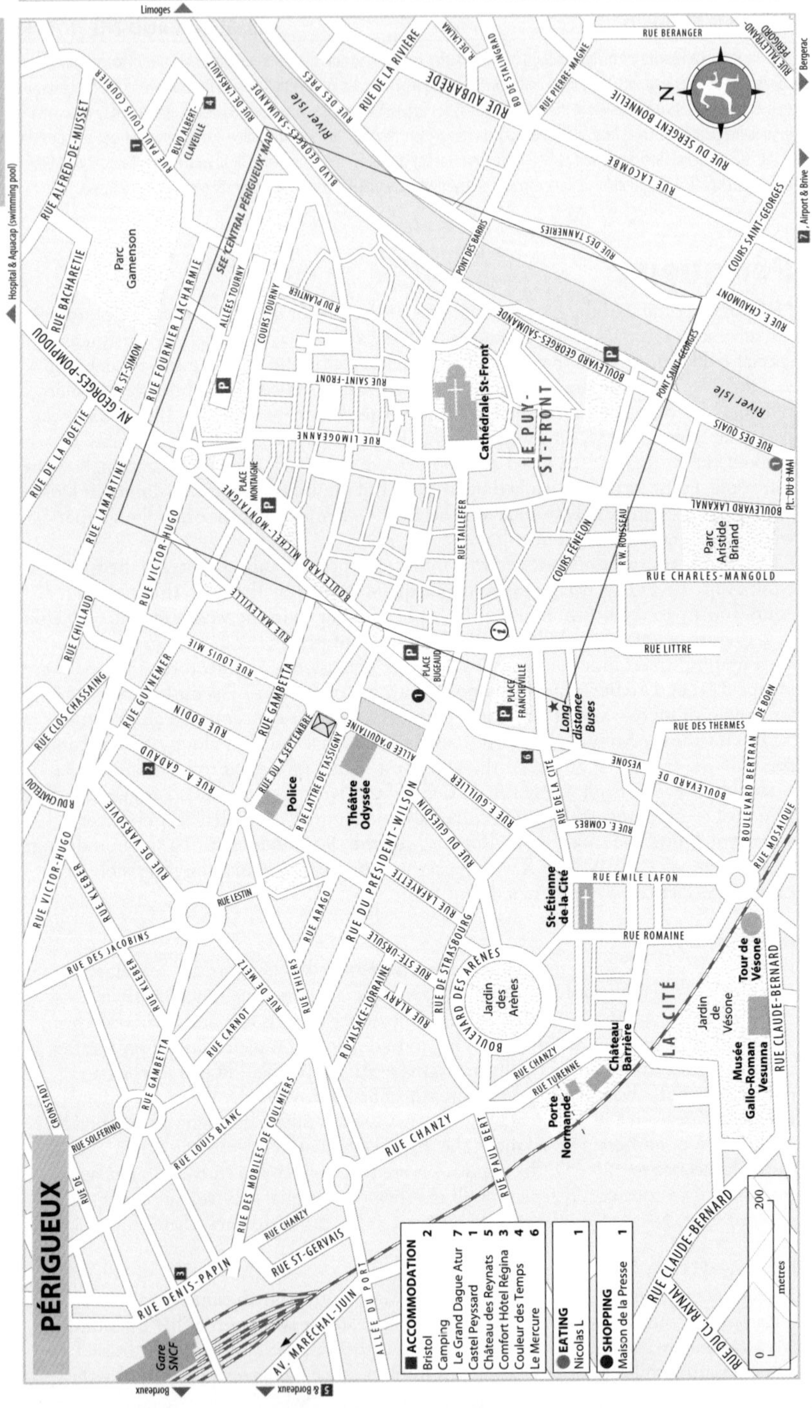

PÉRIGUEUX
ACCOMMODATION
Bristol 2
Camping Le Grand Dague Atur 7
Castel Peyssard 1
Château des Reynats 5
Comfort Hôtel Régina 3
Couleur des Temps 4
Le Mercure 6
EATING
Nicolas L 1
SHOPPING
Maison de la Presse 1
0 200 metres
Limoges
Bergerac
Airport & Brive
Hospital & Aquacap (swimming pool)
Bordeaux
& Bordeaux
River Isle
SEE 'CENTRAL PÉRIGUEUX' MAP
Parc Gamenson
LE PUY-ST-FRONT
Cathédrale St-Front
Parc Aristide Briand
Police
Théâtre Odyssée
Long distance Buses
St-Étienne de la Cité
Jardin des Arènes
Château Barrière
Porte Normande
LA CITÉ
Jardin de Vésone
Tour de Vésone
Musée Gallo-Roman Vesunna
Gare SNCF
PLACE MONTAIGNE
PLACE BUGEAUD
PLACE FRANCHEVILLE
BOULEVARD MICHEL-MONTAIGNE
RUE DU PRÉSIDENT-WILSON
COURS FÉNELON
RUE CHARLES-MANGOLD
BOULEVARD LAKANAL
COURS SAINT-GEORGES
PONT SAINT-GEORGES
PONT DES BARRIS
BOULEVARD GEORGES-SAUMANDE
RUE AUBARÈDE
RUE DE LA RIVIÈRE
AV. GEORGES-POMPIDOU
RUE VICTOR-HUGO
RUE GAMBETTA
RUE CHANZY
RUE CLAUDE-BERNARD
AV. MARÉCHAL-JUIN
RUE DENIS-PAPIN

thirteenth century it had spawned a small but prosperous town of merchants and artisans known as **Le Puy-St-Front**, which began to rival La Cité, now the seat of the counts of Périgord. Though the two communities were joined by an act of union in 1240, they continued to glare at each other over their encircling walls – indeed, at the start of the **Hundred Years War** La Cité sided with the English and Le Puy with France. For a while following the Treaty of Brétigny in 1360, Périgueux, as it was now known, fell under English rule, but the loyal burghers of Le Puy soon rallied to Charles V, and by 1369 Périgueux had been liberated by Bertrand du Guesclin, who then chased the English back towards the coast. Even so, by the early fifteenth century the city was in ruins, its population decimated by war, plague and famine and its buildings crumbling through neglect.

With peace, however, came renewed prosperity and a building boom that left Périgueux its wonderful legacy of **Renaissance** architecture, though much was lost or damaged during the **Wars of Religion**: despite being predominantly Catholic, Périgueux was held by the Protestants for six years after 1575, during which time they vandalized

FESTIVALS, EVENTS AND MARKETS

The list below comprises some of the biggest and more interesting of the **festivals** and **events** in this region. Where we haven't given a specific phone number or website, contact the relevant tourist office.

First weekend in May Bertric Burée, near Ribérac: Snail Festival. Locals celebrate snails by preparing and cooking them in their thousands; they are then consumed throughout the village by locals and tourists alike.

Second weekend in May St-Jean-de-Côle: Les Floralies (ⓦfloralies-saintjean.fr). Longstanding and highly rated festival, where the streets and squares of this pretty village are packed with flower stalls.

Mid-July and August Brive and around: Festival de la Vézère (ⓦfestival-vezere.com). Operas and classical concerts in the open air (bring a picnic) or in various châteaux and churches, including Arnac-Pompadour and Turenne.

July and August Périgueux: La Truffe d'Argent. A festival of French song open to amateurs, which takes place in the streets on Thursday evenings. Entrants are judged and take part in a final on the last night.

Late July Ribérac: Le Grand Souk (ⓦlegrand souk.com). Aimed at fostering young talent from around the world, this five-day international music festival is a vibrant affair.

Late July Périgueux: Mimos, the International Festival of Mime (ⓦmimos.fr). One of the most exciting and innovative contemporary art festivals in France, with

more than 150 artists performing in over fifty shows; mostly street performances but also some ticketed events.

Second week in August Périgueux: New Orleans Music Festival (ⓦmnop-festival.com). Jazz, gospel and blues concerts in a different area of the city each night.

Last week of August Périgueux and around: Sinfonia en Périgord (ⓦsinfonia-en-perigord. com). A five-day celebration of Baroque and Renaissance music, with concerts in various venues in Périgueux, as well as the nearby abbeys of Chancelade and Brantôme and the Château de Bourdeilles.

First weekend in November Brive: La Foire du Livre (❶05 55 92 39 39, ⓦfoiredulivre.net). One of the country's most prestigious literary gatherings. Held in Brive's market hall, it attracts some three hundred authors and artists presenting their new works, and around ten thousand book-lovers keen to snap up signed editions.

Mid-November Périgueux: Salon International du Livre Gourmand (ⓦlivre -gourmand.com). Biennial (2018, 2020 etc) book fair dedicated to wine and gastronomy. Events take place over four days in the theatre (1 allée d'Aquitaine), and include book exhibitions, cooking demonstrations and opportunities to sample the results.

MARKETS

The main weekly **markets** in this region are: Brantôme (Fri); Brive (Tues, Thurs & Sat); Excideuil (Thurs); Périgueux (Wed & Sat); Ribérac (Fri); and Thiviers (Sat). In winter many local towns hold foie gras, truffle and walnut markets, generally on the same day as their weekly market.

1

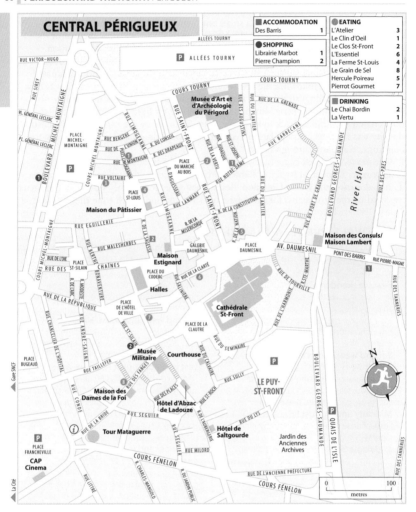

CENTRAL PÉRIGUEUX

■ ACCOMMODATION	
Des Barris	1

● SHOPPING	
Librairie Marbot	1
Pierre Champion	2

● EATING	
L'Atelier	3
Le Clin d'Oeil	1
Le Clos St-Front	2
L'Essentiel	6
La Ferme St-Louis	4
Le Grain de Sel	8
Hercule Poireau	5
Pierrot Gourmet	7

■ DRINKING	
Le Chai Bordin	2
La Vertu	1

many religious buildings, among them St-Étienne de la Cité cathedral. This proved to be the final blow for La Cité, which fell into slow decline, culminating in the transfer of cathedral status to St-Front in 1669.

Modern Périgueux

La Cité and Le Puy-St-Front remained firmly inside their respective walls, separated by open space, up until the beginning of the eighteenth century, after which Périgueux began to expand into today's **modern city**. In the process the medieval walls gave way to wide boulevards, while in the nineteenth century the canal and railway brought further development to what was by then the capital of Périgord. The old city centre was left largely untouched, so that in 1979 some twenty hectares were designated a preservation district. Nevertheless, Périgueux is still the *département*'s most industrialized town: its biggest current claim to fame – a result of 1970s decentralization policies – is the printing works where all French postage stamps are produced.

Le Puy-St-Front

There's still a slight medieval air to **Le Puy-St-Front**, the city's cobbled old quarter. Its confined and cobbled alleys harbour Périgueux's oldest buildings – the former homes of wealthy merchants – as well as the last remaining fragment of the medieval fortifications. Le Puy was originally surrounded by 28 defensive towers, of which only stout, circular **Tour Mataguerre** (July & Aug daily 10am–noon & 2–5pm; €2), protecting the southwest corner, remains. According to legend, it was named after an English captain imprisoned here during the Hundred Years War, but the present structure dates from the late fifteenth century, when it was rebuilt using leper labourers. Although there's little to see inside – just the prison and a simple guardroom above – the views from the roof are worth the climb.

Maison des Dames de la Foi

6 rue des Farges

From beside Tour Mataguerre, rue de la Bride runs into rue des Farges, where you'll find Périgueux's most venerable building, **Maison des Dames de la Foi**, dating from the late twelfth century. The name, "House of the Ladies of Faith", refers to a convent established in the seventeenth century for young Protestant women wishing to convert to Catholicism. Two hundred years earlier, during the Hundred Years War, it's said that du Guesclin stayed here while preparing to liberate nearby Chancelade Abbey from the English. Nowadays, it's a private residence, and you'd be forgiven for walking straight past: the only evidence of its illustrious history is the blocked-in window arches on the ground floor.

Musée Militaire

32 rue des Farges • Mon–Sat 2–6pm • €5 • ☎ 05 53 53 47 36, ⓦ museemilitaire-perigord.fr

At the top of rue des Farges, the **Musée Militaire** contains a vast and rather chaotic array of military memorabilia, one of the foremost such collections in France. Covering everything from the Franco–Prussian War to the Gulf War and today's UN peacekeeping missions, the exhibits are of rather specialized interest, but there are some noteworthy pieces including some poignant sketches of trench life in World War I and memorabilia dating back to the French colonial wars in Indochina (today's Vietnam, Laos and Cambodia), among them a couple of tattered Viet Minh flags.

Rue de l'Aubergerie

Rue de l'Aubergerie is known for its fortified fifteenth-century houses, of which **Hôtel d'Abzac de Ladouze** at no. 16, a typically dour building with an octagonal defensive tower, is the most interesting. The massive blind arch on the wall is evidence of much older foundations, while the incongruous ornamental balustrade above is a Renaissance addition. Note also the cockleshell carving on the side of the tower, indicating that the house once received pilgrims en route to Santiago de Compostela. Further down the street, at no. 6, **Hôtel de Saltgourde** sports an impressive tower complete with a machicolated parapet.

Rue St-Roch to place de la Clautre

Rue St-Roch leads east from below Hôtel d'Abzac past several interesting houses, one retaining its wood-timbered upper storey, others their overhanging latrines or decorative arcaded windows, to **rue du Calvaire**. This was the road that criminals in the Middle Ages climbed on their way to the courthouse, identifiable by its studded Renaissance door. The condemned would then continue to the gallows on **place de la Clautre**, which also served as an execution ground during the Revolution. Nowadays it provides a more peaceful setting for a twice-weekly produce **market** (Wed & Sat mornings) against the backdrop of the cathedral.

Cathédrale St-Front

Place de la Clautre • **Cathedral** Daily 8.30am–6.30pm • Free • **Cloister** Daily 2.15–6pm • €1.50

The domed and coned **Cathédrale St-Front** began life in the sixth century as a simple chapel over the tomb of St Front. Seven hundred years later – by then an important

1

abbey – it was rebuilt after a fire and in the process the architects created one of the most distinctive Byzantine churches in France, modelled on St Mark's in Venice and on Constantinople's Church of the Holy Apostles. Multi-language leaflets available at the cathedral entrance give a concise run-down of its points of interest, and in July and August the tourist office run daily tours of the cathedral in French at 3pm (€7; no booking necessary).

From outside, the cathedral is the very picture of exotica (despite some over-enthusiastic nineteenth-century restoration work). The Byzantine influence is evident in the interior's Greek-cross plan – unusual in France – and in the massive, clean curves of the domes. The bell tower also survived largely intact and is one of the few vestiges of the twelfth-century reconstruction. The adjoining **cloister** has two sides constructed in the Gothic style, and the other two in Romanesque.

North of the cathedral

North of the cathedral crowd the renovated buildings of the **Renaissance** city. The longest and finest street in this part of town is narrow **rue Limogeanne**, leading north from place de la Clautre via rue Salinière. Among the proliferating souvenir shops stand elegant mansions, now turned into swish boutiques, confectioners and delicatessens; its most notable facade belongs to **Maison Estignard** at no. 5, whose elaborate architecture – mullions, dormer windows and ornamental columns – is typical of the Renaissance. It's also worth popping into the more sober courtyard of no. 3 to see a salamander carved above the inner door; this was the insignia of Francis I (reigned 1515–47), who brought Italian Renaissance style to France. Opposite, impasse Limogeanne leads into a series of courtyards and passageways known as **galerie Daumesnil** after the famous general born at 7 rue de la Clarté in 1776.

Though nearby place du Coderc and place de l'Hôtel-de-Ville are both strong contenders, **Place St-Louis**, to the west of rue Limogeanne, is probably the prettiest of Périgueux's squares. In its southeast corner stands the handsome, turreted **Maison du Pâtissier** – built by a man who made his fortune from *pâté en croûte* (pâté in a pastry crust) – with a lovely Renaissance door bearing a fearsome warning on its lintel. There are more fine houses over to the east of rue Limogeanne on rue de la Constitution; from here the lanes begin to drop steeply to the river, where you'll find the semi-fortified fifteenth-century **Maison des Consuls** with the sixteenth-century **Maison Lambert** next door.

DAUMESNIL: THE PEG-LEG GENERAL

A devoted follower of Napoleon Bonaparte, **Baron Pierre Daumesnil** (1776–1832) was fiery, impetuous, loyal, patriotic and, above all, brave. He first distinguished himself during the Italian campaign (1796–97) when he rescued the drowning Napoleon from a river during the Battle of Arcole; then, at Acre in 1799, Daumesnil threw himself in front of his hero when a bomb landed at Napoleon's feet. It failed to explode, but Daumesnil, by now a major, was less lucky at the **Battle of Wagram** in Poland in 1809, when his left leg was so badly mutilated that it had to be amputated. Three years later he was promoted to general and made **governor of the Château de Vincennes** – the country's largest arsenal – which he twice refused to hand over to the allied European armies fighting Napoleon. The second time, in 1815, he declared: "I will give up Vincennes when you give me back my leg." Nevertheless, Daumesnil was forced to retire a few months later following Napoleon's defeat at Waterloo, and he eventually died of cholera in 1832, though his wooden leg was preserved and is now on display in Paris's Musée de l'Armée. In Périgueux you'll find a statue of him towards the south end of boulevard Michel Montaigne, proudly pointing at his peg-leg.

Musée d'Art et d'Archéologie du Périgord

22 cours Tourny • April–Sept Mon & Wed–Fri 10.30am–5.30pm, Sat & Sun 1–6pm; Oct–March Mon & Wed–Fri 10am–5pm, Sat & Sun 1–6pm • €5.50, children €3.50 • ☎ 05 53 06 40 70, ⓦ perigueux-maap.fr

Set in a grand, nineteenth-century building at the top of rue St-Front, overlooking the broad, tree-lined allées de Tourny is the **Musée d'Art et d'Archéologie du Périgord**. First and foremost, the museum houses an extensive **prehistoric collection**, among its most prized exhibits a partially complete 90,000-year-old human skeleton, the oldest yet found in France, and a delicate engraving of a bison's head. However, many of the more fragile items on display are copies, and the museum's old-fashioned layout makes it hard to appreciate what's on offer: the ethnographic exhibit is particularly poorly displayed and looks as if it hasn't been touched since 1897. Of the fine and **decorative arts section** the display of sculpture by the Transylvanian-born French sculptor Étienne Hajdu (1907–96) is worth musing over; his striking, bright-white aluminium structures are loosely based on the work of renowned Romanian sculptor, Constantin Brancusi. Elsewhere, the **cloister** is packed with carved stones and decorative sculptures, some taken from the Cathédrale St-Front, as well as some beautiful Gallo-Roman mosaics.

Look out, too, for the **temporary exhibitions**, often innovative and challenging in their outlook.

La Cité

Remnants of the Roman town of Vesunna, now known as **La Cité**, lie southwest from place Francheville along Le Puy-St-Front's rue de la Cité. Named after a local divinity, Vesunna was an important and prosperous town: by the first century AD it extended over some seventy hectares, complete with a forum, basilica, thermal baths and a 7km-long aqueduct. Today the most visible vestiges – a ruined amphitheatre, the remains of a temple complex and an excavated villa – lie scattered around the hulk of Périgueux's first cathedral, **St-Étienne de la Cité**.

St-Étienne de la Cité

Place de la Clautre • Daily 8.30am–6.30pm, except during Mass

Approaching from the east, the domes of **St-Étienne de la Cité** dominate the surrounding area. The cathedral was founded by St Front in the fourth century, then rebuilt in its present form, with a Romanesque nave comprising big square bays, some six hundred years later. The original building comprised four bays but two were destroyed, along with the bell tower, by Huguenots in 1577, leaving the church's west facade roughly truncated. The first bay you enter is the older of the two, dating from the eleventh century: the dome is more massive, the windows smaller and fewer and the stone less regular. The second bay was added a century later, then restored as an exact copy in the 1600s. Apart from being lighter and higher, its main feature is the line of decorative columns along the walls which stand out in the otherwise unornamented church.

Jardin des Arènes

Bd des Arènes • Daily: April–Sept 7.30am–9pm; Oct–March 7.30am–6.30pm • Free

The pretty **Jardin des Arènes**, a circular garden a few paces northwest of St-Étienne de la Cité, conceals a few remnants – comprising an entrance arch and traces of the foundations – of an enormous **amphitheatre** capable of holding twenty thousand people or more. Built in the first century AD, it was dismantled two hundred years later to construct defensive walls, of which you can see a fragment, the **Porte Normande**, along nearby rue Turenne. In the panic, the walls were cobbled together with whatever came to hand: a column, some capitals, a carved lintel, all pilfered from neighbouring monuments.

For most locals, though, history plays second fiddle to parklife, and the biggest attraction (particularly for children) is the large fountain and kids' paddling pool that stand at the heart of the park.

1

Tour de Vésone

Jardin de Vésone • Daily: April–Sept 7.30am–9pm; Oct–March 7.30am–6.30pm • Free

Southeast of the Jardin des Arènes, past the empty carcass of the twelfth-century **Château Barrière** and across the train lines, you reach the neatly manicured **Jardin de Vésone**, within which stands Périgueux's most imposing Roman monument, the **Tour de Vésone**. This high, hulking circular tower was once the sanctuary of a temple dedicated to Vesunna's eponymous guardian goddess. The gaping breach on the north side is said to have been created when St Front exorcized the pagan gods; more prosaically, the bricks and stones probably went into local building works.

Musée Gallo-Roman Vesunna

Jardin de Vésone • April–June & Sept Tues–Fri 9.30am–5.30pm, Sat & Sun 10am–12.30pm & 2.30–6pm; July & Aug daily 10am–7pm; Oct–March Tues–Fri 9.30am–12.30pm & 1.30–5pm, Sat & Sun 10am–12.30pm & 2.30–6pm • €6, children €4, audioguides (English-language available) €1 • ☏ 05 53 53 00 92, ⓦ perigueux-vesunna.fr

Concealed within a magnificent modern glass building a few paces from the Tour de Vésone is the **Musée Gallo-Roman Vesunna**, an outstanding museum built around the well-preserved remains of a grand Roman villa, which were discovered by chance in 1959. Superbly conceived wooden walkways (note how the layout is cleverly mirrored in the ceiling painting) take you over the walls and into the heart of the site, which is dominated by the garden, ornamented with peristyles of varying height. Indeed, this villa was no humble abode. It was complete with at least sixty rooms, an underfloor central-heating hypocaust, thermal baths and colonnaded walkways. Around the walls you can see the remains of first-century murals of river and marine life, the colours still amazingly vibrant, and here and there, graffiti of hunting scenes, gladiatorial combat and even an ostrich – perhaps the work of some bored Roman teenager. The best views of the site are from the two balconies, which are otherwise laid out with exquisitely crafted pilasters and funerary monuments.

On Thursday evenings in July and August, the museum stages special tours and various family-friendly activities (conducted in French).

ARRIVAL AND DEPARTURE

PÉRIGUEUX

By plane Périgueux has a small domestic airport at Bassilac, 7km east of the city, with just six flights per week to and from Paris Orly with Twin Jet (ⓦ twinjet.fr). There are no facilities – though rented cars can be picked up here if booked in advance – and no bus links, but a taxi into town will take less than 20min and cost around €20.

By train The *gare SNCF* is on rue Denis Papin, a 10min walk from the centre, or you can take bus #3, #4 and #NSe to the city centre (€1.25).

Destinations Bordeaux (7–11 daily; 1hr–1hr 30min); Brive (4–6 daily; 1hr); Neuvic (5–8 daily; 20–30min); St-Astier (6–12 daily; 10–15min); Thiviers (7–11 daily; 20–50min).

By bus Long-distance buses leave from the bus stop on rue de la Cité, behind place Francheville. Most routes are operated by CFTA (☏ 05 53 08 43 13, ⓦ cftaco.fr), which has an information office close to the rue de la Cité bus stop. Tickets (€2 on all routes) are available on board.

Destinations Angoulême (Mon–Sat 2 daily, Sun 1 daily; 1hr 45min); Bergerac (school term Mon–Fri 4 daily; school hols Mon–Fri 3 daily; 1hr); Brantôme (1 daily; 40min); Excideuil (school term Mon–Fri 4–5 daily; school hols Mon–Fri 3 daily; 1hr); Hautefort (Mon–Fri 1 daily; 40min); Neuvic (school term Mon–Fri 1–3 daily; 40min); Ribérac (school term Mon–Fri 4 daily; school hols Mon–Fri 3 daily; 1hr).

By car You can park for free along the river below St-Front Cathedral, or there's plenty of pay-parking along allées de Tourny, to the north of the centre, in place Montaigne to the east and underneath place Francheville.

FOLLOW THE RIVER

Once you've had your fill of tramping the streets, you might like to explore Périgueux's greener side. If you're on a bicycle, or on foot, take to **La Voie Verte** (see p.66), a 15km path winding from Marsac in the west of the city to Trélissac in the east. With car parks, picnic areas and information points along the way, it's popular with both locals and tourists. **La Voie Bleue** is the water-based alternative – a 21km paddle down the River Isle by canoe. For more details on both routes ask at the tourist office; for canoe hire contact the clubs at Trélissac (☏ 05 53 08 63 95), Périgueux (☏ 05 53 04 24 08) or Marsac (☏ 05 53 04 11 57).

GETTING AROUND

Car rental Near the train station, try: Ada-Autoloc 24, 4 bis avenue Henri Barbusse (☎ 05 53 05 40 28); Hertz, 1 Angle rue Puebla et Barbusse (☎ 05 53 54 61 80); Europcar, 7 rue Denis Papin (☎ 05 53 08 15 72), or Avis, 12 rue Denis Papin (☎ 05 53

53 39 02). You can also arrange to pick up cars at the airport.
Taxis Call Allo Taxi Périgueux (☎ 05 53 09 09 09). There are also taxi stands outside the train station and another on place Bugeaud.

INFORMATION

Tourist office 26 place Francheville (Jan–June & Oct–Dec Mon–Sat 9am–12.30pm & 2–6pm; July & Aug Mon–Sat 9am–7pm, Sun 10am–6pm; ☎ 05 53 53 10 63, ⓦ tourisme -perigueux.fr). They offer excellent themed city tours

(April to mid-Sept; €6) covering medieval and Renaissance Périgueux, the Gallo-Roman city or with a focus on music or food and drink. Though the tours are predominantly in French, some guides also speak English; ask in advance.

ACCOMMODATION

Des Barris 2 rue Pierre Magne ☎ 05 53 53 04 05, ⓦ hoteldesbarris.com; map p.50. Just across the river from Le Puy-St-Front, this two-star *Logis* hotel has fourteen simple and fairly small rooms, two with views of the cathedral. The bathrooms are cramped and the furnishings could do with a bit of an overhaul, but otherwise it's fair value. Note that reception closes for a few hours in the middle of the day. Breakfast €7. **€55**

Bristol 37 rue Antoine Gadaud ☎ 05 53 08 75 90, ⓦ bristolfrance.com; map p.48. This welcoming place looks pretty bland from the outside, but inside it's another story with airy, bright and bold part-painted, part-wallpapered en-suite rooms. Breakfast €9. **€80**

Camping Le Grand Dague Atur ☎ 05 53 04 21 01, ⓦ legranddague.fr; map p.48. Lost in the hills 7km southeast of Périgueux, this spacious and immaculate four-star site is worth seeking out if you've got your own transport. A welter of facilities including TV lounge, shop, launderette, playground, swimming pools and slides, plus bike hire. Mobile homes available too (from €70). Closed Sept–May. **€40**

Castel Peyssard 15 rue Paul Louis Courier ☎ 05 53 35 91 90, ⓦ castelpeyssard.com; map p.48. Sitting pretty in the midst of a gorgeous landscaped park, this gleaming-white stone château offers up the most luxurious stay in the city, albeit at a fair whack. Based on the owner's love of cinema (check out the staircase lined with photos of screen divas), each of the four beautifully upholstered rooms is themed – and decorated accordingly – on a famous film: *The Tiger of Bengal*, *Indochina*, *Out of Africa* and *Cleopatra*, while two of these also incorporate the château's corner turrets. To add to the glamour, there's a luxury spa on site too. **€195**

Château des Reynats 15 av des Reynats ☎ 05 53 03

53 59, ⓦ chateau-hotel-perigord.com; map p.48. In the village of Chancelade, roughly 5km northwest of central Périgueux, this nineteenth-century château has plush, immaculately turned out rooms both in the château itself and the Orangerie annexe, with those in the latter fashioned in more contemporary style. There's a top-class restaurant too. Closed Jan. Orangerie **€89**, château **€119**

Comfort Hôtel Régina 14 rue Denis-Papin ☎ 05 53 08 40 44, ⓦ comfort-perigueux.fr; map p.48. The only hotel in the vicinity of the train station worth considering, a pleasant place offering cheerful en-suite rooms with high ceilings with spotlights, and windows to match (double-glazed on the front). Triples and quads available too (€81/€87). Breakfast €10. **€72**

★**Couleurs du Temps** 20 bd Albert Claveille ☎ 06 79 81 83 71, ⓦ couleursdutempsdordogne.blogspot.fr; map p.48. Easily the most imaginatively decorated hotel in town, the two huge attic rooms in this gracious townhouse are a masterpiece of creative thinking, with quirky touches such as lamps made from bike lights and chains, crimson Louis XV-style chairs, curved Perspex mirrors akin to something from a fairground and fabulous photo art. Rooms also have small fridges and coffee-making facilities and a small shared kitchenette is on the way. Best of all, though, are the two very helpful owners. **€75**

Le Mercure 7 place Francheville ☎ 05 53 06 65 00, ⓦ mercure.com; map p.48. Located on the corner of the city's most prominent square, *Le Mercure* is by some distance the smartest hotel in the centre. The classic facade conceals a fairly typical business-style chain hotel with impeccably kept rooms decorated in cream and beige tones, and with a few extras like tea- and coffee-making facilities. Breakfast €16, parking €10. **€90**

EATING

l'Atelier 2 rue Voltaire ☎ 05 53 04 56 71; map p.50. Sweet little restaurant on the edge of the old town, decorated with funky red lamps and photos of rusty bikes. The food, made from fresh market produce, is as entertaining and delightful as the decor and the ever-changing menu might include chicken and lemon tajine or fish of the

day with leek and potato curry. *Menus* from €28. Tues–Sat noon–2pm & 7–9.30pm.

Le Clin d'Oeil 6 rue Puits Limogeanne ☎ 05 53 54 13 08; map p.50. This is one of those charming countryside farmhouse-like bistros that you occasionally stumble upon in French towns. Despite the retro decor, the food is

1

completely modern French and includes delights such as a risotto of *jambon de Bayonne* with Périgord truffles. The service is friendly, the atmosphere cosy and the prices refreshingly low (lunchtime three-course *menu* for €14.90). Daily noon–2pm & 7.30–9.30pm.

Le Clos St-Front 5 rue de la Vertu ☎ 05 53 46 78 58, ⓦ leclossaintfront.com; map p.50. This elegant, brick-walled restaurant has a well-earned reputation for its inventive *menus*, starting at €33. The dishes are beautifully presented, the *menu* changes approximately every six weeks and could include delights such as pigs' feet in garlic cream, which is actually a lot tastier than it sounds, or octopus with a saffron and mussel cream. Tues–Sat noon–2pm & 7.30–10.30pm, Sun noon–2pm.

L'Essentiel 8 rue de la Clarté ☎ 05 53 35 15 15, ⓦ restaurant-perigueux.com; map p.50. As the city's sole Michelin-starred restaurant, *L'Essentiel* is, as you'd expect, a high-class and pretty expensive affair. The service and cooking here, by supermo chef Eric Vidal, are outstanding, and you'll have a tough time choosing from the seasonal menu which includes the likes of spit-roasted pigeon stuffed with foie gras. *Menus* from €59. Tues–Sat noon–2pm & 7.30–10pm.

★ **La Ferme St-Louis** 2 place St-Louis ☎ 05 53 53 82 77; map p.50. By far the most rewarding – and welcoming –of the many restaurants on this square, possessing a homely, stone-walled interior and sunny little terrace. The food is as seasonal as you could wish for and generously portioned, but if it all looks too tempting, try one or two of the house specialities such as sweetbreads with vinegar, or scallops with red pepper and chorizo. The three-course *Menu Terroir* at €25 (lunchtimes and evenings) is terrific value. Tues–Fri

& Sun noon–2pm & 7–9.30pm; July & Aug also open Mon.

Le Grain de Sel 7 rue des Farges ☎ 05 53 53 45 22; map p.50. Tucked away in a narrow street just along from the tourist office, this impeccable little restaurant uses fresh produce from the market to create original dishes, many based around seafood. *Menus* from €24. Tues–Sat noon–1.30pm & 7.30–9.30pm.

Hercule Poireau 2 rue de la Nation ☎ 05 53 08 90 76; map p.50. One of Périgueux's best-known restaurants, located down in a gorgeous, sixteenth-century stone-vaulted room with soft lighting and cheerful red-check fabrics. This is rich fare: house speciality is the luxurious *rossini de canard* (duck with a slice of foie gras in a truffle sauce). *Menus* from €21. Mon, Tues & Thurs–Sun noon–2pm & 7.30–10pm.

Nicolas L 7 place du 8 Mai ☎ 05 53 13 45 02, ⓦ restaurantnicolasl.com; map p.48. This highly regarded gourmet restaurant is a short way out of the city centre. It's the kind of place locals come to when they want to impress and enjoy dishes such as unusually creative dishes such as beef with violet ice cream. *Menus* start at €22 at weekday lunch-times, and €32 for three courses in the evening. Tues noon–2pm, Wed–Sat noon–2pm & 7.30–9.30pm.

★ **Pierrot Gourmet** 6 rue L'Hôtel de Ville ☎ 05 53 53 35 32; map p.50. Although principally a gourmet deli and rotisserie, *Pierrot Gourmet* also has a few attractive-looking tables for daytime diners. The food is crisp and fresh, and includes a range of wonderful yet simple dishes such as mushroom pâté and pears poached in red wine. Wash it down with a glass of Bergerac and you've got yourself a cracking little lunch. Tues–Sat 11am–6pm.

DRINKING

★ **Le Chai Bordin** 8 rue de la Sagesse ☎ 09 81 89 40 65, ⓦ lechaibordin.com; map p.50. Ostensibly a shop, *Le Chai Bordin* is actually a delightful little wine bar that makes for a terrific place to linger for an hour or two. Some six hundred varieties of both French and foreign wines are available, many of these by the glass, with each costing €2–4.50. Tues & Wed 10am–12.30pm & 3–9pm, Thurs–

Sat 10am–12.30pm & 3–10pm.

La Vertu 11 rue Notre-Dame ☎ 05 53 53 20 75; map p.50. Appealingly eccentric bar where, in summer, you can lounge in wooden deck chairs outside in the quiet square. As well as a good choice of wines and beer, *La Vertu* serves cocktails, tapas and ice creams. Note that opening hours can be erratic. Thurs–Sun 7pm–midnight.

THEATRE AND CINEMA

CAP Cinema Place Francheville ☎ 05 53 03 92 91, ⓦ cap-cine.fr/perigueux. The multiscreen CAP Cinema is the place to catch a Hollywood blockbuster as well as some art-house films, screened in the original language.

Théâtre Odyssée (NTP) 1 allée d'Aquitaine ☎ 05 53 53 18 71, ⓦ odyssee-perigueux.fr. Cultural centre which puts on a varied programme of theatre, dance, concerts and variety shows.

SHOPPING

Librairie Marbot 17 bd Michel-Montaigne ☎ 05 53 06 45 20, ⓦ librairiemarbot.com; map p.50. Capacious bookshop which stocks a few English-language novels. Mon–Sat 10am–7pm.

Maison de la Presse 11 place Bugeaud; map p.48. Stocks a wide selection of English-language newspapers and

magazines and has a decent selection of local guidebooks too. Mon–Sat 7am–7pm, Sun 7am–12.30pm.

Pierre Champion 21 rue Taillefer ☎ 05 53 31 37 42; map p.50. Local wines and truffles as well as duck and goose in all its guises. Mon–Sat 10am–12.30pm & 2–7pm.

MARKETS IN PÉRIGUEUX

Périgueux has some great **markets**: the biggest are the fresh-produce markets in the centre of Le Puy-St-Front around **place de la Clautre**, **place du Coderc** and **place de l'Hôtel de Ville** (Wed & Sat mornings), and the clothes and household goods market just to the southeast on **place Bugeaud** (Wed morning). There's also a daily fresh-food market (mornings only) in place du Coderc's covered **halle**. In winter (mid-Nov to mid-March), stalls selling foie gras and truffles set up just north of the Cathedralé St-Front in place St-Louis for the annual **marchés au gras** (Wed & Sat morning).

DIRECTORY

Hospital Central Hospitalier, 80 av Georges Pompidou (☎ 05 53 45 25 25, ⓦ ch-perigueux.fr), to the north of the centre off bd Michel-Montaigne.

Police Commissariat de Police, rue du 4 Septembre (☎ 05 53 06 44 44); Police Municipale, 2A cours Fénelon (☎ 05 53 08 49 33).

Post office The central post office is at rue du 4 Septembre

(Mon–Fri 9am–6pm, Sat 9am–12.30pm).

Swimming pool Aquacap (☎ 05 53 02 90 29, ⓦ aquacap .agglo-perigueux.fr) at Champcevinel, northeast of the city centre, just after the main hospital, is Périgueux's watersports centre, with space for serious swimmers as well as slides, aquagym, swimming for babies, jacuzzi, sauna and hamam.

Brantôme

Thirty kilometres north of Périgueux, the beautiful town of **BRANTÔME** is often described in tourist literature as the "Venice of Périgord". Of course, it's nothing of the sort, though the river walks and the waterside, along with a Benedictine **abbey** and some **troglodyte caves**, certainly help to make it one of the more attractive towns in a region blessed with an overabundance of pretty competitors.

Handsomely located on an almost circular island, which was created around one thousand years ago when local monks dug a mill-stream across a tight meander of the Dronne, Brantôme's **old centre** is seemingly tethered to the surrounding bank by its bridges and is surrounded by leafy gardens and parks such as the waterfront **Jardin Public**, from which you can take in the lively waterborne **jousting competitions** staged on Friday evenings (from 9pm) in July and August. All this scenic beauty attracts masses of tourists, and even though a modern bypass takes the worst of the traffic, in summer it's still a bottleneck along the main road, **rue Gambetta**, which cuts north across the island to place de Gaulle on the far bank of the Dronne. The modern bridge directly in front of the abbey leads into **rue Puy-Joli**, Brantôme's main shopping street, where you'll find a variety of attractive **shops**, while the **café-bars** on place du Marché are a popular spot for a drink. A good day to visit is Friday, when the waterfront and surrounding streets are given over to the weekly **market**, which has been doing a roaring trade for some 450 years. Between December and March the stalls are augmented with truffles, foie gras and walnuts. It's also worth coming here to take to the river: Brantôme is one of the most popular places in the region to hop in a **canoe** or **kayak** for a couple of hours (see p.59). The Dronne is especially pretty here, with its narrow width and overhanging trees, and at times it can feel like you're paddling through an Amazonian rainforest.

Abbaye St-Pierre de Brantôme

Bd de Charlemagne

Brantôme owes its existence to some rock-shelters – where the first hermits set up home around the fifth century – and a **spring**, whose waters are said to be able to cure sick children and treat infertility. The spring is now behind the church and convent buildings of the **Abbaye St-Pierre de Brantôme**, standing on the river's far north bank. The first church was built under the cliffs here sometime before 817 – according to local tradition, it was Charlemagne (742–814) who founded the abbey with the endowment

1

of St Sicaire's relic, one of the infants massacred by Herod. It had a rocky start, but by its twelfth-century heyday the abbey supported 24 parishes and had spawned a thriving town. Nevertheless, things started going downhill again with the Hundred Years War and, after being rebuilt on several occasions, the abbey was finally abandoned after the Revolution. The present buildings, which date from the seventeenth century but were heavily restored two hundred years later, house the **Hôtel de Ville**, whose staring, serried windows still hint at ascetic institutional life.

The abbey **church** recalls some of this history. The death of St Sicaire is the subject of a stained-glass window behind the altar, while bas-reliefs to either side depict the Massacre of the Innocents and Charlemagne offering Sicaire's relic to the church.

Grottes de l'Abbaye de Brantôme and the Musée Desmoulin

Bd de Charlemagne • April & May daily 10am–1pm & 2–6pm; June & Sept daily 10am–6pm; July & Aug daily 10am–7pm; mid-Feb, March & Oct–Dec Mon & Wed–Sun 10am–noon & 2–5pm • €5, children €3; tickets sold at the tourist office (see below) • Caves ☎ 05 53 05 80 63, museum ☎ 05 47 45 30 12

After a quick look at the palm-frond vaulting in the chapterhouse, adjacent to the Benedictine Abbey, head to the **Grottes de l'Abbaye de Brantôme**. Despite being used as a quarry over the years, there's still considerable evidence of the monks' earlier troglodytic existence here. The most interesting of the caves contains a large, rather crude **sculpture** of the Last Judgement, believed to date from the fifteenth century, in the aftermath of the Hundred Years War. Look out, too, for the *pigeonniers*, identifiable by several rows of niches carved into the rock face; not only were pigeons a valuable source of meat, but their droppings were traded as fertilizer.

In the same complex as the caves, the **Musée Desmoulin** is dedicated to the eponymous illustrator and painter. Much of Desmoulin's work was heavily influenced by spritualism, hence his well-known (if slightly spooky) medium drawings, many of which are on display here – typically pencil or charcoal portraits of women, or more specifically, women's faces. The artist later went on to paint more orthodox impressionist works, in particular, landscapes.

ARRIVAL AND INFORMATION

By bus Buses on the Périgueux–Angoulême route, timed to connect with TGV trains in Angoulême, stop on the Champs de Foire, at the south end of rue Gambetta.
Destinations Angoulême (Mon–Sat 3 daily; 1hr); Périgueux (Mon–Sat 2–3 daily, Sun 1 daily; 35min).
Tourist office Église Notre-Dame, 2 rue Puyjoli (April &

May daily 10am–1pm & 2–6pm; June & Sept daily 10am–6pm; July & Aug daily 10am–7pm; mid-Feb to March & Oct–Dec Mon & Wed–Sun 10am–noon & 2–5pm; ☎ 05 53 05 80 63, ⊛ perigord-dronne-belle.fr). Family-friendly guided tours of the town can be organized through the tourist office for €2 per person; reserve in advance.

ACCOMMODATION

Au Nid des Thés 13 rue Victor Hugo ☎ 05 53 02 75 49, ⊛ au-nid-des-thes.fr. There are surprisingly few *chambres d'hôtes* in Brantôme, but this one, on the main shopping street, is a real delight. The four elegant, Edwardian-style rooms are enormous, with modern bathrooms, and there's a cute little tea shop downstairs. Prices drop if you stay more than a night. **€80**
Camping Peyrelevade Av André Maurois ☎ 05 53 05 75 24, ⊛ camping-dordogne.net. Shady and sunny site just 1km east of town beside the River Dronne, with private beach, fishing and heated swimming pool. Children's playground, shop, snack bar and campervan emptying facilities, as well as chalets for rent (€590 weekly). Closed Oct–April. **€26**
Camping Puynadal ☎ 05 53 06 19 66, ⊛ camping -puynadal.com. Small, family-run site offering around

thirty pitches, but it's well equipped with bar, restaurant, children's playground, sports facilities and swimming pool, plus chalets to rent (€449 weekly). Closed Sept–April. **€22**
Chabrol 57 rue Gambetta ☎ 05 53 05 70 15, ⊛ lesfreres charbonnel.com. One of Brantôme's most popular hotels, in a superb location by the Pont des Barris, offering quality rooms decked out in lots of pretty florals combined with fine wood-carved furnishings. The more expensive rooms (€88) have river views. Breakfast €12. Closed mid-Nov to mid-Dec and Feb. **€65**
Coligny 8 place Charles-de-Gaulle ☎ 05 53 05 71 42, ⊛ hotel-coligny.fr. This friendly hotel is the cheapest option in Brantôme, with eight good-sized, a/c rooms painted in strong violet and mauve colours and with marshmallow-puffy sofas and wooden floorboards. Some rooms (€65) have

1

ACTIVITIES IN BRANTÔME

In summer, **boat trips** around Brantôme's island (April to mid-Oct; hourly trips 11am–6pm; 50min; €7.50, children €5) depart from beside the town's old bridge in the Jardin Public. From Brantôme you can also embark on a **canoe** or **kayak** expedition, from a full-or half-day paddle downriver to a spin around the town's waterways for an hour or so. Either way, reservations are recommended in high season: try Allo Canoës, on the road to Bourdeilles (☎05 53 06 31 85, ⓦallocanoes.com) or Brantôme Canoë, just out of the centre on the road east to Thiviers (☎05 53 05 77 24, ⓦbrantome canoe.com); both rent canoes and kayaks from €10/hr, and are open from April to October or thereabouts, depending upon the weather. Brantôme Canoë also runs **rock-climbing classes** (from €25/2hrs) for individuals or small groups, taught by a registered monitor.

The surrounding area is also a good bet for **cycling**. Bikes can be rented from L'Hermitage in Saint Julien de Bourdeilles (☎05 53 08 28 93, ⓦgitehermitageperigord.fr), 4km west of Brantôme, though they can deliver bikes: delivery charge from €15, bike rental from €9.50.

partial river views. Downstairs is an inexpensive and popular restaurant. Breakfast €7.50. Closed Jan & Feb. **€60**

Les Jardins de Brantôme 33 rue Pierre de Mareuil ☎05 53 05 88 16, ⓦlesjardinsdebrantome.com. Just outside the old centre, on the road to Angoulême, *Les Jardins* has eight sparkling rooms, one of which has level access and facilities for disabled persons. Most rooms are set back from the main building at the top of the lush gardens, each with a patio-style door leading onto its own bit of terrace. Other highlights include a swimming pool,

and an exceptionally helpful manageress. Not cheap but worth it. Breakfast €12. **€145**

Moulin de l'Abbaye 1 rue de Bourdeilles ☎05 53 05 80 22, ⓦmoulinabbaye.com. If you're feeling self-indulgent, treat yourself to a night of unbridled luxury in this beautiful old mill to the west of the abbey. Nineteen rooms are spread between three buildings, though there's little to distinguish between them in terms of comfort offered. Sumptuous, but perhaps a little overpriced. Breakfast €22. Closed Nov–Jan. **€190**

EATING AND DRINKING

Cô 'Thé-Café Salon de Thé 30 rue Victor Hugo ☎05 53 06 93 17. With a shady rear courtyard lined with pot plants and guarded by a soft-toy farmer, this little tea shop is a fun place to relax and recharge with one of their huge range of teas as well as various coffees, milkshakes, juices and snacks. Drinks around €3.50, snacks around €6. Mon–Sat 10am–7pm.

★ **Les Frères Charbonnel** 57 rue Gambetta ☎05 53 05 70 15, ⓦlesfrerescharbonnel.com. The restaurant of the *Chabrol* hotel is in the gourmet class, but is still good value with *menus* from €34; for this expect sumptuous dishes like pigeon in smoked milk. The elegant dining room looks

fantastic, as does the adjacent stone terrace – and the views across the water are even better. Daily 12.15pm–1.30pm & 7.30–9.30pm; closed mid-Nov to mid-Dec.

★ **Les Jardins de Brantôme** 33 rue Pierre de Mareuil ☎05 53 05 88 16, ⓦlesjardinsdebrantome.com. The food at this cool, intimate restaurant is consistently superb: pork with blackberries, ginger and pineapple, rabbit salad with pine nuts or grilled octopus with garlic are the sort of mouthwatering dishes you can expect, with many of the ingredients culled from the chef's vegetable garden. *Menus* from €31.50. Mon, Tues & Fri–Sun noon–2pm & 7.30–10pm; Wed & Thurs 7.30–10pm.

SHOPPING

Éric Simonin Souffleur de Verre 11 place Bugeaud ☎05 53 35 24 13, ⓦericsimonin.com. With regular press and TV appearances, Éric Simonin might just be the most famous glass-blower in France. Built into the cliffs close to the abbey, this is as much art gallery and tourist attraction as it is a shop, and if you're lucky (summer weekends

are best), you'll be able to watch Simonin at work – the production process is fascinating. Expect to part with around €3500 for one of his stunning glass jellyfish or mushrooms, though there are also some far less expensive options. Jan–June & Sept–Dec Mon–Sat 10am–noon & 2–7pm; July & Aug daily 10am–7pm.

The lower Dronne valley

The country west of Brantôme and along the **River Dronne** remains largely undisturbed. It's tranquil, very beautiful and restoring, best savoured at a gentle pace, perhaps by bike or, even better, by canoe along the river. Delightful **Bourdeilles**, the first real

1

settlement downstream from Brantôme, was the seat of one of Périgord's four baronies (see p.290), as its great tower testifies, while the Renaissance château next door contains a marvellous collection of furniture. From the foot of the castle, the Dronne meanders through water-meadows to one of the Dordogne's most famous market towns, **Ribérac**. Though Ribérac itself holds little else of interest, it makes an agreeable base from which to visit a crop of Romanesque churches scattered in the countryside around. **Aubeterre-sur-Dronne**, with another extraordinary troglodyte church and a splendid position, represents the final stop along the river.

Bourdeilles

BOURDEILLES, 16km southwest of Brantôme via the pretty D106, is at its best when approached for the first time by canoe. Many visitors only come here on a day-trip from Brantôme, but this sleepy backwater, clustered round its **château** on a rocky spur above the river, is also a good option for an overnight stay, with some enticing accommodation and eating options; the river around Bourdeilles offers some delightful **canoeing** and **kayaking** (see p.61), too.

Château de Bourdeilles

Feb, March, Nov & Dec Mon & Wed–Sun 10am–12.30pm & 2–5pm; April–June, Sept & Oct daily 10am–1pm & 2–6pm; July & Aug daily 10am–7pm • €8.20, children €5.30 • ☎ 05 53 03 73 36, ⓦ semitour.com

The **Château de Bourdeilles** essentially comprises two buildings, the first of which is a thirteenth-century **fortress**. Entered via a heavily cobbled yard, it consists of a now empty banqueting hall – though the two enormous, unadorned fireplaces are worth a peek – and a sturdy octagonal **keep**, the top of which offers lovely views over the town and river below.

The other building, and the main reason for visiting, is the sombre-looking **Renaissance château** begun by the lady of the house, Jacquette de Montbrun, wife of André de Bourdeilles, as a piece of unsuccessful favour-currying with Catherine de Médici – unsuccessful because, though she passed through the area, Catherine never came to stay and so the château remained unfinished. The Renaissance residence is now home to an exceptional collection of **furniture** and religious statuary. Among the more notable pieces are some splendid Spanish dowry chests; the gilded bedroom suite of a former Yugoslav king; and a sixteenth-century Rhenish *Entombment* whose life-sized **statues** embody the very image of the serious, self-satisfied medieval burgher. The showpiece room, however, is the overly elaborate **salon doré** (the room Catherine de Médici was supposed to sleep in), which has retained its original decor, notably a fine oak-panelled wainscot comprising over sixty painted panels depicting the various properties owned by the Bourdeilles family, and the coffered ceiling bearing a riot of paintings, from flowers and insects to sphinxes.

Throughout summer, the château offers **children's activities** such as calligraphy and coin-making; book ahead.

BOATING WITH DAMSELFLIES

Safety precautions mean that children under 5 aren't allowed on the canoes and kayaks available for rent throughout the Dordogne and Lot, but there is an alternative for kids who desperately want to glide down the rivers on a boat. The Maison de la Dronne (June–Sept Mon–Sat 10am–noon & 2–6pm; July & Aug Mon–Sat 9.30am–12.30pm & 2–6pm, ☎ 05 53 91 35 11), 14km southwest of Bourdeilles along the D106 in the village of Montagrier, offer river trips open to all ages aboard silent little **electric paddle boats**, which seat up to four. An hour's motoring will take you up a jungly, narrow river channel where masses of damselflies dance and herons perch like statues on the riverbanks, and there's a deeper part where you can stop for a swim. You can either go it alone (per-person €2/hr with oars, €3/hr with an electric engine; children under 5 free) or with an experienced nature guide (an extra €5/€3 per adult/child).

INFORMATION AND ACTIVITIES

BOURDEILLES

Tourist office Place des Tilleuls, just downhill from the château (June 15–30 & Sept 1–15 daily 10am–noon & 2–5pm; July & Aug daily 10am–noon & 2–6pm; ☏ 05 53 05 62 43, ⓦ perigord-dronne-belle.fr).

Canoe rental Canoës Bourdeilles Loisirs (April–Oct;

☏ 06 77 30 12 77, ⓦ canoesbourdeilleloisirs.fr), by the bridge, offer an array of different routes (from €12) that range from a gentle 1hr downstream paddle back to Bourdeilles (you'll be driven upstream to the starting point) to a full-day trip from Brantôme.

ACCOMMODATION AND EATING

★ **l'Ambroisie** Grand Rue ☏ 05 53 04 24 51, ⓦ ambroisie-dordogne-perigord.com. At the top of the hill leading into the village, this charming *chambre d'hôte* is a place for idle living. Its four rooms (one of which sleeps four; €140) have high ceilings with eighteenth-century wooden beams and elegant furnishings. Add to all this a chatty lady owner, big breakfasts made using local market produce and a little hidden garden and you get a sure-fire winner. **€72**

Hostellerie le Donjon Place de la Halle ☏ 05 53 04 07 50, ⓦ hostellerie-ledonjon.fr. A sweet little family-run residence, directly opposite the tourist office, offering seven modestly sized rooms fitted out in nicely carved wooden furnishings. Whether you're staying here or not, the courtyard restaurant (no credit cards) to the rear of the hotel is a top place to eat, with a menu that's heavily skewed towards North African influences, from Moroccan chicken with herbs to duck tagine; *menus* from €25. The courtyard really comes alive on Thursday evenings throughout the summer, when there's free live music, either blues, jazz or folk. Breakfast €8. Restaurant Mon

& Wed–Sun noon–2pm & 7–9.30pm, closed Mon in July & Aug; hotel closed Oct–April. **€75**

Hostellerie les Griffons Grand Rue ☏ 05 53 45 45 35, ⓦ griffons.fr. About 200m down from *Le Donjon*, the more upmarket *Griffons* occupies a fabulously picturesque spot in a sixteenth-century house beside the humpback bridge. The ten rooms are plushly carpeted in anthracite grey, which looks great set against the partially exposed brickwork and occasional stone fireplace; all have a view of the river, though some are better than others. A small, kidney-shaped pool enclosed within a flowery walled garden rounds things off beautifully. Breakfast €13. Closed mid-Oct to Easter. **€105**

Moulin du Pont ☏ 05 53 04 51 75. If you don't fancy eating in Bourdeilles, head 8km downstream to the *Moulin du Pont*, near the village of Lisle, and grab a seat on a terrace with the river on one side and the restaurant's trout ponds on the other. *Menus* start at €16.50, and feature duck, walnuts, truffles and, of course, trout. March–June & Sept to mid-Nov Tues–Sat noon–2pm & 7.30–9.30pm, Sun noon–2pm; July & Aug daily noon–2pm & 7.30–9.30pm.

Ribérac and around

Surrounded by an intimate, hilly countryside of woods, hay meadows and drowsy hilltop villages, **RIBÉRAC**, 30km downstream from Bourdeilles, is a pleasant if unremarkable town whose greatest claim to fame is its Friday **market**, bringing in producers and wholesalers from all around. The town lies on the south bank of the Dronne: its main street starts in the south as rue Jean Moulin, runs through the central **place Nationale** and then continues northwards as rue du 26 Mars 1944. From place Nationale, rue Gambetta heads east to **place Général de Gaulle** and the vast market square beyond.

There's nothing really in the way of sights, but the country here is dotted with numerous **Romanesque churches** that provide a focus for leisurely wandering – the tourist office (see p.62) has a leaflet detailing these. A couple of hundred metres from Ribérac's centre on the hill to the east of town, the **Collégiale Notre-Dame** (July & Aug Fri–Sun 9am–6pm, ask at tourist office at other times; free), now an exhibition and concert hall, makes a good place to start exploring. It's a pleasing building, with its squat tower and semicircular apse designed on a grander scale than its country cousins, but the west end and interior have been extensively altered; if it's open, it's worth popping in to see the recently restored seventeenth- and eighteenth-century frescoes.

The Romanesque churches

Nowadays many of the **Romanesque churches** in the villages around Ribérac are kept locked, but the route described here takes in a representative sample of those that are more likely to be open – hours tend to be 9am to 6/7pm daily. The **Église de St-Pierre** in the village of **FAYE**, 1km west of Ribérac on the D20, has great charm even though

1

it's no architectural beauty: its diminutive single nave seems barely able to carry the fortress of a tower above. There's more reason to stop at **BOURG-DU-BOST**, 6km further downstream, where the significantly chunkier **Église de Notre-Dame** possesses a similarly haphazard mix of architectural styles and an almost identical tower. It also harbours some very faded twelfth-century **murals**: the four Evangelists inside the dome, and the twelve Apostles around the choir.

From here the route cuts north and climbs to an undulating plateau with good views back over the Dronne's river meadows, then meanders through a string of villages. The first one to aim for is **ST-MARTIAL-VIVEYROL**, roughly 15km due north of Ribérac. Its church more resembles a castle keep; the windows are reduced to narrow slits, there's just a single, simple door at ground level and the belfry doubles as a watchtower with, behind it, a guardroom along the length of the nave big enough to hold the whole village. Looping southeast from St-Martial-Viveyrol, the **Église de St-Pierre-et-St-Paul** in **GRAND-BRASSAC** is unusual in that sculptures were added over its north door. They show Christ in majesty flanked by St Peter and St Paul above a frieze of the Adoration with traces of earlier paintwork.

The last of the Romanesque churches, **St-Pierre-ès-Liens**, is also one of the most prettily sited. It lies in wooded country 6km south of Ribérac and is best approached from the west with the roofs of **SIORAC-DE-RIBÉRAC** clustered behind. From the hastily erected rubble walls it's easy to see where, in the fourteenth century, the nave was raised a couple of metres and a guard tower added at the west end. Again, there are almost no windows and the walls are up to 3m thick – which explains why the nave is so surprisingly narrow.

ARRIVAL AND INFORMATION   RIBÉRAC

By bus Buses for Périgueux and Angoulême stop on place Debonnière, a few paces north of the tourist office.
Destinations Angoulême (Mon & Fri 1 daily; 1hr); Périgueux (Mon–Fri 5 daily; school hols Mon–Fri 4 daily; 1hr).
Tourist office Inside the Palais de Justice on place Général de Gaulle (Mon–Fri 10am–12.30pm & 2–5pm, Sat 9.30am–12.30pm; ☎ 05 53 90 03 10, ⍟ riberac-tourisme.com). The

office doubles as a ticket office for SNCF, and in July and August they organize guided walks and farm visits.
Canoe rental Beside the entrance to Camping de la Dronne (see below), Canoës Ribérac (mid-June to mid-Sept; ☎ 06 77 30 89 63, ⍟ canoriberac.free.fr) rents out canoes and pedal-boats, and also organizes guided day-trips along the Dronne; prices start at €8.

ACCOMMODATION

Camping de la Dronne Rte d'Angoulême ☎ 05 53 90 50 08. Inexpensive, mid-sized but quite basic site just across the Dronne on the Angoulême road, with reasonable facilities, including shower blocks, laundry and play area. Closed mid-Sept to May. **€13.20**
Chambres Florence 5 place Général de Gaulle ☎ 05 53 90 93 38, ⍟ chambres-florence.com. In a spacious and elegant townhouse just across the square from the tourist office, this enthusiastically run chambre d'hôte has two rooms and a suite (€78), variously accommodating exposed

stone walls, lovingly polished parquet floors and roll-top baths, plus there's a gorgeous conservatory for breakfast and a small pool. Elsewhere, the boldly painted walls clearly take their cue from the in-house art gallery. **€60**
Rev'Hôtel Rte de Périgueux ☎ 05 53 91 62 62, ⍟ rev-hotel.fr. Some 1km east of town, this single-storey, two-star hotel won't win any awards for class, but it does offer inexpensive, convenient and comfortable rooms (two wheelchair accessible) and helpful service. Triples and quads (€90/€95) available, too. Breakfast €6.50. **€51**

EATING AND DRINKING

Café des Colonnes 17 place Général de Gaulle ☎ 05 53 90 01 39. You can't beat sitting under the trees with a coffee on the terrace of this venerable café, which has been keeping locals fuelled since 1832 – alternatively, head inside to park yourself on one of the leather seats and admire the old posters and photos dotted around the walls.

The food is classic bistro fare with well-priced mains at €10–15. Daily 8am–11pm.
Le Chabrot 8 rue Gambetta ☎ 05 53 91 28 59. Though sparingly furnished and decorated, this is a terrific local restaurant that offers mainly traditional fare as well as more unusual dishes, such as duck skewer with mash, salmon with

CLOCKWISE FROM TOP LEFT ÉGLISE SOUTERRAINE SAINT-JEAN (P.64), AUBETERRE-SUR-DRONNE; CHÂTEAU DE PUYGUILHEM (P.67); CA BRIVE IN ACTION (P.76) >

1

polenta, and gazpacho with goat's cheese. The gourmet menu marries the various dishes with some first-rate local wines, for example, Montbazillac with the dessert. Express lunch *menu* for €15. Dinner on Sundays is by reservation only. Mon & Thurs–Sun 12.15–2pm & 7.30–9pm, Tues 12.15–2pm.

Le Citronnier 3 place Nationale ☎ 05 53 90 22 72. This refined, Anglo/Swiss-owned restaurant, tucked away in what is probably the oldest house in Ribérac, prepares dishes that you're unlikely to find elsewhere: a filo pastry wrap of black pudding with apples, nuts and caramelized red onion, or sea trout topped with a herb crumble. Everything is seasonal and home-made and there's an extensive wine list, including an impressive two pages of Bergeracs. As pretty as the restaurant is, the rear garden is the place to dine in summer. *Menus* from €28. Mon–Sat noon–2.30pm & 7–10pm, plus Sun 7–10pm July & Aug.

Aubeterre-sur-Dronne

Hanging on a steep hillside above the river, some 30km west of Ribérac (and technically just inside the Charente region rather than the Dordogne), **AUBETERRE-SUR-DRONNE** is a beautiful town of steep, cobbled streets, its ancient galleried and turreted houses overlooking the lazy River Dronne. The town's attractions – including two interesting churches – haven't gone unnoticed, however, and the place can be absolutely packed to the gills with visitors in summer. For a cooling break, head down the hill to the river where you will find a man-made **beach** with swimming area.

Église Souterraine Saint-Jean

Rue St Jean • Daily: June to Sept 9.30am–12.30pm & 2–7pm; Oct to May 9.30am–12.30pm & 2–6pm • €5, children €2; audioguide €1 • ☎ 05 45 98 65 06

Aubeterre-sur-Dronne's principal curiosity is the cavernous **Église Souterraine Saint-Jean**, in the lower town northeast of the village's lime-shaded central square, **place Trarieux**. Carved out of the soft rock by twelfth-century Benedictine monks, it's the largest subterranean church in Europe – it took at least a century to excavate the astonishing 20m-high chamber and gallery above. Accessed via some eighty steps, the gallery offers the best views over the capacious baptismal font, designed for total immersion, and the two-tiered, hexagonal structure, possibly a reliquary, cut from a single piece of rock – its precise arches seem strangely out of place against the rough walls. The side-chapels are riddled with eerie, rock-hewn tombs, while a now blocked-off tunnel connects the gallery with the château on the bluff overhead. The chilly crypt, meanwhile, was discovered by chance after a lorry accidentally demolished this part of the square in 1961.

Église St-Jacques

On the southwestern hillside, the upper town of Aubeterre-sur-Dronne consists of a single street of houses culminating in the **Église St-Jacques**, where only the beautiful, sculpted west facade remains of the original twelfth-century church. The great tiered and decorated arch around the main door is lovely, but don't overlook the frieze of zodiacal signs on the smaller arch to the left: Taurus, Aries and Pisces are easy enough to recognize, then come Capricorn, Aquarius and Sagittarius. The other half of the frieze is missing. The remainder of the exterior is rather humble by comparison. Inside, the cold, but light-coloured brickwork is devoid of ornamentation, though the smooth circular arches separating the nave and aisles, and timber-beamed ceiling, are worth a look.

ARRIVAL AND INFORMATION   AUBETERRE-SUR-DRONNE

By train There's no train station at Aubeterre-sur-Dronne, but Chalais, which is on the Angoulême–Bordeaux train line, is 12km to the west; call ☎ 06 86 80 25 46 if you need a taxi into Aubeterre.

Tourist office Facing the town's main car park on place du Champ de Foire (Jan–June & Sept–Dec Mon–Sat 9.30am–12.30pm & 2–6pm; July & Aug daily 9.30am–1pm & 2–6.30pm; ☎ 05 45 98 57 18, ⊕ sudcharente tourisme.fr).

Canoe hire On weekends in May and June and daily in July and August, there's canoe rental down by the bridge (☎ 05 45 98 51 72; from €7).

ACCOMMODATION AND EATING

1

Camping Aubeterre-Sur-Dronne Rte Ribérac ☎ 05 45 78 29 36, ⓦ camping-aubeterre.fr. Just across the bridge, and adjacent to the river, this three-star site has some good amenities; snack bar and grill, a kids' play area, and a small sandy beach for volleyball and sunbathing. Bungalows for rent, too (from €340 weekly). Closed Sept–May. **€23**

Crêperie de la Source 4 rue St Jean ☎ 05 45 98 61 78, ⓦ creperie-de-la-source.com. On the corner of the main town square, this endearing little crêperie has fab views down onto the plains far below, and an inexpensive three-course *menu* (€14.50) consisting of a melon or charcuterie starter, a savoury *galette* for the main and a crêpe or other dessert to finish up. Mon–Wed & Sun noon–3pm, Thurs–Sat noon–3pm & 7–9pm.

De France 24 place Ludovic Trarieux ☎ 05 45 98 50 43. On the corner of the main square, this lovely nineteenth-century building has rooms of varying sizes and styles, though all feature thick wood-panelled flooring and heavily timbered ceilings; a couple of rooms share bathroom facilities. It's certainly not an unattractive option, though, like most things in this town, it's a little overpriced. Breakfast €6. **€70**

Du Périgord Quartier Plaisance ☎ 05 45 98 50 46, ⓦ hostellerie-perigord.com. An appealing low-rise building down by the bridge on the Ribérac road, the *Périgord* offers bright (though not particularly inspiring) rooms, with the occasional floral wallpaper and wicker furniture, and there's a pool, jacuzzi and sauna for good measure. The in-house restaurant (mains €12) hosts occasional cookery courses (€85). Breakfast €8. Restaurant Tues–Sat 11.45am–1.30pm & 7.45–11.30pm, Sun 11.45am–1.30pm. **€80**

La Double

South of the Dronne valley the landscape and atmosphere change dramatically as you enter the region known as **La Double**. This high, undulating plateau is strewn with lakes and brooding **forests** of oak, chestnut and pine, interspersed with pockets of vines, scattered farmhouses and an abbey at **Échourgnac**. The larger lakes, such as the **Étang de la Jemaye**, have been developed for tourism, and in summer the Double is a popular destination for walkers, cyclists and nature lovers; the best place to pick up information is Ribérac tourist office (see p.62).

GETTING AROUND   **LA DOUBLE**

While there is no public transport in the Double itself, several services on the Périgueux to Bordeaux train line (see p.54) stop daily at Neuvic, to the east of the region.

Échourgnac and around

Until the late nineteenth century, when Napoléon III decreed that the region should be drained and planted with maritime pines in similar fashion to the great Landes forest further south, La Double was largely uninhabited thanks to its poor soils and malarial marshes. The drainage work was partly carried out by Trappist monks who arrived from Port-Salut in 1868. They settled near the only village of any size, **ÉCHOURGNAC**, plumb in the middle of the plateau and nearly 20km southwest of Ribérac, where they founded the **abbey** which still dominates the village today.

Abbaye de Notre-Dame de Bonne-Espérance

La Trappe • **Shop & abbey church** Jan–June & Sept–Dec Sun noon–12.30pm, 2.30–4.45pm & 5.45–6.30pm; July & Aug Sun 2–7pm • ☎ 05 53 80 82 50, ⓦ abbaye-echourgnac.org

Since 1923 the walled **Abbaye de Notre-Dame de Bonne-Espérance** has sheltered a small community of Cistercian sisters – these days numbering about thirty, some under a vow of silence – who not only continued in the monks' spiritual footsteps but also in their role as local cheesemakers. But the enterprising and energetic sisters didn't stop there. In their well-stocked **shop** opposite the church entrance you'll find the original Le Trappe Échourgnac, a firm, orange-crusted cheese with a smoky flavour, and a newer version laced with walnut liqueur, as well as jams, pâté, jellied sweets and handicrafts from missions around the world; you can also watch a video about the convent here. You can also look into the abbey's **church**, which was given a very modern renovation in 2016.

1

Étang de la Jemaye

The large, scythe-shaped and forest-fringed **Étang de la Jemaye**, a few kilometres to the northeast of Échourgnac, offers lots of summertime fun, with its beaches and swimming, watersports, children's playgrounds, fishing and forest walks.

EATING AND DRINKING   ÉCHOURGNAC

Auberge de la Double Échourgnac ☎ 05 53 80 06 65. To fortify yourself before setting off to explore the area, you can eat at this little village inn which serves weekday lunches at €13 and a *menu* at €22 (Fri & Sat eves & Sun lunchtime). Jan–Nov Mon–Thurs 8am–3pm, Sat 8am–9pm.

Ferme du Parcot

May, June & Sept Sat & Sun 2–7pm; July & Aug daily 10am–12.30pm & 2–7pm • Guided visits to farm buildings: May, June & Sept Sat & Sun 2.30pm & 5.30pm; July & Aug daily 10.30am, 2.30pm, 4pm & 5.30pm • Free • ☎ 05 53 81 99 28, ⓦ parcot.org

Some 5km east of Abbaye de Notre-Dame de Bonne-Espérance, on the D41 from Échourgnac, the **Ferme du Parcot** has been preserved as a typical example of the architecture of La Double. With walls of mud and straw on latticed timber frames, protected by a limestone plaster, these farm buildings are quite unlike the sturdy stone houses found elsewhere in the Dordogne. They date from 1841 and, from the grandeur of the barn, it seems the farmer was relatively affluent. In true rural style, however, the house itself, which was inhabited up to 1990, consists of just two very spartan rooms containing a few bits and pieces of furniture and old implements. The farm also marks the start of a gentle **nature trail** (2.5km; accessible all year) through the fields and forest to a fishing lake.

The Northern Périgord Vert

North of Brantôme lies a peaceful, little-populated region with one or two classic tourist attractions (including the superb **Grotte de Villars**), but as much as anything this area is about exploring quiet lanes and picnicking in the countryside. **St-Jean-de-Côle**, a tiny sun-soaked village dominated by its château, makes a good base for exploring nearby attractions such as the ruined Cistercian **Abbaye de Boschaud** and the French Renaissance **Château de Puyguilhem**, while quiet **Thiviers** is another good bet for an overnight stay.

St-Jean-de-Côle

Twenty kilometres northeast of Brantôme, **ST-JEAN-DE-CÔLE** ranks as one of the loveliest villages in the Périgord Vert, and with a couple of restaurants, it makes a good lunchtime stop. Tiny and very picturesque without being twee, St-Jean's unusually open, sandy square is dominated by the charmingly ill-proportioned **Église de St-Jean-Baptiste**, dating from the late eleventh century. The view as you approach is harmonious enough – layers of tiled roofs from the low, square market hall to the steeply pitched belfry – but on

---

LA VOIE VERTE

One of the lesser-known walking and cycling routes in the region is **La Voie Verte** ("Green Way"), an 18km footpath and cycleway that follows a disused train line from Thiviers into the heart of the Périgord Vert. On a warm summer's day it's a delightful outing, taking in pretty villages like St-Jean-de-Côle and Milhac-de-Nontron, as well as rivers and viaducts, before winding up at Saint-Pardoux-la-Rivière. Local tourist offices can provide a handout illustrating the route, and bikes can be hired from Dordogne Cycle Hire in Thiviers (☎ 05 53 52 26 42, ⓦ dordognecyclehire.com; €15/day), who will also deliver throughout the northern Périgord Vert region. Trailer-buggies and child seats are available too.

entering the single, lofty bay it becomes apparent that the nave was never completed, due to a lack of funds. Beside the church stands the rugged-looking **Château de la Marthonie** (no public access), which dates from the twelfth century, but has since acquired various additions in a pleasingly organic fashion. Apart from a huddle of houses round the square, the rest of the village consists of a line of pastel-plastered cottages stretching west to a humpbacked bridge over the River Côle and the inevitable water mill. The whole ensemble makes a perfect backdrop for the Floralies **flower festival**, held on the second weekend in May.

INFORMATION   ST-JEAN-DE-CÔLE

Tourist office 19 rue du Château (mid-June to mid-Sept daily 10am–1pm & 2–6.30pm; mid-Sept to Oct & March to mid-June Wed–Sun 10am–1pm & 2–6pm; Nov–Feb Mon–Fri same times; ☎05 53 62 14 15, ⓦ ville-saint-jean-de-cole.fr). The office runs guided tours of the village (in French) daily at 11am in July and August (€5 per person) or you can go it alone with a multi-language audioguide (€5).

ACCOMMODATION, EATING AND DRINKING

Chez Robert 14 place de l'Église ☎05 53 52 53 09. The setting couldn't be any more simple, with tables set out in the owner's front room (or outside on the square in fine weather), but the food is anything but plain: think lobster salad with pan-fried foie gras and mango sauce, followed perhaps by a turbot soufflé with scallops and vegetables. The view over the château isn't half bad either. *Menu* €43. Tues–Sun 7–10pm.

★**Parenthèses Imaginaires** Fontaine de Cardissou ☎06 10 03 67 04, ⓦparentheses-imaginaires.com. A couple of kilometres outside the quiet village of Milhac-de-Nontron, this is a small, shady and fun glamping site. Accommodation is in a series of pre-erected tents (sleeping 2–4) that are more wooden chalet than canvas, equipped with beds and kitchenettes. The pricier ones are built right beside a carp-filled lake and you can jump straight from your private terrace into the water. With a nature cabin where children are encouraged to make art from pinecones, shells and driftwood, as well as a shallow swimming pool and crazy golf, this is one of the best sites around for families. One-week minimum stay in high season. Closed Nov–March. Weekly rate €490

La Perla Café Place de l'Église ☎05 53 52 38 11. Take a seat at this welcoming outdoor café overlooking the church and fill up with one of their light lunches, for example duck salad or flambéed prawns, or just kick back with a coffee. Mains €8.50–14. May, June & Sept Wed–Sun 10am–6pm; July & Aug daily 10am–9pm.

Le Temps des Mets 1 place du Vieux Pont ☎09 67 78 25 72. With big, puffy paper lampshades hanging from the branches of trees and lime-green chairs on a lawn surrounded by hot pink flowers, *Le Temps des Mets* is a stylish place to eat treats such as roasted cod with a seasonal veg sauce or duck kebab with goats' cheese cream. *Menus* from €30. Daily noon–2pm & 7–9.30pm; closed Nov–Feb.

Château de Puyguilhem

April & Sept 10am–12.30pm & 2–5.30pm; May–Aug daily 10am–12.30pm & 2–6.30pm; Oct–March Wed–Sun 10am–12.30pm & 2–5.30pm • €5.50 • ☎05 53 54 82 18, ⓦ chateau-puyguilhem.fr

About 10km west of St-Jean, just outside the attractive village of **VILLARS**, the **Château de Puyguilhem** is a perfect example of early French Renaissance architecture. It was erected at the beginning of the sixteenth century by the La Marthonie family of St-Jean-de-Côle on the site of an earlier and more military fortress. The lake that once filled the foreground has long gone, but the château still makes an enchanting prospect, with its steep roofs, stone balustrades, mullion windows, carved chimney stacks and an assortment of round and octagonal towers reminiscent of contemporaneous Loire châteaux.

Though the **interior** suffered more from neglect and pillaging, it too has been beautifully restored and contains some noteworthy pieces of furniture and Aubusson tapestries; the most impressive of the latter are located in the Great Hall, one tapestry depicting a rhinoceros, and another, a lion fighting a leopard. Its most remarkable features, however, are two magnificent fireplaces: the first, in the guardroom, depicts three Greek soldiers, while upstairs in the banqueting hall the theme is continued with six of the twelve Labours of Hercules. Both are heavily restored, but no less remarkable for that. The sculptors also went to work on the entrance hall and main staircase, leaving a wealth of oak, vine and acanthus leaves, thistles, fleur-de-lis and

1

a few salamanders for good measure. Right at the top, it was the turn of the master carpenters, whose superb hull-shaped roof timbers have lasted five hundred years. Once done in the château, take a look at the **pigeonnier**, situated amongst the trees to the rear of the castle; it's a fine example of a French medieval pigeon house, this one consisting of hundreds of *boulins* (pigeon holes), each of which typically lodged a pair of birds.

ACCOMMODATION AND EATING   VILLARS

Le Petit Château de Villars Rue de Moulin ☎ 05 53 03 41 58, ⓦ chateaudevillars.com. This glamorous, American-owned grand residence dating back to 1862 sits in five hectares of parkland on the southern fringe of Villars. With five regal rooms, a classy dark-wood panelled bar and an excellent restaurant (mains from €18, *menus* €29) serving local classics as well as more international dishes, from curries to southern US-style barbeque, it offers a taste of rather royal living. Restaurant Wed–Sat noon–2pm & 7–9.30pm, Sun 7–9.30pm. **€110**

Abbaye de Boschaud

Unrestricted access • Free

The ruined Cistercian **Abbaye de Boschaud**, 3km from Villars in the next valley south of the Château de Puyguilhem, merits a quick visit while you're in the area. Standing in the middle of a field, it's reached by a lane not much bigger than a farm track. Though the pure, stark lines of the twelfth-century architecture hold a certain appeal, the abbey's real charm rests in the fact that it is – for once – unfenced and unpampered, and you can explore its tumbledown walls and lifeless shell at will.

Grotte de Villars

40min guided tours daily: April–June & Sept 10am–noon & 2–7pm; July & Aug 10am–7.30pm; Oct to mid-Nov 2–6pm • €8.50, children €5.50 • ☎ 05 53 54 82 36, ⓦ grotte-villars.com

In 1953 speleologists discovered an extensive cave system in the hills 3km north of Villars, now known as the **Grotte de Villars**. To date, around 13km of the system has been explored, and some 600m of caves are open to the public via a guided tour. Villars is unusual in that it boasts a combination of both concretions and paintings. As impressive as these few paintings are – notably of horses and a still-unexplained scene of a man and bison – the main reason for coming here is the variety of **stalagmites** and, in particular, **stalactites**. Some are almost pure white and as fine as needles, others ochre-yellow or tainted red from the soil, and there are also cascades, semicircular basins and hanging curtains of semi-translucent calcium carbonate. The final cave contains the **paintings**, dating from 17,000 years ago, though they're only just discernible under the thick layer of calcite. Look out, too, for the claw marks further back from the entrance, where generations of tiny bear cubs have left their imprints – there are a handful of cave-bear bones, including part of a jaw, on display near the reception area. There's a good chance, too, that you'll encounter one of the many resident pipistrelle bats as they swoop around the caves.

The **parkland** surrounding the cave holds models of prehistoric wildlife and people alongside information panels about life on the hillside then and now; and with a variety and range of activities laid on for children, from making your own "cave painting" to spear-throwing, Villars is arguably the most family-friendly cave complex in the whole of the Dordogne.

Thiviers

Eight kilometres east of St-Jean-de-Côle, and linked by the pleasant Voie Verte cycle route (see box, p.66), the small market town of **THIVIERS** sits on the main road and rail links between Périgueux, 40km to the south, and Limoges. The peaceful old centre comprises a clutch of pretty, aged houses round the church and along pedestrianized rue de la Tour.

Thiviers is at its most lovely during the Saturday **market**, when the streets present a lesson in local agriculture: walnuts, apples, Limousin beef, pork, duck and goose and all manner of associated foodstuffs. From mid-November to mid-March the *foies* come out in force at the *marché au gras*, some of them destined to go into the local speciality, *L'autre fois de Thiviers*, consisting of duck- or goose-liver robed in pâté.

Up until the 1920s, Thiviers was an important centre for **faïence** (tin-glazed pottery), a hundred or so pieces of which are displayed in the town hall (Sat 10am–noon & 3–5.30pm; free). But the pretty blue-and-white faïence plays second fiddle to the town's prime concern: the history and production of **foie gras**, the subject of the small **Maison du Foie Gras** museum (Mon–Fri 10am–1pm & 2–6pm; Sat 9am–1pm & 3–6pm; plus July & Aug Sun 10am–1pm; €3) accessed via the tourist office (which also houses a specialist foie gras shop), though it's expensive for what it is and not particularly stimulating, especially as there's nothing by way of English explanation.

FOIE GRAS

It is generally agreed that it was the Egyptians who first discovered the delights of eating the **enlarged livers** of migratory geese and ducks gorging themselves in the Nile delta, and that it was the Romans who popularized the practice of force-feeding domesticated birds, generally with figs. For many the name (literally, "fat liver") is off-putting enough, let alone the idea of force-feeding the birds, while for others a slice of the succulent, pale rose-coloured liver is a pleasure not to be missed.

DUCK OR GOOSE?

Foie gras is produced throughout southwest France and also in Alsace, Brittany and the Vendée. However, the yellowish-hued livers from the Périgord, where the birds are traditionally fed on local yellow (as opposed to white) maize, and where producers jealously guard their methods of preparation, are particularly sought after. Périgord farmers now favour hybrid Mulard or Barbary **ducks** over the more traditional **geese** for a variety of reasons: they fatten more quickly, are easier to raise and force-feed, and the liver is easier to cook with. The softer goose livers, on the other hand, have a more delicate flavour and smoother texture. They are also larger – 600g to 700g for an average goose liver (*foie gras d'oie*) as opposed to 500g for duck (*foie gras de canard*).

PRODUCTION

The young birds are raised outside to the age of four months, after which they are kept in the dark and fed over one kilo per day of partly cooked maize for between two and three weeks. During this time the livers can quadruple in size. This **gavage**, or force-feeding, was traditionally carried out using a funnel to introduce the grain into the bird's throat and then stroking it down the neck by hand. Modern techniques follow the same principle but use a mechanized feeder. When done carefully, it's not nearly as terrible as it sounds and most small producers go to a lot of trouble not to harm their birds, if for no other reason than that a stressed bird will produce a rancid liver.

WHERE AND WHAT TO BUY?

All round, it's best to **buy** foie gras from small family concerns, either direct from the farm – local tourist offices can advise – or at the region's many *marchés aux gras* that take place from November to March. If you're buying **fresh liver**, choose one which is not too big, is uniform in colour and firm but gives slightly to the touch; the market price averages €30–40 per kilo for foie gras of duck and €50–60 for goose. The alternative is the ready-prepared **preserved** version, of which there is a bewildering variety. The majority is de-veined, seasoned (wherein the secret recipes) and then sterilized by cooking briefly (*mi-cuit*) before being vacuum-packed or sealed in jars, either of which is preferable to the canned varieties; the tin taints the flavour. When choosing, check that it is locally produced and then look for the label *foie gras entier*, in other words consisting of one or more whole lobes, or simply *foie gras*, which is composed of smaller pieces but is still top-quality liver. Next step down is a *bloc de foie gras* made up of reconstituted liver (sometimes *avec morceaux*, visible pieces of lobe) pressed together. Below that come all sorts of *mousses, parfaits*, pâtés and so forth, each of which has to contain a specified minimum percentage of foie gras and to indicate this on the label.

1

By train The *gare SNCF* is located on rue Pierre Sémard, just a few minutes' walk north of Thiviers' centre.

Destinations Bordeaux (4–7 daily; 2hr); Limoges (12 daily; 45min); Périgueux (13 daily; 25min).

Tourist office 8 place du Maréchal Foch (Mon–Fri 10am–1pm & 2–6pm, Sat 9am–1pm & 3–6pm; plus July & Aug Sun 10am–1pm; ☎ 05 53 55 12 50, ⓦ thiviers.fr), also known as La Maison du Foie Gras on account of it housing the foie gras museum.

ACCOMMODATION AND EATING

De France et de Russie 51 rue du Général Lamy ☎ 05 53 55 17 80, ⓦ thiviers-hotel.com. A warm welcome is assured at this ever-so-relaxing English-run hotel, set in a former eighteenth-century coaching inn and popular with pilgrims travelling the route to Santiago. Its rooms retain a pleasingly timeworn ambience, though the whole place is run through with the owner's personal, and occasionally quirky, touch – you can even play chess in the reception area or tinkle on the ivories in the lounge. In the building to the rear, two rooms have been specially adapted for wheelchair users. Breakfast €8. **€74**

Le Repaire ☎ 05 53 52 69 75, ⓦ camping-le-repaire.fr. A well-run three-star campsite beside an artificial lake on the D707 road towards Lanouaille, with lounge bar, pool and playground, plus chalets to rent (from €500 weekly). Closed Nov–March. **€22**

La Sablière 25 Promenade de la Sablière ☎ 05 53 52 47 23, ⓦ la-sabliere-perigord.com. Classy *chambre d'hôte* located around 1km north of town. There are four rooms, basically mini-suites (three of them sleep four): fantastically comfortable beds, fine white linen and brilliant power showers are just some of the little luxuries that await. It's a little tricky to find as there are no signs; head north along the road towards Jumilhac-le-Grand and take a left at the turning for the abbatoir. **€89**

Jumilhac-le-Grand

In its upper reaches the Isle valley narrows down between steep, wooded banks to become a mini-ravine. One of its rocky bluffs, some 20km northeast of Thiviers, is home to the vast Château de Jumilhac, centrepiece of attractive **JUMILHAC-LE-GRAND** village. For more than two centuries Jumilhac has been closely associated with **gold**, and though the nearby mines closed in 2001, you can learn more about the history of gold here and further afield in the **Galerie de l'Or** (Jan–May & Oct–Dec Tues–Fri 2–5pm; June & Sept daily 10am–12.30pm & 2–6pm; July & Aug daily 10.30am–1pm & 2.30–6.30pm; €4, children €2; ☎ 05 53 52 55 43), a succinct but well-presented museum, next to the tourist office and overlooking the grassy square in front of the château. Visit in summer and you can even try your luck **panning for gold** in the River Isle (July & Aug; call the tourist office to reserve a half-day session; €18); it's not uncommon to find tiny specks, but don't expect to make your fortune.

Château de Jumilhac

Place du Château • March–May & Oct daily 2–6pm; June–Sept daily 10am–7pm; Nov–Feb Sun 2–5pm • €7, children €4; €8.40/€5.50 including gardens • Night visits: May, June & Sept Tues 9.30–11.30pm; July & Aug Tues & Thurs 9.30–11.30pm • From €8.50, children €5.50 • ☎ 05 53 52 42 97, ⓦ chateaudejumilhac.com

While elements of the original thirteenth-century **Château de Jumilhac** remain – such as the stone-paved ground-floor rooms and the family chapel – the present structure largely owes its existence to an ironmaster, Antoine Chapelle, later count of Jumilhac, who made his fortune manufacturing arms for the future Henry IV during the Wars of Religion. The body of the château is suitably uncompromising: the hard, grey stone allowed for little decorative detail, and what windows there are mostly consist of narrow slits. But the roof is another matter, adorned with no fewer than eight different **towers**, from great grey-slate wedges to pinnacled turrets and a jaunty pepper-pot, topped off with delicate lead statues depicting the angels of justice or more mundane pigeon-shaped weather-vanes.

Inside, however, austerity reigns once again. This is particularly so in the cramped, ground-floor rooms, which date back to the thirteenth century, but also extends to the medieval rooms above, of which the much-vaunted **spinner's room** provides the focus of the tour. Not so much for its architecture – it's a small vaulted chamber decorated with naive frescoes of animals and flowers – but for the story attached. The spinner in question was **Louise de Hautefort**, wife of the then count of Jumilhac, who was imprisoned here for thirty years (1618–48) for her alleged infidelity. Not one to mope, Louise took to painting the walls and spinning to occupy her time – or so it seemed. The shepherd who regularly called under her window, and from whom she bought her wool, was of course her lover in disguise, and the spindles were used to carry secret messages between them. According to one legend, the story ended in the lover being killed in a duel, while another has him retiring to a monastery. To give you some idea what all the fuss was about, there's a portrait of Louise, supposedly painted at the time of her release but still beautiful, defiantly holding her spindle aloft.

The two wings enclosing the courtyard were added later in the seventeenth century and are gradually being restored by the château's present owners, descendants of Antoine Chapelle, who bought it back from the state in 1927. The interior is demonstrably lighter in tone, thanks to the prevailing use of limestone – witness the handsome staircase – while the flooring is a pebble and stone mosaic encrusted in sand. The outstanding features here are two wooden fireplaces at opposing ends of the **Grand Hall**, which is otherwise dominated by paintings of various hunting scenes. Crossing the balustraded stone balcony to the opposite wing gives you superb views of the steeply sloping tree-lined square straight ahead.

The castle is opened up for **evening visits** in the summer, when the candle-lit gloom adds a suitably spooky aspect, while the beautiful and very formal flower **gardens** are well worth a look, with display panels to identify the plants.

INFORMATION	JUMILHAC-LE-GRAND
Tourist office Place du Château (Jan–May & Oct–Dec Tues–Fri 2–5pm; June & Sept daily 10am–12.30pm &	2–6pm; July & Aug daily 10.30am–1pm & 2.30–6.30pm; ☎ 05 53 52 55 43, ⓦ pays-jumilhac.fr).

ACCOMMODATION

La Chatonnière ☎ 05 53 52 57 36, ⓦ www .chatonniere.com. Beside the Isle just over 1km north of Jumilhac, the three-star *La Chatonnière* campsite is a small, family-oriented affair, with extensive play spaces and a sandy river beach to keep the little ones amused. Closed mid-Sept to June. **€28**

Lieu d'Or 12 rue des Croix Bancaud ☎ 05 53 62 06 36, ⓦ lieudor.com. One of the few places to stay in and around Jumilhac, *Lieu d'Or* is a pretty and very welcoming *chambre d'hôte*, with five classic white-painted rooms with a touch of the past about them. Meals available on request (€20). **€67**

Excideuil

The old route between Périgueux and Limoges used to run up the Isle and Loue rivers to **EXCIDEUIL**, 17km southeast of Thiviers, where two huge medieval keeps still dominate the little market town. The **castle** was one of the region's most heavily fortified and for a while the viscounts of Limoges held court here. Following the Hundred Years War, however, the fortress lay in ruins until relatively recently, when restoration was carried out. It is now privately owned, so you can enter only the (fairly uninteresting) precinct, but it's an impressive sight from afar, particularly if you approach from the west. From the castle, rue des Cendres leads north into the tight knot of streets concentrated around lovely **place Bugeaud**, with its stone duck fountain and the much-restored church, with its Gothic portal. This square and the nearby *halle* are the venue for a lively farmers' **market** on Thursday mornings, augmented in winter (Nov to early March) by an important *marché au gras aux truffes*, dedicated to foie gras and truffles. The tourist office can provide a leaflet outlining a walking tour of the village which, even at an easy pace, should take no more than an hour.

1

THE BLACK DIAMONDS OF PÉRIGORD

The **black truffle** of Périgord, *tuber melanosporum*, is one of those expensive delicacies that many people find overrated. This is mainly because it's usually served in minute quantities or combined with such strong flavours that its own subtle, earthy taste and aroma are completely overwhelmed. Truffle is best appreciated if eaten in a salad, omelette or simple pastry crust.

The truffle is a **fungus** that grows entirely underground, and a fussy one at that. It prefers shallow, free-draining limestone soils rich in organic matter, a sunny position and marked seasonal differences, and requires the presence of certain species of oak, or occasionally lime or hazelnut, around the roots of which it grows. It's greedy, too, absorbing so much of the nutrients and water available that the vegetation overhead often dies. This tell-tale ring of denuded earth is just one of the clues truffle-hunters are on the lookout for. Others include small, yellow truffle-flies hovering just above the soil, and the distinct smell – which is where the pig, or generally these days the more amenable dog – comes in.

Even now the **life cycle** of the Périgord truffle – the most prized out of more than forty different varieties – is not completely understood, and attempts to cultivate them artificially have so far proved unsuccessful. What is clear is that the spores are released in the spring and mature truffles are ready for harvest between December and early March. When ripe, the skin of a Périgord truffle is a deep purple-brown or black, while the lighter-coloured flesh is flecked with fine white veins. It should be firm to the touch and give off a pleasantly earthy aroma; an overripe truffle stinks.

The principal **truffle markets** take place at Périgueux, Sorges, Sarlat and Brantôme, and at Labenque near Cahors in the Quercy. Prices these days average €800–1000 per kilo. In the past, however, truffles were so common that they were considered a pest by vine growers. Ironically, the fungus proved a life-saver for many local farmers when phylloxera hit in the late nineteenth century, ushering in the truffle's "golden age". Since the 1950s, the harvest has declined dramatically for a number of reasons – deforestation and rural depopulation among others – although a revival is well underway with up to 90 hectares of truffle trees being planted each year in the Dordogne since 2000.

If you want to learn more about truffles, then head to Sorges, 17km west of Excideuil, where the **Musée de la Truffe** (Jan to mid-June & Oct–Dec Tues–Sun 10am–noon & 2–5pm; July & Aug daily 9.30am–12.30pm & 2.30–6.30pm; €5; ☎ 05 53 05 90 11) offers detailed explanations (in French only) of the truffle-growing process – from how the fungus forms to how to create your own truffle-oak orchard. There are also many preserved specimens for sale in the downstairs shop (May–Sept Mon–Sat 10am–1pm & 2–6pm, plus July & Aug Sun 9.30am–1pm; Oct–April Thurs–Sat 10am–1pm & 2–6pm), which doubles as the tourist office.

ARRIVAL AND INFORMATION   EXCIDEUIL

By bus Buses stop beneath the castle on place du Château.
Destinations Périgueux (school term Mon–Fri 4–5 daily, school hols Mon–Fri 3 daily; 50min).
Tourist office 1 place du Château, which lies on the main road through town (May–Sept Mon–Sat 10am–1pm & 2–6pm, plus July & Aug Sun 9.30am–1pm; Oct–April Thurs–Sat 10am–1pm & 2–6pm; ☎ 05 53 52 29 79, ⊛ naturellementperigord.fr).

ACCOMMODATION AND EATING

★**Aux Delices d'Excideuil** 2 place Burgeaud ☎ 05 53 62 46 65, ⊛ auxdelicesdexcideuil.fr. The cool stone walls, grey shuttered windows and a delightful wrought-iron balcony mark this out as one of the loveliest buildings on the square. It also conceals a classy *chambre d'hôte*, with four smartly furnished rooms, each furnished in wildly alternating styles. In warm weather, breakfast is served on the flower-strewn garden patio. €88

Hostellerie du Fin Chapon Place du Château ☎ 05 53 62 42 38, ⊛ lefinchapon.com. Next to the tourist office, the *Hostellerie du Fin Chapon* offers rather plain but comfortable rooms in stock *Logis* chain-style fashion. Some have views over the castle that will leave lasting memories. Breakfast €8. €65

★**Kitsch Kafe** 29 rue Jean Jaurès ☎ 05 53 52 21 62. The Anglo–Aussie proprietors of *Kitsch* certainly know a thing or two about coffee, which is lovingly prepared before being served in brightly coloured mugs – to be savoured, perhaps, with one of their sweet or savoury crumpets or home-made cupcakes. Wonderfully mismatched furnishings in the shape of 1960s formica-covered plastic tables and wooden chairs, as well as wall paintings and other cute collectables add to this gorgeous little café's undoubted charm. Mon–Fri 8.30am–4.30pm.

Les Troubadours 29 rue Jean Jaurès ☎ 05 53 62 17 74, ⊛ chambresdhotesexcideuil.info. Hiding behind the front door of this huge old townhouse – parts of which date back to the seventeenth century – are five refined and peaceful rooms with polished wooden furnishings and a taste of the early twentieth century. Downstairs is a billiard room and library as well as an inviting bar, while out the back is a lovely enclosed garden. **€60**

1

Hautefort and around

Southeast of Excideuil you cross the pretty Auvézère valley and enter the limestone plateaux of the Périgord Blanc. The views are magnificent, and nowhere more so than around **HAUTEFORT** and its eponymous **château**, standing on a south-facing promontory some 20km from Excideuil and 40km northeast of Périgueux. Bustling with tourists during the day, Hautefort is a peaceful backwater come evening and is an enjoyable place for an overnight stay, with swallows and cicadas providing the only background noise.

Château de Hautefort

March & Nov 1–11 Sat & Sun 2–6pm; April & May daily 10am–12.30pm & 2–6.30pm; June–Aug daily 9.30am–7pm, plus Wed 9–10pm; Sept daily 10am–6pm; Oct daily 2–6pm • €9.50, children €5 • ☎ 05 53 50 51 23, ⓦ chateau-hautefort.com

The **Château de Hautefort** is a stunning sight from whichever direction you approach, a magnificent example of blue-blood living on a grand scale, endowed with an elegance that's out of step with the usual rough stone fortresses of Périgord. Indeed, when the then marquis de Hautefort rebuilt it in the mid-seventeenth century, his ambition was to create a château worthy of the Loire.

The original fortress was built some time around 1000, and in the twelfth century it belonged jointly to the famous troubadour **Bertran de Born** (see box, p.293) and his brother Constantin, until Bertran persuaded his overlord, Henry II of England, to grant him sole ownership in 1185. The following year Constantin took his revenge and left the place in ruins – at which point Bertran went off to become a monk. The château's recent history has been no less troubled. After decades of neglect, in 1929 Hautefort was bought and meticulously restored by the rather unfortunately named Baron Henri de Bastard and his wife. Then in August 1968, just three years after the work was completed, a **fire** gutted everything except the chapel in the southeast tower. A year later the indomitable baroness – her husband having died before the fire – set about the whole task again, and master craftsmen were called in to recreate everything from the staircases to the ornate chimneypieces. There's no disguising the fact that it's all brand new, but the quality of work is superb – and if you visit in summer you might coincide with various **special events** (mainly aimed at children), from nature and art workshops to a special film-set experience; see the website for details.

The approach to the château lies across a wide esplanade, flanked by immaculate topiary gardens, and over a drawbridge to enter a stylish Renaissance **courtyard** opening to the south. The two wings end in a pair of round towers, whose great bulk is offset by grey-slate domes topped with matching pepper-pot lanterns; the southwestern tower, nearest the entrance, is the only part of the medieval château still standing. While the main building is equally symmetrical, the overall impression is one of rhythm and harmony rather than severity.

About the only furnishings saved from the fire were four sixteenth-century tapestries, now on display inside, but the real highlight is the **great hall**, a monumental room which provides the perfect setting for two huge chimneypieces. Exact copies of the originals and carved from local walnut, each took five thousand hours' work. The **chapel**, meanwhile, is worth a look for its pebble mosaic flooring, representing the family coat of arms, and the trompe l'oeil ceiling.

With open lawns and plenty of grand old trees, the undulating **park** surrounding the château also holds a formal garden and a maze.

1

Musée de la Médecine

Place de Marquis J-F de Hautefort • Daily: March–May, Oct & Nov 10am–noon & 2–6pm; June–Sept 10am–7pm • €6, children €4.50 • ⓦ musee-hautefort.fr

The **Musée de la Médecine** lies in the midst of an open square and is accessed via Hautefort's tourist office. It occupies part of a hospice for the poor founded in 1669 by Marquis Jacques-François de Hautefort, who also built the the Château de Hautefort, as its architecture – particularly the domed central chapel – suggests. One of the ground-floor rooms presents an early-nineteenth-century ward (complete with silly-looking mannequins under the ministration of the Sisters of Charity). Here you'll find a reconstruction of a so-called *tour*, essentially a revolving cupboard in which abandoned children would be placed by mothers who could not, or did not wish to, care for their child – they would then ring the bell to inform the hospice of the new arrival; these could be found in hospices all over the region, including here at Hautefort, until their removal in 1847. As if this wasn't sobering enough, things get worse upstairs among the displays of brutal-looking medical implements through the ages (the gynaecological stuff doesn't bear thinking about), culminating in examples of dental surgeries up to 1970. There's also a section devoted to Louis Pasteur, inventor of the rabies and anthrax vaccines, among many other notable achievements. However, the absence of any English captioning ultimately renders this a rather frustrating visit if you don't read French.

ARRIVAL AND INFORMATION   HAUTEFORT

By bus Public transport to Hautefort is almost non-existent, the only possibility being to catch a late afternoon bus from Périgueux (Mon–Fri at 5.20pm), with the return service departing from Hautefort at 6.30am the following morning.

Tourist office In the north wing of the old hospice on Place du Marquis J-F de Hautefort (Jan–March & Nov–Dec Mon–Fri 9.30am–12.30pm & 2–6pm; April, May & Oct daily 9.30am–12.30pm & 2–6pm; June–Sept daily 10am–7pm; ☎ 05 53 50 40 27, ⓦ ot-hautefort.com).

ACCOMMODATION AND EATING

Auberge du Parc ☎ 05 53 50 88 98, ⓦ aubergeduparc -hautefort.fr. The *Auberge du Parc*, right under the castle walls, has five rooms, which are basic at best and rather on the dowdy side – though they're pleasingly inexpensive. Breakfast €7. Closed mid-Dec to Feb. **€55**

Le Camping du Coucou ☎ 05 53 50 86 97, ⓦ camping ducoucou.com. A lakeside campsite, less than 2km to the south of Hautefort in Nailhac, with superb facilities including a grocery shop, TV lounge, playground, boulodrome

and swimming pool, plus chalets to rent (from €362 weekly). Closed Sept to Easter. **€10.80**

Les Petits Plaisirs Place Eugène Le Roy ☎ 05 53 51 91 86. After visiting the castle, stop by this sweet little café-cum-shop on the pretty little main square just below, where they serve crêpes, salads, gourmet burgers and charcuterie platters; or just indulge in a glass of wine. *Menus* from €19.50. Mon noon–2pm, Wed–Sun noon–2pm & 7–9pm.

Abbaye de Tourtoirac

Museum July & Aug daily 10am–12.30pm & 2.30–6pm • Free

Some 8km west of Hautefort, the village of **Tourtoirac** is best known for its caves, but you can also visit the **Abbaye de Tourtoirac**, parts of which date from the tenth century, and which houses an **archeological museum** containing weapons and tools found during the course of excavations at the site.

Grotte de Tourtoirac

March & Nov Sat & Sun 2–6pm • April & Oct daily 2–6pm; May, June & Sept daily 10am–noon & 2–6pm; July & Aug daily 9.30am–7.30pm & 9–10pm • €8.20, children €5.50 • ☎ 05 53 50 24 77, ⓦ grotte-de-tourtoirac.fr

Some 2km south of Tourtoirac village along the D5, the **Grotte de Tourtoirac** cave system was only discovered in 1995, and opened to the public in 2010. The caves were

CHÂTEAU DE BOURDEILLES (P.60)>

1

never inhabited, but contain a rich array of stalactites and stalagmites, and have the advantage of offering access to for those with limited mobility via a lift.

Brive-la-Gaillarde

A major road and rail junction, **Brive-la-Gaillarde** is the nearest thing to an industrial centre for miles around. That said, its largely pedestrianized old centre, enclosed within a circular boulevard shaded by plane trees, comes as a pleasant surprise after its sprawling suburbs. The town's cultural highlights include the much-restored **Collégiale St-Martin de Brive**, the wide-ranging **Musée Labenche** and the local Resistance museum, the **Musée Edmond Michelet**, along with a handful of very smart restaurants. However, this is very much a town for locals rather than tourists.

It's thought that Brive earned its nickname **la Gaillarde** during the Hundred Years War when, for much of the time, it was a lone French stronghold surrounded by English. Opinions are divided, but the name "la Galliarde" (meaning strong, sprightly or bawdy) refers either to its fortifications or – the generally preferred option – the spirited, valiant nature of its people. The ramparts disappeared after the Revolution to make way for today's gardens and ring road, but the "Brivistes" themselves haven't changed, as they will happily tell you, citing past glories on the rugby field as the prime example. Brive also makes a convenient base for exploring the beautiful towns and villages around, and it's not that far to Lascaux and the upper reaches of the River Dordogne.

Collégiale St-Martin de Brive

Place du Général-de-Gaulle • Daily 10am–noon & 3–6pm • Free

As a focus for wandering Brive's compact old streets, head first to the **Collégiale St-Martin de Brive**, plumb in the middle of town on a square dotted with handsome turreted and towered houses, some dating back to the thirteenth century. The church was originally Romanesque in style; now only the transept, apse and a few comically carved capitals survive from that era. The most striking aspect of the church **interior**, however, is its outwardly slanting columns, which have supposedly given way in this manner due to the sheer weight of the central vault. It's said that St Martin, a Spanish aristocrat, arrived in pagan Brive in 407 AD on the feast of Saturnus, smashed various idols and was promptly stoned to death by the outraged onlookers. Supposedly, St Martin's unmarked tomb is among those in the tiny crypt, which is otherwise crammed with archeological remnants, reliquaries and other religious artefacts.

RUGBY IN BRIVE

Southwest France is without question the heartland of French **rugby**, and Brive one of its major centres. Founded in 1910, **Club Athlétique Brive Corrèze Limousin** (or CA Brive) enjoyed only moderate success until the 1990s, when, somewhat surprisingly, it emerged as a major European force. The club's greatest moment came in 1997, when it won the European Cup, beating Leicester Tigers in Cardiff. The following year they reached the final again, this time narrowly losing to Bath, and in 2000 contested the final of the French Cup, though this proved to be their last taste of success, as that same year they were relegated, following financial mismanagement. Since then they've yo-yoed between the top two divisions, but as of 2016 they play in the Top 14, which comprises the best clubs in the country. CA Brive games take place at the **Stade Amédée Domenech**, twenty minutes' walk east of the centre, usually on a Saturday or Sunday; tickets cost as little as €10 (Ⓦ cabrive-rugby.com).

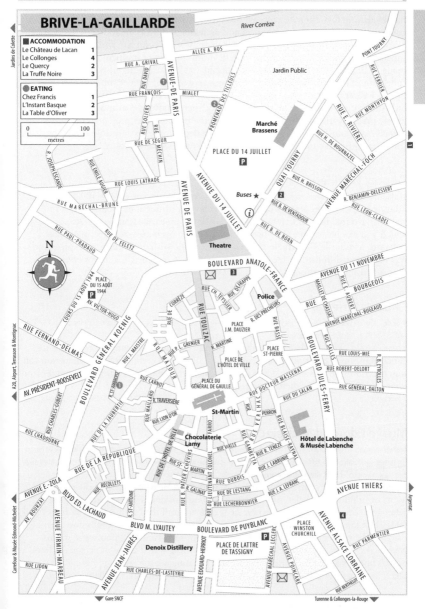

BRIVE-LA-GAILLARDE

■ ACCOMMODATION
Le Château de Lacan	1
Le Collonges	4
Le Quercy	2
La Truffe Noire	3

● EATING
Chez Francis	1
L'Instant Basque	2
La Table d'Oliver	3

Musée Labenche

26 bd Jules-Ferry • Mon & Wed–Sun: May–Sept 10am–12.30pm & 1.30–6pm; Oct–April 2–6pm • €5 • ☏ 05 55 18 17 70,
Ⓦ museelabenche.brive.fr

The most impressive of the buildings on or just off place du Général-du-Gaulle is the sixteenth-century **Hôtel de Labenche**, now housing the enlightening **Musée Labenche**, whose prime focus is local art and history. As you enter, note the busts of the Labenche

1

family leaning forward over each window. The museum's exhaustive collection encompasses wide-ranging geological and archeological finds, including stalagmites and cave-bear bones, some delightful Gallo-Roman bronzes complete with moulds, and a superb ethnographic section featuring a beautiful display of multicoloured accordions made in Brive by the Dedenis factory prior to 1939. The highlight, though, is a rare collection of **Mortlake tapestries**. The Mortlake workshop, under the supervision of Dutch weavers, was founded by James I of England in 1620, and though they were only in business until the end of that century, they produced a number of important, highly prized works. The most interesting of the ten tapestries presented here are *Fête de Nuit*, and *La Chasse au Loup*, the latter depicting a fox-hunting scene – both are still in exceptional condition and have retained their vibrant colours.

Denoix Distillery

9 bd Maréchal Lyautey • Mon 10am–noon & 2.30–7pm, Tues–Sat 9am–noon & 2.30–7pm • Free • ☏ 05 55 74 34 27, ⓦ denoix.com

Founded in 1839, the **Denoix Distillery** is renowned throughout the region for its walnut-flavoured **liqueurs**, notably a very mellow tipple called Suprême Denoix, of which you can have a free taste here. They have also been busy resurrecting a local **mustard**, Moutarde Violette de Brive, which is made with grape must and spices and was first devised in the fourteenth century for Pope Clément VI, a native of Corrèze. Not surprisingly for this area, it goes very well with duck.

Chocolaterie Lamy

5 rue de l'Hôtel de Ville • Mon 2–7pm, Tues–Sat 9am–noon & 2–7pm • Demonstrations mid-June to mid-Sept Thurs 3pm • €4 • ☏ 05 55 18 91 26, ⓦ chocolaterie-lamy.com

Those with a sweet tooth won't want to miss the **Chocolaterie Lamy**. Though just a chocolate shop at heart, it's nonetheless a hive of Wonka-style creativity, where you can watch demonstrations of the delectable chocolates being made during the summer, and even learn how to make them yourself on half-day courses. The shop itself is well worth a browse, too.

Musée Edmond Michelet

4 rue Champanatier • Jan–April & Oct–Dec Mon–Sat 1–6pm; May–Sept Mon–Fri 11am–6pm, Sat 1–6pm • Free • ☏ 05 55 74 06 08, ⓦ museemichelet.brive.fr • To get here take the main rue de la République west from St-Martin church as far as the ring road, from where the museum is signed straight ahead along avenue Émile Zola

A short way west of central Brive, the **Musée Edmond Michelet** occupies the former home of Edmond Michelet, one of Brive's leading *résistants*, who was arrested here in 1943 and deported to Dachau, where he remained until the camp was liberated in April 1945. Not long after, Michelet became a minister in de Gaulle's postwar government, rising to the post of Minister of Justice in 1959. Spread over three floors, the rooms portray the Resistance and deportations during World War II through personal effects, posters and objects of the time, though most affecting are the chilling photographs taken in the concentration camps. A free audioguide in English is available.

Jardins de Colette

April, Oct & Nov Wed–Sun 2–6pm; May, June & Sept Tues–Sun 10am–6pm; July & Aug daily 10am–7pm • €7.50, children €6, audioguide €1 • ☏ 05 55 86 75 35, ⓦ lesjardinsdecolette.com

Ten minutes' drive west of Brive, at **Varetz**, are the lovely **Jardins de Colette**, named after the eponymous and controversial French writer, and generally at their best in June and early July. Between 1912 and 1923, Colette lived next door in Château de Castel Novel (now a hotel) with her second husband, Henry de Jouvenel. By means of plants and landscaping, the gardens aim to represent the places she lived, from her native Burgundy through to the Palais Royal in Paris. There are six in all, the most impressive of which is the **Brittany garden**, distinguished by its various rock formations, and the **Provence garden**, bursting with the typically distinctive colours of the region. The highlight – for kids at least – is an immense butterfly-shaped **maze** (a nod to Collette's beloved butterfly collection), made from double-plaited willow and dotted with educational signs outlining aspects of the writer's life. Once you're done wandering, take a cool drink on the terrace of the *salon de thé* overlooking the gardens.

ARRIVAL AND DEPARTURE   BRIVE-LA-GAILLARDE

By plane Brive airport (Brive-Vallée de la Dordogne; ☎ 05 55 22 40 00, ⓦ aeroport-brive-vallee-dordogne.com) is around 10km to the south of town in Nespouls. There is no public transport into Brive; a taxi should cost around €15; if there aren't any waiting outside, you can call the local company (☎ 05 55 24 24 24) or ask at the airport information desk. There are few other facilities to speak of here, save for a small café.

By train The *gare SNCF*, on the Paris–Toulouse and Bordeaux–Lyon main lines, is located on the south side of Brive, a 10min walk along avenue Jean Jaurès from the centre. Alternatively, bus #3 makes the trip into the centre of town.

Destinations Arnac-Pompadour (3–4 daily; 1hr); Bordeaux (6–7 daily; 2hr 30min); Cahors (6–9 daily; 1hr 10min); Paris

Austerlitz (7–9 daily; 3–4hr 15min); Périgueux (3–6 daily; 1hr); Souillac (5–8 daily; 25min); Toulouse (6–9 daily; 2hr–2hr 30min).

By bus Buses depart from various spots round town, including the *gare SNCF*, though many buses around the *département* leave from place du 14 Juillet, just across from the tourist office; for information on timetables contact CFTA buses (☎ 05 55 86 07 07, ⓦ cftaco.fr).

Destinations Arnac-Pompadour (Mon–Fri 2 daily; 2hr); Beaulieu-sur-Dordogne (school term Mon–Sat 1–3 daily, school hols Mon–Sat 1–2 daily; 1hr–1hr 30min); Collonges-la-Rouge (Mon–Sat 1–4 daily; 25min–1hr); Meyssac (Mon–Sat 1–4 daily; 30min–1hr 5min); Turenne (Mon–Sat 1–3 daily; 20–40min).

GETTING AROUND AND INFORMATION

Car rental Avis, 56 av Jean Jaurès (☎ 05 55 84 34 99); Europcar, 52 av Jean Jaurès (☎ 05 55 74 14 41); National, 59 av Jean Jaurès (☎ 05 55 17 22 23). All of these companies also have desks at the airport.

Taxis Allo Brive (☎ 05 55 24 24 24).

Tourist office Place du 14 Juillet (April–June & Sept Mon–Sat 9am–12.30pm & 1.30–6.30pm; July & Aug

Mon–Sat 9am–7pm, Sun 11am–4pm; Oct–March Mon–Sat 9am–noon & 2–6pm; ☎ 05 55 24 08 80, ⓦ brive -tourisme.com). It occupies an old pumping station and water tower built in the form of a lighthouse, so you can't miss it; for €0.50 you can pop up to the top of the tower and enjoy the views of the market place below.

ACCOMMODATION

Le Château de Lacan Rue Jean Mace ☎ 05 55 22 00 01, ⓦ hotelchateaulacan.com. Hidden away, somewhat incongruously, in a residential area north of the centre, this superbly renovated twelfth-century mansion is the place for a splurge, offering thirteen rooms and two suites of the highest order, each beautifully and thoughtfully integrated into this ancient building. And as well as going that extra mile – bottled water, fresh fruit and pastries in

the rooms – the place is impeccably staffed, too. €123
Le Collonges 3 place Winston Churchill ☎ 05 55 74 09 58, ⓦ hotel-collonges.com. Easily the best value in the centre, offering impressive rooms with smart, dark furniture and impeccable bathrooms. Despite its position on a busy road junction, it's just a few paces from the old centre, and there are a couple of cafés and bars close by as well as pay parking. Breakfast €9. €75

BRIVE'S MARKETS AND FAIRS

The modern **Marché Brassens**, behind the tourist office on place du 14 Juillet, is the venue for a huge **market** on Tuesday, Thursday and Saturday mornings, though the Saturday one is by far the biggest; the hall itself is usually reserved for foodstuffs, while the square itself is taken over with stalls selling clothes, textiles and other knick-knacks. On the first Saturday of each month between December and March, the fabulous *foires grasses* – for foie gras and truffles – are held in the same place. During the first weekend in November, the fruit and veg gives way to one of the country's most important book fairs, **La Foire du Livre** (see p.49), which attracts a number of well-known authors and artists.

1

Le Quercy 8 bis quai Tourny ☎ 05 55 74 09 26, ⓦ hotel duquercy.com. Super-slick hotel in a central location overlooking the marketplace. Each floor is colour themed, so if you really have a preference, there's black and white, lime green and beige, or silver and rose. There are some neat little touches like reading lights on bed headboards. Breakfast €12. **€99**

La Truffe Noire 22 bd Anatole-France ☎ 05 55 92 45 00, ⓦ la-truffe-noire.com. Rather dated both in and out, this nineteenth-century pile could quite easily be transformed into a stupendous boutique hotel, but as it is the rooms are rather forgettable. It does have a quirky charm that some might enjoy, but it's undeniably expensive for what it offers. Breakfast €12. **€120**

EATING AND DRINKING

Chez Francis 61 av de Paris ☎ 05 55 74 41 72. A favourite haunt of writers, actors and artists during Brive's book festival, with its walls, ceilings and lampshades covered with messages of appreciation, which add to the mildly bohemian, occasionally eccentric, flavour of the place. The imaginative seasonal menus feature the best of local ingredients; at lunch you can have two courses with a glass of wine for €18, while the fixed *menus* are priced at €21 and €28. Tues–Sat noon–2pm & 7–10pm.

L'Instant Basque 21 Promenade des Tilleuls ☎ 05 55 23 15 56. For a taste of the far southwest corner of France (and of northern Spain), head to this inexpensive, simple and characterful place, with stone walls and dangling hams. The food is classic Basque all the way: *axoa* (made from mashed veal, onions, tomato and lots of red Espelette pepper), and cod scorched on the *plancha* (hot plate). Tapas (*pintxos* in Basque) are also big here. *Menus* from €19.90. Tues–Sat 10.30am–2.30pm & 5pm–midnight.

★ **La Table d'Oliver** 33 rue St-Ambroise ☎ 05 55 18 95 95. Locals speak about *La Table d'Oliver* in tones of awe, and when you sit down to enjoy finely presented dishes like salmon with a white cheese sorbet or summer truffles you'll understand why. Weekday lunch *menu* €28, dinner *menus* from €43. Wed 7.30–9.15pm, Thurs–Sat noon–1.15pm & 7.30–9.15pm, Sun noon–1.15pm.

Arnac-Pompadour

Some 30km northeast of Brive, among the green fields and apple orchards of the southern Limousin, **ARNAC-POMPADOUR** is a must for anyone remotely interested in horses. The town is dominated by its massive, turreted château – from where Madame de Pompadour got her name – a fitting and stately backdrop to a national **stud farm** and one of the most picturesque **racecourses** in France.

Château de Pompadour

Guided tours: daily April to mid-Sept 10am, 2pm & 4pm; mid-Sept to Oct 11am & 3.30pm; Nov–March Mon–Sat 11am & 3pm • €9.50, children €7

Although there was a fortress of sorts here as far back as the eleventh century, the present **Château de Pompadour** largely dates from the fifteenth century. When the Pompadour line died out in 1745, it was ceded to Louis XV who promptly bestowed the title on his mistress, the **Marquise de Pompadour**. Though she never bothered to visit, the marquise started breeding horses on her estate before being forced to sell for financial reasons in 1760; she nevertheless kept the title. On regaining possession of the castle the following year, Louis founded the Royal Stud, which became a **National Stud** in 1872, and which is open to visitors (see box opposite). In between, the horses were sold off during the Revolution, but Napoleon I soon re-established the stud to keep his cavalry supplied. He sent four Arab stallions, booty from his Egyptian campaign, which were crossed with English thoroughbred mares to produce the first **Anglo-Arabs**. Although historically bred for military purposes, today these magnificent horses are ideally suited to eventing, owing to their powerful combination of speed, stamina and jumping ability.

The **château** was gutted by fire in 1834 and now houses the stud's headquarters. If you want to visit the château itself (albeit just three rooms), you must do so on a **guided tour** organized by Trois Tours de Pompadour. Otherwise, you can explore the formal gardens and parkland independently.

VISITING THE NATIONAL STUD

The **stallions** of Pompadour's National Stud are housed in the **Écurie du Puy Marmont** (April–Sept daily; Oct–March Mon–Sat; €5.50), across the chestnut-shaded esplanade from the château. During the spring breeding season (March–June) there are fewer stallions in the *écurie*, but this is the best time to visit the **mares** (*juments*) at the **Jumenterie de la Rivière** (afternoons only: April–June & Sept Tues–Sun; July & Aug Tues & Thurs; €5.50), 4km southeast, near the village of Beyssac. In late spring (May & June) the fields around are full of mares and foals, the best being kept for breeding, the rest sold worldwide as two-year-olds. To visit both the Écurie du Puy Marmont and the Jumenterie de la Rivière, you have to join a **guided tour** organized by Trois Tours de Pompadour, located inside the gatehouse of the château (☎05 55 98 51 10). Times of the visits vary, so check first. They also sell tickets to the château and a "passport", with which you can visit two of the three sites for €9.50.

At any time of year, you will see horses being exercised round the magnificent oval track in front of the château. On numerous Sundays between May and September, there are **race meetings** (around €6), as well as dressage and driving events, shows and open days. A calendar of events is available from Trois Tours de Pompadour. A good time to be here is August 15, when the Pompadour *fête du cheval* takes place, with various races, dressage and jumping events.

Chapelle St Blaise

45min guided tours (in French only) Tues, Thurs & Sat 11.30am • Free

In the centre of Arnac-Pompadour, just behind the château, lies the town's own parish church, the **Chapelle St Blaise**. Since its restoration in 2008, the chapel is home to over three hundred square metres of paintings depicting Old and New Testament scenes by the contemporary artist, André Brasilier, worth seeing for the scale of the work alone. You're free to explore independently if you don't fancy the guided tour.

Église Prieurale d'Arnac

Rue des Écoles • Daily 9am–6pm • Free

Some 2km northwest of Arnac-Pompadour, in the village of Arnac itself, the Romanesque **Église Prieurale d'Arnac** (part of the Pompadour *domaines*) is chiefly of interest for its carved capitals, which sit atop the inwardly leaning columns, just about perceptible if you stand at the back of the church. Though the columns are exceptionally high, enlarged photos beside each one help identify the striking images, including Daniel in the lions' den.

ARRIVAL AND INFORMATION
ARNAC-POMPADOUR

By train Arnac-Pompadour lies on a minor train line between Brive and Limoges; the *gare SNCF* is 500m southeast of town on the D7 to Vigeois.
Destinations Brive (Mon–Fri 4 daily; 45min); Limoges (Mon–Fri 3 daily; 1hr 15min).
By bus Buses from Brive (Mon–Fri 2 daily; 1hr 15min)

stop by the château.
Tourist office In the gatehouse of the château (April–May & mid-Sept to Oct daily 10am–12.30pm & 2–5.30pm; June daily 10am–12.30pm & 2–6pm; July to mid-Sept daily 10am–6.30pm; Nov–March Mon–Sat 10am–12.30 & 2–5.30pm; ☎05 55 98 55 47, ⓦpompadour.net).

ACCOMMODATION

Auberge de la Marquise 4 av des Ecuyers ☎06 86 03 06 88. Arnac-Pompadour doesn't have much in the way of hotel accommodation, but this friendly place on the southeast edge of town is a good bet, with smallish, somewhat old-fashioned, rooms and a decent restaurant down below. Breakfast €8. **€50**

Camping Les Étoiles Allée du Stade, Saint-Sornin-Lavolps ☎06 30 78 85 47, ⓦcamping-pompadour .com. Spruce, well-shaded campsite by a small lake 2km south of town, with places for both tents and campervans; there are also a handful of chalets sleeping between two and five (from €320 weekly). Closed Nov–March. **€15**

1

Turenne

TURENNE, 16km south of Brive, is the first of two very picturesque villages in the vicinity. In this case, slate-roofed, mellow stone houses crowd under the protective towers of a once-mighty fortress. At their peak during the fifteenth century, the viscounts of Turenne ruled over a vast feudal domain containing some 1200 villages. Virtually autonomous, it was one of the most powerful estates in France. The viscounts retained the right to raise taxes and mint their own coins, amongst other privileges, up until 1738 when Louis XV bought the viscountcy in the aftermath of the Fronde rebellion (see p.297).

Château de Turenne

April–June, Sept & Oct daily 10am–noon & 2–6pm; July & Aug daily 10am–7pm; Nov–March Sun 2–5pm • €5 • ☎ 05 55 80 90 66

Although Louis XV ordered that the **Château de Turenne** be demolished, two towers still sprout from the summit, one of which is occupied by the present owners of the château. From this first tower (known as the **Tour d'Horloge**, or Clocktower), you walk along a gravel pathway through the neatly manicured **gardens** – which is where the main body of the castle once stood – to the round **Tour de César**, where a further 64 steps await. It's well worth climbing for the vertiginous views away over the ridges and valleys to the mountains of Cantal. Although it's a stiff fifteen-minute climb up to the castle entrance, you do pass a number of elegant Renaissance houses and the all-important salt store, as well as a **church** hurriedly thrown up in 1662 during the Counter-Reformation to bring the local populace back to Catholicism; take a peek inside at the gilded altar and unusual mosaic ceiling.

ARRIVAL AND INFORMATION

By bus Buses from Brive (Mon–Fri 4 daily, Sat 1 daily; 25min) stop on the main road near the tourist office booth.

Tourist office Place Belvedere (Easter to June & Sept daily 10am–12.30pm & 2–6pm; July & Aug daily 10am–12.30pm & 2.30–6.30pm; ☎ 05 55 85 59 97, ⓦ brive

-tourisme.com). You can pick up walking maps of the village (€1), which are also available at the souvenir shop next to the lane that leads up to the castle. The office runs guided walks around Turenne in July and Aug (Mon–Fri 9.30am and 11am; €5).

ACCOMMODATION AND EATING

Le Clos Marnis Place de la Halle ☎ 05 55 22 05 28, ⓦ closmarnis.online.fr. Quiet and homely bed and breakfast just a stride or two from the main square, housed within a barn-like building erected by the Guild of White Penitents in 1771. While the five rooms won't set the pulse racing, they're of a decent size and tidily furnished with low-slung beds, and there's a large open garden to chill in. Closed Nov–March. **€69**

La Maison des Chanoines Rue Joseph Rouveyrol ☎ 05 55 85 93 43, ⓦ maison-des-chanoines.com. Along the path leading up to the church, this handsome sixteenth-century house has retained many of its fine Gothic flourishes, some of which have been incorporated into the four rooms and three suites (the latter in the building opposite; €105). There are plenty of thoughtful touches too, like tea- and coffee-making facilities, while all the rooms offer either a castle or countryside

view. There's also a pleasant little courtyard garden and a superb restaurant (*menus* from €41), offering solid French country fare, sometimes featuring truffles. Breakfast €10. Restaurant daily 7–9.30pm; hotel and restaurant closed Nov–Easter. **€80**

La Vicomté Place de la Halle ☎ 05 55 85 91 32, ⓦ lavicomte.com. You can't miss the jolly facade (albeit with two rather disturbing mannequins hanging out of the window) of *La Vicomté*, where the Dutch owner/ chef crafts dishes like Waldorf salad with smoked salmon, ravioli with duck foie gras and grilled pork with violet mustard. The interior has a faintly medieval whiff about it, but if you're going to eat here, grab a seat on the bright stone terrace and take in the views up to the château. Main dishes around €18 or a traditional regional *menu* for €19. Tues–Sat noon–2pm & 7.30–10pm, Sun noon–2pm.

Collonges-la-Rouge

There's a great view back to Turenne as you head southeast from the village on the D20 before cutting eastwards on pretty back lanes through meadows and walnut orchards to reach **COLLONGES-LA-ROUGE**, some 10km on; alternatively, you can walk between the two on the GR446 footpath. The village is the epitome of bucolic charm, with its rust-red – even verging on mauve – sandstone houses, pepper-pot towers and chestnut trees, although it's arguably more touristy than Turenne and crammed with artisan shops and souvenir stalls; it's best to arrive earlier or later in the day if possible. Though small-scale, there is grandeur about Collonges, for this is where the nobles who governed Turenne on behalf of the viscounts built their mini-châteaux, each boasting at least one tower – there's a wonderful view of the bristling roofs as you approach from the west.

On the main square, the twelfth-century **Église St-Pierre** is unusual in having two naves, of which the shorter, north nave – the one used today – was a later addition. They came in handy during the sixteenth century when Turenne supported the Huguenot cause; here at least, Protestants and Catholics conducted their services peacefully side by side. Outside, the timber-framed covered **market hall** still retains its old-fashioned baker's oven, which is fired up just once a year for the annual **Bread Festival** on the first Sunday of August.

Maison de la Sirène

Rue de Barrière • Easter to June & mid-Sept to Oct daily 3–5pm; July to mid-Sept daily 10.30am–12.30pm & 3–6pm • €2 • ☎ 07 82 27 41 39

Diagonally opposite the Collonges tourist office, the sixteenth-century **Maison de la Sirène** is named after the little mermaid sculpted above the entrance. Though battered, she's still charming as she preens herself, comb in one hand and mirror in the other. The only house in the village open to visitors, it contains a small **museum** with archeological remains including a Merovingian sarcophagus, tools relating to local trades, and rooms arranged with typical rural furniture from the eighteenth and nineteenth centuries. The curator is a mine of information on the village and also gives guided tours; book through the tourist office.

ARRIVAL AND INFORMATION
COLLONGES-LA-ROUGE

By bus Buses from Turenne (Mon–Fri 3 daily; 15min) and Brive (Mon–Fri 5 daily, Sat & Sun 2 daily; 25min) pass Collonges on their way to the terminus at Meyssac, stopping on the main road at the northern entrance to the village.

Tourist office Rue de la Barrière (April–June & Sept daily 10am–12.30pm & 2.30–6pm; July & Aug daily 10am–12.30pm & 2–6pm; Oct & March Mon–Sat 10am–noon & 2–5pm; Nov–Feb Mon–Sat 2–5pm; ☎ 05 65 33 22 00).

ACCOMMODATION AND EATING

Camping la Valane ☎ 05 55 25 41 59, ⓦ camping lavalane.com. Just off the main road, halfway between Collonges and Meyssac, this is a large, sunny site with comprehensive facilities, among them a snack bar, lounge, laundry, tennis courts and heated pool with slides, as well as chalets for rent (from €323 weekly). Closed Oct–April. **€19**

Relais du Quercy ☎ 05 55 25 40 31, ⓦ relaisduquercy .fr. Some 2km east of Collonges towards the village of Meyssac is this pleasant *Logis* hotel, which has two categories of room, both in a clean modern style, as well as a brightly coloured garden with pool. Breakfast €7.50.

Closed three weeks in Nov. **€65**

Relais de St-Jacques de Compostelle Rue de la Barrière ☎ 05 55 25 41 02, ⓦ restaurant-relaisstjacques .com. The village's most prominent hotel, just around the corner from the Maison de la Sirène, though it's not quite as grand as it sounds. There are ten rather sparsely furnished rooms, though the views of the narrow streets are lovely and it's fairly priced; there's also a good restaurant with *menus* from €26. Expect combinations such as tandoori breast of guinea-fowl with lemon juice. Breakfast €8.50. Restaurant Mon, Tues & Thurs–Sun noon–1.45pm & 7–8.45pm; hotel and restaurant closed Nov–Feb. **€73**

Bergerac and around

89 Bergerac

96 Monbazillac and around

98 Pécharmant

98 South of Bergerac

104 West of Bergerac

107 East of Bergerac

VILLA MARGUERITE, CADOUIN

2

Bergerac and around

In its lower reaches the Dordogne slides wide and slow through a landscape of vine-planted hills where the scent of wine is thick. This is the heart of the Périgord Pourpre, a major wine-growing area that blends seamlessly into the Bordelais vineyards to the west. For centuries the region's most important market town, port and commercial centre has been Bergerac, the second largest city in the Dordogne *département*, but still a pleasantly provincial place with a clutch of worthwhile sights among its twisting lanes. While lacking the sheer density of big-ticket tourist attractions to be found in other parts of the Dordogne, the outlying areas do offer a rich complement of stately châteaux, attractive *bastide* towns and some outstanding natural heritage.

The foremost sight in the wine region is the Renaissance **Château de Monbazillac**, clearly visible on the ridge to the south of Bergerac and surrounded by its prestigious vineyards, originally planted by monks in the Middle Ages, which produce a very palatable sweet white wine. The high country further south of Bergerac, where the gentle River Dropt marks the border of the Dordogne and Lot-et-Garonne *départements*, wasn't always such a bucolic scene, as a glance at the remaining fortifications of **Issigeac** and **Eymet** – the ramparts built in the run-up to the Hundred Years War – goes to show. The prevailing sense of unease following more than a century of war, plague and famine is caught in the fifteenth-century frescoes of the Last Judgement in the little **Église St-Eutrope** at Allemans-du-Dropt. Further downstream at **Duras**, another semi-ruined château dominates the valley.

To the west of Bergerac the Dordogne valley becomes wider, busier and less attractive. Nevertheless, there are one or two appealing sights, notably the Gallo-Roman remains at **Montcaret** and the nearby **Château de Montaigne**, where the eponymous philosopher wrote his original, wide-ranging *Essais*. North of here, the **Forêt du Landais** stretches north across the top of the Périgord Pourpre. It's a pretty region of wooded hills, meandering streams and sparse habitation, good for wandering, though without any particularly compelling sights.

Upstream of Bergerac, the pure waters of the River Couze, a tributary of the Dordogne, have spawned a paper-making industry at **Couze-et-St-Front**, where traditional, handmade paper is still produced to this day. Further east, the Dordogne has carved two gigantic meanders at **Trémolat** and **Limeuil**, which also happen to be two of the prettier villages in the region. Here also the Périgord Pourpre gradually gives way to wooded hills on the western edge of the Périgord Noir. The change is perhaps most obvious in the landscapes south of the river, where the *bastide* town of **Beaumont** and the nearby abbey of **St-Avit-Sénieur** stand isolated on the edge of a high, open plateau. Just a few kilometres to the northeast, however, **Cadouin**'s abbey church sits in a hidden valley deep among the chestnut forests.

GETTING AROUND
BERGERAC AND AROUND

Overall, exploring this region by public transport is not easy. While the main towns along the Dordogne valley are reasonably well served by trains on the Sarlat–Bordeaux line, anywhere inland requires your own car. What limited bus services do exist are planned around the needs of school children not travellers, and in school holidays many services simply don't operate.

Festivals, events and markets p.89
The wines of Bergerac p.92
Cyrano de Bergerac p.93

The Lord of Montaigne p.106
Grotte de Cussac p.111

Highlights

❶ Bergerac Surrounded by vineyards, this sleepy provincial town of cobbled squares and half-timbered facades makes for an atmospheric day's wander. **See p.89**

❷ Bastides The fortified towns of Issigeac, Eymet and Beaumont, with their arcaded central squares, retain a heady medieval atmosphere. **See p.98, p.100 & p.112**

❸ Église Saint-Eutrope, Allemans-du-Dropt Fifteenth-century frescoes depict the Last Judgement in spine-tingling detail. **See p.101**

❹ Montcaret The elaborate mosaics in a fourth-century villa unearthed here provide ample evidence of luxury living, Roman-style. **See p.105**

❺ Cingle de Trémolat A classic Dordogne River meander, best viewed from the limestone cliffs to the north. **See p.109**

❻ Canoeing the Dordogne Don a life-jacket and take to the waters at Limeuil for a leisurely trip down either the Vézère or Dordogne rivers. **See p.110**

❼ Cadouin An exceptionally pretty village with unusual accommodation options and the main draw of an austere twelfth-century Cistercian abbey. **See p.114**

HIGHLIGHTS ARE MARKED ON THE MAP ON P.88

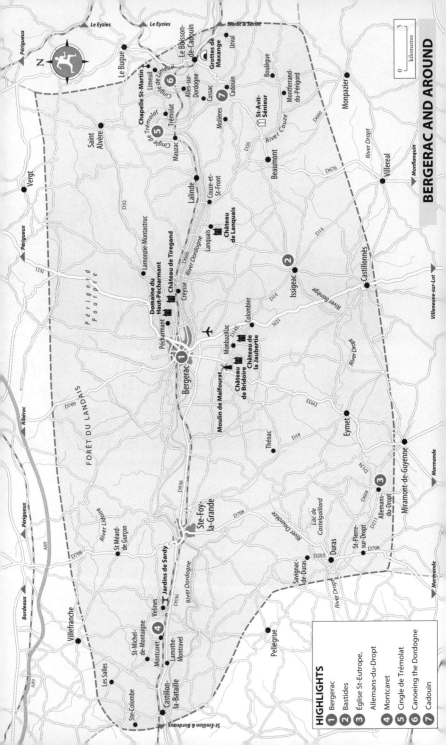

BERGERAC AND AROUND

HIGHLIGHTS

1 Bergerac
2 Bastides
3 Église St-Eutrope, Allemans-du-Dropt
4 Montcaret
5 Cingle de Trémolat
6 Canoeing the Dordogne
7 Cadouin

Bergerac

Lying mostly on the Dordogne's north bank overlooking its wide flood plain, **BERGERAC** is a rather sleepy place for much of the year, but bursts into life for the summer tourist season, when cafés and restaurants spill out into the cobbled squares and alleyways. It suffered particularly badly during the Wars of Religion, but in recent years the old streets fanning out from the former port have been carefully restored to bring out the best in the rows of half-timbered cottages and more bourgeois stone-built residences; main sights are a surprisingly rewarding **museum** devoted to tobacco and a former **monastery** which now houses an information centre on the local wines.

The best place to start exploring is beside the old port where, in season, replica *gabares* (barges) pick up passengers for leisurely **river trips**. A short hop east of the port, the narrow lanes of the **vieille ville** spread gently uphill. A calm and pleasant area to wander, with numerous late-medieval houses and perfect pavement cafés, its main artery is the Grand Rue, which runs north from the central **Église St-Jacques** to join rue de la Résistance, the old town's northern perimeter; these two form Bergerac's principal shopping streets. Just beyond their junction, across the wide place de Lattre-de-Tassigny, stands another useful landmark, the **Église Notre-Dame**.

FESTIVALS, EVENTS AND MARKETS

The list below comprises some of the biggest and more interesting of the **festivals** and **events** in this region. Where we haven't given a specific information number or website, contact the relevant tourist office.

July and August Bergerac: Les Mercredis du Jazz (**W** bergerac.fr). Free concerts by French jazz artists on Wednesday evenings on place de la Myrpe and the Cloître des Récollets.

Third weekend in July Duras: Fête de la Madeleine (**W** paysdeduras.com). The castle grounds in Duras play host to inexpensive or free concerts, a firework display on the Monday night and plenty of wine tasting.

Third Sunday in July Issigeac: Foire aux Paniers. Unique basket-weavers' fair held on the place du Château. Some sixty artisans from all regions of France demonstrate their different techniques and styles.

Late July to mid-August Bergerac and around: Été Musical en Bergerac (**T** 05 53 74 30 94, **W** festivalbergerac.com). Performances of classical music, jazz and ballet in Bergerac, the Château de Biron, Monpazier, St-Avit and Cadouin.

Mid-July to mid-August Castillon-la-Bataille: La Bataille de Castillon (**T** 05 57 40 14 53, **W** batailledecastillon.com). Local citizenry stage a spectacular floodlit re-enactment of the battle that ended the Hundred Years War. Some four hundred actors and forty cavaliers take part, performing for around six weeks each Friday and Saturday evening (plus

Thursdays in the first half of August); tickets are €23 per performance (€12 for children).

August Drop valley: Itinérance Médiévale en Vallée du Drop (**W** medieval.dropt.org). This four-week festival sees all kinds of events – gastronomic markets, parades in medieval costumes, joustings and concerts by torchlight – laid on in towns and villages along the Dropt valley, including Duras, Eymet, Issigeac and Cadouin.

Second or third Sunday in August Duras: Fête du Vin (**T** 05 53 83 63 06, **W** cotesdeduras. com). A one-day wine-fest held beside the château with free tastings (you have to buy a refillable glass at the entrance for €5). The festival features some good music too, with live jazz/blues on the Sunday afternoon.

Mid-Aug Bergerac: L'Assiette de Cyrano (**W** pays-de-bergerac.com). The old town is transformed into a gigantic outdoor restaurant for this magnificent food festival, which also includes free evening concerts.

Late September to mid-October Bergerac: Grain d'Automne (**T** 05 53 63 57 55, **W** vins-bergerac.fr). To coincide and celebrate the *vendanges* (grape harvest), Bergerac hosts classical, jazz and traditional music concerts plus various other festivities.

MARKETS

The main **markets** in this region are at Bergerac (Wed & Sat); Le Buisson-de-Cadouin (Fri); Cadouin (Wed); Eymet (Thurs); Issigeac (Sun); Lalinde (Thurs); Ste-Foy-la-Grande (Sat) and Trémolat (Tues).

2

BERGERAC

```
0        250
    metres
```

Ribérac

1, 2 & Périgueux

Gare SNCF

RUE DU PETIT SOL
RUE DE LA BOÉTIE
RUE ST-MARTIN
RUE DU PETIT SOL
AV. DU 108E RÉGIMENT-D'INFANTERIE
COURS ALSACE LORRAINE
RUE FÉLIX FAURE
RUE DESMARTIS
BOULEVARD VICTOR-HUGO
AVENUE DU PRÉSIDENT-WILSON
RUE CARNOT

BOULEVARD JEAN-MOULIN
BOULEVARD MONTAIGNE
PLACE GAMBETTA
RUE DES FAURES
RUE SAINTE-CATHERINE
BOULEVARD MAINE DE BIRAN
BD. DE VARSOVIE

Notre-Dame

RUE VALETTE
R. MONTAU
RUE CYRANO
PLACE DE LATTRE-DE-TASSIGNY
RUE E. LEROY
RUE DES CARMES
PLACE DE LA RÉPUBLIQUE

RUE DU PONT ST-JEAN
RUE SAINT-ESPRIT
GRAND RUE
RUE DE LA RÉSISTANCE
RUE ROURBARRAUD
RUE DU DRAGON
RUE DE LA BRÈCHE

N

PL. DU MARCHÉ COUVERT
Halle
St-Jacques
R. ST-JAMES
R. GAUDRA
RUE DU PROFESSEUR POZZI
RUE LAKANAL
RUE JULES MICHELET

PLACE PÉLISSIÈRE
RUE DES CONFÉRENCES
PL. DE LA MYRPE
PL. DU DR-CAYLA
RUE NEUVE D'ARGENSON
RUE CANDOLLE
RUE JUNIEN-RABIER
R. PROSPER-FAUGÈRE

Musée du Vin et de la Batellerie
QUAI SALVETTE
Cloître des Récollets

Maison des Vins
Jetty
PLACE DU FEU
Périgord Gabarres
Musée du Tabac
PLACE DU FOIRAIL
RUE ÉMILE-VIEILLEFOND
PLACE DU FOIRAIL

R. DU DR-BARRAUD
R. HYPPOLYTE TAINE
RUE JOUANEL
RUE DU DR. PROF.-TESTUT

River Dordogne
VIEUX PONT
RUE DUGUESCLIN
RUE CLAIRAT

● EATING	
La Cocotte des Halles	2
D'un Terroir l'Autre	1
L'Imparfait	5
Le St Jacques	4
La Table du Marché	3
Le Vin'Quatre	6

■ DRINKING	
Au Plus Que Parfait	1

■ ACCOMMODATION	
La Bonbonnière	5
Camping la Pelouse	7
Le Colombier de Cyrano et Roxane	6
Les Farcies du Pech'	1
De France	4
Inter Hotel de Bordeaux	3
L'Ostal de Pombonne	2

● SHOPPING	
La Colline Aux Livres	1
Godard	2

Airport, Bordeaux, Agen & Monbazillac ▼   ▼ Sarlat, Cahors & Pécharmant

Brief history

The largest town in the Dordogne valley, Bergerac owes its existence and prosperity to the **river**. By the twelfth century it was already an important bridging point and port, controlling the trade between its Périgord hinterland and Bordeaux, particularly the burgeoning **wine trade**. Things began to take off after Henry III of England sought to keep the townspeople sweet by giving them certain privileges in 1254: they were exempted from local taxes, given the right of assembly and allowed to export their wines to Bordeaux unhindered. Local burghers took advantage of the new dispensations to ship their own wines first, while the less privileged were forced to sell later, at disadvantageous prices, and were also charged a tax of five *sous* per barrel. Bergerac's wine aristocracy were thus able to corner the lucrative foreign market until the seventeenth century, when the technique of ageing wines was discovered.

The town's heyday came in the decades preceding the Wars of Religion (1561–98), when Bergerac was among the foremost centres of **Protestantism** in southwest France. One of many truces between the warring factions was even signed here in 1577, but in 1620 the Catholic Louis XIII seized the town and ordered that the ramparts and fortress be demolished. Worse was to come when Catholic priests arrived to bring Bergerac back into the fold. They met with mixed success – the majority of the Protestant population fled, principally to Holland, where they soon established a long and mutually profitable business importing Bergerac wines.

Since then wine has continued to be the staple of the local economy. Up until the railway arrived in the 1870s, the bulk of it was transported by river, leading to a thriving **boat-building** industry all along the Dordogne. Though most have long disappeared, a few sturdy *gabares* are still being built to cater to the tourist trade.

Musée du Tabac

Place du Feu • April & May Tues–Sat 10am–noon & 2–6pm, Sun 2.30–6.30pm; June–Sept daily 10am–1pm & 2–6pm; Oct–March Tues–Fri 10am–noon & 2–6pm, Sat 10am–noon • €4 • ☎ 05 53 63 04 13

Rue de l'Ancien Pont leads northwards from portside rue Hippolyte Taine to the splendid seventeenth-century Maison Peyrarède, which houses the unexpectedly absorbing **Musée du Tabac**. Tobacco used to be a major crop in the Bergerac region (and is still grown hereabouts today), and Europe's major tobacco research centre is based here. While inevitably glossing over the more dire medical effects of smoking, this is nevertheless an impressive collection of pipes, tobacco jars and various tools of the trade, garnered from all over the world. There are wooden graters etched with religious scenes, snuffboxes engraved with the busts of Napoleon and Marie Antoinette, blushing young beauties adorning porcelain pipe-bowls and hunting scenes fashioned out of meerschaum. Among many rare and beautiful pieces, the museum's prize possessions are an incredibly ornate Viennese meerschaum-and-amber cigar holder depicting a Sicilian wedding, and an intriguing machine, invented in the 1860s, for carving fourteen brier pipes at once. Look out, too, for the clay pipe in the ominous form of a skull with glittering glass eyes. The cool 1960s and 70s-era Gitanes posters, meanwhile, hark back to a time when smoking was regarded as a somewhat more glamorous activity.

Cloître des Récollets

Rue des Récollets

Just north of the Musée du Tabac stands the **Cloître des Récollets**. This simple, galleried cloister dates from the early seventeenth century when, in the aftermath of the Wars of Religion, Louis XIII dispatched five monks of the Franciscan Récollets order to bring Protestant Bergerac back to the faith. They were not warmly welcomed – it took a visit by Louis himself, in 1621, to assure their authority – but by the end of the decade the Récollets had succeeded in founding a new chapel and monastery. Not that they had the last word. After the Revolution, Bergerac's remaining Protestant congregation bought the chapel and re-established a temple on the site, which is still used for regular Sunday-morning worship. The monks' vaulted grain and wine cellars now form an unusual setting for Bergerac's **Maison des Vins** (see below), which can be entered through the cloister.

Maison des Vins

2 place du Docteur Cayla • Feb–April & Oct–Dec Tues–Sat 10.30am–12.30pm & 2–6pm; May, June & Sept Tues–Sat 10.30am–12.30pm & 2–7pm; July & Aug daily 10am–7pm • Free • Wine-tasting lessons (reservations required) July & Aug Wed (in French) & Fri (in English) • €5 • ☎ 05 53 63 57 55, ⊕ vins-bergerac.fr

Accessed either through the Cloître des Récollets or at street level on the riverfront, the **Maison des Vins** provides wine-tasting lessons and produces the *Route des Vins de Bergerac*, a handy guide to visiting the vineyards around the town. In addition there are interesting **displays** about the history of the Bergerac *appellation* and, between mid-June and mid-September, a wine grower or expert is on-hand to answer questions and offer wine tastings.

2

THE WINES OF BERGERAC

The **Bergerac wine region** extends along the north bank of the Dordogne from Lamothe-Montravel in the west to Lalinde in the east, and south as far as Eymet and Issigeac. It comprises no fewer than thirteen different *appellations*, of which over half the total output is red wine, although the region's most famous wine is the sweet white Monbazillac.

There is evidence of wine production around Bergerac since Roman times, but the vineyards really began to develop in the thirteenth century to supply the English market. Demand from Holland, for sweet white wines in particular, led to a second spurt in the sixteenth century and then again after the Wars of Religion, when Protestant émigré merchants virtually monopolized the market in Monbazillac wines. By the nineteenth century vines covered 100,000 hectares around Bergerac, only to be decimated by phylloxera in the 1870s; the area under AOP wines today covers a mere 12,000 hectares.

Pre-eminent among the Bergerac wines is **Monbazillac**. This pale golden, sweet white wine is blended from Semillon, Sauvignon and Muscadelle vines grown on the chalky clay soils of the valley's north-facing slopes. As with Sauternes, a key element is the cold, autumn-morning mists which lead to the development of *Botrytis cinerea*, or "noble rot", on the grapes. The result is an intensely perfumed, concentrated wine best consumed chilled with foie gras, desserts or as an apéritif. Though they can't compare to the finesse of Sauternes, even a top-quality Monbazillac is eminently affordable at around €15 a bottle.

Pécharmant, the best of the local reds, is often compared unfavourably to Bordeaux wines, though some now rival a number of less prestigious St-Émilions. Pécharmant wines are produced from Cabernet Sauvignon, Cabernet Franc and small quantities of Malbec or Merlot grapes, grown on the most favourable pockets of sand and gravel soils found to the north and east of Bergerac. They are thus far more complex and full-bodied than other Bergerac reds, and some will age well up to seven years.

You can sample the range of local AOP wines at Bergerac's Maison des Vins. Alternatively, many producers offer **tastings and visits** to their *chais* – for a full list see the brochure *Route des Vins de Bergerac* available at the Maison des Vins (see p.91) or Bergerac tourist office (see p.94).

Place de la Myrpe

On its north side the Cloître des Récollets opens onto Bergerac's most picturesque square, the cobbled, tree-shaded **Place de la Myrpe** (also spelt Mirpe), lined with stone and half-timbered labourers' cottages looking onto a badly weathered statue, erected in 1977, honouring Edmond Rostand's fictional hero **Cyrano de Bergerac** (see box opposite) in typically haughty pose.

Musée du Vin et de la Batellerie

5 rue des Conférences • April & May Tues–Sat 10am–noon & 2–6pm, Sun 2.30–6.30pm; June–Sept daily 10am–noon & 1–6pm; Oct–March Tues–Fri 10am–noon & 2–6pm, Sat 10am–noon • €3 • ☎ 05 53 57 80 92

The small **Musée du Vin et de la Batellerie** (Wine and Inland Waterways Museum), just off place de la Myrpe, contains a collection of items related to viticulture, farming and the town's once bustling river trade. This latter section is the most interesting, with models of the *gabares* alongside some text (French only) on the practicalities of navigating the Dordogne. If you'd been wondering how non-motorized vessels used to make any progress at all going upriver against the flow, the answer is that they did so with difficulty. The river was only navigable upstream on about 150 days per year, and for a long time this relied on men hauling the boats from the riverbank – a practice banned in 1837 for humanitarian reasons.

Église St-Jacques

Rue St-Jacques • Mon–Sat 2–7pm

Uphill from place de la Myrpe stands the patchwork **Église St-Jacques**. A stop on the route to Santiago de Compostela (see p.290), the church has had a chequered past, founded in the twelfth century but plundered and destroyed in the Hundred Years War and the Wars of Religion – only the campanile and balcony remain from the original structure. Today's church is fairly modest, but has a certain grandeur in its narrow, high nave, topped by a precise rib-vaulted ceiling and lit by stained-glass windows.

Rue St-James to the market square

Rue St-James runs east from the Église St-Jacques across the top end of pedestrianized **place Pélissière**, the old tanners' quarter but now dotted with cafés and ice cream parlours. Like the place de la Myrpe, place Pélissière also boasts a statue of **Cyrano de Bergerac** (see box below), this one a recent incarnation from 2005 and bearing an uncanny (and somewhat cartoonish) resemblance to Gérard Depardieu. From here, pretty **rue des Fontaines** continues uphill past prosperous fourteenth- and sixteenth-century houses – no. 29 on the corner with rue Gaudra is particularly noteworthy, with its large, arched windows and carved capitals – to the market square. The covered **Halle** is the focus of a vast market on Wednesday and Saturday mornings, with more stalls on the square outside the Église Notre-Dame.

Église Notre-Dame

Place de Lattre de Tassigny • Mon–Sat 8.30am–6pm

The **Église Notre-Dame** was built in 1865 as the town's congregation grew too large for the church of St-Jacques. Designed by Paul Abadie of Sacré-Coeur fame, it does impress for the resolutely Neo-Gothic style of its architecture, though the twee miniature columns and Nativity-scene sculptures on its main facade border on greeting-card kitsch. The long, high and grey interior does little to inspire, though it's worth a look to view two large oil paintings in the east chapel: *The Adoration of the Shepherds*, attributed to a pupil of Leonardo de Vinci, and *The Adoration of the Magi* from the Venetian School.

ARRIVAL AND DEPARTURE

BERGERAC

By plane Bergerac's airport is in Roumanière (☎05 53 22 25 25, ⓦbergerac.aeroport.fr), 5km southeast of the city on the Agen road. There's a restaurant and an ATM here but nothing else. Moreover, there's no public transport to the centre and taxis (€18–20) are often in short supply. If there aren't any outside, you can call Abeilles Bergerac Taxis (☎05 53 23 32 32).
Airlines Flybe (ⓦflybe.com); Jet2 (ⓦjet2.com); Ryanair (ⓦryanair.com); Transavia (ⓦtransavia.com); Twinjet (ⓦtwinjet.fr).

By train The *gare SNCF* is located at the north end of cours Alsace Lorraine, a 10min walk from the old town.
Destinations Bordeaux (10–12 daily; 1hr 15min–1hr 30min); Le Buisson (5–8 daily; 55min); Castillon-la-Bataille (8–14 daily; 40–50min); Couze (4 daily; 15min); Lalinde

CYRANO DE BERGERAC

In 1897, the poet and playwright Edmond Rostand penned his most successful play, **Cyrano de Bergerac**. It tells the story of a guardsman and poet, renowned for his bravery and intellect, who falls in love with his cousin Roxane, but feels unable to declare his feelings because of his unattractive looks – in particular his large, protruding nose. Instead, he writes letters to her on behalf of one of his cadets, the handsome but dim-witted Christian, who has also fallen for her charms. First attracted by Christian's looks, Roxane falls in love with the soul revealed in the letters – not discovering until it is too late that it is in fact Cyrano's soul. Rostand's play has since been the subject of numerous adaptations, perhaps most famously the 1990 French film version staring Gérard Depardieu.

The lead character was inspired by a seventeenth-century soldier, playwright and free-thinking philosopher called **Savinien de Cyrano**, who was born in Paris and only decided to embellish his name while serving in a Gascon company. It seems Cyrano was well able to match the Gascon reputation for swaggering boastfulness and impetuosity. Not only was he a famous duellist, but many of his works were so outspoken that they had to be withheld from publication until after his death.

(6 daily; 25min); Lamothe-Montravel (4 daily; 35–40min); Libourne (13 daily; 45min–1hr); St-Émilion (14 daily; 40min); Ste-Foy-La-Grande (10–14 daily; 20min); Sarlat (4–6 daily; 1hr 20min–1hr 30min); Trémolat (6 daily; 30min).

By bus Most buses around the region depart from outside the *gare SNCF*.

Destinations Eymet (Mon–Fri 1–2 daily; 50min–1hr

20min); Issigeac (Mon–Fri 1–2 daily; 45min); Lalinde (Mon–Sat 1–2 daily; 40min); Périgueux (school term Mon–Fri 7 daily; school hols Mon–Fri 3 daily; 1hr); Port de Couze (Mon–Sat 1–2 daily; 30min).

By car You'll find free parking in the cobbled area beside the old port and on place du Foirail, a short walk east of the town centre.

GETTING AROUND

Bike rental The friendly and helpful Apolo Cycles, 31 bd Victor-Hugo (☎06 20 64 59 25, ⓦapolo-cycles.com) rent bikes from €15 per day, and can also do drop-offs at your hotel.

Car rental Near the train station, try Avis, 42 Route d'Agen (☎05 53 57 69 83, ⓦavis.fr), and Europcar, 3 av du 108e

Régiment-d'Infanterie (☎05 53 58 97 97; ⓦeuropcar.fr), also at the airport (☎05 53 61 61 61), as is Hertz (☎05 53 27 10 51, ⓦhertz.fr). In town there's also Ucar, 34 av de Gaulle (☎05 53 57 80 57, ⓦucar.fr).

Taxis There's a taxi stand outside the station; otherwise, call Abeilles Bergerac (☎05 53 23 32 32).

INFORMATION AND TOURS

Tourist office 97 rue Neuve d'Argenson, on the south side of place de la République (April–June & Sept–Oct Mon–Sat 9.30am–1pm & 2–6.30pm; July & Aug daily 9.30am–7pm; Nov–March Mon–Wed & Fri–Sat 9.30am–1pm & 2–6pm, Thurs 10am–1pm & 2–6pm; ☎05 53 57 03 11, ⓦbergerac-tourisme.com). There's one internet terminal (15min free), plus free wi-fi. In summer they also open an annexe in the Cloître des Récollets (July & Aug daily 10.30am–1pm & 2.30–6.30pm, closed Sun early July & late Aug; ☎05 53 57 03 11). Both offices organize guided tours of the old town twice a

week (April–Aug Wed 11am & Thurs 3pm; 1hr 30min; €5.50). The Wednesday tour includes a snack at the market.

River trips Périgord Gabarres, Le Quai Salvette (☎05 53 24 58 80, ⓦgabarres.fr), operate replica *gabares* which depart from the old port for leisurely 50min river trips (April–Oct 10am–8pm; €9) along the Dordogne to a nature reserve that is home to herons, cormorants and kingfishers, among other wildlife; commentary is bilingual. Departures are at least four times daily, or up to once an hour in July and Aug.

ACCOMMODATION

For a modestly sized town, Bergerac has a fairly broad range of **accommodation**, offering an appealing mix of hotels and *chambres d'hôtes*, many of the latter clustered in or around lovely place de la Myrpe, as well as some excellent options just a short drive out of town. There's no hostel in Bergerac, though there is a well-located **campsite** very close to the centre.

La Bonbonnière 15 place de la Myrpe ☎05 53 61 82 04, ⓦlabonbonniere.net. Bergerac's loveliest square is full of fine medieval buildings, though few possess as much character as this cosy, cottage-like *chambre d'hôte* run by engaging host, Simone. There are four rooms, one of which is an attic room, and two share a bathroom. Each is replete with beautiful detail, from wooden beams running through the partially exposed stone walls, to colourful handwoven textiles and all sorts of oddball knick-knacks including an array of hanging witches. Breakfast is taken around the communal kitchen table, which only adds to its charm. **€84**

Camping la Pelouse 8bis rue J-J Rousseau ☎05 53 57 06 67, ⓦentreprisefrery.com/camping-la-pelouse. In a beautiful position on the peaceful south bank of the river, a short walk west from the Vieux Pont, this is an inexpensive and friendly municipal site but with fairly basic facilities. As well as tent pitches, there are mobile homes for rent (€485 weekly). Closed Oct–April. **€13.50**

Le Colombier de Cyrano et Roxane 17 place de la Myrpe ☎05 53 57 96 70, ⓦlecolombierdecyrano.fr. This lovely if rather eccentric little *chambre d'hôte* in a flagstone

sixteenth-century cottage is adorned with blue shutters, flower boxes and a tiny blue wooden door. Bursting with colour, the two en-suite rooms offer touches of Baroque extravagance, while one – only a touch more expensive – has its own private terrace with wicker chairs and a hammock. **€77**

★ **Les Farcies du Pech'** Les Farcies Nord ☎05 53 74 16 11, ⓦfarciesdupech.com Wonderful *chambre d'hôte*, some 3.5km northeast of Bergerac centre, occupying part of a château surrounded by rolling parkland and a working vineyard. The walls of the five rooms are adorned with portraits of dapper gentlemen that exude an appropriately grand atmosphere of elegant eighteenth-century high society. The huge home-made breakfasts are eaten communally on one long banquet table, and wine tastings are available in the evenings. **€110**

De France 18 place Gambetta ☎05 53 57 11 61, ⓦhoteldefrance-bergerac.com. This three-star hotel has an unpromising modern exterior, but don't let that put you off; the twenty rooms are pleasing on the eye and there's a high level of comfort on offer. In addition, there's an open-air pool at the back to enjoy. Front rooms overlook the road but are more colourful than those at the quieter rear. Breakfast €10. €69

Inter Hotel de Bordeaux 38 place Gambetta ☎ 05 53 57 12 83, ⓦ hotel-bordeaux-bergerac.com. Set in the middle of the new town, this hotel boasts a retro Art Deco exterior that gives an immediate sense of character. Inside, though, the rooms are disappointingly identikit business-chain-like, but even so in terms of facilities, comfort and price it's arguably Bergerac's top choice, and boasts a sizeable pool and plush bar. Rooms at the back are quieter and have views of

the pool and small garden. Breakfast €9. €65

★ **L'Ostal de Pombonne** 19 rue du Bourg de Pombonne ☎ 05 47 56 01 13, ⓦ ostaldepombonne.fr. Set in the village of Pombonne, some 4km northeast of central Bergerac, this is a delightful four-room *chambre d'hôte* in an old stone-walled farmhouse with a pretty garden. Named after plants and trees found in the garden, the rooms have cool, clean modern accents, while the garden has a swimming pool and childrens' toys (which make this a perfect base for young families). Breakfast is taken at a communal table. €75

EATING

When it comes to places to eat, Bergerac offers a temptation of tasty treats – you'll find a bunch of terrific **restaurants** clustered around place du Marché Couvert, and several more located further down towards the river.

La Cocotte des Halles 14 place du Marché-Couvert ☎ 05 53 24 10 00. Just inside one corner of the market hall, you'll find this easy-going place – all plastic chairs and tables – packed to the gills every lunchtime with locals filling up on surprisingly sophisticated dishes like fresh fish in coconut milk. *Menus* €18. Mon–Sat 9am–2.30pm.

L'Imparfait 8 rue des Fontaines ☎ 05 53 57 47 92, ⓦ imparfait.com. Bergerac's longest-standing and most refined traditional restaurant is an attractive high-ceilinged stone dining room complete with fireplace and a somewhat out-of-place fish tank. In summer diners migrate outside to the well-shaded terrace. The menu changes daily, but revolves around fresh fish and meat, subtly flavoured by a talented chef; the veal sweetbreads are a bit of a house speciality. *Menus* from €24. Mid-Jan to mid-Dec daily noon–2pm & 7–10pm.

Le St Jacques 30 rue St-James ☎ 05 53 23 38 08, ⓦ restaurant-saintjacques-bergerac.com. This place has a charming shaded garden at the back, complete with outdoor fireplace and stone walls strewn with lanterns and candles. The menu is small but varied, from beef in a truffle sauce to *dorade* (bream) with an "Asian air". *Menus* from €22. Mon & Thurs–Sun noon–1.30pm & 7–9pm.

★ **La Table du Marché** 21 place de la Bardonnie ☎ 05

53 22 49 46, ⓦ table-du-marche.fr. If you've only time for one meal in Bergerac, then make it *Table du Marché*, where chef Stéphane Cuzin oversees dazzlingly market-fresh dishes (which are limited to a choice of one meat and one fish main dish a day). The black-and-white decor gives the venue a sharp, contemporary feel, as does the open kitchen where you can watch your food being prepared. *Menus* from €35. Tues–Sat noon–2pm & 7.30–10pm.

D'un Terroir l'Autre 51 rue Ste Catherine ☎ 05 24 10 56 14. A little way out of the centre, and run by a husband-and-wife team who offer up dishes from the Himalayas, such as chicken *momos* (dumplings) as well as cooking closer to the French earth, such as classic *confit de canard*. *Menus* €27–32. July & Aug Tues–Sat 9am–9.30pm; Sept–June Tues–Sat 9am–2.30pm & 4–9.30pm.

Le Vin'Quatre Rue Saint-Clair ☎ 05 53 22 37 26. Although this little place is in the heart of the old town, it's somewhat tucked away down a side-alley, with just a couple of tables inside and three more out on the terrace. Most of the patrons are locals in search of quality, highly creative dishes such as slow-cooked lamb with hummus or a white cream and pineapple piña-colada dessert. *Menus* from €32. Mon, Tues, Thurs & Fri 7pm–9.30pm, Sat & Sun noon–2pm & 7pm–9.30pm.

DRINKING

Bergerac is hardly your typical party town, hence the paucity of **drinking** establishments, though there are one or two bars and cafés where you can linger over a morning coffee or a beer at sundown.

Au Plus Que Parfait 12 rue des Fontaines ☎ 05 53 61 95 11. Great-looking pub across the street from *L'Imparfait*, where you'll receive a warm welcome and a choice of seven or eight Belgian beers on tap and dozens more by the bottle.

There's plenty of entertainment too, from games nights and salsa to occasional live music on Saturday evenings. Tues–Thurs 9am–1am, Fri & Sat 9am–2am.

SHOPPING

As well as the individual **shops** picked out below, Bergerac also has some excellent **markets**. The main event (Wed & Sat morning) spreads out from the central *halle* into the surrounding streeets and squares; the *halle* also has a fresh-produce market (Mon–Sat mornings). There's also a small organic market (Tues morning) in front of the town hall, and a flea market on place de la Myrpe on the first Sunday of the month.

La Colline Aux Livres Place Louis de la Bardonnie ☎ 05 53 57 90 97. This fantastic independent bookshop has a small selection of books in English. Tues–Sat 9.30am–1pm & 2–7pm.

Godard 29 rue des Conférences ☎ 05 53 61 93 49, ⓦ foie-gras-godard.fr. Lovers of the southwest's finest culinary delight, foie gras, will want to pop by Godard in the old town, which is chock-full of jars and blocks of the stuff as well as a few other local culinary products. Tues–Sat 10am–1pm & 3–7pm.

DIRECTORY

Hospital Central Hospitalier Samuel Pozzi, 9 bd du Professeur Albert Calmette, the eastern extension of rue du Professeur Pozzi (☎ 05 53 63 88 88).
Police Commissariat de Police, 37 bd Chanzy (☎ 05 53 74 74 17).
Post office The main post office is at 36 rue de la Résistance (Mon–Fri 8.30am–8pm, Sat 8.30am–12.30pm).

Monbazillac and around

Six kilometres south of Bergerac, **MONBAZILLAC** is the name not only of a village but also, more famously, of a château and a sweet white wine (see box, p.92) similar to those of the Sauternes in the Bordeaux region. After whetting your appetite at Monbazillac, investigate some of the area's private **vineyards**. There are two good options to the east of Monbazillac near the village of **Colombier**.

Château de Monbazillac

Daily: April, May & Oct 10am–12.30pm & 2–6pm; June & Sept 10am–7pm; July & Aug 10am–7.30pm; Nov, Dec & Feb–March 10am–noon & 2–5pm • €7.50 • Guided tours July & Aug daily 11.30am–3pm, additional €5 • ☎ 05 53 63 65 00, ⓦ chateau-monbazillac.com

Visible from miles around, the handsome sixteenth-century **Château de Monbazillac** sits invitingly atop a low hill, surveying the gentle slopes of its long-favoured vineyards below. An eye-catching blend of Renaissance residence and mock-medieval fortress, its corners reinforced by four sturdy towers, the château was a Protestant stronghold during the Wars of Religion. Surprisingly, it has survived virtually intact and now contains many richly furnished rooms; although few original furnishings remain, it is nevertheless an impressive collection. The pick of the rooms are located on the **ground floor**, notably the *grand salon* with its beautifully decorated ceiling, herringbone parquet flooring of oak, pine and cherry wood and a Renaissance fireplace with heraldic sculptures. There's another fine fireplace in the adjoining *petit salon*, this one clad in walnut and featuring an unusual triptych. The so-called **Library Tower**, meanwhile, is just that, well-stocked with books as well as a family tree of the D'Aydies', the founders of the castle. Better still is the superbly vaulted **cellar** with its many wine-related displays including a cabinet full of antique bottles specially labelled for the Dutch market, the oldest of which dates from 1920.

Cave de Monbazillac

Mon–Sat: Jan & Feb 10am–12.30pm & 2–6pm; March–May & Sept–Dec 10am–12.30pm & 1.30–7pm; June 9am–12.30pm & 1.30–7pm; July & Aug 9am–7pm • Free • ☎ 05 53 63 65 06, ⓦ cave.chateau-monbazillac.com • The cave is 2km west of Château de Monbazillac on the D933 Bergerac–Marmande road

The Château de Monbazillac and its vineyards have been under the ownership of the local wine producers' co-operative, the **Cave de Monbazillac**, since 1960. You can taste its famous velvety sweet white wine both at the château or at the main **showroom**, were the helpful staff can offer expert advice on what to buy, too.

Maison de Tourisme

Mon–Wed & Fri–Sat 10am–12.30pm & 2–6.30pm, Thurs 10am–6.30pm, Sun 10am–1pm & 2–6.30pm • Free • ☎ 05 53 58 63 13

Just 500m up the road from the Château de Monbazillac, you can sample (and purchase) a variety of local wines at the **Maison de Tourisme**, which also has a small but interesting exhibition on the local vineyards. Staff can help to arrange château tours, too.

Château de la Jaubertie

Mon–Sat 10am–5pm • Free • ☎ 05 53 58 32 11, ⓦ chateau-jaubertie.com

Some 4km southeast of Monbazillac via the D14E is the sixteenth-century **Château de la Jaubertie**, which was supposedly built by Henry IV for his mistress, Gabrielle d'Estrée, and later belonged to a doctor of Marie Antoinette. Now owned by an English family, the Rymans, the estate produces a variety of very reasonable wines under the Bergerac *appellation*, the most prominent of which is the *Bergerac Blanc Sec*.

Domaine de l'Ancienne Cure

Shop Mon–Sat 9am–6pm, plus Sun with prior reservation • ☎ 05 53 58 27 90, ⓦ domaine-anciennecure.fr

The **Domaine de l'Ancienne Cure** in the village of **COLOMBIER**, overseen by Christian Roche, has won any number of awards for its high-quality, and mostly organic, Monbazillac, Bergerac and Pécharmant wines – their three *cuvées*, namely the Jour du Fruit, L'Abbaye and the highly concentrated L'Extase are all fantastic; a bottle of the latter, which is harvested only in vintage years, will set you back around €20. You can visit the *chais* by appointment, but tastings are available at any time at their shop just below the village on the main N21 Bergerac–Agen road, right by the Issigeac turning.

Château de Bridoire

Daily: April–June & Sept 2–6pm; July & Aug10am–7pm; Oct Sun 2–6pm, plus daily 2–6pm in school hols • €8.50, children €5.50, Vallée Mystèrieuse €5.50/€3.50 • ☎ 05 53 58 11 74, ⓦ chateaudebridoire.com

Four kilometres west of Monbazillac, in Ribagnac, the **Château de Bridoire** has undergone a fabulous partial renovation, and is one of the more interesting – and certainly most family-friendly – of the châteaux around here. A private estate since 1979, the renovation work is still ongoing and some rooms were crashed-out building sites at the time of writing. Of the restored rooms, the **grand salon** is a magnificent example of upper-class eighteenth-century living while the **Salle des gardes** (guardroom) comes complete with a knight in armour mounted on a horse. Other rooms to look out for include the so-called King's bedroom and the main dining room.

There's also lots of fun to be had in the surrounding **grounds**, where dozens of medieval and traditional French games and activities have been laid out, from *Jeu d'Oies* (similar to snakes and ladders, with wooden geese rather than serpents) to archery, croquet and an enormous chess board, as well as the **Vallèe Mystèrieuse** fantasy maze of twisting pathways and obstacle courses, with a few surprises thrown in. Between mid-July and the end of August the château is open on Thursday and Saturday nights for torch-lit visits, musical events and medieval food tastings; see the website for more details.

ARRIVAL AND GETTING AROUND   MONBAZILLAC AND AROUND

By bus Very infrequent buses run between Monbazillac and Bergerac, which are normally timed only to get children to and from school. Once in Monbazillac you'll need your own transport to get to and from sites of interest.

EATING

Tour des Vents ☎ 05 53 58 30 10, ⓦ tourdesvents.com. Some 3km west from the Cave de Monbazillac, the Michelin-starred *Tour des Vents* sits beside the Moulin de Malfourat, a ruined windmill perched on the highest point for miles around. Though it's not an attractive building, the views from the restaurant's picture windows and terrace are superb, and the ever-changing menu might include veal with cashew nuts and panacotta or turbot with

Espelette peppers; *menus* start at €29 and shoot up to €75. Tues–Sat noon–2pm & 7.30–10pm, Sun noon–2pm.

Pécharmant

East of Bergerac, if you leave the river valley at Creysse and head north, you're soon back among vine-covered hills. Some of this region's best red wines are produced around the village of **PÉCHARMANT**, 6km northeast of Bergerac; indeed, the wines here are certainly a cut above the surrounding Côtes de Bergerac and Bergerac *appellations*.

Domaine du Haut-Pécharmant

Signposted north off the D32 between Bergerac and Ste-Alvère • Mon–Sat 9am–6pm • Free guided tours June–Sept Mon–Sat 10.30am & 3.30pm • ☎ 05 53 57 29 50, ⌨ haut-pecharmant.com

Just to the northeast of Pécharmant, the family-run **Domaine du Haut-Pécharmant** stands in the thick of fields of vines, with views across to Monbazillac. It produces a typically full-bodied, aromatic wine, which ages well. Short but informative tours are availble in English (call ahead to be sure an English-speaker is available) that finish with a tasting and the chance to buy.

Château de Tiregand

April–Oct Mon–Sat 9am–noon & 2–6pm; Nov–March Mon–Fri 9am–noon & 2–5.30pm • €5.50 • Guided tours July & Aug Tues & Fri 10.30am, additional €5.50 • ☎ 05 53 23 21 08, ⌨ chateau-de-tiregand.com

Opposite the turnoff from the D32 to Domaine du Haut-Pécharmant, at the end of a long alley, the much grander **Château de Tiregand** offers free tastings, as well as guided tours (in French) of the estate. Their star wine is the delicious Cuvée Grand Millésime.

South of Bergerac

South of Bergerac, you gradually leave the vines behind as you cross an area of high, rolling country, featuring several picturesque small towns and villages that have a low-key but undeniable charm. The region is off the standard Dordogne tourist trail but is very popular with British ex-pats – in fact, some towns can seem to have almost as many British residents as French. First stop, **Issigeac**, is perhaps the most rewarding, with its pretty medieval centre situated on a tributary of the Dropt. From here you can follow quiet backroads southwest along the **Dropt valley** to **Eymet**, a particularly satisfying *bastide* with a well-preserved central square and an abandoned castle, and on to Allemans-du-Dropt, where the focus of interest is a remarkable series of frescoes in its otherwise unassuming **Église St-Eutrope**. Last but not least comes **Duras**, the town from which the twentieth-century novelist Margaret Duras took her pen-name after spending part of her childhood in the region. Duras's semi-ruined but still forbidding castle holds a commanding position on Périgord's southwestern border and is easily the most impressive in the Bergerac region.

GETTING AROUND   **SOUTH OF BERGERAC**

Public transport is almost non-existent. Buses do link Bergerac with Eymet and Issigeac, and Eymet with Allemans, but there are only one or two in each direction daily, none of which allows for a day-trip from Bergerac.

Issigeac

An almost perfectly circular huddle of houses in the midst of pastureland and orchards 8km southeast of Colombier along the D14, **ISSIGEAC** owes its prosperity to the bishops of Sarlat who established a residence here in 1317. Only fragments of the outer walls remain, and in recent years the village has been considerably tarted up, but otherwise its core of half-timbered medieval buildings is largely unspoilt and the narrow streets mercifully traffic-free. On Sunday mornings an animated **market** takes over much of the centre.

The seventeenth-century **bishop's palace**, now containing various administrative offices, and the **Maison des Dîmes**, the former tax office, with its immense roof, command the village's north entrance. Behind the palace, and not much larger, the Gothic **Église de St-Félicien** contains little of interest beyond some polychrome statues. Better instead to wander the old streets, starting with the **Grand Rue**, leading south to Issigeac's most famous building, known as the **Maison des Têtes** for its roughly carved, almost grotesque crowned and grimacing heads. It stands on the corner with rue Cardénal, at the east end of which a house with a half-timbered upper storey on a narrow stone pedestal – allowing carts to pass on either side – resembles nothing so much as a toadstool. From here, take rue Sauveterre circling southwest past more medieval houses and then cross over the southern end of the Grand Rue to find the rue de l'Ancienne Poste, which meanders generally back northwards to the Maison des Dîmes.

2

ARRIVAL AND INFORMATION   ISSIGEAC

By bus Infrequent buses from Bergerac stop on the main road on the southwest side of Issigeac.

Tourist office The office is set in a vaulted cellar beneath the bishop's palace (June–Sept Mon–Sat 10am–12.30pm & 2–6pm, Sun 10am–12.30pm; ☎05 53 58 79 62, ⓦissigeac-tourisme.com). As well as holding temporary exhibitions, which allow you to explore a few rooms of the palace, the office can provide you with a walking guide to the village.

ACCOMMODATION AND EATING

La Brucelière Place Capelle ☎05 53 73 89 61, ⓦlabruceliere.com. Located by the roundabout on the road to Beaumont, the cheery, family-run *Brucelière* offers five light and airy rooms with polished floors, beige curtains, wicker chairs, and crisp white bedlinen. Whether you're staying here or not, it'd be remiss not to give its handsome, yellow and cream stone restaurant a try. *Menus* (from €20) feature devilishly tempting dishes like crayfish and mushrooms in ravioli parcels with shellfish sauce, and crème brûlée with spiced pineapple. Restaurant Mon & Thurs–Sun noon–1.15pm & 7.30–9pm. €62

El Borini Tour de Ville ☎05 53 58 06 03, ⓦelborini .com. Just across the ring road from the bishop's palace, the supremely classy *El Borini* boasts a log fire in winter and a very pretty courtyard with a stone fountain for alfresco dining in summer. The *menus* (starting at €17.90 and going up to €33) feature refined and delicate versions of southwest classics such as duck with honey and spices, or beef fillet with potatoes or frogs' legs with Roquefort. Mon–Sat noon–2pm & 7–10pm, Sun noon–2pm.

★**Passé & Present** 14 Grand Rue ☎05 53 63 35 31, ⓦpasse-et-present.com. You could quite easily miss this wonderful *chambre d'hôte*, such is the mass of pretty foliage enveloping its little grey door. The interior is similarly winsome, with four gorgeous, parquet-floored rooms possessing lots of homely detail: ornamented fire-places, handmade textiles and linens, black-and-white wall prints and shelves of antiques, many of which are for sale. All rooms, one of which sleeps four (€110), offer views of the pretty garden below. €48

Thénac

Take a drive through the vine-striped countryside southwest of Bergerac, close to the blink-and-you'll miss it hamlet of **THÉNAC**, and you may well come across rather incongruous-looking groups of people wearing the maroon robes of Buddhist monks. They're residents of **Plum Village** (aka Les Pruniers; ⓦplumvillage.org), a commune established by two Vietnamese monks in 1982 to provide Buddhist **retreats** (€330–500 weekly per person, including accommodation), as well as shorter stays and **meditation classes** and "Days of Mindfulness (donation expected), which have become very popular over the years. Even if you're not in search of enlightenment, Thénac itself makes for a lovely, quiet rural base from which to explore the countryside south of Bergerac.

Château de Panisseau ☎ 05 53 58 40 03, ⌨ chateau depanisseau.com. Built by the English during the twelfth century, this château just outside Thénac is a good option for families, with well-equipped four- to eight-bedroom *gîtes* (from €150), and very comfortable rooms with shared kitchen facilities; guests can make use of the heated pool, gym and sauna. Tastings of the estate wines and vineyard tours are also available. **€55**

Eymet

In contrast to Issigeac's meandering medieval streets, **EYMET**, 15km to the southwest, is laid out on a typical *bastide* chequerboard plan around a well-preserved arcaded central square, **place Gambetta**. Founded in 1270 by Alphonse de Poitiers (see p.293), Eymet changed hands on several occasions – not always by force – during the Hundred Years War and later joined Bergerac as a bastion of Protestantism. Indeed, locals are still proud of the fact that in 1588 Henry of Navarre, the then leader of the Protestant armies and future King Henry IV, wrote a letter from Eymet to his mistress, Diane d'Andouins. With its distinctive sloping roof, corner tower and trefoil windows, the house in which he supposedly set pen to paper is the grandest on **place Gambetta**; naturally, it's called the **Maison d'Amour**. Otherwise, the square – also known as place des Arcades – is a wonderful confection of rough-hewn stone buildings and timbered medieval houses, their thick beams creaking and curving with age. Three sides of the square shelter broad arcades, variously concealing cafés and shops – the only thing rather spoiling the whole ensemble is the proliferation of cars.

Once you've soaked up the atmosphere here – which will take longer if you chance to be here for the Thursday-morning **market** – head to Eymet's ruined **castle**, just north of the centre. It hasn't been developed as a tourist sight at all, so you're free to wander inside the curtain wall and right up to the largely intact thirteenth-century keep, built shortly before the *bastide* itself. There's plenty of tree-shaded green space around the castle, as well as a children's playground.

The **riverfront** plays a surprisingly low-key role in town life, but it's worth a quick walk along it; look out for the communal village laundry sinks here, which were still in use until surprisingly recently.

By bus Buses from Bergerac and Issigeac stop on the main boulevard, east of the central square.
Destinations Allemans-du-Dropt (school term Mon–Fri 1 daily; 15min); Bergerac (Mon–Sat 1–2 daily; 45min); Issigeac (Mon–Fri 1–2 daily; 25min).

Tourist office 45 place Gambetta, under the arcades on the square's southeastern corner (May–Sept Mon–Sat 10am–12.30pm & 2–6.30pm, plus Sun 10am–12.30pm in July & Aug; Oct–April Tues–Sat 10am–12.30pm & 2–5.30pm; ☎ 05 53 23 74 95, ⌨ eymet-perigord.fr).

ACCOMMODATION AND EATING

52 Eymet 52 rue du Temple ☎ 05 53 22 65 89, ⌨ 52eymet.com. Just back from place Gambetta, the four gorgeous rooms at this English-run *chambre d'hôte* are individually decorated in antiques, dainty china, gold-rimmed chairs and mirrors, and each has its own balcony. They also open up to non-guests for a lovely afternoon tea (€12) with home-made cakes, scones and clotted cream. Two-night minimum stay. Afternoon tea Jan–Easter Mon & Wed 3–5pm. **€85**

Camping du Château Rue de la Sole ☎ 05 53 23 80 28, ⌨ eymetcamping.com. A modest, peaceful little site north of place Gambetta between the château and the river; facilities include decent shower blocks, laundry and wi-fi, plus bike and boat rental. Closed Oct–April. **€14.50**

★ **L'Cour d'Eymet** 32 bd National ☎ 05 53 22 72 83. Set inside an elegant old building with a shady summer courtyard, this is the locals' choice when it comes to eating out in Eymet. The food is based on local products used in a refreshingly modern way and includes dishes like prawn crumble with a carrot and celery fondant, and white truffles or beef cooked for seven hours in a chocolate sauce. *Menus* €22–45. Mon, Tues & Thurs–Sat noon–2pm & 7.30–9pm, Sun noon–2pm; closed mid-Feb to mid-March and last week of June.

Maison 20 20 rue Traversière ☎ 06 32 32 13 24, ⌨ maison20.com. On a quiet street one block west of place Gambetta and running parallel to boulevard National, is this very stylish French/Kiwi-run boutique *chambre d'hôte*. The two rooms are a cool mix of contemporary and antique, with quirky bits and pieces gathered from all over the world by the exuberant owner; there's also a self-contained apartment (€90). **€70**

La Maison d'Amour 37 place Gambetta ☎05 53 22 34 64. Place Gambetta has plenty of places to eat, the best of which is this always-busy crêperie and *salon de thé*

located on the bottom floor of the square's most appealing building. You'll have a tricky time choosing from a mouth-watering menu of stuffed *galettes* (€8–100), like *canard à la Royale* (duck breast with honey and vinegar) and *Normande* (chicken with mushrooms and cider), but there are also some decent veggie options and salad platters. The interior is nicely done, but you can't beat sitting out on the colourful terrace. Tues–Sun noon–2pm & 7–9.30pm.

2

Église St-Eutrope

Daily 9am–6pm • Free

Some 10km downstream from Eymet lies the tiny village of **ALLEMANS-DU-DROPT**, not much more than a central square and the **Église Saint-Eutrope**. The church's top-heavy lantern tower (topped with a carp as opposed to a cock) and grand west door are both nineteenth-century additions to this much-altered tenth-century building. The interior, meanwhile, would be unremarkable were it not for some recently restored fifteenth-century **frescoes** depicting the Crucifixion and Last Judgement. A number of scenes have been lost or damaged over the years, but on the whole the paintings, which were only rediscovered in 1935, are unusually complete. They read from left to right as you enter, starting with the Last Supper and ending with a particularly graphic view of Hell. Despite the best efforts of St Michael, clad in medieval armour, a mere two souls seem bound for heaven while the damned are being carried off by the basket-load, or skewered on a spit, to be thrust into a boiling cauldron.

ARRIVAL AND INFORMATION

ALLEMANS-DU-DROPT

By bus Buses stop on place de la Mairie, southwest of the church.

Tourist office 13 place de la Liberté (April–June, Sept & Oct Tues–Sat 2–5pm; July & Aug Tues–Sat 11am–1pm &

2–5pm; ☎05 53 20 25 59, ⓦallemansdudropt.com) opposite the church. Though Allemans is easy enough to find your way around, it's still worth picking up an English-language walking guide.

ACCOMMODATION AND EATING

Camping Municipal ☎05 53 20 23 37. Allemans-du-Dropt has a tiny, low-key municipal campsite beside the river, north across the old stone bridge from the village. Closed Sept–April. **€9**

L'Étape Gasconne Place de la Mairie ☎05 53 20 23 55, ⓦletapegasconne-hotel.com. Just across from the market hall, this is a peaceful hotel whose comfortable rooms rather

belie the dowdy, old-fashioned bar downstairs. Three rooms have balconies looking onto the outdoor pool, and in the absence of anywhere else to eat in the village, there's a reasonable restaurant serving traditional cuisine; *menus* from €11.80. Breakfast €8. Restaurant May–Sept daily noon–2pm & 7.30–10pm; Oct–April Mon–Thurs & Sat noon–2pm & 7.30–10pm, Sun noon–2pm. **€51**

Duras and around

From Allemans, the Dropt winds its way northwest for 10km to where the castle-town of **DURAS** lords it over the valley from its rocky outcrop. The château towers were truncated during the Revolution, but they still afford fine views beyond the Dropt to the country around, an enchanting region of rolling hills topped with windmills, of pasture, orchards, woods and, particularly to the north, of vines. The town of Duras sits at the heart of an interesting **wine region**, worthy of its own *appellation*. Sandwiched between Bergerac and the Entre-Deux-Mers region, Duras wines come in all shades: reds, dry whites, and some sweet whites that are lighter than those of Monbazillac.

Château des Ducs de Duras

Feb, March, Nov & Dec daily 2–6pm; April–June, Sept & Oct daily 10am–1pm & 2–6pm; July & Aug daily 10am–7pm • €8, children €4–€5.50 • ☎ 05 53 83 77 32, ⓦ chateau-de-duras.com

The chequered history of Duras is evident in the mix-and-match architecture of the **Château des Ducs de Duras**, which dominates the town. The château was founded in 1137, but then rebuilt after 1308 by Bertrand de Goth, nephew of Pope Clément V; it is said he used money confiscated from the Templars. Rebuilt again after the Hundred Years War, it was then extensively remodelled during the more peaceful and prosperous late sixteenth and seventeenth centuries. The finishing touches were added in 1741, just in time to be thoroughly ransacked during the Revolution, after which the château was left to crumble until the commune bought it in 1969. Since then, it has been thoroughly restored, allowing you to visit almost the whole building, from the basements, where the bakery is still recognizable, to the panoramic ramparts at the top. On your way round, look out for wells cut straight through the bedrock and freshwater tanks in case of siege, and a monstrous kitchen fireplace big enough to roast a whole ox. The dukes obviously liked to build on a grand scale – across a wide, open courtyard the entrance hall is impressive enough, and the ceremonial hall above has no fewer than eleven chimneys.

The château is probably the single best day out for families in the Bergerac area (where so many of the attractions are aimed more at adult visitors). In summer they also stage occasional **medieval shows** with jousting, sword fights, knights in armour and more.

Moulin de Cocussotte

May–Sept Wed–Sun 2–6pm • €4 • ☎ 05 53 83 83 44, ⓦ moulin-de-cocussotte.fr

Three kilometres southeast of Duras, back on the banks of the River Dropt just north of the town of St-Pierre-sur-Dropt, the **Moulin de Cocussotte** and its surrounding garden are a haven of bucolic calm. As well as the ivy-covered thirteenth-century mill and its slowly turning water-wheel, the garden has a wide variety of trees and plants and a shop-cum-café selling some rustic local produce including wine and honey.

Maison de Vins

On the D668 just south of Duras • April–Sept Mon–Fri 10am–1pm & 2–6.30pm, Sat 2–6.30pm; Oct–March Mon–Fri 10am–12.30pm & 2–6pm • Free • ☎ 05 53 94 13 48, ⓦ cotesduras.com

The best place to find out more about the local wines is the tremendously innovative **Maison de Vins**, just downhill from Duras. As well as the standard opportunity to taste and buy, this showcase also has interactive displays on the history of the local wine region, and its own small sample vineyard, planted with different types of vine.

ARRIVAL AND INFORMATION   DURAS AND AROUND

By car Sadly, Duras is pretty much inaccessible without your own transport – the closest station is at Ste-Foy-la-Grande (see p.104), which is 27km to the north.

Tourist office 14 bd Jean-Brisseau (July & Aug Mon–Sat 9am–12.30pm & 2–5.30pm, Sun 10am–1pm; Sept–June Mon–Fri 9am–noon & 2–5.30pm; ☎ 05 53 93 71 18, ⓦ paysdeduras.com).

ACCOMMODATION AND EATING

Camping Municipal ☎ 05 53 83 70 18. The only campsite in Duras is this extremely basic municipal site right under the château's north wall; the sole facilities are showers and toilets. Closed Sept–June. €12

Hostellerie des Ducs Bd Jean-Brisseau ☎ 05 53 83 74 58, ⓦ hostellerieducs-duras.com. A few paces back along from the tourist office, this rather grand-looking building, complete with ostentatious turret hovering near the entrance, makes for a most comfortable stay; variously priced rooms are available, either with a shower or bath, and some with a/c. In addition to a pool, spa/sauna and flower-filled terrace, there's also an excellent conservatory

restaurant (*menus* €22–59) serving upmarket regional cuisine; ox-cheek in belly of pork and local duck prepared in "different ways". There's also a small selection of vegetarian dishes. Breakfast €9.50. Restaurant Tues–Fri noon–2pm & 7.30–9pm, Sat 7.30–9pm, Sun noon–2pm. **€94**

Vue de Duras Gargot Sud ☏ 05 53 83 24 86, ⊛ vuede duras.com. Three kilometres north of Duras along the

D203 and atop a hill with, as the name suggests, views across the valley to Duras, is this wonderful English-run *chambre d'hôte* in a converted farmhouse. There are four rooms and a two-bedroom *gîte* (€925 per week), all with exposed stone walls and clean, simple decor. Outside is a big pool and a large grassy garden with a couple of children's climbing frames and toys. **€72**

2

West of Bergerac

Downstream from Bergerac, the steep north slopes of the Dordogne valley are clothed in vines all the way along to the more illustrious vineyards of St-Émilion. The valley here is flat and uninteresting, dominated by a major road and rail line, but there are a few worthwhile diversions en route. First is **Ste-Foy-la-Grande**, which – with its excellent Saturday market and medieval traces – is the most interesting town on this stretch. From here, it's a short drive to the well-preserved mosaics at **Montcaret**'s Gallo-Roman villa, which is by far the biggest draw in these parts; and to the **Château de Montaigne**, where the influential Renaissance thinker and confirmed sceptic, Michel de Montaigne, wrote most of his famous *Essais*.

GETTING AROUND

Public transport along this stretch of the Dordogne is limited to trains on the Sarlat–Bordeaux line. With just a couple of services per day between some of these towns, it requires careful planning and a fair bit of walking to reach the area's more interesting sites.

Ste-Foy-la-Grande

Heading west from Bergerac along the River Dordogne, the first place of any size is the prosperous town of **STE-FOY-LA-GRANDE**. The central **place Gambetta** retains some of its original arcades, now shading lively café terraces, while **rue de la République** also boasts several fine, timbered medieval houses, the most grandiose of which, with its corner tower, now houses the tourist office. However, it's the soaring, jagged spire of the **Église Notre-Dame** that marks this particular building out as the street's most prominent edifice. The bulk of this present incarnation dates from the mid-seventeenth century, its beautifully proportioned interior pure Gothic, with tall, slender pillars reaching upwards to a fine rib-vaulted ceiling. Take a look, too, at the stained-glass windows, depicting characters from the Old and New Testaments.

Also worth a wander is the riverside esplanade a short walk to the north, from where you can cross the river via the pont Michel Montaigne to visit Ste-Foy's modest museum, the **Maison du Fleuve et du Vin** (June–Sept Tues–Sun 2–5.30pm; Oct–May Mon, Tues, Thurs & Fri 2.30–4.30pm; €3), covering the role played by river trade in the town's history and providing information on the wine produced around Ste-Foy. Even if that doesn't tempt you, it's definitely worth timing your visit to Ste-Foy to catch the Saturday-morning **market**, one of the region's biggest and most important, when the whole town centre is closed to traffic.

ARRIVAL AND INFORMATION

By train The *gare SNCF* is a 5min walk south of Ste-Foy; from the station, turn left along avenue de la Gare then walk north along avenue Paul Broca and then rue Victor Hugo, the town's major shopping street.

Destinations Bergerac (3–10 daily; 20min); Bordeaux

(4–10 daily; 1hr); Castillon-la-Bataille (3–10 daily; 15–20min); Lamothe-Montravel (1–3 daily; 15–20min); St-Émilion (3–5 daily; 30min).

Tourist office 102 rue de la République (Jan–June & Sept–Dec Mon–Sat 9.30am–12.30pm & 2.30–5.30pm;

July & Aug Mon–Sat 9.30am–1pm & 2.30–6.30pm, Sun 10am–1pm; ☎05 57 46 03 00, ✆tourisme-dordogne-paysfoyen.com).

Boat trips In July and August Bateau de Promenade Rivesdo offer 45min riverboat trips (€6) along the Dordogne; departures take place from Quai de la Brèche, a short walk down from the tourist office (see opposite), which also handles all bookings.

Canoe rental In July and Aug you can rent canoes (from €9) from Canoe Kayak (☎05 53 24 86 12), on the north side of the river opposite *Camping de la Bastide* (see below).

ACCOMMODATION AND EATING

Le 8 8 rue Marceau ☎05 57 41 31 49. A couple of blocks back from the main square, this very cosy, vine-festooned place is one of those delightful hidden restaurants that only locals seem to know about. The husband-and-wife team serve dishes that vary with the season but might include hake with lemon cream and, for something a little richer, steak with truffle and foie-gras sauce *Menus* €18.50–51. Thurs–Sat noon–2pm & 7.30–9pm, Sun noon–2pm.

★**Au Fil de l'Eau** 3 rue de la Rouquette ☎05 53 24 72 60, ✆restaurantaufildeleau.com. On the north side of Pont Michel Montaigne, the smart *Au Fil de l'Eau* is one of the best-regarded fish restaurants in the region; specials include eels with parsley (*menus* €17–37). Be sure to grab a table out in the conservatory, which affords marvellous views across the water. Tues–Sat noon–2pm & 7–9pm, Sun noon–2pm.

Camping de la Bastide Allée du Camping ☎05 57 46 13 84, ✆camping-bastide.com. Set about 500m east of town along the river's south bank on avenue Georges Clemenceau – the extension of rue de la République – this is a small and very comfortable three-star site, with modern shower blocks, a laundry, play area, games room and pool; mobile homes are also available to rent (€490 weekly). Closed Nov–March. €25

Grand Hôtel 117 rue de la République ☎05 57 46 00 08, ✆grandhotelstefoy.com. Not nearly as grand as its name implies, this is nevertheless a decent enough hotel, with airy, high-ceilinged rooms, albeit just a touch old-fashioned and slightly frayed around the edges. Still, it's handily located smack bang in the centre and fairly priced. Breakfast €6. Closed two weeks in Dec & Feb; reception closed noon–5pm and Sept–June. €55

Le Victor Hugo 101 rue Victor Hugo ☎05 57 41 35 43. Just on the edge of the old centre as you're coming in from the train station, the ten spotlessly clean, generously sized rooms here are painted in warm, predominantly burgundy colours, and come with beautifully styled wood-carved furnishings. Breakfast €7.90. €59

Around Ste-Foy-la-Grande

The area **around Ste-Foy-la-Grande** holds several worthwhile excursions, though in order to reach any of them, you will require your own wheels. One attractive option, particularly if you don't have a car, would be to rent a bike in Ste-Foy (see opposite) and then follow the flat, quiet side roads running parallel to the D936.

Jardins de Sardy

June–Sept daily 10am–6pm • €6 • ☎05 53 27 51 45, ✆jardinsdesardy.com

West from Ste-Foy on the D936, you can make a brief detour after about 10km up into the hills north of the river to visit the **Jardins de Sardy** in Vélines. The entry fee is a bit steep, but the gardens – a combination of English and Italian style – occupy a pretty, sheltered spot overlooking the Dordogne. The centrepiece is an informal pond garden set against the wisteria-covered farmhouse.

Villa Gallo Romaine de Montcaret

June–Sept daily 9.45am–12.30pm & 2–6.30pm; Oct–May Mon–Fri & Sun 10am–12.30pm & 2–5.30pm • €3 • ☎05 53 58 50 18, ✆villa-montcaret.fr

Twelve kilometres west of Ste-Foy-la-Grande, at the tiny village of **MONTCARET**, the remains of the fourth-century **Villa Gallo Romaine de Montcaret** lie randomly scattered around the village church. The first mosaic of this Gallo-Roman villa was discovered in 1827, but it wasn't until the early twentieth century that major excavation works took place, carried out by local villager Pierre-Martial Tauziac. Still, only about one-tenth of the villa has been fully excavated, but it's more than enough to demonstrate the occupants' affluent lifestyle, from underfloor heating and a variety of hot and cold baths to a grand reception room measuring 350 square metres. The floors, baths and

2

covered walkways were laid with elaborate mosaics, of which large areas have survived relatively intact, most notably in the **cold bath**, which is superbly decorated with shellfish, dolphins and octopuses – the only figurative decorations remaining. No less impressive is the "dining room", or **Cruciform Room**, housed within a glass building adjoining the reception; here, you can see the more abstract pattern of shields and fish scales, alongside a couple of skeletons; note, however, that from mid-November to mid-April those mosaics outdoors are covered to protect them from frosts and are therefore not on view. The reception area houses a small **museum** displaying some of the many objects found on the site, such as pottery fragments, bits of axes, amphorae and oil lamps.

ACCOMMODATION   MONTCARET

A l'Olivier 7 rue de la Villa Gallo Romaine ☎ 05 53 61 65 87, ⓦ bandbalolivier.com. Right opposite Montcaret's village church and Roman villa, this child-friendly *chambre* *d'hôte* has large, peaceful gardens and comfortable but rather plain rooms, and offers a very relaxed place to stay. €52

Château de Montaigne
45min guided tours: Feb, March, Nov & Dec Wed–Sun 10am–noon & 2–5.30pm; April–June, Sept & Oct Wed–Sun 10am–noon & 2–6.30pm; July & Aug daily 10am–6.30pm • €8 • ☎ 05 53 58 63 93, ⓦ chateau-montaigne.com

Back lanes lead 3km northwest from Montcaret to the sleepy village of **ST-MICHEL-DE-MONTAIGNE**, where Montaigne (1533–92) wrote many of his chatty, digressive and influential essays on the nature of life and humankind. Even if you haven't read any of his works, it's worth making the pilgrimage to the **Château de Montaigne**, just beyond the village to the north, to learn more about this engaging, if somewhat quirky and complex, character. Montaigne's castle residence burned down in 1885, and its modern reconstruction is closed to the public. You can, however, go on a guided tour (in French only) of the fourteenth-century **tower** where Montaigne closeted himself away after 1571 to work on his three volumes of essays. On the ground floor was his private chapel, the first floor is the room where he died and the final storey held the library. Unfortunately his priceless collection of more than a thousand books, all carefully annotated, was dispersed immediately after his death, but some traces of his thought can still be found in the Greek and Latin maxims he inscribed on the beams.

THE LORD OF MONTAIGNE

The third son of a Catholic father and a mother from a wealthy Spanish-Portuguese Jewish family, Michel Eyquem, **Lord of Montaigne**, had an unusual education which involved everyone, including the servants, speaking to him in Latin, and being woken by a musician to ensure "his brain not be damaged". It certainly seems to have caused no harm, since Montaigne went on to become a councillor and later mayor of Bordeaux, and was highly respected for his tolerance, wisdom and diplomacy. There is evidence that he also possessed a mischievous sense of humour – throughout the bitter Religious Wars, the Catholic Montaigne apparently took pleasure in ringing his chapel bell as loudly and as often as possible to annoy his Protestant neighbours. On the other hand, it must also be said that Montaigne, who held the Protestant leader Henry of Navarre in great esteem, played an important role in resolving the conflict, though he didn't live to see peace restored in 1598.

Though he attended Mass regularly before his death, and received the last sacrament, Montaigne's **writings** are renowned for their scepticism; in a typical outburst he declares, "Man is insane. He wouldn't know how to create a maggot, and he creates Gods by the dozen." His philosophical standpoint was essentially an argument for introspection – "if man does not know himself, then what can he know?" While it is criticized as being inconclusive, his legacy is rather his great originality of thought and his essays' wide-ranging questioning of generally accepted truths.

East of Bergerac

The real interest and beauty of the Bergerac region lies upstream of the city, where the Dordogne river makes two great meanders near **Trémolat** and **Limeuil**: here, castles, abbeys and pretty villages of soft stone crowd the hilltops and valley floors. There are two main tourist routes: along the Dordogne river itself, or looping inland up the heavily wooded **Couze valley** to the village of **Cadouin**, with its austere abbey church and elaborately carved cloister.

GETTING AROUND **EAST OF BERGERAC**

Transport along the Dordogne valley is provided by trains on the Bergerac–Sarlat line, with the stations at Lalinde, Trémolat and Le Buisson served fairly regularly. To get to the towns and churches on the inland route, you need your own car or bike – though it's hilly country for cycling.

Along the Dordogne

Following the Dordogne east from Bergerac, the first sight of any interest is the half-completed **Château de Lanquais**, as much for the story behind its architecture as for its somewhat dilapidated interiors. The working paper mills at **Couze-et-St-Front** also merit a quick stop, while **Lalinde** provides hotels, transport and other tourist facilities, before you meet the first of the Dordogne's great loops, the **Cingle de Trémolat**. At the top of the second meander, the feudal village of **Limeuil** marks where the River Vézère flows into the Dordogne and where you pass into the Périgord Noir, while the final destination, **Le Buisson-de-Cadouin**, sits on an important rail junction on the Bergerac–Sarlat and Agen–Périgueux lines.

Château de Lanquais

April–June & Sept–Oct Mon & Wed–Sun 2.30–6pm; July & Aug daily 10am–7pm • €8 • ☎ 06 10 79 12 69, ⓦ chateaudelanquais.fr

Some 15km east of Bergerac and just outside the village of the same name, the **Château de Lanquais** is described in tourist literature as "Périgord's unfinished Louvre", and its isolation and rugged charm make for an enjoyable little excursion; come in July or August and you might coincide with regular special events such as medieval fairs, night markets and antique roadshows.

In the mid-sixteenth century, when Bergerac and much of the surrounding country was under Protestant sway, Lanquais was owned by a Catholic, Isabeau de Limeuil, cousin to Catherine de Médici. In a brave – or foolhardy – move, Isabeau commissioned the architects of the Louvre in Catholic Paris to add a wing in similar style to her castle. Before the work could be completed, however, the Protestant armies besieged the château in 1577 and left the facade pitted by cannonballs. They didn't destroy it, though, and you can still discern the change in styles where the Renaissance wing, with its dormer windows and ornamentation, was grafted onto the medieval fortress. It's an imposing rather than an attractive building and some of the **interiors** are in need of restoration. As in many Périgord châteaux, it's the fireplaces that steal the show, notably that occupying one whole wall of the "blue salon" with its two enigmatic bulls'-skull carvings. The difference between medieval and Renaissance styles is perhaps most discernible in the kitchen, where the large stone slabs of the former give way to the Italian *pisé* style of mosaic flooring, whereby stones are dug into the earth. Underneath the kitchen are the extensive cellars, part of which once functioned as a prison – as evidenced by the one remaining gloomy cell. The adjoining pavilion, meanwhile, was a nineteenth-century addition by a local abbot.

Couze-et-St-Front

Two kilometres east of Lanquais, the road drops down to the Dordogne again at what was once an important paper-making centre, **COUZE-ET-ST-FRONT**. Head down a side street in the northwest corner of the town to see a series of beautiful old mill buildings, some cut into the cliff face itself, all profiting from the source of power provided by the River Couze. During the industry's heyday in the late fifteenth century – when some thirteen mills were in operation here – *gabares* would carry the paper along the river to Bordeaux, from where it would be exported abroad, principally to the Netherlands.

Moulin de la Rouzique

1hr guided tours April–June & Sept–Oct Mon–Fri 2–6pm; July & Aug daily 10am–7pm • €8 • ☎ 05 53 24 36 16, ⓦ moulin-de-la-rouzique.com

The only water-wheel still turning in Couze-et-St-Front is that of the fifteenth-century **Moulin de la Rouzique**, where you can see how paper is made in time-honoured fashion, using rags. Note that it is only possible to visit on a **guided tour**, for which there are no set times, so you'll just have to turn up and wait until there are enough people for a small group. Tours begin inside the *chiffonerie* (rags room), itself hewn into the rock face, where the rags were stored to make the paper pulp – a mix of plant fibres and water. Here, the crushing machine would set to work, its hammers crushing the rags, which would eventually soften and decompose following several weeks in large vats of water. Today, though, a far more efficient Dutch machine is used, which is able to convert around 30kg of rags into paper pulp in around ten hours, a process so powerful that it renders decomposition unnecessary. The metal water-wheel still turns at quite a lick, having replaced the old wooden wheel (still on view) some years ago. The tour concludes in the drying room, where you can examine a beautiful collection of antique watermarked papers.

In July and August, there's a free daily paper-making workshop for children (and adults, if they want, too) at 10am.

Lalinde

The only town of any size along this stretch of the Dordogne, **LALINDE** guards an important river-crossing 3km upstream from Couze and 23km from Bergerac. In 1267 Henry III of England chose the little settlement on the river's north bank to become the first English *bastide*. The central square, grid plan and fragments of wall remain, but Lalinde today is mainly of interest as a place to stay or have a bite to eat, and to visit its **market** (Thursday is the main trading day, and there's also a smaller farmers' market on Saturday), though the **Église Sainte-Colombe** and gardens on its balustraded riverfront and a large canal basin immediately to the north are worth a quick stop. The **canal** was built in the nineteenth century to bypass a dangerous set of rapids, made more hazardous in legendary times by the presence of a dragon, La Coloubre, which lurked in a cave on the opposite bank. According to legend, St Front (see p.47) got rid of the monster in the fourth century by burning it on an enormous bonfire on the hill above its lair – grateful citizens later erected the tiny clifftop **Chapelle de St-Front** in his honour. You can get to the chapel in ten minutes on foot by crossing the bridge and then scrambling up the steep marked path in the hillside.

ARRIVAL AND INFORMATION   LALINDE

By train The *gare SNCF* is a 5min walk across the canal on avenue du Général Leclerc.
Destinations Agen (2–10 daily; 1hr 50min–3hr 45min); Bergerac (7 daily; 25min); Le Bugue (2 daily; 50min); Couze (3 daily; 5min); Les Eyzies (2–6 daily; 1hr–2hr 45min); Périgueux (2–7 daily; 1hr–2hr 30min); Sarlat (7 daily; 45min); Trémolat (7 daily; 10min).
By bus Buses to Bergerac depart from the central place de la Halle.

Destinations Bergerac (school term Mon–Sat 1–2 daily, school hols Tues–Thurs & Sat 1–2 daily; 40min); Port de Couze (as for Bergerac; 15min).
Tourist office In the Jardin Public, by the old bridge (May & Oct–April Mon–Fri 9.30am–12.30pm & 2–5pm, Sat 10am–12.30pm; June & Sept Mon–Fri 9.30am–12.30pm & 2–6pm, Sat 9.30am–12.30pm & 2–5.30pm; July & Aug Mon 2–6pm, Tues–Sat 9.30am–12.30pm & 3–7pm, Sun 9.30am–12.30pm; ☎ 05 53 61 08 55, ⓦ pays-des-bastides.com).

ACCOMMODATION AND EATING

★**Côté Rivage** Badefols-sur-Dordogne ☏05 53 23 65 00, ⓦcote-dordogne.com. Some 3km east of Lalinde, on the south side of the river in Badefols-sur-Dordogne, this refined hotel offers seven beautifully thought-out rooms, each styled according to a different theme: wine, chocolate, the *bastide* and so forth. The restaurant (*menus* €19–32) is a joy too; it not only looks superb, with fantastic view across the river, but the food is first-class; melon gazpacho, prawn risotto or slow-cooked lamb are typically tantalizing dishes. Breakfast €13. Restaurant Mon–Fri noon–2pm & 7–9pm, Sat & Sun 7–9pm; hotel and restaurant closed Jan. **€85**

Le Forêt 2 place Victor-Hugo ☏05 53 27 98 30, ⓦleforet-hotel-dordogne.com. Located at the western end of Lalinde next to a chunk of the original old town wall and gate, this pleasant little hotel boasts considerable charm, from its range of good-looking rooms – a couple have four-poster beds, while those on the top floor have retained their original beams – to the plethora of paintings and antiques dotted around. The wonderful, olde-worlde *salon de thé* on the ground floor is by far the best place in town for an afternoon tea and cake (€7). Breakfast €9.50. Salon de thé daily 8am–7pm. **€51**

Trémolat

Some 8km upstream from Lalinde the Dordogne snakes its way through two huge meanders, of which the first you come to, the **Cingle de Trémolat**, is the tighter and therefore more impressive. A bend in the river might not sound like a very worthwhile sight, but this is where one of the most beautiful rivers in France puts on its prettiest face. The best views are from the limestone cliffs to the north of the village – follow signs to the Panorama de Trémolat, or on upwards to the Bélvèdere de Rocamadour – from where the whole meander is visible. Over to the east, a heavily fortified church tower pinpoints the village of **TRÉMOLAT**, one of the more picturesque in the area and home to one of the finest hotel-restaurants in the Dordogne, as well as a boulangerie and small supermarket where you could stock up on picnic supplies.

ARRIVAL AND INFORMATION   TRÉMOLAT

By train The *gare SNCF* is located just over 1km to the south of the village.
Destinations Agen (2–6 daily; 1hr 45min–3hr 45min); Bergerac (7 daily; 45min); Le Bugue (2 daily; 45min); Couze (3 daily; 25min); Les Eyzies (2–4 daily; 50min); Lalinde (7 daily; 15min); Périgueux (2–4 daily; 1hr 20min–2hr

45min); Sarlat (7 daily; 35min).
Tourist office Tucked away in one corner just behind the church (July & Aug daily 10am–1pm & 3–6pm; Sept–June Mon–Fri 9am–noon & 2–6pm; ☏05 53 22 89 33, ⓦtourisme.tremolat.fr).

ACCOMMODATION AND EATING

★**Bistrot de la Place** Le Bourg ☏05 53 22 80 06. Operated by the *Vieux Logis* (see below), the sprightly *Bistrot de la Place*, just on the corner of the main square, is the less expensive version of the hotel's upscale restaurant, but it doesn't scrimp on quality. This apparently simple, workaday place offers a superb take on old Périgord classics: expect dishes such as cream of asparagus with prawn curry or guinea-fowl with leek and hazelnut crumble. *Menus* from €18 at lunchtime and from €25 for dinner. June–Sept daily noon–1.30pm & 7–9.30pm; Oct–May noon–1.30pm & 7–9.30pm.

Camping de Trémolat ☏05 53 22 81 18, ⓦsemitour .com. On the banks of the Dordogne, this is a good-sized campsite, also with mobile homes to rent (from €540 weekly). There's a restaurant/bar, pool and some excellent sports facilities, including canoeing and kayaking. Closed Oct–April. **€12.10**

★**Vieux Logis** ☏05 53 22 80 06, ⓦvieux-logis.com. Having served as a place of worship and a tobacco farm, this is now one of the best hotels in the Dordogne and one of the original members of the upmarket Relais & Châteaux chain. There are 23 utterly swish rooms with a 1920s feel, and though all differ somewhat most have carved wooden furnishings and portraits of dour Victorian-era families on the walls. In addition, there are two cosy lounges, a smoking room, large pool surrounded by formal gardens and a lovely terrace for summer dining at the hotel's phenomenal, Michelin-starred gastronomic restaurant (weekday lunch *menu* €49, dinner *menus* from €90), offering a creative modern take on local classics courtesy of renowned chef Vincent Arnould. Restaurant mid-April to mid-Oct daily noon–1.30pm & 7–9.30pm; closed Wed & Thurs mid-Oct to mid-April. **€200**

Limeuil

The D31 east from Trémolat takes you over a ridge for a bird's-eye view of the second meander in the Dordogne, the **Cingle de Limeuil**. But this pretty loop is only half the

2

story; the road drops down to the gorgeous honey-stoned village of **LIMEUIL**, which straggles down a steep hillside leading to the confluence of the Vézère and Dordogne rivers. Limeuil reached its first peak in the Middle Ages, thanks to its strategic location, and then another in the nineteenth century when local craftsmen built boats for the booming river trade. Today, the flower-filled village relies on tourism for its bread and butter, and can be over-run in high season, but with an ideal combination of waterborne river activities, pretty streets with an arty, hippy air and good places to eat, it offers something for everyone.

Limeuil's willow-shaded riverbank makes a good picnic spot, and also has a pebbly **beach** from which you can go for a dip in the river, though it's too shallow and fast-flowing to allow serious swimming. This is also the base for all canoeing and kayaking trips on the river.

Jardins Panoramiques de Limeuil

Rue du Port • Easter–June, Sept & Oct Mon–Fri & Sun 10am–12.30pm & 2–6pm; July & Aug daily 10am–8pm • €8, children €5.50 • ☎ 05 53 73 26 13, ⓦ jardins-panoramiques-limeuil.com

Passing under Limeuil's old gate and huffing and puffing up the narrow, central and impressively steep rue du Port will bring you to the hilltop **Les Jardins Panoramiques de Limeuil**, where the feudal château once stood. The gardens here are pleasantly leafy, with some pretty water features, and it does monopolize the best river views, but since the entry fee is about as steep as the hill it's on, you might prefer to head for the classic viewpoint of the Cingle de Limeuil near Trémolat (see p.109). In high summer there are various activities laid on for children which make it more tempting for families.

Atelier du Verre Soufflé

Rte de la Poste • Free • ☎ 05 53 63 38 96, ⓦ nicolas-guittet-verrier.com

Down on the main road at the bottom of the village is the **Atelier du Verre Soufflé** glass-blowing workshop, where you can marvel as glass vases in a dozen different shades appear like magic out of the flames and, of course, buy one of the beautiful pieces to take home. There are no set opening hours, as these are governed by whenever the owner feels like turning up.

ARRIVAL AND INFORMATION   LIMEUIL

By car As Limeuil isn't on the train line and the bus service is scanty at best, you'll need a car to get here.

Tourist office Jardin de la Mairie, just up rue de Port and through a little gateway on your left (April & Oct Mon–Fri 10am–1pm & 2–5pm; May, June & Sept daily 10am–1pm & 2–5pm; July & Aug daily 10am–1pm & 2–6pm; ☎ 05 53 63 38 90, ⓦ limeuil-en-perigord.com). Pick up one of their informative walking leaflets, which guide you around the village in about an hour and a half.

Canoe and kayak rental Canoës Rivières Loisirs (☎ 05 53 63 38 73, ⓦ canoes-rivieres-loisirs.com), based

on Limeuil's beach, offers a 1hr trip along the Dordogne river to Buisson (6km), which costs €9.50 in a canoe and €11.50 in a kayak, while canoe/kayak trips up the Vézère river to Le Bugue (8km) cost €11.50 and €13.50 respectively. You can also hire canoes and kayaks for longer periods.

Horseriding There's an excellent riding centre, La Haute Yerle (☎ 05 53 63 35 85, ⓦ rando-equestre-hauteyerle .com), a little to the southwest of Limeuil off the D2 road in Alles-sur-Dordogne, which offers treks from half a day (from €80) up to a week's circuit of the Périgord Noir.

ACCOMMODATION AND EATING

Au Bon Accueil Rue du Port ☎ 05 53 63 30 97, ⓦ au-bon-accueil-limeuil.com. Small, friendly hotel-restaurant positioned towards the top end of this pretty cobbled street. In a separate building to the restaurant, the hotel has five tidy, violet/mauve and slate-grey-coloured rooms, though they're rather on the sparse side, with smallish beds and boxy little bathrooms. The restaurant, meanwhile, not only looks great – one room

has bright-orange walls, the other exposed stone walls, plus there's a vine-covered terrace with views along the valley – but the food is outstanding; sublime dishes like pork in a rich mustard sauce, and rabbit fricassée, in addition to half a dozen daily home-made desserts chalked up on a board. *Menus* start at just €16. Restaurant April–Oct noon–2pm & 7–10pm; hotel closed Nov–March. **€80**

★**Port de Limeuil** Rue du Port ☎ 05 53 63 29 76, ⓦ leportdelimeuil.com. Campers are extremely well catered for at this excellent four-star site just across the river from the village. Facilities include shaded pitches, cabins (from €690 weekly), a laundry, restaurant/snack bar, lots of sporting activities including pool, plus bike and canoe hire. Closed Sept–May. **€30.20**

★**Garden Party** Place des Fossés ☎ 06 83 48 36 61.

Right by the entrance to the Jardins Panoramiques at the very top of town, this is a fun, poppy place to eat and the terrace is the most convivial spot in town for an evening *apéro*. The frequently changing menu is limited to three or four light, creative dishes (one of which is normally vegetarian) such as cod with rosemary, tomato, peppers, garlic and lemon. *Menus* €26, mains €14–18. Tues–Sat 7–9pm, Sun noon–2pm.

Chapelle St-Martin
Daily 9am–7pm • Free

One kilometre northeast of Limeuil on the Le Bugue road is the **Chapelle St-Martin**; opening hours can be as up and down as the building's history – if it's locked, you can get the key from the house opposite. A Latin inscription inside this dumpy little Romanesque chapel records that it was dedicated to St Thomas à Becket, the archbishop of Canterbury murdered by Henry II's courtiers in 1170 after the king famously asked who would rid him of "this turbulent priest". The inscription goes on to relate that the chapel was founded in 1194 by Henry's son and successor, Richard the Lionheart, together with Philippe II (Philippe Auguste) of France on their return from the Third Crusade, "to beseech the pardon of God". There are also the remnants of fifteenth-century frescoes in the choir: to the right a Crucifixion scene and the Descent from the Cross; to the left the Flight from Egypt.

Le Buisson-de-Cadouin

LE BUISSON-DE-CADOUIN, 5km south of Limeuil, is the last stop on this stretch of the Dordogne river. Other than the **Grottes de Maxange**, the town is no great shakes when it comes to tourist attractions, but it has convenient transport links and a few other facilities.

Grottes de Maxange
40min tours Daily: April–June & Sept 10am–noon & 2–6pm; July & Aug 9am–7pm; Oct 10am–noon & 2–5pm • €8.50, children €5.90 • ☎ 05 53 23 42 80, ⓦ lesgrottesdemaxange.com

Just 1km southeast of Le Buisson-de-Cadouin, the **Grottes de Maxange** were discovered completely by chance in 2000 by the owner of the quarry in which they are located. The caves were opened to the public in 2003, while a newly discovered and equally impressive gallery was revealed in 2009; tours take in around 350m of the cavern. The Grottes de Maxange are particularly unusual in that they hide extensive displays of *excentriques*. These delicate limestone formations, some looping round on

---

GROTTE DE CUSSAC

In September 2000, great excitement broke out among art historians and archeologists when a speleologist nosing around Cussac, near Le Buisson-de-Cadouin, stumbled on a previously unknown decorated cave containing more than one hundred **prehistoric engravings**. So important is Marc Delluc's discovery that it's been dubbed the "Lascaux of engraving", in reference to the famous Vézère-valley cavern (see p.148).

The Grotte de Cussac is particularly significant because of the number and size of the engravings. The biggest is a 4m-long bison, while some scenes comprise as many as forty figures. They are also unusually well preserved, the outlines etched deep into the clay by artists sometime between 25,000 and 30,000 years ago. **Horses**, **bison**, **mammoths**, **rhino** and **deer** all feature strongly, but there are also very rare representations of **birds**, as well as **female silhouettes**, **fertility symbols** and a strange long-snouted animal that has yet to be identified.

Because of the vulnerability of these caves (see box, p.149), it is unlikely that Cussac will ever be opened to the public, but you can get a glimpse of what all the fuss is about at ⓦ www .culture.gouv.fr/culture/actualites/index-cussac.htm.

themselves, others suddenly veering off in a different direction, are believed to occur where water evaporates from extremely fine fissures in the rock. Here and there the walls glitter with star-like formations known as *aragonites*. Look out, too, for the cave-bear scratches on the walls. Maxange is also one of the more accessible caves in the region, with no stairs or narrow passages to negotiate – and little in the way of queuing for tickets.

ARRIVAL AND INFORMATION — LE BUISSON-DE-CADOUIN

By train Le Buisson-de-Cadouin is a junction on the Bordeaux–Sarlat and Agen–Périgueux train lines; its *gare SNCF* is a couple of minutes' walk north of the town centre; for a taxi call Taxi Morante (05 53 22 06 51).

Destinations Agen (4–6 daily; 1hr 30min); Bergerac (4–6 daily; 30–40min); Le Bugue (2 daily; 8min); Couze (3–4 daily; 25min); Les Eyzies (4–6 daily; 15min); Lalinde (6 daily; 20min); Périgueux (4–6 daily; 50min); Sarlat (5–7 daily; 40min); Trémolat (5 daily; 10min).

Tourist office Place André Boissière, 150m down from the train station (July & Aug Mon–Sat 10am–1pm & 6pm, Sun 10am–1pm; Sept–June Mon–Fri 10am–12.30pm & 2–5.30pm; 05 53 22 06 09, dordogne-vezere.com).

ACCOMMODATION AND EATING

Manoir de Bellerive 05 53 22 16 16, bellerivehotel.com. Just under 2km east of town on the road to Siorac, the *Manoir de Bellerive* is an elegant little château, built on the orders of Louis-Napoleon in 1830 and housing a charming luxury hotel set in an English-style park on the banks of the Dordogne. Some of the rooms in the original manor have river views, while those in the quieter *orangerie* annexe have private terraces. There's also a tennis court, pool and a perfect breakfast spot on the terrace overlooking the river. Its Michelin-starred restaurant serves meals "inspired by the seasons and the surrounding countryside", which translates as fresh market and farm produce used to create dishes such as scallops in a cream of mushroom sauce or duck with walnut sauce (*menus* €39–57). Breakfast €15. Restaurant Feb–Dec Tues–Sat noon–1.30pm & 7.15–9.30pm, Sun noon–1.30pm; hotel closed Jan. **€140**

Le Pont de Vicq Av de la Dordogne 05 53 22 01 73, campinglepontdevicq.com. Around 2km beyond the train station, on the road to Le Bugue, this large and tidy three-star campsite has a heated pool, as well as a long river-beach for bathing, cabins for rent (€570 weekly) and canoe and kayak hire on site; in summer there's also a snack bar where you can drink and eat barbecued food till late. Closed Nov–March. **€27.80**

The Couze valley

The **Couze valley**, striking southeast of the paper-making town of Couze-et-St-Front, has provided an important thoroughfare since Gallo-Roman times. It's a region of thickly wooded hills and pastoral valleys, interspersed with comely villages, such as **Beaumont**, and hilltop churches, none finer than those at **St-Avit-Sénieur** and **Montferrand-du-Périgord**.

Beaumont

Part of Edward's I's motivation for founding **BEAUMONT** in 1272, on a dominant spur 10km upstream along the Couze from its confluence with the Dordogne, was to guard the trade routes along the valley. As in many such *bastides*, the fourteenth-century **Église St-Laurent-et-Saint-Front** was built for military as well as religious reasons – a final outpost of defence in times of attack – hence the two bulky towers either side of the entrance, and the well inside. The north tower, to the left of the entrance, is the old clocktower; it is lower by some 30m than the south tower, a brooding presence complete with battlements. The largely Gothic interior is a hollow, single-nave structure, and is fairly ordinary save for its impressive vaulted ceiling.

The main focus of the town, however, is the attractive **place Centrale**, which once held sixteen arcades, of which seven now remain. The square's most notable building is **Maison Lafitte**, a fine timbered house on the south side, which used to sit above a covered market; note the cross of St Andrew set between the windows. The modern-day market takes place here on Tuesdays and Saturdays. Off to the west of the square stands the Porte de Luzier, one of the original sixteen town gates.

INFORMATION

By car There's no reliable public transport to Beaumont, so you'll need a car to get here.

Tourist office Place Centrale (July & Aug Mon–Sat 10am–12.30pm & 2–6pm, Sun 10am–12.30pm; Sept–June Mon–

Fri 10am–noon & 2–5pm; ☎05 53 22 39 12, ⓦpays-des-bastides.com). They stock an impressive selection of English-language history and architecture leaflets on Beaumont, St-Avit and Montferrand.

ACCOMMODATION AND EATING

Hostellerie de St-Front 3 rue Romieu ☎05 53 22 30 11, ⓦhostellerie-de-saint-front.com. A short walk along from the church, the *Hostellerie* has six simple rooms, some with shared bathroom facilities; those at the back have private terraces with good views over the countryside. The commendable restaurant here (*menus* €20–30) cooks up excellent traditional food. On Saturday mornings outside of high-season they run a half-day pâtisserie-making course for €45 a head. Breakfast €7. Restaurant Mon & Wed–Sun noon–2pm & 7–10pm. **€53**

★**Moulin de la Ville** ☎05 53 22 47 35, ⓦmoulin delaville.com. A steep half-kilometre downhill from

the town centre (exit the town via the Porte de Luzier and carry straight on down into the valley), the former town mill has been reborn by its English owners (one an interior decorator, the other a Michelin-starred chef) to match most people's idea of the dream French getaway. The rooms are light, airy and flavoured with sunny Mediterranean vibes, the gardens are a planned exercise in dishevelled art and, not surprisingly, dinner (*menu* €25; open to outside guests with pre-booking) is a gourmet affair of local fare, with the added bonus that chef Steve loves to patiently explain how he created each dish. **€70**

St-Avit-Sénieur

Church Daily 10am–noon & 2–6pm • Free

On the other side of the Couze valley from Beaumont, roughly 4km by road, the semi-ruined abbey of **St-Avit-Sénieur** stares across the countryside from another rocky knoll. It grew up around the burial place of a fifth-century hermit, Avitus, who was born at Lanquais and later served in the Visigoth army until taken prisoner in 507 by the Frankish king Clovis, a recent convert to Christianity. At some point during his fourteen years' captivity in Paris, Avitus followed suit, and was then instructed in a vision to return to Périgord, where he lived as a hermit until his death in 570. Tales of his miracles soon attracted pilgrims and the simple chapel grew into a monastery; the present **church** was founded in the early twelfth century, and an inscription records that the saint's bones were brought here in 1117.

Montferrand-du-Périgord

Upstream of St-Avit-Sénieur, the D26 continues southeast up the narrowing valley for another 8km to the tiny village of **MONTFERRAND-DU-PÉRIGORD**. With a clutch of typical Périgord houses sheltering beneath a semi-ruined château, this is one of those gorgeous lost hamlets that seems to have stopped moving forward in time about a hundred years ago; and if its looks weren't reason enough to make the minor detour out to Montferrand-du-Périgord, the excellent *Lou Peyrol* restaurant (see p.114) might sway you. A single street leads up past the village's superb sixteenth-century **market hall** – bigger, and sturdier it seems, than some of the surrounding houses – to where a footpath takes off west, past the château, its crumbling walls and a panoramic **viewpoint**. If you fancy stretching your legs a bit more then stick with the footpath, which then wends its way through the woods. Roughly a kilometre later it comes out near the hilltop **Église de St-Christophe**, standing on its own in a cemetery. It used to be the parish church but has gradually been diminished over the years to little more than a stocky bell tower, so it's surprising to find that the twelfth- and fifteenth-century **frescoes** have survived. There's some wonderful detail to admire, not least on the north wall (to your left as you enter), where you can just about make out a sea monster, mouth agape as it readies itself to swallow the damned, next to which is a woman riding a lion, supposedly the symbol of lust. The oldest painting is on the north wall of the choir, portraying St Leonard releasing prisoners (the little building below symbolizing the prison), while St Christopher himself makes an appearance on the west wall, carrying the Infant Jesus upon his shoulder.

ACCOMMODATION AND EATING — MONTFERRAND-DU-PÉRIGORD

★**Lou Peyrol** La Barrière 05 53 63 24 45, hotel-loupeyrol-dordogne.com. Owned by a friendly English–French couple, this small, creeper-covered country hotel is down on the main road and has five rustic and simple rooms (think wrought-iron beds with floral-patterned bedspreads) and an excellent restaurant (*menus* €21–39) serving traditional Périgord cuisine, such as smoked duck salad or foie gras in Montbazillac wine. Breakfast €8. Restaurant Mon, Tues & Thurs–Sun 12.30pm–2pm & 7.30–9pm; hotel and restaurant closed Oct–Easter. **€57**

Cadouin

At the same time that Augustinian monks were busy building their church in honour of St Avit (see p.113), the Cistercians founded a typically austere **abbey** in what is now the village of **CADOUIN**, 8km to the northeast of Montferrand-du-Périgord, up the D25. The abbey aside, Cadouin's handsome confection of honey- and gold-coloured stone buildings is a big draw for many tourists, as is the busy Wednesday morning **market**, which spreads out over much of the town centre. Moreover, there's no shortage of terrific places to sleep and eat here, most of which are on or just off **place de l'Abbaye**, the pretty main square. Leaving Cadouin, most people drop straight down to the Dordogne at Le Buisson, from where the caves around Les Eyzies (see p.132) are within easy striking distance.

Abbaye de Cadouin

Place de l'Abbaye • April–June, Sept & Oct Mon & Wed–Sun 10am–1pm & 2–6pm; July & Aug daily 10am–7pm; Nov, Dec, Feb & March Tues–Sun 10am–12.30pm & 2–5pm • €6.80, audioguide €3 • 05 53 63 36 28, semitour.com

The efforts of the Cistercians were given a boost when, in 1117, crusaders returning from the Holy Land brought them a piece of cloth believed to have been part of Christ's shroud. For eight hundred years it drew flocks of pilgrims – including Eleanor of Aquitaine, Richard the Lionheart and King Louis IX – until in 1935 the two bands of embroidery at either end were shown to contain an Arabic text from the early eleventh century. The original cloth is no longer kept at the **Abbaye de Cadouin**, but a replica is displayed in the small museum at the entrance to the flamboyant Gothic **cloister**, which is accessed via a separate entrance to the north of the church door. In any case, the cloth plays second fiddle to the finely sculpted but badly damaged capitals around the cloister, most of which are concentrated along the north wall; the first one you come to is of two monks opening a book, beyond which are two merchants squabbling over a goose. Next to this, above the abbot's seat, is a superb bas-relief, showing Jesus carrying the cross while two soldiers dice for his tunic, and a procession of monks alongside a prostrate Mary Magdalene – the remains of a Crucifixion scene. A little further along you can just make out the traces of a fifteenth-century fresco, the only one remaining. Scattered along the east side of the cloister, meanwhile, are some twenty-five pendants, representing prophets and evangelists.

Adjacent to the cloister stands the contrastingly austere Romanesque church, **La Paroisse de Cadouin**, with its stark, monumental west wall and unusual double-tier belfry roofed with chestnut shingles. Inside, the triple nave is equally spartan and so high that the pillars appear to bulge outwards. You can still see the chains above the altar where the shroud was suspended in its casket, but the main point of interest is the stained glass in the north aisle, installed around a century ago, which recounts the story of the shroud's journey from Jerusalem.

ARRIVAL AND DEPARTURE — CADOUIN

By train The only way to get here by public transport is to take the train to Le Buisson-de-Cadouin (see p.111) and then a taxi for the final 6km (count on around €20).

ACCOMMODATION

L'Ancienne Gendarmerie Rte de Beaumont ☎ 05 53 58 39 84, ⓦ anciennegendarmerie.com. Situated some 300m from the main square on the Beaumont road, this *chambre d'hôte* is set in Cadouin's former police station. There are four lovely en-suite rooms, each possessing warm stone walls, exposed beams and colourful floor tiling; two have their own balcony overlooking the garden. There's also an elegant communal sitting room, with an open hearth, books aplenty and a DVD player complete with a selection of films. The Dutch/French breakfast is excellent. Closed mid-Dec to mid-Jan. €69

★ **Auberge de Jeunesse** Abbaye de Cadouin ☎ 05 53 73 28 78, ⓦ fuaj.org. Adjacent to the cloister, the monks' dormitories have been turned into an excellent and very friendly HI youth hostel, with five-, seven- and ten-bedded dorms, as well as private rooms with shower, basin and mezzanine-floor sleeping area. There's also a well-equipped kitchen and laundry facilities. Picnics and hot evening meals can be provided upon request, though breakfast is included in the price. Closed mid-Dec to end Jan. Dorms €23.40, doubles €53.20

Les Jardins de l'Abbaye Rte de Monpazier ☎ 05 53 61 89 30, ⓦ jardinsabbaye.com. Out on the Montferrand road just above the village, this is a calm, shady site which also has some attractive mobile homes (from €480 weekly) set above the camping area on a series of picturesque ridges. Snack bar and outdoor pool. Closed Oct–April. €19.90

Les Songes de l'Abbaye Place de l'Abbaye ☎ 05 53 63 94 18, ⓦ songesdelabbaye.com. Situated plum on the main square, this charming hotel has four exceptionally cool, gloriously colourful rooms (yellow, salmon, mauve and grey), all furnished in gorgeous French oak and chestnut wood. The bathrooms are similarly snappy, featuring huge showers, glass basins and wood-framed mirrors, as is the dining area with its red-painted wooden beams running across the ceiling. The owners are bio-farmers and the breakfast (included in the rates) is an organic feast. €80

★ **Villa Marguerite** Place Géraud de Salles ☎ 05 53 27 28 73, ⓦ villa-marguerite-cadouin.com. One of the Dordogne's most memorable *chambres d'hôtes*, the *Villa Marguerite* is so rammed with antique memories it might as well be a museum. Each of the five rooms is individually styled, one themed on ancient Greece, another the jungles of Central Africa, with tribal masks and decorated calabashes lining the walls. Everything is immaculately well-kept, the owner loves a good chat and there's a cute little garden. It's just back from the main road at the western end of the village. €95

EATING

Restaurant de l'Abbaye Place de l'Abbaye ☎ 05 53 63 40 93. Cadouin's best restaurant offers tasty, traditional *menus* from €15.50, from rabbit terrine with chestnuts to a terrific chocolate-nut pie; it's also renowned for its garlic soup. The predominantly bare brick interior, with a beautiful stone fireplace at its centrepiece, looks fabulous, though dining alfresco looking across to the abbey is no less inviting. April–Oct Tues–Sun noon–2pm & 7–9pm; Nov–March daily noon–2pm, plus Sat 7–9pm.

Un Air de Campagne Av Republique ☎ 05 53 27 37 66. A short walk up the main road from place de l'Abbaye, *Un Air* is a charming restaurant with a very short menu consisting of not much more than a few omelettes, juicy salads and a cracking little two-course *menu* (€12.50) of duck with home-made potato fritters, followed by a bowl of Périgordin vanilla and walnut ice cream. You eat at dinky wooden tables topped with chequered tablecloths. Daily 11am–6pm.

2

Sarlat and the Périgord Noir

121 Sarlat-la-Canéda and around

129 The Vézère valley and around

151 The middle Dordogne

CANOEING NEAR LA ROQUE-GAGEAC

Sarlat and the Périgord Noir

The central part of the Dordogne valley and its tributary, the valley of the Vézère, form the heart of the Périgord Noir. This is the classic Dordogne countryside of tourist brochures: rivers meandering through deep-cut valleys framed by limestone cliffs; dense, dark oak woods; orchards of walnut trees; and flocks of ducks and low-slung grey geese. This rich, fertile land has provided food and shelter since the earliest times, and the first settlers left behind them the world's greatest concentration of prehistoric sites. Later generations built the beetling medieval castles and huddled villages that now provide the region's iconic images. It is rich fare, best taken at a gentle pace, concentrating on a few sites rather than trying to see everything.

3

The focal point of the Périgord Noir region is its capital, **Sarlat-la-Canéda**. Though this medieval town boasts no great monuments, Sarlat is not to be missed, with a warren of old lanes, hidden courtyards and fine architecture – the background for many a period drama – not to mention its excellent weekly markets.

Sarlat is within spitting distance of the two iconic river valleys which have come to define the whole region. First up is the **Vézère valley**, cutting diagonally across the region from the northeast. The valley's immense, overhanging cliffs have been worn away by frost action over the millennia to create natural rock shelters where humans have sought refuge for thousands of years, leaving an incredible wealth of archeological and artistic evidence from the late Paleolithic era. The two unmissable highlights are the outstandingly preserved polychrome paintings of the **Grotte de Font-de-Gaume**, which you can still visit in the original, and the reproductions at **Lascaux**, near Montignac. The valley has more than cave paintings to offer, however: several sites show how cliff shelters were lived in throughout the Middle Ages up until relatively recently, while some breathtaking chasms like the **Gouffre de Proumeyssac** are the work of nature alone.

South of Sarlat, in the sublime, château-studded **Dordogne valley**, it's the region's medieval, feudal history that's most palpable. **Beynac** and **Castelnaud**, two semi-ruined fortresses on either side of the river, are without doubt the most spectacular. Closer to river level, **La Roque-Gageac** presents a more homely scene. From a distance, save for its red-tiled roofs, the village is barely distinguishable from the vertical cliff into which it nestles. This is also one of the best spots in the whole country to hop on a **canoe** and take a leisurely trip downstream.

With so many first-class sights in such a compact area, it's not surprising that this is one of the most heavily visited inland areas of France, and as a result has all the concomitant

The Dordogne and Lot's best cave art p.121
Festivals, events and markets p.122
Building blocks p.129
Visiting the Vézère valley prehistoric caves p.132
Canoeing the Vézère p.133
Cave art p.135

Tickets for Abri du Cap Blanc, Abri du Poisson, Font-de-Gaume and des Combarelles p.136
The Grotte de Lascaux and Lascaux II–IV p.149
The lighter side of Beynac p.156
Périgord walnuts p.160
Josephine Baker and the Rainbow Tribe p.161

THE GARDENS AT THE MANOIR D'EYRIGNAC

Highlights

❶ Sarlat-la-Canéda Wander the cobbled lanes of this beautifully preserved medieval town, which hosts one of the region's best markets. See p.121

❷ Manoir d'Eyrignac The formal gardens, with their manicured hornbeam hedges and trompe l'oeil parterre, are as much a work of art as of nature. See p.128

❸ Vézère valley Prehistoric artists left moving testimony of their skill in myriad decorated caves here, among them the magnificent friezes of Lascaux and Font-de-Gaume, the bas-reliefs of the Abri du Cap Blanc and the drawings of the Grotte de Rouffignac. See p.129

❹ La Roque-St-Christophe Multistorey living medieval-style in these dozens of rock shelters cut into the limestone cliffs. See p.144

❺ Château de Castelnaud This archetypal feudal fortress lording it over the Dordogne valley contains a superb museum of medieval warfare and offers lots of summertime family fun. See p.158

❻ La Roque-Gageac One of the region's most picturesque villages, with its jumble of roofs and the towering cliffs above mirrored in the slow-moving waters of the Dordogne, which you can explore by boat. See p.162

HIGHLIGHTS ARE MARKED ON THE MAP ON P.120

problems of crowds, high prices and tat. If you can't come out of season, seek accommodation away from the main centres, visit places first thing in the morning and always drive along the back roads, even when there is a more direct route available. On the plus side, the competition for tourism revenue has resulted in some outstandingly good-value places to stay.

GETTING AROUND

By train Though you'll need your own transport for exploring much of the Périgord Noir, two train lines cut through the area. Sarlat is the terminus of a line from Bordeaux via Bergerac, while trains between Agen and Périgueux stop at Le Bugue and Les Eyzies; the best place to change between the two lines is Le Buisson (see p.111). In addition, the northern Vézère valley can be accessed from Terrasson, on the Brive–Bordeaux main line.

By bus The region is served by a minimal smattering of bus routes, though even these early-morning school services can fizzle out entirely in the school holidays.

THE PÉRIGORD NORD

By bike In addition to bike rental outfits in Sarlat, Les Eyzies and Castelnaud-la-Chapelle (see p.125, p.132 & p.160), Bike Bus, based at Castelnaud (☎05 53 31 10 61, ⊚bike-bus .com), offers a range of bikes, including mountain bikes, tourers and children's bikes, with prices starting at €20 per day. They deliver free to Sarlat, Beynac, La Roque-Gageac, Vitrac and most other towns in the immediate region so long as a minimum rental fee is met. Similarly Aquitaine Bike (☎05 53 30 35 17 or ☎06 32 35 56 50, ⊚aquitainebike .com), based in the Périgord Noir at Le Coux-et-Bigaroque, offers free deliveries within 20km, or further afield for a fee.

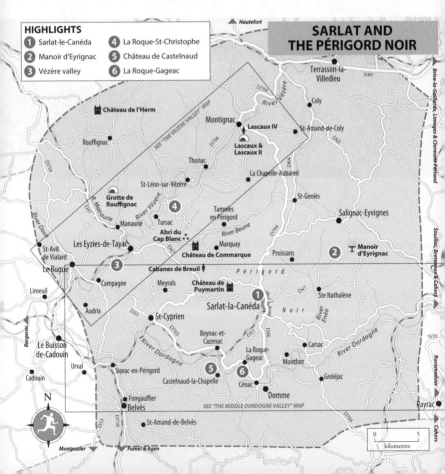

HIGHLIGHTS

1 Sarlat-le-Canéda
2 Manoir d'Eyrignac
3 Vézère valley
4 La Roque-St-Christophe
5 Château de Castelnaud
6 La Roque-Gageac

SARLAT AND THE PÉRIGORD NOIR

THE DORDOGNE AND LOT'S BEST CAVE ART

Lascaux IV Superb replica of the summit of Cro-Magnon art. See p.140

Grotte de Font-de-Gaume Beautifully preserved paintings and engravings in a narrow tunnel. See p.134

Abri du Cap Blanc Sculpted frieze of life-size horses and bison. See p.137

Grotte de Pech-Merle "The chapel of mammoths" stands out among more than five hundred drawings. See p.219

Grotte de Rouffignac Hop on an electric train to view drawings of mammoths and woolly rhinos in a 1km-long cave. See p.138

Grotte du Sorcier Mystifying engraving of a human – the "Sorcier" – among many animals. See p.142

Sarlat-la-Canéda and around

Very picturesque and very touristy, **SARLAT-LA-CANÉDA** (usually known just as Sarlat) sits in a green hollow between hills 10km or so north of the River Dordogne. You hardly notice the modern suburbs, as it is the mainly fifteenth- and sixteenth-century houses of the old town in mellow, pale ochre-coloured stone that draw the attention. Unless you're here for the Wednesday and Saturday **markets**, Sarlat's main draw is its architectural harmony and its foodie-oriented shops; there's also a large range of **accommodation**, both in and just outside the town, making it the most natural base for exploring the Périgord Noir. The ramparts surrounding old Sarlat were torn down in the late 1800s, at about the same time that the north–south **rue de la République** was cut through the centre to create its main thoroughfare. The streets to the west remain relatively quiet; the east side is where you'll find the majority of interest.

The hills above Sarlat also contain a number of sights, such as the topiary gardens of the **Manoir d'Eyrignac**, with perhaps a detour to the picturesque village of **St-Geniès**. Heading westwards, the still-occupied **Château de Puymartin** tends to be overshadowed by the more famous castles along the Dordogne, but contains some unusual interior decorations, while the nearby **Cabanes de Breuil**, a harmonious group of what were probably shepherds' huts, represent a completely different architectural tradition. With the exception of St-Geniès, which, with an early start, is accessible on the Sarlat–Périgueux bus route, you'll need your own **transport** to reach any of these places.

Brief history

Though it started life as a Gallo-Roman settlement, Sarlat really came to prominence in the late eighth century when Benedictine monks established an **abbey** here, later dedicated to a former bishop of Limoges, St Sacerdos. In 1147 **Bernard of Clairvaux** also left his mark when he preached the Second Crusade – according to legend he miraculously cured the sick by offering them bread he had blessed. In spite of this, the townspeople were keen to gain independence from Church rule, and in 1298 were eventually granted the right to elect their own consuls by Louis VIII. In return, they remained loyal to the French Crown during the Hundred Years War and staunchly Catholic in the Wars of Religion, when the town suffered considerably at the hands of the Protestants. The fine **Renaissance** facades visible today date from a period of prosperity in between these two wars. That they are so well preserved is largely due to the fact that the town went into slow decline after the late 1700s. By the early twentieth century the centre was in a pretty poor state, but was saved from further decay by the vision of **André Malraux**, the novelist, Resistance hero and politician who launched the concept of the *secteur sauvegardé* ("protected area") in 1962. Sarlat's town centre was a pilot for this initiative, saving it from excessive postwar renovation and providing funds for a huge restoration project. Today, the 65 **protected monuments** in the medieval centre make it the most popular tourist destination in the whole of Dordogne, packed to the gunwales in summer, though still relatively undisturbed during the winter months.

3

FESTIVALS, EVENTS AND MARKETS

The list below comprises some of the biggest and more interesting of the **festivals** and **events** in this region. Where we haven't given a specific information number or website, contact the relevant tourist office.

Late March, April or early May Sarlat: La Ringueta (☎06 88 96 73 84, ⓦringueta -sarlat.fr). At Pentecôte (Whit Sunday) in even-numbered years, place de la Grande-Rigaudie is the venue for traditional games and sports of the Périgord.

Mid-July to early August Sarlat: Festival des Jeux du Théâtre (☎05 53 31 10 83, ⓦfestival -theatre-sarlat.com). One of the most important theatre fests in France, covering a wide range of material from Shakespeare to the avant-garde Theatre of the Absurd, as well as several productions for children. The open-air performances take place over two weeks in various venues around town.

Mid- to late July Montignac: Festival de Montignac (☎05 53 51 86 88, ⓦfestivalde montignac.fr). Major arts festival featuring local and international folk groups from as far afield as South America and China. As well as ticket-only events, there are street performances, food stalls, exhibitions and crafts demonstrations during the week.

Late July to late September St-Léon-sur-Vézère and around: Festival du Périgord Noir (☎05 53 51 95 17, ⓦfestivalduperigordnoir.fr). Baroque and classical music concerts in the atmospheric churches of St-Léon, St-Amand-de-Coly, Sarlat and in other venues throughout the region.

Early August Les Eyzies and around: Festival Musique en Périgord (☎05 53 30 36 09, ⓦmusiqueenperigord.fr). Interesting mix of medieval and classical works alongside jazz and traditional music from around the world. Concerts take place over two weeks in the Romanesque churches of Les Eyzies, Campagne and Audrix, among other venues.

Late July to early August Belvès and Cadouin: Festival Bach (ⓦfestivalbach.fr). Dedicated to the composer and comprising a handful of concerts generally held in Belvès church and the abbey at Cadouin.

Early November Sarlat: Festival du Film (ⓦfestivaldufilmdesarlat.com). One-week festival previewing films from around the world, including special screenings of student productions.

MARKETS

The main **markets** in this region are at Belvès (Sat); Le Bugue (Tues & Sat); Domme (Thurs); Les Eyzies (April–Oct Mon); Montignac (Wed & Sat); St-Cyprien (Sun); St-Geniès (Sun); Sarlat (Wed & Sat); and Terrasson (Thurs).

Place de la Liberté

Sarlat's labyrinthine lanes fan out from **place de la Liberté**, the central square where the big Saturday **market** spreads its stands of flowers, foie gras, truffles, walnuts and mushrooms, according to the season; it's mostly foodstuffs in the morning and general goods after lunch.

Hôtel de Maleville

Place de la Liberté • Closed to the public

The finest building on place de la Liberté is the **Hôtel de Maleville,** tucked into its southwest corner. The facade facing onto the square consists of a tall, narrow building in French Renaissance style with ornate window surrounds; turn down the lane beside it to see its more classical Italianate frontage, with a balustraded terrace and two medallions above the door representing Henry IV and, according to popular belief, his mistress Gabrielle d'Estrée.

Maison de La Boétie

Place du Peyrou • Ground floor occasionally open for art exhibitions

The lane beside the Hôtel de Maleville continues through a series of passages and geranium-filled courtyards to emerge beneath Sarlat's most famous house, the **Maison de**

La Boétie. Though its prominent gables and tiers of mullion windows, each within a sculpted frame, are certainly eye-catching, much of the building's renown derives from the fact that the poet and humanist **Étienne de La Boétie**, a close friend of Michel de Montaigne (see p.106), was born here in 1530. He went on to study law in Orléans, where he wrote his most famous work, *Discourse on Voluntary Servitude*, though it wasn't published until after his premature death at the age of 33. A treatise on the tyranny of power, and thus a very early expression of anarchism, the *Discourse* later struck a chord with Rousseau and other radical thinkers in the run-up to the Revolution.

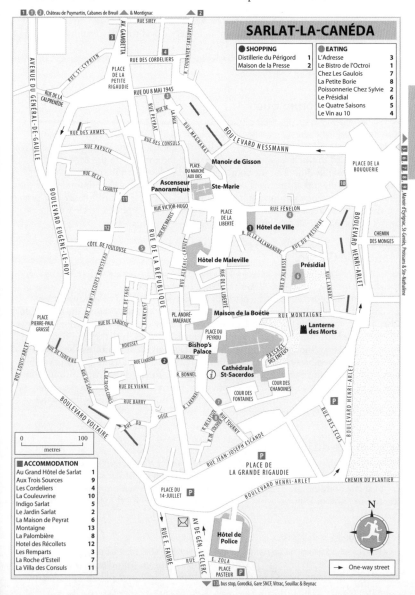

SARLAT-LA-CANÉDA

● SHOPPING	
Distillerie du Périgord	1
Maison de la Presse	2

● EATING	
L'Adresse	3
Le Bistro de l'Octroi	1
Chez Les Gaulois	7
La Petite Borie	8
Poissonnerie Chez Sylvie	2
Le Présidial	6
Le Quatre Saisons	5
Le Vin au 10	4

■ ACCOMMODATION	
Au Grand Hôtel de Sarlat	1
Aux Trois Sources	9
Les Cordeliers	4
La Couleuvrine	10
Indigo Sarlat	5
Le Jardin Sarlat	2
La Maison de Peyrat	6
Montaigne	13
La Palombière	8
Hotel des Récollets	12
Les Remparts	3
La Roche d'Esteil	7
La Villa des Consuls	11

Cathédrale St-Sacerdos and around

Opposite the Maison de La Boétie, the former **Bishop's Palace**, with its Renaissance gallery and windows, is now home to the tourist office and is attached to the large and unexciting **Cathédrale St-Sacerdos** (daily 9am–6pm), which mostly dates from a seventeenth-century renovation. More interesting are the two pretty courtyards to the south of the cathedral – **cour des Fontaines**, filled with the sound of playing water, and **cour des Chanoines**, surrounded by a pleasing assembly of buildings – and the **Passage des Enfeus** around the chevet, where Sarlat's nobles were laid to rest in arched niches (*enfeus*) let into the wall. Less illustrious mortals were buried in the cemetery above, presided over by a curious bullet-shaped tower, the **Lanterne des Morts**, built in the twelfth century. Its exact purpose remains a mystery. Local tradition maintains that it commemorates St Bernard's visit in 1147 (see p.121).

Further north along the same slope you come to the **Présidial**, the former seat of royal justice, now a restaurant (see p.127).

Ascenseur Panoramique

Rue des Consuls • April–Dec daily 9am–9pm, though check with the tourist office (see opposite) for the latest hours; closed in wet weather • April–Oct €5, Nov–March €4, children €1 all year • Tickets available at the tourist office, or on-site by credit card only • ☎ 05 53 31 45 42

Just off place de la Liberté, behind the back of the church of Ste-Marie (now a covered market accessed through massive metal doors) lies the entrance to the **Ascenseur Panoramique**, a lift built into the church tower. The glass-sided lift takes you up 35m to peer out of the top of the tower, which was never roofed, for ten minutes, while the guide points out Sarlat's more famous monuments, including some of its 22 towers and remnants of the medieval walls. From up here you also get a bird's-eye view of the town's many *lauze* roofs (see box, p.129).

Manoir de Gisson

Place du Marché-aux-Oies • Daily: mid-Feb to end March & Oct to mid-Nov 10am–6pm; April–June & Sept 10am–6.30pm; July & Aug 10am–7pm; mid-Nov to mid-Jan 11am–5pm • €7 • ☎ 05 53 28 70 55, ⓦ manoirdegisson.com

Dominating the north side of the place du Marché-aux-Oies – a delightful corner decorated by three bronze geese in tribute to the square's name – stands the **Manoir de Gisson**. This impressive building, with its hexagonal tower and stone-mullion windows, offers a rare chance to see inside one of Sarlat's noble houses. It dates from the thirteenth century, though was considerably enlarged in the fifteenth by the Gisson family, whose members most famously served as consuls in charge of the town's public order. You'll find their portraits inside, presiding over rooms decked out with furniture from medieval times to the seventeenth century, much of it fashioned in local walnut. At the top of the lovely circular stone staircase don't miss the chance to admire the internal structure of the heavy *lauze* roof (see box, p.129).

West of rue de la République

It's worth crossing over **rue de la République** to wander the western sector of Sarlat, particularly **rue Jean-Jacques Rousseau**. There's nothing particular to see, beyond more cobbled lanes and ornate doorways or the odd defensive tower, but this side of town is less touristy and quieter.

Gorodka

La Canéda • Daily: July & Aug 10am–midnight; Sept–June 2–6pm • €10 • ☎ 05 53 31 02 00, ⓦ gorodka.com

Just outside Sarlat, 4km south off the D704 to Gourdon, **Gorodka** provides a complete break from Sarlat's medieval monuments. The home of conceptual artist

Pierre Shasmoukine, it's a rambling place with various galleries crammed full of inventive pieces of art, enlivened by a strong dose of irony. The extensive grounds serve as an offbeat gallery of the weird and wonderful, including a giant dragonfly made from the body of a helicopter and bizarre, sinister-faced plastic totems that glow in the dark.

ARRIVAL AND DEPARTURE
SARLAT-LA-CANÉDA

By train Sarlat's *gare SNCF* is just over 1km south of the old town on the road to Souillac.
Destinations Bergerac (5–7 daily; 1hr 30min); Bordeaux (5–7 daily; 2hr 50min); Le Buisson (5–7 daily; 30min); Castillon-la-Bataille (5–7 daily; 1hr 40min–2hr); Lalinde (5–7 daily; 45min–1hr 30min); St-Cyprien (5–7 daily; 15min); Ste-Foy-la-Grande (5–7 daily; 1hr 20min–2hr 10min); Siorac-en-Périgord (5 daily; 20min); Trémolat (5–7 daily; 20–50min).

By bus Buses from Périgueux and Souillac pull into place Pasteur, immediately south of the centre. Souillac buses also call at the train station. As well as the routes covered below, there are also services to Montignac, Périgueux and St-Geniès, though as these run during school term-time only to coincide with childrens' pick-ups and drop-offs,

they're not really a viable option for visitors.
Destinations Carsac (2–4 daily; 20min); Souillac (2–4 daily; 50min–1hr).

By car It's normally easy to find a metered parking space in central Sarlat, though more difficult on market days and in July and August. Paid parking is also available all around Sarlat's ring road, the most convenient being on place de la Grande-Rigaudie. Prices and the maximum stay vary by season; check the instructions on the meter. Note that Sarlat's medieval core is mostly closed to traffic in July and August (daily 11am–6am) and at weekends from mid-April to end June & Sept (8pm Sat to 6am Mon). Free parking is available at any time in most streets just beyond the central part of town.

GETTING AROUND

Car rental Europcar (☎05 53 30 30 40, ⌨europcar.co.uk), on place de Lattre-de-Tassigny, near the train station.
Taxis Call Allo Philippe Taxi (☎06 08 57 30 10, ⌨allo philippetaxi.com), or Brajot Taxi (☎05 53 59 41 13).
Bike rental Liberty-cycle at Zone de Madrazes (☎07 81

24 78 79, ⌨liberty-cycle.com; from €22 per day), on the edge of Sarlat and the start of the Voie Verte cycle path, offer bike rental and half-, full- and multi-day guided bike rides around the region (half-day €25, full day €45).

INFORMATION AND ACTIVITIES

Tourist office In the heart of the old centre at 3 rue Tourny (April Mon–Sat 9am–noon & 2–6pm, Sun 10am–1pm & 2–5pm; May, June & Sept Mon–Sat 9am–6pm, Sun 10am–1pm & 2–5pm; July & Aug Mon–Sat 9am–7.30pm, Sun 10am–1pm & 2–6pm; Oct Mon–Sat 9am–noon & 2–5pm, Sun 10am–1pm; Nov–March Mon–Sat 9am–noon & 2–5pm; ☎05 53 31 45 45, ⌨sarlat-tourisme.com). As well as stocking the *Sortir à Sarlat* leaflet, which gives a run-down of the town's cultural calendar, including its excellent theatre and film festivals (see box, p.122), the office sells maps of hiking and mountain-bike trails around the Périgord Noir (€1.50 per map; €14.90 for all 27 maps).

Guided tours The tourist office runs a wide array of French-language guided tours in Sarlat, from a straightforward trot through local history (€6) to themed tours with a guide in fancy dress; most run from Easter to October only, but check with the office for exact times and tour types. There are also standard historical tours in English (mid-May to mid-Oct Thurs 2pm; €6), and the office sells a booklet (€0.50) which lists self-guided tours of Sarlat.
Canoe rental Head to Vitrac, 7km south of Sarlat, where Périgord Aventure et Loisirs (☎05 53 28 23 82, ⌨canoe-copeyre.com) offers canoe and kayak rental (from €18/€22).

ACCOMMODATION

Note that during the peak holiday season (July–Sept) it's advisable to book several weeks in advance and to consider the quieter places outside the town centre. If you arrive without a **reservation**, it's worth asking for help at the tourist office.

IN SARLAT
Au Grand Hôtel de Sarlat 97 av de Selves ☎05 53 31 50 00, ⌨au-grand-hotel-de-sarlat.com. Impressive five-star hotel just outside the town centre, this is all old-fashioned elegance with grand four-poster beds, soft lighting and bright colours. Other perks include a

covered heated pool, sauna and jacuzzi. Garage parking €12, breakfast €12. Book online in advance for big discounts. **€69**
Les Cordeliers 51 rue des Cordeliers ☎05 53 31 94 66, ⌨hotelsarlat.com. You'll need to book early for this excellent English-run *chambre d'hôte* in an elegant

eighteenth-century townhouse just outside the historic centre, decked out with period furnishings (including a floor-to-ceiling hallway mirror). Spacious rooms are equipped with a/c and impeccable bathrooms. Those on the top floor are tucked under the eaves, and one boasts its own roof terrace. Two nights' minimum stay required, though it's worth double-checking. Closed Nov–Feb. €110

La Couleuvrine 1 place de la Bouquerie ☎05 53 59 27 80, ⓦla-couleuvrine.com. One of Sarlat's more atmospheric hotels, *La Couleuvrine* partly occupies one of the town's defensive towers and has twenty-six comfortable rooms with exposed stone walls and sweet-smelling polished wooden floorboards. Downstairs is a big fireplace and a good restaurant (*menus* from €24) and a lunchtime bistro (*formules* from €13). Breakfast €9.50. Restaurant daily noon–2pm & 7.30–9pm. €65

Indigo Sarlat Rue Jean-Gabin ☎05 53 59 05 84, ⓦcamping-Indigo.com. Sarlat's closest campsite is on a terraced hillside 1km northeast of the centre up rue Jean-Jaurès. It's small, intimate and well equipped – facilities include heated indoor pool, outdoor pool, washing machines, tennis courts and grocery shop, plus mobile homes to rent (€128, two-night minimum stay). Closed Oct–March. €32.50

Le Jardin Sarlat 14 rue du Jardin-de-Madame ☎05 53 29 22 67, ⓦlejardin-sarlat.com. A highly rated English-owned *chambre d'hôte* tucked down a quiet backstreet a short walk from the town centre. It's set in a lush country-cottage garden with a vine-covered terrace, fruit trees, a splash-pool and an outdoor jacuzzi. Inside is a residents' lounge and four cute, airy, en-suite bedrooms. The generous breakfast will set you up for the day. Closed mid-Dec to Feb. €103

★**La Maison des Peyrat** Le Lac de la Plane ☎05 53 59 00 32, ⓦmaisondespeyrat.com. High on a hill, a 10min walk from the town centre, this gorgeous property, parts of which date back to the fourteenth century, has served as a farmhouse, a hospital and place of worship; it's now a unique hotel of higgledy-piggledy corridors, low wooden beams, whitewashed walls and bathrooms big enough for a knight in armour. The surrounding gardens are an idyllic spot for an alfresco breakfast, and there's a nice pool and a big, friendly dog. They have rooms suitable for families (€112) as well as appealing doubles. €69

Montaigne Place Pasteur ☎05 53 31 93 88, ⓦhotel montaigne.fr. This three-star hotel occupies an imposing building just south of centre. The rooms, in cool creams, have less character than the grand exterior might suggest but are well equipped for the price, including double-glazing and a/c. Breakfast €9. Closed mid-Nov to mid-Feb. €85

Hotel des Récollets 4 rue Jean-Jacques Rousseau ☎05 53 31 36 00, ⓦhotel-recollets-sarlat.com. Offering great value, this budget hotel on a very quiet street has a range of different rooms which retain some unusual features like arched stone doorways. The cheapest are very small and it's worth splashing out another €10 for something a little more expensive. Breakfast (€10) is served on the patio in fine weather. €69

Les Remparts 48 av Gambetta ☎05 53 59 40 00, ⓦhotel-lesremparts-sarlat.com. Cheap and cheerful little hotel in a convenient location offering 25 fuss-free rooms, some of which are wheelchair accessible. Though lacking somewhat in decor, all rooms come with TV and a/c. Secure parking available (€8.50). Breakfast €8.50. Closed Dec–Feb. €69

La Villa des Consuls 3 rue Jean-Jacques Rousseau ☎05 53 31 90 05, ⓦvillaconsuls.fr. Neatly positioned on a quiet side-street next to a seventeenth-century chapel, this place has taken an old, stone building with wobbly chimneys and converted it into a pleasantly modern hotel complete with a massage centre. The studios and apartments (€95/€109) are good for travelling families, while the standard rooms are spacious and bright. €95

AROUND SARLAT

Aux Trois Sources Pech-Lafaille ☎05 53 59 08 19, ⓦhebergement-sarlat.com. A very well-priced *chambre d'hôte* in a handsome seventeenth-century manor house 3km east of Sarlat on the road to Ste-Nathalène. Five charming but very simple en-suite rooms, with wooden floors, rugs and original hearths, are squeezed into a converted barn, and there are three small studios (€50). It's surrounded by an attractive park, with chestnut trees and pond full of frogs, not to mention the three springs. €45

★**La Palombière** Ste-Nathalène ☎05 53 59 42 34, ⓦlapalombiere.fr. A five-star job, this is one of the region's best campsites, roughly 10km east of Sarlat on the D47. In a lovely, peaceful location in an extensive area of mature woodland, it's very well equipped – including restaurant, bar, grocery store, pools and tennis courts – and puts on all sorts of kids' events in summer. Mobile homes available, too (€1045 weekly). Closed mid-Sept to April. €36.70

★**La Roche d'Esteil** ☎05 53 29 14 42, ⓦlaroche desteil.com. Run by a welcoming young family, this magical *chambre d'hôte* is one of the most appealing in all of the Dordogne. Set in a converted old farmhouse of warm, dry-stone walls, rooms are painted in pastel colours and decorated in natural, home-made art. There's lots of space outside, with a large, sun-drenched pool, plenty of shade-giving trees and a whole load of peace and tranquillity. A couple of evenings a week in season, excellent dinners are cooked up by the owner. It's 1km or so outside the hamlet of Ste-Nathalène. €97

EATING

During the main tourist season Sarlat is chock-a-block with **restaurants**. In winter pickings are thinner as many places close up for a few months, but those that do stay open tend to be the better-quality places patronized by locals. You'll find foie gras, duck and walnuts in various guises everywhere, alongside another local staple, *pommes sarladaises*: potatoes crispy-fried in duck fat with lashings of garlic, parsley and, sometimes, mushrooms.

L'Adresse 8 rue du 8 Mai 1945 ☎ 05 53 30 56 19. This small, glass-fronted place on the edge of the old quarter offers an eclectic mix of Asian and Dordogne flavours, including Thai-style wok vegetables with rice noodles and a duck-heavy selection of local dishes. It's a real favourite with locals. *Menus* €18–34. Mon 7–9pm, Tues–Sat noon–1.30pm & 7–9pm.

Le Bistro de l'Octroi 111 Av de Selves ☎ 05 53 30 83 40, ⓦ lebistrodeloctroi.fr. A couple of minutes' walk from the town centre, *l'Octroi* sells itself as a simple bistro, but with deer steaks, prawn risotto and duck in walnut sauce on the menu it's clear that it's far from ordinary. *Menus* €14–36. Daily noon–2pm & 7.15–9.30pm.

★**Chez Les Gaulois** 1 rue Tourny ☎ 05 53 59 50 64. Not one for vegetarians, but charcuterie addicts will love this authentic and welcoming restaurant where cured Savoy, Corsican and Spanish hams and sausages hang from the ceiling. They're served, along with Savoy cheeses, on a choice of platters and in salads (€11–14), or you can buy to take away. April–June & Sept–Feb Tues–Sat noon–2pm & 7–8.30pm; July, Aug & school hols daily noon–2pm & 7–9pm.

La Petite Borie 4 rue Tourny ☎ 05 53 31 23 69. Friendly and consistently reliable restaurant offering good service and classic Périgord cuisine at affordable prices. The majority of ingredients are sourced locally, with home-made foie gras featuring strongly. The *menus* (€14.80–€28.50) offer excellent value for money, each starting with a traditional garlic soup. July & Aug daily noon–2.30pm & 7–9.30pm; Sept–June Tues–Sat noon–2.30pm & 7–9.30pm, Sun noon–2.30pm; closed two weeks in Nov or Jan.

★**Poissonnerie Chez Sylvie** 21 av Gambetta ☎ 05 53 28 55 25. A fishmongers' shop moonlighting as a fabulous restaurant, there's nothing fancy about the setting here (think strip lights and plastic chairs), but the fish, seared on a *plancha* (hot plate) is perfectly cooked and the unpretentious atmosphere is great. What's on offer depends on what came into the Atlantic coast ports that morning, but oysters and prawns are a standard, with mains costing €14–16. Mon–Thurs noon–1.30pm, Fri & Sat noon–1.30pm & 7–10pm.

Le Présidial 6 rue Landry ☎ 05 53 28 92 47, ⓦ lepresidial.fr. Classy restaurant in the former court building, with a walled garden and airy, elegant dining rooms. While the setting is more spectacular than the food, especially when floodlit on a summer's evening, it's a reliable choice, offering dishes such as duck breast with blackcurrant sauce. *Menus* €19.50–39.50. Tues 7–9pm, Wed–Sun noon–2pm & 7–9pm.

Le Quatre Saisons 2 Côte de Toulouse ☎ 05 53 29 48 59. Escape the hubbub of central Sarlat to this small, refined restaurant, up a steep flight of stairs from the west side of rue de la République. Menu highlights include poached eggs with cèpes and foie gras, and they have some luscious desserts. *Menus* €16–28. April–June & Sept–Nov Mon & Thurs–Sun noon–1.30pm & 7–8.30pm; July & Aug daily noon–1.30pm & 7–8.30pm.

Le Vin au 10 10 rue Fénelon ☎ 05 53 29 47 80. Arrive early or book ahead for this stylish wine bar with a handful of tables on a quiet street leading up from Sarlat's main square. They serve a carefully selected range of wines from the region and further afield, with inventive and tasty food to accompany them. Try nems (Vietnamese spring rolls) filled with *confit de canard* (preserved duck) and iced soufflé with walnuts to follow. Lunch *menu* €16, dinner €33, or feast on the €60 truffle *menu* in summer. Mon–Sat noon–1.30pm & 7–9pm, Sun 7–9pm.

SHOPPING

While the **markets** are the best place to buy foie gras, walnuts, walnut oil, prunes and other local foods straight from the farmer, place de la Liberté, rue de la Liberté and rue des Consuls are full of **speciality shops**.

Distillerie du Périgord Place de la Liberté ☎ 05 53 59 20 57, ⓦ distillerie-perigord.com. Delectable liqueurs from walnut to plum, as well as fruits in alcohol – try their Guinettes, containing local morello cherries. Mon–Sat 10am–12.30pm & 2–7pm.

Maison de la Presse 34 rue de la République. You'll find English papers and magazines on sale all around Sarlat, but this is a good central option. Mon–Sat 8am–noon & 2–7pm.

DIRECTORY

Hospital The Centre Hospitalier is on rue Jean-Leclaire (☎ 05 53 31 75 75) to the northeast of the centre.
Police Sarlat's Gendarmerie is at 1 bd Henri-Arlet (☎ 05 53 29 18 71).
Post office The main post office is on place du 14-Juillet.

Manoir d'Eyrignac

Gardens Daily: April 10am–7pm; May–Sept 9.30am–7pm; Oct 10am–dusk; Nov–March 10.30am–12.30pm & 2.30pm–dusk • €12, children €6.50–8.50, under 5s free; family ticket €39 • ☎ 05 53 28 99 71, ⓦ eyrignac.com • The gardens are 14km northeast of Sarlat, signed along backroads via Ste-Nathalène

Northeast of Sarlat, the River Enéa rises among oak woods on a plateau to the north of the hamlet of Ste-Nathalène. Though the hills appear scrubby and dry, one of the Enéa's tributaries is fed by seven springs, the same springs that prompted a seventeenth-century noble, Antoine de Costes de la Calprenède, to build a manor house here, the **Manoir d'Eyrignac**. The house itself isn't open to the public, but you can explore the glorious **gardens**.

The gardens aren't huge, but, consisting of lush evergreens – mainly hornbeam, box, cypress and yew – clipped and arranged in formal patterns of alleys and borders, achieve remarkable effects with almost no colour. The regimented lines are softened by the occasional pavilion or fountain and by informal stands of trees framing the countryside around. The original formal garden was laid out by an eighteenth-century Italian landscaper, and later converted to an English romantic garden according to the fashion of the times. What you see today is the work of the last forty years, the creation of the present owner's father in a combination of Italian and French styles.

The complex also contains a small **exhibition hall** next to the ticket office, where you can watch a video about the garden and its history, and a restaurant-cum-snack bar. You can also bring your own food and take advantage of their picnic tables.

St-Geniès

Some 14km north of Sarlat, the cluster of buildings known as **ST-GENIÈS** is worth a detour. It's a typical Périgord Noir village, with its partly ruined château and fortress-like church all constructed from the same warm-yellow stone under heavy *lauze* roofs. Unless it's market day (Sun morning), it won't take long to explore, the only sight being the **Chapelle de Cheylard**, standing on its own on a small knoll to the east. The fourteenth-century frescoes inside have suffered over the years – at one time the chapel served as a dance hall – but a number remain visible, including a particularly manic bunch pelting St Stephen with stones.

Château de Puymartin

45min guided visits: April–June & Sept 10.30–11.30am & 2–6pm; July 1–15 10am–noon & 2–6.30pm; mid-July to Aug 10am–6.30pm; Oct to mid-Nov 2–5.30pm • €8, children €4–6 • ☎ 05 53 59 29 97, ⓦ chateau-de-puymartin.com

Eight kilometres northwest of Sarlat on the D47, the **Château de Puymartin** stands guard over the headwaters of the Petite Beune River, which flows down to join the Vézère at Les Eyzies (see p.130). The castle, which underwent extensive remodelling in the seventeenth and nineteenth centuries, has been in the same family since 1450 and is remarkably well preserved.

Among a large collection of family heirlooms, most noteworthy are the **tapestries**, particularly those in the grand hall, depicting the Siege of Troy. The Classical theme continues in the seventeenth-century trompe l'oeil paintings on the chimneypiece here and in the guest bedroom, where Zeus visits Danaë in a shower of gold – presumably he would have been surprised to find her clothed and holding a cross, a liberty taken in the more puritanical 1800s.

The same sensibilities demanded that a number of naked figures in the **mythological room** also be dressed. To preserve the original, visitors now only see a replica, but it is still an extraordinary sight. The room, though not large, is completely covered in monochrome scenes from mythology: snake-haired Medusa, Argus with his hundred eyes and Althaea murdering her son Meleager by burning a brand. The general

> **BUILDING BLOCKS**
>
> The hallmarks of the Périgord region are the primitive-looking stone huts called **bories**, and the mottled-grey roofs made of limestone slabs – **lauzes** – used on cottage and château alike. Although they are now protected, the cost of maintaining these roofs – the stones weigh on average 500kg per square metre – means that many have been replaced with terracotta tiles. A floor made out of *lauzes* is called *pisé*, and is commonly found in châteaux and chapels, the stones inserted upright into a bed of clay and lime. While you'll find *lauze* roofs and, to a lesser extent, *pisé* floors in evidence throughout the region, *bories* are less common. The best examples are at the Cabanes du Breuil, near Sarlat (see below).

consensus is that the room was a place of meditation, though surprisingly it also served as a children's nursery for some time.

Like all good castles, Puymartin also has its **ghost**, in this case La Dame Blanche, who supposedly haunts the north tower. In real life she was Thérèse de St-Clar, the lady of the household during the sixteenth century, who, on being surprised in the arms of a lover, was walled up in the tower until she died fifteen years later. More prosaically, it's worth climbing up into the roof here to admire the elaborate timber framework supporting the *lauzes*.

Cabanes du Breuil

April–Sept daily 10am–7pm; Oct daily 10am–noon & 2–6pm; Nov 1–11 daily 2–5pm; mid-Nov to March by reservation only • €5, children €2.50 • ☎ 06 80 72 38 59, ⓦ cabanes-du-breuil.com

At the opposite end of the architectural scale to Puymartin are the **Cabanes du Breuil**, a couple of kilometres up in the hills to the northwest of the château. You'll find these dry-stone circular huts under conical *lauze* roofs scattered throughout the region, but none so picturesque as this group belonging to a small, working farm. Known locally as *bories*, the huts were originally used for human habitation, then for animals or storage. In season (June–Sept) there's a video presentation explaining how the huts are made, but really these beautiful structures speak for themselves.

The Vézère valley and around

Billed as the "Vallée de l'Homme", the **Vézère valley** is home to the greatest concentration of **prehistoric sites** in Europe. They are by no means the oldest, but the sheer wealth and variety are quite stunning. It was here also that many important discoveries were made in the nineteenth and early twentieth centuries.

Now listed by UNESCO as a World Heritage site, and for many the top attraction in all of the Dordogne, the Vézère valley draws more than two million visitors a year. The epicentre of all this activity is **Les Eyzies-de-Tayac**, where the Musée National de la Préhistoire contains an almost overwhelming display of important finds. The choice of sites nearby is bewildering, but at the very least you should visit the **Grotte de Font-de-Gaume** and the **Abri du Cap Blanc**, both in the Beune valley to the east of Les Eyzies and harbouring the best cave paintings and bas-relief sculptures still open to the public. Also within striking distance of Les Eyzies, this time to the north, are the **Grotte de Rouffignac**, one of the area's largest caves, with a breathtaking array of animal engravings accessible only by an underground electric train, and the **Château de l'Herm**, an evocative ruined castle with literary associations.

Back on the River Vézère, the market town of **Le Bugue** gives access to the **Grotte du Sorcier**, with its highly significant human image, and the stunning chasm of the **Gouffre de Proumeyssac**.

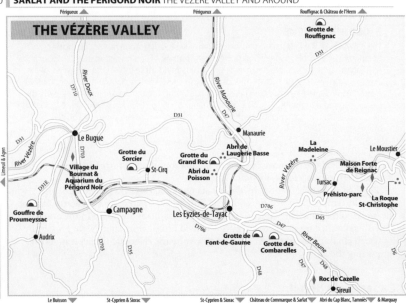

North along the river from Les Eyzies is a more diverse collection of sights, ranging from the semi-troglodytic settlements at **La Madeleine** and **La Roque St-Christophe** – where a whole town was built into the cliff face – to prehistoric theme parks and the appealing Renaissance castle, the **Château de Losse**. Finally there's the pretty town of **Montignac**, just a couple of kilometres from the valley's biggest name, the cave of **Lascaux**. Lascaux itself has been closed to the public since 1963, but its legendary paintings – with all their exceptional detail, colour and realism – have been faithfully reproduced in the brand-new, showstopping **Lascaux IV**.

GETTING AROUND	THE VÉZÈRE VALLEY

As far as transport is concerned, Le Bugue, Les Eyzies and Terrasson, the latter being the northern gateway to the valley, are all accessible by train, while you can get to Montignac by bus from Sarlat and Brive (via Terrasson) if you plan carefully – however many bus services are aimed at schoolchildren and are generally timed for the start and the end of the school day, so aren't very convenient for visitors. Note also that as many of the area's sights are at least a couple of kilometres away from these transport hubs, you'll rely heavily on walking or taxis if you don't have your own vehicle.

Les Eyzies-de-Tayac and around

The principal base for visiting the Vézère valley is **LES EYZIES-DE-TAYAC**, 20km northwest of Sarlat, its one main street dramatically located between the river and a towering cliff into which is built the **Musée National**, home to the largest collection of Paleolithic art in France. While it offers a good choice of hotels and restaurants out of season, Les Eyzies gets completely overrun in summer.

Pôle International de la Préhistoire

30 rue du Moulin • Jan–April & Oct–Dec Mon–Fri 9.30am–5.30pm, Sun 10.30am–5.30pm; May, June & Sept Mon–Fri 9.30am–6.30pm, Sun 10.30am–6.30pm; July & Aug daily 9.30am–6.30pm • Free • ☎ 05 53 06 06 97, ⌨ pole-prehistoire.com

Before tackling the Vézère-valley sites, you might want to pop to the **Pôle International de la Préhistoire** information centre, on the east side of town, for a quick introduction to what's on offer. All the prehistoric sites in the Dordogne region are marked on a

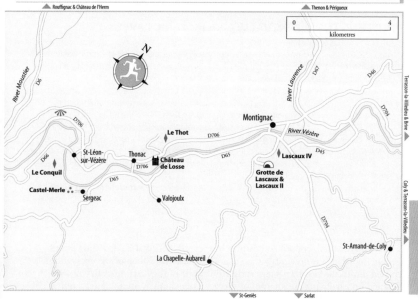

3-D model, with interactive displays, and two slide presentations show how the area has evolved over the last 400,000 years. Knowledgeable staff are available to answer questions and can help plan an itinerary; they also organize various events and temporary exhibitions.

Musée National de la Préhistoire
June & Sept Mon & Wed–Sun 9.30am–6pm; July & Aug daily 9.30am–6.30pm; Oct–May Mon & Wed–Sun Tues 9.30am–12.30pm & 2–5.30pm • €6; free first Sun of the month, and to EU students under 25 • ☎ 05 53 06 45 65, ⓦ musee-prehistoire-eyzies.fr

Under the jutting limestone cliff that dominates Les Eyzies, Paul Dardé's 1930 statue of Neanderthal man, portrayed as an ape-like hunk, stands staring out over the Vézère. Beside him, the **Musée National de la Préhistoire** occupies the remains of a castle built into the rock as well as a striking new building constructed around it. This stunning museum is a vital first stop on any tour of the region's prehistoric sites, and contains a vast array of increasingly sophisticated stone tools of the Paleolithic era (two million to ten thousand years ago). There is so much to see that it can get a bit overwhelming; allow at least two hours for a visit.

The **first floor** is devoted to blades found at various archeological sites; the spear- and axe-heads appear as delicate and perfect as the day they were made, and are accompanied by some engaging short films showing how these blades were made and then used. Look out also for a life-sized giant elk. **Upstairs** are some good re-creations (and the odd original) of engravings and sculptures from the era; highlights include a bison head carved into a stone (now the symbol of the museum); and an oil-burning torch used to illuminate the caves when painting took place.

Musée de l'Abri Pataud
45min guided visit: April & Oct 1–15 Mon–Fri 10am–noon & 2–6pm; May, June & Sept Mon–Thurs & Sun 10am–noon & 2–6pm; July & Aug daily 10am–noon & 1–6pm • €5 • ☎ 05 53 06 92 46

In the late nineteenth century, local farmer Martial Pataud discovered prehistoric remains when he was cutting a new road beside what is now Les Eyzies' Musée National. The rock shelter (*abri*), which had been occupied for over 15,000 years before the roof collapsed around 20,000 years ago, yielded a rich hoard of finds,

VISITING THE VÉZÈRE VALLEY PREHISTORIC CAVES

Visitor numbers to most caves are severely restricted, either for conservation reasons or simply because the site can only hold a certain number of people at a time. At the most popular, including the Grotte de Font-de-Gaume (see p.134) and Grotte des Combarelles (see p.136), you have to buy **tickets** in advance by phoning the ticket office or visiting in person, though in some cases it's now also possible by email. If you can, buy your tickets several weeks in advance, sometimes longer during peak periods. The new Lascaux IV (see p.148) had not opened to the public at the time of writing, but given the scale of the new complex, queues are likely to be less of an issue here than they were at Lascaux II.

In all cases you have to join a **guided tour**, which usually lasts around 45min. Some are offered in English, while others provide a translated text, but they are tiring – and the talks get repetitive. Unless you're a real prehistory buff, limit yourself to just two or three sites, rather than risk losing that sense of magic.

The remote location of the caves makes them hard to access for **travellers with disabilities**. As a reconstruction, Lascaux IV is more accessible, as are the copies at Le Thot. But if you're in doubt, it's best to ask.

a selection of which are now on display in the next-door **Musée de l'Abri Pataud**, occupying what was previously the Patauds' wine cellar. Much of the excavation was carried out in the late 1950s and early 1960s, one of the first "modern" digs which enabled unusually precise analysis of the successive human occupations – unless you're an archeology buff this may not seem hugely exciting, but the guide's explanations help sort out all the different eras mentioned at other sites.

The site is still being explored, but the most famous find so far is a female "Venus" figurine discovered in 1958. The small bas-relief you see today, with her pendulous breasts and rounded belly, is a copy. Archeologists also found six skeletons, including a young mother with her newborn baby and a pearl necklace; again, you see a copy here alongside a bronze statue modelled from her bone structure, while the original pearls are in the town's Musée National (see p.131). Look out, too, for the enchanting little ibex (*bouquetin*) carved on the museum's rock ceiling 17,000 years ago.

Fortified church of Tayac

If you're here in summer and feel the need to get a bit of space from the crowds on the Les Eyzies' street, head down to the riverbank, where there's a nice picnic area and riverside path, or 500m past the railway station to the twelfth-century **fortified church of Tayac**. Nobody ever went to much effort to prettify it, but it's a forbidding defensive structure, with no steeples, but two broad parapets to give archers a proper shot at any attackers.

ARRIVAL AND INFORMATION

By train A stop on the Périgueux–Agen train line, Les Eyzies' *gare SNCF* lies about 500m northwest of the centre, just off the main road before you cross the river.

Destinations Agen (2–5 daily; 1hr 50min); Belvès (2–4 daily; 30min); Le Bugue (2–7 daily; 7min); Le Buisson (2–7 daily; 15min); Périgueux (4–7 daily; 30–50min); Siorac-en-Périgord (2–5 daily; 25min).

Tourist office On the main road right in the town centre (Jan–March, Nov & Dec Mon–Fri 10am–12.30pm & 2–5pm; April & Oct Mon–Sat 9.30am–12.30pm & 2–6pm; May, June & Sept Mon–Sat 9.30am–12.30pm & 2–6pm, Sun 9.30am–12.30pm; July & Aug daily 9am–6.30pm;

☎ 05 53 06 97 05, ⓦ lascaux-dordogne.com). In addition to plentiful information on local sights and *chambres d'hôtes*, they also offer free wi-fi access and bike rental (€20/day; reserve in advance in high season), and there's a 24hr ATM outside.

Hiking The tourist office sells hiking maps of the area (€2.50) and gives out a leaflet describing the "Chemins de la Préhistoire", two hikes up the valley to Laugerie-Basse (8km round trip) and beyond to La Madeleine (15km round trip). Along the route you'll find information panels in English.

ACCOMMODATION

While there are some great **accommodation** options in Les Eyzies, they can be pricey, especially in high season, when it's better to stay out of the main centre or in one of the villages around. Note that most places close in winter, so it's wise to book ahead if you're visiting between October and April.

IN LES EYZIES

Le Centenaire 2 av Cingle ☎ 05 53 06 68 68, ⓦ hotel ducentenaire.fr. There's a lot to like about this recently renovated hotel, from the bright, blinged-out rooms to the classy restaurant (*menus* €26–62) with its traditional Périgord dishes, but the real highlights are the park-like grounds and impressive swimming pool. Restaurant April–Oct Mon–Fri 7–9pm, Sat & Sun noon–2pm & 7–9pm. **€150**

Le Cro-Magnon 54 av de la Préhistoire ☎ 05 53 06 97 06, ⓦ hostellerie-cro-magnon.com. The *Cro-Magnon* is a sunny, inviting building with yellow shutters and vine-covered walls built into the cliff on the north side of town. Rooms are bright with writing desks and walls hung with oil paintings of roses. There are good communal areas, with open hearths, armchairs and a small library, as well as a pool. The restaurant serves one daily *menu* (€29) with a choice of seasonal dishes. Breakfast €11. Restaurant Tues–Sun noon–2pm & 7–9pm; hotel and restaurant closed mid-Nov to mid-March. **€85**

Des Falaises 35 av de la Préhistoire ☎ 05 53 06 97 35, ⓦ hotel_des_falaises.monsite-orange.fr. The best-value rooms in Les Eyzies, located behind a central café-bar run by a friendly owner, are bright, cheerful, clean and well-kept. All are en-suite (though there's no TV) and the marginally more expensive ones (€43) at the back of the building have their own balconies. Breakfast €5. **€40**

★ **La Ferme de Tayac** 14 rue de Tayac ☎ 05 53 06 04 61, ⓦ fermedetayac.com. Though only 1km from Les Eyzies, this welcoming Dutch/English-run *chambre d'hôte* in twelfth-century buildings beside Tayac church is a real delight. The six beautifully appointed rooms and spacious communal areas are full of artistic touches, as are the flower-filled gardens. There's a pool and bikes available for guests to borrow. Three-night minimum stay required, though it's always worth checking. No children. Closed Nov–March. **€100**

De France 1 rue du Moulin ☎ 05 53 06 97 23, ⓦ hotel defrance-perigord.com. Right next to the Musée National entrance, this place has the advantage of being away from the main road and has quiet and comfortable rooms that gather a lot of sunlight. Unfortunately the bathrooms are a bit dated. Breakfast (€10) is taken at the terrace-café opposite. **€67**

★ **Les Glycines** 4 av de Laugerie ☎ 05 53 06 97 07, ⓦ les-glycines-dordogne.com. Les Eyzies' most beguiling hotel by some distance stands on the main road just north of the centre. It's a romantic place, with light, airy rooms, full of drapes and frills, and a beautiful garden behind, criss-crossed by shady paths, with a swimming pool in the middle. The nicest rooms open directly onto the garden (€199). There's also a spa centre and a bistro in addition to the main restaurant (see p.134). Book online in advance for discounts. Breakfast €17. Closed mid-Oct to May. **€129**

Hostellerie du Passeur Place de la Mairie ☎ 05 53 06 97 13, ⓦ hostellerie-du-passeur.com. The vine-covered *Du Passeur* is in a prime spot right in the centre beside the tourist office, but set back from the road. The rooms are pleasant enough, many decked out in rich ochre hues, and have three-star comforts. Downstairs is a smart restaurant (*menus* from €16) with a super terrace by the river. Breakfast €11. Unusually, it's cheaper to book directly with the hotel rather than through a third-party site. Restaurant daily noon–2.30pm & 7.30–9.30pm; hotel and restaurant closed Nov–Feb. **€95**

★ **Le Moulin de la Beune** Rue du Moulin-Bas ☎ 05 53 06 94 33, ⓦ moulindelabeune.com. A pretty, converted mill building on the southern edge of Les Eyzies, this

---

CANOEING THE VÉZÈRE

Les Eyzies is the main base for **canoeing trips** on the Vézère River, which is narrower and quieter than the Dordogne, cutting a thin channel between high cliffs and wooded banks. The scenery is perhaps less dramatic than the château-studded stretch of the Dordogne around Beynac (see p.156), but you do pass beneath several of the troglodytic forts and dwellings lining the valley. Three **companies** cluster around the bridge just north of the town centre, operating from Easter to late September, depending on the weather; all will drive you upstream so you can canoe back down to Les Eyzies; prices (€9–26) rage depending on starting point and rental time.

CANOE RENTAL COMPANIES

Les 3 Drapeaux ☎ 05 53 06 91 89, ⓦ canoes -3drapeaux.fr.

AVCK ☎ 05 53 06 92 92, ⓦ vezere-canoe.com.

Canoës Vallée Vézère ☎ 05 53 05 10 11, ⓦ canoes valleevezere.com.

old-fashioned hotel has simple, spacious and well-priced rooms, some looking out onto its peaceful garden and the rushing stream. There is also a lovely restaurant, *Au Vieux Moulin* (see below), so it's well worth considering the half-board option. Breakfast €11. Closed Nov–March. **€68**

La Rivière 3 rte du Sorcier ☎ 05 53 06 97 14, ⓦ lariviere leseyzies.com. A good, inexpensive choice about 1km from Les Eyzies on the Périgueux road. There are just six unfussy rooms, all en suite, in a typical Périgord farmhouse with access to a pool, bar, laundry and a simple restaurant. There's also a well-tended, four-star campsite, which shares the same facilities as the hotel. Breakfast €9. Closed Nov–March. Camping **€29**, doubles **€55**

AROUND LES EYZIES

La Grange du Mas Le Mas-de-Sireuil ☎ 05 53 29 66 07, ⓦ grange-du-mas.com. Welcoming *chambre d'hôte* with five cutesy rooms on a working farm just outside the village of Sireuil, 5km east of Les Eyzies. For the full French rural experience it's a hard one to top. They only offer half-board, but it's good value, comprising produce from the farm and including drinks. There's also a pool and tennis court. Closed Oct–March. Half-board for two adults **€112**

Laborderie Tamniès ☎ 05 53 29 68 59, ⓦ hotel -laborderie.com. Perched 13km up the Beune valley, northeast of Les Eyzies, this geranium-decked hotel on the edge of a pretty hamlet occupies four separate buildings, with a big choice of rooms – the best are those in the newer blocks with balconies or terraces overlooking the extensive garden and pool – and a good restaurant (see below). Early booking is advisable in summer. Breakfast €9.80. Closed Nov–March. **€84**

EATING

IN LES EYZIES

★**Au Vieux Moulin** Rue du Moulin-Bas ☎ 05 53 06 94 33, ⓦ moulindelabeune.com. Attached to the *Moulin de la Beune* hotel (see p.133), this is one of Les Eyzies' best restaurants. You can enjoy great dishes like green risotto with snails, sitting either in the old-fashioned stone-walled dining room, or outside in the garden where the tiny River Beune rushes past. The prices are decent too, with full *menus* costing €21–58. April–Oct Mon, Thurs, Fri & Sun noon–1.30pm & 7–8.30pm; Tues, Wed & Sat 7–8.30pm.

Les Carottes Sont Cuites 7 rue du Moulin ☎ 06 45 39 25 52. Close to the entrance of the Musée National, this is a boon for vegetarians, whipping up ornate salads and simple dishes of the day without a single bit of duck or beef in sight. With mains starting at just €11, it's also an inexpensive option for lunch. Mon–Fri noon–2pm.

Les Glycines 4 av de Laugerie ☎ 05 53 06 97 07, ⓦ les -glycines-dordogne.com. For a gastronomic treat try the restaurant at the *Les Glycines* hotel (see p.133). There is a strong emphasis on local and seasonal produce, including vegetables and salads from the hotel garden. The Sunday lunch *menu* is €49 or you can splash out on the tremendous truffle *menu* at €110. Reservations highly recommended. June & Sept to mid-Oct Mon & Tues 7.30–9pm,

Wed–Sun 12.15–1.30pm & 7.30–9pm; July & Aug daily 12.15–1.30pm & 7.30–9pm.

AROUND LES EYZIES-DE-TAYAC

Auberge de Layotte ☎ 05 53 06 95 91, ⓦ auberge layotte.com. It's worth searching out this rustic *auberge* lost in the middle of nowhere – signed off the D47 north of Les Eyzies, at the end of a dirt track – for a taste of old-style country cooking. Run by an extrovert and enthusiastic young couple, there's just one five-course *menu* (€32 including drinks) offering such delights as nettle soup, home-cured hams, beef stew and walnut cake. Everything but the wine, bread and cheese is home-made. By reservation only. March–June & Sept–Dec Thurs–Sat noon–1pm & 7–8pm, Sun noon–1pm; July & Aug Tues–Sat noon–1pm & 7–8pm, Sun noon–1pm.

Laborderie Le Bourg ☎ 05 53 29 68 59, ⓦ hotel -laborderie.com. This hotel restaurant is equally popular for its pretty country setting in the village of Tamniès en Périgord as its good-value *menu*, a cut above the standard local fare. Choose between Aquitaine sturgeon in truffle cream and quail stuffed with mushrooms, followed perhaps by iced walnut soufflé. *Menus* €28–49, or count on €45–50 à la carte. April–Oct Mon–Wed 7–8.30pm, Thurs–Sun noon–1.30pm & 7–8.30pm.

Grotte de Font-de-Gaume

1hr guided visits Mon–Fri & Sun: mid-May to mid-Sept 9.30am–5.30pm; mid-Sept to mid-May 9.30am–12.30pm & 2–5.30pm • €7.50, combined ticket with Grotte des Combarelles & Abri du Cap Blanc €18 • ☎ 05 53 06 86 00, ⓦ sites-les-eyzies.fr • The caves are just over 1km east of Les Eyzies along the D47 to Sarlat

Since they were first discovered in 1901, over two hundred Magdalenian-era (18,000–10,000 years old) polychrome paintings and engravings have been found in the narrow tunnel of the **Grotte de Font-de-Gaume**. In order to preserve the artwork, only 78 people are allowed to enter the cave each day (26 allocated to advance bookings, and 52 available on the day), and numbers may be further restricted in the future (see box, p.132).

CAVE ART

Thousands of years ago, early inhabitants of the Dordogne and Lot region created some of the most expressive and moving prehistoric **paintings**, **engravings** and **reliefs** seen anywhere in the world. While these stunning works of art lie scattered throughout the area, hidden deep within limestone caves and on cliff walls, by far the greatest concentration is in the **Vézère valley** in the heart of the Dordogne.

The **Cro-Magnon people** who swept across Europe 40,000 or so years ago are responsible for the earliest cave art in the region. Named after a rock shelter near Les Eyzies, where the first skeletons were discovered, they were a nomadic people, who tracked herds of reindeer across what was then steppe, occasionally settling in riverside rock shelters under overhanging cliffs. They developed increasingly sophisticated tools using bone, ivory and antlers and later crafted ornaments such as necklaces. Some 20,000 years ago, the Cro-Magnon had honed their artistic skills sufficiently to depict supremely realistic animals on the walls of their rock shelters, by means of engraving and sculpting with flints or painting with dyes made from charcoal, manganese dioxide and red ochre.

Approximately 17,000 years ago, during what is now known as the **Magdalenian** period – named after another site in the Vézère valley – there was a real explosion in the quantity and level of sophistication of prehistoric art. It was prompted by the use of the tallow lamp, fuelled with reindeer fat, which allowed artists to penetrate deep within the limestone caves. They covered the walls of passages and cavern ceilings with hundreds of drawings, paintings and engravings. In some places artists used the natural contours of the rock to produce supremely realistic, almost 3-D representations of horses, bison and other animals. Some of the drawings are almost like caricatures, in which mammoths are portrayed by just a couple of lines. Occasional human figures also appear, most spectacularly in the Grotte du Sorcier (see p.142).

The question of why these cave-dwellers dedicated such skill and time to their art evokes endless debate. While it's likely that the significance of the caves was in some way spiritual, the exact nature of the relationship between Cro-Magnon people and their art remains opaque. Some scholars believe that the paintings and engravings were some form of **ritual practice** or **magic** to evoke a successful hunt, while others think they have a **shamanistic role**, with the animals advancing into the caves as into the afterlife.

You'll often hear guides at the sites lament the fact that we know so little, but perhaps the desire for categorical meaning misses the point – that the paintings and engravings reveal a desire to capture elusive, transcendent beauty – or in other words, "art for art's sake". Whatever the truth, not knowing certainly adds to the wonder and magic of these caves.

TICKETS FOR ABRI DU CAP BLANC, ABRI DU POISSON, FONT-DE-GAUME AND DES COMBARELLES

Because of the limit on visitor numbers allowed to enter Abri du Cap Blanc, Abri du Poissons and the caves of Font-de-Gaume and des Combarelles, it is essential to **book tickets ahead** by phone (☎05 53 06 86 00) or online (🖥 sites-les-eyzies.fr) several weeks or, if you can, months in advance at any time of year, and as early as possible if you plan on visiting in July and August, especially for Font-de-Gaume. Tickets go on sale in January for the coming year. Note that you have to pay for your tickets by credit card at least fifteen days in advance, and there's a €1.50 booking fee. If you haven't got a ticket, you can try queuing up at the Font-de-Gaume ticket office first thing in the morning for one of the few tickets for all three sites which are sold on the day, but you'll need to get there early. Given the high demand for tickets, it's worth considering a visit to one of the valley's less popular caves instead; note also that none of the above caves are really suitable for children.

3

The cave mouth is no more than a fissure concealed by rocks and trees above a small, lush valley. Inside is a narrow twisting passage of irregular height over 100m long, where you quickly lose your bearings in the dark. The majority of the **paintings** depict bison, but also horses, mammoths, reindeer and wild cats, and many unexplained signs such as the so-called "**tectiforms**", comprising a very gently inclined, upside down "V" with vertical lines beneath.

The first painting you come to is a frieze of bison at about eye level: reddish-brown in colour, massive, full of movement and an almost palpable force. Further on, a horse stands with one hoof slightly raised, resting; another appears to be galloping or jumping and, in a breathtakingly tender depiction, one reindeer gently licks another's nose. But the most miraculous painting of all is a **frieze of five bison** discovered in 1966. The colour, remarkably sharp and vivid, is preserved by a protective layer of calcite. Shading under the belly and down the thighs is used to add volume, with a sophistication that seems utterly modern.

Another panel consists of **superimposed drawings**, a fairly common phenomenon in cave-painting, sometimes the result of work by successive generations, but here an obviously deliberate technique: a reindeer in the foreground shares legs with a large bison to indicate perspective.

Grotte des Combarelles

1hr guided visits Mon–Fri & Sun: mid-May to mid-Sept 9.30am–5.30pm; mid-Sept to mid-May 9.30am–12.30pm & 2–5.30pm • €7.50, combined ticket with Grotte de Font-de-Gaume & Abri du Cap Blanc €18 • Tickets available from Font-de-Gaume booking office (see box above) • ☎05 53 06 86 00, 🖥 sites-les-eyzies.fr • The caves are 2km southeast of Les Eyzies, just along the D47 from Font-de-Gaume

The myriad engravings of the **Grotte des Combarelles** were discovered in 1901, a few days before those at the Font-de-Gaume. Only five decorated caves had been found prior to this, and with the jury still out on primitive man's artistic abilities, they were an incredibly significant discovery. As with Font-de-Gaume, visitor numbers are restricted: just 42 people are allowed in per day, with seven tickets sold in advance and 35 on the day.

You make your way down a long, claustrophobic tunnel, stopping every now and then while the guide picks out a tiny selection of the six-hundred-plus **engravings** identified so far. It is a veritable Magdalenian menagerie: mostly horses, but also bison, reindeer, mammoths, rhinos, bears, ibex, aurochs and wild cats; stylized human figures and geometric symbols also feature.

A good deal of imagination is required to recognize some of the fainter outlines, often superimposed one upon another, while others are astounding in their simplicity and realistic treatment – among the finest are the heads of a horse and a lioness, where the dips and projections in the rock provide eyes, nostrils and even bone structure.

Roc de Cazelle

Daily: Feb–April & Oct to mid-Nov 10am–6pm; May, June & Sept 10am–7pm; July & Aug 10am–8pm; Dec & Jan 11am–5pm • €8, children €4.50 • ☎ 05 53 59 46 09, ⓦ rocdecazelle.com • The caves are 2.5km southeast of Les Eyzies, some 2km further along the D47 from the Grotte des Combarelles

Arriving at **Roc de Cazelle**, a theme park that reconstructs life 12,000 years ago, you'll be greeted by mammoths roaring and the sound of people chipping flints. It's great for children, and the imaginative design helps bring the surrounding caves to life. Various scenes – from hunting and gathering to painting and sculpting – are scattered around a wooded valley once occupied by prehistoric man, culminating in a real troglodyte fortress and a troglodyte farm that was inhabited up to the 1960s.

Abri du Cap Blanc

45min guided visits Mon–Fri & Sun: mid-May to mid-Sept 10am–6pm; Sept 16–May 14 10am–12.30pm & 2–5.30pm • €7.50, combined ticket with Grotte de Font-de-Gaume & Grotte des Combarelles €18 • Tickets available from Font-de-Gaume booking office (see box opposite) • ☎ 05 53 06 86 00, ⓦ sites-les-eyzies.fr • The site is about 7km east of Les Eyzies, signed left off the D47 shortly after the Grotte des Combarelles

Not a cave but a natural rock shelter, the **Abri du Cap Blanc** lies on a steep wooded hillside above the River Beune. The shelter contains a superb **sculpted frieze** of horses and bison dating from the middle Magdalenian period (16,000–13,000 years ago), discovered in 1909 behind thick layers of sediment. Visitor numbers are limited to 105 people a day, with 35 tickets sold in advance and 70 on the day (see box, p.132).

Unfortunately, the excavation was carried out in such a hurry that the frieze had been badly damaged before anyone realized it was there. Even so, it is quite remarkable, mainly for its scale – the middle horse, which closely resembles the wild Przewalski horse of Central Asia, is virtually life-size – but also the depth of some of the sculptures. The bodies were obviously polished to set them off against the rough background, while traces of ochre and manganese pigments indicate that they were also painted at one time.

Château de Commarque

Daily: April–June & Sept 11am–7pm; July & Aug 10am–8pm; Oct to mid-Nov 11am–6pm • €8, children €4–6 • ☎ 05 53 59 00 25, ⓦ commarque.com • The château is 10km east of Les Eyzies, and drivers must approach from the south, following signs from the D47 Sarlat road; there's a 600m walk from the car park to the entrance, though anyone with reduced mobility can drive right to the site

Southeast along the Beune valley from Abri du Cap Blanc you come to the elegant sixteenth-century Château de Laussel (closed to the public) and, on the opposite side, the romantic ruins of the **Château de Commarque**. Dating from the twelfth century, Commarque was a **castrum** – a fortified village made up of six separate fortresses, each belonging to a different noble family, of which the best preserved is that built by the powerful Beynac clan in the fourteenth century. The site was abandoned some 200 years later, then left to moulder until the late 1960s when the present owner, Hubert de Commarque, came to the rescue.

The ruins have now been made structurally sound and it's possible once again to climb the Beynac's 30m-high tower for **views** over the surrounding countryside. In summer, the site makes a spectacular setting for concerts, plays and other events, including child-friendly activities such as archery, cave-painting and sculpture.

Grotte du Grand Roc

40min guided visits: Feb–Easter & mid-Nov to Dec Mon–Thurs & Sun 10am–noon & 2–5pm; Easter–June & Sept to mid-Nov daily 10am–6pm; July & Aug daily 10am–7pm • €7.20, combined ticket with Laugerie Basse €9.50 • ☎ 05 53 06 92 70, ⓦ semitour.com • The caves are 2km north of Les Eyzies on the D47 to Périgueux

The entrance to the **Grotte du Grand Roc** lies under the cliffs that line much of the Vézère valley. There's a great view from the mouth of the cave, which was discovered in 1924 in the continuing search for prehistoric art. Instead, they found a fantastic array of **rock formations** along some 80m of tunnel. Most unusual are the still-unexplained *excentriques* growing in all directions, and triangles formed by calcite crystallizing in still, shallow pools.

Abri de Laugerie Basse

Feb–Easter & mid-Nov to end Dec Mon–Thurs & Sun 10am–noon & 2–5pm; Easter–June & Sept to mid-Nov daily 10am–6pm; July & Aug daily 10am–7pm • €6.50, combined ticket with Grotte du Grand Roc €9.50 • ☎ 05 53 06 92 70 • The site is 5km northwest of Les Eyzies

Sixty years before the discovery of the Grotte de Grand Roc (see p.137), Edouard Lartet and Henry Christy had identified a rock shelter further along the same cliff. The **Abri de Laugerie Basse** was inhabited almost constantly over the last 15,000 years – most recently in the form of farmhouses built against the rock – and yielded hundreds of **engravings** and **sculptures**, not on the rock face but on pieces of bone or fashioned out of individual stones. The majority date from the late Magdalenian period (13,000–10,000 years ago) when prehistoric art reached its peak.

They include a mysterious engraving of a heavily pregnant woman lying under a reindeer, and a sculpted female torso, the first so-called "Venus figure" discovered in France – both are obviously symbols of fertility, though it's not known whether they relate to fertility rites; the originals are displayed in the Musée National de la Préhistoire at Les Eyzies. These and other important finds are covered in a short film before visiting the shelter; there's little to see otherwise, though during the visit you learn a lot about the history of the excavations and what conditions were like during the Magdalenian era.

Abri du Poisson

1hr guided visits Mon–Fri & Sun, by advance booking only via the Font-de-Gaume ticket office (see box, p.136), or by phone • €3 • ☎ 05 53 06 86 00, ⊚ sites-les-eyzies.fr • The site is 4km northwest of Les Eyzies, just before the Grotte du Grand Roc

More interesting than the nearby Abri de Laugerie Basse (see above) is the **Abri du Poisson**, a rock shelter – one of many along a side valley – that contains one of the very few **sculpted fish** in prehistoric art. It's a real beauty too, a 1m-long male salmon, complete with gills and beak, probably carved about 25,000 years ago. The deep-cut rectangular outline is not a prehistoric picture-frame, however, but the remains of an abortive attempt by a Berlin museum to acquire the salmon soon after it was discovered in 1912. Since then the shelter has been kept sealed up and can now be visited by a maximum of twenty people per day.

Grotte de Rouffignac

1hr guided visits daily: March 20 –June, Sept & Oct 10–11.30am & 2–5pm; July & Aug 9–11.30am & 2–6pm • €7.50, children €4.80, English-language audioguide €1.50 • ☎ 05 53 05 41 71, ⊚ grotationderouffignac.fr • The site is 20km north of Les Eyzies

North of the Grotte du Grand Roc (see p.137), the D47 turns northwest to follow the Manaurie valley. Seven kilometres beyond the village of **Manaurie**, you'll pass a right turn signed to the **Grotte de Rouffignac**, another 7km uphill among dense woods. One of the best caves in the region for children, the visit here kicks off with a 1km-ride on a little **electric train** along the bed of an underground river that dried up about three million years ago. On the way the guide points out where hibernating bears scratched their nests and human visitors left their mark in the form of graffiti – including a priest, Abbé de la Tour, in 1808. In fact, records show that the cave was known about in the sixteenth century, but it took until 1956 before the 13,000-year-old monochromatic drawings and engravings were recognized. Over 260 **animal figures** have been identified so far, the vast majority of which are mammoths, including a superb patriarch, his great tusks arcing under a piercing eye. Most dramatic is the final chamber, when you descend from the train to wander around beneath a ceiling covered with mammoths, woolly rhinos, horses, bison and ibex. When these drawings were done, the cave here was less than 1m high – proof that the authors were prepared to suffer for their art, and of their mysterious obsession with penetrating as deep into these caves as possible.

Rouffignac

Some 5km north of the Grotte de Rouffignac and 25km from Les Eyzies, **ROUFFIGNAC** was destroyed by German troops in 1944, who drove everyone out before torching

CLOCKWISE FROM TOP RIVER DORDOGNE AT SARLAT-LA-CANÉDA (P.121); SARLAT MARKET (P.122); LA ROQUE-ST-CHRISTOPHE (P.162) >

the town. Rouffignac was subsequently rebuilt – the only buildings to survive from the original village were the **Église Saint-Germain de Rouffignac**, with its carved portal and unusual twisted columns inside, and three nearby houses.

Château de l'Herm

April, May & July–Sept daily 10am–7pm • €6.50 • ☎ 05 53 05 46 61, ⓦ chateaudelherm.com • The château is 4km north of Rouffignac and 22km from Les Eyzies

The **Château de l'Herm** has an unhappy history, a complicated tale of murders, forced marriages and disputed inheritance rights. In the end the castle was abandoned and left to crumble away for more than three centuries to leave an atmospheric ruin engulfed by trees. Since 2000, however, a massive restoration project has been under way, initially to protect the existing structure from further decay.

Two big round towers and some decorative touches from the fifteenth and sixteenth centuries remain: a late Gothic doorway opens onto a spiral stone staircase, at the top of which is a beautifully worked palm-tree vault, while three sculpted fireplaces cling one above the other to the wall of an otherwise empty shell. At the bottom of the keep, you can still distinguish the castle's grim-looking dungeons. It was these evocative ruins, looking out over the thickly wooded country where rural rebels thrived, which inspired Eugène Le Roy for his novel *Jacquou le Croquant* (see p.303), in which a nineteenth-century rebellion culminates in the Château de l'Herm being burned to the ground.

Le Bugue and around

LE BUGUE lies on the north bank of a meander in the Vézère, 11km downstream from Les Eyzies, and though tourist facilities are thinner on the ground it makes a reasonable alternative base, especially for the family-friendly historical theme park and zoo just outside town and the Proumeyssac and du Sorcier caves, slightly further afield. Le Bugue itself is fairly attractive with a riverfront setting and scattering of old houses along the River Doux, which flows into the Vézère here. On Tuesdays and Saturdays, it comes alive with one of the better **markets** in the area.

The heart of Le Bugue is **place de la Mairie**, the town centre and market square, from where there are good views in both directions along the river. From here, **rue de Paris**, the main shopping street, heads north towards Le Bugue's old quarter around the generously named **Grande Rue**.

Village du Bournat

Daily: April–June & Sept 10am–6pm; July & Aug 10am–7pm • €13.80, children €9.90, family ticket €44 • ☎ 05 53 08 41 99, ⓦ lebournat.fr • The village is just inder 1km southeast of Le Bugue

Younger children will have a whale of a time at the **Village du Bournat**. This is a fair re-creation of a Périgord village in the early 1900s complete with *lauze*-roofed cottages, chapel, schoolhouse, baker, flour-mill, fairground rides and so forth. The entry price seems expensive, but there's a lot to see, including demonstrations of local crafts, such as clog- and barrel-making, potting and basketry, and you can come and go as you please within a day. There's a restaurant and snack bar on site.

Aquarium du Périgord Noir

Mid-Feb to March & Oct to mid-Nov Mon–Sat 2–6pm, Sun 10am–6pm; April–June & Sept daily 10am–6pm; July & Aug daily 10am–10pm • €12.50, children €8.70 • ☎ 05 53 07 10 74, ⓦ aquariumperigordnoir.com • The aquarium is just inder 1km southeast of Le Bugue, adjacent to the Village du Bournat

The **Aquarium du Périgord Noir** is home to one of the largest collections of freshwater fish in Europe, as well as numerous reptiles and an impressive new alligator park. At set times each day you can watch – and children can assist with – the feeding of the more benign species.

Labyrinthe Préhistorique

April–June & Sept daily 10am–noon & 1.30–6.30pm; July & Aug daily 10am–9pm • €12, children €8.20 • ☏ 05 53 07 10 74,
ⓦ labyrinthe-prehistorique.com • Just under 1km southeast of Le Bugue, adjacent to the aquarium

If you've young children in tow, you might want to head to Le Bugue's newest attraction, the **Labyrinthe Préhistorique**, a theme park centred on the history of the region's caves which opened in spring 2016. Kids will enjoy a trek through the maze of mirrors in pursuit of Cro-Magnon man, the cave inhabited by models of prehistoric beasts, and can try their hand at cave-painting.

ARRIVAL AND DEPARTURE

LE BUGUE

By train Trains on the Périgueux–Agen line pull into Le Bugue's *gare SNCF*, roughly 2km southeast on the D703; call Taxis Sourbier (☏ 05 53 07 41 35) if you need a taxi. Note that the station is unstaffed, so you'll need to buy tickets from the machine.

Destinations Agen (3–6 daily; 1hr 30min); Belvès (3–6 daily; 25min); Le Buisson (3–7 daily; 8min); Les Eyzies (4–7 daily; 7min); Périgueux (4–7 daily; 45min); Siorac-en-Périgord (3–6 daily; 20min).

INFORMATION AND ACTIVITIES

Tourist office Bang In the town centre at 22 place de l'Hôtel de Ville (Jan–March & Nov–Dec Mon–Fri 10am–12.30pm; April & Oct Mon–Sat 9.30am–12.30pm & 2–5pm; May, June & Sept Mon–Sat 9.30am–12.30pm & 2–5pm, Sun 9.30am–12.30pm; July & Aug daily 9am–12.30pm & 2–6.30pm; ☏ 05 53 07 20 48, ⓦ lascaux-dordogne.com).

Canoe rental Canoëric (☏ 05 53 03 51 99, ⓦ canoe -perigord.com), beside the Village du Bournat.
Horseriding Ferme Équestre de Belle Oreille (☏ 05 53 07 80 61, ⓦ belleoreille.com) is a few kilometres to the northwest of Le Bugue in the village of St-Avit de Vialard; 2hr children's rides are €33.

ACCOMMODATION

IN LE BUGUE

Le Cygne 2 rue de Cingle ☏ 05 53 06 01 16, ⓦ lecygne -perigord.com. Though it's on the main road, this good-value place on the edge of the town centre is the most appealing hotel in Le Bugue. It offers comfortable, if plain, rooms, most of them with double-glazed windows. There's also a very good restaurant (see below). Breakfast €5.50. Closed mid-Dec to mid-Jan. **€58**
Le Royal Vézère Place de l'Hôtel-de-Ville ☏ 05 53 07 20 01, ⓦ hotel-royal-vezere.com. Once Le Bugue's grandest hotel, this three-star occupies a prime position on the river right in the town centre. Its other main draws are a rooftop swimming pool and good restaurant (see p.142). Cheaper rooms face onto the road (€60), but it's worth upgrading to one with river views (€105). Garage €7. Breakfast €9.50. Closed mid-Oct to March. **€60**
Les Trois Caupain Le Port ☏ 05 53 07 24 60, ⓦ camping -des-trois-caupain.com. A welcoming and well-equipped three-star campsite located on the riverbank 1km east of town. Among its facilities, it boasts two pools, one of them heated, and a bar-restaurant in season. Mobile homes available too (€475 weekly). Closed Nov–March. **€23.90**
Vézère Lodge 10 rte de Campagne ☏ 05 53 05 56 57, ⓦ vezerelodge.com. Set slightly back from the D703, 1.5km southeast of Le Bugue, this is a cheap-and-cheerful

option run by a friendly young couple. It has just six simple en-suite rooms, a pool and a decent restaurant (*menus* from €24.50). Breakfast €8. Restaurant Mon–Wed 7.30–9.30pm, Thurs–Sun noon–2pm & 7.30–9.30pm; hotel closed Oct to mid-March. **€57**

AROUND LE BUGUE

★**L'Auberge Médiévale** Audrix ☏ 05 53 07 24 02, ⓦ auberge-medievale.fr. In the tiny, picturesque hamlet of Audrix, 6km from Le Bugue past the Gouffre de Proumeyssac, is this delightful, bargain-priced traditional country hotel. With its eight simple but pretty rooms, all with en-suite facilities and views either of the Romanesque church or the valley below, it really is one of the most peaceful and idyllic spots in the region. Breakfast €7. Closed Nov to mid-March. **€45**
Brin d'Amour St-Cirq ☏ 05 53 07 23 73, ⓦ brindamour camping.com. Up in the hills north of St-Cirq, midway between Le Bugue and Les Eyzies, this three-star campsite is an excellent choice if you've got your own transport: small, friendly, well-run and lacking the regimented feel of so many sites. Facilities include a heated pool, tennis court, grocery store (April–Sept) and restaurant (July & Aug), plus mobile homes for rent (€580 weekly). Closed mid-Oct to Easter. **€24**

EATING

IN LE BUGUE

Le Cygne 2 rue du Cingle ☏ 05 53 06 01 16,

ⓦ lecygne-perigord.com. While this hotel restaurant is lacking in atmosphere, it serves excellent food, with a choice of regional *menus* (weekday lunch €15, evenings and weekends €25). Alternatively, you can eat from the limited *carte*. Mid-Jan to May & Oct to mid-Dec Mon–Thurs noon–1.30pm & 7.30–9pm, Sat 7.30–9pm, Sun noon–1.30pm; June–Sept Mon–Thurs & Sat–Sun noon–1.30pm & 7.30–9pm, Fri 7.30–9.30pm.

Le Pha 25 rue du Jardin-Public ☎ 05 53 08 96 96, ⓦ lepha.fr. Friendly little place opposite *Le Cygne* (see p.141); in fine weather, get here early or phone ahead to reserve a table overlooking the river. It serves an unusual mix of Asian and French dishes: everything from the regular *magret* (duck breast) and local salads to king prawns in peanut sauce, beef and ginger soup or *banh bao* (Vietnamese steamed dumplings). *Menus* €15–26. Daily: Feb–June & Sept to mid-Dec noon–1.30pm & 6.30–8.15pm; July & Aug noon–2.30pm & 6.30–9.30pm.

Le Royal Vézère Place de l'Hôtel-de-Ville ☎ 05 53 07 20 01, ⓦ hotel-royal-vezere.com. The restaurant at the *Royal Vézère* hotel is in a prime position in the town centre, with a terrace jutting out over the river. It offers nicely presented traditional cuisine on a wide choice of *menus* (€18–25). April to mid-Oct daily noon–2pm & 7–9pm.

AROUND LE BUGUE

Du Château Campagne ☎ 05 53 07 23 50, ⓦ hotel campagne24.fr. If you're looking for somewhere to eat between Le Bugue and Les Eyzies, try this traditional hotel-restaurant in the attractive village of Campagne. You can opt for the lunch-only bistro (*menu* at €16), or the more formal restaurant (*menus* €24–39) serving Périgordin cuisine, plus a choice of fish dishes. Easter to mid-Oct daily noon–2pm & 7–9.30.

★ **La Vieille Treille** Audrix ☎ 05 53 07 24 02, ⓦ auberge -medievale.fr. The restaurant of Audrix's charming hotel (see p.141) serves delicious and well-priced regional cuisine from a broad range of four- to five-course *menus* at €15–€31. House specialities include warm scallops with truffles, and langoustine ravioli. In summer you can sit out in the shade of a vine-draped trellis. Mid-March to June, Sept & Oct Mon, Tues & Thurs–Sat noon–2pm & 7–9pm; July & Aug daily noon–2pm & 7–9pm.

Gouffre de Proumeyssac

45min guided visits daily: Feb, Nov & Dec 2–5pm; March & mid-Sept to Oct 9.30am–noon & 2–5.30pm; April–June & Sept 1–15 9.30am–6pm; July & Aug 9am–7pm • €9.90, children €6.60; basket descent €18.70 per person; audioguide €0.90 • ☎ 05 53 07 85 85, ⓦ gouffre-proumeyssac.com • In July & Aug reserve well in advance by phone or online to save queuing; to descend in the basket, phone ahead at any time of the year (online reservations not accepted) • The caves are 5km south of Le Bugue on the D31E2

High-tech has hit the Vézère in a big way at the **Gouffre de Proumeyssac**, a vast and spectacular limestone cave. Its 40m-high vault dripping with multicoloured stalactites, ranging from fine needles to massive petrified waterfalls, is dubbed the "crystal cathedral". To heighten the sense of atmosphere you enter in the dark, then the music builds as lights pick out various formations before revealing the whole chamber in a grand finale.

It's cleverly done, though some will find it too commercialized, even down to stacks of calcite-coated pottery souvenirs, and a far cry from when the cave was first opened in 1907. At that time the only way in was via a basket lowered through a hole in the roof under flickering torchlight – you can still make the descent by eleven-person **basket**, which rotates as it makes its way down.

Even before the chasm was fully explored and its size and beauty discovered, it had a gruesome notoriety in local folklore: it gets a mention in Eugène Le Roy's 1899 work *Jacquou le Croquant* as the "*Trou de Pomeissac*" near Le Bugue, into which so many people had been thrown after being murdered on the neighbouring highway, that the hole had to be blocked up..."

Grotte du Sorcier

30min guided visits daily: April & Sept to mid-Nov 10am–6pm; May & June 10am–6.30pm; July & Aug 10am–7.30pm • €7, children €3.50 • ☎ 05 53 07 14 37, ⓦ grottedusorcier.com • The cave is 6km east of Le Bugue

South from Le Bugue via the D703, a left turn down a quiet back road just before the road crosses the train line takes you eventually to the village of **ST-CIRQ**, halfway to Les Eyzies. St-Cirq is known above all for the **Grotte du Sorcier**, a shallow cave with some thirty **engravings** dating from between 17,000 and 19,000 years ago.

The majority of engravings depict animals (look at the tremendous image of the horse turning its head back towards the entrance), but the most significant is the "**Sorcerer**" himself, a rare image of a human being in Magdalenian cave art.

The enigmatic figure has been interpreted in countless ways: as a fertility symbol, half man and half pregnant woman; as a shaman or spiritual leader, with his musical instrument and dancing legs; or indeed as a man's head with the body of a horse. However you choose to see him, he makes a fascinating counterpoint to the supremely realistic animals you see elsewhere: the Sorcerer is compelling evidence of ancient cave art's figurative or metaphorical purpose.

After the guided tour of the cave, have a quick look around the site's **museum**, a collection of blades and fossils dating from the different eras in which it was occupied. Then, if you're feeling athletic, climb up to explore the vestiges of a **medieval fortress** and look-out posts in the rock face beyond the museum.

The central Vézère valley

To the northeast of Les Eyzies, the D706 follows the River Vézère all the way to Montignac, taking you past a range of sights appealing to all ages, from the rock-shelters of **La Madeleine** and **La Roque St-Christophe** to the Renaissance splendour of the **Château de Losse** and **Le Thot**, a wildlife park with a prehistoric theme. On the way, you'll pass the prettiest village in the whole valley – **St-Léon-sur-Vézère**.

Tursac

The village of **TURSAC** sits astride the main D706 road 5km upstream from Les Eyzies. Though there's nothing remarkable to see here, the village boasts a recommended restaurant and makes a good base for campers exploring this stretch of valley.

ACCOMMODATION AND EATING   TURSAC

La Ferme du Pelou ☎ 05 53 06 98 17, ⓦ lafermedu pelou.com. Of the two good campsites near Tursac, this two-star site signed off the D706 to the south of the village is the more basic but is spectacularly located, perched on the hilltop overlooking La Madeleine (see below) and its meander from the east. Pitches are spacious, grouped around an old Périgordin farmhouse with chickens running around amid the flowers. There are two pools and lots of walks around, plus mobile homes to rent (€290 weekly). No internet access. Closed mid-Nov to mid-March. **€15.60**
★**La Source** Lieu-dit Le Bourg ☎ 05 53 06 98 00, ⓦ restaurant-la-source.fr. Tursac's central square, just off the main road, is home to this well-regarded restaurant with a pleasant garden and imaginative daily specials, including wild salmon in a shellfish sauce, or beef slow-cooked in beer. There's a two-course *menu du jour* at €14 and other *menus* at €17–25. They'll also provide vegetarian options if you phone a day ahead. Reservations recommended. March–June & Sept–Dec Mon & Thurs–Sun noon–2pm & 7–9pm; July & Aug Mon, Tues & Thurs–Sun noon–2pm & 7–9pm.
Le Vézère Périgord ☎ 05 53 06 96 31, ⓦ levezere perigord.com. Just over 1km north of Tursac, this is a well-run, spacious and good-value campsite set back from the main road among trees. Facilities include a decent-sized pool with water slides, a tennis court and a fitness room. There's also a bar, restaurant and grocery store in season (May–Sept), plus mobile homes to rent (€440 weekly). Closed Nov–Easter. **€27**

La Madeleine

April & Oct daily 10am–6pm; May, June & Sept daily 10am–7pm; July & Aug daily 9.30am–8pm; Nov–March Sat, Sun & school hols 10am–6pm • €6, children €3.50 • ☎ 05 53 46 36 88, ⓦ la-madeleine-perigord.com • The site is 3km northwest Tursac on the opposite side of the river

The semi-troglodytic medieval settlement of **La Madeleine** lies near the neck of a huge meander in the Vézère, where the river takes a 3km loop to cover less than 100m as the crow flies. The cliffs here have been inhabited on and off for the last 15,000 years. Indeed, the prehistoric rock shelter down by the water's edge yielded such a wealth of late-Paleolithic tools and engravings that archeologists named the period Magdalenian; one of the more intriguing finds was a carving of a man with a bestial head, believed to be a mask, now on display at Les Eyzies' Musée National (see p.131). There's a copy here, too, along with copies of other important finds, such as a bison with its finely engraved head looking back over a powerful shoulder.

Further up the cliff subsequent settlers constructed a whole **village** complete with fortress, drawbridge, square and chapel, all dating back to the tenth century. La Madeleine was inhabited until 1920, and the Resistance (see p.300) used it as a hideout, but now the chapel is the only building completely intact. Nevertheless, enough remains to give a good sense of what such cliff-dwellings were like.

Préhisto-parc

Daily: Feb, March, Oct & Nov 10am–5.30pm; April–June & Sept 10am–6.30pm; July & Aug 10am–7pm • €7, children €3.50–5.50 • ☎ 05 53 50 73 19, Ⓦ prehistoparc.fr • The park is 2km northwest of Tursac, just beyond the turning to La Madeleine on the D706

Plastic Neanderthals hunting mock mammoths to an accompanying soundtrack won't be everyone's cup of tea, but the **Préhisto-parc**, will probably please the kids. A woodland walk takes you past tableaux of encampments as well as costumed staff making flints, painting, sculpting and generally being busy in a prehistoric sort of way.

Maison Forte de Reignac

Daily: Feb, March, Oct, Nov & during Christmas school hols 10am–6pm; April–June & Sept 10am–7pm; July & Aug 10am–8pm • €6.50, children €3.50 • ☎ 05 53 50 69 54, Ⓦ maison-forte-reignac.com • Maison Forte de Reignac is adjacent to the Préhisto-parc, 2km northwest of Tursac and just beyond the turning to La Madeleine on the D706

A fortified, semi-troglodytic feudal residence whose knights owed allegiance to the superior lord at St-Christophe (see below), the **Maison Forte de Reignac** was occupied throughout the Middle Ages and into the twentieth century. It presents an intriguing combination of primitive cave-dwelling (some of the rooms occupy the old rock shelters) and medieval opulence.

The three storeys of the house are furnished with items from different periods of its occupation and contain interesting **displays** on the feudal system (pick up the English leaflet at the entrance for full translations). The most interesting **rooms** are the grand reception room on the ground floor, with its authentic *pisé* floor, monolithic washbasin and smoking wood fire, and the last room you see, the former bedroom of the countess of Reignac, which is very elegantly furnished. Above the house, you can climb to higher rock shelters to appreciate the defensive nature of the site, and admire the views along the valley. The visit ends with rather a gruesome display of instruments used for torture and punishment.

La Roque St-Christophe

Daily: Jan 10am–5pm; Feb, March & Oct to mid-Nov 10am–6pm; April–June & Sept 10am–6.30pm; July & Aug 10am–8pm; mid-Nov to Dec 10am–5.30pm • €8.50, children €4.50 • ☎ 05 53 50 70 45, Ⓦ roque-st-christophe.com • The site is 3km upriver from Tursac

The enormous natural refuge of **La Roque St-Christophe** is made up of about one hundred **rock shelters** on five levels, hollowed out of the limestone cliffs. The whole complex is nearly 1km long and up to 80m above ground level, where the River Vézère once flowed.

The earliest traces of **occupation** go back over 50,000 years, although permanent settlement dates from around the ninth century when the site's natural defences really came into their own. At its peak during the Middle Ages, the settlement had grown into a veritable town clinging to the rock face – with its own marketplace, church, prison, abattoir, baker and artisans' workshops – and was able to shelter over one thousand people in times of trouble. And there was no shortage of those, culminating in the Wars of Religion when Protestant sympathizers took refuge here. After they were kicked out in 1588, Henri III ordered the town and fortress demolished – which means you need a good imagination to re-create the scene from the various nooks and crannies hacked into the rock.

In summer, there are frequent **guided visits** (in French only). Although instructive they're long and can get a bit tedious – better to take one of their English-language leaflets and wander at your own pace. The second half of the set **trail through the site** is perhaps the more interesting, with its re-creation of a medieval kitchen, weapons of war and, below that, a Neolithic cave scene complete with unlikely attacking bears.

St-Léon-sur-Vézère and around

With its gurgling river and honeycomb-coloured stone buildings, **ST-LÉON-SUR-VÉZÈRE**, 6km above Tursac, is by far the most attractive village in the whole Vézère valley. It sits off the main road in a quiet bend of the river guarded by two châteaux – one topped by a fairytale array of turrets – and boasts one of the region's most harmonious Romanesque churches, **Église de St-Léon-sur-Vézère**; the tree-shaded riverfront outside makes for a perfect picnic spot. In summer the church serves as one of the principal venues, along with St-Amand-de-Coly (see p.150), for classical music concerts during the **Festival du Périgord Noir** (see box, p.122). For the best views of the village, walk over the iron-girder bridge and turn left along a footpath on the opposite bank.

Le Conquil

Park Daily: April–Aug 10am–7.30pm; Sept–Oct 11am–6pm • €8, children €5.80 • **Zip-wire** Same hours • Children 3–6yrs €11.80, over 6yrs €14.80, anyone over 1.5m tall €19.80 • ☎ 05 53 51 29 03, ⓦ parc-aux-dinosaures.com

Up the hill on the far side of the bridge from St-Léon-sur-Vézère lies **Le Conquil**, an attraction largely aimed at families with its "dinosaur park" and a nicely situated tree-top obstacle course, with **zip-wires** running along the bank of the Vézère. It also includes a series of shallow **troglodytic shelters**, the most interesting of which contains dozens of niches in the rock, used for housing pigeons in the Middle Ages. Otherwise the caves don't have much to see, but children will enjoy wandering through the woods trying to spot the full-size model dinosaurs and other animals lurking in the trees, before you get up to the clifftop belvedere. Overall, Le Conquil can't really compare to some of the other attractions in the valley, but it's a good (if expensive) bet if you're after something of interest to suit all ages.

INFORMATION AND ACTIVITIES   ST-LÉON-SUR-VÉZÈRE

Tourist office There's a summer-only office opposite the municipal campsite at the entrance to St-Léon (May, June & Sept Tues–Sat 10am–noon & 4–6pm; July & Aug Tues–Sun 10am–1pm & 2–7pm; ☎ 05 53 51 08 42, ⓦ saint-leon-sur-vezere.fr).

Canoe rental APA (☎ 05 53 50 67 71, ⓦ canoevezere .com), by the bridge in St-Léon, operates from Easter to mid-Nov (depending on the weather), and offers various route options from €19; the whole stretch from Montignac to St-Léon, and then St-Léon to Les Eyzies, takes two days (total 30km) and costs from €56.

ACCOMMODATION AND EATING

Auberge du Pont Le Bourg ☎ 05 53 50 73 07. A lovely wisteria-covered restaurant with a shady summer terrace beside the bridge. It serves a wide choice of dishes in generous portions, including fresh salads, Limousin beef and a selection of vegetarian options, plus wood-fired pizzas and a wicked array of home-made ice creams and sorbets. *Menus* start at €16.80. Mid-March to mid-Nov & school hols Mon & Thurs–Sun noon–2.30pm & 7–9pm, Tues & Wed noon–2.30pm.

★**Le Clos des Songes** Place de l'Église ☎ 05 53 42 25 72, ⓦ leclosdessonges.com. Opposite the church, this *chambre d'hôte* is set in a beautifully renovated village house of soft-coloured stone with four very different, artfully decorated rooms, such as the "Voyage" with its blissed-out Buddhas and smiling Hindu deities, or the earthy tones of the "Nature". The fab breakfast featuring local produce is a highlight. **€99**

★**Déjeuner sur l'Herbe** ☎ 05 53 50 69 17. Tucked down beside the church you'll find this tiny shop selling top-notch local produce to eat at picnic tables along the riverbank or to take away. A platter of cheese or charcuterie, for example, with a hunk of country bread, costs around €12.70 and a salad €7.90, while open toasted sandwiches start at €4.80. March–June & Sept–Nov Mon–Fri & Sun 10.30am–6.30pm; July & Aug daily 9am–9pm.

Camping Municipal ☎ 05 53 50 73 16. St-Léon's small municipal campsite, with just 26 pitches, is right on the river beside the bridge. There are no frills, but it is beautifully quiet and well maintained. Closed Oct–April. **€10.50**

Le Paradis ☎ 05 53 50 72 64, ⓦ le-paradis.fr. Excellent five-star campsite, 3km south of St-Léon on the D706, where thick hedges separate the pitches. Facilities include four nicely designed pools set among luxuriant vegetation; a restaurant, bar and shop; wi-fi and a communal herb garden. You can rent bikes and canoes, and they also organize canoe trips. Not surprisingly, you need to book early for the summer season. They have a whole host of permanent accommodation available to rent by the week in the high season. Closed Nov–March. **€39**

Castel-Merle

30min guided tours: April–June 10am–noon & 2–5pm; July & Aug 10am–6pm; Sept 2–5pm • €6.50, children €3.50 • T 05 53 42 30 09, W castel-merle.com

Southeast across the valley from St-Léon-sur-Vézère, just beyond the village of **SERGEAC**, the rock shelters of **Castel-Merle** have yielded a terrific number of flints, bones and beads over the years, including a necklace of shells from the Atlantic, presumably obtained by trade. In 2007, excavation teams also discovered the earliest evidence so far of mural wall art, a series of animal engravings dating from around 37,000 years ago, during the early Aurignacian period.

Guides take you on a fascinating French-language tour (thorough English-language booklet available) visiting five of the ten shelters. Only one of these still contains any **cave art**, including three rather poorly preserved bison sculptures, but you learn a lot about the history and significance of the site, and the lives of the people who once lived here. You can also try throwing a spear using a prehistoric propelling device – it's not easy, bur adds some interest for those with children.

3

ACCOMMODATION SERGEAC

Auberge de Castel-Merle Sergeac T 05 53 50 70 08, W hotelcastelmerle.com. A handsome country inn perched on the hill above the Castel-Merle rock shelters and still run by the descendants of Marcel Castanet, who first excavated the site. The rooms are cheerful, but its main attribute is its clifftop terrace, where guests can eat dinner overlooking the Vézère on fine evenings. The friendly, English-speaking owners can also provide a wealth of information about the area. Breakfast €9. Closed Oct–March. **€64**

Château de Losse

40min guided visits daily: May–Sept noon–6pm • €9.50 • T 05 53 50 80 08, W chateaudelosse.com

Of several castles along the Vézère valley, the Renaissance **Château de Losse** stands out as the most striking. It occupies a rocky bluff 4km upstream from St-Léon on the main D706, though the best views are from the opposite bank, where the D65 provides a quiet and picturesque back-road from St-Léon to Montignac (see opposite).

The present castle was constructed in the 1570s by **Jean II de Losse**, royal tutor and the governor of Guyenne, on medieval foundations. It has changed little since then, and is a well-proportioned L-shaped building surrounded by dry moats and watchtowers. Inside, the château's present owners have established an impressive collection of sixteenth- and seventeenth-century **furniture** and **tapestries**. Among the latter, the Florentine *Return of the Courtesan* is particularly successful in its use of perspective, while the colours of this and the Flemish rendition of knights preparing for a tournament remain exceptionally vibrant. There's also a rare, tulip-decorated tapestry dating from around the time of the Dutch tulipomania in 1634, when tulips cost more than gold.

On your way out, note the inscription over the unusually imposing gatehouse which quotes one of Jean II's favourite maxims: "When I thought the end was in sight, I was only beginning." His perhaps jaundiced view is forgivable – of his five sons, four were killed in war and the fifth had no heirs to inherit the family estates. After the tour you are free to wander the beautifully tended **gardens**, including beds of lavender and rosemary and a charming little knot garden.

Le Thot

Mid-Feb to March & Nov–Dec Tues–Sun 10am–12.30pm & 2–5.30pm; April–June & Sept–Oct daily 10am–6pm; July & Aug daily 10am–7pm • €9, children €5.90 • T 05 53 50 70 44, W lascaux-dordogne.com • Le Thot is 1km into the hills to the west of the Château de Losse

A combination of museum and animal park, **Le Thot** focuses on prehistoric art, not only the technical aspects but also some of the **wildlife** that provided inspiration: Przewalski horses with their erect manes, plus ibex, deer and European bison are all resident here. You'll also see **aurochs**, though these primitive wild cattle really died out in the 1600s – the beasts here are a close approximation achieved through selective breeding in the early twentieth century.

The **museum** explains the different techniques and styles of cave art, and allows you to appreciate how skilfully the artists depicted these same animals. But the most interesting aspect is the reproduction of four **friezes** from the Lascaux caves, including a rotund black cow who seems almost to be dancing on her slender legs, and two powerful bison back-to-back. Experts then explore the paintings and speculate on their meaning in three video presentations, unfortunately in French only.

Montignac and around

Some 26km upstream from Les Eyzies, **MONTIGNAC** is an attractive town, with a vibrant annual **arts festival** in July (see box, p.122). The town serves as the main base for exploring the Vézère valley's northern sights, foremost of which is the spectacular new complex containing reproductions of the renowned **Lascaux** cave paintings, though the Romanesque abbey church of **St-Amand-de-Coly** is also worth a visit.

Montignac straddles the Vézère; to the north of the river lies the **old town**, home to numerous timbered fourteenth- to sixteenth-century houses and centred on pretty **place d'Armes**, a harmonious square of warm, sun-bathed stone, adorned by hanging creepers and smart blue shutters. Nearby is **place Carnot**, where a **market** is held on Wednesday and Saturday mornings, beneath the dominant spire of the square's somewhat unexciting twentieth-century church. To the west of the two squares, the narrow alleyway of **rue des Jardins** leads uphill to give a view of the town's abandoned feudal castle (not open to the public), which was the abode of the once powerful counts of Périgord (see p.290).

Home to the tourist office and most hotels, the **Faubourg** area south of the river is less attractive, though it does have some elegant buildings, including the galleried former **hospice** immediately south of the bridge, where the town's municipal offices are now housed, and a number of older timbered structures on **rue de la Pégerie**.

ARRIVAL, INFORMATION AND ACTIVITIES
MONTIGNAC

By bus Buses from Périgueux, Sarlat and Brive via Terrasson stop on place Carnot and place Tourny, at the north end of rue du 4-Septembre. Those serving St-Léon only stop on place Tourny. However as all these services are aimed at schoolchildren, and run once or twice a day during term-time only, they're not really a viable option for visitors.

Tourist office Place Bertran-de-Born (Jan–March & Nov–Dec Mon–Fri 10am–12.30pm & 2–5pm; April & Oct Mon–Sat 9.30am–12.30pm & 2–6pm; May, June & Sept Mon–Sat 9.30am–12.30pm & 2–6pm, Sun 9.30am–12.30pm; July & Aug 9am–6.30pm; ☎ 05 53 51 82 60, ⍾ lascaux-dordogne .com). They sell a map (€2.50) detailing 31 walking routes around Montignac.

Canoe and kayak rental Montignac has two outlets: Les 7 Rives (☎ 05 53 50 19 26) beside the more northerly Pont de la Paix; and Kanoak (☎ 06 75 48 60 47; ⍾ c.farcache .free.fr) below the old bridge. Both open roughly June to September; possible routes include the 2hr descent from Thonac or the 3hr paddle from St-Léon, and prices start at €12 for canoes, €15 for kayaks.

ACCOMMODATION

De la Grotte 63 rue du 4-Septembre ☎ 05 53 51 80 48, ⍾ hoteldelagrotte.fr. A quirky, old-fashioned place with a fair amount of charm and an attractive garden; many rooms are in a modern annexe, though all have pleasingly old-fashioned decor. It also offers a traditional restaurant serving meals either in the garden or among a riot of frills and flounces in the dining room (*menus* from €11.90). Breakfast €9. Restaurant Tues–Sun noon–2pm & 7.30–9pm; hotel and restaurant closed two weeks in Jan & one in Feb. €52

★**Hostellerie la Roseraie** Place d'Armes ☎ 05 53 50 53 92, ⍾ laroseraie-hotel.com. In a characterful ivy- and wisteria-clad building on a quiet square, this is the nicest place to stay in Montignac. The fourteen rooms are decorated with period furniture and floral touches and there's an unusual mechanical piano in the lounge. The spacious garden has a landscaped springwater pool and an abundance of roses. La Roseraie is also home to one of Montignac's best restaurants (see p.148) – if you're staying here, it's well worth considering the *demi-pension* option. Breakfast €14. Closed Nov–March. €89

Le Lascaux 109 av Jean-Jaurès ☎ 05 53 51 82 81, ⍾ hotel-lascaux.fr. About 300m out of Montignac on the Sarlat road, this welcoming three-star offers bright, modern rooms, not huge at the cheaper end but equipped with nice touches such as a tea-maker and music station.

There's a sizeable garden and a restaurant (*menus* from €24.80), in addition to secure parking. Breakfast €9.50. Restaurant Mon–Sat 7.45–11.30pm; hotel closed mid-Nov to mid-Feb. **€69**

★**La Licorne** Valojoulx ☎ 05 53 50 77 77, ⊛licorne-lascaux.com. In the picturesque village of Valojoulx, 7km south of Montignac via a turnoff from the D65 towards St-Léon, you'll find this beautiful and welcoming *chambre d'hôte*. It offers five homely rooms, filled with accents of the countryside, in buildings dating back to the thirteenth century that overlook a garden and heated pool. The best are the huge "Mélilots", complete with a four-poster bed, and "Les Templiots", which opens onto the garden. Breakfasts are generous, and it also offers excellent home-cooked dinners (Mon, Thurs & Sat evening on request; €28). **€85**

Le Moulin du Bleufond Av Aristide Briand ☎ 05 53 51 83 95, ⊛bleufond.com. A well-tended three-star campsite on the riverbank 500m downstream from Montignac, where each pitch is sheltered behind a thick hedge. Facilities include a heated pool, tennis court and sauna. There's also a snack bar in season (April–Sept). Closed early Oct to March. **€23**

Le P'tit Monde 54 rue du 4-Septembre ☎ 05 53 51 32 76, ⊛hotellepetitmonde.com. A short walk from the centre along the Sarlat road, this is the least expensive option in town, offering simple, well-priced rooms with TV and either shared or en-suite facilities. It also has a small garden, mostly taken up by a plunge-pool. Breakfast €8.50. **€49**

EATING

For consistent quality and gracious surroundings, you can't beat the hotel-restaurant at *La Roseraie*, but if your priority is the setting, head to the northern riverbank where a number of **restaurants** – with not a lot to choose between them – have outside seating right on the river, beneath medieval timbered supports.

La Chaumière 53 rue 4-Septembre ☎ 05 53 50 14 24. If you're looking for something different, head for this cosy little place serving hearty meat and cheese specialities of the Savoie. Try *chiffonnade* (ultra-thin slices of ham), *raclette* (melted cheese served with boiled potatoes and cold meats) or *tartiflette* (potatoes cooked with onions, bacon and lashings of cheese). Portions are generous and everything is home-produced. There is one *menu* at €18.90, or you can eat from the *carte* at €20–25 for a full meal. July & Aug daily noon–2pm & 7–9pm; Sept–June Tues–Sat 7–9pm.

Hostellerie la Roseraie Place d'Armes ☎ 05 53 50 53 92, ⊛laroseraie-hotel.com. The restaurant of this aptly named hotel, with its rose-flanked terrace, serves a seasonal *menu* (from €39). Dishes might include local beef or duck or strawberries from Les Eyzies. April–Oct Mon, Wed–Fri & Sat 7.30–9.30pm, Sun noon–1.30pm & 7.30–9.30pm.

Lascaux IV

Daily: Jan–March & Oct–Dec 10am–7pm; April–June & Sept 9.30am–8pm; July & Aug 9am–10pm, last tickets sold 2hr before closing time • €16, children 6–12yrs €10.40 • ☎ 05 53 51 95 03, ⊛ lascaux.fr • The complex is just outside Montignac along the road to Lascaux II and the original cave system

Opened in December 2016, the incredible **Lascaux IV** (also known as the Montignac-Lascaux Parietal Art International Centre or CIAP) has replaced Lascaux II as the main monument to the caves' original glory. Costing around €60 million to build, the complex has taken prehistory into the digital age: the entire Lascaux complex has been reproduced in perfect form, and there are also museums, 3D visualizations, films and interactive displays. The reproductions of the **cave paintings** are undeniably impressive, carried out over two years by a dedicated team of 25 specialists in mineral reproduction of prehistoric art, mostly fine-art painters alongside moulders and resin sculptors. Their completed work was deemed to pass muster by independent experts who compared the new paintings with the originals to ensure that the visitor experience is as close to the real thing as possible.

Visits start by being whizzed 21,000 years back in time to a period when the Dordogne was cold steppe and wolves, reindeer and mammoths roamed the tundra. You then follow in the footsteps of the boys who first discovered Lascaux in the 1940s and enter the "**cave**" itself, where sounds are muffled and the atmosphere damp and dark – while it can't offer the excitement of the real thing, the reproduction is still breathtaking. Highlights of the cave art include the **Hall of Bulls**, where five huge aurochs – one 5.5m long with an astonishingly expressive head and face – dominate the ceiling, while the **Axial (Painted) Gallery** is covered with more cattle surrounded by deer, bison and horses rendered in distinctive Lascaux style, with pot-bellies and narrow

THE GROTTE DE LASCAUX AND LASCAUX II–IV

Arguably the most spectacular cave in the Dordogne, and certainly the most well-known, the **Grotte de Lascaux** was discovered in 1940 by four teenagers in search of their dog, which had fallen into a deep cavern on a hill just south of Montignac. The cave was found to be decorated with marvellously preserved **animal paintings**, executed by Cro-Magnon people some 17,000 years ago, which are among the finest examples of prehistoric art in existence. Lascaux was opened to the public in 1948, and over the next fifteen years the humidity created by more than a million visitors caused algae and then an opaque layer of calcite to form over the paintings. The algae was cured by disinfection, but even though access to the cave was strictly controlled from 1963 onwards, limited only to scientists and others with special permission, **fungal contamination** continues to threaten the paintings today. In 2001, feather-shaped patches of white mould, later identified as *Fusarium solani*, common in agricultural areas, began spreading rapidly throughout the cave. In a controversial emergency measure, the authorities sprayed it with antibiotics and fungicides and, when they failed to halt the spread of the mould, covered the floors with quicklime. This controlled the contamination, but soon created other problems in this incredibly fragile environment. The quicklime was eventually removed in 2004.

Then, while attempts to formulate a global conservation programme were proceeding, new **black stains** were discovered on the ceilings in 2006. By 2007 they had spread to some of the paintings, most notably the Black Cow. The stains appear to be a complex contamination which is not yet fully understood. This time the Scientific Committee authorized localized chemical treatment, after which the cave was sealed off for three months. According to the latest surveys, the contamination seems at least to be stabilized, and a climate-control system installed in 2012 may help stop further degradation.

As to what is causing these contaminations, no one yet knows for sure. Various theories put forward include global warming, rising humidity, badly designed or inadequate climate-control systems and the presence of humans. To complicate matters further, these prehistoric caves are very poorly understood, and every treatment so far has led to unexpected side-effects.

3

THE REPLICA CAVES

After the Lascaux caves were closed to the public in 1963, the authorities decided to build a **replica** so that visitors could continue to enjoy the remarkable artwork. Opened in 1983, just 200m from the original and 2km south of Montignac, **Lascaux II** was the result of ten years' painstaking work by twenty artists and sculptors, using the same methods and materials as the original cave painters. After thirty-plus years in service, however, the sheer number of visitors and the erosion and vibrations they and their vehicles were causing had started to create problems within the real cave system, and the rather cramped and uninspiring Lascaux II was itself replaced by the lavish state-of-the-art **Lascaux IV** complex (see opposite), built well away from the real cave system on the outskirts of Montignac; visit Ⓦ projet-lascaux.com for more on the project's inception. Even though Lascaux IV has now opened, it's still possible to visit Lascaux II, but only by advance reservation; see Ⓦ lascaux.fr for more information. And in case you're wondering, there is a **Lascaux III**, though it's a travelling exhibition about the caves rather than a static site.

heads. Some are shaded or spotted with different coloured pigments, while others, like the bulls, are drawn in black outline. One particularly dynamic series is of three horses appearing to be in the different phases of breaking into a gallop. You don't have to be an expert to appreciate the incredible skill employed by the prehistoric artists, who would have painted these animals from memory by the light of flickering oil lamps; nor to appreciate their sense of perspective and movement, and the sheer energy they manage to convey.

In high season visitors enter this part of the complex with a guide in groups of thirty at a time (in low season you can go it alone with just a torch). Emerging from the cave, you enter the **Interpretation area**, where the history and formation of the cave is explained alongside the story behind the paintings. Finally, there's a 3D digital tour of the original cave followed by various temporary exhibitions.

St-Amand-de-Coly

Nine kilometres east of Montignac, the village of **ST-AMAND-DE-COLY** boasts the superb fortified Romanesque **Abbaye de St-Amand-de-Coly**. Despite its size and bristling military architecture, the twelfth-century abbey church manages to combine great delicacy and spirituality. It is supposedly built over the burial place of the sixth-century St Amand, who gave up soldiering to become a hermit. Despite a promising start, however, the abbey never really prospered and had largely been abandoned by the late 1400s. In 1575 a Protestant garrison withstood a heavy siege here for six days, after which the building continued to crumble until 1868, when it was classified as a historic monument; since then it has been entirely restored.

With its purity of line and simple decoration, the church is at its most evocative in the low sun of late afternoon or early evening. Its **defences**, added in the fourteenth century, left nothing to chance: the church is encircled by ramparts, its walls are 4m thick, and a passage once skirted the eaves, with numerous positions for archers to rain down arrows and blind stairways to mislead attackers. Walk up the hill behind the church to admire its vast *lauze* roof and defensive elements.

If you're lucky enough to be here in the autumn you might catch a classical music concert in the church during the **Festival du Périgord Noir** (Aug to early Oct; see box, p.122).

ACCOMMODATION AND EATING ST-AMAND-DE-COLY

Manoir d'Hautegente Coly ☎05 53 51 68 03, ⓦmanoir-hautegente.com. A very grand – but not standoffish – creeper-clad manor house some 3km north of St-Amand, beyond the village of Coly. Set in its own grounds well back from the road, the hotel has a pool, sumptuous rooms overlooking the grounds to the river and one of the region's best restaurants. In fine weather, tables are set up on the terrace, overlooking the water; it's magical at night. *Menus* start at €39, rising to €75 for the *menu dégustation*. Dishes include eggs with truffles, rabbit stuffed with dried tomatoes and basil or inside-out lemon meringue pie. Breakfast €16. Restaurant May to mid-Oct Tues–Fri 7–9pm, Sat & Sun noon–1.45pm & 7–9pm; hotel closed mid-Oct to April. **€95**

Table de Jean Coly ☎05 53 51 68 08. Beside the road in the village of Coly, the same team behind the *Manoir d'Hautegente* (see above) have opened a convivial bistro, popular with both locals and tourists for its well-presented but fresh, affordable dishes. There's a lunch *menu* at €14.50, which changes daily, and two more elaborate options at €20 and €30, or you can eat from the *carte* for around €30. Old photos and exposed stone walls set the scene. May to mid-July & mid-Aug to early Oct Tues–Fri noon–2pm & 7–9pm, Sat 7–9pm, Sun noon–2pm; mid-July to mid-Aug daily noon–2pm & 7–9pm.

Terrasson-la-Villedieu

Beyond Montignac the prehistoric sites die out and the Vézère valley becomes busier and more industrialized as it opens out towards **TERRASSON-LA-VILLEDIEU**, 15km upstream, and Brive (see p.76). The old part of Terrasson, a knot of lanes on the river's south bank, merits a quick wander; head up from the arched stone bridge to the ramparts for panoramic views, and to the sixteenth-century **Eglise St-Sour** beyond. But the main reason for coming here is to visit its resolutely contemporary garden, **Les Jardins de l'Imaginaire** on a terraced hillside to the west of the church.

Les Jardins de l'Imaginaire

Place de Genouillac • 1hr 15min guided visits: April–June, Sept & Oct Mon & Wed–Sun 10–11.30am & 2–5pm; July & Aug daily 10am–6pm • €7.50 • The ticket office is on place de Genouillac, below the garden entrance, and opens April–June, Sept & Oct Mon & Wed–Sun 9.30–11.30am & 1.30–5pm; July & Aug daily 9.30am–6pm • ☎05 53 50 86 82, ⓦjardins-imaginaire.com

Designed by American landscaper Kathryn Gustafson, the **Jardins de l'Imaginaire** explore common themes found in gardens throughout history and among different cultures, from the Romans' sacred groves and the Hanging Gardens of Babylon to moss, water and rose gardens, the last a magnificent display of nearly two thousand varieties. In this respect this is much more than "just" a garden, which is why they insist you go with a guide to explain the complicated symbolism (though this can be rather tedious if you just wanted to relax under a tree in some pretty gardens); English-language texts are available. The gardens are full of imaginative touches: a forest of wind chimes, a stark line of weather-vanes and, above all, the use of water to splendid effect.

ARRIVAL AND INFORMATION — TERRASSON-LA-VILLEDIEU

If you're travelling by public transport, you might find yourself passing through Terrasson since it lies on the Brive–Bordeaux train line; buses hereabouts, however, are timed primarily for schoolchildren, so aren't of much use. While the Brive-Vallée de la Dordogne airport is not that far away (see p.79), there is no direct public transport to Terrasson; you have to travel via Brive.

By train Terrasson's *gare SNCF* lies on the north side of town at the far end of avenue Jean-Jaurès.
Destinations Bordeaux (1–2 daily; 2hr–2hr 30min); Brive (3–7 daily; 15–20min); Périgueux (4–7 daily; 35–50min).
Tourist office Rue Jean-Rouby, immediately west of place de la Libération (May & June Mon–Fri 9am–noon & 2–6pm, Sat 9am–noon & 2–5.30pm; July & Aug Mon–Sat 9.30am–12.30pm & 2–6pm, Sun 9.30am–12.30pm & 2–5.30pm; Sept–April Mon–Sat 9am–12.30pm & 2–5.30pm; ☎ 05 5350 37 56, ⌨ ot-terrasson.com).

ACCOMMODATION AND EATING

L'Imaginaire Place du Foirail ☎ 05 53 51 37 27, ⌨ l-imaginaire.fr. Just seven large, plush rooms, including one suite, in this classy hotel near the Jardins de l'Imaginaire. The rooms are decked out in cool creams, with wooden floors and minimalist bathrooms with roomy showers or baths. There's also a very well-regarded restaurant (*menus* €60–90). Breakfast €15. Restaurant Tues–Sun noon–2pm & 7–9pm; hotel and restaurant closed mid-Nov to early Dec. **€175**

★**La Mandragore** Place de l'Abbaye ☎ 05 53 51 34 17. Perched above the river near the abbey church, this restaurant has unbeatable views from its terrace. The chef cooks up unusual takes on local produce, such as Chinese-style duck with bamboo shoots and glass noodles, and early strawberries with basil-flavoured *fromage blanc*, all beautifully presented and often garnished with flowers. In addition to a short *carte* (around €45 for three courses), it offers three good-value *menus*, from an €18 weekday lunch, presented on a single platter, or a €20 *menu* which changes every day, up to the €55 *menu dégustation*. Mon & Thurs–Sun noon–2pm & 7–9pm, Tues noon–2pm.

The middle Dordogne

The stretch of river to the south of Sarlat sees the Dordogne at its most appealing, forming great loops between rich fields, wooded hills and craggy outcrops. This is also castle country, where great medieval fortresses eyeball each other across the valley. Most date from the Hundred Years War, when the river marked a frontier of sorts between French-held land to the north and English territory to the south.

For the visitor today, things start slowly in the west with the service town of **St-Cyprien** and nearby **Belvès**, the latter a sleepy little place where people once lived in troglodyte houses beneath its streets, but châteaux come thick and fast thereafter. The first you reach on the river's north bank is at **Beynac-et-Cazenac**, a stunning village of russet-hued, stone-roofed cottages cascading to the river, and overlooked by one of the most photogenic châteaux in the Dordogne. A short distance further upstream, the **Jardins Suspendus de Marqueyssac** provide respite from the history among Italian-style terraced gardens and woodland promenades, with views of both Beynac and its archrival over on the south bank, the craggy **Château de Castelnaud**. Then a brief diversion westwards brings you to the far-from-militaristic château of **Les Milandes**, once owned by the cabaret artist Josephine Baker and now set up as a museum in her honour.

Heading back upstream, the next stop is **La Roque-Gageac**. This lovely village caught between the river and the rock face is up there with Beynac and Castelnaud as one of the Dordogne's most photographed – and visited – sights. Across on the

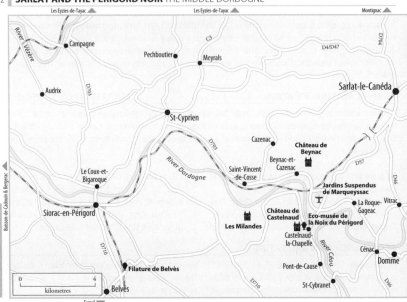

south bank, **Domme**, a fortified *bastide* town perched on the cliff edge, is no pushover on either the tourist stakes or in terms of its views. From up here you can take in a 10km sweep of the river, giving you a foretaste of the **Cingle de Montfort**, a particularly picturesque meander set off by yet another glorious château to the east. Before you cross from the Dordogne *département* into the Lot, the **Château de Fénelon** is an attractive blend of medieval and Renaissance architecture with good collections of furniture and weaponry.

GETTING AROUND   **THE MIDDLE DORDOGNE**

You can just about forget about public transport in this area. St-Cyprien, Siorac-en-Périgord and Belvès are accessible by train, but the picturesque Sarlat line runs past all the prime sights around Beynac without stopping. The only place accessible by bus is Carsac, a village with a pretty church just east of Montfort, which is a stop on the Sarlat–Souillac bus route.

St-Cyprien and around

Despite its location, just 20km west of Sarlat and 10km south from Les Eyzies, **ST-CYPRIEN** remains a refreshingly workaday place set back from the busy D703. Admittedly, it hasn't got much in the way of sights, but the whole place really comes to life on Sunday mornings for one of the area's best **markets**. The hillside setting is also attractive and, although the town itself has few accommodation options, hotels and *chambres d'hôtes* in neighbouring villages make it a possible base. The old centre's narrow lanes of medieval houses and labourers' cottages, a good number still unprettified, hold the greatest interest. They zigzag up from the modern, lower town towards the austere **Église St-Cyprien** on rue Bertrand de Got, founded by twelfth-century Augustinian monks. You certainly can't accuse the church of being pretty either, though there's a certain robust grandeur about its Romanesque tower and the echoing nave. The interior is worth a look for some fine eighteenth-century sculpted wooden statues on its retables, and is an evocative setting for classical music concerts in summer.

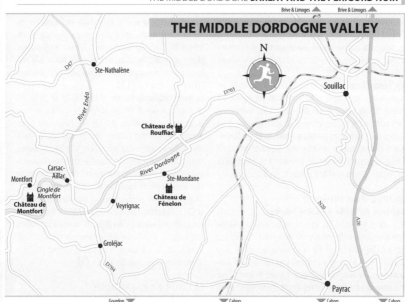

THE MIDDLE DORDOGNE VALLEY

Brive & Limoges ▲   Brive & Limoges ▲

N

Ste-Nathalène

River Enéa

D47

D703

Souillac

Château de
Rouffiac

River Dordogne

Carsac-
Aillac

Montfort

Cingle de
Montfort

Château de
Montfort

Ste-Mondane

Veyrignac

Château de
Fénelon

N20

A20

Groléjac

D704

Payrac

Gourdon ▼   Cahors ▼   Cahors ▼   Cahors ▼

ARRIVAL AND INFORMATION

ST-CYPRIEN

By train St-Cyprien's train station, on the Bordeaux–Sarlat line, is located about 1km south of the centre. There's no ticket office, so buy your tickets on the train or from the station machines.

Destinations Bergerac (4–6 daily; 1hr–1hr 30min); Bordeaux (3–6 daily; 2hr 15min); Le Buisson (4–6 daily; 15min); Sarlat (4–6 daily; 25min); Siorac-en-Périgord (1–2 daily; 8min).

Tourist office Place Charles-de-Gaulle, in the centre of the lower town (Jan–April & Oct–Dec Mon–Fri 9.30am–12.30pm & 1.30–5.30pm; May–Sept Mon–Fri 9.30am–12.30pm & 1.30–6pm, Sat 10am–12.30pm & 1.30–5pm, Sun 10am–12.30pm; ☎ 05 53 30 36 09, ⊛ perigordnoir-valleedordogne.com). The office produces a good (free) walking map of St-Cyprien and coordinates an active programme of concerts, events and activities in summer.

ACCOMMODATION AND EATING

There are no particularly good **accommodation** options in St-Cyprien, but you'll find plenty of choice scattered in the hills and villages around. There is a cluster near the typical Périgord village of Meyrals, 5km to the north; the other option is to head 8km downstream to Siorac-en-Périgord – a junction, albeit infrequently served, on the Sarlat–Bordeaux and Agen–Périgueux train lines. Across the river from Siorac, the village of Le Coux-et-Bigaroque also has a good place to stay.

ST-CYPRIEN

★**Le Cro-Marin** Rue Gambetta ☎ 05 64 28 58 74. On St-Cyprien's high street, just along from the tourist office, this fishmonger doubles up as a restaurant, with a few tables inside, spreading onto the pavement in summer. The menu changes daily, but seafood platters are a popular choice (mains start at €11). Reservations recommended. Tues–Thurs & Sun 12.15–1.30pm, Fri & Sat 12.15–1.30pm & 7.15–9.30pm.

MEYRALS

Le Chèvrefeuille Pechboutier ☎ 05 53 59 47 97, ⊛ lechevrefeuille.com. English-owned, family-friendly *chambre d'hôte* in a hamlet 2.5km west of Meyrals. It has

five pretty en-suite rooms, a pool and spacious garden, plus additional facilities including a well-equipped shared kitchenette, laundry room and bikes. Two nights' minimum stay required. Closed Nov–Easter. **€75**

★**Domaine de la Rhonie** Boyer ☎ 05 53 29 29 07, ⊛ domainedelarhonie.com. You're assured a warm welcome at this beguiling country inn lost in the middle of nowhere, 3.5km northeast of Meyrals off the C3. A working farm, it offers twelve cheerful, modern rooms set in extensive grounds with a covered and heated pool, and an excellent restaurant, which focuses on traditional Périgord cuisine. Expect dishes using geese fattened on the farm itself and their walnuts, in addition to other local produce. This means meat-heavy *menus* (€23–31), featuring dishes such as melt-in-the-mouth foie gras and succulent *magret* (grilled breast of goose) served with *pommes sarladaises* (potato in a creamy sauce). Breakfast €10. Restaurant Easter to mid-Nov Mon–Sat 7.30–8pm; hotel closed mid-Nov to Easter. **€89**

La Ferme Lamy Boyer ☎ 05 53 29 62 46, ⊛ ferme-lamy.com. You'll need to book early to get one of the twelve stylish rooms at this three-star hotel surrounded by woods and fields. The whole place is immaculate, from the en-suite bathrooms to the big infinity pool and flower-filled garden, not to mention the breakfast-spread of home-made jams and breads. Breakfast €14, other meals on request. Closed early Nov to March. **€125**

SIORAC-EN-PÉRIGORD

Auberge du Trèfle à Quatre Feuilles 173 rue de la Gare ☎ 05 53 31 60 26, ⊛ letrefle4feuilles.com. In the centre of Siorac, with seven good-value rooms located in a separate building to the rear of a popular restaurant. They are functional but bright and well kept, all with en-suite bathrooms, TV and double-glazing. It's wise to book ahead to sample the delights of the restaurant. Working with fresh, mostly local produce, it offers well-priced four-course *menus* (€26.50–41), which might feature home-made foie gras, *tartare* of pollock with lemon and beetroot, and rounded off by strawberry tart with a green-apple sorbet. Breakfast €8. Restaurant Mon 7–9pm, Tues & Thurs–Sun noon–1.30pm & 7–9pm; hotel and restaurant closed first two weeks of Jan. **€47**

Camping du Port ☎ 05 53 31 63 81, ⊛ campingduport.net. An inexpensive and relaxed two-star campsite on the riverbank beside the bridge; to reach it, turn down behind the Carrefour supermarket. Mature trees provide plenty of shade, there's an on-site snack bar in July and August, and caravans are available to rent (€225 weekly). Closed Nov–March. **€15.50**

Le Petit Chaperon Rouge La Faval ☎ 05 53 29 37 79, ⊛ chaperonrouge.fr. On the north side of the river from Siorac, set on a hillside just off the D703, this is an inexpensive, peaceful country inn. In high season you'll need to book early to stay in one of its nine homely rooms: nothing fancy but impeccably maintained. Their restaurant is authentic and good value, with a summer terrace shaded by lime trees. In winter, meals are served in an old-fashioned, floral dining room among gleaming tableware. *Menus* start at €14 for weekday lunches, or €22–27.50 for four courses weekends and evenings. Breakfast €7. Restaurant July & Aug daily 12.30–1.30pm & 7.30–9pm; Dec–June & Sept to mid-Oct Mon & Thurs–Sun 12.30–1.30pm & 7.30–9pm; hotel closed mid-Oct to Nov. **€55**

LE COUX-ET-BIGAROQUE

Manoir de la Brunie ☎ 05 53 31 95 62, ⊛ manoirdelabrunie.com. Characterful *chambre d'hôte* in a fifteenth-century manor house 1km northwest of Le Coux-et-Bigaroque, signed off the D703. The more expensive rooms (€100–110) are huge, with high ceilings and period furniture. There's a saltwater pool and extensive parkland with splendid views over the Dordogne valley. Evening meals on request (Mon–Sat; €27). Closed Dec & Jan. **€85**

Belvès

Accessible by public transport, and a possible base before you reach the most touristy stretch of the Dordogne valley, the picturesque hilltop town of **BELVÈS** is 12km south of St-Cyprien. There's no mistaking the town's strategic importance, encircled by ramparts on a promontory above the Nauze valley and bristling with seven towers – even the central square is called **place d'Armes**. These days, however, the only battles likely to take place here involve haggling over prices at the Saturday-morning **market** under the old *halle*, or a hotly disputed game of *boules*.

Several fine streets, lined with handsome houses from various eras, lead off place d'Armes: **rue Rubigan**, reached under the old stone gateway, is a narrow, winding medieval street, while on **rue des Filhols** you can see the imposing tower of the Maison des Consuls and, further up, a battered ornate Renaissance facade slapped on the twelfth-century Hôtel Bontemps.

Rue Jacques-Manchotte, on the other side of the square, leads past shops and cafés towards the imposing thirteenth-century **Église de Notre-Dame**, an interesting example of early, undecorative Gothic architecture, where recently discovered medieval frescoes are currently being restored.

On the way, if it's open, you could also pop into the **Organistrum**, 14 rue Jacques-Manchotte (no fixed hours; free; ☎ 05 53 29 10 93), a combined museum and workshop producing medieval instruments. Music-lovers might also be interested in Belvès' principal annual event, the **Festival Bach**, dedicated to the composer, with at least one concert in the church during the first fortnight of August (see box, p.122).

Troglodyte houses

Place d'Armes • 35min guided tours (minimum four people): mid-June to mid-Sept eight daily (three in English) 10.30am–6pm; mid-Sept to mid-June Mon–Sat bilingual visits at 11am, 3pm & 4pm, but confirm times with the tourist office (see below) • €5.50, children €2.50, tickets sold at the tourist office • T 05 53 29 10 20

In 1907 the wheel of a cart crossing place d'Armes broke through the roof of a warren of **troglodyte houses**. Hollowed into the rampart wall, these damp, dark and insalubrious dwellings were inhabited from the twelfth century up to the mid-1700s, after which they were blocked up and forgotten. So far eight "houses" have been opened, consisting of single rooms averaging a mere twenty square metres apiece for a family plus animals. It's hard to imagine what they must have been like to live in, even if the more sophisticated dwellings boast chimneys, raised sleeping areas and shelves cut into the soft rock.

Filature de Belvès

Fongauffier • 45min guided visits: mid-Jan to June & Sept to late Dec Mon–Fri & Sun 2–6pm; July & Aug daily 10am–7pm • €8, children €5.50 • T 05 53 57 52 64, W filaturedebelves.com

3

In the Nauze valley just below Belvès, on the D710, the former woollen mill of **Filature de Belvès** produced top-quality yarn for the Aubusson tapestry workshops until the 1990s. It has now been opened as a museum, where you learn about the history of wool in the area and how the raw fleeces were processed into various grades of yarn.

The machines you see today date from the late 1940s, when electricity replaced water-power, and though none of them is working, films of similar machines in action give the general idea. The visit ends with the chance to try felt-making, weaving or using vegetable dyes. It makes for a fun hour or so, particularly if you have children in tow.

ARRIVAL AND INFORMATION — BELVÈS

By train Belvès lies on the Agen–Périgueux line, with the *gare SNCF* down on the main road below the town.

Destinations Agen (3–5 daily; 1hr–1hr 15min); Le Bugue (3–5 daily; 25min); Le Buisson (3–5 daily; 15min); Les Eyzies (3–5 daily; 30–40min); Périgueux (3–5 daily; 1hr–1hr 15min); Siorac-en-Périgord (3–5 daily; 6min).

Tourist office On the ground floor of the fifteenth-century Maison des Consuls, just off the market square at 1 rue des Filhols (April to mid-June Mon–Sat 10am–12.30pm & 2.30–6pm; June 15–30 & Sept 1–15 daily 10am–12.30pm & 2.30–7pm; July & Aug daily 10am–1pm & 2.30–7.30pm; Oct–March Mon–Sat 10am–12.30pm & 2.30–5.30pm; T 05 53 29 10 20, W perigordnoir-valleedordogne.com).

ACCOMMODATION AND EATING

Hôtel Clement V 15 rue Jacques Manchotte T 05 53 28 68 80, W clement5.com. Halfway up the main shopping street, this is an eighteenth-century former grocery turned boutique hotel, with palatial rooms decorated in puffy claret-red furnishings, four-posters beds, stone floors and lots of old black-and-white pictures on the walls. The bathrooms are particularly impressive. It's somewhat expensive compared to similar places in the region, however. Breakfast €12. **€135**

Le Home 3 place de la Croix-des-Frères T 05 53 29 01 65, W lehomedebelves.fr. This friendly, one-star hotel really has the feel of old-fashioned, small town France, and you half expect prices to be quoted in francs. There are ten no-frills rooms, the cheapest with tiny bathrooms. The restaurant is popular at lunchtime for its good-value traditional cuisine, with *menus* starting at €14.70 on weekdays. Breakfast €7.50. Restaurant April–Sept daily noon–2pm & 7–9.30pm; Oct–March Mon–Thurs noon–2pm & 7–9.30pm, Fri 7–9.30pm. **€50**

Manoir de la Moissie Bd de la Moissie T 05 53 29 93 49, W lamoissie.fr. On the western edge of Belvès by the municipal tennis courts, signed off the D53 Monpazier road, this sixteenth-century manor house is now a stylish *chambre d'hôte*. Four beautifully decorated and spacious rooms sit under the eaves, while guests also have access to an enormous communal room downstairs, a TV room and washing machine, as well as the surrounding park. Secure parking available. **€56**

Les Nauves Le Bos Rouge T 05 53 29 12 64, W lesnauves.com. Belvès' nearest campsite is in a quiet spot 4km southwest off the D53 Monpazier road. They offer good-size plots and a pool, and organize various kids' activities in July and August. From June to September and at weekends they also open a grocery store, bar and restaurant, and cabins are available (from €644 weekly). Closed Nov–March. **€27.90**

Beynac-et-Cazenac

Clearly visible on an impregnable cliff-edge along the Dordogne's north bank, with its **château** soaring above the valley and standing sentry over a bend in the river, the eye-catching village of **BEYNAC-ET-CAZENAC** was built in the days when the Dordogne was the only route open to traders and invaders. Nowadays the busy main road squeezes between the cliffs and the water, creating a horrible bottleneck in midsummer (arrive first thing in the morning to beat the coach groups), but nonetheless postcard-perfect Beynac is easily a highlight of the region.

Château de Beynac

1hr guided tours (in French only) daily: April–Sept 10am–6.30pm; Oct to mid-Nov & mid-Dec to March 10am–dusk, though times can vary so it's best to check • €8, children €6 • ☎ 05 53 29 50 40, ⊕ beynac-en-perigord.com

It's three kilometres by road from the Beynac-et-Cazenac waterfront to the **Château de Beynac**; alternatively, you can walk up the steep lane among the *lauze*-roofed cottages in fifteen minutes. The lichenous-grey castle is protected on the landward side by double walls and ditches; elsewhere the sheer drop of almost 150m does the job. The redoubtable Richard the Lionheart nevertheless took and held Beynac for a decade, until a gangrenous wound ended his term of blood-letting in 1189; apparently the heart-shaped keys and keyholes were fashioned in his memory. Though the English regained the castle briefly – thanks to the Treaty of Brétigny rather than any military prowess – in essence Beynac remained loyal to the French Crown during the Hundred Years War.

THE LIGHTER SIDE OF BEYNAC

Particularly in summer, the tiny village of Beynac-et-Cazenac, cramped between road and cliff-face, can get oppressively crowded. Thankfully there are a number of ways to escape and enjoy a more peaceful perspective on the countless castles in the area.

RIVER TRIPS

Gabarres de Beynac (daily: April & Oct 11am–5pm; May–Sept 10am–6pm; €8, children €4.50; ☎ 05 53 28 51 15, ⊕ gabarre-beynac.com), based on a jetty next to the riverside car park, offer 50min **river cruises** on their replica *gabarres*, the traditional wooden river-craft, affording excellent views of castle and village. During holidays and high-season you can expect at least one departure an hour, but at other times and on wet days you might have to wait a while for the boat to fill up.

CANOEING

The stretch of the Dordogne between Vitrac and Beynac, taking you past a breathtaking parade of castles, is the most stunning **canoe-trip** in the region. If you hire a canoe in Beynac, the company will drive you upriver before you canoe back down to your vehicle; prices start at €16. In town, you'll find Copeyre Canoë (May–Sept; ☎ 05 53 28 95 01, ⊕ canoe-copeyre.com), while Canoës Roquegeoffre (☎ 05 53 29 54 20, ⊕ canoe-roquegeoffre.com), based 3km downstream near Saint-Vincent-de-Cosse, offers the best value around and is open all year.

HOT-AIR BALLOONING

The ultimate slow-paced activity, **hot-air ballooning** is also a possibility here: if you phone ahead, Montgolfière et Châteaux (☎ 06 71 14 34 96, ⊕ montgolfiere-chateaux.fr; from €180 per adult per hour) will collect you from Beynac's riverside car park to take you to the launch site.

WALKING

The cheapest way to get away from the crowds around Beynac's port and castle is to **walk** inland away from the river; the tourist office (see opposite) sells maps (€1.50) which detail five suggested **routes** around Beynac from 4km to 10km, with the longer itineraries taking you to the beautifully unspoilt fifteenth-century church of Cazenac, where some unusual modern stained-glass windows depict scenes from daily life in this area in the nineteenth century. For another pretty walk, head roughly south along the riverbank, starting next to the campsite; there are lots of perfect picnic stops along the way.

The buildings are in surprisingly good condition thanks to a mammoth **restoration project** over the last forty years, which is scheduled to continue until at least 2030. If the French-language guided tour is too much for you, you can go it alone with a rather brief English-language leaflet, available from the ticket office. You enter into a **guardroom**, one of the castle's more atmospheric rooms along with the **great hall**, where the nobles of Beynac, Biron, Mareuil and Bourdeilles – the four baronies of Périgord (see p.290) – met; note the unusual ox-skull motif over the fireplace, also found at the Château de Lanquais (see p.107). The twelfth-century **kitchens** have a cobbled ramp allowing horses access to the central courtyard, and are kitted out with no-nonsense tables, vats, meat-hooks and great pulleys. If it looks familiar, that's because it featured in Luc Besson's epic, *Jeanne d'Arc*.

For most people, however, it's the **views** that steal the show, notably from the top of the keep, where you get a stupendous – and vertiginous – sweep over the surrounding châteaux: Marqueyssac (see below), Fayrac (see p.161) and Castelnaud (see p.158).

ARRIVAL AND INFORMATION   BEYNAC-ET-CAZENAC

By car You need your own vehicle to get to Beynac. Parking is available down by the river, in three car parks (daily 9am–noon & 2–7pm) on the road up to the castle and beside the castle itself. Other than the last of the three on the road to the castle, all charge a fee (€2.50/2hrs, €4/day); once you've bought a ticket, you can move to the other car park if you choose.

Tourist office At the bottom of the road up to the château (Feb, March, Oct, Nov & Christmas hols Fri 2–5pm, Sat 10am–1pm & 2–5pm; April–June & Sept daily 10am–1pm & 2–5pm; July & Aug daily 10am–1pm & 2–6pm ☎ 05 53 29 43 08, ⊚ beynac-en-perigord.com).

ACCOMMODATION AND EATING

Le Capeyrou ☎ 05 53 29 54 95, ⊚ campinglecapeyrou .com. A three-star campsite on the riverbank immediately east of Beynac, with unbeatable views up to the château. The best plots are those lined up along the river, though they could do with more hedges around. There's a good-size heated pool and well-equipped children's play area, plus a bar. Closed Oct–March. **€27.50**

Du Château Le Bourg ☎ 05 53 29 19 20, ⊚ hotel-beynac -dordogne.com. A two-star hotel on a rather busy junction, where the road heads up to the castle. The rooms are a bit of an after-thought to the main business of the restaurant, but they're bright and impeccably clean, equipped with satellite TV; those at the front have double-glazing and a shared terrace with river views, best appreciated in the quiet of the evening. There's a tiny pool and one of Beynac's better restaurants, which has a broad range of *menus*, ranging from a €12.90 weekday lunch *menu* to €39 for a four-course extravaganza. House specialities include *tourin* (the local garlic soup), eggs baked with truffles, and sturgeon in a Monbazillac sauce. They also offer large salads, omelettes and a few vegetarian dishes. Breakfast €8.50. Restaurant daily noon–2pm & 7.30–9.30pm. **€69**

La Petite Tonnelle Le Bourg ☎ 05 53 29 95 18. This well-respected restaurant is surprisingly relaxed, despite its location on the road up to the château, opposite *Pontet*. In addition to daily specials, it offers an array of *formules* and *menus*, ranging from €19.50 for two courses and €42 for four, plus a fine choice of local wines. Everything is home-made, including home-smoked duck breast and Scottish salmon; try the John Dory in a shellfish sauce. Reservations recommended. Daily noon–1.30pm & 7–9.30pm.

Pontet Rue la Balme ☎ 05 53 29 50 06, ⊚ hostellerie -maleville.com. With the benefit of being off the main drag, on the road leading up to the château, this little place offers thirteen very comfortable rooms, all a/c, with en-suite bathrooms and TV. Breakfast €8. Closed Jan. **€52**

Jardins Suspendus and Château de Marqueyssac

Daily: Feb, March & Oct to mid-Nov 10am–6pm; April–June & Sept 10am–7pm; July & Aug 9am–8pm; mid-Nov to Jan 10am–5pm • €8.80, children €4.40, combined ticket with Château de Castelnaud €16.80/€8.40 • Candlelit evenings July & Aug Thurs 7pm–midnight • €14.50, children €7 • ☎ 05 53 31 36 36, ⊚ marqueyssac.com

Three kilometres east of Beynac, the Dordogne loops south round a long and narrow wooded promontory, at the tip of which the **Château de Marqueyssac** presides over its terraced "hanging" gardens, the **Jardins Suspendus de Marqueyssac**. A few rooms of the château, a typically mellow Périgord mansion of the late eighteenth century, are now open to the public, but it is the surrounding gardens and the **views**, encompassing the châteaux of Beynac, Fayrac and Castelnaud, that are the star attractions.

The **gardens** were first laid out in the 1600s by the then owner, Bertrand Vernet de Marqueyssac, under the inspiration of Le Nôtre, the landscaper responsible for Versailles. However, most of the features you see today were added two centuries later when the 500m-long **Grande Allée** was established – thousands of box trees clipped into plump cushions – and 6km of woodland walks opened up along the ridge to the east. In recent years, landscape gardeners have added more modern touches, including sculptures and the "boxwood chaos" resembling angular stone blocks. All paths lead to a 130m-high **belvedere**, from where you can see La Roque-Gageac nestling under its cliff (see p.162). The gardens are also the best in the Sarlat area for children, with a **maze**, **playground** and various kid-friendly activities such as mask-making. The gardens are also home to **Via Ferrata**, an exhilarating **cliff-walk** suspended 100m up along a narrow path and a series of ropes, beams and brackets attached to the rock face, to which you are secured by a safety line. It's restricted to those over 8 years old and 1.3m in height, and entry is included in the main ticket price; however hours vary so phone ahead or check the website for the current schedule.

On Thursday evenings in July and August thousands of **candles** and **fairy lights** give the gardens a magical touch. Between Easter and mid-November, the restaurant-*salon de thé* serves meals and light refreshments; note that in high season **picnicking** within the gardens is forbidden – you have to go and eat in the dedicated area just by the entrance gate, which can be a bit of a pain.

Castelnaud-la-Chapelle

Rivals for centuries, the feudal fortresses of Beynac and **CASTELNAUD-LA-CHAPELLE**, on the Dordogne's south bank some 4km upriver of Beynac, now vie over visitor numbers. There's no question that Beynac has the edge, with its more dramatic location and arguably the better views, but the **Château de Castelnaud** provides the more entertaining and informative visit; allow at least a couple of hours.

Château de Castelnaud

Daily: Feb, March & Oct to mid-Nov 10am–6pm; April–June & Sept 10am–7pm; July & Aug 9am–8pm; mid-Nov to Jan 2–5pm • €9.60, children €4.80, combined ticket with Jardins Suspendus de Marqueyssac €16.80, children €8.40 • Evening guided visits, in French only: mid-July to Aug Mon–Wed at 8.15pm and 10pm • €14.50, children €9 • ☎ 05 53 31 30 00, ⓦ castelnaud.com • There's a €3.50 charge for the upper car park, closest to the château, from where it's still a fair walk down; alternatively, you can park for free in the lower car park on the main road, and then walk up

Like Beynac, the **Château de Castelnaud** was founded in the twelfth century and bitterly fought over on many occasions, starting with the bellicose Simon de Montfort, who seized it as early as 1214 during his Cathar crusades (see p.292). During the Hundred Years War the lords of Castelnaud sided with the English, slugging it out for nearly four decades with the French at Beynac until Charles VII besieged Castelnaud in 1442. After holding out for three weeks, a treacherous English captain handed over the keys in return for his life and the princely sum of four hundred crowns.

Heavily restored in the last decades, the château now houses an excellent **museum of medieval warfare**. Its core is an extensive collection of original weaponry, including all sorts of bizarre contraptions, such as an "organ" which sprayed lead balls from its multiple barrels, and a fine assortment of armour.

This is easily the most enjoyable château in the area for families. Throughout the year, but particularly during school holidays, staff give demonstrations of iron forging, weaponry and firing the trebuchet siege engine. Evening visits led by guides in period costume are also on offer.

PÉRIGORD WALNUTS

According to archeological evidence, **walnuts** have formed part of the Périgordin diet for more than 17,000 years. In medieval times, walnut oil was so valuable that it was sometimes used as a form of currency, and in the seventeenth century it was exported by river (via Bordeaux) to Britain, Holland and Germany. Walnuts are still central to the local economy today: rich in polyunsaturated fats, potassium, magnesium and vitamin E, both nuts and oil are marketed for their health-giving properties – they're said to help reduce cholesterol, stimulate the memory and protect against the effects of ageing. The nuts are also incorporated into bread, cakes, tarts and ice cream, or served whole with salads and the local *Cabécou* cheese. Green walnuts are often pickled in vinegar, but can also be made into jam or used to flavour wines and liqueurs. Not even the leaves are wasted: picked young, they give a distinctive tang to walnut apéritif.

In recognition of the walnut's importance to the economy – and indeed culture – of the region, four varieties (Grandjean, Marbot, Corne and Franquette) were granted an **Appellation d'Origine Contrôlée** (AOC) in 2002, to guarantee that you're buying only premium-quality, locally grown produce. Walnuts are grown in the Lot, Corrèze and Charente *départements*, but the heart of the industry is the Dordogne, with more than 40 square kilometres of orchards. To capitalize on the AOC label, the local authorities have put together a **Route de la Noix**, along the Dordogne valley from Argentat to Beynac and north to Hautefort. Free leaflets outlining the suggested itineraries are available from tourist offices, indicating producers and traditional oil mills open for visits as well as specialist patisseries and restaurants serving dishes with a nutty theme.

Eco-musée de la Noix du Périgord

April & Sept to mid-Nov daily 10am–noon & 2–7pm; May–Aug daily 10am–7pm • €5 • ☎ 05 53 59 69 63, ⊛ ecomuseedelanoix.fr • The park is on the D57 south of Castelnaud, by the turning up to the Château de Castelnaud

The **Eco-musée de la Noix du Périgord** is considerably more interesting than it might sound. This part of the Dordogne is prime walnut-growing country, and as well as detailing oil pressing, the exhibits here reveal all kinds of unexpected nut-related titbits, such as the fact that Louis XI's beard was trimmed using heated walnut shells, and that walnuts were used in the insulation of American spaceships. They also point out the nuts' many health benefits, before you're shepherded through to the well-stocked shop, which makes a good place to pick up some unusual – and completely organic – walnut souvenirs. If you're lucky the mill itself will be working (July & Aug Tues, Wed & Thurs afternoons), but otherwise there's a self-explanatory video. The adjacent orchard, scattered with picnic tables and giant walnuts rendered in cement, might appeal to young children.

ACTIVITIES   CASTELNAUD-LA-CHAPELLE

Bike rental From Castelnaud-la-Chapelle you can follow the quiet Voie Verte cycle route along the lovely Céou valley to Daglan and L'Abbaye-Nouvelle, in the Lot. Bike Bus (☎ 05 53 31 10 61, ⊛ bike-bus.com), at the Voie Verte car park charge around €20 per day.
Canoe rental On the riverfront, beside the bridge, you can rent canoes at the Base Municipale Canoë-Kayak (daily 9am–6pm; ☎ 05 53 29 40 07; €4/hr).

ACCOMMODATION

Lou Castel ☎ 05 53 29 89 24, ⊛ loucastel.com. While there are no hotels in Castelnaud, you'll find this lively and well-equipped four-star campsite set among oak woods on the plateau roughly 3km to the south. It has several pools, water slides, a grocery store, bar and restaurant, as well as children's activities in July and August. There are also fixed tents and chalets to rent (from €90). Closed Oct–March. **€29**

★**La Tour de Cause** Pont-de-Cause ☎ 05 53 30 30 51, ⊛ latourdecause.com. High-quality *chambre d'hôte* in a lovely Périgordin manor house in the hamlet of Pont-de-Cause, 2km south of Castelnaud on the D57. There's a choice of three rooms downstairs and two up in the eaves, all different (1950s style in one, and tropical bird in another) and all with their own charm. Guests also have access to a communial living room and kitchen area and a saltwater pool. The Belgian owners, who worked as chefs in their homeland, go out of their way to make you comfortable, and prepare copious breakfasts; fabulous evening meals (guests only; €35) are also available. Closed mid-Oct to May. **€100**

Les Milandes

Daily: April & May 10am–6.30pm; June to mid-July & Sept 10am–7pm; mid-July to Aug 9.30am–7.30pm; Oct 10am–6.30pm; early Nov 10am–6pm • €10, children €6.50 • ☎ 05 53 59 31 21, ⓦ milandes.com

From Castelnaud-la-Chapelle it's a scenic drive 5km west along the river past **Château de Fayrac** (not open to the public) with its slated pepper-pot towers – an English forward position in the Hundred Years War, built to watch over Beynac – to **Les Milandes**. Built in the late 1400s, the château was the property of the Caumont family (the lords of Castelnaud) until the Revolution, but its most famous owner was the Folies Bergère star, **Josephine Baker** (see box below), who fell in love with it while visiting friends in the area in 1937.

It's easy to see why she liked it so much. The Renaissance château, sitting high above the Dordogne, has all the necessary romantic ingredients: towers, machicolations, balustrades, gargoyles, ornate dormer windows and terraced gardens shaded by great, glossy-leafed magnolias. After she bought Les Milandes in 1947, Josephine set about modernizing it, adding creature comforts such as the en-suite **bathrooms**, whose decor was inspired by her favourite perfumes – Arpège-style black tiles with gold taps and ceiling in one, Dioresque pink marble with silver-leaf in another. But it's really the stories surrounding Josephine and Les Milandes that are more intriguing than the château itself. Her roller-coaster life story is enough to fill a book, but you can trace the broad outlines from the collection of **photos** and **posters**. The few **costumes** that escaped the auctioneer's hammer in 1968 are also on display, though these are somewhat moth-eaten after mouldering in the cellar for 25 years.

3

JOSEPHINE BAKER AND THE RAINBOW TRIBE

Born on June 3, 1906, in the black ghetto of East St Louis, Illinois, **Josephine Baker** was one of the most remarkable women of the twentieth century. Her mother washed clothes for a living and her father was a drummer who soon deserted his family, but despite such humble beginnings Baker was the most celebrated cabaret star in France by the late 1920s, primarily due to her role in the legendary **Folies Bergère** show in Paris. On her first night, de Gaulle, Hemingway, Piaf and Stravinsky were among the audience, and her notoriety was further enhanced by her long line of illustrious **husbands and lovers**, which included the crown prince of Sweden and the crime novelist Georges Simenon. She also mixed with the likes of Le Corbusier and Adolf Loos, and kept a pet cheetah, with whom she used to walk around Paris. During the war, she was active in the **Resistance**, for which she was awarded the Croix de Guerre. Later on, she became involved in the civil rights movement in North America, where she insisted on playing to non-segregated audiences, a stance that got her arrested in Canada and tailed by the FBI in the US.

By far her most bizarre and expensive project was the château of **Les Milandes** (see above), which she rented from 1938 and then bought in 1947, along with three square kilometres of land, after her marriage to the French orchestra leader Jo Bouillon. Having equipped the place with two hotels, three restaurants, a mini-golf course, tennis court and an autobiographical wax museum, Baker opened the château to the general public as a model multicultural community, popularly dubbed the "village du monde". Unable to have children of her own, in the course of the 1950s she adopted babies (mostly orphans) of different ethnic and religious backgrounds from around the world. By the end of the decade, she had brought twelve children to Les Milandes, including a black Catholic Colombian and a Buddhist Korean, along with her own mother, brother and sister from East St Louis.

Over 300,000 people a year visited the château in the 1950s, but her more conservative neighbours were never very happy about Les Milandes and the so-called **Rainbow Tribe**. In the 1960s, Baker's financial problems, divorce and two heart attacks spelt the end of the project, and despite a sit-in protest by Baker herself (by then in her sixties), the château and its contents were auctioned off in 1968. Still performing and as glamorous as ever, Josephine died of a stroke in 1975 and was given a grand state funeral at La Madeleine in Paris, mourned by thousands of her adopted countryfolk.

After visiting the château, you can explore the gardens, where they hold daily **falconry demonstrations** (check the website for exact times). From the terrace, there are views down on the J-shaped swimming pool belonging to one of the many fun-parks that Josephine established in the area.

La Roque-Gageac

The village of **LA ROQUE-GAGEAC**, on the Dordogne's north bank 5km east of Beynac, is almost too perfect, its ochre-coloured houses overlooking the lazy-flowing river and sheltering under dramatically overhanging rust-coloured cliffs. Regular winner of France's prettiest village contest, it inevitably pulls in masses of tourist buses, and since the main road separates the village from the river, the noise and fumes of the traffic can become oppressive. The best way to escape is to slip away through the lanes and alleyways that wind up through the terraced houses. The other option is to rent a canoe and paddle over to the opposite bank, where you can picnic and enjoy a much better view of La Roque than from among the crowds milling around beneath the village, at its best in the burnt-orange glow of the evening sun.

INFORMATION AND ACTIVITIES

LA ROQUE-GAGEAC

Tourist office Occupies a hut by the main car park on the Sarlat side of town (daily: Easter to June & Sept 10am–1pm & 2–5pm; July & Aug 10am–1pm & 2–6pm; ☎ 05 53 29 17 01). On Friday evenings between mid-June and mid-September at 9pm they organize guided tours of the village (€5).

Boat trips An almost compulsory activity in La Roque-Gageac is to take a boat trip down river in a *gabarre* (traditional flat-bottomed river craft). They're lots of fun and offer good views of the village, passing through a pretty stretch of riverbank forest where birds of prey and waterbirds are common, then pressing on to Castelnaud-la-Chapelle before returning along the same route. The 1hr

trips (April–Oct; €9) are run by Gabares Norbert (☎ 05 53 29 40 44, ⓦ gabarres.com) and Gabarres Caminades (☎ 05 53 29 40 95, ⓦ gabarrecaminade.com), both based beside the main car park on the east side of La Roque and offering live (and often quite amusing) commentary in French or a pre-recorded, rather more dry English version on a headset.

Canoe rental Canoë Dordogne (☎ 05 53 29 58 50, ⓦ canoesdordogne.fr), which is based just at the eastern end of the car park, and Canoë Vacances (☎ 05 53 28 17 07, ⓦ canoevacances.com), which is 1km or so further east of La Roque in the direction of Vitrac and Sarlat. Rates at both start at €7/hr.

ACCOMMODATION AND EATING

La Belle Étoile ☎ 05 53 29 51 44, ⓦ belleetoile.fr. The nicest of the town's hotels is the family-run *La Belle Étoile*, on the main road below the fort, with fifteen airy and perfectly adequate rooms. It's worth paying extra for one at the front with river views (€80). The hotel also boasts La Roque's best restaurant which, with its shady terrace and river views, makes a great place for a splurge, though you'll need to book ahead. It offers a varied selection of regional specialities, with three-course *menus* starting at €28, all beautifully presented, and attentive service. Breakfast €12. Restaurant April–Oct Tues & Thurs–Sun 12.30–1.30pm & 7.15–9pm, Wed 7.15–9pm; hotel closed Nov–March. **€65**

La Ferme Fleurie Le Colombier ☎ 05 53 28 33 39, ⓦ fermefleurieperigord.com. For a peaceful place to stay, head 5km northwest of La Roque (just off the D703), to this

auberge surrounded by flower-filled gardens. The floral theme is continued in the eight simple en-suite bedrooms. They also offer more basic accommodation in shared dorms (breakfast included) in their *gîte d'étape*, and there's a good-value guests-only restaurant serving evening meals at communal tables. Closed Nov–March. Dorms **€24**, doubles **€60**

Manoir de la Malartrie Vézac ☎ 05 53 29 03 51, ⓦ chambresdhotes-lamalartrie.com. This *belle époque* château offers luxurious *chambre d'hôte* accommodation on the D703 just west of La Roque. Even if the faux-medieval exterior isn't quite your cup of tea, the stately interiors are sumptuous and it's in a perfect setting, with a heated pool, beautiful formal gardens and terraces overlooking the river. The only slight hiccup is the proximity of the road. Three-night minimum stay in high season. Closed Jan & Feb. **€151**

Domme and around

High on the scarp on the south bank of the Dordogne, 5km southeast from La Roque-Gageac and 10km due south of Sarlat, **DOMME** is an exceptionally well-preserved, terribly pretty *bastide*, now wholly given over to tourism;

fortunately, though, most of the village is pedestrianized so crowds never seem quite as heavy as in La Roque-Gageac. Architecturally beautiful it might be, but Domme's foremost attraction, however, is its position. From the chestnut-shaded **Esplanade du Belvédère** at the town's northern edge, you look out over a wide sweep of river country encompassing everything from Beynac to the Cingle de Montfort (see p.164). The drop here is so precipitous that fortifications were deemed unnecessary when the *bastide* was founded in 1281. They lived to regret it: in 1588 a small band of Protestants scaled the cliffs at dawn to take the town completely by surprise. The intruders stayed four years, during which time they destroyed the church amongst other buildings, before they were forced to abandon the town again to Catholic control.

Thursday morning is **market** day, when stalls spill out of the central square south down the main commercial street, the **Grande-Rue**, itself lined with souvenir shops.

Porte des Tours
Closed for restoration at the time of writing; check with the tourist office to see if their guided tours have resumed

Much of Domme's thirteenth-century walls and three of the gateways they skirted remain. Of the latter, the best-preserved and most interesting is easterly **Porte des Tours**, flanked by two round bastions. In 1307 a group of Templar knights was imprisoned here for eleven years. Tours of the gateway reveal traces of the graffiti they carved on the walls depicting Crucifixion scenes, the Virgin Mary, angels and various secret signs. Alternatively, you can see photos of the carvings in the town's Musée des Arts et Traditions Populaires (see below).

Musée des Arts et Traditions Populaires
Place de la Halle • May, June & Sept daily 10.30am–12.30pm & 2.30–6pm; July & Aug Mon–Fri & Sun 10.30am–7pm, Sat 10.30am–12.30pm & 2.30–7pm • €4, combined ticket with Grotte de Domme €8.50 • ☎ 05 53 31 71 00, 🖳 tourisme-domme.com

Located on Domme's central square, the **Musée des Arts et Traditions Populaires** focuses on local life in the nineteenth and twentieth centuries. The displays are nicely done, if not wildly interesting, but are worth a quick glance.

Grotte de Domme
Place de la Halle • Daily: mid-Feb to March, Oct–Nov & winter school hols 2.30–4.30pm; April & May 10.15am–noon & 2.30–5.30pm; June & Sept 10.15am–noon & 2.15–6pm; July & Aug 10.15am–6.30pm • €8.50, children €6 • Tickets cover entry to the Musée des Arts et Traditions Populaires, and are available at Domme's tourist office (see p.164)

Extending for hundreds of metres under the village from beneath the timbered market hall, the **caves** of Domme definitely can't compete with most Dordogne caverns, but you're likely to have them to yourself and the way out from the caves is enjoyable in itself: a lift takes you up the cliff-face from the exit, affording panoramic views, then there's a pleasant stroll back to town along the promenade de la Falaise.

Jardin Public
Rue du Vieux Moulin • No set hours • Free

For perhaps the most calm and tranquil viewpoint in Domme, follow the lanes westward from the tourist office to the small but perfectly formed **Jardin Public**. The gardens also hold a very heavily restored twelfth-century **mill**, used to grind the wheat for the town's bread.

Cénac

On the way to or from Domme, it's worth making a brief stop in **CÉNAC**, down by the river some 1km from town, to admire its Romanesque church, the **Chapelle St-Julien**, located a short distance along the D50 to St-Cybranet. Apart from a lovely *lauze* roof, its main draw is the remarkably distinct carving on the capitals, featuring various animals and demons, including Daniel taming the lions.

INFORMATION AND ACTIVITIES
DOMME

Tourist office Place de la Halle (mid-Feb to April & Sept daily 10am–noon & 2–6pm; May & June daily 10am–12.30pm & 1.30–6pm; July & Aug daily 10am–7pm; Oct to mid-Nov & Christmas hols daily 10am–noon & 2–5pm; mid-Nov to mid-Feb Mon–Fri 10am–noon & 2–4.30pm;

☎ 05 53 31 71 00, ⓦ tourisme-domme.com).
Canoe and kayak rental Beside the bridge below Domme, Cénac Périgord Loisirs (☎ 05 53 29 99 69, ⓦ canoe dordogne.pro) offer a 2hr, 12km descent from Beynac to Cénac (€16 in a canoe, €18 in a kayak).

ACCOMMODATION AND EATING

Le Belvédère Esplanade de la Belvédère ☎ 05 53 31 12 01. This café-restaurant has unbeatable views from its terrace, located at the cliff edge. Your best bet is to come for a drink or ice cream, served all day, though it also offers standard brasserie fare, such as omelettes, salads and regional dishes, with *menus* starting at €16 and main dishes priced between €10 and €15. April–Sept daily 11.30am–3.30pm & 6–8.30pm.

Cabanoix et Châtaigne 3 rue Geoffroy-de-Vivans ☎ 05 53 31 07 11, ⓦ restaurantcabanoix.com. Cosy little restaurant just off the Grande-Rue with a well-deserved reputation for its creative takes on traditional local cuisine. Foie gras features strongly, though there are always a couple of fish and vegetarian dishes. There's a broad range of *formules* and *menus* to choose from, with three-course options at €25 and €39. No views, but a quiet courtyard or tables by the fire in winter. Reservations recommended. Mid-Feb to mid-Dec Mon–Thurs & Sun noon–2pm & 7.15–9pm.

L'Esplanade Esplanade de la Belvédère ☎ 05 53 28 31 41, ⓦ esplanade-perigord.com. The smartest place to stay in Domme, right on the cliff edge. The spacious and elegant rooms are prettily decked out in soft pastels, and it has an excellent restaurant, where the chef dishes up delights such as scallops with green asparagus. *Menus* are €35–70; in winter, there's a sublime *menu de truffes* costing €100, and in summer, cheaper midday meals are available on the terrace. Note that opening days can vary, especially in winter – phone ahead to be sure. Breakfast €9–16. Restaurant mid-Feb to Nov & mid-Dec to mid-Jan Mon 7.15–9pm, Tues–Sun 12.15–2pm & 7.15–9pm; hotel closed Nov to mid-Dec & mid-Jan to mid-Feb. **€99**

Le Nouvel Hôtel 1 Grande-Rue ☎ 05 53 28 38 67. Simple, reasonably priced if slightly old-fashioned en-suite rooms in this little hotel above a restaurant, just down from Domme's central square. Breakfast €7. Closed mid-Nov to mid-Dec & Jan. **€59**

Upstream towards Souillac

If you're taking the prettier north bank of the Dordogne from Domme, the spectacular, white-walled **Château de Montfort** (not open to the public) soon swings into view atop its well-defended promontory. The distinctive, Disneyesque turrets (which are a nineteenth-century reconstruction) make the whole thing look like a Snow White fantasy. To complete the picture it overlooks the almost perfect curve of the **Cingle de Montfort**, not the biggest but certainly the tightest of the Dordogne's many meanders.

Carsac-Aillac

Two kilometres east of the Château de Montfort, the inviting little Romanesque **Église de Saint-Caprais** below the village of **CARSAC-AILLAC** makes a good place to pause. Though the meadow setting is delightful, the church's **carvings** are the main point of interest: in this case Arabic-influenced capitals around the choir and some later keystones. Note, too, the Stations of the Cross made by Russian abstract artist Léon Zack, who was a refugee here during World War II. Carsac also has some decent **accommodation** options, which could be used as a base for Sarlat (see p.121), only 10km to the northwest.

ARRIVAL AND DEPARTURE
CARSAC-AILLAC

By bus Buses on the Sarlat–Souillac route stop outside the post office in Carsac-Aillac.

Destinations Sarlat (2 daily; 15–20min); Souillac (2 daily; 45min).

ACCOMMODATION AND EATING

Delpeyrat ☎ 05 53 28 10 43. In the centre of Carsac, the likeable family-run *Delpeyrat*, with old-fashioned rooms, most of them set back from the road overlooking a small

garden, is one of those classic roadside hotels that must have been running for years with nothing much changing (except the arrival of wi-fi). Downstairs is a restaurant serving equally homely cooking (*menus* from €14.50). Breakfast €6.50. Restaurant Mon–Fri 11.30am–1.30pm & 7.45–11.30pm, Sat 7.45–11.30pm, Sun 11.30am–1.30pm; hotel and restaurant closed mid-Oct to mid-Dec. €40 **L'Ombrière** Montfort ☎ 05 53 28 11 38, ⦾ lombriere .com. You'll need to book early for this hospitable, Italian-owned *chambre d'hôte* in an eighteenth-century manor house perched above the Cingle de Montfort, 2km west of Carsac and only 5km southeast of Sarlat. Its four light, airy rooms are tastefully decorated and very reasonably

priced, and breakfasts are generous. There's also a cosy lounge and fine views from the terrace. Evening meals – with an Italian twist – are available on request (€30). €98 **Le Relais du Touron** Le Touron ☎ 05 53 28 16 70, ⦾ lerelaisdutouron.com. Set in extensive grounds 500m along the Sarlat road from Carsac, the *Relais* makes a peaceful place to stay. The rooms are fairly functional but spacious and well-kept, occupying a modern block beside an outdoor pool and a lily-filled pond. Restaurant meals also available. Breakfast €9.50. Closed Nov–Easter. €88

Château de Fénelon

Ste-Mondane • April–June & Sept Mon, Wed–Fri & Sun 10.30am–12.30pm & 2.30–6.30pm; July & Aug Mon–Fri & Sun 10.30am–6.30pm; Oct Mon, Wed–Fri & Sun 2–5pm • €9, children €6 • ☎ 05 53 29 81 45, ⦾ chateau-fenelon.fr • The château is on the south bank of the Dordogne, along the D50 some 5km from Carsac-Aillac

Clamped to its own rocky outcrop, with triple walls and great round towers topped with *lauzes*, the **Château de Fénelon** exudes all the might of the original medieval fortress. As you get closer, however, the Renaissance-era additions and other, later embellishments become more apparent – the large mullion windows and the gallery closing the interior courtyard, for example.

The castle's most illustrious occupant was **François de Salignac de la Mothe-Fénelon**, who was born here in 1651. Private tutor to the heir to the throne and later archbishop of Cambrai, he fell from grace when King Louis XIV interpreted his work *Télémaque* – which recounts the adventures of Ulysses' son – as a thinly veiled attack on the Crown. His intention had been to teach the young prince the finer points of kinghood, but for his pains Fénelon was banished to Cambrai, where he died in 1715. He is remembered with much pride at Fénelon today. There's a mock-up of his study and numerous portraits, but the present owners have also amassed a worthwhile collection of period furniture, tapestries and medieval weaponry. The ornate walnut chimneypieces are also eye-catching.

The Upper Dordogne valley and Rocamadour

170 Souillac and around

175 Rocamadour and around

182 Martel and around

185 Carennac and around

187 Bretenoux and around

188 Beaulieu-sur-Dordogne and around

191 St-Céré and around

ROCAMADOUR

The Upper Dordogne valley and Rocamadour

In its upper reaches the Dordogne river cuts a green swathe through the rocky limestone plateau of Haut-Quercy, as the northern sector of the Lot *département* is traditionally known. This is a land of walnut orchards and strawberry fields and although the cliffs rise to considerable heights in places, the valley here lacks the drama of the perched castles and towns immediately downstream. Instead, away from the main towns, it offers a slow, lazy river and a pace of life to match: quieter lanes, more modest castles and a succession of unspoilt riverside villages that proudly proclaim their status as among the most beautiful in France.

The main gateway to the Upper Dordogne valley is **Souillac**, a busy little town whose major attraction is its domed abbey church. A short distance upstream, an attractive back road strikes off along the River Ouysse, a minor tributary of the Dordogne, heading southeast to the spectacular pilgrimage town of **Rocamadour**, whose seven religious sanctuaries are built almost vertically into a rocky backdrop.

Back on the Dordogne, near the little village of **Lacave**, the river meanders in a northeasterly direction through walnut forests and dozing villages to the dramatic crags around **Gluges**, where it has carved the **Cirque de Montvalent** out of the plateau. North of here, the market town of **Martel** sees surprisingly few tourists despite its medieval centre full of turreted mansions, while to the east, **Carennac** merits a stop for its picturesque lanes and the twelfth-century carved portal adorning its church. Carennac also lies within striking distance of the **Gouffre de Padirac**, where a collapsed cavern has left a gaping hole in the limestone plateau. Upstream of Carennac the Dordogne valley begins to open out to form a broad plain around its confluence with the Cère. **Bretenoux**, the main town guarding the Cère valley, isn't itself a particularly engaging place, but it's more than compensated for by the nearby **Château de Castelnau**, which still dominates the country for miles around. North of Bretenoux is the pleasing town of **Beaulieu-sur-Dordogne**, while south is **St-Céré**, which provides a good base for exploring the region. Beneath the brooding towers of its ruined château, a scattering of stone and half-timbered townhouses attests to the St-Céré's fifteenth- and sixteenth-century heyday, while there's more Renaissance architecture on show at the **Château de Montal**, a few kilometres to the west. The nearby villages of **Autoire** and **Loubressac**, meanwhile, are rooted firmly in the Quercy soil, their houses sporting little pigeon-lofts and the red-tiled roofs splayed gently above the eaves, which are typical of the region.

GETTING AROUND
THE UPPER DORDOGNE VALLEY

By train Souillac, Rocamadour, St-Denis-près-Martel (for Martel) and Bretenoux can be reached by train. Gignac (Cressensac-Gignac station) is also on the train line, and is just 5km from the Brive-Vallée de la Dordogne airport (see p.79).

By bus Most small towns have no public bus service and can only be reached by car, but daily bus services run between Souillac, St-Denis-près-Martel (for Martel), St-Céré and Bretenoux. However they are aimed at schoolchildren and run

Festivals, events and markets p.171
Hiking the GR6 from Lacave to
    Rocamadour p.174
Walk with the animals p.180

The tale of Young King Henry p.182
La Môme Piaf and the Église de
    Gluges p.185

GOUFFRE DE PADIRAC

Highlights

❶ Église Ste-Marie The image of the prophet Isaiah in Souillac's abbey church is a masterpiece of Romanesque art. **See p.171**

❷ Rocamadour One of France's top pilgrimage sites defies gravity in its spectacular cliff-edge location. **See p.175**

❸ Carennac Wander the lanes of this typical Quercy village and then peek inside its serene cloister. **See p.185**

❹ Gouffre de Padirac Take a boat trip on an underground river, accessed via an immense cavern. **See p.186**

❺ Château de Castelnau Fans of military architecture shouldn't miss this brooding fortress. **See p.188**

❻ Beaulieu-sur-Dordogne Laidback market town on the banks of the Dordogne that sees fewer tourists than it deserves. **See p.188**

❼ Château de Montal Admire some of the region's finest Renaissance carvings on the facade and staircase of this magnificent stately home. **See p.193**

❽ Autoire A picture-perfect village, encircled by limestone cliffs and serving up some impressive views. **See p.194**

HIGHLIGHTS ARE MARKED ON THE MAP ON P.170

at school drop-off and pickup times during term-time only, so are an inconvenient option for travellers. Nonetheless, a comprehensive timetable, *Les Bus du Lot*, is published annually and available at tourist offices; you can also get bus information by contacting the transport information desk of the Conseil Général du Lot (☎ 05 65 53 43 91, ⓦ lot.fr).

Souillac and around

Traffic-ridden **Souillac** suffers from being the major gateway to both Sarlat and the Périgord Noir to the west and the upper reaches of the Dordogne valley to the east, and though the nearby A20 *autoroute* brings some relief, it will never be a particularly pretty place. Souillac's main attraction is the **Église Ste-Marie**, with its exquisite carvings, but the town also has a small enclave of old streets, which are worth a quick wander. A handy landmark to aim for is the semi-ruined **belfry** of the disused **Église St-Martin**, partially destroyed in the Wars of Religion, on the southeast corner of the old centre; you can get a good view down into the nave from of a window inside the tourist office (see p.172).

Immediately upstream from Souillac, the valley is dominated by the A20 road-bridge, but a few meanders of the river later and you're back among quiet lanes and unspoilt scenery. One place to head for is **Lacave**, a village on the south bank with some passably interesting limestone caves. From Lacave you can take an attractive detour south along a tributary river, the Ouysse, as it cuts its way through a mini-gorge in the limestone plateau, to visit a 600-year-old working flour mill, the **Moulin de Cougnaguet**. Continue on this route and you will eventually find yourself in Rocamadour (see p.175).

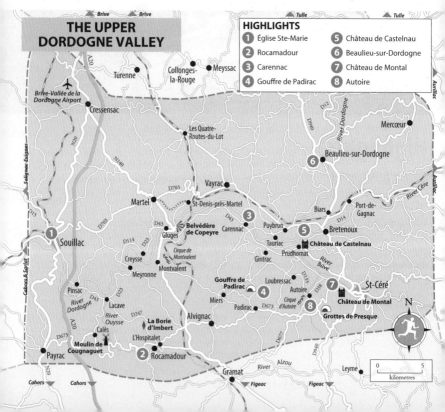

THE UPPER DORDOGNE VALLEY

HIGHLIGHTS
1. Église Ste-Marie
2. Rocamadour
3. Carennac
4. Gouffre de Padirac
5. Château de Castelnau
6. Beaulieu-sur-Dordogne
7. Château de Montal
8. Autoire

FESTIVALS, EVENTS AND MARKETS

The Upper Dordogne hosts a wide range of **festivals** and **events** throughout the summer season, and many of the villages host special markets and small fêtes to celebrate the autumn harvest. The main festivals are detailed below, but for the full schedule, pick up the free *Calendrier des Fêtes des Villes et Villages* booklet from tourist offices. Where we haven't given a specific information number or website, contact the relevant tourist office.

Second Sunday in May Beaulieu-sur-Dordogne: Fête de la Fraise. France's strawberry capital gets down to some serious baking with an 800-kilo strawberry tart. There's a great strawberry market, too.

Late May or early June Rocamadour: Fête des Fromages Fermiers (☎ 05 65 23 22 05, ⓦ fromages.rocamadour.free.fr). At Pentecôte (Whit Sunday) artisan cheese producers gather above the town at L'Hospitalet to show off their wares, while folk concerts are staged around town.

June–Sept Rocamadour: Spectacles Équestres de Durandal (☎ 06 19 39 18 00, ⓦ rocamadour-horseshow.com). Medieval jousting, horseback stunts and vaulting displays on the hilltop behind the château. Performances are held regularly between June and September; tickets start at €8/children €7 (under 4s free).

Mid-July to mid-August St-Céré and around: Festival de St-Céré et du Haut-Quercy (☎ 05 65 38 28 08, ⓦ festival-saint-cere.com). Three weeks of opera, recitals, orchestral works and chamber music in St-Céré

(including the châteaux of Montal and Castelnau), Beaulieu, Martel, Cahors and Souillac. Tickets required.

August Rocamadour: Cantica Sacra (☎ 06 52 74 01 06, ⓦ rocamadourfestival.com). Ten days of sacred singing performances and workshops in an exceptional setting.

Third weekend in July Souillac: Souillac en Jazz (☎ 05 65 37 04 93, ⓦ souillacenjazz.fr). International jazz acts let rip in the streets of Souillac for six days of concerts, films, exhibitions and a feast on the final night. The big-name, ticket-only events take place outdoors next to the abbey church.

Early September Rocamadour: Semaine Mariale. The week dedicated to the Virgin Mary is celebrated with pilgrimages, prayers and Masses, including torchlight processions to the Chapelle Notre-Dame.

Third weekend in September Rocamadour: Rassemblement Européen de Montgolfières. Hot-air balloons take off from the valley below Rocamadour; for the best views, take up position early on the Belvédère in L'Hospitalet.

MARKETS

The main **markets** in this region are at Beaulieu-sur-Dordogne (Wed & Sat); Bretenoux (Tues & Sat); Martel (Wed & Sat); St-Céré (Sat & first and third Wed of the month); and Souillac (Fri). In addition to the weekly market, an annual truffle market takes place in Martel (Wed & Sat mornings) betwen mid-December and the end of January.

Église Ste-Marie

Place de l'Abbaye • Daily 8am–12.30pm & 3.30–7.30pm • ☎ 05 65 37 34 34

One block west of the belfry of St-Martin lies a wide, open space dominated by the beautiful Romanesque **Église Ste-Marie**. The Byzantine domes of this abbey church are reminiscent of the cathedrals of Périgueux and Cahors, though on a smaller scale, while its largely unadorned interior conveys a far greater sense of antiquity. The first church on this site belonged to a priory founded in the tenth century, which became an abbey five hundred years later. Badly damaged during both the Hundred Years War and Wars of Religion, the church was restored in the seventeenth century before being abandoned during the Revolution. Sadly, only fragments of the **Romanesque sculptures** that once graced the main (west) portal have survived, but those that do remain – now reassembled inside the west door – are superb. Those on the tympanum tell the story of a local monk, Théophile, who was dismissed from the treasury for corruption. Desperate to regain his position, he is said to have made a pact with the Devil, but then fell seriously ill and, full of remorse, besought the Virgin Mary for forgiveness. His luck was in: the final scene depicts Théophile's dream of the Virgin accompanied by St Michael driving the Devil away. The greatest piece of craftsmanship is the **bas-relief of the prophet Isaiah** to the right of the door. Fluid and supple, it appears that the elongated, bearded figure clutching his parchment and with one leg extended is dancing for joy as he proclaims news of the coming of the Messiah.

Musée de l'Automate

Place de l'Abbaye • Jan–March, Nov & Dec Tues–Sun 2.30pm–5.30pm; April–June & Sept–Oct Tues–Sun 10am–noon & 2–6pm; July & Aug daily 10am–12.30pm & 2–6.30pm • €7 • ☎ 05 65 37 07 07, ⊛ musee-automate.fr

Behind the Église Ste-Marie, to the west, the **Musée de l'Automate** contains an impressive collection of nineteenth- and twentieth-century mechanical dolls and animals that dance, juggle and perform magical tricks. Most come from the once-famous Rouillet-Decamps workshops in Paris and include such pieces as a life-size 1920s jazz band, Charlie Chaplin and a woman doing the twist.

ARRIVAL AND INFORMATION   SOUILLAC

By air Brive-Vallée de la Dordogne airport (☎ 05 55 22 40 00, ⊛ aeroport-brive-vallee-dordogne.com; see p.79) is a 25min drive north of Souillac; the nearest train station is Cressensac-Gignac (see p.168). For taxis call Bernard Mauvais (☎ 05 65 37 88 40).

By train Getting to Souillac by train is not a problem since it lies on the main Paris–Toulouse line. The *gare SNCF* is just over 1km northwest of town; take av Jean Jaurès and then av Martin-Malvy, which will bring you out at the west end of av Gambetta, the old quarter's main east–west artery. Destinations Brive (6–9 daily; 25min); Cahors (6–9 daily; 40min–1hr); Cressensac/Gignac (1–2 daily; 15min);

Gourdon (4 daily; 15min); Montauban (2–4 daily; 1hr 30min); Paris (4–6 daily; 4hr 30min); Toulouse (4–6 daily; 1hr 55min).

By car Place du Foirail provides the most convenient car parking for the centre.

By bus Buses to and from Souillac are aimed at schoolchildren, and hence aren't a viable option for visitors.

Tourist office Bd Louis-Jean Malvy, across the road from place du Foirail (July & Aug Mon–Sat 9.30am–12.30pm & 2–7pm, Sun 10am–noon & 3–6pm; Sept–June Mon–Sat 10am–12.30pm & 2–6pm; ☎ 05 65 37 81 56, ⊛ tourisme-vallee-dordogne.com).

GETTING AROUND

Car rental RSL (☎ 05 65 32 64 72, ⊛ location-vehicule-souillac.fr) is at 38 av Général-de-Gaulle, the northern extension of bd Louis-Jean Malvy.

Bike rental Carrefour du Cycle, 23 av Général-de-Gaulle (☎ 05 65 37 07 52, ⊛ carrefourducycle.com), has bike

rental from €16 a day.

Canoe rental Copeyre Canoë (☎ 05 65 32 72 61, ⊛ copeyre .com), next to *Les Ondines* campsite (see below), has bikes (from €17/day), canoes (from €16/day) and kayaks (from €20 /day).

ACCOMMODATION

Chastrusse Nadaillac-de-Rouge ☎ 05 65 37 60 08, ⊛ hotel-restaurant-chastrusse.com/accueilfrance.htm. Delightfully unpretentious place some 10km southwest of Souillac, with homely rooms looking out over a flower-lined terrace and a well-sized pool. There's a restaurant serving specialties like garlic-stuffed snails and walnut tart. Half- and full-board options are available; otherwise breakfast is €8. Restaurant Feb to mid-Oct Mon–Fri & Sun noon–2.30pm & 7.30–9pm, Sat 7.30–9pm. **€55**

Domaine de la Paille Basse ☎ 05 65 37 85 48, ⊛ lapaillebasse.com. Some 9km northwest of Souillac, signed off the D15 to Salvignac, this swish five-star campsite offers cosy bungalows (€269 weekly), chalets (€219 weekly), "glamping" tents (€389 weekly) and ample grassy camping spots. A great choice for families, there are also two swimming pools with water slides, children's playgrounds, tennis courts and a discotheque. Minimum one-week stay for chalets/bungalows. Closed

mid-Sept to mid-May. **€33**

Grand Hotel 1 allée de Verninac ☎ 05 65 32 78 30, ⊛ grandhotel-souillac.com. Exceedingly friendly staff, comfortable modern rooms and a handy location next door to the tourist office make this well-priced hotel a top choice. The downstairs restaurant is always packed, with *menus* from €22 and ample seating on the shady terrace; buffet breakfast €8. Restaurant daily noon–2.30pm & 7–9.30pm. **€55**

Les Ondines Rue des Ondines ☎ 05 65 37 86 44, ⊛ camping-lesondines.com. Huge three-star campsite in a tranquil riverside location. The heated pool, splash pools and multiple playgrounds make it a convenient option for young families. Closed Oct–April. **€22**

★ **Le Pavillon Saint-Martin** 5 place St-Martin ☎ 05 65 32 63 45, ⊛ hotel-saint-martin-souillac.com. Housed in a sixteenth-century stone-and-brick mansion, *Le Pavillon Saint-Martin* has bags of character and it's easily Souillac's most stylish hotel. The eleven rooms each have their own unique flair, with the decor ranging from nostalgic florals to modern colour-blocking and colour schemes from pastel pink to eye-popping tangerine. Breakfast is served in the atmospheric vaulted cellar and free private parking is available on site. Breakfast €12. €81

La Vieille Auberge 1 rue de la Recège ☎05 65 32 79 43, ⓦla-vieille-auberge.com. An upmarket option located in Souillac's old quarter at the west end of avenue Gambetta. Rooms are spotless and modern, there's private parking available (€7 a night) and a swimming pool out back. Stick around to dine at the hotel restaurant, where evening *menus* start from €25. Breakfast €12. Restaurant Tues–Sun noon–2pm & 7–9pm. €79

EATING

Along with the places listed below, don't forget Souillac's hotel **restaurants** (see opposite), which are all worth trying. There are also several delightful **cafés** offering more basic food. Head west into the old quarter, well away from the traffic-ridden centre, where the streets are cobbled and the town pump still works; you may see Souillac in a new light.

Le Beffroi 6 place St-Martin ☎05 65 37 80 33. With a prime location right on place St-Martin, *Le Beffroi* makes a lively spot for people-watching: grab a seat on the terrace beneath the lamp-lit wisteria. Simple *plats du jour* are around €9, while *menus* start from €22. Tues–Sat noon–2.30pm & 7–9pm, Mon noon–2.30pm.

L'Entracte 32 rue de la Halles ☎05 65 32 76 56. The best spot in town to grab lunch on a budget – set *menus* start from as little as €12, and change daily according to what's in season. Be sure to sample the home-made ice cream or passionfruit sorbet. Mon–Sat noon–2pm.

Lycée d'Hôtellerie Av Roger Couderc ☎05 65 27 03 00. Sample the skills of Souillac's future generation at the *Lycée* (college), situated on a hill to the west of the old quarter, where you can act as a guinea-pig for trainee chefs and waiters/waitresses. Don't be put off, though – with the *menus* set in advance and the trainees trying hard to impress, the food is typically excellent. Expect to pay €17 for a lunch *menu* or €35 in the evening. Reservations essential. Mon–Fri noon–2pm & 7–9.30pm; closed during school summer hols.

Lacave

Following the Dordogne upstream along the D43 you soon leave the *autoroute* behind as you crest the hill and drop down to **LACAVE**, on the river's south bank and 14km southeast of Souillac. It's a tranquil base-camp for those visiting nearby Rocamadour and boasts some excellent Michelin-star restaurants to splash out on, but there's no public transport so you'll need your own vehicle.

Grottes de Lacave

1hr 15min guided tours daily: mid-Feb to March & Oct to mid-Nov 10am–noon & 2–5pm; April–June & Sept 9.30am–noon & 2–5.30pm; July & Aug 9.30am–12.30pm & 1.30–6pm • €9, children €5.50 • ☎05 65 37 87 03, ⓦ grottes-de-lacave.com

A cavernous hole in the limestone cliffs overshadowing Lacave village marks the entrance to a series of underground lakes, together making up the **Grottes de Lacave**, which can be visited on guided tours. You travel the first few hundred metres by electric train, after which there's a lift up to the kilometre-long gallery, resplendent with all manner of stalactites and stalagmites, from petrified "waterfalls" to great organ pipes. But the highlight here is the magical reflections in the lakes' mirrored surfaces – at one point they also use ultraviolet light to reveal the glittering fluorescence of the "living" water-filled formations, while the older, dry deposits remain lost in the darkness.

ACCOMMODATION AND EATING   LACAVE

★**Château de la Treyne** ☎05 65 27 60 60, ⓦchateau delatreyne.com. Set high above the Dordogne valley, 6km west of Lacave on the Souillac road, this idyllic château strikes the perfect balance between timeless luxury and modern creativity. The foundations are traditional – inlaid wood ceilings, regal tapestries and twinkling chandeliers – but there are plenty of surprises: an opulent gold and marble bathroom, an eye-popping red boudoir or whimsical print-on-print decor, while each of the seventeen rooms is infused with its own character. There's also a Michelin-starred restaurant, where chef Stéphane Andrieux whips up dishes like beef and foie gras millefeuille, followed by

HIKING THE GR6 FROM LACAVE TO ROCAMADOUR

The **GR6 long-distance hiking route**, one of France's *Grandes Randonnées* (🌐 gr-infos.com), runs all the way from Sainte Foy-la-Grande, near Bordeaux on the west coast, to Fouillouse in the Haute-Alps, crossing the entire width of France. The 1,100km route also passes through the heart of the Lot valley, offering ample opportunities for day-hikes or longer walks, with marked trails connecting towns like Souillac, Lacave, Rocamadour and Gramat.

The most scenic stretch for a day hike is the route **from Lacave to Rocamadour** (some 14km), stopping along the way at the Moulin de Cougnaguet (see below). From Cougnaguet, the route runs alongside the River Ouysse past another mill – this was once big wheat country and even in high summer the Ouysse, part of which flows underground, never dries up – before turning eastwards along the River Alzou. Gradually the valley closes in until you round a bend and see the pilgrimage town of Rocamadour clinging to the cliff like a lost city. From Rocamadour, it's possible to continue along the GR6 or veer south along the GR46.

coconut and strawberry mousse. All that, plus a a pool, tennis courts and some 300 acres of parks and gardens. *Menus* from €96, breakfast €24. Restaurant April–Oct Tues 7.30–9pm, Wed–Sun noon–2pm & 7.30–9pm. **€200**

Ferme-Auberge Calvel ☎ 05 65 37 87 20. Just 2km northeast of Lacave, on the D23 toward Meyronne, this friendly little place offers basic *camping à la ferme*, with space for just a handful of tents, and rustic, home-cooked cuisine, available by reservation only (*menus* €12). No credit cards. Closed mid-Sept to April. **€15**

Le Pont de l'Ouysse ☎ 05 65 37 87 04, 🌐 lepontde louysse.fr. A stylish country hotel, 1km west of Lacave on the Souillac road, with a Michelin-starred restaurant offering delights such as lobster or caramelized pigeon, and a terrace overlooking the river. The twelve immaculate rooms each have hardwood floors, chic furnishings and individual touches, and the pastoral views from the windows are nothing short of magnificent. *Menus* from €60, breakfast €17. Restaurant April–Oct daily noon–2pm & 7.30–9pm. **€140**

Calès

From where the River Ouysse empties into the Dordogne just west of Lacave, a minor road heads south along the tributary, winding its way up the valley side to the plateau near the village of **CALÈS**, 5km later. The village is a neat and tidy place with little more than a couple of decent hotels in its centre, but it's a quiet alternative to Rocamadour and the nearby **Moulin de Cougnaguet** makes a worthy detour. There are no buses so you'll need your own transport to get here.

ACCOMMODATION AND EATING   CALÈS

Le Petit Relais Le Bourg ☎ 05 65 37 96 09, 🌐 hotel -petitrelais.fr. Well-kept, family-run hotel with a pleasingly rustic atmosphere, spick-and-span rooms and a pretty, flowery terrace where you can enjoy above-average cuisine,

with *menus* from €29.50. Breakfast €11. Restaurant May– Sept daily noon–1.30pm & 7–8.30pm; Oct & mid-March to April Sat & Sun noon–1.30pm & 7–8.30pm; hotel closed mid-Nov to mid-March. **€77**

Moulin de Cougnaguet

Visit by guided tour (30min) April to mid-Oct daily 10am–noon & 2–6pm • €4.50, children €2.50 • ☎ 05 65 38 73 56, 🌐 cougnaguet.com

At Calès the road from Lacave joins the D673 and turns east before dropping back down to the river, which has here carved out a mini-gorge. For an interesting diversion, turn left just after crossing the river and wind along the gorge for about a kilometre until you reach the **Moulin de Cougnaguet**. The fourteenth-century fortified mill only ceased working commercially in 1959 and is now open to visitors for **guided tours**. During the tour, the enthusiastic owner points out its many defensive features – including arrow slits and sluice gates which, when opened from inside the mill, unleashed a torrent of water to sweep away anyone attempting to ford the millrace – and also puts the mill through its paces. Standing close to 1.5 tonnes of stone spinning at eighty revolutions per minute, you get a real feel for the pent-up power of the water waiting calmly upstream.

Rocamadour and around

Halfway up the northern cliff face of the deep and abrupt canyon of the River Alzou, the spectacular setting of **ROCAMADOUR** is hard to beat, with the turrets and spires of the **Cité Religieuse** at its heart, sandwiched between the jumbled roofs of the medieval town and the château's crenellated walls above. However, as you draw closer the spell is broken by the constant stream of pilgrims and more secular-minded visitors, particularly in summer, who fill lanes lined with shops peddling incongruous souvenirs. The main reason for Rocamadour's popularity – going back centuries – is the supposed miraculous properties of the statue of the **Black Madonna**, enshrined in the Cité's smoke-blackened **Chapelle Notre-Dame**. Modern tourists are also courted with a number of secondary attractions, including two wildlife parks, scattered on the plateau to the north and east of town. Even if those don't appeal, it's worth venturing up to the hamlet of **L'Hospitalet**, on the cliff (1.5km by road) east of Rocamadour, for the finest views of the town.

Brief history

The first mention of Rocamadour's Chapelle Notre-Dame dates from 1105, although evidence suggests pilgrims started coming here as early as the ninth century. However, things really got going when a perfectly preserved body was discovered in a rock-hewn tomb beside the chapel in 1166. It was promptly declared to be that of Zacchaeus, later **St Amadour**; according to one legend, Zacchaeus – a tax-collector in Jericho at the time of Christ – was advised by the Virgin Mary to come to France and lived out his years in Rocamadour as a hermit. As tales of the saint and associated miracles spread, the faithful began to arrive in droves from all over Europe. St Bernard, numerous kings – including Henry II of England and Louis IX of France (St Louis) – and thousands of ordinary mortals crawled up the **Grand Escalier** (the pilgrims' staircase) on their knees to pay their respects and to seek forgiveness or cures. Others came simply to plunder the shrine – among them the Young King Henry (see box, p.182) – but they were easily outclassed by the Huguenots, who, in 1562, tried in vain to burn St Amadour's corpse and finally resigned themselves to hacking it to bits instead. In the meantime, centuries of warfare and plague led to a decline in the number of pilgrims. The buildings gradually fell into ruin until the bishops of Cahors, hoping to revive the flagging pilgrimage, financed a massive reconstruction in the early nineteenth century and so gave us the Rocamadour we see today.

Old Town

Rocamadour's **old town** is easy enough to find your way around since there's just one street, pedestrianized **rue de la Couronnerie**, which runs west from **Porte du Figuier** – one of Rocamadour's four medieval gateways – to the wide stone staircase leading up to the sanctuaries, roughly 300m later.

La Cité Religieuse

The steep hillside above rue de la Couronnerie supports no fewer than seven chapels, known collectively as "Les Sanctuaires", or the **Cité Religieuse**. There's a lift dug into the rock-face (see p.180), but it's far better to climb the 216 worn and pitted steps of the **Grand Escalier**, up which the devout once dragged themselves on their knees to the doors of the Cité. Inside lies a small square, place **Parvis**, completely hemmed in by the various chapels.

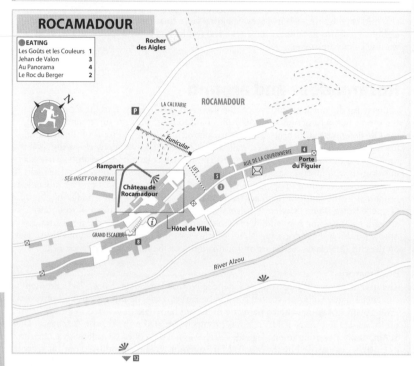

Basilique St-Sauveur

Daily: July & Aug 8am–9pm; Sept–June 8.30am–6.30pm, though these times can vary

The largest chapel in the Cité Religieuse is the **Basilique St-Sauveur**, a vaulted Romanesque-Gothic hall which, up until 1900, provided lodgings for pilgrims who couldn't afford anything better. An unusual and rather rickety-looking twentieth-century wooden gallery covers the rock-face wall and there are several paintings of notable visitors on the other walls. The slightly sparse altar has a fine bronze frontal of the Ascension, surmounted by a rather gruesome sixteenth-century Christ on the Cross.

Chapelle Notre-Dame

Daily: July & Aug 8am–9pm; Sept–June 8.30am–6.30pm, though these times can vary

The little **Chapelle Notre-Dame** is nestled against the rock and the wall of the Basilique St-Sauveur, and is where the miracle-working twelfth-century **Black Madonna** resides. The crudely carved statue, less than 70cm tall, still wears a faint smile despite her mutilated state, though the adult-featured Jesus balanced on her knee looks decidedly out of sorts. The rest of the chapel is unremarkable, but note the empty recess in the rock outside, where St Amadour's body was found, and a rusty sword protruding from the cliff above. According to local tradition this is **Durandal**, the trusty blade of the legendary Roland whose heroic exploits are recorded in the twelfth-century *Chanson de Roland* (*The Song of Roland*), though it's not revealed exactly how it got here from northern Spain, where Roland supposedly died in battle against the Moors in 778. Beside the chapel's ornately carved door there are also some faded fifteenth-century **frescoes** depicting a macabre fight between the Living and the Dead.

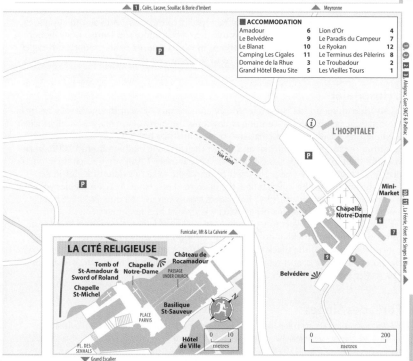

ACCOMMODATION (within map):
Amadour 6
Le Belvédère 9
Le Blanat 10
Camping Les Cigales 11
Domaine de la Rhue 3
Grand Hôtel Beau Site 5
Lion d'Or 4
Le Paradis du Campeur 7
Le Ryokan 12
Le Terminus des Pèlerins 8
Le Troubadour 2
Les Vieilles Tours 1

Chapelle St-Michel

Accessible only by guided tours of the Cité (see p.79)

Opposite the Chapelle Notre-Dame, tucked tightly into a corner of the place Parvis with one long wall of overhanging rock, the twelfth-century **Chapelle St-Michel** is home to two incredibly well-preserved twelfth-century polychrome paintings of the Annunciation and the Visitation.

Château de Rocamadour

Ramparts daily 8am–8pm • €2

East of the Cité Religieuse there's a sandy esplanade and the funicular (see p.180) that will take you to the top of the cliff. Alternatively, you can walk up the shady zigzag path, *La Calvarie*, past tableaux depicting the Stations of the Cross, or take a more direct and steeper path to come out near the **Château de Rocamadour**, a full 150m above the river below. While the château itself, a mostly nineteenth-century reconstruction, is private, you can walk round the **ramparts** and soak up dramatic views over the valley.

Rocher des Aigles

Daily: April, May & Sept 2–5pm; June 12.30–7pm; July & Aug 1–8pm; last entry 2hrs before closing • €10, children €6 • Flying demonstrations daily: April, May & Sept 2.30pm & 4pm; June 1pm, 2.30pm & 4pm; July & Aug daily noon–5pm, roughly every hour • ⊕ 05 65 33 65 45, ⓦ rocherdesaigles.com

The road leading west from Rocamadour's château brings you almost immediately to the **Rocher des Aigles**, a wildlife park and breeding centre for birds of prey. The cages seem uncomfortably small, but with a production rate of nearly a hundred chicks a year the birds can't be overly stressed about it. There's a film explaining the breeding programme, which aims to reintroduce a number of rare species to the wild, and you can also see the hatching room where scrawny chicks warm themselves under sun lamps. Best, though, are the thirty-minute **flying demonstrations**, in which a dozen or so condors, fish eagles and other such majestic birds are allowed to soar free over the valley.

L'Hospitalet

It's worth coming up to **L'Hospitalet** for the tremendous views of the medieval Cité from the cliff-edge belvedere. It's stunning at any time, but particularly magical at night when the buildings are illuminated (March–Nov & Christmas hols). To get to the area, head east from the top of the funicular and follow the cliff-edge road for around 700m until you join the D673 from Calès (see p.174). After another 150m you'll reach the modern, plate-glass **tourist office** (see p.180), which marks the western extent of L'Hospitalet. From the bottom of the valley, follow the main road east from Porte du Figuier which winds up the valley side to L'Hospitalet; pedestrians can use the quieter Voie Sainte, a narrow lane which branches off left after a couple of hundred metres.

L'Hospitalet's name refers to a pilgrims' hospital founded on the clifftop here in the thirteenth century, of which only a few ruined walls and the **Chapelle Notre-Dame**, containing a copy of the Black Madonna, remain. A crossroads lying immediately to the northeast of the chapel represents the centre of modern L'Hospitalet, which consists of a scattering of hotels, cafés and shops.

Forêt des Singes

Mid-March to April & Sept 1 to Sept 15 daily 10am–noon & 1–5.30pm; May & June daily 10am–noon & 1–6pm; July & Aug daily 9.30am–6.30pm; Sept 16–Sept 30 Mon–Fri 1–5.30pm, Sat & Sun 10am–noon & 1–5.30pm; Oct & Nov Mon–Fri 1–5pm, Sat & Sun 10am–noon & 1–5pm • €9, children €5.50 • ☎ 05 65 33 62 72, ⓦ la-foret-des-singes.com

About 300m east of L'Hospitalet, the **Forêt des Singes** wildlife park is one of the better such parks, with some 150 Barbary apes roaming twenty hectares of oak and scrubland in relative freedom. The aim is conservation – so far around six hundred young monkeys have been reintroduced to North Africa. The best time to visit is during the cool of the early morning or evening and in early summer when the youngsters are frolicking about.

La Borie d'Imbert

Daily mid-March to Sept 10am–7pm • Free; special events €5, children €3 • ☎ 05 65 33 20 37, ⓦ laboriedimbert.com

An attraction worth visiting, particularly for those with children, **La Borie d'Imbert** is a small country farm situated on the D247 in the direction of Souillac. The old farmhouse, La Maison de Justine, has countrified rooms complete with traditional cookware and furniture, while the baby farm animals are a sure winner for the very young. The goats are milked every day from 5 to 6pm, and in the farm shop you can taste and buy the Rocamadour goat's cheese (see p.181) and home-produced charcuterie. There's also a busy schedule of special events throughout the summer, including wine tasting, cheese-making workshops or hands-on animal workshops for kids.

ARRIVAL AND INFORMATION   ROCAMADOUR

By car Rocamadour is pedestrianized, so unless you have access to hotel parking you'll have to park in L'Hospitalet at the top of the hill. There is a large, free car park at the top of the funicular or else paid parking (daily 10am–7pm; €1 per hour) outside the tourist office in L'Hospitalet. Otherwise you can park in the valley several hundred metres below,

and rather than walking into town from the valley car park, you could take Le Petit Train (see p.181).
By train Getting to Rocamadour by public transport is awkward. There are no buses, and the rather confusingly named Rocamadour-Padirac *gare SNCF*, on the Brive–Figeac line, lies 3km away to the northeast of Rocamadour

CLOCKWISE FROM TOP BEAULIEU-SUR-DORDOGNE (P.188); CIRQUE D'AUTOIRE (P.194); SOUILLAC (P.170) >

WALK WITH THE ANIMALS

If you're a keen walker and happen to be in the area in the last week of April, you might like to join in the **Transhumance**, a five-day, 70km walk spearheaded by a flock of sheep. Open to the public, the route starts off in Rocamadour and heads to Luzech (see p.232), via narrow country lanes and rolling fields. Unlike in mountainous regions in France, transhumance is not yet a tradition in the Lot, but local associations, as well as the Conseil Général (w lot.fr), are actively promoting it in the hope that it will become so. There's a practical side to the idea, too: as the sheep traverse fields lent by local landowners, they will eat down the grass, in a demonstration of ecological land maintenance.

(and some way from the town of Padirac itself). If you don't want to trek into Rocamadour alongside the main road, you can call Taxi Herbert (t 05 65 50 14 82 or t 06 81 60 14 60). Note that the station is rarely staffed, and there's no ticket machine, so check the times of return trains carefully on arrival and buy a return ticket beforehand.

Tourist office Rocamadour has two tourist offices, both with the same hours and contact details (Sept–June daily 10am–12.30pm & 2–6pm; July & Aug daily 9.30am–7pm; t 05 65 33 22 00, w tourisme-vallee-dordogne.com); the main one is located on the western outskirts of L'Hospitalet, the second on rue de la Couronnerie next to the Hôtel de Ville. Both offer guided tours of the Cité and sell tickets to regional attractions.

GETTING AROUND

By lift In the village centre, a lift (daily: May, June & Sept 9am–7pm; July & Aug 9am–10pm; Oct–April 9am–6pm; €2.10 one-way, €3.10 return) links the town's main street, rue de la Couronnerie, with the Cité Religieuse above.

By funicular A funicular (daily: May, June & Sept 9am–7pm; July & Aug 9am–10pm; Oct–April 9am–6pm; €2.60 one-way, €4.20 return) departs from just east of

the Cité to emerge on the clifftop near the château and the upper car parks.

Le Petit Train As well as running a circular route from the Porte du Figuier (April–Sept departures every 15min; €2.50 one-way, €3.50 return; w lepetittrainderocamadour.com), Le Petit Train also offers two 30min evening tours around the Cité with a commentary (April–Sept 9.30pm & 10pm; €5).

ACCOMMODATION

One of the benefits of staying over in Rocamadour is that you can enjoy the town at its quietest in the early morning and late evening, and the **hotels** here are not too expensive. The downside is that everywhere is completely booked up in summer for miles around, and most places close during the winter months. Outside these periods, there are some good options, with a choice between central Rocamadour, the modern places in L'Hospitalet or somewhere in the surrounding countryside.

OLD TOWN

★**Grand Hôtel Beau Site** Rue de la Couronnerie t 05 65 33 63 08, w bestwestern-rocamadour.com. Chic, modern rooms with wood floors, spacious bathrooms and tasteful splashes of colour make this the top choice is town. Best of all is the setting: a lovely old mansion with its original beams, plus an annexe across the street overlooking the valley. There's also an excellent restaurant, *Jehan de Valon* (see opposite), a bistro and free parking right outside. Breakfast €14. Closed mid-Nov to mid-Feb. €84

Lion d'Or Porte du Figuier t 05 65 33 62 04. Just inside the old city gate at the east end of rue de la Couronnerie, this old-fashioned, family-run hotel is one of the cheaper options in the old quarter. Expect to get what you pay for though – the en-suite rooms are small but adequate, and wi-fi is only available in public areas. There' also a decent on-site restaurant. Closed mid-Dec to March. Breakfast €8. €50

Le Terminus des Pèlerins Place de la Carreta t 05 65 33 62 14, w terminus-des-pelerins.fr. Friendly, good-value hotel in a great location at the bottom of the Grand

Escalier. The brightly painted rooms are well-furnished and comfortable, and the best ones have terraces overlooking the valley. Their restaurant is also a safe bet, popular for its traditional and regional cuisine, with *menus* from €19. Breakfast €8. Restaurant April to mid-Nov noon–2.30pm & 7–9.30pm. €64

L'HOSPITALET AND AROUND

Amadour Place de l'Europe, L'Hospitalet t 05 65 33 73 50, w amadour-hotel.com. Sleek modern rooms with tasteful decor and a pop of colour make this a stylish choice. The best rooms have a private terrace, while the family rooms (sleeping 4–5; from €90) are spacious and great value. Breakfast €8.50. Closed mid-Oct to March. €59

Le Belvédère L'Hospitalet t 05 65 33 63 25, w hotel-le-belvedere.fr. This busy, well-located hotel looks out across the valley and it's worth paying extra for a room with a view. Doubles are roomy and comfortable, with parquet floors and floor-to-ceiling windows, plus there's a pool and an excellent restaurant with *menus* from €26.

Breakfast €8.50. Restaurant Feb–Dec daily noon–2pm & 7–9pm. €58

Le Blanat ☎ 05 65 33 68 27, ⓦ leblanat.fr. In a tiny hamlet, 4km east of Rocamadour just across the N140, this is a useful place to find in this area, as unlike most options it remains open all year (reservations are required out of season). Set in a pretty garden, it offers five simple *chambre d'hôte* rooms. The GR6 runs close by. €55

Camping Les Cigales ☎ 05 65 33 64 44, ⓦ camping -cigales.com. This well-equipped three-star campsite east of the *Amadour* (see opposite) has plenty of shady plots, plus two swimming pools, sports fields, mini golf and a restaurant. Closed Sept–May. €22

Domaine de la Rhue ☎ 05 65 33 71 50, ⓦ domainede larhue.com. This family-run *chambre d'hôte* has bags of character, with its ivy-covered facade, wood-beamed interiors and rustic furnishings. There are five rooms available, housed in a converted stable block, plus a studio flat (€600 weekly), a swimming pool and beautiful gardens. It's 6km northeast of Rocamadour, off the D840; hikers can head to town on foot (60min); otherwise it's 10min by car. €95

Le Paradis du Campeur ☎ 05 65 33 63 28, ⓦ leparadis ducampeur.com. This fairly basic two-star campsite offers ample space for campers, a heated pool and children's playground. Situated next to the *Amadour* (see opposite). Closed Sept–April. €19

Le Ryokan Mages ☎ 05 65 11 63 67, ⓦ leryokan.com. Inspired by a Japanese country inn, this chic *chambre d'hôte* occupies a converted stone barn decked out in a Japanese theme. Rooms have a homely vibe, dotted with mementos of the hosts' travels in Asia, and you'll be assured a warm welcome. It's just south of Rocamadour and signed off the D32. Closed Nov–March. €65

Le Troubadour Belveyre ☎ 05 65 33 70 27, ⓦ hotel -troubadour.com. A kilometre north of L'Hospitalet on the D673, this is a pocket of tranquillity away from the crowds of Rocamadour, offering ten rooms with comfy beds and country-style decor. The real highlight is the garden setting, complete with pool, bikes and a guests-only restaurant (*menus* €33), where you can tuck into regional delights like *cassoulet périgourdin* flavoured with herbs from the hotel garden. Breakfast €12. €70

Les Vieilles Tours Lafage ☎ 05 65 33 68 01, ⓦ vtrocamadour.com. Luxe furnishings and polished wood floors bring this beautifully restored country home bang up to date, while original beams and pigeon towers retain a touch of authenticity. There's also a pool and an excellent restaurant, with some intriguing dishes such as walnut-stuffed snails, crayfish risotto and chocolate figs; *menus* from €35. Breakfast €12; half-board obligatory July & Aug. It's located 3km west of L'Hospitalet just off the D673. Restaurant April to mid-Nov & Christmas hols daily 7.30–9.30pm. €80

4

EATING

Eating in Rocamadour is a mixed bag and there are a good few greasy fast-food joints and tourist traps. In general, the best **restaurants** are those attached to the hotels (see above), along with a few more everyday recommendations; note that most places are closed in winter. The local speciality, which you'll find on most menus, is **Rocamadour**, a round disc of goat's cheese, often served on toast or with a walnut salad, or occasionally flambéed in brandy or drizzled with honey. Elsewhere in the region it is known as *Cabécou*, but cheeses produced around Rocamadour warrant their own special *appellation* – and even their own festival (see box, p.171). You can buy it at shops selling the inevitable foie gras and other regional produce.

Au Panorama L'Hospitalet ☎ 05 65 40 67 36. The simple but tasty food at this bright, modern restaurant is a hit with both locals and in-the-know tourists. Opt for a seat on the terrace and tuck into perfectly cooked *galettes* (from €7.50), a hearty portion of steak and fries (€9.50) or a generous salad (from €9.80). April–Sept daily noon– 2pm & 7–9pm.

Les Goûts et les Couleurs Pech de Bardy ☎ 06 46 84 74 81, ⓦ goutsetcouleurs.fr. A short drive out of town, 1.5km from Rocamadour toward Pauillac, and worth seeking out on a sunny summer afternoon to cool off with a delicious ice cream or sorbet in the relaxing garden. Home-made with milk (goat and cow) from the owners' farm, there are almost forty flavours to choose from, including passionfruit, pistachio, blueberry and *spéculoos* (gingerbread biscuits), plus home-made cream and caramel sauce to top it off. May–Sept daily 11am–7pm.

★**Jehan de Valon** Rue de la Couronnerie ☎ 05 65 33 63 08. In a spectacular setting overlooking the Alzou valley, this elegant terrace restaurant is the most romantic spot in town. Impeccable service, beautifully presented dishes and a scrumptious lemon meringue *tarte* add to the effect. Splash out on the seasonal *menu* (€36) and sample delicacies like langoustines, quails' eggs and Rocamadour cheese. Mid-Feb to Nov daily 12–2pm & 7–9pm, closes 9.30pm in July & Aug.

Le Roc du Berger Bois de Belvyre ☎ 05 65 33 19 99, ⓦ rocduberger.fr. A wooden country inn, 1.5km from Rocamadour in the direction of Pauillac and situated in the middle of a truffle orchard. Traditional dishes such as *confit de canard* and lamb steaks are given extra flavour by being cooked over an open fire; *menus* €19–28. Reservation strongly advised in high season. April–Sept daily noon–2.30pm & 7.15–9pm; Oct Sat & Sun noon–2.30pm & 7.15–9pm.

Martel and around

Fifteen kilometres east of Souillac, **MARTEL**'s medieval centre is built in a pale, almost white, stone, offset by warm reddish-brown roofs. A Turenne-administered town (see p.82), its heyday was during the thirteenth and fourteenth centuries when the viscounts granted certain freedoms, including the right to mint money, and established a royal court of appeal here. The good times ceased, however, when the wars showed up: Martel was occupied briefly by English forces during the Hundred Years War and suffered again at the hands of the Huguenots in the sixteenth century.

Despite the town's rather turbulent past, on the whole the compact old centre has survived remarkably intact, with the exception of the ramparts, which have been dismantled to make way for the wide boulevard that now rings Martel's pedestrianized centre. Take any of the lanes leading inwards and you will soon find yourself in the cobbled main square, **place des Consuls**. It is mostly taken up by the eighteenth-century *halle*, scene of a busy market on Wednesday and Saturday mornings, but on every side there are reminders of the town's illustrious past: most notable is the grand Gothic **Palais de la Raymondie** on the square's east side, now occupied by the *mairie*. Begun in 1280, it served as both the Turenne law courts and fortress, hence the large square tower – one of seven that gave the town its epithet, *la ville aux sept tours*. On the square's south side is another one of the towers – a circular five-storey turret belonging to the **Maison Fabri**. According to tradition, this striking building is where Young King Henry, son of Henry II, died in 1183 (see box below).

One block south of here, rue Droite leads east to the town's main church, **St-Maur**, built in a fiercely defensive, mostly Gothic style, with a finely carved Romanesque tympanum depicting the Last Judgement above the west door.

ARRIVAL AND INFORMATION MARTEL

By train The *gare SNCF* is at St-Denis-près-Martel, 7km to the east of Martel, on the Brive La Gaillarde and Rodez lines. For taxis into town, call Mme Daubet (☎05 65 37 34 87).

Destinations Figeac (5–6 daily; 1hr); Gramat (5–6 daily; 20–30min); Rocamadour-Padirac (4–5 daily; 15–20min); Souillac (4–5 daily; 25min); Vayrac (2 daily; 5min).

By tourist train In season, a tourist train runs along a splendid stretch of decommissioned line from Martel towards St-Denis and back – but not as far as St-Denis

station – along cliffs 80m above the Dordogne (departures by diesel train: April–June & Sept Tues & Thurs 3pm; July Mon, Tues, Thurs & Fri 11am, 2.30pm & 4pm, Sat 2.30pm; Aug Sat 2.30pm; €8 return; departures by steam train: April–June & Sept Sun & hols 11am, 2.30pm & 4pm; July & Aug Mon–Fri & Sun 11am, 2.30pm & 4pm; €10.50 return; ☎05 65 37 35 81, ⌨trainduhautquercy.info). It departs from the otherwise disused station 200m south of town; reservations are recommended.

THE TALE OF YOUNG KING HENRY

At the end of the twelfth century, Martel provided the stage for one of the tragic events in the internecine conflicts of the **Plantagenet** family. When Henry Plantagenet (King Henry II of England) imprisoned his estranged wife Eleanor of Aquitaine, his sons took up arms against their father. The eldest son, also **Henry** (nicknamed the Young King since he was crowned while his father was still on the throne), even went so far as to plunder the viscountcy of Turenne and Quercy. Furious, Henry II immediately stopped his allowance and handed over his lands to the third son, Richard the Lionheart. Financially insecure, and with a considerable army to maintain, Young King Henry began **looting** the treasures of every abbey and shrine in the region. Finally, he decided to sack the shrine at Rocamadour (see p.175). This last act was to mark his downfall, for shortly afterwards he fled to Martel and fell ill with a fever. Guilt-ridden and fearing for his life, he confessed his crimes and asked his father for forgiveness. Henry II was busy besieging Limoges, but sent a messenger to convey his pardon. On the messenger's arrival in Martel, Young Henry died, leaving **Richard the Lionheart** heir to the English throne.

Tourist office Palais de la Raymondie, on place des Consuls (April–June, Sept & Oct Mon–Sat 9am–noon & 2–6pm; July & Aug daily 9am–7pm; Nov–March Mon–Fri 9am–noon & 2–5pm; ❶ 05 65 37 43 44, ❿ martel.fr); staff can provide further information about the tourist train and Martel's events.

ACCOMMODATION

Auberge des 7 Tours Av de Turenne ❶ 05 65 37 30 16, ❿ auberge7tours.com. The rooms at this *auberge* are small, but the size is compensated for by tasteful decor, modern bathrooms and a leafy terrace restaurant with great views over the town. The food is simple but tasty, with mains including veal and tuna steak, and menus from €19. Breakfast €9. Restaurant July & Aug daily 12.30–2.30pm & 7.30–9.30pm; April–June & Sept–Oct Mon–Fri 12.30–2.30pm & 7.30–9.30pm; Nov–March Mon–Fri 12.30–2.30pm. **€66**

★ **Château des Termes** ❶ 05 65 32 42 03, ❿ chateau -de-termes.com. An idyllic 7.5-acre plot high in the hills, 3km north of St-Denis-prés-Martel, allowing you to get back to nature without losing the comforts of home. There are cosy wooden cabins (€119) and ten self-contained *gîtes* (€100), all with a kitchen and lounge, plus three *chambre d'hôte* rooms with spectacular views over the valley. Kids and adventurous adults will be in their element with tennis courts, go-karts, a trampoline, zip-line swing and fishing lessons, but best of all is the communal atmosphere – bring-your-own barbecues and shared lounges mean you can mingle with other travellers, plus the hosts are exceedingly friendly and you can even help yourself to fresh eggs from the chicken pen. Breakfast (€8.50) and daily bread delivery available on request. **€82**

★ **Relais Ste-Anne** Rue du Pourtanel ❶ 05 65 37 40 56, ❿ relais-sainte-anne.com. This gorgeous hotel occupies a former girls' boarding school and is set in immaculate gardens with its own chapel, pool and beautifully appointed rooms. There is an excellent restaurant (lunch and dinner by reservation only) where chef Rimet-Mignon whips up delectable dishes like shrimp with orange marmalade or lobster with foie gras ravioli. *Menus* from €30. Breakfast €13. Hotel closed mid-Nov to mid-March. **€95**

EATING AND DRINKING

Au Hazard Balthazar Rue Tournemire ❶ 05 65 37 42 01, ❿ lesbouriettes.com. Tuck into wholesome home-made dishes like lamb stew or *magret de canard* in rustic surroundings, then pick up local products like foie gras, truffle oil and fruit chutney in the shop downstairs. *Menus* from €18.90. Tues–Thurs & Sat noon–1.45pm & 7–9pm, Fri 7–9pm, Sun noon–1.45pm.

Ferme Auberge Moulin à Huile de Noix ❶ 05 65 37 40 69, ❿ moulin-martel.com. Some 3km east of Martel, off the D703 to St-Denis and Bretenoux, this family-run restaurant oozes character. It's attached to a working walnut-oil mill (demonstrations on Mon and Thurs afternoons in July and Aug), and you can expect authentic home-cooked cuisine made with fresh seasonal ingredients. *Menus* from €21; reservations essential. April–Nov Tues–Sun 12.30–2pm & 7.30–9pm.

★ **Le Petit Moulin** Rue Droite ❶ 06 59 59 27 66, ❿ lepetitmoulinmartel.com. This chic little restaurant in the heart of Martel is beloved by locals and tourists alike, and for good reason. Expect fresh, seasonal dishes with a personal touch and highlights including home-made foie gras, local specialty Quercy lamb and indulgent millefeuille. There's also a great kid's *menu* (€11.50), vegetarian options and an excellent regional wine list. *Menu* €26.50. Mon–Sat 9am–midnight, Sun 9am–11pm.

Plein Sud Place des Consuls ❶ 05 65 37 37 77. This humble locals' haunt is well situated in the centre of town and offers a surprisingly wide menu, including a good selection of pizzas from €10, some regional dishes and a choice of salads (from €12.50). April–Sept Tues–Sun noon–2.30pm & 7–9.30pm.

★ **Le Pourquoi Pas?** Le Barry ❶ 05 65 32 46 79, ❿ lepourquoipas.fr. Tucked away in the pretty village of Floirac, 4km south of St-Denis-près-Martel, *Le Pourquoi Pas?* might have only one thing on the menu – crêpes – but the choice is remarkable. Opt for a savoury crêpe with cheese, smoked salmon or ratatouille (from €5.50); indulge your sweet tooth with fillings like nutella, caramel or coconut (from €3); or go all-out with a Cointreau-doused crêpe *flambée*. There's a sunny garden terrace open in summer, plus a range of Belgian beers on tap (from €4). July & Aug daily noon–2pm & 7–9pm; Sept–June Wed–Fri noon–2pm & 7–9pm, Sat 7–9pm.

Meyronne

Roughly 10km south of Martel as the crow flies, the sleepy hilltop village of **MEYRONNE** is certainly worth a lunchtime stop. In the eleventh century the bishops of Tulle, northeast of Brive, built a château here to defend what was then an important bridging point over the River Dordogne. The château has since been transformed into a hotel-restaurant (see p.184), but its brooding facade still presides over the town, affording spectacular views along the valley from its terrace.

ACCOMMODATION AND EATING — MEYRONNE

★**La Terrasse** Place de l'Église ☎ 05 65 32 21 60, ⓦ hotel-la-terrasse.com. Housed in the town's château, *La Terrasse* is charmingly eclectic, with its sloping ceilings, oak beams and spiral stairwell jazzed up with colourful bed linen and mismatched furniture. The creative flair extends to the restaurant, which has *menus* from €29 and great views from the terrace. Breakfast €13. Restaurant mid-March to Oct Mon, Tues & Thurs–Sun 12.15–1.15pm & 7.15–9pm, Wed 7.15–9pm. €95

★**Le Virage** Rue de la Poutine, Montvalent ☎ 05 65 37 47 53. This aptly named restaurant, 6km east of Meyronne, offers magnificent views over the valley from its breezy terrace. Head here in the evening when you can watch the sunset while listening to live music and dining on delicious, well-priced cuisine. Expect classic French dishes like *confit de canard* or chocolate fondant cake, prepared to perfection. Mains from €8.50. June–Sept daily noon–2pm & 7–10pm.

Creysse

CREYSSE, some 3km northeast of Meyronne, is an idyllic hamlet – with a dinky market hall and fast-running stream – that sits in the lee of a knuckle of rock, where a fortified gate and scraps of wall are all that remain of a château once owned by the viscounts of Turenne (see p.82). Their twelfth-century **chapel**, standing immediately above the village, has fared rather better (ask for the key at the *mairie*), and is worth a look for its *pisé* floor and unique arrangement of two apsidal chapels.

ACTIVITIES — CREYSSE

Bike and canoe rental On the riverside by the bridge, Port Loisirs (☎ 05 65 32 27 59, ⓦ portloisirs.com), offers canoes (from €8/hr, children €6/hr) and mountain bikes (from €12 per half-day).

ACCOMMODATION AND EATING

Auberge de L'Île ☎ 05 65 32 22 01, ⓦ auberge-de-lile .com. With its stone-and-brick facade, gabled windows and leafy riverside plot on the main street, just east of the canal, it's hard to resist this charming country hotel. Inside, rooms are simple but surprisingly modern with wood floors and sparkling bathrooms. There's also a decent restaurant which serves tasty dishes such as Quercy casserole and *tartiflette de Rocamadour*, and plenty of seating on the tree-shaded terrace (*menus* from €14). Breakfast €11. Restaurant mid-March to Nov daily 12.15–1.30pm & 7.30–8.30pm. €75

Camping du Port ☎ 05 65 32 20 82, ⓦ campingduport .com. Excellent three-star campsite by the Dordogne River, 100m east of Creysse. A good spot for kids, with a riverside beach, pool, small restaurant and a range of five person cabins for rent by the week (from €525). Closed Sept–June. €18

Gluges

The cliffs lining the Dordogne valley are more dramatic upstream from Creysse. For the most impressive scenery, follow the D23 northeast for a good 2km and then branch off right along the D43. The road quickly narrows down to a single track – with passing spaces – cut into the rock. You emerge 2km later at another huddle of houses, **GLUGES**, whose prime attraction is its location under the cliffs and its views south to the **Cirque de Montvalent**. Here, the meandering river has carved a great semicircle out of the cliffs; for a sweeping panorama, climb up to the hilltop **Belvédère de Copeyre**, signed off the main road 1km above Gluges to the east. In the lee of the great cliff you can still see the ruined troglodyte chapel of **Saint-Pierre-ès-Liens**, founded by Gaillard Mirandol on his return from the First Crusade in 1095. It was eventually superseded by the little village **church**, which is worth a quick peek on its own account, as there's a fascinating tale attached to it (see box opposite).

ACTIVITIES — GLUGES

Bike and canoe rental Copeyre Canoë (☎ 05 65 32 72 61, ⓦ copeyre.com), down by the *Les Falaises* campsite (see below).

ACCOMMODATION

Les Falaises ☎ 05 65 37 37 78, ⓦ camping-lesfalaises .com. This two-star campsite is simple but well kept, with a leafy riverside location opposite the village and canoe rental. Closed mid-Sept to mid-June. €15

LA MÔME PIAF AND THE ÉGLISE DE GLUGES

Édith Giovanna Gassion was one of the most enigmatic figures of twentieth-century France. Born in 1916 in the backstreets of Paris, she rose to fame and became a cultural icon. She was nicknamed "La Môme Piaf", a colloquialism meaning "the little sparrow" in reference to her diminutive size – she was 142cm tall – by nightclub owner Louis Leplée, who first discovered her in the Pigalle area of Paris in 1935. Despite her subsequent success, Piaf led a troubled and turbulent life, gradually becoming more and more reclusive. She liked to escape whenever possible to the peaceful atmosphere of the Dordogne valley, and the tiny troglodyte village of Gluges became one of her favourite spots; she would come here to wander the lanes and pray in the little **Église de Gluges**. One evening as the *curé*, Monsieur Delbos, was locking the doors he turned to find Piaf standing behind him. He told her that he would soon have to close the church permanently, as the repair bills were more than the congregation could afford – the two stained-glass windows particularly were badly damaged and no longer safe. Piaf offered to fund the replacement windows on condition that the donation would remain anonymous until after her death. The windows were duly replaced and the *curé* kept his promise. In 1963, after Piaf's untimely death at the age of 47, he finally revealed her secret to his congregation. A special Mass was held for her, and the tiny square in front of the church was renamed **place Edith Piaf** in her honour.

Carennac and around

CARENNAC is without doubt one of the most beautiful villages along this part of the Dordogne valley. It sits on a terrace above the river's south bank 16km or so east of Martel; backtrack to Gluges and then head upstream on the D43 for the prettiest route in – as you approach from the west, you'll get one of the best views of Carennac's towers and higgledy-piggledy russet-tiled roofs. Carennac is best known for its typical Quercy architecture and the richly carved tympanum of its Romanesque priory church, the **Église St-Pierre**. Founded in the eleventh century by Benedictine monks, the priory grew rich from pilgrims en route to Santiago de Compostela. Sacked during the Hundred Years War (see p.293), it then enjoyed a second renaissance in the late fifteenth and sixteenth centuries, when the church was restored and the **Chateâu des Doyens** was built alongside it. But by the 1700s, the rot had set in as the monks became lazy and corrupt, and the priory was finally closed after the Revolution.

Église St-Pierre

Daily: May–Sept 9am–noon & 2–7pm; Oct–April 10am–noon & 2–5pm • Free

Tucked in behind the **Château des Doyens**, the **Église St-Pierre** is set in a small cobbled courtyard, with houses clustered so tightly round the priory buildings that it's hard to tell them apart: follow the road along the riverbank and you'll soon find the gateway. Straight ahead of you, the church's twelfth-century tympanum – in the style of Moissac and Cahors – dominates its recessed west door, with its carvings in exceptionally good condition.

South of the church, still inside the courtyard, you can gain access to the **cloister and chapter house**. The cloister's Romanesque and flamboyant Gothic galleries were somewhat mutilated during the Revolution, but they are in any case overshadowed by the late-fifteenth-century, life-size *Mise au Tombeau* ("*Entombment of Christ*") on display in the chapterhouse. So supremely detailed is the sculpture that you can even see the veins in Christ's hands and legs. Joseph of Arimathea and Nicodemus, holding either end of the shroud, are richly attired as a fifteenth-century nobleman and pilgrim respectively, while behind them Mary Magdalene, her hair a mass of ringlets, ostentatiously wipes away a tear.

4

Château des Doyens and the Espace Patrimoine

May, June & Sept Mon–Fri 10am–noon & 2–6pm, Sat & Sun 2–6pm; July & Aug Mon–Fri 10am–noon & 2–7pm, Sat & Sun 2–7pm; Oct–Nov Mon–Fri 10am–noon & 2–6pm • Free • ☎ 05 65 33 81 36, ⓦ pays-vallee-dordogne.com

In the sixteenth century the *doyens* (deans) in charge of Carennac's priory and its dependent churches built themselves a grand residence abutting the church's north wall, referred to nowadays as the **Château des Doyens**. A few stone chimneypieces and the great hall's painted ceiling remain from this era, but little else, since the building has been partially modernized to serve as an **Espace Patrimoine**. Displays cover the geography, history, architecture and economy of the Dordogne valley from Bretenoux downstream to Souillac, and provide a good overview of what the region has to offer. Staff here also organize a broad range of guided visits (to Carennac, Martel and Souillac, for example, some in English) and workshops based on the art and history of the Dordogne valley; call or visit the website for further information.

ARRIVAL AND INFORMATION

CARENNAC

By train Carennac's nearest *gare SNCF* is at Vayrac, 8km northwest on the other side of the river, on the Brive–Aurillac line; note that there are no ticket sales at this station, but you can buy tickets from the conductor on board the train. Call ☎ 05 65 32 40 32 if you need a taxi. Services are more frequent to St-Denisprès-Martel, 10km to the west (see p.182), on the Brive–Figeac line.

Tourist office In the priory courtyard (April–June & Sept–Oct Mon–Sat 10am–12.30pm & 2–6pm, Sun 2–6pm; July & Aug Mon–Sat 10am–12.30pm & 2–7pm, Sun 2–7pm; ☎ 05 65 10 97 01, ⓦ tourisme-vallee -dordogne.com).

Canoe rental You can rent canoes from Saga Team (June–Oct; ☎ 05 65 10 97 39, ⓦ dordogne-soleil.com) at the *L'Eau Vive* campsite (see below).

ACCOMMODATION AND EATING

L'Eau Vive ☎ 05 65 10 97 39, ⓦ camping-lot-eauvive .com. Kid-friendly campsite 1km east of Carennac with shady plots, a swimming pool, mini golf and a snack bar. Wi-fi available at reception. Closed Nov–April. **€22**

Hostellerie Fénelon Le Bourg ☎ 05 65 10 96 46, ⓦ hotel-fenelon.com. Carennac's only hotel is efficiently run, with clean, comfortable standard rooms (plus cheaper ones with bath only for those on a budget) as well as a pool. There's also a decent restaurant serving up regional cuisine (*menus* from €19). Breakfast €10. Restaurant May–Sept daily noon–2pm & 7–9.30pm. **€71**

La Petite Vigne Le Bourg ☎ 05 65 50 25 84, ⓦ lapetitevigne-carennac.com. A cosy, English-style *chambre d'hôte* run by a British couple, this is a home away from home. The three rooms are spotless, airy and modern, plus there's a flower-filled terrace and a guest lounge. Book ahead and be sure to stick around for the delicious lunch (guests only, *menus* from €13.50). Closed Oct–March. **€65**

Relais de Gintrac Gintrac ☎ 05 65 38 49 41, ⓦ lerelais degintrac.com. A very popular, if isolated place – about 3km from Carennac southeast along the D30 – offering wholesome country cooking washed down with well-priced wines. Lunchtime *formules* from €10; evening *menus* from €20. Wed–Sun noon–1.45pm & 7–9pm.

Gouffre de Padirac

1hr 30min guided tours daily: April–June 9.30am–5pm; July 9.30am–6pm; Aug 8.30am–6.30pm; Sept & Oct 10am–5pm • €12, children €8.50, under 4s free • ☎ 05 65 33 64 56, ⓦ gouffre-de-padirac.com • The nearest *gare SNCF* is Rocamadour-Padirac, more than 10km to the west, from where you could take a taxi (☎ 05 65 33 63 10)

Local legend holds the Devil responsible for opening the gaping mouth of the **Gouffre de Padirac** in the middle of the limestone plateau 10km south of Carennac. The hole is over 30m wide and 75m deep, its sides festooned with dripping ferns and creepers, though the sense of mystery is somewhat diminished these days by the presence of a lift-cage built against the side. Rather than the Devil, the chasm was probably formed by a cave roof collapsing centuries ago; locals took refuge here during the Hundred Years War and probably long before. The cave system was not properly explored, however, until 1889 when spectacular **stalactites** – the biggest a staggering 75m tall – and lakes were discovered. Even today teams are still exploring the caves and passages.

The visit starts with a **boat trip** along an underground river, after which you walk on past barrages and massive cascades formed by calcite deposits over the millennia.

The lakes are pretty, but the most notable feature here is the sheer scale of the formations and the height of the passages carved out of the rock, reaching nearly 100m at their highest. Be warned, though: it is very, very touristy and it's best to pre-book your tickets if you plan to visit in peak periods – otherwise, expect a long wait. In wet weather you'll need a waterproof jacket.

ACCOMMODATION AND EATING   GOUFFRE DE PADIRAC

Giscard Le Bourg ☎ 05 65 11 68 62, ⓦ hotel-giscard .com. About 2km back from the Gouffre de Padirac towards Rocamadour, in the medieval village of Thegra, this simple but friendly little hotel-restaurant has a cool terrace, a pool and basic but spotless rooms. The restaurant is a good place to try classic French delicacies like frogs' legs and snails, plus some less intimidating options such as salmon or duck. *Menus* from €13 at lunch and €16.50 in the evening; dinner is by reservation only. Breakfast €5.50. Restaurant May–Sept daily noon– 2pm & 7–9pm; Oct–April Mon–Fri & Sun noon–2pm & 7–9pm. **€50**

Bretenoux and around

Some 10km east of Carennac, the *bastide* town of **BRETENOUX**, founded in 1277 by the barons of Castelnau, sits on the south bank of the River Cère just upstream from where it joins the Dordogne. It was obviously a pretty little place at one time – the cobbled and arcaded **place des Consuls** behind the tourist office is a delight, especially on **market** days (Tues & Sat mornings) – but these days the town suffers from a busy main road and modern development. With its good transport connections, however, Bretenoux is a useful staging post for the nearby towns of St-Céré and Beaulieu-sur-Dordogne (see p.191 & p.188). East of here, the journey to Aurillac takes you through a very picturesque and otherwise inaccessible landscape, popular with walkers and cyclists.

ARRIVAL AND INFORMATION   BRETENOUX

By train Bretenoux's *gare SNCF*, on the Brive–Aurillac line, is officially known as Bretenoux-Biars since it is located some 2km north of the River Cère in the town of Biars. Taxis wait outside the station, or call ahead (☎ 05 65 10 90 90). Destinations Aurillac (3–4 daily; 45min–1hr); Brive (3–4 daily; 45min–1hr); St-Denis-près-Martel (3–4 daily; 20min). **Tourist office** Avenue de la Libération, just south of the bridge (July & Aug Mon–Sat 9.30am–7pm, Sun 10am–1pm; April–June & Sept–Oct Mon–Sat 10am–noon & 2–6pm; ☎ 05 65 38 59 53, ⓦ tourisme-vallee-dordogne .com).
Bike rental Cycles Bladier on avenue de la Libération (☎ 05 65 38 41 56).
Canoe rental Available in July and Aug at the *Bourgnatelle* campsite (see below), down by the river at Bretenoux (☎ 05 65 10 89 04).

ACCOMMODATION AND EATING

There are no **hotels** in Bretenoux itself, but there are a few options in the countryside around the village, as well as in Port-de-Gagnac, 6km northeast on the D14 on the north bank of the Cère.

BRETENOUX

La Bourgnatelle ☎ 05 65 10 89 04, ⓦ dordogne -vacances.fr/camping-la-bourgnatelle. A great spot for families, this grassy three-star campsite is located on an island just north of Bretenoux and has a pool, table tennis and various organized activities, as well as cabins for rent (from €230 weekly). Closed mid-Oct–April. Camping **€19.70**

★ **Domaine de Granval** ☎ 05 65 11 24 55, ⓦ domaine degranval.com. A charming *chambre d'hôte*, 2km south of Bretenoux on the D803, with five lovely rooms all at ground level. There's a pool, and breakfast is served on the terrace (evening meals available for €25); but it's the typical French hospitality and quiet country atmosphere that makes it a winner. Closed mid-Oct to April. **€80**
Les Saveurs Place des Consuls ☎ 05 65 39 72 39. A lively suntrap on the main square, *Les Saveurs* serves a steady stream of locals; its popularity is well deserved, with good-value *menus* from €18. March–Oct Mon–Thurs 12.30– 2pm, Fri & Sat 7.30–9.30pm.

PORT-DE-GAGNAC

Auberge du Vieux Port ☎ 05 65 38 50 05, ⓦ auberge -vieuxport-lot.com. Cosy *auberge* right on the waterfront with spotless rooms, modern bathrooms and welcoming, English-speaking staff. The restaurant serves great-value regional cuisine like pan-fried lamb sweetbreads and Quercy-style *flambée; menus* from €16, breakfast €9. Restaurant Tues–Sun 12.30–2pm & 7.30–9.30pm. **€65**

★**Hostellerie Belle Rive** ☎05 65 38 50 04, ⓦ bellerive-dordogne-lot.com. The twelve individually decorated rooms at riverside *Hostellerie Belle Rive* are

bright, sunny and full of personal touches. Stick around for dinner – the chef is a local celebrity and the focus is on fresh local ingredients. *Menus* from €25, breakfast €10. Restaurant Easter to mid-Oct daily 12.20–1.45pm & 7.30–9pm; mid-Oct to Easter Mon & Sun 12.20–1.45pm. **€80**

Château de Castelnau

April & Sept daily 10am–12.30pm & 2–5.30pm; May & June daily 10am–12.30pm & 2–6.30pm; July & Aug daily 10am–7pm; Oct–March Mon & Wed–Sun 10am–12.30pm & 2–5.30pm • €7.50, under 18s free (guided tour included in entry price) • ☎ 05 65 33 20 37, ⓦ castelnau-bretenoux.monuments-nationaux.fr

Bretenoux lies within striking distance of the **Château de Castelnau**, 2.5km to the southwest – one of this region's most outstanding examples of medieval military architecture. The great fortress dominates an abrupt knoll to the east of the village, its sturdy towers and machicolated red-brown walls visible for miles around. It dates from the mid-tenth century, but took on its present form – a triangular fort with a massive square keep and three round towers, the whole lot surrounded by ramparts and dry moats – during the Hundred Years War under the ownership of the powerful barons of Castelnau. By the early eighteenth century, however, the Castelnau family had died out. Their abandoned château was sacked during the Revolution, sustained even greater damage in a fire in 1851 and was left to rot until it was salvaged, somewhat bizarrely, in 1896 by a celebrated tenor of the Parisian Comic Opera, **Jean Mouliérat**. He threw his fortune into its restoration and into amassing the valuable but rather dry collection of religious art and furniture from the fifteenth to eighteenth centuries, which populates the handful of rooms you see on the guided tour. The **views** from the ramparts, though, are extremely impressive; on a clear day you can just make out the towers of Turenne, nearly 30km to the north (see p.82).

As you exit the castle's inner enclosure, turn left along the walls to take a quick look in the **Collégiale St-Louis**. Built of the same red stone and with powerful buttresses, this little Gothic church contains a fine fifteenth-century polychrome statue of the Baptism of Christ – note the startled expression of the angel holding his clothes – and a macabre treasure in the form of a bone from the arm of St Louis (alias King Louis IX of France). In 1970 the relic was taken to St Louis in America to commemorate the founding of the city.

Beaulieu-sur-Dordogne and around

At Bretenoux the River Dordogne turns northwards to Biars; the valley here is wide and industrial, with factories such as Andros churning out sufficient quantities to make this the "jam capital" of Europe. Aspects improve 8km north of Biars at **BEAULIEU-SUR-DORDOGNE**, beautifully situated on a wide bend in the river. It's a perfectly proportioned town, with an **abbey church** that boasts another of the great masterpieces of Romanesque sculpture, and yet is refreshingly untouristy.

Arriving from Bretenoux, the main road skirts south of Beaulieu's compact and semi-pedestrianized core of old streets. On its way it passes through a large square, **place Marbot**, which represents the town's modern centre, off which rue de la République leads north to **place du Marché** and the **Église St-Pierre**. It won't take long to cover the rest of Beaulieu, but it's worth devoting half an hour or so to wandering its maze of lanes. In particular, there are a number of half-timbered houses along **rue Ste-Catherine**, running east from place du Marché, while if you head northwest along rue de la République and rue de la Chapelle you'll pass some handsome sculpted facades before

emerging beside the **Chapelle des Pénitents** in an attractive spot on the riverbank. This twelfth-century chapel now makes a splendid venue for the occasional art exhibition or concert; if it's open, it's worth popping in to see the collection of religious art.

Église St-Pierre

Place du Marché • Daily 9am–noon & 3–6pm

Place du Marché boasts some nicely faded stone and half-timbered buildings, along with the twelfth-century **Église St-Pierre**, a surprisingly large abbey church whose architecture reflects its position on the border between Limousin and Languedoc. The pairs of rounded arches piercing the belfry, for example, are typical Limousin styling, while the subject matter and style of carving on the magnificent **south portal** belongs firmly to the south. The **tympanum** is presided over by an oriental-looking Christ with one arm extended to welcome the chosen on the Judgement Day. Around him a mass of angels and apostles, even the dead rising from their graves below, seem ready to burst with vitality.

ARRIVAL AND INFORMATION   BEAULIEU-SUR-DORDOGNE

By train It's just over 6km from Beaulieu-sur-Dordogne to the Bretenoux-Biars *gare SNCF* (see p.187). Unfortunately there are no connecting buses, but you could call a taxi to get into Beaulieu (☏ 05 55 91 02 83).

Tourist office On the south side of place Marbot (April–June & Sept–Oct Mon–Sat 10am–12.30pm & 2–6pm;

July & Aug daily 10am–12.30pm & 2–7pm; ☏ 05 55 91 09 94, ⓦ tourisme-vallee-dordogne.com).

Boat trips From May to October traditional wooden *gabares* depart from the riverbank near the Chapelle des Pénitents for a 1hr jaunt upstream (adults from €7.50, children under 11 €6); contact the tourist office (see above) to book.

ACCOMMODATION

★**Auberge de Jeunesse** Rue de la Chapelle ☏ 05 55 91 13 82. Welcoming hostel set in a striking half-timbered and turreted building, with surprisingly modern dorms inside and a well-equipped kitchen. Meals are available on request for groups of ten or more. Breakfast €5.50. Closed mid-Oct to Easter. Dorms **€15.50**

Camping des Iles ☏ 05 55 91 02 65, ⓦ campingdesiles .com. Leafy riverside campsite, on the island to the north of the town's main road-bridge, with plenty to keep the kids entertained, including a pool, splash-pool, playground, ping-pong and kayaks for hire. Closed mid-Sept to mid-April. **€26**

★**Les Charmilles** 20 bd St Rodolphe de Turenne ☏ 05 55 91 29 29, ⓦ auberge-charmilles.com. Country-chic decor, comfy beds and welcoming staff will have you feeling at home as soon as you step through the door of *Les Charmilles*. Each of the eight rooms – named after regional varieties of strawberry – has it's own unique style, while the riverfront terrace restaurant focuses on fresh, seasonal produce. *Menus* change daily and start from €21; breakfast is €9. Restaurant Wed–Sun noon–2pm & 7–9pm. **€74**

Les Flots Bleus Place du Monturu ☏ 05 55 91 06 21,

ⓦ hotel-flotsbleus.com. This friendly riverside hotel offers generously sized rooms in a tranquil location, but the real highlight is the waterfront restaurant (see opposite). Opt for a room with a view over the Dordogne. Breakfast €10. Closed mid-Nov to March. **€74**

Relais de Vellinus Place du Champ-de-Mars ☏ 05 55 91 11 04, ⓦ vellinus.com. Let down by its rather uninspiring facade, this friendly hotel is nonetheless comfortable, well-furnished and spotless, and it's the top pick for those on a budget. The in-house restaurant is excellent, serving elegantly presented dishes and mouth-watering desserts. *Menus* start at €15, breakfast €10. Restaurant daily March–Sept noon–2pm & 7–9pm. **€50**

★**Le Turenne** 1 bd St Rodolphe de Turenne ☏ 05 55 91 94 72, ⓦ leturenne.com. With its bold colour palette and innovative decor, *Le Turenne* is the kind of hotel that puts a smile on your face. The smart and stylish rooms are jazzed up with giant Buddhas, faux-fur bed runners and embossed wallpaper, while the staff go out of their way to make you welcome. There's also a recently opened restaurant serving delicious gourmet cuisine (*menus* from €22.50, breakfast €10). Restaurant daily noon–2pm & 7–9pm. **€85**

EATING AND DRINKING

★**Café Douceur** 34 rue du Général-de-Gaulle ☏ 05 55 28 67 05. Across the road from *Chez Collette*, this delightful café serves a wide choice of teas and coffees as well as innovative lunchtime platters (€9–13) such as *pissaladière* tart

with onions, thyme, tomatoes and olives, to eat in or take away, and some great vegetarian options. The atmosphere is pleasant and relaxed, with armchairs for lounging in. Mon, Tues, Thurs, Fri & Sun 9am–6pm, Wed 9am–2pm.

Chez Collette 27 rue du Général-de-Gaulle ☎ 05 55 28 22 71. Red-and-white checked tablecloths, cutesy knick-knacks and smiley staff ensure a warm welcome at this homely café. There's a small and often-changing menu, with excellent salads, and everything is home-made. *Menus* from €19. Tues–Sat noon–2pm & 7–9pm, Sun noon–2pm.

Les Flots Bleus Place du Monturu ☎ 05 55 91 06 21, ⓦ hotel-flotsbleus.com. The most romantic restaurant in town, with a perfect riverside setting and a summer terrace that faces Beaulieu's Chapelle des Pénitents. The cuisine is just as impressive, with creative use of seasonal ingredients

and beautifully presented dishes that will have you reaching for your camera. *Menus* from €32. Reservations advised in high season. March–June & Sept to mid-Nov Tues–Sun 12.15–2pm; July & Aug Mon 7–8.30pm, Tues–Sun 12.15–2pm & 7–8.30pm.

Velouté Place de la Bridolle ☎ 05 55 91 14 51. A worthy alternative to the hotel restaurants, this Scottish-run restaurant serves up classic French cuisine according to the seasons. It's well-priced too, with three-course *menus* from €17.50. March–July & Sept to mid-Dec Wed–Fri noon–2.30pm & 7–10pm, Sat noon–2.30pm; Aug Mon–Sat noon–2.30pm & 7–10pm, Sun noon–2.30pm.

Argentat

Upstream from Beaulieu, the Dordogne valley becomes wilder as you enter the first forest-covered foothills of the Massif Central. It makes for a lovely drive along the D12 as far as **Argentat**, the last town of any size on the river, where it's easy to while away an hour or so sitting at one of the waterside cafés. Beyond Argentat, however, the Dordogne changes character entirely, due to a series of hydroelectric dams that turn the river into a succession of huge reservoirs.

St-Céré and around

About 9km south of Bretenoux on the River Bave, a minor tributary of the Dordogne, you come to the medieval town of **St-Céré**, dominated by the brooding ruins of the **Château de St-Laurent-les-Tours**, whose powerful twin keeps are the first things you see when arriving in the town from the north. Once part of a fortress belonging to the viscounts of Turenne (see p.82), the château is now home to an engaging museum dedicated to local tapestry designer Jean Lurçat, who revitalized contemporary French tapestry. However, St-Céré's prime attraction is its old centre, peppered with picturesque half-timbered houses. The town sits in the valley to the southwest where the old houses cluster round place du Mercadial and place de l'Église. These two squares lie north and south respectively of rue de la République, the main shopping street cutting through the old centre which, at its southeast end, comes out into **place de la République**, a big, open square where you'll find car parks, cafés and the town's main tourist facilities, as well as its Sunday-morning **market**; a much larger market spreads throughout the old town on the first and third Wednesdays of the month.

St-Céré makes a useful base for exploring the surrounding area. The town lies on the border between the empty but glorious wooded hills of the Ségala to the east and south, and the dry limestone *causse* to the west. However, the region's most impressive sight, and one not to be missed, is the Renaissance **Château de Montal**, 2km west of St-Céré, with its sculpted facade and grand staircase. From here you can loop south via the **Grottes de Presque** – a limestone cave with a tremendous variety of unusually colourful concretions – to arrive at the lip of the Cirque d'Autoire for dramatic views over the russet-red roofs of **Autoire** village, which provide a splash of colour in the valley far below. On the way back to St-Céré the route passes through another captivating little village, **Loubressac**, which can hardly have changed for centuries.

Brief history

St-Céré owes its existence to the martyrdom of **Ste Spérie** in 780. Born the daughter of the then lord of St-Laurent, Sérenus, Spérie pledged her life to God at an early age, and when later she refused to marry a local nobleman, she was beheaded by her brother and buried on the riverbank. Later a chapel was erected on the spot around which the town began to develop in the tenth century. It lay initially under the jurisdiction of the counts of Auvergne, but was transferred to the Turenne viscounts in 1178. They beefed up the fortress and, as usual, granted the town a certain degree of autonomy. Its heyday didn't arrive, however, until after the fifteenth century when St-Céré's wealthy **merchants** began investing in the noble houses that can still be seen around the town today.

Place du Mercadial and around

The best of St-Céré's fifteenth-century townhouses lie in the streets to the north of rue de la République, notably around **place du Mercadial**, which is particularly appealing; to find it, walk one block north from rue de la République and turn left along rue du Mazel. You come out opposite the town's most eye-catching building, the **Maison des Consuls**, where the administrative council used to meet – it now hosts various free art exhibitions in summer. Beneath the pitched tile roof, the building's most striking feature is the slightly overhanging upper storey of neatly layered brick in a timber frame. The same design is echoed in the **Maison Arnoud**, on the north side of the square, whose ground floor is a mere 3m wide. **Rue St-Cyr**, the lane to the right of this house, takes you east and then south past several elegant Renaissance buildings and into a recently renovated area of courtyards and alleys.

Église Sainte-Spérie

12 rue Paramelle • Daily 9am–6.30pm • ☎ 05 65 38 15 04

There's not much of interest on the south side of rue de la République, though the **Église Sainte-Spérie**, largely rebuilt after the Wars of Religion, is worth a quick peek for its eighteenth-century altarpiece with a statue of Ste Spérie standing on the left. It was carved by a local monk who received 240 *livres* and, for some reason, four handkerchiefs for his pains.

Atelier-Musée Jean Lurçat

Mid-April to Sept Tues–Sun 10.30am–12.30pm & 2.30pm–6.30pm • €4 • ☎ 05 65 38 28 21, ⊛ musees.lot.fr • 1km or so above St-Céré – take avenue du Docteur Roux heading northeast past the hospital and then follow the signs winding uphill

Only the ramparts and two square towers of the **Château de St-Laurent-les-Tours** remain, the smaller one dating from the late twelfth century and the taller, eastern tower from the 1300s. The rest of the castle was destroyed during the Wars of Religion, but around 1895 the then-owner built himself a Neo-Gothic mansion between the two towers. It is this building in which Jean Lurçat (1892–1966) set up his studio in 1945 and which is now the **Atelier-Musée Jean Lurçat**. Locally born Lurçat is best known for his big, bold tapestries, of which the most famous is the eighty-metre-long *Chant du Monde* ("*Song of the World*"), now on display in Angers, but you can get an idea of his distinctive style – typically incorporating animals and birds, both real and fantastic, against dark blue or black backgrounds – in the Atelier. Alongside his sketches and illustrations, a slideshow of the *Chant du Monde* and a short biographical film, the museum's highlight is the artist's unmistakable paintings, which cover the ceilings and doors.

ARRIVAL AND INFORMATION
ST-CÉRÉ

By train The nearest *gare SNCF* to St-Céré is Bretenoux-Biars (see p.187), a good 10km to the north, from where there are buses on two days a week (Wed & Sat; Delbos ☎ 05 65 38 24 19) on to St-Céré.

Tourist office On the north side of place de la République

(daily: July & Aug 9am–noon & 2–7pm; Sept–June 10am–noon & 2–5.30pm; ☎ 05 65 38 11 85, ⊛ tourisme-vallee-dordogne.com).

Bike rental Cycles St-Chamant, 45 rue Faidherbe (☎ 05 65 38 03 23), to the west of place de la République.

ACCOMMODATION

De France 139 av François-de-Maynard ☎05 65 38 02 16, ⓦlefrance-hotel.com. Light, airy rooms, spacious balconies and a pool make this a great choice, plus there's a restaurant where you can sample regional specialties like *moutarde violette* (a purple mustard made with sweet grapes) truffles and Rocamadour cheese. *Menus* from €28.50, breakfast €10. Restaurant Mon–Thurs & Sat–Sun 12.30–2pm & 7.30–9.30pm. €65

Le Soulhol Quai Salesses ☎05 65 38 12 37, ⓦcamping -le-soulhol.e-monsite.com. Three-star campsite, beside the river and a short walk east of the *Victor-Hugo*, offering a heated pool, BBQ area, bike rental and free wi-fi throughout the site. Closed Oct–March. €18.10

Les Trois Soleils de Montal Les Prés de Montal ☎05 65 10 16 16, ⓦ3soleils.fr. The Michelin-starred restaurant (see below) is the undisputed star here, but *Les Trois Soleils* is also St-Céré's most elegant hotel. Expect timeless luxury with well-furnished rooms, garden views and a wonderfully romantic terrace. Breakfast €13. Closed Nov–Feb. €115

★**Victor-Hugo** 7 av des Maquis ☎05 65 38 16 15, ⓦhotel-victor-hugo.fr. Behind the quintessentially French facade, with its traditional wooden shutters and flowery terrace overlooking the river, *Victor Hugo* is all modern, with sunny, spacious rooms. Add to that an excellent restaurant (which serves a perfect steak), welcoming staff and a convenient location, just minutes from place de la République, and it's the best deal in town. *Menus* from €18.90, breakfast €9. Private covered parking €10. Restaurant daily noon–2.30pm & 7–9.30pm. €70

EATING

In addition to the *Trois Soleils* (see below), the best places to eat in St-Céré are the **restaurants** at the *De France* (see above) and *Victor-Hugo* hotels (see above). Otherwise, try the cafés and brasseries around place de la République and place du Mercadial.

L'Instant T 3 place du Mercadial ☎05 65 10 66 82. This charming café serves delicious quiches, salads and *tartines* on its covered terrace and courtyard, with lunchtime *menus* starting from €12. In the afternoons from May to Sept it turns into a cosy tearoom. Mon–Sat noon–2pm & 7–9.30pm.

Pizzeria du Mercadial 4 place du Mercadial ☎05 65 38 35 77. Tasty food and generous portions are the order of the day at this rustic pizzeria, and the terrace seating is ideal for people-watching. Pizza (from €9) is the obvious choice, but there's also a wide selection of pasta dishes (from €12) and grills (from €15). *Menus* from €16 at lunch;

in the evenings it's à la carte. Feb–Dec Tues, Wed & Fri–Sat noon–2pm & 7–9.30pm, Thurs 7–9.30pm, Sun noon–2pm,.

★**Les Trois Soleils de Montal** Les Prés de Montal ☎05 65 10 16 16, ⓦ3soleils.fr. A Michelin-starred treat with candlelit tables set amid beautiful gardens and creative dishes whipped up from local ingredients; specialities include roasted pigeon and miso-marinated foie gras. The lunchtime weekday *menu* at €32 is a bargain, while evening *menus* start from €52. March–Oct Mon 7.30–9pm, Tues–Sun noon–1.45pm & 7.30–9pm.

Château de Montal

April & Sept daily 10am–12.30pm & 2–6.30pm; May–Aug daily 10am–12.30pm & 2–6.30pm; Oct–March Wed–Sun 10am–12.30pm & 2–5.30pm • €7.50 • ☎05 65 38 13 72, ⓦchateau-montal.fr

Two kilometres west of St-Céré, the **Château de Montal** is a superb example of French Renaissance architecture, and has recently reopened after extensive renovations. Its fascinating history began in 1523 when **Jeanne Balzac d'Entraygues**, the widow of Amaury de Montal, started transforming the medieval fortress into a Renaissance palace, as was all the rage. But then came news that her eldest son, Robert, had been killed in Italy and poor Jeanne lost the heart to continue. Nevertheless the de Montal family continued to own the château up to the Revolution, after which it was bought by a certain Monsieur Macaire who gradually sold off the chimneypieces, sculptures and even the carved window surrounds. Rescue was at hand, however, in the form of **Maurice Fenaille**, a rich industrialist and patron of the arts, who bought the château in 1908 and began to restore it to its former glory. In just five years he managed to track down nearly everything that had been sold, including some of the original wall-coverings, and also filled the rooms with a fine collection of Renaissance and Louis XIII furnishings, before giving the whole caboodle to the state in 1913. Later, during World War II, Montal was chosen as a hiding place for thousands of paintings from the Louvre, including the *Mona Lisa*, which were moved from Paris for safekeeping.

The inner courtyard

The rear of the château, which you see first on approach, still exudes a thoroughly medieval air with its small windows, steep *lauze* roof and pepper-pot towers, but turn the corner into the **inner courtyard** and you're immediately transported to sunny Italy. The lovely pale stone of the two facades is worked into delicate carvings, including a frieze of mermaid-like sibyls and, above, busts representing three generations of the de Montal family: Jeanne is flanked by her husband and son Robert on the west wing, while her parents take pride of place over the front door.

The interior

The craftsmen went to work inside as well as on the outside, particularly on a magnificent **staircase** made from the same local limestone. As you climb up, notice the carving on the panels above, each bearing a different design, which gets finer and more elaborate towards the top. The rest of the interior can't quite compare, but there are some massive old oak tables, a good, homely kitchen and an excellent collection of tapestries, including a rare example featuring a pastoral scene with descriptive boxes of text, like an early cartoon.

Grottes de Presque

45min guided tours daily: mid-Feb to March & Oct 10am–noon & 2–5pm; April–June & Sept 9.30am–noon & 2–6pm; July & Aug 9.30am–6.30pm • €8, children €4 • ☎ 05 65 40 32 01, ⓦ grottesdepresque.com

About 3km southwest from the Château de Montal, the D673 cuts through a hillside as it climbs up onto the *causse*. When this road was dug in 1825, engineers discovered the entrance to the **Grottes de Presque**. The cave system is not only unusually accessible, with just a few stairs, but it also contains a marvellous variety of **stalactites** and **stalagmites**, some up to 10m high, as well as columns, semi-translucent curtains and glistening crystalline cascades. The other notable feature is the sheer amount of **colour**, from pure white to grey, yellow and deep orange. This is the result of rainwater picking up iron, manganese and other minerals as it percolates through the 90m of rock above, minerals that are then deposited along with the calcite, drip by drip, inside the cave.

Autoire

Eight kilometres by road west of the Grottes de Presque (follow the D673 southwest for another 4km and then turn right on the D38), the River Autoire has carved an impressive canyon and waterfall, the **Cirque d'Autoire**, into the limestone plateau. The D38 brings you in above the *cirque* – for the best views, walk west from the car park (€2/day) for about five minutes, following the footpath across a bridge and up onto the opposite hillside. In the valley bottom, some 2km below you, lies the extremely pretty little village of **AUTOIRE** where the ochre-hued houses, including several rather grand piles built by nobles from St-Céré in the fifteenth and sixteenth centuries, snuggle round a very plain, solid Romanesque church.

ACCOMMODATION AND EATING   AUTOIRE

Auberge de la Fontaine ☎ 05 65 10 85 40, ⓦ auberge-de-la-fontaine.com. This lovely little hotel is on Autoire's main street opposite the church. It's a simple country inn offering basic but well-kept rooms and a restaurant with good regional country cooking washed down with local Coteaux de Glanes wines; *menus* from €11.50 at lunch and €21.90 in the evenings, breakfast €7.50. Restaurant July & Aug daily noon–1.45pm & 7.30–8.30pm; March–June & Sept–Nov Tues–Fri noon–1.45pm, Sat 7.30–8.30pm. **€60**

La Cascade ☎ 06 07 85 90 62. Autoire's longest-running crêperie has been serving up delicious home-made crêpes and *galettes* since 1976. Take a seat on the pretty terrace looking out over the valley, or cosy up inside, and enjoy *menus* from €15.90. March–June & Sept–Nov Mon & Wed–Sun noon–2pm; July & Aug daily noon–2pm & 7.30–9pm.

Loubressac

It's 8km back to St-Céré from Autoire, but it's worth taking a short diversion 6km northwest along the D135, little more than a country lane, to **LOUBRESSAC**. The narrow lanes of this fortified hilltop village are full of flowers and typical Quercy houses. You can't visit the château standing on the cliff edge, but there are grand **views** from the lookout point immediately to the east of the village, taking in the whole sweep of the Dordogne, Bave and Cère valleys across to St-Céré and the châteaux of Castelnau and Montal.

INFORMATION
LOUBRESSAC

Tourist office In season a tourist office opens up just outside Loubressac's southern gateway (mid-June to Sept Mon–Fri 10am–12.30pm & 2–6pm; ☎ 05 65 33 22 00, ⓦ tourisme-vallee-dordogne.com).

ACCOMMODATION AND EATING

La Garrigue ☎ 05 65 38 34 88, ⓦ camping-lagarrigue .com. Small but pleasant three-star campsite with a pool, 200m south of the village. Closed Oct–March. €22

Lou Cantou La Place ☎ 05 65 38 20 58, ⓦ loucantou .com. Simple but comfortable rooms in a tranquil location, offering beautiful views over the valley from the communal terrace. There's also a restaurant that serves regional specialties like Quercy lamb and walnut salad, with lunch menus from €14. Breakfast €9. Restaurant April to mid-Nov daily 12.30–2pm & 7.30–8.30pm; Dec–March Tues–Sat 12.30–2pm & 7.30–8.30pm. €60

Relais de Castelnau Rte de Padirac ☎ 05 65 10 80 90, ⓦ relaisdecastelnau.com. Looking out over the Dordogne valley, the modern *Relais de Castelnau* boasts dramatic views as well as a swimming pool and a quality restaurant with *menus* from €18.50. Breakfast €10. Restaurant Easter to Oct daily 7.30–9pm, plus Sun 12–2pm; hotel closed Nov–Easter. €95

4

The Lot valley and around

200 Cahors

210 East along the Lot

218 The Célé valley

220 Figeac

225 The Causse de Gramat

228 Gourdon

230 The Bouriane

231 West along the Lot from Cahors

240 Villeneuve-sur-Lot and around

243 The bastide country

PONT VALENTRÉ, CAHORS

5

The Lot valley and around

Like the Dordogne, the River Lot rises in the foothills of the Massif Central and is dammed in its upper reaches to form huge reservoirs. It begins to get more interesting, however, where it enters the Lot *département*, the boundaries of which roughly coincide with the old province of Quercy. Here the serpentine river carves its way through the immense limestone plateau – encompassed by the Parc naturel régional des Causses du Quercy – that characterizes the region.

The largest town in the Lot valley, and capital of the *département*, is **Cahors**. It may lack the higgledy-piggledy charm of Sarlat or Bergerac, but compensates with a pleasingly workaday atmosphere and a wonderful riverside location. It also boasts the best example of a fortified medieval bridge left in France, the **Pont Valentré**, while the country round about produces an extremely distinctive dark, almost peppery red **wine**.

The Lot valley is at its most picturesque upstream from Cahors. The scenery may not be as dramatic as the middle reaches of the Dordogne, but the sheer cliffs here host their fair share of perched fortresses and feudal villages. Foremost among these is spectacular **St-Cirq Lapopie**, while the nearby **Grotte de Pech-Merle**, with its glittering rock formations and prehistoric cave art, draws almost as many visitors. Pech-Merle lies in the hills above the wild and pretty **Célé valley**, which leads northeast to lovely, medieval **Figeac**, the Lot's second largest town.

North and west of Figeac stretches the **Causse de Gramat**, the biggest and wildest of the region's limestone *causses*. With its huge vistas, it makes a welcome change from the confining valleys and a great place for walking or cycling, though it has few notable sights beyond the village of **Assier**, in the far southeast, with its extraordinary church. On its western edge the Causse de Gramat suddenly gives way to a lovely area of gentle wooded hills known as the **Bouriane**. Again, there are no must-see sights, though its capital, **Gourdon**, a once-prosperous town built of butter-coloured stone, is worth a stop-off, and the nearby **Grottes de Cougnac**, with a smattering of prehistoric cave paintings and some exceptionally delicate limestone concretions, repay a visit.

Returning to the Lot valley, the river south of Cahors wriggles its way westwards through vineyards and past ancient towns and villages. By far the most striking of these is **Puy-l'Évêque**. An outpost of the bishops of Cahors, the town's medieval and Renaissance houses jostle for space on a steep incline, reaching upwards like trees for light, though none is equal to the bishop's thirteenth-century keep towering above. An even more dramatic sight lies in store in the country northwest of Puy-l'Évêque, where the **Château de Bonaguil** is an outstanding example of late-fifteenth-century military architecture, its great bulk silhouetted against the wooded hillside.

Further downstream things begin to quieten down again as the valley flattens out towards **Villeneuve-sur-Lot**. Despite unattractive modern suburbs, the town has a decent supply of hotels and restaurants, and with the river sliding through an old centre built of stone and warm red brick, it's a pleasant and convenient place to stay. Villeneuve – as its

Festivals, events and markets p.202
Jacques Duèze and Châteauneuf-du-Pâpe p.204
Léon Gambetta p.205
Les Jardins Secrets p.206

The wines of Cahors p.209
Quercy saffron p.216
The legend of Monkey's Leap p.217
Champollion and the Rosetta Stone p.223
Bastides p.244

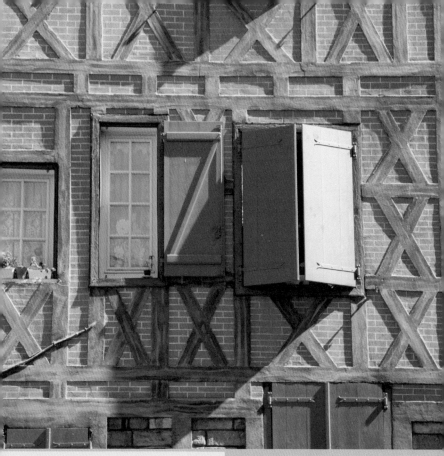

HALF-TIMBERED HOUSE, FIGEAC

Highlights

❶ Pont Valentré Cahors' signature sight is the fortified medieval bridge guarding the town's western approaches, at its most atmospheric at sunset. **See p.206**

❷ Wine tasting in Cahors Sample the distinctive, full-bodied wines of Cahors, dark enough to merit the nickname of "black wines". **See p.209**

❸ St-Cirq Lapopie Perched high above the River Lot, this former feudal stronghold boasts stunning views and lovely, labyrinthine alleys to explore. **See p.212**

❹ Quercy saffron The Lot's signature spice is more than just a cooking ingredient – it's the focal point of the harvest festival at Cajarc, one

of the region's largest. **See p.216**

❺ Grotte de Pech-Merle The combination of dazzling limestone formations and more than five hundred prehistoric drawings make this cave unmissable. **See p.219**

❻ Figeac A laidback riverside town with plenty of medieval architecture and a fascinating museum of writing. **See p.220**

❼ Château de Bonaguil One of the last medieval fortresses built in France, and now a magnificent ruin. **See p.238**

❽ Bastides Monpazier provides an almost perfect example of the region's myriad fortified towns. **See p.244**

HIGHLIGHTS ARE MARKED ON THE MAP ON PP.200–201

5

name indicates – was also one of the many "new towns", or *bastides*, founded in this area in the thirteenth and fourteenth centuries. You'll find the best examples of *bastide* architecture in the hills to the north, where the villages of **Monflanquin** and **Monpazier** seem hardly to have changed since the Middle Ages. The same can't be said for the **Château de Biron**, lying between the two, which was altered and expanded extensively during the Renaissance, but its superb hilltop location makes it hard to resist.

GETTING AROUND   THE LOT VALLEY AND AROUND

By car Given the paucity of public transport, you'll need your own vehicle for exploring much of the Lot valley, and a car is essential for the Célé valley, the Bouriane and other places off the beaten track.

By train SNCF trains between Brive-la-Gaillarde and Toulouse, via Gourdon and Cahors and to Rodez, stop at Gramat, Assier, Figeac and Capdenac, while the Figeac–Cahors line passes Cajarc. Funel is also connected to Cahors, Agen and Penne D'Agenais.

By bus The only regular SNCF bus services in the region

run east from Cahors to Figeac and west to Fumel – timetables are available at tourist offices. Many smaller towns have no public bus service, and though there are buses from Cahors and Figeac to Gramat and Gourdon, these are aimed at school drop-offs and pickups, and are not a viable option for visitors. Nonetheless, a comprehensive bus timetable, *Les Bus du Lot*, is published annually and available at tourist offices; otherwise contact the transport information desk of the Conseil Général du Lot (☎ 05 65 53 43 91, ⊚ lot.fr).

Cahors

A sunny southern backwater built in a tight meander of the River Lot, **CAHORS** was the chief town of the old province of Quercy and is now the modern capital of the Lot *département*. Its somewhat troubled history has left a warren of dark medieval lanes,

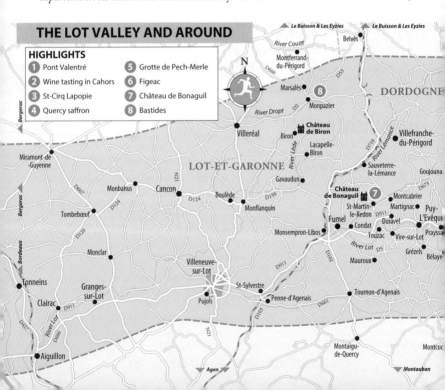

THE LOT VALLEY AND AROUND

HIGHLIGHTS

1. Pont Valentré
2. Wine tasting in Cahors
3. St-Cirq Lapopie
4. Quercy saffron
5. Grotte de Pech-Merle
6. Figeac
7. Château de Bonaguil
8. Bastides

a rather knocked-about cathedral and impressive fortifications, among them Cahors' famous landmark, the turreted **Pont Valentré**. Another reason to come here is to sample the local **wines**, heady and black but dry to the taste (see box, p.209).

Compact and easily walkable, Cahors is surrounded on three sides by the River Lot and protected to the north by a series of fourteenth-century fortifications. Most sights of interest lie within the cramped confines of the medieval streets on the peninsula's eastern edge, focused around the twin domes of the **Cathédrale St-Étienne**. From here, **rue Nationale** leads south past the former homes of wealthy merchants to the flood-prone artisans' quarter, while north of the cathedral the land continues to slope gently upwards along **rue du Château-du-Roi**, where bankers and aristocrats once lived, towards the old town gate with its guardhouse and tower. Of medieval Cahors' three fortified bridges, only westerly **Pont Valentré** remains – one of the finest surviving bridges of its time. More recent history is commemorated in a couple of passably interesting **museums** and, on a fine day, there are good views from the summit of **Mont St-Cyr**, which overlooks the town from the southeast.

Brief history

Both the names Quercy and Cahors derive from the area's first-known inhabitants, the local Gaulish tribe known as the **Cadurci**. At some time between the seventh and fifth centuries BC they founded their settlement near a sacred spring, immediately across the river to the southwest of modern Cahors, which the Romans, who arrived in over-whelming force in 51BC, later called **Divona Cadurcorum**. Following successive Vandal and Frankish invasions after the fifth century, only a few fragments of Roman stonework remain, as well as the spring, which continues to supply Cahors' drinking water.

It wasn't until the seventh century that the then Bishop (later Saint) Didier finally erected a wall to protect the nascent town and his rapidly growing cathedral. The

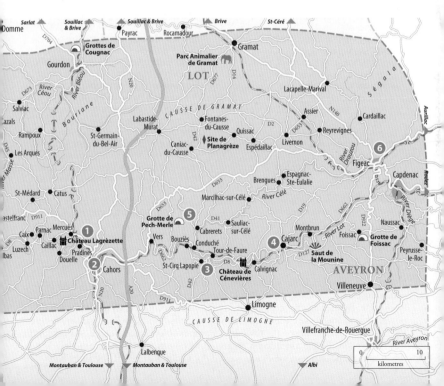

5

FESTIVALS, EVENTS AND MARKETS

Festivals and **events** are held throughout the Lot valley during the summer season, and many of the villages host special markets and small fêtes to celebrate the harvest season. The principal festivals are detailed below, but for the full schedule, pick up the free *Calendrier des Fêtes des Villes et Villages* booklet from tourist offices. Where we haven't given a specific information number or website, contact the relevant tourist office.

Late April to early May Capdenac: Le Chaînon Manquant (☎05 34 51 48 88, ⊛reseau-chainon.com). Two weeks of contemporary performance art introducing up-and-coming talent from France and around the world. There's a mix of street performances and ticketed events.

May Albas: La Fête du Vin (☎05 65 36 28 93, ⊛albas.fr). The area's largest wine festival is held biennially (next due in 2017, then 2019), kicking off with a barrel of wine being paraded through the village and including various wine-tasting and dinner events starting from around €15 a head.

Mid-July Monpazier: Fête Médiévale (☎05 53 22 68 59, ⊛pays-des-bastides.com). In addition to its many small summer events, Monpazier steps back in time for five days, with banquets, concerts and equestrian displays.

Mid-July Cahors: Blues Festival (☎05 65 35 99 99, ⊛cahorsbluesfestival.com). A week of blues, jazz and rock, where French and international artists bare their souls in the streets: head to Les Docks, Théâtre de Verdure, rue Wilson and Boulevard Gambetta. The early performances are free, later ones are ticketed. The tourist office has a leaflet with all details.

Mid-July to mid-August Cahors: Festival de St-Céré et du Haut-Quercy (☎05 65 38 28 08, ⊛festival-saint-cere.com). Three-week festival of opera, orchestral works and chamber music, with ticketed concerts in Cahors' cathedral and Musée Henri-Martin.

Late July Cajarc: Africajarc (⊛africajarc.com). Cajarc moves to an African beat during three days of concerts, exhibitions, craft displays,

markets and food stalls. Tickets required for the main concerts.

First weekend in August Gourdon: Grande Fête Médiévale (☎05 65 27 52 50, ⊛medievalesdegourdon.jimdo.com). Gourdon lets rip with two days of junketing complete with jugglers, fire-eaters, musicians and the works.

Early August Puy-l'Évêque: Fête Votive. One of the area's most important local fêtes, lasting five days with a free dance every night, a funfair and a fireworks spectacular with music on the Sunday.

Early to mid-August Château de Bonaguil: Festival du Bonaguil Fumel (☎05 53 71 17 17, ⊛festivaldebonaguil-fumel.fr). Bonaguil's inner court and moats make a spectacular venue for this festival of French theatre, held over eight or nine days. There's a play or musical event every night (tickets required), as well as workshops, street theatre and lectures.

Mid-August Monflanquin: Journées Médiévales (☎05 53 36 40 19). Two days of mead, minstrels and merry japes as Monflanquin goes medieval. Jousting, banquets, siege engines – you name it. You can even rent costumes.

First weekend in September Peyrusse-le-Roc: Spectacle Pyrosymphonique. The ruined towers of Peyrusse make a spectacular setting for a son-et-lumière-cum-fireworks display.

Late October Cajarc: Fête du Safran (⊛safran-du-quercy.com). Cajarc hosts the region's biggest saffron fair, featuring an array of saffron-infused products, cooking demonstrations and a growers' competition.

MARKETS

The region's main **markets** take place at Aiguillon (Tues & Fri); Cahors (Wed & Sat); Cajarc (Sat); Duravel (Sat); Figeac (Sat); Fumel (Sun); Gourdon (Tues & Sat, also Thurs in July & Aug); Gramat (Tues & Fri); Luzech (Wed); Monflanquin (Thurs); Monpazier (Thurs); Monsempron-Libos (Sun); Prayssac (Fri) and Villeneuve-sur-Lot (Tues & Sat).

bishops of Cahors gradually spread their net until they not only ruled over a vast area extending down the Lot as far as Puy-l'Évêque but also controlled the all-important river trade. By the early thirteenth century Cahors was entering its **golden age**, as powerful local merchants known as Caorsins, together with Lombard bankers fleeing the Cathar crusades, turned the town into Europe's chief banking centre – a wealth that was reflected in the gentrification of various townhouses, bridges and cathedral. When the local bishop, Jacques Duèze, was named **Pope John XXII** in 1316, Cahors had reached its apogee. His greatest legacy was a university, which remained one of the most important in France for the next four centuries.

By now, however, the English and French armies were at loggerheads. Cahors was never attacked during the Hundred Years War, but the end result was the same: under the Treaty of Brétigny (1360) it succumbed reluctantly to **English occupation**. When French rule was eventually restored around 1440, the Cadurciens set about rebuilding their ravaged town, adding a few Italianate flourishes and developing a distinctive decorative style comprising carved or moulded rose blossoms, flaming suns and the so-called "*bâtons écotés*" ("pruned branches"), which is still in evidence today.

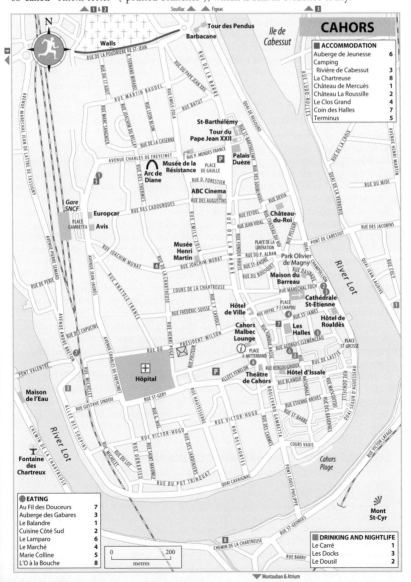

CAHORS

◼ ACCOMMODATION	
Auberge de Jeunesse	6
Camping	
Rivière de Cabessut	3
La Chartreuse	8
Château de Mercuès	1
Château La Roussille	2
Le Clos Grand	4
Coin des Halles	7
Terminus	5

◼ EATING	
Au Fil des Douceurs	7
Auberge des Gabares	3
Le Balandre	1
Cuisine Côté Sud	2
Le Lamparo	6
Le Marché	4
Marie Colline	5
L'O à la Bouche	8

◼ DRINKING AND NIGHTLIFE	
Le Carré	1
Les Docks	3
Le Dousil	2

0   200
metres

Montauban & Atrium

5

Unlike several of its neighbours, Cahors remained staunchly Catholic during the **Wars of Religion**. As a consequence it was sacked by the Protestant Henry of Navarre, the future King Henry IV of France, when he seized it after a brief battle in 1580. Later the same year, however, one of many peace treaties saw the town returned to the Catholic fold. By way of recompense, Henry later donated six thousand *livres*, half of which went towards restoring the cathedral.

Over the years Cahors gradually expanded to fill the entire peninsula, though it was not until the nineteenth century that Bishop Didier's ramparts were finally razed. They were replaced by a tree-lined boulevard that was later named after Cahors' most famous son, the politician **Léon Gambetta** (see box opposite). The heart of present-day Cahors is **place François Mitterrand**, named after yet another politician, a recently renovated wide open square. During the renovation process, and excavation of the car park housed underneath, a staggering amount of ancient ruins were uncovered. Work was stopped, archeologists called in and part of a **Roman amphitheatre** emerged. The much-needed car park was still built, but it contains a semicircle of the amphitheatre (the rest is under the old college), carefully lit for public display – a parking facility and a day out in one.

Cathédrale St-Étienne

Place Jean-Jacques Chapou • Mon–Sat 10am–noon & 2–7pm, Sun 2–7pm • Free • ☎ 05 65 35 27 80

The oldest and simplest of the region's Périgord-style Romanesque churches, the **Cathédrale St-Étienne** dates largely from the early twelfth century, when Bishop Didier's original cathedral was rebuilt in part to house the relic of the Holy Coif, said to have covered Christ's head in the tomb. According to local legend, it was brought back from the Holy Land around this time by Bishop Géraud de Cardaillac.

Numerous reconstructions of the building have been carried out over the centuries, meaning St-Étienne's exterior is rather unexciting, with the notable exception of the elaborately decorated portal above the **north door**. Carved in around 1140, it depicts Christ's Ascension. Side panels show scenes from the life of St Stephen (St Étienne), the first Christian martyr, who was stoned to death around 35 AD, while the outer arch portrays people being stabbed and sliced with axes.

Inside, the cathedral is much like Périgueux's St-Étienne (see p.53), with a nave lacking aisles and transepts, roofed with two monumental domes. High in the west dome, original fourteenth-century frescoes again depict the stoning of St Stephen, encircled by eight giant prophets. In 1988 further paintings from the same era were discovered behind layers of plaster just inside and above the west door. They consist of faded but beautiful Creation scenes, including Adam and Eve in the Garden of Eden and many finely observed birds and animals.

To the right of the choir, the aptly named **Chapelle Profonde** ("Deep Chapel") bears scars from the Wars of Religion, when Protestant armies hacked away at its carvings. They also caused irreparable damage to the **cloister**, accessed by a door next to the Deep Chapel, though the flamboyant Gothic colonnades still retain some intricate craftsmanship. The door surrounds are also beautifully carved, if rather battered; that on the northeast wall

---

JACQUES DUÈZE AND CHÂTEAUNEUF-DU-PÂPE

Cahors' home-grown cleric, **Jacques Duèze**, was immensely fond of his native town, and no less fond of its powerful black wines. So much so that when elected to the papacy, as John XXII, and forced to move his episcopal seat from Cahors to the Holy See in Avignon, he devised a wheeze for continuing to imbibe his favourite tipple. Rather than having the wine transported 400 kilometres from the Cahors vineyards to the papal palace, he built a new summer palace on the banks of the Rhône and planted his beloved Malbec vine-stock around it. Thus a new wine was born, which the locals christened **Châteauneuf-du-Pâpe** – in essence a Cahors wine in all but name.

LÉON GAMBETTA

Heralded as the "father of the Republic", **Léon Gambetta** was born in Cahors in 1838. After graduating as a lawyer, he specialized in defending republican sympathizers accused of political crimes against Emperor Napoléon III. The republicans soon rallied around Gambetta – a charismatic man and a great orator – and, when Napoléon was forced to surrender to an invading Prussian army in 1870, he was among those who quickly proclaimed the **Third Republic**, the regime which continued to govern France until 1940. It had a rocky start, however. With the Prussians besieging Paris, Gambetta fled the capital by balloon to organize the war effort in the provinces. While he opposed the armistice signed in 1871, Gambetta and his band of moderate republicans, or "Opportunists", were able to keep the Republic afloat despite constant attacks from both the monarchist majority and the radical Left. He served as president of the National Assembly from 1879 to 1882, but later that year his career was cut short when he accidentally shot himself with a revolver, and died soon after.

leads into the **Chapelle St Gausbert** (only accessible as part of the guided tours run by the tourist office; see p.208), which holds the **Holy Coif** – a decidedly unimpressive, rather grubby looking piece of padded cloth – among chalices, gilded statues and other treasures.

Place Jean-Jacques Chapou

The square on which Cathédrale St-Étienne stands, **place Jean-Jacques Chapou**, commemorates a local Resistance leader killed in a German ambush in July 1944. On its west side, look for a sign above what is now a bank announcing *Bazar Gênois: Gambetta Jeune et Cie*. This is where **Léon Gambetta** (see box above), the son of an Italian grocer, spent his childhood. At its southern end the square extends into place Galdemar, popularly known as place de la Halle. The covered **Les Halles** at its centre, built as a corn exchange in 1865, provides the focus for Cahors' lively markets. There's a fresh food **market** in here (Tues–Sat 7.30am–12.30pm & 3–7pm, Sun 9am–noon), and a more extensive market on Wednesday and Saturday mornings spreading north into the cathedral square; in winter (Nov to mid-March), the *halle* plays host to a Saturday morning *marché au gras*, selling all manner of duck and goose products. Nearby place François Mitterrand also hosts an antiques fair-cum-flea market on the first and third Saturdays of the month.

Medieval Cahors

A warren of narrow lanes and alleys fills the area between boulevard Gambetta and the eastern riverbank, where the majority of houses, turreted and built with flat, thin southern brick, have been handsomely restored during recent decades. From the market square, **rue Nationale** cuts almost due south through the heart of medieval Cahors to where the old Roman bridge once stood – the foundations are still just visible when the water level is low. Other roads worth exploring in the area are canyon-like **rue Bergougnioux** and its easterly extension **rue Lastié**, which comes out among a pretty group of brick and timber buildings around **place St-Urcisse**.

One of Cahors' most attractive corners lies just north of the cathedral along **rue Daurade**, where a lovely row of buildings overlooks a little park named after the sixteenth-century poet Olivier de Magny, who lived at no. 12. His house is overshadowed, though, by the thirteenth-century **Maison du Bourreau** (no public access), the "executioner's house", with its big arched openings and line of double windows above. The name dates from the Revolution, when the public executioner lived here; naturally, the building is said to be haunted.

Continuing north along rue Daurade you reach the southern end of **rue Château-du-Roi** and its extension, **rue des Soubirous**. This is the "upper town", where the houses become distinctly grander. One of the most imposing is the fourteenth-century

5

Château du Roi itself, built by cousins of Pope John XXII but later taken over by the king's emissary when the bishops lost their stranglehold on Cahors in the fifteenth century. Its massive, featureless walls can be easily seen from the eastern riverbank, though there's no public access to the interior.

Wealthy Caduriciens were very fond of adding turrets to their homes and there are a number of examples scattered through the Soubirous quarter. To see them properly it's best to head down to the river – rue du Four-Ste-Catherine provides the most interesting route – to a vantage point across **Pont de Cabessut**. Cahors' skyline stretches in front of you from the cathedral domes in the south via Collège Pélegry, with its crenellated hexagonal turret, and the square, solid tower of the Château du Roi. In the far distance the **Tour du Pape Jean XXII** and the **Tour des Pendus** pinpoint Cahors' northern ramparts, which still stretch partway across the peninsula.

Musée de la Résistance

Place Charles-de-Gaulle • Daily 2–6pm • Free • ☎ 05 65 22 14 25

In a small building on the north side of place Charles-de-Gaulle, the **Musée de la Résistance** documents the history of the local Resistance movement against the broader context of German occupation, deportations and, finally, Liberation in 1945. The most interesting section, on the ground floor, deals with local history, where you can read about Jean-Jacques Chapou, after whom the cathedral square is named (see p.205), and about the *Mona Lisa*'s sojourn in the area (see p.193).

Musée Henri Martin

792 rue Émile-Zola • Closed for restoration until 2018 • ☎ 05 65 20 88 66, ⓦ mairie-cahors.fr/musee

Housed in a seventeenth-century former episcopal palace, the **Musée Henri Martin** was closed for extensive renovations at the time of writing – check the website or ask at the tourist office for an update. Its permanent collection ranges from Gallo-Roman pots to works by nineteenth- and twentieth-century artists such as Dufy, Vlaminck and Utrillo, and comprises over two thousand documents, photographs, sculptures and paintings. Highlights include seventeen oil paintings by local artist **Henri Martin** (1860–1943), whose mix of Impressionism and Pointillism perfectly evokes the lazy sun-filled landscapes of this part of France; and an important collection dedicated to **Léon Gambetta**.

Pont Valentré

The main reason most people venture to Cahors is to see the dramatic **Pont Valentré**, which guards the western river crossing. Its three powerful towers, originally closed by portcullises and gates, made it an independent fortress, which was so imposing, in fact, that the bridge was never attacked. Building it was a problem, however: work started in 1308, but the bridge was not completed for another seventy years. According to legend, the Devil was to blame – at least in part. The story goes that the architect, exasperated at the slow progress, sold his soul in exchange for the Devil's assistance. As the bridge was nearing completion, he tried to wriggle out of the deal by giving the Devil a sieve with

---

LES JARDINS SECRETS

A quirky way to unearth Cahors' history is to find the **Jardins Secrets**, a series of around thirty gardens making use of otherwise vacant patches of land dotted around the old town and the river. Medicinal herbs, vines and fruit orchards all feature, laid out as they would have been by monks or local gardeners. Pick up a map of the garden locations from the tourist office (see p.208) or at the boat-tour ticket booths near Pont Valentré; all the descriptions are in English.

5

which to carry water for the masons. The Devil took revenge by creeping up the central tower every night to remove the last stone, thus ensuring that the bridge would never be finished. If you look carefully at the top of the tower's east face, you'll see a little devil, which was added when Pont Valentré was renovated in 1879.

Maison de l'Eau

Chemin de la Chartreuse • June–Aug daily 10am–1pm & 3–7pm; Sept–Dec Mon & Fri–Sun 11am–1pm & 3–6pm • €3 • ☎ 05 65 53 04 99

At the west end of the Pont Valentré, the old **Maison de l'Eau** pumping station is now home to a small museum detailing the bridge's history. Most of the information is in French, but you can pick up a leaflet that has the basics in English. Glass floors show off the pumping mechanism below, while the café makes for a pleasant, if rather pricey, riverside spot.

Mont St-Cyr

All around Cahors rise the dry, scrubby uplands of the *causse*. These valley-sides were carpeted with vines from Roman times until the nineteenth century when phylloxera set in, after which the land was used for grazing sheep; now, however, only the lines of tumbled-down stone walls and abandoned farmhouses remain. One of the few landmarks around is the red-and-white TV mast on the summit of **Mont St-Cyr**, overlooking Cahors to the southeast. At 264m, this is the place to head for bird's-eye views of the town: the division between medieval and seventeenth-century Cahors becomes very apparent from the summit, particularly in summer when tree-lined boulevard Gambetta picks out the former course of the ramparts.

It's a stiff but straightforward **climb to the summit** of Mont St-Cyr. From the southern end of boulevard Gambetta, cross Pont Louis-Philippe, then take the steps behind the Virgin's statue and keep going up for about twenty to thirty minutes. Though you can drive, it takes almost as long, as the road winds for about 5km among stunted oaks and pines across the plateau. Apart from the views, there are picnic tables at the top and a summer-only café-bar.

Cahors Plage

Place de l'Acacias • First week of July to second week of Aug daily 1pm–7pm • Free

Landlocked Cahors might be miles from the coast, but in high season you can still cool off at the free riverside **Cahors Plage** beside Pont Louis Philippe. The lively beach comes complete with imported sand, straw parasols and picnic tables, while beach bars and a bouncy castle make it the perfect spot for families on a sunny afternoon.

ARRIVAL AND DEPARTURE   CAHORS

By train The *gare SNCF* sits 500m northwest of the centre of town, on place Jouinot Gambetta.
Destinations Brive (7–12 daily; 1hr 10min); Gourdon (6–10 daily; 30min); Montauban (up to 16 daily; 45min–1hr); Paris-Austerlitz (5 daily; 5–6hr); Souillac (6–10 daily; 45min); Toulouse (7–14 daily; 1hr 25min).
By bus The *gare SNCF* is the terminus for many buses, while others stop on place de Charles-de-Gaulle at the north end of rue de la Barre. The tourist office (see p.208) stocks bus timetables.

Destinations Albas (4–10 daily; 30min); Bouziès (3–6 daily; 30min); Cajarc (3–6 daily; 1hr); Figeac (3–6 daily; 1hr 45min); Fumel (3–8 daily; 1hr–1hr 15min); Luzech (3–10 daily; 20min); Monsempron-Libos (3–8 daily; 1hr 15min–1hr 30min); Puy-l'Évêque (4–10 daily; 45min); Tour-de-Faure (3–6 daily; 40min); Vers (3–6 daily; 15–20min).
By car The most convenient places to park are in the Parking de l'Amphithéâtre under the allées Fénelon or on place de Gaulle.

GETTING AROUND

Car rental Avis, opposite the train station on av Jean Jaurès (☎ 05 65 30 13 10).

Taxis There are taxi stands outside the train station and on bd Gambetta, or call Allo Taxi (☎ 05 65 22 19 42).

5

Bike, kayak and boat rental V-lot, just south of the Pont Valentré on Quai Valentré (☎06 18 46 76 05, ⓦv-lot.fr) rent bikes (adult €15/day, children €10/day) and electric bikes (€35/day), plus saddle-bags, trailers, emergency phones and even GoPro cameras (€15/day).

Alternatively, Base Nautique (July & Aug only; ☎05 65 21 11 78, ⓦbase-nautique-lot.com) in Douelle, about 10km west of Cahors, rent bikes for €18 per day, plus kayaks, pedalos and motorboats.

INFORMATION AND TOURS

Tourist office Cahors' tourist office (Nov–March Mon–Sat 9am–12.30pm & 2–6pm; April, May & Oct Mon–Sat 9am–12.30 & 1.30–6.30pm; July & Aug Mon–Sat 9am–7pm; May–Sept Sun 10am–6pm; ☎05 65 53 20 65, ⓦtourisme-lot.fr) occupies a handsome building on the north side of place François Mitterrand. It provides detailed walking maps of the town, and can help booking tours and wine tastings.

Boat rental and tours Babou Marine (☎05 65 21 07 86) rent motor-boats for up to twelve people, with

prices starting from €30 for an hour. Les Croisières Fénelon (☎05 65 30 16 55, ⓦbateau-cahors.com) put on a varied programme of excursions such as a day-trip to St-Cirq Lapopie (€62) which includes a meal. There are ticket booths for both companies beside the Pont Valentré jetty.

Canoe tours Departing from the jetty below Pont Valentré, Safaraid (April–Oct; ☎05 65 37 44 87, ⓦcanoe-kayak-dordogne.com) offer half- and full-day tours from €22 around the Cahors meander of the Lot, with English commentary.

ACCOMMODATION

Cahors has a broad range of **hotels** and some good options for those on a budget, although the choice, particularly in the middle price categories, is not particularly inspiring. Instead, there's better value for money in the surrounding region, though you'll need your own transport to get there.

CAHORS

Auberge de Jeunesse 222 rue Joachim Murat ☎05 65 35 64 71, ⓦfuaj.org/cahors. Pleasantly situated in a quiet building behind a park, this hostel is not far from the *gare SNCF* and is popular with walkers. There are also washing and drying facilities. Breakfast €5, evening meals from €12. **€15.30**

La Chartreuse Chemin de la Chartreuse ☎05 65 35 17 37, ⓦhotel-la-chartreuse.com. Modern, minimalist rooms and a prime riverside location just a 5min walk from the city centre make *La Chartreuse* a good choice. There's also a pool, terrace and a well-appointed restaurant serving evening *menus* from €25. Breakfast €10. **€90**

Coin des Halles 30 place St-Maurice ☎05 65 30 24 27, ⓦlecoindeshalles-hotel.com. Right in the heart of the old town in the corner of the market square, this hotel offers clean, bright rooms, though some are a little on the small side. The bar-restaurant teems with life all day long (*plat du jour* €9.50, *menu* €16). Breakfast €8. **€77**

Terminus 5 av Charles de Freycinet ☎05 65 53 32 00, ⓦbalandre.com. Housed in a nineteenth-century bourgeois residence and once one of Cahors' grandest hotels, *Terminus* is looking a little scuffed around the edges these days. Nonetheless, the rooms are spotless and spacious, staff are exceedingly friendly and quirky touches like a piano on the landing help make it nostalgic rather than shabby. The excellent in-house restaurant *Le Balandre* (see opposite) is reason alone to stay. Private parking €10. Breakfast €10. **€75**

AROUND CAHORS

Camping Rivière de Cabessut Rue de la Rivière ☎05 65 30 06 30, ⓦcabessut.com. Three-star campsite in a quiet spot beside the river just over 1km from Cahors across Pont de Cabessut; facilities include a shop, snack bar, small pool and canoe rental. Closed Sept–April. **€20**

Château de Mercuès Mercuès ☎05 65 20 00 01, ⓦchateaudemercues.com. High on its promontory 6km to the northwest of Cahors, this thirteenth-century castle was once the residence of the bishops of Cahors. It is now a glamorous four-star hotel with pool, tennis courts, excellent wine cellars (free tastings for guests in July & Aug) and a good restaurant with evening *menus* from €89. Breakfast €27. Closed Dec–Feb. **€350**

Château la Roussille Chemin du Moulin, Labéraudie ☎05 65 22 84 74, ⓦchateauroussille.com. A welcoming *chambre d'hôte*, a 5min drive from Cahors centre; take the D8 in the direction of Moulin de Labéraudie. There are four equally delightful rooms to choose from, plus a lounge, billiard room and solar-heated pool. Closed Nov–April. **€95**

Le Clos Grand 12 rue des Claux Grands, Labéraudie ☎05 65 35 04 39 ⓦleclosgrand.fr. Cahors' best budget option is located in Pradines, a suburb 5km northwest of the city. It's a welcoming spot, with a pool, a pleasant shady garden and en-suite rooms equipped with balconies or small terraces. The restaurant is also a popular haunt of locals, serving good-value *menus* from €16 at lunch. Breakfast €8. Restaurant July & Aug daily noon–1.30pm & 7.30–8.45pm; Sept–June Tues–Sat noon–1.30pm & 7.30–8.45pm, Sun noon–1.30pm. **€50**

EATING

Cahors has no shortage of good places to **eat**, many of which make full use of the excellent local produce. Most are concentrated in the streets of the medieval town, though you'll also find **brasseries**, **pizzerias** and **cafés** along boulevard Gambetta. There are also plenty of boulangeries and patisseries, and the *halles* has a splendid *fromagerie*.

Au Fil des Douceurs 32 av Andre Breton ☎ 05 65 22 13 04. In a prime location opposite the Pont Valentré, this much-loved local institution is famed for its haute cuisine, adding its own stamp to typical regional dishes. Don't pass on dessert – the mouthwatering home-made pastries and flaky millefeuille are sublime. *Menus* from €26. Reservations recommended – ask for a table with a riverside view. Tues–Sat noon–1.30pm & 7.30–9pm.

★ **Auberge des Gabares** 24 place Champollion ☎ 05 65 53 91 47. A rare find in the city, this authentic family-run *auberge* serves up rustic country cuisine on a wisteria-covered terrace overlooking the Lot. There's a single *menu* that changes daily, with the emphasis on hearty, no-fuss cuisine – think tasty soups, casseroles and meat dishes, with generous servings. Weekday *menus* are great value at €15,

while there's a €21 *menu* available on Saturday evenings. Tues–Sat noon–1.30pm & 7.30–8.30pm.

★ **Le Balandre** 5 av Charles de Freycinet ☎ 05 65 53 32 00, ⓦ balandre.com. The star attraction of *Terminus* hotel, *Le Balandre* serves up timeless dishes like roast pigeon, steamed cod and ratatouille, all with a fresh modern twist: the results are undeniably delicious. Cap it off with the *café gourmand* – coffee accompanied by an array of bite-size desserts. There are also cooking classes held at the restaurant, starting from €100 per person. *Menus* from €23. Tues–Sat noon–1.30pm & 7.30–9.30pm.

Cuisine Côte Sud 24 place Champollion ☎ 05 65 53 15 16, ⓦ cuisine-cotesud.com. A small but chic restaurant by the riverside serving above-par cuisine, this is the ideal spot for a stylish lunch date. Opt for the delicious foie gras served

---

THE WINES OF CAHORS

So dark that they're often referred to as "black wines", the **red wines of Cahors** are by far the most distinctive of the southwestern wines, full-bodied with lots of tannin, and they generally need long ageing to bring out their best: the accepted period is about ten years; longer than that and many are past their peak. The dominant **grape variety** is Malbec (also known as Auxerrois or Cot), which gives the wine its rich tannin content, its colour and its ability to age. Up to thirty percent of another grape variety is permitted for AOC Cahors, usually Merlot and Tanat – Merlot for roundness and aroma, Tanat to help the ageing process. However, most of the very best wines are 100 percent Malbec. The distinctive bite of a young Cahors wine goes well with charcuterie and stews, while the more aromatic older wines usually accompany red meats, game and the local goat's cheese, *Cabécou*.

VINEYARDS

There are approximately 43 square kilometres under vines in the *appellation*, which stretches from Cahors west along the Lot for 30km to Soturac, producing on average 240,000 hectolitres (roughly 32 million bottles) per annum. Before **visiting the vineyards**, pick up a copy of the free *Cahors and La Vallée du Lot et du Vignoble*, which details the two hundred or so producers in the *appellation*; it's available from the tourist office (see opposite) and from wine merchants in Cahors (see below).

BUYING AND SAMPLING WINE

In general you can expect to pay between €10 and €20 for a decent Cahors, although some of the region's prestige wines fetch €70 or more. For an introduction to what's on offer, head for the imposing **Château Lagrézette** (Mon–Sat 10am–7pm; ☎ 06 52 20 94 37, ⓦ chateau-lagrezette .tm.fr), 10km northwest of Cahors on the D12 midway between Douelle and Mercuès. In addition to sampling their award-winning wines, you can visit the magnificent, state-of-the-art *chais* dug into the hillside, though it's best to call in advance to arrange this. South of the city, on the N20, the **Atrium** (☎ 05 65 20 80 80, ⓦ g-vigouroux.fr) outlet sells wines from the Châteaux de Mercuès and arranges vineyard visits. Also worth a visit for its reliably good wines – if not for its ambience – is the **Côtes d'Olt** co-operative (April–Oct Mon–Sat 9am–12.30pm & 1.30–6pm; Nov–March Mon–Fri 9am–noon & 2–6pm, Sat 9am–noon; ☎ 05 65 30 57 80; ⓦ cavedecahors. com) on the river's south bank about 17km west of Cahors on the D8 in the commune of Parnac. In the city itself, the **Cahors Malbec Lounge** (mid-June to Sept daily 11am–7pm; Oct to mid-June Mon–Sat 11am–1.30pm & 4–7pm; ☎ 05 65 23 82 38) on place François Mitterrand by the tourist office, offers wine-tasting sessions (starting from €5; no reservation necessary).

5

with *petit pain aux figures*, followed by the lamb moussaka. *Menus* from €19.25. Tues–Sat noon–2pm & 7.30–9pm.

Le Lamparo 76 rue Georges Clemenceau ✆ 09 70 35 13 97, ⓦ le-lamparo.fr. Large, bustling restaurant that spills out onto the square in summer. It's justifiably popular for its generous portions, slick service and very reasonable prices. Though the speciality is pizza (from €9), there's plenty of variety, including mountainous salads and local dishes such as *confit de canard*, plus enticing desserts to follow – try the indulgent *café gourmand* taster selection. *Menus* €18.50. Mon–Sat noon–2pm & 7–10.30pm.

Le Marché 27 place Chapou ✆ 05 65 35 27 27, ⓦ restaurantlemarche.com. Excellent service and elegant surroundings help put *Le Marché* up among Cahors' most popular restaurants, but the real star is the cuisine. As the name suggests, the focus is on fresh, local produce and the seasonal *menus* start from €25 at lunch and €27 at dinner. Tues–Sat noon–2pm & 7.30–9pm.

Marie Colline 173 rue Georges Clemenceau ✆ 05 65 35 59 96. Vegetarian restaurants are in short supply in France, and this one is unsurprisingly popular, so it's best to reserve a table in advance. Choices are limited: two entrées and two main dishes (*plat du jour* €9) which change daily – but it's all freshly made, using locally grown vegetables. July & Aug Mon–Sat 12.30–2.30pm; Sept–June Mon–Fri 12.30–2.30pm.

★ **L'O à la Bouche** 56 allées Fénelon ✆ 05 65 35 65 69, ⓦ loalabouche-restaurant.com. Cahors' favourite fine-dining restaurant occupies a chic open-plan space in the centre of town, with tables billowing out onto place François Mitterrand in summer. Here you can watch chef Dive conjure up such delectable treats as smoked duck with marinated courgettes and ratatouille terrine. Lunchtime *menus* start from €21.50, while evening *menus* are from €28. April–Oct & mid-Nov to mid-March Tues–Sat noon–1.30pm & 7–9.30pm.

DRINKING AND NIGHTLIFE

Cahors is not exactly a hub for **nightlife**, but there's more here than meets the eye, especially in season. For events, ask at the tourist office, which publishes lists of the many festivals (see box, p.202), exhibitions, concerts and plays taking place in the city. Classical concerts are also held in the cathedral.

Le Carré Quai Jean Lagrive ✆ 90 80 44 48 72, ⓦ carre -club.com. This little nightclub on the east bank of the river plays a mix of French and international pop music, with a crowd mostly of under 30s. On Fridays the entrance fee for men is €5, while women get in free; on Saturdays it's €10 for all. €2 compulsory bag check. Fri & Sat 11.30pm–6.30am.

Les Docks 430 allées des Soupirs ✆ 06 65 22 36 38, ⓦ lesdocks-cahors.fr. Down on the waterfront, *Les Docks* serves as a youth venue, skate park and events space, with

live bands playing each Friday. Ticket office Tues–Fri 9am–noon & 2–6pm, Sat 2–6pm.

Le Dousil 124 rue Nationale ✆ 05 65 53 19 67. This wine bar is a great place to sample local reds before setting off on the wine trail. They dish up good food, too, including cheese or charcuterie platters (from €12.90), tapas (from €3.20) and *tartines* (from €3.60). Wine is sold by the glass or bottle. July & Aug daily 11am–3pm & 6pm–1am; Sept–June Tues–Sat 11am–3pm & 6pm–1am.

ENTERTAINMENT

ABC Cinema 24 rue des Augustins ✆ 05 65 35 03 11, ⓦ abc-cahors.fr. Shows a range of international movies and new releases – check ahead for English screenings.

Théâtre de Cahors Place François Mitterrand ✆ 05 65

20 88 60, ⓦ mairie-cahors.fr. For plays, the principal venue is this very plush Neoclassical theatre, which puts on a varied programme of theatre, dance, concerts and opera.

DIRECTORY

Hospital Centre Hospitalier Jean Rougier, 449–335 rue du Président Wilson (✆ 05 65 20 50 50). Emergencies should head round the back of the building.

Police Commissariat de Police, 1 rue de l'Ancienne Gendarmerie (✆ 05 65 23 17 17).

East along the Lot

Upstream from Cahors the Lot valley becomes narrower and the cliffs higher. The river is confined to ever-tighter turns and castles sprout from inaccessible knuckles of rock, often with red-tiled villages clinging to their flanks. Delightful **St-Cirq Lapopie**, 30km or so east of Cahors, perched precariously on the edge of a 100m drop, is the most dramatic sight in the whole valley. Further along the river's south bank on the D8, the Renaissance **Château de Cénevières** boasts an interesting history, as well as some unusual frescoes and a good collection of period furniture. The only major settlement along this stretch of river is **Cajarc**, an important market town with an incongruous modern art gallery; the town is also a stop on the pilgrims' road to Santiago de Compostela. Continuing upstream, the scenery takes over once again as the Lot winds its way past more medieval villages and castles, and beneath a 300m-high belvedere, the **Saut de la Mounine**, on the valley's southern lip. There's nothing particular to stop for along the last stretch of river heading northeast to **Capdenac**, near **Figeac**. Instead, you could take a diversion south across the *causse* to where the **Grotte de Foissac** harbours some prehistoric remains alongside a varied and colourful array of stalactites and stalagmites, and then continue on across country to the atmospheric ruins of **Peyrusse-le-Roc**.

GETTING AROUND   **EAST ALONG THE LOT**

The Lot valley is unusually well served by **public transport**, with an SNCF bus (see p.207 & p.224) running along the river's north bank from Cahors to Figeac. It stops at almost every village en route, though you'll have to walk across the river to villages on the south side, and will need your own transport to explore the high country on either side.

Vers

Immediately east of Cahors, the Lot valley is taken up with a busy main road, train tracks and scattered modern developments, above which soars the bridge for the A20 *autoroute*. However, things improve dramatically after the village of **VERS**, some 15km upstream, where the main D653 to Figeac strikes off northeastwards. Vers itself doesn't merit a stop, unless you are in search of overnight **accommodation**.

ARRIVAL AND DEPARTURE   **VERS**

By bus Buses stop near *La Truite Dorée* hotel.

ACCOMMODATION AND EATING

La Truite Dorée Rue de la Barre ☎ 05 65 31 41 51, ⓦ latruitedoree.fr. At the entrance to the village overlooking the River Vers where it flows into the Lot from the north, *La Truite Dorée* is the most attractive accommodation option in Vers. Rooms in the modern annexe have balconies over the river and there's an excellent restaurant, much patronized by locals, offering *menus* from €16 at lunch and €24.50 in the evenings. Breakfast €9.50. Restaurant daily March to mid-Nov noon–1.30pm & 7.30–9pm. **€79**

Bouziès

East of Vers, the D662 hugs the north bank of the River Lot as it meanders back and forth beneath cliffs that loom ever higher as you near **BOUZIÈS**, located on the south bank across a narrow suspension bridge. The main reason for coming here is to walk along the **chemin de halage**, a towpath cut into the cliff just above water level on the river's south bank. In pre-railway days it was used by men hauling produce-laden *gabares* boats upstream; it now forms part of the GR36 long-distance footpath, indicated by red-and-white markers, which you can join at the car park on the east side of Bouziès. The rock-hewn section starts after about 500m and extends for some 300m; if you're feeling energetic, you can then continue on to St-Cirq Lapopie (see p.212).

Another way of exploring the riverbank is to take to the water. Bouziès is a **boating** and **canoeing** centre, with several companies setting up shop on the south side of the bridge in the summer.

ARRIVAL AND ACTIVITIES   **BOUZIÈS**

By bus SNCF buses stop on the main road near the bridge. Destinations Cahors (3–6 daily; 45–50min); Cajarc (3–6 daily; 40min); St-Cirq Lapopie (3–6 daily; 10min).

Boat rental You can hire canoes from various outlets along the river during the summer months; prices typically start at €5 per hour. Lot Navigation (April–Oct; ☎ 05 65 24 32 20, ⓦ lot-navigation.com) rents houseboats for up to ten people (from €971 per week, or €630 for a three-day weekend).

5

ACCOMMODATION AND EATING

Les Falaises Le Bourg ☎05 65 31 26 83, ⊛hotel-falaises-bouzies.federal-hotel.com. The sole choice if you want to stay in Bouziès, *Les Falaises* offers clean albeit outdated rooms, a swimming pool and a decent restaurant (*menus* from €22), right in the village centre. Breakfast €10. Restaurant April–Oct daily noon–2pm & 7–9pm. **€75**

St-Cirq Lapopie

The gravity-defying village of **ST-CIRQ LAPOPIE** sits 5km east of Bouziès, clinging to the cliffside above the south bank of the Lot. Blessed with quaint cobbled lanes, half-timbered houses and gardens virtually unspoilt by modern intrusions, it's easy to see how it earned itself the title of *Village préféré des Français* ("France's favourite village") back in 2012, though the honour has since been passed on to Cordes-sur-Ciel (see p.280). Today, St-Cirq remains an irresistible draw for visitors and tour-bus crowds overwhelm its narrow streets during the summer months, but it's still worth the trouble, especially if you visit early or late in the day.

With a warren of alleyways snaking off from a single main street, St-Cirq is easy to navigate: simply follow the steep **rue de la Peyrolerie** downhill between the medieval gates of Porte de la Peyrolerie and Porte de Pélissaria, in between which it's variously known as **rue Droite** and **rue de la Pélissaria**. Along the way, stop off to stroll the central square, **place du Sombral**, where a small market is held on Wednesday mornings throughout summer, and admire the jumble of stone and half-timbered houses with their steeply pitched and gabled Quercy roofs.

Brief history

There has been a **castle** on this rocky protuberance, known as **La Popie**, since Gallo-Roman times, if not before. It was such a strategically important site that in the Middle Ages it was owned by not only the viscount of St-Cirq but also the other three viscounts of Quercy (Gourdon, Cardaillac and Castelnau). A feudal town soon grew up within the protection of its walls, although it wasn't a particularly safe haven: St-Cirq took a battering from the English during the Hundred Years War, while in the Wars of Religion it was seized by the Protestant Henry of Navarre, who ordered the castle to be destroyed in 1580 to keep it from the Catholics. Undaunted by these events, local craftsmen built up a reputation for their skill in **wood turning**, specifically of boxwood, which they fashioned into goblets, furniture and taps for casks. They continued to ply their craft into the nineteenth century, but following industrialization St-Cirq went into steep decline until it was rediscovered in the early twentieth century by the artistic fraternity, most famously **Henri Martin** (see p.206), **Man Ray** and the surrealist poet **André Breton**, who came to live here in the 1950s. The fame of St-Cirq has been spreading ever since.

Château and Église St-Cirq

The first place to seek out in St-Cirq Lapopie is the ruined **château** to the north of place du Sombral. Precious little remains of the castle, but the site is fantastic, plunging down to the river 100m below. Further east along the cliff edge, the fortified **Église St-Cirq** is now the village's dominant building. It's in a pretty sorry state itself, though you can still make out faint traces of thirteenth-century murals where the original Romanesque chapel was incorporated into a larger church three hundred years later.

Musée Rignault

Le Bourg • March–Oct Mon & Wed–Sun 10am–12.30pm & 2.30–6pm, open until 7pm July & Aug • €2 • ☎ 05 65 31 23 22

Below the Église St-Cirq, to the east, the **Musée Rignault** occupies a lovely fortified mansion with a romantic little rock garden and various other embellishments added by an art dealer who came to live here in 1922. A few pieces of his wide-ranging art collection are on display, while the rest of the space is given over to temporary exhibitions.

Maison Daura

Le Bourg • ☎ 05 65 40 78 19, ⓦ magp.fr

5

Maison Daura, near the entrance to St-Cirq Lapopie, was once the home of Catalan painter **Pierre Daura**. It's an exceptionally beautiful example of Gothic architecture, with archetypal windows and perfectly preserved doors, a fit setting for the purpose it now serves – a residence for international artists. It hosts frequent **modern art exhibitions**, which are open to the public and well worth a look; the tourist office (see below) will have all details of what's on.

ARRIVAL AND INFORMATION
ST-CIRQ LAPOPIE

By bus Buses on the Cahors–Figeac route drop you across the river from St-Cirq in the hamlet of Tour-de-Faure; from here you can call a taxi (Philippe Merle; ☎ 06 03 15 41 67) or leg it up the steep hill for the last 2km.

By car There are three car parks for St-Cirq: the lowest, 800m below the village, is free; the one closest to the village centre charges €4 per day; and the third sits 300m above the village and costs €3.50 per day.

Tourist office Place du Sombral (April, May & Oct Mon–Sat 10am–1pm & 2–6pm, Sun 11am–1pm & 2–5pm; June & Sept daily 10am–6pm; July & Aug Mon–Sat 10am–7pm,

Sun 10am–6pm; Nov–March Mon–Sat 9.30am–12.30pm & 2–5.30pm; ☎ 05 65 31 31 31, ⓦ saint-cirqlapopie.com); staff can furnish you with a handy English-language walking guide to St-Cirq.

Activites Kalapca Loisirs (☎ 05 65 24 21 01, ⓦ kalapca .com) at the *Camping de la Plage* (see below) offer a host of different activities, including canoeing (1.5hr guided tours €15; rentals €6/hr), guided walks (€220 per day), rock climbing (half-day €26 per person) and canyoning (full-day €49 per person).

ACCOMMODATION

There are various **accommodation** options in the village itself, all of which get booked up weeks ahead in summer. The best bet if you don't have a pre-booked room is to look in **Tour-de-Faure**, on the other side of the river.

Auberge du Sombral Place du Sombral ☎ 05 65 31 26 08, ⓦ lesombral.com. Spotless, albeit sparsely furnished, rooms in the heart of the village, plus a decent restaurant with *menus* from €17 at lunch and €26 in the evening. Breakfast €9. Restaurant April–June & Sept to mid-Nov Mon, Wed–Thurs & Sun noon–2pm, Fri & Sat 7.30–9pm; July & Aug Mon–Thurs & Sun noon–2pm, Fri & Sat 7.30–9pm. **€85**

Camping de la Plage ☎ 05 65 30 29 51, ⓦ camping plage.com. Well-run three-star campsite down by the bridge, offering a restaurant/snack bar and canoe and bike rental (see above). Closed mid-Oct to April. **€24**

Les Gabarres Le Roucayral ☎ 05 65 30 24 57, ⓦ hotel lesgabarres.com. The functional rooms at this hotel in Tour-de-Faure are more than compensated for by friendly, welcoming staff and a wonderful setting including a pool, flower-filled terrace and garden. Breakfast €9.90. **€98**

Le Mas de Laval ☎ 06 32 66 21 68, ⓦ masdelaval.fr. Some 3km southeast of St Cirq, this charming *chambre d'hôte*

is full of rustic charm, plus there's a large pool, delicious all-organic cuisine (reservations required) and horse riding tours available. **€110**

Maison Redon La Combe ☎ 05 65 30 24 13, ⓦ maison redon.com. A quiet and peaceful *chambre d'hôte* in an ivy-covered house, with five spacious, well-appointed rooms and a lovely garden. Closed Sept–May. **€84**

★**St Cirq** Tour-de-Faure ☎ 05 65 30 30 30, ⓦ hotel -lesaintcirq.com. St Cirq's most lavish hotel is perched at the top of the valley, offering spectacular views over the town. There are a range of well-furnished rooms and romantic suites to choose from, plus an indoor pool, hamam and spa. Free shuttles to the village are also available. Breakfast €13.80. Closed Feb to mid-Nov and two weeks at Christmas. **€108**

La Truffière ☎ 05 65 30 20 22, ⓦ camping-truffiere .com. A spacious, well-managed campsite on the plateau 3km southeast of St-Cirq via the D42. There's a restaurant (July & Aug only), plus a heated pool and children's play area. Closed Sept to mid-April. **€18.80**

EATING

The nearest food shop is a small grocer down in Tour-de-Faure. If you're self-catering you might like to head 12km south to the charming little town of Limogne where you'll find everything you need, including a Sunday morning **market**.

★**Le Canton** Rue de la Pélissaria ☎ 05 65 35 59 03, ⓦ lecantou.net. St-Cirq's top restaurant offers limited options but executes each dish to perfection, blending some unusual ingredients into tasty creations. Tuck into

green asparagus and pesto panna cotta, savour monkfish in a coconut-milk sauce, then indulge in gingerbread and walnut tiramisu. *Menus* from €18.50. Mon noon–2pm, Tues–Sun noon–2pm & 7–9pm.

5

Le Gourmet Quercynois Rue de la Peyrolerie ☎05 65 31 21 20, ⓦrestaurant-legourmetquercynois.com. Take a table on the leafy terrace or cosy up by the open fire at this traditional restaurant and enjoy dishes such as pork with honey and herbs, or duck with truffles; evening *menus* at €27.80. Mid-Feb to Dec daily noon–2pm & 7–9pm.

Lou Bolat Just inside Porte de la Peyrolerie ☎05 65 30 29 04. Reliably good food with a terrace overlooking the valley and a choice of crêpes, omelettes (from €8.50) and salads (from €9.50) on offer. July & Aug daily noon–9pm; Sept–June Mon & Wed–Sun noon–2pm.

L'Oustal Rue de la Pélissaria ☎05 65 31 20 17. A tiny but atmospheric little place tucked in a corner at the top end of rue de la Pélissaria, just south of the church. The food is fresh from the market and organic, with dishes varying according to the season. Three-course *menus* from €19. Easter–June & Sept to mid-Oct Mon & Thurs–Sun noon–2pm & 7–9pm; July & Aug daily noon–2pm & 7–9pm.

Château de Cénevières

Guided tours May–Sept Mon–Sat 10am–noon & 2–6pm, Sun 2–6pm; April & Oct Mon–Sat 2pm–5pm • €7, children €3.50 • ☎05 65 31 27 33, ⓦ chateau-cenevieres.com • The nearest bus stop is in St-Martin-Labouval, a good 1km downstream and across on the north bank

Seven kilometres out of St-Cirq Lapopie, along the quiet D8 road (avoid the main D662), is the **Château de Cénevières**, perched on a rocky spur just beyond Cénevières village. The château, which largely dates from the sixteenth century in its present form, belonged to the **de Gourdon** family for nine hundred years until the line petered out in 1616. The last in line, Antoine de Gourdon, was a fervent supporter of the Reformation, so much so that the Protestant leader Henry of Navarre stayed here before attacking Cahors in 1580. Antoine brought back a rich haul that included the cathedral's principal altar – the boat carrying it, however, capsized and the altar is now somewhere at the bottom of the Lot. The château was saved from being torched during the Revolution by a quick-thinking overseer who opened the wine cellars to the mob, though he couldn't save the library, nor the coat of arms and other carvings on the facade. Cénevières was sold only once during its long history, to the ancestors of the present owners in 1793. Over the years they have uncovered several unusual Renaissance-era **frescoes**: notably, a frieze of the Istanbul skyline in the grand salon, and scenes from Greek mythology alongside what is believed to be a representation of an alchemist's fire and the philosopher's stone adorning a little vaulted chamber.

Cajarc

CAJARC, which lies on the river's north bank 9km upstream from Calvignac, is the biggest town on the Lot between Cahors and Capdenac. It consists of a small core of old lanes encircled by the **boulevard du Tour-de-Ville**, where you'll find a cluster of cafés, brasseries and small shops. A lively **market** takes place each Saturday afternoon on place du Foirail, off Tour-de-Ville opposite the tourist office (see p.216), while the town is also the focus of the region's **saffron** production (see box, p.216), hosting the annual Fête du Safran each October.

Maison des Arts Georges-Pompidou

134 av Germain Canet • Wed–Sun 2–6pm • Free • ☎05 65 40 78 19, ⓦ magp.fr

Cajarc's only sight as such is the **Maison des Arts Georges-Pompidou**, on the northeastern outskirts on the D19 Figeac road. The gallery is named in honour of the former French prime minister, who bought a holiday home near here in 1963, and hosts three or four major contemporary art exhibitions a year.

ARRIVAL AND INFORMATION	CAJARC

By bus SNCF buses stop on the north side of town on place du Foirail.

By train The train station is on avenue de la Gare, just north of the riverfront.

Destinations Bouziès (3–6 daily; 40min); Cahors (3–6 daily; 1hr).

5

QUERCY SAFFRON

Saffron was originally introduced to the Quercy region by returning crusaders in the twelfth century, and quickly became a major source of income. However, production of the spice declined drastically in the eighteenth century, largely due to the significant manpower requirements. Obtained from the dried stigmas of the saffron crocus, the spice can only be picked by hand early on autumn mornings. It takes 200,000 flowers and over forty hours' labour to obtain a kilogram of dried saffron, and pound for pound it's more expensive than gold. Historically the spice has been used in sweet and savoury dishes, particularly in central Asia, as well as for dyeing cloths, as a hangover remedy and to cure tuberculosis and measles. It's also supposed to have cancer-suppressing properties.

Around seventy farms in the Lot valley area now produce saffron commercially, and many of them can be visited, particularly around harvest time in **October**. Their organization's website, ⓦ safran-du-quercy.com, details recipes using saffron, and they host a major **saffron fair** at Cajarc (see p.202) at the end of October to celebrate the harvest, with plenty of opportunities for tasting and buying.

Tourist office Housed in a converted chapel on boulevard du Tour-de-Ville (April–June & Sept Mon–Sat 3–6pm, Sun 10am–12.30pm; July & Aug daily 10am–12.30pm & 2.30–7pm; ☎ 05 65 40 72 89).

ACCOMMODATION

Gîte d'Étape Place du Foirail ☎ 06 14 66 54 89. A great-value *gîte d'étape* with comfortable rooms and individual shower and kitchen facilities on each floor. No wi-fi, and no meals served, but there are restaurants within walking distance. **€12.35**

Mas de Garrigue La Garrigue, Calvignac ☎ 05 65 53 93 31, ⓦ masdegarrigue.com. A few kilometres back from Carjac towards Cahors lies this delightful *chambre d'hôte*, set in a restored fifteenth-century hunting lodge. It offers five beautifully appointed bedrooms, plus evening meals (€37) available on Mon and Thurs by reservation only. **€120**

La Peyrade Rte de Cahors ☎ 05 65 10 42 03. This simple, sparsely furnished hotel is nonetheless a welcoming option for budget travellers. As well as rooms there are small apartments sleeping up to four (from €120), plus a restaurant with good-value *menus* from

€13.50. Breakfast €7. Restaurant April–Sept Mon–Sat 7–9pm, Sun 12.30–2pm; Oct–March Mon, Tues & Thurs–Sun 7–9pm. **€57**

La Ségalière 380 av François Mitterrand ☎ 05 65 40 65 35, ⓦ lasegaliere.com. The smartest hotel in town, around 400m east on the D662 to Capdenac. Expect bright, well-furnished rooms, some with balconies, plus a swimming pool and ample grassy gardens. There's also a decent restaurant with *menus* from €22. Breakfast €10. Restaurant April–Oct Mon–Fri 7–9.15pm, Sat & Sun noon–2.30pm & 7–9.15pm. **€85**

Le Terriol ☎ 05 65 40 72 74. A basic two-star municipal campsite, beside the river roughly 200m southwest of the centre. It offers laundry facilities and a communal freezer; the municipal swimming pool is next door. Closed Sept–May. **€16.36**

EATING

L'Allée des Vignes 32 bd du Tour-de-Ville ☎ 05 65 11 61 87, ⓦ alleedesvignes.com. Part bistro (lunchtimes Mon–Sat), part gastronomic restaurant (evenings and Sun lunch), Cajarc's latest addition is a swish, modern affair, hung with the works of local artists. Tempt your taste buds with delicacies like foie gras carpaccio or wild truffles, with *menus* from €34. June–Oct Thurs–Sat noon–2pm & 7.15–9pm, Sun 12–2pm.

Cajarc Gourmand Place de L'Église ☎ 05 65 40 69 50, ⓦ cajarcgourmand.com. Hidden away in a quiet square beside the church, *Cajarc Gourmand* is a safe bet for a good meal, with classic French dishes accompanied by some more creative fare. There are various *formules* and *menus* available ranging from €12.50 up to €32 – be sure to try the delicious foie gras ravioli. March–June & Sept–Nov Wed & Fri–Sun noon–2pm & 7.30–9.30pm; July & Aug daily same hours.

Upstream to Capdenac

Upstream from Cajarc, the Lot twists through one more giant meander and then straightens out until you reach the next big loop at Capdenac. Buses follow the northerly route past a succession of picturesque villages and castles, but if you've got your own transport, the less-travelled roads along the river's south bank make for a more interesting journey through walnut orchards and past weathered farm buildings, then up on to the flat, empty *cause* with little sign of habitation, save for the occasional dolmen or *cabane*, the traditional, stone-built shepherds' huts.

A few kilometres further on you drop back down to the river along tiny lanes that wend their way northeastwards for about 15km before hitting the main D922. Turn left here and you'll be in Figeac (see p.220) in about ten minutes. Alternatively, if you cross over and follow the D86 along the river, another 7km will bring you to **CAPDENAC**, a major railway town on the south bank of the River Lot. There's a great view from the high ridge above the town and river to the north, but otherwise Capdenac is of little interest.

Grotte de Foissac

1hr guided tours: April, May & Oct Mon–Fri & Sun 2–5pm; June & Sept daily 10–11.30am & 2–6pm; July & Aug daily 10am–6pm • €9 • ☎ 06 19 12 98 28, ⓦ grotte-de-foissac.fr

One of the area's less-frequented caves, the **Grotte de Foissac** lies about 3km west across the *causse* from Foissac village. The cave was discovered in 1959 by a local pot-holing club, who found not only a huge cavern of colourful and varied concretions – including delicate needles, some bulging out into onion shapes – but also evidence of human activity going back at least four thousand years. From the number of **skeletons** and their positions, it seems that, unusually, the cave was used as a cemetery. It was also a source of clay – you can still see where people dug it out with their hands, and they also left large and beautifully fashioned pots, probably for storing grain. But the most moving evidence is the lone footprint left by a child deep inside the cave.

Peyrusse-le-Roc

Twenty kilometres east of Foissac village, via beautiful back lanes through Naussac and along a scenic brook, the ruined towers of **PEYRUSSE-LE-ROC** are well worth a look. The "modern" village, a tiny weatherworn huddle of half-timbered houses gathered round a seventeenth-century church, sits above a narrow valley. On the valley sides, hidden in the steep woods, lie the scattered remains of a fortified medieval town which once sheltered some 4500 people – a sizeable population in those days – who were seeking their fortunes in the local silver mines. But their luck ran out in the early sixteenth century, when silver from the recently discovered Americas began to flood the market, and the town was eventually abandoned around 1700. The site is gradually being tidied up and some of the buildings restored, but it still remains an atmospheric place.

THE LEGEND OF MONKEY'S LEAP

Around 7km east of Cajarc, where the D127 first climbs up from the Lot river, the road skirts along the edge of a 300m-high cliff formed by the meander. The spot is known as the **Saut de la Mounine** ("Monkey's Leap"), after a legend concerning a local lord who ordered his daughter to be thrown off the cliff when she fell in love with a boy he disapproved of. A hermit took pity on the girl and secretly dressed a monkey in her clothes instead. When the poor beast was chucked over the edge, the lord of course repented, and was only too relieved to discover he'd been outwitted. He apparently forgave his daughter, but history doesn't relate whom she married. Whatever the outcome, it's a marvellous **view** from up here, taking in the meander filled with patchwork fields and the ruined Château de Montbrun on the far hillside – where the lord and his fortunate daughter once lived.

5

A path leads from the northwest corner of the church square to a pinnacle of rock crowned by **twin towers**, all that's left of the medieval fortress that protected the town. If you've got a head for heights, you can scramble up the iron ladders for a vertiginous view of the gorge. From here a cobbled mule trail leads steeply down through the woods, where the stones of a Gothic church, synagogue and hospital stand roofless, to the river and a little thirteenth-century chapel, complete but not open to the public. To return to the modern village, follow the river downstream and pick up another path, which takes you past the old market hall to the village gate. It's possible to do shorter circuits simply by following the signs, or you can buy a guidebook and map (€4) from the **tourist office** beside the church (Mon–Sat 10am–noon; ☎05 65 80 49 33).

The Célé valley

Instead of following the River Lot east from Cahors, you can take an alternative route to Figeac along the wilder and narrower **Célé valley**, which joins the Lot 1km or so upstream from Bouziès (see p.211). A single road winds through the luxuriant canyon-like valley, frequented mainly by canoeists and walkers on the GR65 footpath, which runs sometimes close to the river, sometimes on the edge of the *causse* on the north bank. The major settlement along here is **Cabrerets**, a village not far upstream from the Célé's confluence with the Lot, which serves as a base for the nearby cave system of **Grotte de Pech-Merle**. Continuing northeast, the valley is punctuated by a succession of villages and hamlets built against the cliff face. Of these, two in particular stand out: **Marcilhac-sur-Célé**, about halfway along the valley, for the atmospheric ruins of its abbey; and the tiny hamlet of **Espagnac-Ste-Eulalie** in the north, where another, more substantial church sports a delightfully whimsical belfry.

GETTING AROUND   **THE CÉLÉ VALLEY**

By canoe There's no public transport along the Célé but it's possible to traverse the valley by canoe; rental outlets in St-Cirq (see p.213) and Marcilhac (see p.220) can organize pick-up and drop-off along the river.

Cabrerets

CABRERETS lies 4km up the Célé from its confluence with the Lot, the approach guarded by the sturdy **Château de Gontaut-Biron** (closed to the public), on a small flood plain where the River Sagne joins the Célé. It's a pretty enough spot, but the only real reason to linger in Cabrerets is to take advantage of its tourist amenities.

INFORMATION   **CABRERETS**

Tourist office There's a small seasonal tourist office in the village centre (May Sat & Sun 10am–1pm & 2–6pm; July & Aug Tues–Sat same hours; June & Sept Thurs–Sat same hours; ☎05 65 31 27 12) that sells handy guides detailing walks in the area.

ACCOMMODATION AND EATING

Auberge de la Sagne ☎05 65 31 26 62, ⓦhotel -auberge-cabrerets.com. The small, smart and absolutely spotless *Auberge de la Sagne*, 1km west of Cabrerets on the road to the Grotte de Pech-Merle, is perhaps the best of the accommodation options hereabouts. There's a pool, a well-tended garden and a restaurant offering good-quality home cooking, with *menus* for €18. Breakfast €8. Restaurant mid-April to mid-Oct daily noon–1.30pm & 7–9pm. **€59**

Le Cantal Cabrerets ☎05 65 31 26 61. Petite and very basic two-star campsite immediately north of Cabrerets on the other side of the Célé. Closed mid-Oct to mid-April. **€10.50**

Des Grottes Le Bourg ☎05 65 31 27 02, ⓦhotel desgrottes.com. Modern, well-furnished rooms with either a bath or shower at this central hotel overlooking the Célé. There's also a pool, a pretty terrace and a good restaurant (*menus* from €16), but wi-fi is only available in communal areas. Breakfast €9. Closed Nov–March. **€65**

Grotte de Pech-Merle

1hr guided visits, English written commentary available: April–Sept daily 9.30am–noon & 1.30–5pm; Nov–March selected dates (see website) 2–4pm • €11, children €7 • ☎ 05 65 31 27 05, ⓦ pechmerle.com

5

Up in the hills 3km west of Cabrerets by road, or 1km via the footpath from beside the *mairie*, the **Grotte de Pech-Merle** takes some beating. Discovered in 1922 by two local boys, the galleries are not only full of the most spectacular limestone formations – structures tiered like wedding cakes, hanging like curtains, and shaped like discs or "cave pearls" – but also contain an equally dazzling display of more than five hundred **prehistoric drawings**. To protect the drawings, tickets are restricted to seven hundred per day (it's advisable to book four or five days ahead in July and August, and at least one day ahead at other times; online bookings must be made at least a week in advance), and the guides make sure you're processed through in the allotted time. If possible, it's worth allowing yourself time to visit the **museum**, located beside the ticket office (same hours and ticket as the cave), before your scheduled tour. A twenty-minute film, subtitled in English, provides an excellent overview of Pech-Merle and its prehistoric art.

Chapelle des Mammouths

The Grotte de Pech-Merle's drawings date mostly from the early Magdalenian era (10,000–17,000 years ago), contemporaneous with much of the cave art in the Vézère valley (see p.135), with which they share many similarities. The first drawings you come to are in the so-called **Chapelle des Mammouths**, executed on a white calcite panel that looks as if it's been specially prepared for the purpose; note how the artists used the contour and relief of the rock to do the work, producing utterly convincing mammoths with just two lines. In addition to the mammoths, there are horses, oxen and bison charging head down with tiny rumps and arched tails; the guide will point out where St-Cirq's André Breton (see p.212) added his own mammoth – he was fined but the damage was done.

The horse frieze

After the Chapelle des Mammouths comes a vast chamber containing the glorious **horse frieze**, the oldest of the drawings (at around 25,000 years). Two large horses stand back to back, the head of one formed by a natural protuberance of rock, and their hindquarters superimposed to provide perspective. The surface is spattered with black dots of some unknown symbolic significance and silhouettes of hands, while the ceiling is covered with finger marks preserved in the soft clay. On the way you pass the skeletons of cave-hyena and bears that have been lying there for thousands of years, and, finally, the footprints of an adolescent preserved in a muddy pool some eight thousand years ago.

Musée de l'Insolite

Lieu dit Liauzu • April–June & Sept–Oct daily 9am–7pm; July & Aug daily 9am–8pm; rest of the year by appointment • €3 • ☎ 05 65 30 21 01, ⓦ museedelinsolite.com

Don't miss the gloriously eccentric **Musée de l'Insolite** (Museum of the Quirky), situated on the D41 heading up the Célé some 9km from Cabrerets. After about 3km you emerge from a tunnel and are suddenly confronted by old bikes, mannequins and even the shells of cars hanging from the rock face. They belong to a sculptor with an engaging sense of humour, and are mostly based on wordplay and puns in French. There's an outdoor garden and an indoor gallery, both full of bizarre montages fashioned out of tree stumps, old machines and other bits of scrap.

Marcilhac

MARCILHAC, 16km upstream from Cabrerets, is home to the partly ruined **L'Abbaye de Marcilhac** (guided tours by advance booking only: July to mid-Sept 2–4.30pm; €3; ☎ 05 65 40 65 52). Founded some time prior to the ninth century, this Benedictine

5

abbey had the good fortune to be in charge of the modest sanctuary at Rocamadour (see p.175), in which St Amadour's body was discovered in 1166. The subsequent revenue from pilgrims and benefactors led to a brief golden age, which came to an end when English troops laid waste to the building in the Hundred Years War. It never really recovered and was abandoned after the Reformation. Entering the abbey from the south, a rather primitive and badly damaged ninth-century Christ in Majesty decorates the tympanum over the ruined door. In the damp interior of the **church** itself are late-fifteenth-century frescoes of the Apostles and another Christ in Majesty, with the local nobility's coats of arms below. The few religious treasures that survived – such as a seventeenth-century polychrome pietà and a nicely rendered statue of a pilgrim – are now on display in the small **Musée d'Art Sacré** (mid-June to mid-Sept 10.30am–12.30pm & 2.30–5.30pm; free) in a handsome half-timbered house immediately west of the abbey church.

INFORMATION AND ACTIVITIES   MARCILHAC

Tourist office The Musée d'Art Sacré (see above) doubles as a seasonal tourist office (mid-June to mid-Sept 10.30am–12.30pm & 2.30–5.30pm; ☎ 05 65 40 68 44, ⓦ marcilhac.fr).

Bike and boat rental Passion Aventure (☎ 06 10 73 73 12, ⓦ location-canoe-cele.com), along the river by the bridge, offer canoe and kayak tours through the Célé valley from €15 per person for a 3hr tour.

ACCOMMODATION

Le Pré de Monsieur ☎ 05 65 40 77 88, ⓦ lepredemonsieur .e-monsite.com. Two-star municipal campsite just north of

Marcilhac village, with a pool, tennis, volleyball, badminton and its own restaurant. Closed Oct–April. __€16.80__

Espagnac-Ste-Eulalie

The tiny and beautiful hamlet of **ESPAGNAC-STE-EULALIE** lies about 12km upriver from Marcilhac and is reached via an old stone bridge. Immediately across the bridge, an eye-catching octagonal lantern crowns the belfry of the **Prieuré Notre-Dame-du-Val-Paradis**; visits can be organized via the Mairie on Chemin des Dames (☎ 05 65 40 09 17). The building itself is strangely ill-proportioned, a result of the nave being truncated in the Hundred Years War, which somehow adds to its charm. Inside, apart from a typically over-the-top altarpiece from the Counter-Reformation, the most interesting features are the ornate **tombs** of the church's thirteenth-century benefactor, Aymeric d'Hébrard de St-Sulpice, a local man who became bishop of Coimbra in Portugal, and those of the duke of Cardaillac and his wife, who financed the rebuilding of the choir in the fourteenth century.

ACCOMMODATION AND EATING   ESPAGNAC-STE-EULALIE

Gîte d'Étape ☎ 05 65 11 42 66. An ancient fortified gateway south of the church now houses a *gîte d'étape* offering very good-value accommodation, including dormitories for four or eight people. Kitchen and dining facilities are also available to guests. Closed Oct–March. Dorms __€12__, doubles __€30__

Le Moulin Vieux ☎ 05 65 40 00 41, ⓦ camping -lemoulinvieux.com. A good three-star campsite in Brengues, 3km back downstream from Espagnac. Facilities include a restaurant (July & Aug), pool, mini-golf and canoe hire. Closed Nov–March. __€15.50__

Figeac

Situated on the River Célé some 70km east of Cahors, **FIGEAC** is a very appealing town with an unspoilt medieval centre that, surprisingly, is not encumbered by tourism. Its principal church, the **Église St-Sauveur**, contains a sumptuous rendition of the Passion of Christ in a side chapel, and there's an excellent **museum** devoted to famed locally born Egyptologist Jean-François Champollion. Apart from these two sights, it's a

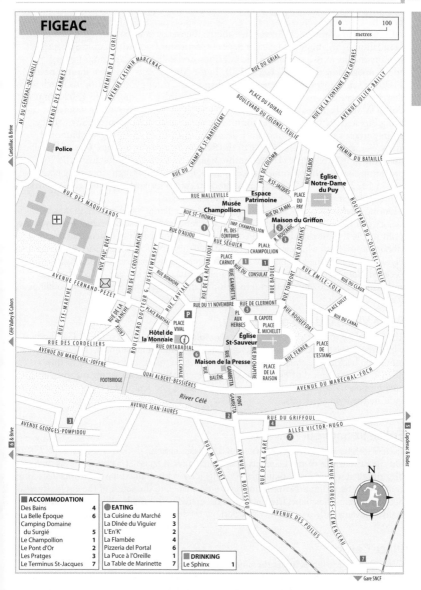

FIGEAC

5

ACCOMMODATION		**EATING**		
Des Bains	4	La Cuisine du Marché	5	
La Belle Époque	6	La Dînée du Viguier	3	
Camping Domaine		L'En'K'	2	
du Surgié	5	La Flambée	4	
Le Champollion	1	Pizzeria del Portal	6	
Le Pont d'Or	2	La Puce à l'Oreille	1	
Les Pratges	3	La Table de Marinette	7	**DRINKING**
Le Terminus St-Jacques	7			Le Sphinx	1

pleasure just to wander the narrow lanes, lined with a delightful array of houses, both stone and half-timbered, adorned with carvings, ornate colonnaded windows and elaborate ironwork.

Figeac's old quarter sits on the north bank of the Célé, its ramparts and ditches now replaced with a ring of boulevards. From the southern boulevard, the town's main artery and principal shopping street, pedestrianized **rue Gambetta**, leads north from the old stone bridge, **Pont Gambetta**, through place aux Herbes, to **place Carnot**, where a food market is held each Saturday, and to neighbouring **place Champollion**.

5

Brief history

Like many other provincial towns hereabouts, Figeac owes its beginnings to the foundation of an **abbey** in the early days of Christianity, one which quickly became wealthy thanks to its position on the pilgrim roads to both Rocamadour (see p.175) and Santiago de Compostela (see p.290). In the Middle Ages the town flourished as a trading centre, exporting wine and woollen fabrics throughout Europe, so much so that the wealthy merchants began to challenge the abbey's authority. In 1302 King Philip IV (the Fair) resolved the issue by sending his representative, the **Viguier**, to bring Figeac directly under royal control. At the same time he granted the town the all-important right to mint money. Figeac's fortunes declined during the Hundred Years War, then revived at the time of the Renaissance, but it was the Wars of Religion that pushed it into eclipse. The town threw in its lot with the Protestants in 1576, providing them with an important safe-haven, until it was brought forcefully back into line in 1622. Figeac later became an important centre for tanning hides, and received a further boost with the arrival of the railway in 1862.

During **World War II** the Germans converted Figeac's Ratier metal workshop into a factory churning out propellers for Luftwaffe bombers. When the Resistance destroyed the plant in 1944, more than five hundred local men were carted off to concentration and labour camps, from which at least 120 failed to return at the end of the war. By the 1960s Figeac's old quarter had declined to such an extent that the majority of buildings were declared uninhabitable. It was designated a preservation zone in 1986, since when the authorities have put a lot of effort into restoring the medieval and Renaissance buildings.

Place Vival and the old quarter

The best place to start exploring Figeac is on **place Vival** to the west of rue Gambetta, where the tourist office occupies the eye-catching **Hôtel de la Monnaie**. The building's origins go back to the thirteenth century when the city's mint was located in this district, and it's typical of Figeac's medieval merchants' houses, starting off with arcaded openings on the ground floor, while the colonnaded and sculpted windows above indicate the living quarters.

Église St-Sauveur

6 rue Ferrer • Daily 9am–noon & 2.30–7pm • Free • ☎ 05 65 34 11 63, ⓦ paroissedefigeac.fr

On the eastern side of rue Gambetta, the much-altered **Église St-Sauveur** stands on a big, gravelled square overlooking the river. Its lofty yet restrained nave provides a striking contrast to the intimate **Notre-Dame de la Pitié** chapel, to the south of the choir. The real highlight lies in the chapel itself, which is decorated with heavily gilded but dramatically realistic seventeenth-century carved wood panels depicting the Passion of Christ.

Place Carnot

Cafés spread their tables under the nineteenth-century *halle* in the middle of **place Carnot**, at the top of rue Gambetta, surrounded by a delightful range of stone and half-timbered houses. Some sport open wooden galleries at the top; another typical feature of this region, these *solelhos* were used for drying and storing foodstuffs. On the eastern side lies *Le Sphinx* café, where the father of Jean-François Champollion (see opposite) had his bookshop, while the *halle* springs to life each Saturday morning, when it hosts a sizeable food **market**.

Place Champollion

Place Carnot opens into the grander but equally alluring **place Champollion**, named after **Jean-François Champollion**, who finally cracked Egyptian hieroglyphics by

5

CHAMPOLLION AND THE ROSETTA STONE

Jean-François Champollion was born in Figeac in 1790, the son of a bookseller who opened a shop on place Carnot, in what is now *Le Sphinx* café. His interest in Egypt was first sparked by news coming back from Napoleon Bonaparte's 1798 Egyptian adventures, and when an acquaintance showed him the ancient Egyptians' so-far indecipherable script two years later, he became hooked. Declaring that he would solve the puzzle, Champollion set about studying ancient and Middle Eastern languages – he eventually mastered a mind-boggling total of twenty – and poring over hieroglyphs. One of the most important resources available was the **Rosetta Stone**. A slab of black basalt measuring around 120cm in height and 80cm wide, the stone was discovered in 1799 by French soldiers building fortifications around the town of Rosetta in the Nile delta; three years later it fell into British hands when they seized Egypt from the French, and it now resides in London's British Museum.

The crucial significance of the Rosetta Stone is that the same text – a decree issued in 196 BC recording the honours to be accorded to the young Pharaoh Ptolemy – is repeated in three different scripts: **hieroglyphics**, **demotic** (an abbreviated, cursive form of hieroglyphics used for everyday affairs) and **Greek**. By being able to translate the Greek, scholars then had fresh clues, but it took until 1822 before Champollion made the final breakthrough when he realized that hieroglyphs were, broadly, not pictograms but phonetic characters. Within two years he had identified the majority of symbols, and all this without having set foot in Egypt. He made his one and only voyage to the country in 1828, but died of a stroke four years later at the age of 41.

deciphering the Rosetta Stone (see box opposite). The square's south side is dominated by a stunning, white-stone Gothic mansion with a row of handsome ornamental windows, filled with lacy trefoil stonework. Opposite, on the corner with rue de Colomb, the **Maison du Griffon** is far less ostentatious, but this is Figeac's oldest house, built in the twelfth century and named after a barely visible griffin carved on the left-hand window arch (now blocked up) on the third floor.

Musée Champollion

Place Champollion • April–June & Sept–Oct Tues–Sun 10.30am–12.30pm & 2–6pm; July & Aug daily 10.30am–6pm; Nov–March Tues–Sun 2–5.30pm • €5, 13–18 year-olds €2.50, under 12s free • ☎ 05 65 50 31 08, ⓦ musee-champollion.fr

Jean-François Champollion was born in a house off place Champollion, to the northwest of the square, which now contains the fascinating **Musée Champollion**, dedicated not only to Champollion's life and work but also to the history of writing, with displays on Egyptian, Chinese, Mayan and Hebraic systems. In addition to many beautiful examples of hieroglyphic script, the museum houses an excellent collection of Egyptian funerary objects from the sixth and seventh centuries BC: sarcophagi, amulets and statues of the gods and goddesses, such as Bastet, a superb bronze cat, and an exquisitely crafted head of the god-king Osiris.

Place des Écritures

At the west end of impasse Champollion, a gigantic reproduction of the Rosetta Stone – the work of American artist Joseph Kossuth – forms the floor of the tiny **place des Écritures**, above which is a little garden with medicinal herbs and tufts of papyrus in pots. If it's open, you can cut through the **Espace Patrimoine** (April to early July & late Sept to end Oct Tues–Sun 2–6pm; early July to late Sept daily 10am–12.30pm & 3–7pm; free), a one-room exhibition illustrating Figeac's history and architecture, to rue de Colomb.

Église Notre-Dame du Puy

1 rue Victor Delbos • Daily: April–Oct 8am–noon & 3–8pm; Nov–March 9am–noon & 3–7pm • Free • ☎ 05 65 50 31 08

The large square tower looming over rue Delzhens is the last vestige of the fourteenth-century residence of the Viguier, royal representative of King Philip IV (the Fair). You'll

5

get a better view of it if you continue on up the hill to the **Église Notre-Dame du Puy**. Transformed into a veritable fortress by the Protestants in the late 1500s, then partially destroyed by Catholic reprisals, it now contains little of interest, but its cedar-shaded terrace is a peaceful spot from which to look down on the roofs of Figeac. When you're done, take cobbled rue St-Jacques, twisting and turning down the hillside back to rue de Colomb and place Champollion.

ARRIVAL AND DEPARTURE   FIGEAC

By train Figeac's *gare SNCF* – on the Toulouse–Clermont-Ferrand and Toulouse–Figeac–Brive lines – lies about 600m south of the town centre.
Destinations Assier (4–7 daily; 25min); Brive (5–7 daily; 1hr 20min); Cordes (4–5 daily; 1hr 20min); Gramat (4–5 daily; 30min); Laguépie (3–5 daily; 1hr); Najac (3–5 daily; 50min); Paris-Austerlitz (1–7 daily; 7hr); Rocamadour (4–5 daily; 40min); St-Denis-lès-Martel (3–5 daily; 55min); Toulouse (3–5 daily; 2hr 20min); Villefranche-de-

Rouergue (3–6 daily; 45min).
By bus SNCF buses stop at the train station. For details of all bus routes, call the central information desk (☎ 05 65 53 43 91).
Destinations Bouziès (3–6 daily; 1hr 10min); Cahors (3–6 daily; 1hr 45min); Cajarc (3–6 daily; 30–35min).
By car If you're arriving by car, note that the old quarter is largely pedestrianized. The most convenient parking is along the riverbank, where it's free, or on place Vival.

GETTING AROUND AND INFORMATION

Bike rental Office Intercommunal du Sport du Pays de Figeac/Cajarc, 2 av du Général-de-Gaulle (☎ 05 65 34 52 54, ⊚ oisgrandfigeac.com).
Car rental ADA, on the road west to Cahors (☎ 05 65 35 10 07); Avis, 1 av Georges-Pompidou (☎ 05 65 30 13 10). Both offer station pick-ups on request.
Taxis Bernard Taxis (☎ 05 65 50 00 20).
Tourist office Place Vival, in the Hôtel de la Monnaie

(April & Oct Mon–Sat 9am–12.30pm & 2–6pm; May, June & Sept Mon–Sat 9am–12.30pm & 2–6pm, Sun 10am–1pm; July & Aug daily 9am–7pm; Nov–March Mon–Fri 10am–12.30pm & 2–6pm, Sat 10am–12.30pm & 2–5pm; ☎ 05 65 34 06 25, ⊚ tourisme-figeac.com). They sell a do-it-yourself *Keys to Figeac* guide (30¢), which follows "keys" marked around the city.

ACCOMMODATION

Des Bains 1 rue du Griffoul ☎ 05 65 34 10 89, ⊚ hotel desbains.fr. Far nicer than its two stars would lead you to believe, *Des Bains* is one of the best choices in town for well-priced, central accommodation. Rooms are spotless and the more expensive ones have a/c and balconies. What makes the hotel special, though, is the friendly and energetic hosts, who are a mine of information about the local area. Breakfast €8.50. **€67**
★**La Belle Époque** Le Coustal, Camboulit ☎ 05 65 40 04 42, ⊚ domainelabelleepoque.com. Buried deep in the heart of the countryside, off the D19 7km southwest of Figeac, this fabulous *chambre d'hôte* is a home away from home, set on a restored seventeenth-century farm. The five individually decorated rooms are full of artful touches, with doors opening out onto the tranquil garden, where camping spots are available. There's also a pool and an acclaimed restaurant (*menu* €25) where highlights include succulent *filet mignon de porc* and the sublime profiteroles. Restaurant July & Aug daily noon–2pm & 7–9pm; Sept–June Wed–Sat noon–2pm & 7–9pm. Camping **€15**, doubles **€80**
Camping Domaine du Surgié Le Terrier ☎ 05 65 34 83 76 or ☎ 05 61 64 88 54, ⊚ domainedusurgie.com. Well-equipped four-star campsite 2km east of Figeac on the riverside that has a restaurant, a good shop, several pools and a leisure programme in high season. Closed Sept–April. **€32**

Le Champollion 3 place Champollion ☎ 05 65 34 04 37. This welcoming place offers ten surprisingly modern en-suite rooms above a popular café right in the centre. Try and snag one of the two rooms overlooking the square. Breakfast €7.50. **€50**
Le Pont d'Or 2 av Jean-Jaurès ☎ 05 65 50 95 00, ⊚ hotelpontdor.com. Traditionally decorated with spick-and-span rooms and spacious bathrooms, this well-situated hotel offers a restaurant (*menus* from €19), bar, rooftop pool and gym. For the best views, opt for a room with a balcony overlooking the riverfront. Breakfast €12. **€101**
Les Pratges/Les Maisons de Marie 6 av Jean-Jaurès ☎ 05 65 50 01 42, ⊚ maisonsdemarie.com. These five charming *chambre d'hôte* rooms and six well-equipped *gîtes* set in tranquil grounds make an excellent alternative to the city centre. There's also a pool, and a small park on the doorstep. Breakfast (€6.50) isn't included in the rates. **€100**
Le Terminus St-Jacques 27 av Georges-Clemenceau ☎ 05 65 34 00 43, ⊚ hotel-terminus.fr. Opposite the train station and just a short walk from the town centre, this friendly, family-run hotel is quiet, comfortable and never short of a warm welcome. Rooms are well turned out with easy-on-the-eye colour schemes and huge beds, while there's also private parking, a communal lounge area and a restaurant (*menus* from €24.50). Breakfast €8.50. **€62**

EATING

Figeac's old centre offers plenty of choice, with **restaurants** serving everything from pizza to haute cuisine. For picnic food, there's a handy supermarket on the corner of rue Gambetta and rue de Clermont, and the charcuterie at 20 quai Bessières sells a wide range of salads as well as meats.

La Cuisine du Marché 15 rue de Clermont ☎ 05 65 50 18 55, ⓦ lacuisinedumarchefigeac.com. A family-run fine-dining establishment, serving fresh local produce, as the name suggests. Menus change with the seasons and feature regional specialties like Quercy lamb and smoked wild salmon. Expect to pay €19 for the midweek lunch *menu* and €32 in the evenings and weekends. Mon 7–9.30pm, Tues–Sun noon–1.45pm & 7–9.30pm.

★ **La Dînée du Viguier** 4 rue Boutaric ☎ 05 65 50 08 08, ⓦ ladineeduviguier.fr. A luxurious setting, impeccable service and a menu of timeless French gastronomy add up to make this one of Figeac's top restaurants. You won't have to break the bank to eat there either – there's a great-value midday *menu* from €19, and evening *menus* start from €29. Reservations are essential. Mid-Feb to mid-Jan Tues–Fri 7.30–9.30pm, Sat 7.30–9.30pm, Sun noon–2pm.

L'En'K 3 rue Boutaric ☎ 05 81 24 06 40. Located opposite *La Dînée du Viguier*, this cheerful locals' haunt serves a mouthwatering range of burgers (from €7.50) with organic buns and home-made sauces. Try the *bécou* burger with Rocamadour cheese or the delicious fish burger. Tues–Sat noon–1.45pm & 7.30–10pm, Sun 7.30–10pm.

La Flambeé 28 rue Caviale ☎ 05 65 34 72 12, ⓦ restaurant-flambee-figeac.fr. Tuck into delicious chargrilled meats and pastas, or sample more adventurous dishes like *escargots* or shrimp flambéed in whisky at this popular local haunt. The great-value *menus* are €13 at lunch and from €16.50 in the evenings, but beware: it gets very busy, so it's best to book ahead. Mon, Tues & Thurs–Sat noon–2pm & 7–9pm, Wed noon–2pm.

Pizzeria del Portel 9 rue Ortabadial ☎ 05 65 34 53 60. Pizza isn't the only option at this lively central restaurant – there are also generously portioned salads and no fewer than seven varieties of *moules-frites* including pesto and Roquefort. The outside terrace is an added bonus. Evening *menus* from €19.50. Tues–Sun noon–2pm & 7–9pm.

★ **La Puce à l'Oreille** 5 rue St-Thomas ☎ 05 65 34 33 08. Located north of place Carnot in a handsome fifteenth-century residence with an interior court for fine weather, and walls adorned with work by local artists, this place serves rich Quercy fare, including succulent pan-fried lamb. Make sure you leave room for one of their indulgent desserts – the lemon tiramisu is a hit. *Menus* from €16 at lunch and up to €39 in the evenings, and there's an extensive regional wine list. Tues–Sat noon–1.30pm & 7.15–9.30pm, Sun noon–1.30pm.

La Table de Marinette 51 allée Victor-Hugo ☎ 05 65 50 06 07, ⓦ latabledemarinette.com. It's worth venturing south across the river to this stylish Art Deco restaurant. *Menus* start from €18 and include some tasty meat and fish dishes – the veal is particularly good. Mon–Thurs noon–2pm & 7–9pm, Sat 7–9pm.

DRINKING

Le Sphinx 7 place Carnot ☎ 05 65 14 05 81. An elegant cocktail bar situated right on the market square, *Le Sphinx* makes the ideal spot for a post-sightseeing *apéro*. There's also a decent selection of traditional food with *menus* from €13. April–June Mon–Sat noon–3pm & 7–9.30pm; July & Aug daily noon–3pm & 7–9.30pm; Sept–March Mon–Sat noon–3pm.

DIRECTORY

Hospital Centre Hospitalier, 33 rue des Maquisards (☎ 05 65 50 65 50).

Police Commissariat de Police, Cité Administrative, place des Carmes (☎ 05 65 50 73 73).

The Causse de Gramat

After the intimate beauty of the Lot and Célé valleys, the wide horizons of the **Causse de Gramat** to the north make a refreshing change. It's an empty land with few people or villages, filled only with the sound of sheep bells and the cicadas' persistent clamour during the tinderbox-dry summers. Across the gently undulating landscape of scrubby pines and oaks, and close-cropped grass spattered with orchids and aromatic plants, you'll come across dolmens, shepherds' dry-stone huts and strange *lacs de St-Namphaise* – water holes hacked out of the rock – but little else to make you want to stop. The exceptions are mostly along the *causse*'s southern boundary, starting off in the far southeast with **Assier**, a small village put on the map by a vainglorious military man who built a château and

5

church here. From Assier the route tracks westwards through a series of picturesque villages to the even more diminutive **Caniac-du-Causse**, last resting place of the hermit St Namphaise. At Caniac the route turns northwards into the wildest part of the *causse* towards the busy market town of **Gramat**, home to an above-average wildlife park.

GETTING AROUND **CAUSSE DE GRAMAT**

Assier and Gramat both lie on main train lines, but to do the *causse* justice you really do need your own means of getting about. With few roads and only a sprinkling of villages, this is a great area for walking or mountain biking; most tourist offices have maps of recommended routes.

Assier

If it weren't for the immoderate – and immodest – nature of Galiot de Genouillac, **ASSIER**, some 17km northwest of Figeac, would probably have remained an insignificant village. Chief of artillery under François I and an inspired tactician, de Genouillac earned his stripes during the decisive French victory at Marignano in 1515 during the Italian wars, after which he returned to his native village bathed in glory to erect a **château** befitting his status.

You can get a better idea of de Genouillac's decorative tastes from the **Église Sainte-Pierre**, which he also had built in the village square. It's an extraordinary edifice, not just because of its size and the feeling that it was built to the glory of de Genouillac rather than God, but mainly due to a frieze running round the exterior depicting Roman centurions, guns being hauled across the Alps, flame-spewing cannon and cities under siege – all beautifully realized but hardly normal church ornamentation. Less surprisingly, the most interesting feature inside is the great man's tomb in an intricately vaulted chapel near the west door. He appears twice: as a bearded man lying with his feet on powder sacks, and as a soldier leaning nonchalantly against a cannon.

Château d'Assier

May & June Mon & Wed–Sun 10am–12.30pm & 2–6.45pm; July & Aug daily 10am–12.30pm & 2–6.45pm; Sept–April Mon & Wed–Sun 10am–12.30pm & 2–5.30pm • €3 • ⓣ 05 65 40 40 99, ⓦ assier.monuments-nationaux.fr

Built in the latest Renaissance style, the **Château d'Assier** was said to rival the châteaux of the Loire, with its vast interior courtyard flanked by four round towers, its galleries, loggias and carved friezes – and liberal repetition of de Genouillac's motto: *J'aime fortune* ("In love with chance/success"). After 1768, however, the château and its contents were sold off lock, stock and barrel to raise money, leaving only part of the west wing – and even that is in a pretty poor state. It's still worth taking a peak inside, where there are some wonderful frescoes to admire.

ARRIVAL AND INFORMATION **ASSIER**

By train Assier is a stop on the main Figeac–Brive train line. The *gare SNCF* lies nearly 1km west of the village. Destinations Brive (9–10 daily; 1hr); Figeac (4–7 daily; 25min); Gramat (3–8 daily; 10–15min).

Tourist office On the northeast corner of place de l'Église (mid-June to mid-Sept Mon–Sat 10am–12.30pm & 3–6pm; ⓣ 05 65 40 50 60, ⓦ assier.quercy-tourisme.com).

ACCOMMODATION AND EATING

L'Assiérois ⓣ 05 65 40 56 27, ⓦ lassierois.com. This humble country hotel offers six basic but spotless rooms at the heart of the village, while the attached restaurant offers above-par fare, with friendly service (evening *menus* €29). Breakfast €6.50. Restaurant June–Aug Tues–Sat noon–1pm & 7–9.30pm, Sun noon–1pm; Sept–May Tues & Thurs–Sat noon–1pm & 7–9.30pm, Sun noon–1pm. **€39**

The southern causse

With your own transport, you can take a circuitous route from Assier through **the southern causse** before cutting northeast to Gramat. There are a few scattered sights to aim for, but on the whole it's the scenery that takes precedence in this high, open country with its grand vistas.

Five kilometres southwest of Assier on the D653, **LIVERNON** is the first of a string of attractive villages, in this case distinguished by a particularly appealing Romanesque belfry, with its rhythmically spaced arches. The route then meanders further south via **ESPÉDAILLAC** – a cluster of crumbling towers and pigeon-lofts – to **QUISSAC**, roughly 10km from Livernon. The main claim to fame of this tiny village is that the ninth-century soldier-turned-hermit **St Namphaise** lived in a nearby grotto. He's a very important person on the *causse*, since it was he who, according to legend, dug the shallow ponds in the rock that are characteristic of this region, thus providing water for flocks of sheep; ironically, he is said to have been killed by an irate bull. There's a statue of Namphaise dressed as a soldier in Quissac church, and you can see one of his famous *lacs* about 1km south of the village beside the Coursac road.

The dying Namphaise supposedly threw away his hammer – with which he presumably created the ponds – and declared that he would be buried wherever it came to rest; it landed 8km away in what is now the village of **CANIAC-DU-CAUSSE**. It's a sleepy, flowery place, undisturbed by the trickle of visitors coming to view Namphaise's small, unadorned sarcophagus lying in a diminutive twelfth-century crypt beneath the village church.

From Caniac cut north across country on the D42, keeping a lookout on the right for signs down a dirt track to the **Site de Planagrèze**, a couple of kilometres later. At the end of the track various footpaths and biking trails strike out across the *causse*, while one of the more accessible dolmens stands a short walk south. On the way you pass a fenced-off area, in the middle of which is another typical feature of the *causse*, a limestone sinkhole, the **Igue de Planagrèze**; in this particular case potholers have so far explored 800m of tunnels.

From here the D42 continues north to Fontanes-du-Causse, where there's a choice of routes to Gramat: you can either stick to the back lanes, or cut west to the faster D677.

Gramat

The biggest town on the *causse*, and its capital, **GRAMAT** developed at the junction of two major Roman roads. Its fortunes increased further when pilgrims started passing through en route to Rocamadour (see p.175), and it received another boost when the railway came here in 1863. Even today it's an important market town, with two weekly **markets** (Tues & Fri morning) and bigger *foires* on the second and fourth Thursdays of each month. Though a few vestiges of the medieval town remain, Gramat is mostly of interest as somewhere to base yourself for a day or so; as well as being an ideal starting point for exploring the *causse*, it's within easy striking distance of Rocamadour, only 9km away to the northwest, and fairly convenient for sights in the upper Dordogne valley (see p.168).

Gramat would be more appealing if it weren't for the busy N140 and D677 funnelling through **place de la République**, a big square on the east side of town. If you walk west from here along the **Grande Rue**, though, you'll suddenly find yourself among the narrow lanes of the old quarter. There's not a lot to see here, but both the place de l'Hôtel de Ville, at the top of the Grande Rue, and the market square, south of the Grande Rue down rue Notre-Dame, are attractive corners.

Jardins du Grand Couvent

33 av Louis Mazet • Daily: June, Sept & Oct 2–6pm; July & Aug 10am–7pm; private visits available in May • €5 • ☏ 05 65 38 73 29

South out of Gramat, head to the flourishing **Jardins du Grand Couvent**, laid out behind a convent complex. Spread over 30-odd acres, it's an idyllic spot for a picnic, with ample grassy lawns hemmed in by colourful flowerbeds. As you stroll around the gardens, you can also see the lovely old wash house and bread ovens used by the nuns until fairly recently; they also run a small shop and a tea room.

5

Parc Animalier de Gramat

Daily: April–June & Sept 10am–6pm; July & Aug 9.30am–7pm; Oct–April 2–6pm • €11.50, children €7 • ☎ 05 65 38 81 22, ⓦ gramat-parc-animalier.com

The main reason for most people's visit to Gramat is the **Parc Animalier de Gramat**, a couple of kilometres south of the Jardins du Grand Couvent, on the D14. Encompassing half a square kilometre of the *causse*, the park is home to an unusually varied selection of animals: the 150 mostly European species include wolves, otters, bears, ibex – with their magnificent curved horns – and *mouflon*, a type of goat crowned with four horns. Allow at least two hours if you want to cover the whole park.

ARRIVAL AND INFORMATION

GRAMAT

By train The *gare SNCF* is 1km south of the centre; if no taxis are waiting, call Adgié (☎ 05 65 38 75 07 or ☎ 06 71 92 67 00).
Destinations Assier (3–8 daily; 10–15min); Brive (6 daily; 50min); Figeac (4–5 daily; 30min); Paris-Austerlitz (2 overnight; 7hr); Rocamadour (4–8 daily; 8min); St-Denis-

lès-Martel (4–8 daily; 25min).
Tourist office Place de la République (April–June & Sept–Nov Mon–Sat 9.30am–1pm & 2–6.30pm; July & Aug Mon–Sat 9.30am–1pm & 2–7pm, Sun 10am–1pm; Nov–March Mon–Sat 10am–12.30pm & 2–5.30pm; ☎ 05 65 33 22 00, ⓦ vallee-dordogne.com).

ACCOMMODATION AND EATING

Le Centre Place de la République ☎ 05 65 38 73 37, ⓦ lecentre.fr. Bold artworks and pops of colour lend a cheerful vibe to the otherwise rather basic rooms at *Le Centre*. It's nonetheless comfortable, friendly and good value, plus there's a decent on-site restaurant, with evening *menus* from €25.90. Breakfast €9.90. Restaurant March–Oct daily noon–2pm & 7.15–9pm; Nov–Feb Mon–Thurs noon–2pm & 7.15–9pm, Fri & Sun noon–2pm. €73
La Cuisine d'Alain 2 rue de la Liberté ☎ 05 65 38 87 87, ⓦ lacuisinedalain.com. Decked out like an American diner with chequerboard floors, a vintage jukebox and Route 66 memorabilia, *La Cuisine d'Alain* offers the perfect setting to dig into a hearty home-made burger and fries (from €9). Mon–Sat noon–2pm & 7–9pm.
Lion d'Or Place de la République ☎ 05 65 10 46 10, ⓦ liondorhotel.fr. With an excellent location right on the main square, *Lion d'Or* has fifteen comfy rooms to its

name, but the real selling point is the restaurant. Expect innovative and tasty cuisine at reasonable prices – *menus* start from €25. Breakfast €9.90. Restaurant July–Sept daily noon–2pm & 7.30–8.30pm; Oct–June Tues–Sat noon–2pm & 7.30–8.30pm, Sun noon–2pm. €75
★ **Relais des Gourmands** 2 av de la Gare ☎ 05 65 38 83 92, ⓦ relais-des-gourmands.fr. The most appealing place to stay in Gramat and surprisingly quiet, despite its close proximity to the train station. Rooms are simple but elegant, with wood floors, tasteful colour schemes and modern bathrooms. There's also a well-kept pool, a flowery terrace and an excellent restaurant serving a mix of traditional fare and more creative dishes (*menus* from €20). Breakfast €9. Restaurant daily July & Aug 12.30–2pm & 7.30–9pm; Sept–June Tues–Sat 12.30–2pm & 7.30–9pm, Sun 12.30–2pm; hotel closed Jan–March. €72

Gourdon

Thirty-five kilometres west of Gramat, **GOURDON** is an attractive town, its medieval centre of butter-coloured stone houses attached to a prominent hilltop, neatly ringed by shady modern boulevards, known collectively as the Tour-de-Ville. While it has no outstanding sights, Gourdon makes a quiet, pleasant base, not only for the nearby **Grottes de Cougnac**, with their prehistoric paintings, but also for the **Bouriane** (see p.230) to the south. Gourdon also has good produce **markets** on Tuesdays beside the church in place St-Pierre, and on Saturdays beside the post office. In July and August, a large farmers' market takes place on Thursday mornings in place St-Pierre, while the Tour-de-Ville is closed off on the first and third Tuesdays of each month for a traditional **country fair**.

The Tour-de-Ville

Where the ramparts once stood, Gourdon's medieval centre is now entirely surrounded by the **Tour-de-Ville**. The best-preserved gateway into the centre is southwesterly Porte du

Majou, which stands guard over the old town's main street, **rue du Majou**, lined with mellow stone-built houses, some, like the **Maison d'Anglars** at no. 17, with its ogive arches and mullion windows, dating back as far as the thirteenth century; look out on the right, as you go up, for the delightfully – and accurately – named rue Zig-Zag.

At its upper end, rue du Majou opens onto a lovely cobbled square beneath the twin towers of the massive fourteenth-century **Église St-Pierre**. Note the traces of fortifications, in the form of machicolations, over the west door, but you'll find nothing of particular interest inside, beyond some seventeenth-century gilded bas-reliefs by a local sculptor depicting the life of the Virgin Mary. The **Hôtel de Ville** – a handsome if unpretentious building whose arcaded ground floor once served as the market hall – stands on the west side of the square, while east of the church in place des Marronniers an ornately carved door marks the home of the Cavaignac family, who supplied the nation with numerous prominent public figures in the eighteenth and nineteenth centuries.

From the north side of the church, a path leads to the top of the hill where Gourdon's castle stood until it was razed in the early seventeenth century in the wake of the Wars of Religion. At 264m in height, it affords superb **views** over the wooded country stretching north to the Dordogne valley.

ARRIVAL AND INFORMATION GOURDON

By train The *gare SNCF* is located roughly 1km northeast of the old centre. From the station, walk south on avenue de la Gare, then turn right onto avenue Gambetta to come out on the south side of the Tour-de-Ville. If you want a taxi, call Taxi Brice (☏ 05 65 32 17 25).

Destinations Brive (4–7 daily; 45min); Cahors (6–10 daily; 30min); Montauban (6 daily; 1hr 10min); Paris-Austerlitz (3 daily; 5hr); Souillac (7 daily; 15min); Toulouse (6 daily; 1hr 45min).

GETTING AROUND AND INFORMATION

Car rental ADA 101 av Gambetta (☏ 05 65 41 40 08).
Bike rental Nature Evasion, 73 av Cavignac (☏ 05 65 37 65 12), out on the west side of town, rents bikes from €14 a day.
Tourist office 24 rue du Majou (March–May & Oct Mon–Sat

10am–noon & 2–6pm; June & Sept Mon–Sat 10am–noon & 2–6pm, Sun 10am–noon; July & Aug Mon–Sat 10am–7pm, Sun 10am–noon; Nov–Jan Mon–Sat 10am–noon & 2–5pm; ☏ 05 65 27 52 50, ⓦ tourisme-gourdon.com).

ACCOMMODATION AND EATING

Domaine le Quercy ☏ 05 65 41 06 19, ⓦ domaine quercy.com. Well-equipped three-star campsite, 1.5km north of Gourdon on the D704 Périgueux road, set beside a leisure lake with a pool and summer-only restaurant. Closed Sept–April. **€13**
Hostellerie de la Bouriane Place du Foirail ☏ 05 65 41 16 37, ⓦ hotellabouriane.fr. An elegant choice with spacious rooms and chic decor, this country inn is the best bet in town. There's also private parking and a restaurant serving traditional fare, with *menus* from €28. Breakfast €13. Restaurant May to mid-Oct Mon–Sat

7–9pm, Sun 12.15–1.30pm; mid-Oct to April Tues–Sat 7–8.30pm. **€85**
De la Promenade 48 bd Galiot-de-Genouillac ☏ 05 65 41 41 44, ⓦ lapromenade-gourdon.fr. The ten cheerfully decorated rooms at this small hotel are immaculate and each follow a different theme, from "British" to Japanese-inspired "Zen". There's also a bar/pub with Guinness on tap, cocktails and tapas, and a well-priced restaurant (*menus* from €13.50 at lunch). Breakfast €7.50. Restaurant April–Sept daily noon–2pm & 7–9.30pm; Oct–March Mon–Sat noon–2pm & 7–9.30pm. **€67**

The Grottes de Cougnac

1hr guided tours daily: April–June & Sept 10–11.30am & 2.30–5pm; July & Aug 10am–5.45pm • €8, children €5.50 • In-depth 2hr-long tours Wed at 9am • €12 • ☏ 05 65 41 47 54, ⓦ grottesdecougnac.com

Signed off the Sarlat road a couple of kilometres north of Gourdon, the **Grottes de Cougnac** were discovered in 1949 by a local water-diviner. To begin with, all the subsequent explorers found only rock formations – notably ceilings festooned with ice-white needles like some glitzy ballroom decoration – but three years later they hit gold when they came across **prehistoric paintings**. These date from between 25,000 and 19,000 years ago, when Cro-Magnon people ventured deep inside the caves to paint panels of ibex, reindeer and

5

mammoths in elegant outline, using the rock's undulating surface to provide a sense of form and movement. They also left hundreds of mysterious signs – mostly dots and pairs of short lines – in addition to two human figures seemingly pierced by spears, a motif also found in Pech-Merle (see p.219). The temperature inside is 13°C, so take a coat.

The Bouriane

The tranquil **Bouriane** region lies south of Gourdon, a large and very pretty area of luxuriant woods and valleys merging into neighbouring Périgord, and a striking contrast to the sparse upland *causses* to the east. It's primarily a place to wander, with no particular destination in mind, but anyone interested in twentieth-century art should visit **Les Arques**, in the south of the region, where a number of powerful, sometimes disturbing, sculptures by Russian exile Ossip Zadkine are on display.

Salviac

Some 14km south of Gourdon, the first place of any size along the D673 is the fortified village of **SALVIAC**, whose Gothic church (known as the **Abbaye Nouvelle**) was built in the late thirteenth century by Jacques Duèze of Cahors, the future Pope John XXII (see p.202), and still contains fine stained-glass windows from that era. It's worth a brief stop for the location as much as anything, but is sadly rarely open to the public; call ☎05 65 41 25 24 to arrange a visit.

Cazals

Seven kilometres southeast of Salviac, the *bastide* town of **CAZALS** has seen better days: its feudal château and ramparts were largely destroyed during the Hundred Years War, though its big central square remains, giving the town character and hosting a splendid Sunday **market**. On the southern outskirts there is a small multi-sport leisure lake which doubles as a pleasant spot for a picnic.

ACCOMMODATION AND EATING CAZALS

La Caminade ☎05 65 21 66 63, ⓦlacaminade.com. A lovely *chambre d'hôte* housed in part of the Cazals ramparts and surrounded by three peaceful gardens. There are four well-appointed rooms to choose from, a salt-water pool and an appetizing home-made breakfast served on the terrace. **€98**

Rampoux

From Cazals, you can work your way 9km eastwards through enticing back lanes to **RAMPOUX**. This unusually scattered hamlet is home to a Romanesque priory **church** in which one of the original frescoes can still be seen – a very faded Christ in Majesty in the apse. Better preserved are those from the fifteenth century in the south chapel, portraying the life of Jesus.

Les Arques

LES ARQUES sits buried in the countryside 10km southwest of Rampoux and 6km south of Cazals. It's a higgledy-piggledy village on a hillock above the River Masse, but its main draw is the **Musée Zadkine** (Feb, March, Nov & Dec Tues–Sun 2–6pm; April–Oct Tues–Sun 10am–1pm & 3–7pm; €3, children under 13 free; ☎05 65 22 83 37). A Russian émigré and well-known sculptor, **Ossip Zadkine** set up a studio in Les Arques in 1934 and worked on and off in the village until his death in 1967, producing big, powerful statues full of restless energy. Many are on a mythological or musical theme, such as those of Orpheus and Diana, the latter metamorphosing from tree to woman, and there's a strong Cubist influence, although Zadkine's work grew more abstract towards the end of his life. Some of his most compelling pieces are displayed inside the Romanesque **Église Saint-Laurent des Arques** opposite the museum, whose cool stone interior provides the perfect foil for a passionate rendering of Christ on the Cross and, in the crypt, the *Pietà*. During his time in Les Arques, Zadkine also discovered some twelfth-century frescoes in the nearby **Église St-André** – you can get a key from the museum.

EATING LES ARQUES

★La Récréation ☎05 65 22 88 08, **ⓦ**restaurant -traiteur-lot.com. In season, it's worth timing your visit to the Zadkine museum in order to have lunch in the old schoolhouse at the entrance to the village, now home to an attractive restaurant. *Menus* start from €26 for lunch and €36 in the evening– a snip for five splendid courses.

Expect some intriguing flavours, like roasted duck breast with lychee or wild seabass with a pink grapefruit sauce. On Thursday evening in season they knock up delicious tapas dishes, while cooking classes are also available. Reservations essential. Mon & Fri–Sun noon–3.15pm & 7.30–9.15pm.

Goujounac

A good place for an overnight stay or tasty meal, charming little **Goujounac**, with its butter-coloured stone houses, lies 5km southwest of Les Arques. Its **Église Saint-Pierre** has rather worn Romanesque carvings of Christ in Majesty and the four Evangelists over the south door.

ACCOMMODATION AND EATING GOUJOUNAC

Camping 46 Rainettes ☎05 87 75 73 70, **ⓦ**camping 46rainettes.com. Good-value three-star campsite immediately west of Goujounac on the D660 Villefranche road. Facilities include a large pool with water slides, tennis, and children's play area, making it an ideal spot for families with young children. There's also cabins for rent (€357 weekly). Closed Oct–April. **€16**

Hostellerie de Goujounac ☎05 65 36 68 67, **ⓦ**goujounac.com. Opposite the church, this Dutch-owned hotel with five simple rooms offers honest country cooking (*menus* from €15), plus a pool and tennis courts available at an extra cost. Breakfast €9. Reservations advised. Restaurant April–Sept Tues–Sat noon–2pm & 7–8.30pm, Sun noon– 2pm; Oct–March Wed–Sat noon–2pm & 7–8.30pm. **€65**

St Médard

About 7km southeast of Goujounac, the picturesque medieval hamlet of **St Médard** sits pillowed against a forested hill. Apart from a renowned restaurant and the twelfth-century church, with its particularly decorative stone stoup, there is little to see, unless you should bump into Leon the peacock – the village pet, and a lordly bird that struts the narrow streets in a regal fashion.

EATING ST MÉDARD

★Le Gindreau ☎05 65 36 22 27, **ⓦ**legindreau.com. With a deservedly stellar reputation, this Michelin-starred restaurant is a rare treat for foodies. Sample delights like seafood bisque with a shellfish gratin, or local lamb with Rocamadour cheese, potatoes and pickled pork rind; the desserts in particular are real works of art and include

cherries soaked in Cahors wine. Opt for the reliably brilliant *découverte menu* (€59). Reservations essential in high season. April, May & Nov to mid-March Wed–Sat noon– 2pm & 7.30–9.3pm, Sun noon–2pm; May–Sept Wed– Sun noon–2pm & 7.30–9.30pm.

West along the Lot from Cahors

The Bouriane's southern boundary is marked by the River Lot, which follows a particularly convoluted course downstream of Cahors as it doubles back on itself again and again between cliffs that gradually diminish towards the west. Standing guard over one of the

5

larger meanders is **Luzech**, whose main claim to fame is the scant remains of a Roman encampment on the hill above the town. Continuing downstream, the route winds through a series of villages perched above the river, culminating in one of the most beautiful along the entire Lot valley, **Puy-l'Évêque**. A castle-town built on a terraced cliff, it dominates the last of the river's meanders, and its wandering lanes, tunnels, staircases and fountains together compensate for the lack of any first-rate sights. The area around **Duravel**, further west again, with its fine selection of hotels and restaurants, provides a good base for visiting the impressive **Château de Bonaguil** in the hills to the north of the Lot. The last of the medieval castles to be constructed in France, and now partially in ruins, it still bristles with sophisticated defensive devices. Back on the Lot, **Fumel** is a major transport hub and service centre, though otherwise contains nothing to make you dally – better to hurry on downriver to where **Penne-d'Agenais**, with its striking basilica, lords it over the valley.

GETTING AROUND   WEST ALONG THE LOT

Public transport along this stretch of the river consists of an SNCF bus that threads along the valley from Cahors via Luzech, Prayssac, Puy-l'Évêque and Fumel to terminate at Monsempron-Libos, on the Agen–Périgueux train line. On the way it also passes through or close by most of the smaller villages cited below, but you'll need your own transport to reach the Château de Bonaguil and Grézels.

Luzech

Twenty kilometres downriver from Cahors, **LUZECH** is situated on the narrow neck of a particularly large meander in the River Lot, overlooked by a twelfth-century **keep**. Little remains of the fortress beyond a few foundation stones, but it's worth trekking up for a splendid view over the Luzech meander. It's 1.5km by road, or you can walk up in about ten minutes from the north end of rue de la Ville; follow signs for the GR36 footpath past the castle keep and then just keep climbing. For a less strenuous jaunt, head south for about 2km to visit a tiny chapel, **Notre-Dame de l'Isle**, surrounded by vines and walnut trees on the very tip of the meander.

The town itself has a small area of picturesque alleys to the north of **place du Canal**, the central square spanning the isthmus.

Maison des Consuls

Grande Rue de la Ville • **Ammonite collection** June–Sept Mon–Fri 10am–1pm & 3–7pm, Sat 3–7pm • **Musée Armand Viré** Feb, March & Oct Mon–Thurs 10am–1pm & 2–5pm, Fri 10am–noon; May–Sept Mon–Sat 10am–1pm & 2pm–6pm; winter opening times variable and restricted to three days a week • Joint ticket for Ammonite Collection & Musée Armand Viré €3, or €5 with Ichnospace • ☎ 05 65 30 58 47

In the centre of town, you'll find the **Maison des Consuls**, built in 1270. The building is home to the tourist office, as well as two of Luzech's three museums. The first houses a fascinating collection of **ammonites**, dating back millions of years and separated into displays that chronicle their evolution.

The **Musée Armand Viré** displays archeological finds from around Luzech. The majority come from the fortress above the town, which has been occupied since the early Iron Age; the Romans reinforced it and erected a temple on the site, which is now known as the Oppidum d'Impernal. Though there are some delicate Gaulish safety-pins and needles which, alongside other exhibits, demonstrate the huge leap in craftsmanship ushered in by the Romans in the first century BC: look out for the unusual folding spoon and the coins chopped in half for small change.

Ichnospace

Grande Rue de la Ville • June–Sept Mon–Fri 10am–1pm & 3–7pm, Sat 10am–1pm & 2–6pm • €3, or joint ticket with the Musée Armand Viré and Ammonite Collection €5 • ☎ 05 65 20 17 27

You can continue in the prehistoric vein with a trip to the **Ichnospace** in the *médiathèque*, just north of the tourist office (see opposite). A must for anyone with an interest in palaeontology, highlights include 140-million-year-old dinosaur footprints from nearby

5

Crayssac and various fossils unearthed in the region, displayed over an area of around sixty square metres.

ARRIVAL AND INFORMATION   LUZECH

By bus Buses from Cahors pull in beside a roundabout at the east end of place du Canal.

Destinations Albas (3–10 daily; 10min); Cahors (3–10 daily; 25min); Monsempron-Libos (3–7 daily; 1hr); Prayssac (3–10 daily; 25min); Puy-l'Évêque (3–10 daily; 30min).

Tourist office Maison des Consuls (Feb, March & Oct Mon–Thurs 10am–1pm & 2–5pm, Fri 10am–noon; May–Sept Mon–Sat 10am–1pm & 2pm–6pm; winter opening times restricted to three days a week, and variable; ☎ 05 65 20 17 27, ⓦ ville-luzech.fr).

Boat rental Luzech marks the end of the navigable river descending from St-Cirq Lapopie. Naviglot, based a couple of kilometres north of Luzech near the village of Caix (mid-May to mid-Sept; ☎ 05 65 20 18 19), rents pleasure boats, canoes (from €6 an hour) and bikes and organizes river-trips (from €30 for a half-day tour).

ACCOMMODATION AND EATING

Gîte d'Étape Luzech ☎ 05 65 30 72 32. A good bet for a stopover if you're walking, this *gîte d'étape* is located just before the bridge to the west of town. As well as basic but comfortable rooms, guests can make use of the kitchen, living area and washing facilities. **€12.50**

Le Vinois Caillac ☎ 05 65 30 53 60, ⓦ levinois.com. Some 10km east of Luzech, in the small village of Caillac, this is a sophisticated hotel with trendy Japanese-inspired decor, a well-tended garden and a pool. The on-site restaurant is also excellent, with Chef Jean-Claude Voisin whipping up delectable dishes concocted from the best local ingredients (*menus* from €21.80). Curious gourmands can even sign up for cooking classes (from €95 for a half-day course). Breakfast €13.90. Restaurant Tues 7.30–9pm, Wed–Sat noon–1.30pm & 7.30–9pm, Sun noon–1.30pm. **€96**

Zotier 750 La Sole ☎ 05 65 30 54 22, ⓦ zotier.com. A welcoming *chambre d'hôte* on the western edge of town, with five prettily decorated bedrooms, a shady garden and delicious evening meals using local produce and fruit from the orchard. **€55**

Albas

The prettiest route downstream from Luzech – which is followed by the bus – is the D8 along the River Lot's south bank. It's especially beguiling in summer when the intense green of the vines and walnut trees in the valley bottom is offset against the dark-grey cliffs. The river loops back and forth across the flood plain, with a village at the bottom of each meander. The first you come to, and the most attractive, is **ALBAS**, 5km from Luzech, instantly recognizable by its tall church spire. The church is nineteenth-century and otherwise uninteresting, but the steep lanes below retain a few noble fourteenth- and fifteenth-century facades, a reminder of when the bishops of Cahors maintained a residence here. The arched double doors of the houses lining the streets conceal deep cellars, reminders of the days when the Lot was fully navigable and Albas was the main port for Cahors wine; hundreds of barrels were stored here to be shipped downstream to Bordeaux and onwards to the world. At the riverside esplanade you can see the spot where the boats were loaded, and it's here that the biennial **fête du vin** (see box, p.202) kicks off, with a barrel brought downstream, unloaded and ceremoniously paraded through the village. Cross the river by the narrow bridge and look back up at the village for a view that graces a million postcards.

EATING AND DRINKING   ALBAS

Auberge d'Imhotep ☎ 05 65 30 70 91. Two kilometres east of Albas, the *Auberge d'Imhotep* is a friendly little restaurant named after the ancient Egyptian who supposedly discovered the art of *gavage* – the process of force-feeding ducks for foie gras – in 2600 BC. Naturally, duck features strongly and they also offer an excellent Cahors wine list and a generous helping of jazz. *Menus* from €16. Reservations advised in season. April–Oct Tues–Sun noon–1.30pm & 7.30pm–3.30am.

Castelfranc

Three kilometres west of Albas, at the little hamlet Le Mayne, the bus turns north to cross the river at engaging little **CASTELFRANC**, a riverside *bastide* village built on a grid

5

pattern around a pretty central *place* by the indefatigable bishops of Cahors. On the northern side of the square lies Castelfranc's main attraction, the thirteenth-century **Église Notre-Dame de l'Assomption** with its four-bell *clocher mur*, whilst on the southern side there's a good little restaurant (see below). Wander a couple of hundred metres further south and you'll find yourself back at the river, where Castelfranc has another surprise attraction, a river beach complete with picnic tables.

EATING AND DRINKING   CASTELFRANC

La Vigne Haute 1 av Tonneliers ☎05 65 53 08 45, ⓦrestaurant-la-vigne-haute.com. A comfortable, traditionally furnished restaurant known for its soufflés and grills, which are executed over a charcoal fire in the dining room itself. The chef is Vietnamese, so there is likely to be an exotic kick to the *menu du jour*. Lunch *menu* from €14, from €25.50 in the evening. Mon, Tues & Thurs–Sun noon–2pm & 7–10pm; closed Christmas hols and two weeks in Feb.

Prayssac

Heading west from Castelfranc the road hugs the cliff, affording ravishing glimpses of the fertile Lot valley. After a scant couple of kilometres you roll into the bustling little town of **PRAYSSAC**. It isn't the prettiest town in the valley, nor the most historically interesting, but in summer there's a real buzz about it, with a string of great cafés along the plane-tree-lined place d'Istrie, spilling out over shady pavements. Outside the tourist office is a stern statue of **Marechál Bessières**, Prayssac's most famous son, born here in August 1768. Bessières was a brilliant commander and a great friend of Napoleon Bonaparte. He died in 1813 after a direct hit from a cannonball, which turned out to be a lucky stroke for Wellington and the allies; Napoleon reputedly asserted that had Bessières been with him he would have prevailed at Waterloo.

The real reason for visiting Prayssac is its main **market**, the best in the area, filling the centre around the place de l'Église and spreading into neighbouring streets every Friday morning. In high summer it's difficult to get anywhere near it – it's best to leave your car at the side of the road (along with five hundred others), then walk in and soak up the atmosphere.

There's also a lovely **riverside walk** between Prayssac and Castelfranc (around 40min), also useful if you're on foot and want to visit the Castelfranc restaurants from Prayssac, as you can't easily walk along the main road.

ARRIVAL AND INFORMATION   PRAYSSAC

By bus SNCF buses from Cahors stop in the rue Colonel Pardes in front of the place d'Istrie. From Monsempron-Libos they stop in front of the post office.
Destinations Albas (3–10 daily; 15min); Cahors (3–10 daily; 55min); Fumel (3–8 daily; 25min); Luzech (3–10 daily; 25min); Monsempron-Libos (3–8 daily; 35min); Puy-L'Évêque (3–8 daily; 10min).
Tourist office 3 bd de la Paix (July & Aug Mon–Sat 9.30am–1pm & 2–6pm, Sun 9.30am–1pm; Sept–June Mon 2–5pm, Tues–Sat 9.30am–12.30pm & 2–5pm; ☎05 65 21 37 63, ⓦtourisme-prayssac.com).

ACCOMMODATION AND EATING

Prayssac has several options for eating. For picnic food there are two good supermarkets, one on the western outskirts towards Puy-L'Évêque, the other on the southern side opposite the *pompiers*. Boulangeries abound, but the best of the bunch is Lasjournias, on the place d'Istrie. There is also a very good *fromagerie* and delicatessen, next door.

Les Catounes 14 place d'Istrie ☎05 65 36 04 86. Possibly the best of the cafés around the *place*, with its courtyard decorated in mellow terracotta and lavished with Mediterranean plants, and a stylish interior that doubles as a boutique. Tables burst out through the gates on market days, so get there early or be prepared for a wait. The food is simple but well executed, with some tasty omelettes and *galettes*. Menus from €15. Tues–Sat 9am–9.30pm, food served noon–2.30pm & 7–9.30pm.
Clau del Loup Métairie haute, Juillac ☎05 65 36 76 20, ⓦclaudelloup.com. A beautifully renovated hotel set among walnut orchards in the hamlet of Juillac, 2km south

5

of Prayssac on the D8. As well as four tastefully decorated rooms, they have a charming garden, a covered pool and a stylish restaurant serving excellent regional dishes; evening *menus* from €29.50. Breakfast €12. Restaurant daily noon–1.30pm & 7–9pm. **€150**

0 Plaisir des Sens 50 bd Aristide Briand ☎05 65 22 47 12, ⓦo-plaisir-des-sens.com. This quirky little restaurant in a corner of place de la Liberté delivers unexpectedly elegant food. Those seeking a change from straight-up French cuisine will find plenty to tempt them, including paella, ossobucco and gazpacho. Menus €13.50

at lunch, €26.50 in the evening. Tues 7–9pm, Wed–Sat noon–1.30pm & 7–9pm.

La Vénus Place la Vénus ☎05 65 22 47 10, ⓦrestaurant-la-venus.com. A reliably good little restaurant with an Italian flavour and some excellent fish and seafood options, situated on the eastern side of town. The chef is French and the waitress English, and *La Vénus* is extremely popular with both French locals and British visitors. *Menus* from €19.50. Wed–Sat noon–1.30pm & 7–9pm, Sun noon–1.30pm.

Belaye and Grézels

Around 5km south of Prayssac, just off the D8, lies the precipitous medieval hamlet of **BÉLAYE**, worth a quick trip for the stunning views of the Lot valley alone. Some 4km further west you arrive at the little village of **GRÉZELS**, another episcopal seat, though in this case its château – a very sober affair – has survived thanks to a seventeenth-century rebuild. The prime attraction here, on the main road through the village, is the *La Terrasse* restaurant (see below).

EATING   **GRÉZELS**

La Terrasse ☎05 65 21 34 03. Renowned for its jovial host and no-nonsense cuisine: there's only one *menu* (€30), including wine), which changes daily. Make sure you've

got a healthy appetite as portions are huge and the owner likes to see clean plates. Reservations recommended. Oct to mid-Sept Tues–Sun noon–1.30pm & 7.30–9pm.

Puy-l'Évêque

On the north bank of the River Lot, and 5km from Prayssac, **PUY-L'ÉVÊQUE** contends with St-Cirq Lapopie (see p.212) as the valley's prettiest village. After 1227 it marked the western extremity of the Cahors bishops' domains and it's the remains of their thirteenth-century **château**, a big square keep like that at Luzech, that provide the town's focal point. Puy-l'Évêque changed hands any number of times during the Hundred Years War, but then withstood a prolonged Protestant siege in 1580 during the Wars of Religion. Ardent anti-clerics tried to change the name to Puy-Libre during the Revolution, then to Puy-sur-Lot, but the locals weren't convinced and it soon reverted to Puy-l'Évêque (which loosely translates as "bishop").

There are no great sights to speak of, just lanes of medieval and Renaissance houses built in honey-coloured stone. Beside the castle keep at the top of the town, the **place de la Truffière** is the venue for the main weekly **market** (Tues morning); in summer there's also a small Saturday farmers' market in the lower town on place Georges Henry, at the west end of rue des Platanes. From place de la Truffière, **rue du Fort** leads steeply down then flattens out beneath an imposing fourteenth-century building distinguished by its Gothic windows, which served as the bishops' audience chamber. As it curves round the hill, rue du Fort becomes rue Bovila and then peters out beside a staircase descending to rue des Capucins. This road heads back east along the hillside to **place Guillaume-de-Cardaillac** and then **place de la Halle**, the town's two most picturesque corners. Downhill from place de la Halle again, you come to rue de la Cale, with the dark alleys of the artisans' quarter off to the left, and the old **port** just beyond. For the best **view** of the whole ensemble walk out onto the modern bridge which crosses the Lot here. Alternatively, head for the belvedere in front of the **Église St-Sauveur** that guards Puy-l'Évêque's northeast quarter – literally, since it once formed an integral part of the fortifications; look carefully and you can still see where cannonballs found their target during the siege of 1580.

ARRIVAL AND INFORMATION | PUY-L'ÉVÊQUE 5

By bus SNCF buses from Cahors stop in front of the church on place du Rampeau and down on rue des Platanes to the southeast of the old centre.
Destinations Albas (3–10 daily; 15min); Cahors (3–10 daily; 1hr); Fumel (3–8 daily; 15–20min); Luzech (3–10 daily; 25–30min); Monsempron-Libos (3–8 daily; 20–25min);

Prayssac (3–10 daily; 10min).
Tourist office 12 Grande Rue (July & Aug Mon–Sat 9.30am–1pm & 2–6pm, Sun 9.30am–1pm; Sept–June Mon–Fri 9.30am–12.30pm & 2–5pm, Sat 9.30am–12.30pm; ☎ 05 65 21 37 63, ⊛ puy-leveque.fr).

ACCOMMODATION AND EATING

Belle Vue Place de la Truffière ☎ 05 65 36 06 60, ⊛ hotel bellevue-puyleveque.com. Perched on the cliffside with views extending over the valley, this hotel certainly lives up to its name. Room standards vary: older ones look a little faded, while others have been given a contemporary makeover. It's worth dining in the restaurant just for the view – menus are €19.50 at lunch or €36 in the evening. Breakfast €10. Restaurant Tues & Thurs–Sat noon–1.30pm & 7.30–9pm, Wed & Sun noon–1.30pm. **€85**

★ **Camping Les Vignes** ☎ 05 65 30 81 72, ⊛ camping -lesvignes.fr. Some 3km south of Puy-l'Évêque, along the river via the D28 (and signed off the road to the bridge from town), you'll find this superb three-star campsite, with exceptionally friendly owners. There's also a small shop, activities for children such as sports and games, plus canoe rental at the supervised river beach in summer. To top it all off they'll give you a discount if you produce a copy of this book. **€15.15**

Franck Tonel 49 rue Ernest Marcouly ☎ 05 65 21 32 56.

If you want to try a true local speciality, Franck Tonel is the place to go. The eponymous owner, an artisan boulanger and patissier, is renowned throughout the region for his delicious tarte aux noix. Tues–Sat 9am–12.30pm & 2.30–6pm, Sun 9am–noon.

Henry 23 rue du Docteur Rouma ☎ 09 70 35 17 37, ⊛ hotel-henry.com. Pleasant rooms at a budget price, though you should try and get one at the back to avoid road noise. The restaurant serves reliable regional cuisine with generous portions and menus from €15. Breakfast €6. Restaurant mid-April to mid-Sept daily noon–2pm & 7–10pm; mid-Sept to mid-April Mon–Thurs & Sun noon–2pm & 7–10pm, Fri noon–2pm. **€42**

Le Pigeonnier ☎ 05 65 21 37 77. A lively café-cum-bistro on the south bank of the river offering huge salads, grills and galettes, with an unbeatable view of the village thrown in. Plats from €7. May–Oct Tues–Sat noon–2pm & 7–9.30pm, plus July & Aug 2–6pm for ice creams and drinks.

Martignac

One of the best excursions from Puy-l'Évêque is to the hamlet of **MARTIGNAC**, 2.5km north, where the much-altered Romanesque **Église St-Pierre-ès-Liens** contains some remarkable late-fifteenth- and early-sixteenth-century **frescoes**; hidden under plaster until 1938, they are reasonably well preserved. Characters on the north wall represent the Seven Deadly Sins being escorted to the mouth of Hell, each mounted on a different animal: Lust on a billy goat, Gluttony scoffing ham and wine and riding a pig, and scruffy Sloth on a donkey bringing up the tail. The Seven Virtues surround the apse, their grey robes tumbling about them, with Courage and Temperance being the easiest to recognize – the former holds a serpent, while Temperance carefully waters down her wine.

Duravel

Downstream of Puy-l'Évêque, the Lot valley begins to open out as the hills along the southern bank fade away. Those to the north continue a while longer, providing a green backdrop for the pretty eleventh-century **Église Saint-Hilarion** at **DURAVEL**, 6km from Puy-l'Évêque. Its crypt contains the remains of no fewer than three saints – Poémon, Agathon and Hilarion, their bodies having been brought back from the Holy Land in the eleventh century. The village is unfortunately spoilt by the busy main road passing through its centre, but it's a lively spot on a Saturday morning when a market is held on the **place de la Mairie**.

ACCOMMODATION AND EATING | DURAVEL

Le Clos Bouyssac ☎ 05 65 36 52 21, ⊛ campingby theriver.eu. A quiet, shady and very friendly two-star campsite, located just south of Duravel along the riverbank.

Facilities include a small shop and snack bar (July & Aug only), pool, riverside beach, canoe hire and volleyball. Closed Sept–April. **€21**

5

Montcabrier

With your own transport, you can cut northwest across country from Duravel to visit the magnificent ruined castle of Bonaguil (see below). On the way it's worth taking a short detour to **MONTCABRIER**, just over 5km north of Duravel, if for no other reason than this tiny *bastide* seems to have been forgotten by the renovators and tourist authorities. There's a clutch of once-noble residences around the chestnut-shaded main square, but the village is best known for a diminutive statue lodged in the north nave of its quietly crumbling **Église St-Louis**. It is one of the first stone representations of the saint, formerly King Louis IX, showing him as a bearded figure wearing a painted crown. It's also slightly macabre: when Louis died on a crusade in 1270, his body was immediately chopped into pieces and dispatched around Europe to meet the demand for relics. Apparently, one unspecified piece of the king now resides inside this little statue.

Château de Bonaguil

Daily: March–June & Sept–Oct 10am–5.30pm; July & Aug 10am–7pm; Nov–Feb bank hols & school hols 2–5pm • €8, children €4 • Guided tours 1hr 30min; English-language tours available in July & Aug • ☏ 05 53 71 90 33, ⊚ chateau-bonaguil.com • From Montcabrier take the D673 from below the village heading southwest, then turn west through the delightful hamlet of St-Martin-Le-Redon and start climbing

As the D673 from Montcabrier crests the ridge above St-Martin-Le-Redon you get a stunning view of the **Château de Bonaguil**, perched at the end of a wooded spur some 7km from Montcabrier. The castle dates largely from the fifteenth and sixteenth centuries when Bérenger de Roquefeuil, from a powerful Languedoc family and by all accounts a nasty piece of work, inherited the partially ruined castle. Fearing revolts by his vassals, he decided to transform it into an impregnable fortress, just as his contemporaries were abandoning such elaborate **fortifications**. It took him around forty years to do so, constructing a double ring of walls, six huge towers, a highly unusual, narrow boat-shaped keep and sophisticated loopholes with overlapping lines of fire. Perhaps because of such elaborate precautions, Bonaguil was never attacked, and although some demolition occurred during the Revolution, the castle still stands, bloodied but unbowed.

The site attracts up to two thousand tourists per day in July and August. It's best to arrive first thing in the morning to avoid the worst of the crush, and rather than joining the **guided tours**, which get tedious when it's very busy, it's preferable to buy a guidebook from the ticket gate and do it yourself. The château provides the backdrop for a **firework** extravaganza on the Friday following July 14, and then in early August makes a stunning venue for a **festival** of theatre (see box, p.202).

EATING AND DRINKING   CHÂTEAU DE BONAGUIL

Auberge les Bons Enfants ☏ 05 65 71 23 52, ⊚ lesbons enfants-bonaguil.net. There are a couple of eating places below the castle, including this English-run restaurant, which serves drinks and snacks all day in high season, as well as a more substantial regional *menu* at €16.80. Feb–June & Sept–Oct Mon–Tues & Fri–Sat noon–2.30pm & 7–9pm, Wed noon–2.30pm, evenings by reservation only; July & Aug daily noon–2.30pm & 7–9pm.

Fumel

Eight kilometres southwest of Bonaguil and 12km west of Duravel, **FUMEL** – an important stronghold in medieval times – is now a busy industrial town, which holds little of interest beyond its transport facilities and a decent hotel. It lies on the north bank of the Lot, spilling along the main road from its old centre – focused around **place du Postel** – in the east, past a huge factory making car parts, and then merges 4km later with the western suburb of **MONSEMPRON-LIBOS**. There is little to say about Monsempron either, except that it happens to be a terminal for both trains and buses. Perhaps for that reason it also hosts a huge, rambling – and often inexpensive – **market**, on the place du Marché, every Sunday.

ARRIVAL AND DEPARTURE   FUMEL

By train You'll find the *gare SNCF* in Monsempron-Libos, set back from the river near the road-bridge at the end of avenue de la Gare.

Destinations Agen (1–3 daily; 40–55min); Le Bugue (3–4 daily; 50min–1hr); Les Eyzies (3–4 daily; 55min–1hr 10min); Penne-d'Agenais (3–5 daily; 15–20min); Périgueux (4–6 daily; 1hr 30min).

By bus SNCF buses from Cahors terminate at the *gare SNCF*, having first called in Fumel at place du Postel.

Destinations (from Monsempron-Libos) Cahors (3–7 daily; 1hr 15min); Fumel (4–7 daily; 6–10min); Luzech (3–8 daily; 50min–1hr); Prayssac (3–8 daily; 35min); Puy-l'Évêque (4–8 daily; 30min).

GETTING AROUND AND INFORMATION

Bike rental AJF Cycles, 2 av de l'Usine (☎ 05 53 71 14 57) offers bike rental from €15 a day.
Taxis Call Fumélois (☎ 05 53 71 39 50).
Tourist office Place Georges Escandes (July & Aug daily

10am–noon & 2–6pm; Sept–June Mon & Wed–Fri 10am–noon & 2–5.30pm, Tues & Sat 2–5.30pm; ☎ 05 53 71 13 70, ⓦ tourisme-fumel.com).

ACCOMMODATION AND EATING

Camping les Catalpas ☎ 05 53 71 11 99, ⓦ les-catalpas.com. A friendly little place located 3.5km east of Fumel, just past the village of Condat. Facilities include a restaurant/bar (May–Sept only), pool, river beach and *pétanque*. SNCF buses stop 1.5km up the road in Condat itself. Closed mid-Nov to March. **€14.50**
Hostellerie Le Vert ☎ 05 65 36 51 36, ⓦ hotellevert

.com. Six beautifully refurbished rooms set on a lovely old farm just east of Mauroux, 9km southeast of Fumel, off the D5 Puy-l'Évêque road. It also boasts a heated pool and an excellent restaurant serving upmarket regional cuisine, with *menus* from €28. Breakfast €10. Restaurant April–June Mon–Wed & Fri 7.30–8.30pm; July–Oct daily 7.30–8.30pm. **€110**

Penne-d'Agenais

The last place worth a stop along the valley before Villeneuve-sur-Lot is the beautiful but touristy old fortress-town of **PENNE-D'AGENAIS**, 15km downstream from Fumel on the river's south bank, where the silver-domed **Notre-Dame-de-Peyragude** teeters on the cliff edge. The church dates back to 1000, but had the misfortune to be built on a particularly strategic pinnacle of rock. After Richard the Lionheart erected a castle right next door in 1182, the church found itself in the crossfire on any number of occasions; in 1412 Penne changed hands no fewer than four times. The most recent construction was only completed in 1949; there's nothing particular to see inside, and the neighbouring castle was razed during the Wars of Religion, but the climb is rewarded with panoramic views.

From **place Gambetta**, the main square immediately south of the old town, **rue du 14-Juillet** ducks under a medieval gate. From here just follow your fancy uphill along narrow lanes lined with an alluring mix of brick-and-stone houses – all incredibly spick and span. A few twists and turns later you emerge beside the basilica.

ARRIVAL AND INFORMATION   PENNE-D'AGENAIS

By train Penne's *gare SNCF* is located a couple of kilometres southeast of the city centre, along the D103 to Agen. For taxis call Andrée Garcia (☎ 06 15 27 05 91).

Destinations Agen (10–12 daily; 20min).

Tourist office Rue du 14-Juillet, just inside the medieval gate (Mon–Sat 9am–12.30pm & 2–6pm, Sun 2–6pm; ☎ 05 53 41 37 80, ⓦ penne-tourisme.com). Staff can supply comprehensive lists of *chambres d'hôtes* and *gîtes* in the area.

ACCOMMODATION AND EATING

Le Bombecul Place Paul Fromet ☎ 05 53 71 11 76, ⓦ bombecul.free.fr. Above-average restaurant serving up delicacies like stuffed quails, suckling pig and salmon gravadlax, with some unique flavours. *Menus* from €17 at lunch, €30 in the evenings. March, Oct & Nov Fri & Sat noon–2pm & 7.30–9pm, Sun noon–2pm; April–June

& Sept Wed–Sat noon–2pm & 7.30–9pm, Sun noon–2pm; July & Aug daily noon–2pm & 7.30–9pm.
Camping Municipal Les Berges du Lot ☎ 05 53 41 22 23. A small, two-star riverside campsite near the bridge over the Lot in St-Sylvestre; facilities include a pool and a children's play area. Closed Sept to mid-May. **€9.50**

5

Camping Municipal Lac Férrié ☎05 53 41 30 97. A three-star campsite beside a lake just north of Penne's *gare SNCF*, with a pool, children's play area and *pétanque*. Closed Sept–June. **€16.50**

La Maison sur la Place 10 place Gambetta ☎06 83 49 21 28, ⓦ lamaisonsurlaplace.com. Recently transformed from a restaurant to a *chambre d'hôte*, this welcoming townhouse is a model of chic. There was only one room available at the time of writing (more are set to open), but it's a delightful haven with white-painted brick, neutral furnishings and an upmarket bohemian vibe. **€105**

Villeneuve-sur-Lot and around

Straddling the river 10km west of Penne-d'Agenais, **VILLENEUVE-SUR-LOT** is a pleasant, workaday sort of town. It has no terribly compelling sights, but the handful of attractive timbered houses in the old centre goes some way to compensate. Founded in 1251 by Alphonse de Poitiers, Villeneuve was one of the region's earliest *bastide* towns (see box, p.244), and in no time it developed into an important commercial centre, which it remains to this day. As elsewhere, its ramparts have given way to encircling boulevards, but the distinctive chequerboard street-plan survives, along with two medieval gates and the old, arched bridge.

As for excursions further afield, the nearby hilltop village of **Pujols** makes for an enjoyable trip, while further down the Garonne, **Aiguillon** provides a clutch of picturesque medieval lanes perfect for a wander.

Porte de Paris and place Lafayette

The principal entrance to Villeneuve-sur-Lot's *bastide* was northerly **Porte de Paris**, also the prison – one of whose occupants was an unfortunate – and incompetent – baker incarcerated for the heinous crime of turning out substandard bread. From here the semi-pedestrianized rue de Paris leads south to Villeneuve's main square, **place Lafayette**; surrounded by arcaded townhouses in brick and stone, it bursts into life on **market** days (Tues & Sat mornings).

Église Ste-Catherine

Rue Ste-Catherine • Daily 8am–noon & 3–7pm • ☎05 53 40 02 09

Villeneuve-sur-Lot's most striking landmark is the 55m-high, octagonal red-brick tower of the **Église Ste-Catherine**, east of rue de Paris. The church was founded at the same time as the *bastide*, but then rebuilt in the late nineteenth century when it was in danger of collapse. In addition to an unusual north–south axis, the new architects chose a dramatic neo-Byzantine style, with a line of three domes above the nave, mosaic portraits of the six St Catherines – including St Catherine of Alexandria, to whom the church is dedicated, third from the left – and a multitude of saints on a frieze inspired by early Christian art. A few relics of the old church remain, notably some attractive stained-glass windows, the oldest dating from the fourteenth century.

Pont des Cieutats and Notre-Dame du Bout-du-Pont

The road running parallel to rue de Paris to the west, **rue des Cieutats**, leads to the thirteenth-century **Pont des Cieutats**, originally topped with three towers reminiscent of Cahors' Pont Valentré (see p.206), and, just beside it on the north bank, a tiny chapel full of candles and votive plaques. The sixteenth-century **Notre-Dame du Bout-du-Pont** enshrines a small wooden statue of the Virgin holding Jesus gingerly in her arms. It was found in the river here by a sixteenth-century boatman when his craft mysteriously stopped midstream – or so the legend goes.

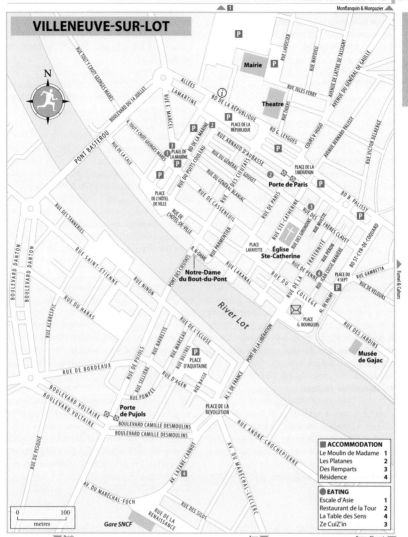

Musée de Gajac

2 rue des Jardins • April–Oct Tues–Fri 10am–noon & 2–6pm, Sat & Sun 2–6pm; Nov–March Tues–Fri 10am–noon & 2–5pm, Sat & Sun 2–5pm • €5 • ☏ 05 53 40 48 00, ⓦ ville-villeneuve-sur-lot.fr

It's worth checking what's on at the **Musée de Gajac**, which has interesting temporary exhibitions that change seasonally, ranging from fine art to photography and archeology. Guided tours are possible if booked in advance – ask at the tourist office (see p.242) for details.

ARRIVAL AND INFORMATION VILLENEUVE-SUR-LOT

By bus SNCF runs regular bus services from Agen calling at Villeneuve's former *gare SNCF* (where there's an SNCF ticket office), a 5min walk south of the centre, and terminating at the Hôtel de Ville.
Destinations Agen (8–10 daily; 45–50min).
By car Villeneuve-sur-Lot is easily accessible by car, although

5

most of the centre operates on a one-way system. There is ample open-air and covered parking all around the city, with the most convenient car parks located at place de la Marine, place de la Libération and along bd de la République.

Tourist office 3 place de la Libération (July & Aug Mon–Sat 9.30am–1pm & 2–6pm; Sept–June Mon–Sat 9.30am–noon & 2–6pm; ☎ 05 53 36 17 30, ⊛ tourisme -villeneuvois.com).

ACCOMMODATION

★ **Le Moulin de Madame** Route de Casseneuil ☎ 05 53 36 14 40, ⊛ moulindemadame.com. A stunning hotel housed in a restored eighteenth-century mill overlooking the Lot, complete with luxury spa, jacuzzi and fitness area. The sumptuous rooms feature plush furnishings, gleaming bathrooms and espresso machines, while the riverfront restaurant is worth a visit for the views alone. *Menus* from €19. Breakfast €12. Restaurant Tues–Fri 12.30–2.30pm & 7.30–9.30pm, Sat 7.30–9.30pm, Sun 12.30–2.30pm. **€90**

Les Platanes 40 bd de la Marine ☎ 09 70 35 63 09, ⊛ hoteldesplatanes.com. Located in the northwest corner of the old quarter, this great-value hotel has been spruced up with bright paintwork and contemporary furniture.

Rooms follow suit, many with recently refurbished bathrooms and all spotlessly clean. Breakfast €9. Closed late-Dec to mid-Jan. **€57**

Des Remparts 1 rue Étienne Marcel ☎ 05 53 70 71 63, ⊛ hotel-des-remparts.eu. For a budget option in the heart of the city, this old-fashioned hotel is a welcoming choice. The cheerfully decorated rooms are comfortable despite being a bit on the small side. Breakfast €7. **€50**

Résidence 17 av Lazare Carnot ☎ 05 53 40 17 03, ⊛ hotellaresidence47.com. A quiet spot not far from the train station with well-kept rooms, friendly staff and a generous continental breakfast (€8). Private parking €5. Closed Christmas to mid-Jan. **€50**

EATING

★ **Escale d'Asie** 8 rue Tout y Croit Georges Marès ☎ 05 53 71 89 48, ⊛ restaurant-asiatique-villeneuve-sur -lot.fr. Tasty and beautifully presented Asian cuisine with a wide choice of dishes and excellent-value *menus* starting from as little as €12. Try the spicy grilled prawns or beef satay, with a side plate of nems (spring rolls), then finish with the banana *flambée* with sake. Takeaway is also available. Tues–Sun noon–2pm & 7–10.30pm.

Restaurant de la Tour 5 rue Arnaud d'Aubasse ☎ 05 53 71 89 70. A great spot to tuck into regional cuisine – opt for *l'assiette de sud-ouest* (€23), laden with duck, foie gras and seasonal vegetables. Alternatively, there's a variety of crêpes, salads and vegetarian dishes to choose from, plus a decent wine list. Tues–Sat noon–2pm & 7–9.30pm.

★ **La Table des Sens** 8 rue de Penne ☎ 05 53 36 97 04, ⊛ www.latabledessens.com. An elegant choice for fine dining, where you'll find French favourites like snails and foie gras, and mains featuring yellowfin tuna, lobster and rabbit. Expect tip-top service, perfectly cooked dishes and some truly showstopping desserts – for a treat, try the Grand Marnier soufflé. *Menus* from €26 at lunch and €46 in the evening. Wed–Sat noon–1.30pm & 7.45–9.30pm, Sun noon–1.30pm

Ze CuiZ'in 38 rue des Frères Clavet ☎ 05 53 36 08 95, ⊛ ze-cuiz-in.fr. Hard to miss, with its bright-red facade, *Ze CuiZ'in* is the go-to place for a spot-on burger (from €13.50); there's plenty of choice, with evocative names like the "Yankee", the "Bollywood" and the "Snob", the last featuring duck and foie gras. There's also a range of salads to balance it out. *Formules* from €14.50. Tues–Sat noon– 2pm & 7–9.30pm.

Pujols

Three kilometres south of Villeneuve, the two-street village of **PUJOLS** stands high above the plain behind its thirteenth-century ramparts. The town is a popular excursion destination, partly because it's a beguiling little place, with its flowery nooks and crannies, and partly for **views** over the surrounding country – for locals, though, the main reason to come to Pujols is gastronomic, with one of the region's best Michelin-starred restaurants on the outskirts of town.

Immediately inside Pujols' main north gate, it's hard to tell where the fortifications end and the Gothic **Église St-Nicolas** begins. It contains nothing of particular note, whereas the **Église Ste-Foy** (open for temporary exhibitions, which take place most of the time between April and October; free), on the far side of the market square, is decorated with fifteenth- and sixteenth-century frescoes. Though faded, many are still visible: around the apse, you can pick out St George poised over the dragon and St Catherine with her wheel of torture. Look out, too, for a painting in the baptismal chapel (first on the left as you enter), depicting the old bridge at Villeneuve-sur-Lot sporting its three towers.

Aux Délices du Puits Rue de la Citadelle ☎ 05 53 71 61 66. A casual dining spot ideal for families, with a range of pizzas (from €8), salads (from €8.50) and ice creams to tempt all tastes. Reservation required for evenings in low season. June–Aug daily 10.30am–10pm, hot food served noon–2.30pm & 6.15–9.30pm; Sept–May Mon & Thurs–Sat 10.30am–10pm, hot food served noon–2.30pm.

★**La Toque Blanche** ☎ 05 53 49 00 30, ⓦ la-toque -blanche.com. Expect stellar service and heavenly cuisine at this Michelin-starred jewel, just south of Pujols with views back to the village. Diners can indulge in lobster, truffle and foie gras salad, or sample more adventurous dishes like stuffed pigs' trotters. Evening *menus* start from €39. Mid-July to end-Oct & mid-Nov to end-June Tues–Sat noon–2pm & 7.30–9pm.

Aiguillon

Around thirty kilometres west of Pujols, the hilltop town of **AIGUILLON** stands guard over the confluence of the Lot and Garonne rivers as it has done at least since Roman times. Nowadays Aiguillon's most imposing building is the eighteenth-century, Neoclassical **Château des Ducs** – now a school – which dominates the western approach to the town. It was built by the duc d'Aiguillon who, having served as an army chief and governor of Brittany under Louis XV, returned to transform his medieval château into a mini-Versailles, though the grand balls and other festivities were soon cut short by the Revolution. The small area of medieval lanes with their half-timbered houses to the north of the château is worth a wander, and the church next to the château boasts a lovely, delicate organ. The town's lively food **markets** are held each Tuesday and Friday on place du 14-Juillet.

ARRIVAL AND INFORMATION AIGUILLON

By train Aiguillon's *gare SNCF*, on the Agen–Bordeaux train line, lies a 2min walk below the château to the southwest along avenue de la Gare.
Destinations Agen (12–14 daily; 18min); Toulouse (12–14 daily; 1hr 45min).

Tourist office Beside the château on the central place du 14-Juillet (June–Aug Tues–Fri 9am–noon & 2–6pm, Sat 10am–noon; Sept–May Tues–Fri 9am–noon & 2–6pm; ☎ 05 53 64 65 31, ⓦ ville-aiguillon.eu).

The bastide country

Although *bastides*, or medieval new towns (see box, p.244), are by no means unique to this stretch of country north of the Lot, it's here that you'll find the two finest examples. The more southerly of the pair is **Monflanquin**, which makes a good place to start thanks to its museum outlining the history, architecture and daily life of the *bastides*. Northeast, skirting round the flanks of the imposing **Château de Biron**, lies **Monpazier**. This is the most typical of the *bastides*, with virtually no modern development around. There's a small museum here, too, but Monpazier's prime attraction is its atmosphere, "like a drowsy yellow cat, slumbering in the sun" as Freda White so aptly describes it in her classic book *Three Rivers of France*.

Nevertheless, some effort is required to explore the area. Neither the Château de Biron nor Monpazier are accessible by **public transport**, so having your own vehicle is essential.

Monflanquin

Some 17km north of Villeneuve-sur-Lot, pretty **MONFLANQUIN**, founded in 1252 by Alphonse de Poitiers, is nearly as perfectly preserved as nearby Monpazier, though less touristy and impressively positioned on top of a hill that rises sharply from the surrounding country, visible for miles. Despite being constructed on a steep slope, it conforms to the regular pattern of right-angled streets leading from a central square to the four town gates. The ramparts themselves were demolished on Richelieu's orders

BASTIDES

From the Occitan *bastida*, meaning a group of buildings, **bastides** were the new towns of the thirteenth and fourteenth centuries. Although they are found all over southwest France, from the Dordogne to the foothills of the Pyrenees, there is a particularly high concentration in the area between the Dordogne and Lot rivers, which at that time formed the disputed "frontier" region between English-held Aquitaine and Capetian France.

That said, the earliest *bastides* were founded largely for **economic and political** reasons. They were a means of bringing new land into production – this was a period of rapid population growth and technological innovation – and thus extending the power of the local lord. But as tensions between the French and English forces intensified during the late thirteenth century, so the motive became increasingly **military**. The *bastides* now provided a handy way of securing the land along the frontier, and it was generally at this point that they were fortified.

As an incentive, anyone who was prepared to build, inhabit and defend the *bastide* was granted various perks and concessions in a founding **charter**. All new residents were allocated a building plot, garden and cultivable land outside the town. The charter might also offer asylum to certain types of criminal or grant exemption from military service, and would allow the election of **consuls** charged with day-to-day administration – a measure of self-government remarkable in feudal times. Taxes and judicial affairs, meanwhile, remained the preserve of the representative of the king or local lord under whose ultimate authority the *bastide* lay.

The other defining feature of a *bastide* is its **layout**. They are nearly always square or rectangular in shape, depending on the nature of the terrain, and are divided by streets at right angles to each other to produce a chequerboard pattern. The focal point is the market square, often missing its covered *halle* nowadays, but generally still surrounded by arcades, while the church is relegated to one side, or may even form part of the town walls.

The busiest *bastide* founders were **Alphonse de Poitiers** (1249–71), on behalf of the French Crown, after he became count of Toulouse in 1249, and **King Edward I of England**, Edward Plantagenet (1272–1307), who wished to consolidate his hold on the northern borders of his duchy of Aquitaine. The former chalked up a total of 57 *bastides*, including Villeneuve-sur-Lot (1251), Monflanquin (1252), Ste-Foy-la-Grande (1255) and Eymet (1270), while Edward was responsible for Beaumont (1272), Monpazier and Molières (both 1284), among others.

in 1630, but otherwise Monflanquin has experienced few radical changes since the thirteenth century.

The main square, tree-shaded **place des Arcades** – where the **market** still takes place on Thursdays as decreed in the *bastide*'s founding charter – derives a special charm from being on a slope. Its grandest building is the Gothic **Maison du Prince Noir** in the northeast corner, where the Black Prince is said to have stayed, as well as the **Musée des Bastides** (see below).

After a quick wander through Monflanquin's old centre, it's worth heading north past the **Paroisse de Monflanquin** church, which took on its pseudo-medieval look in the early twentieth century, to end up on a terrace with expansive views northeast to the Château de Biron (see opposite).

Musée des Bastides

Place des Arcades • April–June & Sept–Oct Mon–Sat 9.30am–12.30pm & 2–5pm; July & Aug daily 9.30am–6.30pm • €4, under-12s free • ☎ 05 53 36 40 19, ⓦ monflanquin-museedesbastides.com

On the north side of the place des Arcades, above the tourist office, the high-tech **Musée des Bastides** is a treasure trove of information about the life and history of *bastides*. Most of the text is translated into English, but the video and multimedia displays are mostly in French only. Nonetheless, there's plenty of interest, with displays spread over two floors, and the collection serves as a comprehensive introduction to the region's medieval past.

INFORMATION

Tourist office Place des Arcades (April–June & Sept Mon–Sat 9.30am–12.30pm & 2–5.30pm; July & Aug daily 9.30am–6.30pm; Oct–March Mon–Wed & Fri–Sat 9.30am–12.30pm & 2–5pm, Thurs 9.30am–12.30pm; ☏ 05 53 36 40 19, ⓦ monflanquin-tourisme.com). They can furnish you with details of the many events taking place here in summer (see box, p.202).

ACCOMMODATION AND EATING

La Bastide Place des Arcades ☏ 05 53 36 77 05. In a prime location right on the main square, this popular British-run crêperie serves salads and crêpes (from €7.50) on their lovely terrace, which offers splendid views down the length of rue Ste-Marie. Tues–Sat noon–11pm, Sun noon–3pm.

La Bastide des Oliviers 1 tour de Ville ☏ 05 53 36 40 01, ⓦ labastidedesoliviers.fr. The best spot to stay in Monflanquin with light, modern rooms equipped with king-size beds, tea- and coffee-making facilities and English TV channels. There's also a restaurant and brasserie on-site, with lunchtime *menus* starting from a very reasonable €12.50. Breakfast €9. Restaurant June–Sept daily noon–2pm & 7–9.30pm. **€65**

Le Bistrot du Prince Noir Place des Arcades ☏ 05 53 36 63 00, ⓦ lebistrotduprincenoir.fr. A welcoming bistro in the southwest corner of the main square, where you'll find a varied menu of European foods, complimented by a great wine list. Vegetarians might opt for the aubergine and mozzarella lasagne, while the fish and chips are (almost) as good as back home. *Menus* from €22. May–Sept daily noon–2pm & 7–9pm.

Le Café de Gavaudun Gavaudun ☏ 05 53 40 99 34, ⓦ lecafedegavaudun.com. Some 10km east of Monflanquin, this humble little restaurant is a popular haunt for locals, with delicious cuisine whipped up from fresh market produce. The menu changes depending on what's in season, but an average *plat du jour* is about €14. Mon, Tues & Thurs–Sun noon–2pm & 7.30–9pm.

SHOPPING

Cave des 7 Monts Lidon ☏ 05 53 36 33 40. Just south of town, off the D124, the Cave des 7 Monts is the best spot to buy regional wines. The wine co-operative represents some two hundred local vineyards producing some very palatable and reasonably priced wines; tastings are available free of charge. Mon 2–6pm, Tues–Fri 9am–noon & 2–6pm, Sat 9am–noon.

Château de Biron

Feb, March, Nov & Dec Tues–Sun 10am–12.30pm & 2–5pm; April–June & Sept–Oct daily 10am–12.30pm & 2–6pm; July & Aug daily 10am–7pm • €8.10, children €5.20 • Guided tours in French only 45min–1hr • ☏ 05 53 63 13 19, ⓦ semitour.com

Twenty-two kilometres northeast of Monflanquin, via a picturesque route along the River Lède, the vast **Château de Biron** dominates the countryside for miles around. It was begun in the eleventh century and added to piecemeal over the years by the Gontaut-Biron family, who occupied the castle right up to the early twentieth century. The biggest alterations were made in the fifteenth and early sixteenth centuries, when Pons de Gontaut-Biron started reconstructing the eastern wing. The result is an architectural primer, from the medieval keep through flamboyant Gothic and Renaissance to an eighteenth-century loggia in the style of Versailles.

Rather than the guided tour (in French only), at busy times it's better to borrow the English-language text from the ticket desk and wander at will. The most striking building in the grassy **lower court** is the Renaissance chapel, where lie the sarcophagi of Pons and his brother Armand, bishop of Sarlat. Though their statues were hacked about during the Revolution, the Italianate biblical scenes and three Virtues carved on the sides still show fine craftsmanship. On entering the cobbled and confined **inner courtyard** around its twelfth-century keep, the route takes you to a dungeon and through the lord's apartments, with their Renaissance chimney and wood-panelled hall, to a vast reception room and an equally capacious stone-vaulted refectory. If the rooms decked out as a tannery, torture chamber and weavers' workshop make you feel as though you're walking through a film set, you are – Biron is a favourite for period dramas.

Auberge du Château Château de Biron ☎ 05 53 63 13 33, ⓦ auberge-chateau-biron.fr. The pretty terrace is overflowing with flowers at this tranquil restaurant, perched on the path up to the castle. There's not much choice, but it's all expertly executed and good value, with lunch *menus* at €14 and evening *menus* at €26. March–Oct daily noon–2pm & 7–9pm.

Le Moulinal Lacapelle-Biron ☎ 05 53 40 84 60, ⓦ lemoulinal.com. Around 6km south of Château de Biron off the D255, Lacapelle-Biron boasts one of the region's best campsites and it's a paradise for kids, with indoor and outdoor pools, a range of water slides and toboggans, plus

mini-golf, tennis courts and a splash pool for toddlers. There's also a restaurant, bar and bikes for rent, and chalets (from €245 weekly). One-week minimum stay in July & Aug. Closed mid-Sept to April. **€17**

Le Palissy Place du Monument aux Morts, Lacapelle-Biron ☎ 05 53 75 04 08, ⓦ lepalissycheznorbert.fr. Head 5km southeast of Château de Biron – by road or on the GR36 footpath – to Lacapelle-Biron and you'll find this friendly bistro-style restaurant on the main road. It has a Dutch chef and consequently rather a polyglot atmosphere, plus some great regional dishes. Mains from €12. May–Oct daily 9am–11pm; Nov–April Mon & Wed–Sun noon–9.30pm.

Monpazier

From the Château de Biron it's 8km north to **MONPAZIER**, the finest and most complete of the surviving *bastides*, made up of a lovely warm-coloured stone on a hill above the River Dropt. Founded in 1284 by King Edward I of England on land granted by Pierre de Gontaut-Biron, and picturesque and placid though it is today, Monpazier has a hard and bitter history, being twice – in 1594 and 1637 – the centre of **peasant rebellions** provoked by the misery that followed the Wars of Religion (see p.295). Both uprisings were brutally suppressed: the 1637 peasants' leader was broken on the wheel in the square and his head paraded around the countryside. In an earlier episode, Sully, the Protestant general, describes a rare moment of light relief in the terrible **Wars of Religion**, when the men of Catholic Villefranche-de-Périgord planned to capture Monpazier on the same night as the men of Monpazier were headed for Villefranche. By chance, the two sides took different routes, met no resistance, looted to their hearts' content and returned congratulating themselves on their luck and skill, only to find that things were rather different at home. The peace terms were that everything should be returned to its proper place.

During the summer, Monpazier puts on all sorts of **events** to draw the tourists, from book fairs to medieval jamborees (see box, p.202). Outside these occasions, however, there's not much else to do here beyond soak up the sun at a café on the market square.

Place des Cornières

Given Monpazier's turbulent past, it comes as something of a surprise to find that it has survived so well. Three of its six **medieval gates** are still intact and its central square, **place des Cornières**, couldn't be more perfect, with an oak-pillared *halle* and time-worn, stone-built houses, no two the same. Deep, shady arcades pass beneath all the houses, which are separated from each other by a small gap to reduce fire risk; at the corners the buttresses are cut away to allow the passage of laden pack animals. On Thursday mornings the square comes to life for the weekly **market**, which expands on the third Thursday of each month into a fair. In mushroom season (roughly Aug & Sept depending on the weather) people also come here in the afternoons to sell their pickings, while in December there's a truffle market.

Monpazier's main north–south axis is **rue Notre-Dame**, which brings you into the northeast corner of place des Cornières, past the much-altered **church**. The thirteenth-century building opposite is a bit battered, but this is Monpazier's oldest house, where the tax collector received his share of the harvest.

Ateliers des Bastides

Rue Jean-Galmot • May–Oct Mon & Wed–Sun 10am–12.30pm & 2.30–7pm • Free • ☎ 05 53 22 60 38

The **Ateliers des Bastides** museum sits west of place des Cornières, and boasts a few prehistoric remains and other historical bits and pieces. However, it is largely devoted to local adventurer Jean Galmot, who was born in Monpazier in 1879 and was assassinated in 1928 in French Guiana, then a penal colony, where he was aiding its fledgling independence movement. There is, however, no information in English. During the summer months the museum also hosts a number of temporary **art exhibitions**.

INFORMATION

MONPAZIER

Tourist office Place des Cornières (Feb–May & Oct–Dec Tues–Sat 10am–12.30pm & 2.30–6pm, Sun 10am–12.30pm; June & Sept daily 10am–12.30pm & 2.30–6.30pm; July & Aug daily 10am–12.30pm & 2–7pm; ☎ 05 53 22 68 59, ⊛ pays-des-bastides.com). Among all sorts of useful information, they produce a free booklet outlining a DIY tour of the town, with information in English and games for children, as well as a book of eleven waymarked walks in the area (€3).

ACCOMMODATION

Camping de Véronne ☎ 05 53 22 65 50. Pleasantly located next to a lake, 3km northwest of Monpazier in Marsalès, this small campsite has two sailboats for children (free) and a restaurant/bar. Closed mid-Sept to mid-June. **€35**

Edward 1er 5 rue Saint-Pierre ☎ 05 53 22 44 00, ⊛ hoteledward1er.com. Luxurious rooms, some more modern than others, in an authentic nineteenth-century château in the heart of the city. There's also a restaurant (dinner by reservation only) and a bistro (see below) to choose from, and half-board available. Breakfast €12.50. **€133**

De France 21 rue St-Jacques ☎ 05 24 10 45 33, ⊛ hotel defrancemonpazier.fr. Occupying a fine medieval building on the southwest corner of place des Cornières, *De France* has nine cosy, cheerfully decorated rooms. The restaurant serves decent regional cuisine and brasserie-style fare, with *menus* from €18. Breakfast €7.50. Restaurant Mon–Thurs noon–2pm & 7–9pm, Fri noon–2pm, Sat noon–2pm & 7–9pm, Sun noon–2pm; closed Nov. **€58**

Le Moulin de David ☎ 05 53 22 65 25, ⊛ moulinde david.com. Deluxe four-star campsite in the Dropt valley that's a favourite with tourists, so reserve well in advance. The eco-friendly facilities include a huge pool, a restaurant, snack bar and shop plus children's play areas. Weekly bookings only in July & Aug. Closed Oct–March. **€30**

EATING AND DRINKING

You'll eat very well in the two hotel **restaurants**. Alternatively the **cafés** and **bars** around place des Cornières are perfect for a sunny lunch or cool afternoon drink; you could also turn north and wander along rue Notre-Dame, where there are more options.

Bistrot 2 Foirail Nord ☎ 05 53 22 60 64, ⊛ bistrot2.fr. Just outside the town walls, this little bistro is owned by the same people as the *Edward 1er* (see above); you can sit out on the terrace watching the world go by as you sample tasty local dishes. *Menus* from €15.75. Daily 9am–10pm.

Le Privilège du Périgord 58 rue Notre-Dame ☎ 05 53 22 43 98, ⊛ privilegeperigord.com. Dine on delicacies like duck with roasted pineapple and sweet potato, or truffle and prosciutto bruschetta at this good-value restaurant, and grab a table in the sunny courtyard. *Menus* from €22.50. April–Oct Tues–Sun noon–2.30pm & 7.30–9.30pm.

South of the River Lot

252 Agen and around

261 Moissac and around

266 Quercy Blanc

271 Montauban

275 The Gorges de l'Aveyron and around

CORDES-SUR-CIEL

South of the River Lot

South of the River Lot, the River Garonne in the west and the rivers Tarn and Aveyron in the east define the southern border of the Dordogne and Lot region. On the whole, this area offers less dramatic scenery than further north, but by the same token it sees fewer tourists. It is a fertile land, full of sunflowers and fruit orchards, particularly along the Garonne and spreading over the hills to the north: plums, pears, peaches, cherries, apples, apricots and nectarines all grow here, as well as melons, strawberries and the succulent *chasselas* grapes.

The first of the region's two gateways is **Agen**, the only major town on the Garonne between Bordeaux and Toulouse and more pleasant than it first appears, with an old centre built of pink-mottled brick and a fine local museum. Southwest of Agen, what's left of **Nérac**'s castle and its riverside pleasure gardens – where King Henry IV misspent his youth – still exude a slightly decadent air. The river here is the Baïse, which flows north to join the Garonne near **Buzet-sur-Baïse**, in the centre of a small wine region.

Upstream from Agen, the region's unmissable sight is the abbey church at **Moissac**, with its wonderful carvings. The Garonne valley here is at its flattest and most featureless, but north of Moissac things improve as you climb up onto the low, rolling plateau of the **Quercy Blanc**, which stretches north almost to Cahors. It's a region of white-stone farmhouses, sun-drenched hilltop villages, windmills and *pigeonniers* – pigeon houses, often raised on stilts – by the hundred. Of these, the prettiest village is **Lauzerte**, but **Montpezat-de-Quercy** also merits a visit for its display of religious art, including a series of superb tapestries.

Near Montpezat the N20 and the A20 *autoroute* mark the eastern extent of the Quercy Blanc and funnel traffic south to **Montauban**. This brick-red city, not far north of Toulouse and on the Paris railway line, is the region's second gateway, and justifies a few hours' exploration thanks to its art museum and central square surrounded by elegant townhouses. It sits on the banks of the Tarn in the midst of an alluvial plain which, in the east, gives way abruptly to hills. Running through them, the stunning **Gorges de l'Aveyron** are punctuated with ancient villages perched high above the river, while **St-Antonin-Noble-Val**, with its core of medieval lanes, lies in the valley bottom caught between soaring limestone crags. Beyond St-Antonin, it's worth making a short detour south across the plateau to the aptly named **Cordes-sur-Ciel**, where noble facades line the steeply cobbled lanes, before rejoining the Aveyron beneath **Najac**'s much-contested fortress. The gorge opens out to the north of Najac, but it's worth travelling the last few kilometres to **Villefranche-de-Rouergue**, in the centre of which, in the monstrous shadow of its church tower, lies a perfectly preserved arcaded market square.

GETTING AROUND	SOUTH OF THE RIVER LOT

By train Three major train lines fan out across this region from Toulouse: along the Garonne valley to Montauban, Moissac and Agen; north to Cahors; and northeast through Cordes, Najac and Villefranche en route to Figeac.
By bus Bus services in the region are limited and patchy, often running only at school times, and many small villages have no buses at all. There is one regular SNCF service between Agen and Nérac, while private buses (aimed at schoolchildren) link Montcuq and Villefranche-de-Rouergue with Cahors, though they're not much use to visitors.

Festivals, events and markets p.255
Boat trips along the Canal de Garonne p.256
Pruneaux d'Agen p.257
Agen's markets and fairs p.258
Montcuq Monopoly p.269

CLOISTER AT THE ÉGLISE ABBATIALE ST-PIERRE, MOISSAC

Highlights

❶ Moissac The carvings decorating the south porch and cloister of Moissac's abbey church are masterpieces of Romanesque art. **See p.261**

❷ Quercy Blanc Take time to savour the bucolic countryside between the Garonne and Lot valleys, dotted with vines, sunflowers and sleepy hilltop villages. **See p.266**

❸ Lauzerte Set on a hilltop amid the fruitful fields of the Quercy Blanc, this perfectly preserved *bastide* village offers outstanding views. **See p.266**

❹ St-Antonin-Noble-Val A compact and charming medieval town set against the limestone cliffs of the Gorges de l'Aveyron. **See p.278**

❺ Cordes-sur-Ciel Perched on its knuckle of rock, this fortified town is the jewel of the Tarn and a favourite haunt of artists and artisans. **See p.280**

❻ Château de Najac Climb the tower of Alphonse de Poitier's erstwhile stronghold for vertiginous views over the Aveyron valley. **See p.283**

❼ Villefranche-de-Rouergue The arcaded and sloping central square makes a superb setting for the weekly market. **See p.284**

HIGHLIGHTS ARE MARKED ON THE MAP ON PP.252–253

Agen and around

Agen, capital of the Lot-et-Garonne *département*, lies on the broad, powerful River Garonne halfway between Bordeaux and Toulouse. Close to the A62 *autoroute* and connected to both cities by fast and frequent train services, and to Paris by train and plane, it provides a useful gateway to the southern reaches of the Dordogne and Lot region. However, Agen is more than just a transport hub. Inside the ring of hypermarkets and industrial estates lies a core of old lanes lined with handsome brick houses, several churches worth a look and a surprisingly good fine arts museum, topped off with a number of excellent restaurants and a good choice of hotels. Make sure you try some prunes while you're there – **pruneaux d'Agen** (see box, p.257) are world famous and the basis for many local desserts.

Agen makes for a pleasant half-day's exploration, or a base from which to cover the surrounding country. The most interesting jaunts take you southwest to **Nérac**, where kings and queens disported themselves on the Baïse's wooded banks, and west to the wine town of **Buzet-sur-Baïse**.

Agen

The old centre of **AGEN** lies on the east bank of the Garonne. It is quartered by two nineteenth-century boulevards – **boulevard de la République**, running east–west, and north–south **boulevard du Président-Carnot** – which intersect at place Goya and make for easy navigation. To the northeast stands **Cathédrale St-Caprais**, somewhat misshapen but worth a look for its finely proportioned Romanesque apse and radiating chapels.

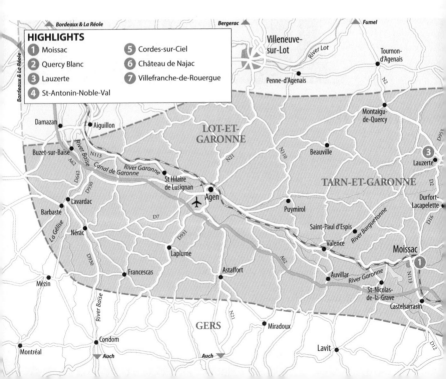

HIGHLIGHTS

1. Moissac
2. Quercy Blanc
3. Lauzerte
4. St-Antonin-Noble-Val
5. Cordes-sur-Ciel
6. Château de Najac
7. Villefranche-de-Rouergue

Musée des Beaux-Arts

Place Dr-Esquirol • Mon & Wed–Sun: 10am–12.30pm & 1.30–6pm • €5.40 • ☎ 05 53 69 47 23, ⓦ www.agen.fr

Beside the exuberant, Italianate municipal theatre, the **Musée des Beaux-Arts** is magnificently housed in four adjacent sixteenth- and seventeenth-century mansions adorned with stair turrets and Renaissance window details. Inside you'll find a rich variety of archeological exhibits, furniture and paintings – among the latter, a number of Goyas and a Tintoretto rediscovered during an inventory in 1997. Best, though, are the basement's Roman finds, which include intricate jewellery and a superb white-marble Venus.

6

Église des Jacobins and around

To the west of place Dr-Esquirol, a clutch of brick and timber houses – the bricks forming neat zigzags within the timber frame – represent Agen's most attractive corner. From here a short and narrow alley, **rue Beauville**, cuts through to rue Richard Coeur de Lion, with more eye-catching facades and the **Église des Jacobins**. This big, brick Dominican church was founded by Dominican monks in the thirteenth century, then served as the Protestants' headquarters before being used as a prison during the Revolution. It now forms an annexe of the Musée des Beaux-Arts (see above) and hosts temporary art exhibitions (Mon & Wed–Sat 2–6pm; ☎ 05 53 69 47 64; prices vary). Inside, you can see unusual Gothic frescoes of leaves and geometric patterns in trompe l'oeil on the walls and ceiling.

West of the church is the river and the public gardens of **Esplanade du Gravier**, where a footbridge crosses the Garonne – from it you can see a 550m **canal bridge** dating from 1843 further downstream.

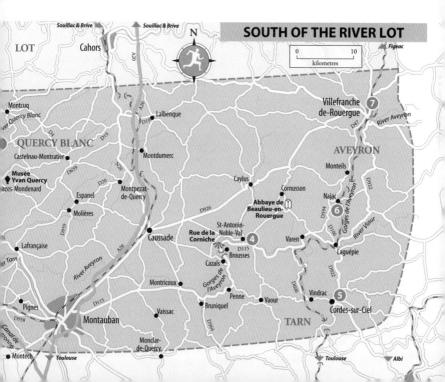

AGEN

Theâtre du Jour, Moissac, Cahors & Toulouse

Moissac

Hospital & Villeneuve-sur-Lot

ACCOMMODATION
Des Ambans	2
Camping	1
Moulin de Mellet	3
Château de Cambes	6
Domaine de Touille	5
Des Jacobins	4
Le Provence	

EATING
Côte Sud	7
Le Margoton	5
Monsieur Jeannot	3
Osaka	1
La Part des Anges	2
Philippe Vannier	4

Locaboat Plaisance

Théâtre du Jour

Halle du Pin

Cap Cinéma

PONT DE LA LIBERATION

RUE DE POMPEYRIE

AVENUE ROBERT SCHUMAN

IMPASSE DE PANOT

RUE DE L'ÉCOLE NORMALE

RUE DE ROMAS

RUE PAULIN RÉGNIER

AVENUE HENRI-BARBUSSE

RUE ROUGET DE L'ISLE

AVENUE JEAN-JAURES

RUE PRUNE

PLACE DU 14 JUILLET

RUE DE LA TOUR

COURS DU 14 JUILLET

Cathédrale St-Caprais

QUAI DUNKERQUE

Gare SNCF

BOULEVARD SYLVAIN-DUMON

RUE SAINT-FIARY

RUE RASPAIL

Gare Routière

RUE DE L'ABREUVOIR

RUE LAMARTINE

RUE S. SANTINI

RUE DE BELFORT

RUE KLEBER

RUE CAMILLE-DESMOULINS

RUE NEUVE

PLACE GOYA

RUE DES AMBANS

RUE MOLINIER

RUE DE RAYMOND

RUE LA FAYETTE

CARNOT

RUE JOSEPH BARA

RUE DES BOURS-SAINT-JEAN

RUE DES AUTAS

RUE LASSAIGNE

BOULEVARD EUGÈNE-PELLETAN

RUE ÉMILE ZOLA

BOULEVARD DE LA LIBERTÉ

AVENUE M. LUXEMBOURG

RUE JEGUN DE MARANS

RUE SAINT-MARTIN

RUE DES FLEURUS

RUE PHILIPPE TAUZIN

RUE D'A PÉPINIÈRE

RUE DE LA COLONNE

RUE ERNEST SARROU

RUE PAUL BERT

AV. MICHELET

VICTOR HUGO

RUE DANTON

COURS DU PRÉSIDENT

BOULEVARD DU PRÉSIDENT

COURS WASHINGTON

RUE LEDRU-ROLLIN

RUE MONTESQUIEU

RUE DE STRASBOURG

Halle

PLACE WILSON

PLACE J-B-DURAND

Théâtre Municipal

Musée des Beaux-Arts

MARCHÉ-AU-BLÉ

RUE GARONNE

PLACE DES LAITIERS

RUE DE CESSAC

PLACE DR-ESQUIROL

RUE BEAUVILLE

RUE MIRABEAU

RUE PALISSY

RUE DES CORNIÈRES

RUE DES AUGUSTINS

BOULEVARD SCALIGER

RUE DE CONTENSOU

RUE DE CALABET

QUAI DU CANAL

Canal

RUE GABRIEL GNIFFON

RUE GRANDE HORLOGE

BOULEVARD DE LA RÉPUBLIQUE

RUE VOLTAIRE

PLACE DES JACOBINS

RUE RICHARD-CŒUR-DE-LION

RUE HENRI MARTIN

Église des Jacobins

RUE BÉRANGER

RUE AUGUSTE GUÉ

RUE LOMET

RUE LOUIS-VIVENT

AVENUE DU GÉNÉRAL-DE-GAULLE

COURS GAMBETTA

Esplanade du Gravier

PÉRISTYLE DU GRAVIER

RUE BAUDIN

QUAI BAUDIN

RUE DES ILES

RUE LAGRANGE

RUE BONIS

RUE GÉRARD DUVERGÉ

Airport, A62 Autoroute & Nérac

1 & Bordeaux

River Garonne

N

0   200   metres

SHOPPING
Confiserie P. Boisson	1
Dalla Vecchia Philippe	4
Joel Manaud	3
Maison Mauferon Raynal	2

DRINKING
L'Endroit Bar	2
La Karafe	4
Le Takeoff	3
Quarts Coffee Kitchen	1

6

ARRIVAL AND DEPARTURE

AGEN

By plane Flights from Paris arrive at Agen's La Garenne airport (☎ 05 53 77 00 88, ⊛ aeroport-agen.com), around 3km southwest of town; taxis wait outside the airport and a trip into the centre costs roughly €20.

Destinations Paris Orly (3 daily Mon–Fri, 1 on Sun; 1hr 30min).

By train The gare SNCF is located on the north side of town, on boulevard Sylvain-Dumon. From in front of the station, boulevard du Président-Carnot leads south to place Goya, where it crosses the town's other main thoroughfare, the east–west boulevard de la République.

Destinations Bordeaux (up to 20 daily; 1hr–1hr 20min); Moissac (5–9 daily; 25–45min); Monsempron-Libos (4–9 daily; 35–45min); Montauban (up to 16 daily; 40–50min); Périgueux (3–5 daily; 2hr–2hr 20min); La Réole (7–10 daily; 50min); Toulouse (12–17 daily; 1hr–1hr 15min).

6

FESTIVALS, EVENTS AND MARKETS

The list below comprises some of the biggest and more interesting of the **festivals** and **events** in this region. Where we haven't given a specific information number or website, contact the relevant tourist office.

Mid-May Montauban: Alors, Chante! (☎ 05 63 04 92 82, ⊛ alorschante.com). Over Ascension weekend various well-known (and not-so-well-known) artists take part in this festival of French song (tickets required).

Late May or early June Moissac: Fêtes de Pentecôte (☎ 05 63 04 63 63). A traditional fair on the banks of the Tarn over the Whitsun weekend, with fireworks on the Monday night.

July and August Moissac: Les Soirs de Moissac (☎ 05 63 04 06 81). Varied programme of concerts, choral works and recitals, including world music, held in the cloister or the church of St-Pierre (tickets required).

Mid-July Cordes-sur-Ciel: Fête du Grand Fauconnier (☎ 05 65 56 34 63, ⊛ grandfauconnier.com). This two-day medieval festival converts the town into a costumed extravaganza, complete with exhibitions on medieval crafts and falconry. Daily admission to the old town is €9, and you can hire medieval costumes for the occasion.

Late July Cordes-sur-Ciel: Musique sur Ciel (☎ 05 63 56 00 75, ⊛ festivalmusiquesurciel. com). Ten days of classical concerts, some by featured contemporary composers, in the church of St-Michel.

Late July to mid-August Lauzerte and around: Festival du Quercy Blanc (☎ 05 65 22 90 73, ⊛ festivalduquercyblanc.com). Concerts of classical and chamber music held mostly in churches around the region, including Lauzerte, Montcuq,

Montpezat-de-Quercy and Castelnau-Montratier. Tickets available from local tourist offices.

End of July or start of August Lauzerte: Les Nuits de Lauzerte (☎ 05 63 94 61 94, ⊛ nuitsdelauzerte.free.fr). Over the space of a weekend, Lauzerte becomes an art installation and performance space, through which you walk at night, taking your time and wandering at your own pace past street theatre, contemporary dance, music and projections. Tickets from the tourist office (€12).

Early August Villefranche-de-Rouergue and around: Festival en Bastides (☎ 05 65 45 76 74, ⊛ espaces-culturels.fr). Five days of contemporary theatre and performance art animate the streets of Villefranche and Najac, amongst other places. Some ticketed events, information from any participating tourist office.

Third weekend in September Moissac: Fête du Chasselas and Fête des Fruits et des Légumes (☎ 05 63 04 63 63). Every year the Fête du Chasselas celebrates the local grape, with tastings on offer and a competition to find the pick of the bunch; the event takes place in the market hall. Every two years (in the odd years) the whole range of local fruits plus vegetables are also on display and there are all manner of related events throughout the town.

Second weekend in October Auvillar: Marché Potier (☎ 05 63 39 57 33). Some forty exhibitors take part in this important pottery fair held on the place de la Halle.

MARKETS

The main **markets** in the region are at Agen (Wed & Sat); Cordes (Sat); Laguépie (Wed & Sun); Lauzerte (Wed & Sat); Moissac (Sat & Sun); Montauban (Wed & Sat); Montcuq (Sun); Nérac (Sat); St-Antonin-Noble-Val (Sun); St-Nicolas-de-la-Grave (Mon); and Villefranche-de-Rouergue (Thurs).

6

BOAT TRIPS ALONG THE CANAL DE GARONNE

The Canal de Garonne (formerly known as the Canal latéral à la Garonne) was once part of a heaving artery of commerce, forming part of the great Canal de Deux Mers, which links the Canal du Midi at Toulouse with the Garonne River. This in turn finally connected the Mediterranean to the Atlantic. Today the peaceful waterways are given over to pleasure, the canal is clean and overhung with trees, and flotillas of ducks replace the commercial barges. **Locaboat Plaisance** (☎ 03 86 91 72 72, ⌨ locaboat.com) offers cruises along the canal from March to October; prices vary from €934 to €1600 per week for a three- to five-person boat, depending on the season and the level of comfort.

By bus The *gare routière* is next to the *gare SNCF*. For up-to-date bus schedules ask at the tourist office or phone the transport desk of the Conseil Général on ☎ 05 53 69 42 03.

Destinations Nérac (Mon–Sat 5–7 daily; 40min); Villeneuve-sur-Lot (3–10 daily; 45min).
By car Free car parking can be found along the riverbank and on place du 14-Juillet.

GETTING AROUND AND INFORMATION

Bike rental Comptoir du Deux Roues, 18–20 av du Général-de-Gaulle (☎ 05 53 47 76 76, ⌨ comptoir-du-deux-roues.fr; closed Sun); from €9 per half-day.
Car rental Avis, 12 bd Sylvain Dumon, near the train station and at the airport (☎ 05 53 47 76 47, ⌨ avis.com); Europcar, 120 bd du Président-Carnot and near the train station (☎ 05 53 47 37 40, ⌨ europcar.com)

Taxis There is a taxi stand at the train station, or call Agen Taxis (☎ 06 09 37 07 74).
Tourist office 38 rue Garonne (July & Aug Mon–Sat 9am–7pm, Sun 9.30am–12.30pm; Sept–June Mon–Sat 9am–12.30pm & 2–6.30pm ☎ 05 53 47 36 09, ⌨ ot-agen .org).

ACCOMMODATION

Des Ambans 59 rue des Ambans ☎ 05 53 66 28 60. No frills but good value, this friendly hotel nonetheless boasts an excellent central location. There are nine small but clean rooms to choose from and all but the most expensive lack an en-suite toilet. Book well ahead for the summer season. Breakfast €6.50. Closed some weekends Oct–March. **€47**
Camping Moulin de Mellet ☎ 05 53 87 50 89, ⌨ camping-moulin-mellet.com. Eight kilometres west of Agen in St Hilaire de Lusignanlies, this friendly campsite boasts two swimming pools, a restaurant, a small petting zoo and plenty of games and activities for kids. **€24.50**
★**Château de Cambes** Cambillou ☎ 05 53 95 38 73, ⌨ chateau-de-cambes.com. Set in five hectares of magnolia forests and gardens, with a swimming pool, sauna and orangery, this *chambre d'hôte* is a little pocket

of paradise, 6km east of of Agen. There are five luxurious rooms to choose from, each with a unique theme and dotted with antique furnishings. **€160**
Des Jacobins 1 place des Jacobins ☎ 05 53 47 03 31, ⌨ chateau-des-jacobins.com. A fancy hotel with lavishly decorated rooms full of antique furniture and historic knick-knacks. The elegant nineteenth-century townhouse and beautiful gardens are a treat, but don't expect the standard of service that you'd get at a hotel. Breakfast €10. **€130**
Le Provence 22 cours de 14 Juillet ☎ 05 53 47 39 11, ⌨ hotel-leprovence-agen.com. Smart, modern hotel with well-furnished, spacious rooms, friendly staff and a convenient location just a short walk from the centre. Breakfast €8. **€74**

EATING

The best place to look for somewhere to **eat** in Agen is within the rough semicircle between boulevard de la République, rue des Cornières and rue Emile Sentini, plus along rue La Fayette and its extension rue Camille Desmoulins running east from boulevard Carnot. **Ethnic restaurants** and **fast-food** outlets sit on rue Voltaire and rue Garonne further west, while there are a couple of decent **cafés** on boulevard de la République and at its western junction with avenue du Général-de-Gaulle.

Côte Sud 36 cours Gambetta ☎ 05 53 96 16 67. A modern take on a traditional family restaurant, stylishly decorated in subdued mauves, with comfortable seating

and down-lighting. Expect typical French cuisine with a few surprises along the way; *menus* from €22. Mon–Sat noon–1.30pm & 7.30–9pm, Sun 7.30–9pm.

Le Margoton 52 rue Richard-Cœur-de-Lion ☎ 05 53 48 11 55, ⓦ lemargoton.com. The emphasis is on quality cuisine and fresh local ingredients at this stylish restaurant. The salmon smoked in-house is delicious, while the unique mojito soufflé offers a flavoursome finish. *Menus* start at €17 for lunch and go up to €35 in the evening. Early Jan to mid-July & Aug to mid-Dec Tues–Fri noon–1.30pm & 7.45–9.45pm, Sat 7.45–9.45pm.

Mariottat 25 rue Louis Vivent ☎ 05 53 77 99 77, ⓦ restaurant-mariottat.com. With its romantic setting in a grand old villa, sumptuous dining room adorned with crystal chandeliers and fresh-cut flowers, and a Michelin-starred chef, there's no doubt that *Mariottat* is Agen's most elegant restaurant. The beautifully presented *menus* change seasonally, starting at a very reasonable €27 and rising to €87 for the highly recommended evening *dégustation menu*. Tues–Fri noon–1.15pm & 8–9.15pm, Sat 8–9.15pm, Sun noon–1.15pm.

★**Monsieur Jeannot** 18 rue des Cornières ☎ 05 40 40 12 24. Rustic French cuisine is the name of the game here, with dishes like *fricassée du lapin* (rabbit stew) or *moules* with red-pesto sauce, served on traditional wooden platters. Lunchtime *menus*, at just €15, are understandably popular with locals, while the €25 tasting *menu* is ideal for hungry gourmands. Tues–Sat noon–2pm & 7–9.30pm.

Osaka 38 bd Sylvain Dumon ☎ 05 53 66 31 76, ⓦ osaka-agen.fr. If you're craving a change from French food, *Osaka* is the place, serving top-notch Japanese cuisine. Indulge in delicious sushi, sashimi, teppanyaki and noodle soups, with *menus* from €15. Tues–Sat noon–2pm & 7–10pm.

La Part des Anges 14 rue Emile Sentini ☎ 05 53 68 31 00. This refined little restaurant is the place to go for well-prepared and presented local dishes, such as black Gascon pork, beef from Duras and cheeses aged on the premises. In summer they put a few tables outside on the pedestrianized street; *menus* from €20. Jan to mid-Feb, March–Aug & mid-Sept to mid-Dec Tues–Sat noon–1pm & 7–9.30pm.

Philippe Vannier 66 rue Camille Desmoulins ☎ 05 53 66 63 70, ⓦ philippe-vannier.com. A stylish restaurant with a cool, art-adorned dining room. The inventive menu includes langoustines marinated in lime, and a range of indulgent desserts such as chocolate mousse with orange and mango jam. There's also a range of home-made burgers (from €6.30) to eat in or take away, and a good-value lunchtime *formule* for €16.50, rising to €23 in the evenings. Note that reservations are essential on Sundays. Mon 7.45–9pm, Tues–Sat noon–1pm & 7.45–9pm, Sun noon–1pm.

Quarts Coffee Kitchen 63 rue Molinier ☎ 05 53 96 63 74. One of few places serving food and drinks non-stop throughout the day, Quarts Coffee Kitchen welcomes a steady stream of locals and it's easy to see why. There's good coffee (from €1.60), a range of smoothies (€5.50) and a selection of burgers, panini and cakes to tempt you. The free wi-fi for customers is handy, too. Mon–Sat 8.30am–7.30pm.

6

PRUNEAUX D'AGEN

Agen grew rich during the seventeenth century thanks to the trade of manufactured goods, such as cloth and leather, flowing through its river port, but the industrial revolution put paid to all that. Since then the town's prosperity has been based on agriculture – in particular, its famous **prunes**. Plums (*prunes* in French) were introduced to France by crusaders returning from Syria in the eleventh century. It is believed that Benedictine monks at Clairac, near the confluence of the Lot and Garonne, were the first to cultivate the fruit, a variety known as *prune d'Ente*, which thrives on sun, high humidity and chalky soils and is also excellent for drying thanks to its size and high sugar content. Though plums now grow throughout the region, the dried fruit (*pruneaux*) were originally exported via the port at Agen – and are thus known as **pruneaux d'Agen**.

Nowadays these prunes are one of the region's principal money-spinners and in late August the orchards are a hive of activity as the ripe fruit are shaken from the trees. They are dried slowly in hot-air ovens to retain the flavour – during which process they lose three-quarters of their weight. Even so, the biggest prunes weigh in at 20g.

You can learn more facts and figures about prune production in the specialist *confiseries* of Agen (see p.258) and also at an enjoyable farm-museum, **Au Pruneau Gourmand** (mid-March to mid-Oct daily 9am–noon & 2–7pm, Sun 3–7pm; mid-Oct to mid-Jan & Feb to mid-March Mon–Sat 9am–noon & 2–6.30pm, Sun 2–6.30pm; €4, under-12s free; ☎ 05 53 84 00 69, ⓦ musee-du-pruneau.com), in the village of Granges-sur-Lot, 10km northeast of Aiguillon (see p.243). In mid-September, the village of St-Aubin, near Monflanquin (see p.243) hosts a fair devoted to the prune, lasting several days; call Monflanquin tourist office (☎ 05 53 49 55 80) for information.

6

DRINKING

L'Endroit Bar 20–22 rue des Cornieres ☎ 05 53 48 18 22. An atmospheric cocktail bar that serves excellent mojitos (from €7) and a range of tasty tapas (from €8), with seating spilling out onto the street. Wed–Sat 6pm–2am.

La Karafe 32 rue Voltaire ☎ 05 53 96 32 39, ⊚ lakarafe .fr. Stylish wine bar stocked with over 150 wines to sample

(from €2.50), plus a range of *pintxos* (bite-sized tapas) from €3 to nibble on. Mon–Sat 6.30pm–2am.

Le Takeoff 26 rue Voltaire ☎ 06 70 88 64 48, ⊚ thetakeoffbar.com. Funky lounge bar with a space-age vibe and a great cocktail menu (€7–8) that features all the usual favourites. Mon–Thurs & Sun 6.30pm–2am, Fri & Sat 6.30pm–3.30am.

ENTERTAINMENT

Agen has a reputation for its thespian activities; there are several **theatre groups** that perform in the open air, both in Agen and nearby towns; ask at the tourist office (see p.256). There's also a **cinema** screening all the latest Hollywood movies alongside French-language films.

Théâtre du Jour 21 rue Paulin-Régnier ☎ 05 53 47 82 08, ⊚ theatredujour.com. Stages innovative works and doubles as a drama school.

Théâtre Municipal Place Dr-Esquirol ☎ 05 53 66 26 60, ⊚ agen.fr. Puts on a varied programme of theatre, dance,

concerts and opera by local, national and international artists.

Cap cinema d'Agen 9 rue de la Prune ☎ 05 53 47 06 95, ⊚ cap-cine.fr. A huge multiscreen cinema in the centre of town; tickets from €9.20.

MARKETS AND SHOPPING

Agen's main **shopping streets** are boulevard de la République and boulevard du Président-Carnot, while pedestrianized rue Molinier, south of the cathedral, has a few smarter boutiques. The thing to buy in Agen is prunes (see box, p.257); you'll find them in the markets and at a number of specialist shops, including those listed below.

Confiserie P. Boisson 171 bd du Président-Carnot ☎ 05 53 66 20 61. Opened in 1835 and still using traditional methods to produce chocolate prunes, truffle prunes, prunes in armagnac and stuffed prunes, among other delicacies. You can also ask to see a short explanatory film of the production processes in English. Mon–Sat 9am–noon & 2–7pm.

Dalla Vecchia Philippe 62 bd du Président-Carnot ☎ 05 53 66 28 82. A good *boucherie*, a few doors down from the bakery; if you're looking for barbecue fodder this

would be a good bet. Mon–Fri 7.30am–noon & 4–7pm, Sat 7.30am–noon.

Joel Manaud 37 rue Voltaire ☎ 05 53 66 67 63. The place to go for charcuterie; they also stock a wide range of tempting salads. Mon–Sat 9am–noon & 2–6pm.

Maison Mauferon Raynal 165 bd du Président-Carnot ☎ 05 53 66 37 65. For picnic supplies, try this lovely bakery at the junction of boulevard du Président-Carnot and cours Washington. Tues–Sat 7.30am–12.30pm & 3–7.30pm, Sun 8am–12.30pm.

DIRECTORY

Hospital Centre Hospitalier, rte de Villeneuve (☎ 05 53 69 70 71), located 1.5km northeast of central Agen on the N21 to Villeneuve-sur-Lot.

Police Commissariat de Police, 4 rue Palissy (☎ 05 53 68 17 00), situated to the south of the old quarter.

Post office 72 bd du Président-Carnot.

AGEN'S MARKETS AND FAIRS

A **fresh-produce market** takes place in the covered market on place Jean-Baptiste Durand (Tues–Sun 7am–1pm). There is also a large **farmers' market** held on Wednesday and Sunday mornings in the Halle du Pin, beside place du 14-Juillet, as well as a smaller one on Saturday mornings on the Esplanade du Gravier, and an **organic market**, also on Saturdays, on place des Laitiers, off boulevard de la République. The most interesting of several **agricultural fairs** are the *foire de la prune* (first or second Mon after Sept 15), devoted to plums and prunes, and the *foire aux oies et canards gras* (second Sun in Dec) for foie gras and all manner of products made from duck and goose. The fairs take place in varying locations around the town centre; contact the tourist office (see p.256) for further information.

Nérac

Thirty kilometres across high, rolling hills to the southwest of Agen, you come to the château town of **NÉRAC** on the banks of the River Baïse. It's hard to believe that this drowsy backwater, seat of the **d'Albret** family, once matched the Parisian court in its splendour and extravagance, or that the bitter rivalries between Protestant and Catholic were played out here. Nowadays, it's an attractive and prosperous little place, where you can happily spend a few hours wandering the riverbanks and what's left of the d'Albrets' **castle**.

The d'Albrets first came to Nérac around 1150 and over the next three centuries grew to become one of Aquitaine's most powerful dynasties – largely through a talent for marrying well. First they gained the Pyrenean kingdom of Navarre when John d'Albret married Catherine of Foix, and then in 1527, their son Henry II d'Albret wed **Marguerite d'Angoulême**, sister to King Francis I of France. Intelligent and cultured, Marguerite filled her Nérac court with scholars and proponents of the new Protestant faith, including Jean Chauvin (John Calvin), who stayed here briefly in 1534. Neither Henry nor Marguerite converted, but their determined and ambitious daughter, **Jeanne d'Albret**, did so in 1560, thus making Nérac an important Protestant stronghold. Jeanne's son, also Henry, for his part married the young and beautiful **Marguerite de Valois**, sister of the king of France and Catherine de Médici, in 1572 and so ushered in Nérac's golden era. Their court glittered with eminent writers, diplomats and nobles, poets and musicians, while Henry indulged in the innumerable amorous conquests that earned him the nickname *Le Vert Galant*; Queen Margot, as she was called, was no retiring violet either, and the marriage was eventually annulled in 1599, by which time Henry had become **Henry IV** of France and removed his court to Paris.

Château de Nérac

April–Sept daily 10am–6pm; Oct–March Tues–Thurs 10am–6pm, Sat & Sun 2–6pm • €4, under-12s free • ☏ 05 53 65 21 11

Throughout their glory days, the d'Albrets added to their **château** on the river's west bank, at the far end of the bridge coming into Nérac from Agen. By the sixteenth century they had made it into a comfortable palace, of which only the north wing with its Renaissance gallery still exists, the other three having been partially destroyed in 1621 and finished off during the Revolution. It now houses the **Musée Henri IV**, of which the most interesting displays relate to Henry, Queen Margot and their larger-than-life relatives.

Église St-Nicolas and around

North of the château stands the Neoclassical **Église St-Nicolas**, which was built in the mid-eighteenth century and contains some attractive nineteenth-century stained-glass windows, depicting scenes from the Old and New Testaments. From the terrace here you get good views of the triple-arched **Pont-Vieux** and the ancient roofs of the area known as **Petit-Nérac** on the opposite side of the river. It's worth wandering over the bridge and turning right along rue Séderie, where the wooden balconies of old tanneries overhang the river, to come out beside the **Pont-Neuf** by Nérac's former port, now a marina bustling with cruise boats in summer.

La Garenne

South from Nérac's port across the main road, avenue Georges Clemenceau, a shady woodland path, leads 1.5km along the riverbank. **La Garenne**, as the area here is known, was laid out as a royal pleasure park in the sixteenth century. The aviaries of exotic birds, the arbours and minstrels have long gone, but it's still a pleasant place to stroll or picnic. Not far from the entrance, look out for the **Fontaine de Fleurette**, marked by a statue of a prostrate and scantily clad young woman. According to legend, Fleurette was a gardener's daughter who had the misfortune to be seduced by *Le Vert Galant* and, when his attentions drifted elsewhere, drowned herself in the river. The inscription reads: "She gave him all her life. He gave her but one day."

6

Cap Cauderoue

April–May & Sept–Oct Sat, Sun & school holidays 1.30–6pm; June Sat & Sun 11am–6pm; July & Aug daily 10am–7pm • €8–17 depending on the course, activities €8–18 • ☎ 05 53 65 52 74, ⓦ cap-cauderoue.com

Cap Cauderoue, 5km west of Nérac, is a treetop adventure playground, where visitors make their way, via ropes and swings, around an obstacle course high above the ground. It's popular with older children and teens, and a little muscle is required. The site also offers **activities** such as mountain biking, horseback rides, ATV rides, canoeing and archery.

ARRIVAL AND INFORMATION   NÉRAC

By bus Buses from Agen (Mon–Sat 5–7; 40min) stop on the central place de la Libération, next to the château.
Tourist office Avenue Mondenard (Sept–June Tues–Sat 9am–noon & 2–6pm, July & Aug Mon–Sat 9am–1pm & 2–6pm, Sun 10am–1pm & 3–5pm; Oct–April Tues–Fri 9am–noon & 2–6pm, Sat 9am–noon & 2–5pm; ☎ 05 53

65 27 75, ⓦ albret-tourisme.com).
Boat rental Les Croisières du Prince Henry (☎ 05 53 65 66 66, ⓦ croisieresduprincehenry.com) offer cruises with French-language commentary on a traditional *gabare* (April–Oct; 1hr; €8.80).

ACCOMMODATION AND EATING

Chocolaterie Artisanale la Cigale 2 rue Calvin ☎ 05 53 65 15 73, ⓦ chocolaterie-la-cigale.fr. Just a couple of minutes' walk south of the *gare SNCF*, this *chocolaterie* is heaven for chocolate lovers, crammed with delicious hand-made goodies. Tues–Sat 9am–noon & 2–6pm.
L'Escadron Volant 7 rue Henri IV ☎ 05 53 97 19 04. Conveniently situated opposite the château entrance, this popular brasserie has a far-reaching menu of traditional French fare, salads and crêpes. *Menus* from €18. May–Aug Mon–Sat noon–2pm & 7–9.30pm; Sept–April Tues–Sat noon–2pm & 7–9.30pm.
★ **Hotel Henri IV** 4 place du Général Leclerc ☎ 05 53 65 00 63, ⓦ hotelhenriiv.fr. Easily Nérac's best hotel, the eleven rooms at *Henri IV* are the epitome of chic, with wood floors, modern bathrooms and tasteful decor. There's also a small pool, a bar, bikes for hire and a well-stocked breakfast buffet. Opt for a deluxe room if your budget allows – the standards are a little on the small side. Breakfast €8.50. **€59**

★ **Le Relais de la Hire** Francescas ☎ 05 53 65 41 59, ⓦ la-hire.com. Located 10km southeast of Nérac in the lovely village of Francescas, *Le Relais* is probably the best place to eat in the area. You can feast on such dishes as roast spiced turbot with caramelized onions, or *canette à l'orange* (roast duckling in an orange sauce) in an elegant eighteenth-century house or its flower-filled garden. *Menus* from €30. Tues–Sat noon–2pm & 7.30–10pm, Sun noon–2pm & 7.30–10pm; closed early Nov.
Le Vert Galant 11 rue Séderie ☎ 05 53 65 31 99. This canalside restaurant is the perfect spot for lunch, with a great selection of *tartines* (from €6.70); the house speciality is one with duck *confit*, pear and bacon. Also on the menu are over fifty flavours of ice cream, including some wacky options like pumpkin, or tomato and basil sorbet. April–June & Sept–Oct Mon & Wed–Sun noon–2pm & 7.30–9.30pm, Tues 7.30–9.30pm; July & Aug daily noon–2pm & 7.30–9.30pm.

Buzet-sur-Baïse

BUZET-SUR-BAÏSE lies roughly 30km west of Agen, in the shadow of the Château de Buzet (not open to the public), which stands high on the green hillside, now separated from its village by the *autoroute*. Buzet itself is rather dull, but as the vines on this south bank of the Garonne indicate, you're in wine country and you shouldn't miss the chance to visit the local **wine co-operative**.

Les Vignerons de Buzet

July & Aug Mon–Sat 9am–12.30pm & 2–7pm; Sept–June Mon–Sat 9am–noon & 2–6pm • Free • 1.5hr guided tour July & Aug daily 10am & 3pm; Sept–June by appointment only • €3 including wine tasting, or free with purchases • For English-language tours call ☎ 05 53 84 17 16 • ☎ 05 53 84 74 30, ⓦ vignerons-buzet.fr • The co-op is around 1.5km east of Buzet-sur-Baïse on the D642

Founded in 1953, **Les Vignerons de Buzet** is France's largest wine cooperative, with around three hundred growers producing an average of fourteen million bottles per year. The majority are strong red wines, which benefit from ageing – Grande Réserve, Baron d'Ardeuil and Château de Gueyze stand out among the many award-winning wines produced by the co-operative, which also offers free tastings. It's also well worth arranging for one of their exceptionally informative **guided tours** of the vinification plant and **chais**.

ACTIVITIES   BUZET-SUR-BAÏSE

Boat trips Aside from wine, the other reason to visit Buzet is to rent a boat for a trip along the Canal de Garonne, or the Baïse or Lot rivers. Aquitaine Navigation (☏ 05 53 84 72 50, ⊕ aquitaine-navigation.com), based at the *halte nautique* on the canal below Buzet village, has small pleasure boats for rent hourly (€40 for a four-person boat) and by the half-day or day, as well as houseboats for longer excursions (from €971 for a two- to three-person boat, but prices vary seasonally).

EATING

★ **Le Vigneron** 20 bd de la République ☏ 05 53 84 73 46. The nicest eating option in Buzet is on the broad main street and offers a four-course *menu du jour* for a mere €15. There's also a special Sunday lunch *menu* (€24) including an hors-d'oeuvre buffet and a trolley stacked with delectable home-made desserts. The house speciality is a confection of crêpes layered with *crème patissière*, coated in meringue and baked. Tues–Sat noon–2pm & 7.30–9.45pm, Sun noon–2pm.

Moissac and around

There is little of historical interest left in the modern town of **Moissac**, some 40km southeast of Agen, largely because of the terrible damage wreaked by the flood of 1930, when the Tarn, swollen by a sudden thaw in the Massif Central, burst its banks, destroying 617 houses and killing more than a hundred people. Masterpieces of Romanesque sculpture and the model for dozens of churches throughout the region, the cloister and porch of the Benedictine **Église Abbatiale St-Pierre** have made Moissac a household name in the history of art; more prosaically, the town also offers plenty of choice in terms of accommodation and eating.

The flat plains to the south and west of Moissac are less exciting, not least because of the looming presence of a nuclear power plant, but there are, nevertheless, a couple of places worth visiting along the banks of the Garonne: **St-Nicolas-de-la-Grave**, for its nature reserve and little museum devoted to the founder of Detroit, after whom Cadillac cars were named; and **Auvillar**, for its exquisite market square.

Moissac

MOISSAC sits with its back to the old river cliffs on the north bank of the Tarn just before its confluence with the Garonne. The town's compact centre is bordered to the south by the Canal de Garonne, to the east by boulevard Camille Delthil and to the west by boulevard Lakanal, at the south end of which Pont-Napoléon carries road traffic over the Tarn. Moissac's main east–west thoroughfare, named rue Gambetta in the west, rue Ste-Catherine and then rue Malaveille, brings you into the central market square, **place des Récollets**, home to the town's covered *halle*, where a fresh-produce **market** is held (Tues–Sat), spilling over into the square on the weekends.

Église Abbatiale St-Pierre

6 place Durand de Bredon • April–June & Oct daily 9am–noon & 2–6pm; July & Aug daily 9am–7pm; Sept daily 9am–6pm; Nov–March Mon–Fri 10am–noon & 2–5pm Sat & Sun 2–5pm • €6.50, guided visit €9 • Tickets are sold at the tourist office (see p.263) and cover entry to the Musée d'Arts et Traditions Populaires (see p.263)

From Moissac's central place des Récollets, rue de la République leads north towards the red-brick belfry of the **Église Abbatiale St-Pierre**. Legend has it that Clovis first founded a church here in 506, though it seems more probable that its origins belong to the seventh century, which saw the foundation of so many monasteries

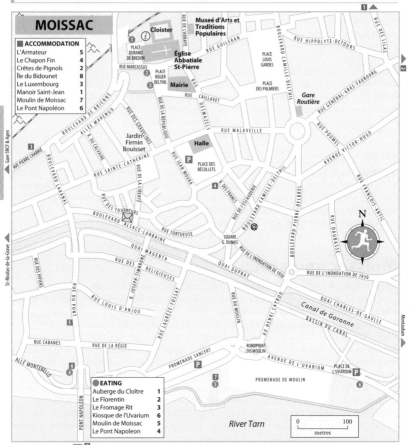

MOISSAC

■ **ACCOMMODATION**

L'Armateur	5
Le Chapon Fin	4
Crêtes de Pignols	2
Île du Bidounet	8
Le Luxembourg	3
Manoir Saint-Jean	1
Moulin de Moissac	7
Le Pont Napoléon	6

●**EATING**

Auberge du Cloître	1
Le Florentin	2
Le Fromage Rit	3
Kiosque de l'Uvarium	6
Moulin de Moissac	5
Le Pont Napoleon	4

River Tarn

0   100
metres

throughout Aquitaine. The first Romanesque church on the site was consecrated in 1063 and enlarged the following century when Moissac became a stop on the Santiago de Compostela pilgrim route. Since then the church has survived countless wars, including siege and sack by Simon de Montfort in 1212, during the crusade against the Cathars. Indeed, the fact that it is still standing at all is something of a miracle. During the Revolution the cloister was used as a gunpowder factory and billet for soldiers, who damaged many of the carvings, while in the 1850s it only escaped demolition to make way for the Bordeaux–Toulouse train line by a whisker.

The south porch

Apart from the dumpy, red-brick belfry, the first thing you see approaching the church from the town centre is the great stone arc of the **south porch**, with its magnificent **tympanum**, completed in 1130. It depicts Christ in Majesty, right hand raised in benediction, the Scriptures resting on his knee, surrounded by the Evangelists and the 24 elders of the Apocalypse – every one different – as described by St John in the Book of Revelation. Below, the central pillar bears the figures of St Paul and St Jeremiah, the latter with the most beautifully doleful face imaginable, in the same elongated style as at Souillac (see p.170).

The interior

There is fine carving on the capitals inside the porch, and the **interior** of the church, which was remodelled in the fifteenth century, is painted with intricate patterns and filled with interesting wood and stone **statuary**. The most outstanding are those in the second chapel on the right as you enter: a lovely stone *Pietà* in which Mary, enveloped in pastel blue, holds her son gently in her arms, and an equally compelling statue of Mary Magdalene with one arm outstretched and a thick tress of hair falling round her knees.

6

The cloister

The **cloister** is accessed through the tourist office, behind the church to the west, where you can see a ten-minute video (in English on request) describing its main features. The cloister surrounds a **garden** shaded by a majestic cedar, and its pantile roof is supported by 76 alternating single and double marble **columns**. Each column supports a single inverted wedge-shaped block of stone, on which are carved, with extraordinary delicacy, all manner of animals and plant motifs, as well as 46 scenes from the Bible and the lives of the saints, among them Daniel in the lions' den, the Evangelists, fishermen on Lake Galilee, St Peter being crucified upside down and the decapitation of John the Baptist. Despite the damage done during the Revolution, they are in amazingly good shape. An inscription on the middle pillar on the west side explains that the cloister was constructed in the time of the Abbot Ansquitil in the year of Our Lord 1100.

Musée d'Arts et Traditions Populaires

Rue de l'Abbaye • Daily: June & Sept–Oct 2–6pm; July & Aug 10am–1pm & 2–6pm • €3, or combined ticket with Église Abbatiale St-Pierre €6.50; tickets are sold at the tourist office (see below) • ☎ 05 63 04 03 08

Immediately northeast of Église Abbatiale St-Pierre, and rather less interesting, the **Musée Marguerite Vidal d'Arts et Traditions Populaires** is housed in the former abbots' palace. Apart from a good collection of local ceramics, including faïence from Auvillar (see p.265), it contains a hotchpotch of furniture, ecclesiastical robes and religious treasures, portraits of old Moissac residents and a mock-up of a Quercy farmhouse interior.

ARRIVAL AND INFORMATION   MOISSAC

By train Moissac's *gare SNCF* lies about 500m west of the centre along avenue Pierre Chabrié; from the station follow this road east and, where it curves northwards, you'll see steps leading down to the church square.

Destinations Agen (6–7 daily; 30min); Montauban (5–7 daily; 20min); Toulouse (4–7 daily; 45min).

By bus Run by Bus Gerla (☎ 05 63 04 55 50), the bus to Lauzerte (Wed & Sat 1–2 daily; 30min) stops outside the Tribunal but services are limited – you need to book in advance.

Tourist office At the western end of the Église Abbatiale

St-Pierre, 6 place Durand-de-Bredon (April–June & Oct Mon–Fri 9am–noon & 2–6pm, Sat & Sun 10am–noon & 2–6pm; July & Aug daily 9am–7pm; Sept daily 9am–6pm; Nov–March Mon–Fri 10am–noon & 2–5pm, Sat & Sun 2–5pm; ☎ 05 63 04 01 85, ⍵ moissac.fr). Staff have details of Moissac's festivals (see box, p.255) and of concerts taking place in the church and cloister in the summer months.

Bike rental Moissac-Loisirs, 29 rue Malaveille (☎ 05 63 04 03 48), on the north side of the market square; prices start at €13 per half-day.

ACCOMMODATION

★ **L'Armateur** 22 rue du Pont ☎ 05 63 32 85 10, ⍵ hotelarmateur.fr. An excellent choice, offering chic and spacious rooms with big comfy beds, plus friendly staff and a quiet location in an elegant eighteenth-century mansion just a short stroll from town. There's also a swimming pool, private parking and a fine restaurant, with *menus* from €17 for lunch, heading up to €45 for the evening *dégustation*.

Breakfast €12. Restaurant Tues–Fri 12.30–2pm & 7.30–9pm, Sat 7.30–9pm. **€110**

Le Chapon Fin 3 place des Récollets ☎ 05 63 04 04 22, ⍵ hotelchaponfin.fr. This clean and comfortable two-star hotel is now run by the Inter-Hotel chain. Rooms are simply furnished with no frills, but the staff are welcoming and the location, right on the market square, is unbeatable for

6

the price. Breakfast €9. **€64**

Crêtes de Pignols 1167 chemin de Lacapalette ☎ 05 63 04 04 04, ⓦ cretesdepignols.com. Twelve smart, well-appointed rooms are available at this friendly, family-run inn, some 4km northeast of Moissac off the D927. There's also a pool and a pleasant sun terrace, and a restaurant serving tasty regional cuisine, with evening *menus* from €21. Breakfast €8. Restaurant daily 7.30–9pm. **€54**

Île du Bidounet ☎ 05 63 32 52 52, ⓦ camping-moissac.com. A good-value, shady three-star campsite on a little island 2km from central Moissac across the Pont-Napoléon. Facilities include a pool, bar and children's play area. Closed Sept–April. **€17.50**

Le Luxembourg 2 av Pierre Chabrié ☎ 05 63 04 00 27, ⓦ luxembourg82.com. A nice, albeit old-fashioned hotel, close to the station, *Le Luxembourg* offers good value, and has a decent restaurant with dinner *menus* from €18. Breakfast €8. Private parking €6. Restaurant mid-Jan to mid-Dec Mon–Fri 7.30–8.45pm. **€56**

Manoir Saint Jean Saint-Paul d'Espis ☎ 05 63 05 02 34, ⓦ manoirsaintjean.com. A stunning country manor located 9km north of Moissac, *Saint Jean* offers beautiful

gardens, a pool and nine suites, all individually decorated with plush furnishings, paintings and chandeliers. There's also a first-rate restaurant serving delicious seasonal produce – organic wines, meat and wild-caught fish with fresh herbs from the garden (*menus* from €39). Breakfast €15. Restaurant June–Sept daily noon–1.15pm & 7.30–9.15pm; Oct–May Tues to Sat noon–1.15pm & 7.30–9.15pm, Sun noon–1.15pm. **€140**

★**Le Moulin de Moissac** Esplanade du Moulin ☎ 05 63 32 88 88, ⓦ lemoulindemoissac.com. Occupying a former watermill just east of the Pont-Napoléon, this is the sleekest hotel in town. It's a large, imposing building, but the inside has been beautifully refurbished and the rooms have very comfortable beds, pristine bathrooms and extras such as DVD players. It also boasts a spa, a terrace overlooking the river and a gorgeous restaurant (see below). Breakfast €14. **€105**

Le Pont Napoléon 2 allée Montebello ☎ 05 63 04 01 55, ⓦ le-pont-napoleon.com. A few very classy rooms above a fine restaurant (see below). The hotel overlooks a busy road beside the bridge, but inside it is a haven of tranquillity and the prices are extremely reasonable. Opt for a room with a view of the river. Breakfast €8. **€62**

EATING AND DRINKING

Auberge du Cloître Place Durand-de-Bredon ☎ 05 63 04 37 50. The magnolia-shaded terrace at *Auberge du Cloître* makes an idyllic spot to spend a sunny lunch hour and it's in a prime location right by the tourist office. The focus is on fresh local produce, much of it grown in the chef's own garden. *Menus* from €22. Mid-May to mid-Sept Tues–Sun 12.15–2pm & 7.30–9.30pm; mid-Sept to mid-May Tues & Thurs–Sat 12.15pm & 7.30–9.30pm, Wed & Sun 12.15–2pm.

★**Le Florentin** 6 place Roger Delthil ☎ 05 63 04 19 18, ⓦ leflorentin-bistrotgourmand.fr. An elegant but unpretentious restaurant that will appeal to adventurous foodies. Surprise your taste buds with specialities like foie gras "ice cream" or smoked salmon and grapefruit salad, accompanied by a carefully selected wine list. Most shocking are the low prices, with *menus* starting from €17. Daily noon–2pm & 7–10pm.

Le Fromage Rit 4 place Roger Delthil ☎ 09 67 47 28 42. Popular with local gourmands, this friendly little establishment serves delicious home-made cuisine made with fresh seasonal ingredients. Save some space for the truly indulgent chocolate mousse. *Menus* from €19. Wed–Sat noon–2pm & 7.30–9pm, Sun noon–2pm.

Kiosque de L'Uvarium Av de L'Uvarium ☎ 05 63 94 88 14. A casual place with a large terrace, serving grills, salads and pastas, with a *menu du jour* at €14. The adjoining outdoor entertainment space hosts a variety of events on summer evenings, such as theatre, Latin dance displays and even hip-hop gigs. May–Sept Mon & Wed–Sun noon–3pm & 6.30–10pm.

★**Le Moulin de Moissac** Esplanade du Moulin ☎ 05 63 32 88 88, ⓦ lemoulindemoissac.com. This sumptuous hotel restaurant is one of the best in the area, tempting the palate with dishes such as locally reared guinea-fowl simmered in ginger and teamed with a mushroom risotto. Lunch *menus* from €16.50 and evening *menus* from €36. Mon–Fri & Sun noon–1.45pm & 7.30–9.15pm, Sat 7.30–9.15pm.

Le Pont Napoléon 2 allée Montebello ☎ 05 63 04 01 55, ⓦ le-pont-napoleon.com. This excellent restaurant is attached to *Le Pont Napoléon* hotel (see above), and it's worth eating here at least once, just for a treat. Grab a seat on the riverside terrace and tuck into a hearty plate of roast lamb with artichoke, followed by mandarin soufflé. Evening *menus* from €35. Daily noon–2pm & 7.30–9.30pm.

St-Nicolas-de-la-Grave

Eight kilometres southwest of Moissac, the small *bastide* of **ST-NICOLAS-DE-LA-GRAVE** is dominated by a four-square château atop a low rise on the south bank of the Garonne. The château's oldest tower – the fattest of the four, on the northeast corner – is attributed to Richard the Lionheart, who passed through here on his return from the Third Crusade in the late 1100s. Nowadays, however, it houses the *mairie*, and there's nothing to see inside.

Musée Lamothe-Cadillac

Place du Château • July & Aug daily 10am–noon & 3–6pm; Sept–June ask at the tourist office (see below) • Free • ☎ 05 63 95 92 55

St-Nicolas is proud of its claim to fame as the home town of **Antoine Laumet**, founder of Detroit in America, who was born here in 1658. His birthplace, just southwest of the central square, now contains the **Musée Lamothe-Cadillac**, worth a quick look as much for the story of Laumet's life as for any of the exhibits, which comprise mock-ups of a period bedroom and kitchen, and masses of documentation, some of it in English. Laumet was an adventurer who, on leaving for Canada in 1683, adopted the upper-crust name of de Lamothe-Cadillac. He later turned up in America in the service of King Louis XIV, where he founded a number of forts, among them a cavalry outpost called *le détroit* between lakes Erie and Huron in 1701. Two hundred years later, a Detroit car company was looking for a name at the same time as the city was celebrating its anniversary. They decided to honour Detroit's founding father, and thus were Cadillacs born.

| ARRIVAL AND INFORMATION | ST-NICOLAS-DE-LA-GRAVE |

By car There's no public transport to St-Nicolas, so you'll need a car to get here.

Tourist office Place du Platane (July & Aug daily 9.30am–12.30pm & 2–6pm; Sept–June Mon 9.30am–12.30pm, Tues–Thurs 2–5pm, Fri 9.30am–12.30pm & 2–5pm; ☎ 05 63 94 82 81, ⓦ www.stnicolasdelag.online.fr). When the office is closed, the *mairie* on rue du Champs de l'Église will provide local information.

ACCOMMODATION

Camping Plan D'Eau ☎ 05 63 95 50 00. Decent two-star campsite 2km north of the village, where the Garonne and Tarn rivers form a large lake; the campsite is part of a leisure complex with snack bar and canoe and bike rental among other facilities, and you can also go birdwatching in the adjacent nature reserve. Closed mid-Dec to mid-June. **€15.50**

Chambres d'hôte au Château 1 bd des fossés de Raoul ☎ 05 63 95 96 82, ⓦ au-chateau-stn.com. A lovely *chambre d'hôte* in an old *maison de maître* surrounded by olive trees and flower-filled gardens. There are six beautifully decorated rooms and suites to choose from, plus a private swimming pool. **€70**

Auvillar

AUVILLAR, 14km west of St-Nicolas, is perched on a cliff on the Garonne's south bank. Its feudal château and ramparts were demolished in the eighteenth and nineteenth centuries, but thankfully the wonderful old village centre remains. From the main road skirting south of the village, you duck under the seventeenth-century **Tour de l'Horloge** to find yourself in the gently sloping triangular-shaped **place de la Halle** surrounded by a harmonious ensemble of brick and timber buildings with arcades running all around. At the square's cobbled centre stands a pleasing circular stone-pillared market hall, built in the early nineteenth century.

Musée du Vieil Auvillar

Place de la Halle • Mid-April to mid-Oct Mon & Wed–Sun 2.30–6.30pm; mid-Oct to mid-April Sat & Sun 2.30–5.30pm • €2.50 • ☎ 05 63 29 15 65

It's worth poking your nose into the **Musée du Vieil Auvillar**, on the place de la Halle's north side, for its collection of local pottery. Auvillar was already known for its pottery production in the sixteenth century, but in the following century they began making faïence of sufficiently high quality to rival that imported from Holland and Italy. Local potters still have a good reputation, as witnessed by the big pottery fair held every October (see box, p.255).

ARRIVAL AND INFORMATION   AUVILLAR

By car There's no public transport to Auvillar, so you'll need your own vehicle.

Tourist office Place de la Halle (April & May daily

10am–12.30pm & 2–5.30pm; June to mid-Oct till 7pm; mid-Oct to March Tues–Sun 2–5.30pm; ☎ 05 63 39 89 82, ⓦ auvillar.com).

ACCOMMODATION AND EATING

De l'Horloge 2 place de l'Horloge ☎ 05 63 39 91 61, ⓦ hoteldelhorlogeauvillar.com. A convenient spot to sleep or eat in Auvillar, *De l'Horloge* is located right beside the gate tower. Rooms are spacious but simple and sparsely furnished, but the hotel restaurant offers a shady terrace

looking out over the main street, with *menus* from €15 at lunch and €25 in the evening. Buffet breakfast €11. Restaurant mid-Jan to mid-Dec Sat 8–9.30pm, Sun–Thurs noon–1.45pm & 8–9.30pm; hotel closed mid-Oct to mid-April. **€62**

Quercy Blanc

North of Moissac, the land gradually rises to gently undulating, green and woody country, cut through by parallel valleys running down to meet the Garonne and planted with vines, sunflowers and maize, as well as apple and cherry orchards. It's a very soft landscape, the villages are small and widely scattered, and the pace of life seems about equal with that of a turning sunflower. This is the **Quercy Blanc**, named after the area's grey-white soils and building stone, a region with few sights, but one which lives up to the image of deepest rural France. The single most interesting place to head for is **Lauzerte**, atop a river bluff 25km north of Moissac. Further north again, **Montcuq** distinguishes itself with its solid square keep, the remnants of a twelfth-century fortress, standing guard over the medieval village, while way over to the southeast, **Montpezat-de-Quercy** is home to a Gothic church with a surprising collection of art treasures, including a beautiful and complete set of Flemish tapestries. Further east still, **Lalbenque** is the truffle centre of the south and a name that reverberates around the high temples of gastronomy.

GETTING AROUND   QUERCY BLANC

Public transport Options are very limited in the Quercy Blanc: there's no train line, and though there are bus services between Lauzerte from Moissac, and Montcuq and Lalbenque from Cahors, you have to book in advance for

them all, as they run by reservation only.
By car Given the paucity of public transport in the Quercy Blanc, you'll really need your own vehicle to get around.

Lauzerte

The sleepy hilltop village of **LAUZERTE** stands on a promontory between two rivers, a press of white-walled houses contained within its medieval ramparts, with the "new" town spilling down the south and eastern slopes. The site's strategic importance was not lost on the counts of Toulouse, who took control of Lauzerte in the late twelfth century and granted it the status of a *bastide* in 1241, with all the rights and privileges that entailed. The other notable event in Lauzerte's history took place fifty years later, when the townspeople threw out the English occupiers. By way of reward the French king, Philip IV, elevated Lauzerte to capital of the Bas Quercy (Lower Quercy) region and seat of the royal seneschal (the king's representative). However, its heyday came to an end in the late sixteenth century when Lauzerte was demoted to a mere district capital in the aftermath of the Wars of Religion.

Nevertheless, a few vestiges of these glory days remain in the old town, which lies clustered around the pretty, arcaded central square, **place des Cornières**, where Lauzerte's **market** is held each Wednesday and Saturday, and the **Église St-Barthélémy**. The church's origins go back to the thirteenth century, but it was largely rebuilt after the Protestants wreaked their havoc, and its main point of interest nowadays is the

gilded Baroque altarpiece, dedicated to the Virgin Mary and depicting scenes from her life, which fills the north chapel. Behind the church, there are good views of the patchwork landscape all around from the **place du Château**, where the castle once stood on the promontory's northern tip. From here **rue de la Garrigue**, and its extension **rue de la Gendarmerie**, double back south of the church, running along the ridge past a number of thirteenth- and fourteenth-century merchants' houses with their big ground-floor arches and colonnaded windows above.

6

ARRIVAL AND INFORMATION   LAUZERTE

By bus There is a bus service run by Bus Gerla (☎ 05 63 04 55 50) to Lauzerte from Moissac, but it only operates on Wednesdays and Saturdays, returning to Moissac at 2pm; a reservation is necessary. Buses leave from outside the Crédit Agricole bank.

By car There is car parking in the lower section of the town, from where you can walk up to the medieval town via a series of steps, or you can drive to the top and park just outside the ramparts, where there is a large car park.

Tourist office Place des Cornières (July & Aug daily 9am–7pm; Sept–June Mon–Sat 9am–noon & 2–6pm; ☎ 05 63 94 61 94, ⌨ lauzerte-tourisme.fr).

ACCOMMODATION AND EATING

Aube Nouvelle Durfort-Lacapelette ☎ 05 63 04 50 33, ⌨ aubenouvelle.com. Located 9km south of Lauzerte on the D2, this Belgian-run hotel is set in a lovely manor house with beautiful gardens. There's also a good restaurant serving delicacies like rabbit in brown ale and *cassoulet d'escargots*, with evening *menus* from €24. Breakfast €8. Restaurant mid-Jan to mid-Dec Sat 7.30–9pm, Sun–Fri noon–1.30pm & 7.30–9pm. **€71**

★**Le Belvédère** Montagudet ☎ 05 63 95 51 10, ⌨ lebelvedere.biz. For a touch of luxury, head to *Le Belvédère*, where highlights include a spa and an infinity pool looking out over the valley towards Lauzerte. Rooms are sunny and spacious, with huge comfy beds and private balconies, while the excellent restaurant offers "slow food" cuisine and an impressive wine list. *Menus* from €32. Breakfast €15. Restaurant daily noon–2pm & 7.15–10pm. **€100**

Le Quercy Faubourg d'Auriac ☎ 05 63 94 66 36, ⌨ hotel -du-quercy.fr. *Le Quercy* offers a handful of old-fashioned but perfectly comfortable rooms, but the real draw is the restaurant. In addition to traditional local dishes, such as *cassoulet*, farm-raised chicken cooked in Cahors wine and *confit de canard* – the latter stuffed with foie gras – they serve a good range of fish and seafood dishes, and game in season; *menus* start at €20. Reserve a table in advance. Breakfast €7. Restaurant Tues–Sat 12.15–2pm & 7.30–9pm, Sun 12.15–1.30pm; hotel closed Nov–March. **€96**

La Table des Trois Chevaliers Place des Cornières ☎ 05 63 95 32 69 ⌨ latabledes3chevaliers.fr. Situated in the beautiful central square, this is a popular spot for relaxed weekend dining, serving dishes like goat's cheese lasagne and gourmet fish and chips. *Menus* from €22.50; reservations advised. Fri 7–9pm, Sat & Sun noon–2pm & 7–9pm.

Musée Yvan Quercy

Opening times vary, so phone to check • €5 • ☎ 05 63 95 84 02 • The museum is 8km southeast of Lauzerte, at the end of a long lane signed off the D16 Molières road 2km east of Cazes-Mondenard

Just outside the village of **Cazes-Mondenard**, with its pretty Gothic church, the quirky **Musée Yvan Quercy** is centred on its collection of **hearses**, which was kick-started in 1970 when Monsieur Quercy was given an old hearse. Once he'd acquired a second one, word spread, and nearby parishes rushed to offer him theirs. By the time of his death, he had amassed nearly a hundred different models, some horse-drawn, others pulled by hand, from the seventeenth century up to the first motorized model manufactured by Peugeot in 1949. His family now continue his work. The collection also includes a large number of regular carriages, all in excellent condition, and some early farm machinery. After the tour, you are offered tastings of wine, pâtés and other local produce, and in season they also serve regional meals if you book in advance.

Montcuq

Thirteen kilometres northeast of Lauzerte along the Petite-Barguelonne valley, **MONTCUQ** – pronounce the "q" if you don't want to be saying "my arse" – is built around the flanks of a conical hill, on top of which stands a huge square keep.

MONTCUQ MONOPOLY

In 2007, Hasbro, makers of **Monopoly**, opened an internet voting site to decide which towns would feature on a new French version of the game. As a joke, web users started a campaign to feature Montcuq, reasoning that most foreigners would rudely mispronounce the name. It took off, and Montcuq won – but Hasbro decided to overrule the popular vote and use Dunkerque instead. The outcry was, predictably, huge. To make up for the lack of democratic compliance, Hasbro agreed to issue a special Montcuq version of Monopoly. The town was allowed to choose which streets would be used, and a local artist provided images. Look out for this unusual souvenir in shops around town.

6

Like Lauzerte, Montcuq guarded the ancient road to Cahors and lies on the Santiago de Compostela pilgrim route, but it seems to have had the knack of picking the wrong cause: it sided with the Cathars, was condemned for collaborating with the English and later became a Protestant stronghold. As a result, there's not much in the way of sights, though it's an attractive little place and has a very good Sunday morning **market** on place de la République.

Torre de Montcuq

July & Aug 10am–12.30pm & 3.30–7pm · €3, under-6s fre · ☎ 05 65 31 80 05

To get the lie of the land in Montcuq, the best thing to do is climb up the **Torre de Montcuq**. Any of the lanes leading uphill from rue de la Promenade, the wide boulevard to the south of the old town, will take you there. It was built at the turn of the eleventh century as part of a larger fortress, and although Louis IX ordered the ramparts destroyed, the ditches filled in and the tower's top knocked off in the aftermath of the Cathar crusades, at 24m, it's still a fair climb. The effort is rewarded with all-round views – and even when the tower is closed, the pinnacle of rock it stands on is high enough to give a good panorama, looking down over the maze of stone and half-timbered houses, and the **Église St-Hilaire**.

ARRIVAL AND INFORMATION

MONTCUQ

By bus Raynal Voyages (☎ 05 65 23 28 28) run buses to Cahors, though you need to book in advance. They stop on rue de la Promenade near the tourist office.

Tourist office 8 rue de la Promenade (April–June &

Sept–Oct Mon–Sat 9am–12.30pm & 3–6pm, Sun 10am–12.30pm; July & Aug Mon–Sat 9am–12.30pm & 3–6pm, Sun 10.30am–1pm; Nov–March Tues–Sat 9am–noon; ☎ 05 65 22 94 04, ⓦ tourisme-quercy-blanc.com).

ACCOMMODATION

Du Parc ☎ 05 65 31 81 82, ⓦ auberge-du-parc.com. A comfortable, albeit somewhat old-fashioned hotel with a large garden and a guests-only restaurant (*menus* from

€18), located on the Belmont road, 500m west of Montcuq. Breakfast €8.90. **€65**

Castelnau-Montratier

The D4 southeast of Montcuq takes you on a roller-coaster ride across the valleys and intervening hills, on one of which stands **CASTELNAU-MONTRATIER**, 20km from Montcuq, with its incongruous neo-Byzantine church and spacious market square.

Lalbenque

If you happen to be in the Quercy Blanc on a Tuesday between December and March, head to the village of **LALBENQUE**, some 22km east along the D19 from Castelnau-Montratier. Its eleventh-century **Église Saint-Quirin** deserves more than a passing glance for its gilded wooden altarpiece, said to have been purchased in the late eighteenth century by a local carter from revolutionaries in Cahors for the paltry sum of 50 francs.

6

Knowing he'd purchased a looted sacred treasure at a bargain price, he began to suffer twinges of conscience and confessed to his local priest, who immediately absolved the penitent and claimed the prize for his church, where it's been ever since.

At any other time of year, once you've inspected the church, that's just about it – Lalbenque is a sleepy little white-stone town, barely distinguishable from all the others in the Quercy Blanc. However, pull in at around 2pm on a Tuesday afternoon between December and March, and you'll witness a market like no other, the **Marché aux Truffes**, when trestle tables laden with **black truffles** line the main street, and a long rope stretches the length of them, holding back a seething mass of buyers, locals and tourists. At 2.30pm sharp, a bell rings and the rope is hauled away as buyers from all over France surge forward to begin negotiations. A price per kilo is announced for the day, but that's just a guide, with some pretty sharp bargaining being necessary before all parties are satisfied. Truffles are rare and capricious, resisting every effort at widespread cultivation – the majority are still found in the wild. It's therefore the intrepid hunters who have the advantage; and before long only a few small specimens remain for the tourists to savour in a sumptuous truffle omelette that night.

ARRIVAL AND INFORMATION

LALBENQUE

By bus Raynal Voyages (☎ 05 65 23 28 28) run buses to Cahors, though you need to book in advance. They stop on place de la Bascule, just north of the tourist office, and Ateliers municipaux.

Tourist office Place de la Bascule (May & June Tues–Sat 9am–12.30pm & 2–5.30pm, Sun 9.30am–12.30pm; July & Aug Mon–Sat 9am–12.30pm & 2–6pm, Sun 9.30am–12.30pm; Sept–April Tues, Thurs & Fri 9am–12.30pm & 2–5.30pm, Wed 2–5.30pm, Sat & Sun 9am–12.30pm; ☎ 05 65 31 50 08, ⊕ lalbenque.net).

ACCOMMODATION AND EATING

Lion d'Or 104 rue du Marché aux Truffes ☎ 05 65 31 60 19, ⊕ le-lion-d-or-lalbenque.com. A modest little café-restaurant that serves delicious *moules*, pizzas and burgers. Head there on Tuesdays during the Marché aux Truffes for the special truffle *menus* (from €45). Mon & Wed noon–2pm, Tues & Thurs–Sun noon–2pm & 7.30–9pm.

Le Logis de Reyjade Place de République, Montdumerc ☎ 05 65 22 89 56, ⊕ lelogisdereyjade.com. A few kilometres southwest of Lalbenque just off the D10, this *chambre d'hôte* is dotted with beautiful eighteenth-century antiques and boasts a pretty garden, but the decor leans on the side of old-fashioned rather than timeless. *Table d'hôte* €29 (reservation only). **€98**

Montpezat-de-Quercy

Ten kilometres southwest of Lalbenque through twisty country lanes lies the interesting hilltop village of **MONTPEZAT-DE-QUERCY**. Traces of its medieval heyday remain in the arcaded central square and lanes of half-timbered houses, but the main reason to stop here is the **Collégiale St-Martin**, with its unusually rich hoard of treasures, standing at the southeast end of the promontory on which the village is built.

Collégiale St-Martin

No set hours • Free

The **Collégiale St-Martin** was founded in the early fourteenth century by Cardinal Pierre des Prés (1281–1361), a local who grew wealthy in the service of the Avignon popes. With its high and severe single nave, the interior of the church is unexciting, at least in comparison with the fourteenth- to sixteenth-century **artworks** arrayed in the side chapels. Best are the battered but still lovely *Vierge aux Colombes*, her face framed by golden ringlets, in the second chapel on the left; a polychrome *Pietà* in the first on the right; and, next door, an English alabaster triptych depicting the Birth, Resurrection and Ascension of Christ – in the last only his feet are visible as he's whisked heavenwards. The Collégiale St-Martin's finest treasures, though, are the five Flemish **tapestries** grouped around the choir. They were made especially for the church in the early sixteenth century, a gift from Jean IV des Prés, bishop of Montauban, and portray events from the life of

St Martin de Tours, to whom the church is consecrated. The most famous scene is that in the first panel, where the future saint – at the time in the service of the Roman army – shares his cloak with a crippled beggar. The workmanship throughout is of superb quality, while the colours remain amazingly vibrant. Also in remarkably good condition is the white-marble sarcophagus and statue of Pierre des Prés, to the right of the choir, with his feet resting on a lion while his well-fed face is bathed in a contented grin.

ARRIVL ND INFORMATION MONTPEZAT-DE-QUERCY

By car There's no public transport to Montpezat, so you'll need your own vehicle. The best place to park is on place de la Résistance, but there is also ample street parking outside the tourist office (see below).

Tourist office Bd des Fossés (April & Oct Tues–Fri 10am–12.30pm & 2–5.30pm; May Tues–Fri 10am–1pm & 2–7pm; June & Sept Tues–Thurs & Sun 10am–1pm &

2–7pm; July & Aug Mon 2–6pm, Tues–Sun 10am–1pm & 2–7pm; Nov–March Tues, Thurs & Sun 11am–5pm; ☏05 63 02 05 55, ⊛ tourisme-montpezat-de-quercy .com). The office doubles as a Maison des Vins where you can buy the local Côteaux du Quercy wines and pick up a brochure listing vineyards to visit, though they don't offer tastings.

ACCOMMODATION AND EATING

Camping Révéa le Faillal ☏05 63 02 07 08, ⊛ revea-vacances.fr. A well-tended two-star municipal campsite in a leisure park on Montpezat's northern outskirts. Facilities include a pool, tennis, mini-golf, and basketball and volleyball courts. Closed Sept–April. **€21.30**

Ferme-Auberge de Coutié ☏05 63 67 73 51. You'll eat very well at this atmospheric *ferme-auberge* on a Quercy farm surrounded by ducks and orchards; it's on the D20, 9km southwest of Montpezat and signed to the east of Espanel hamlet. *Menus* €22–35, including wine. Reservations essential. Daily 12.30–1pm & 7–8pm.

Montauban

Lying 20km east of Moissac and 50km north of Toulouse, **MONTAUBAN** is a prosperous, middle-sized provincial city and the capital of the largely agricultural *département* of Tarn-et-Garonne. The most interesting area is the small kernel of streets based on the original *bastide*, a harmonious ensemble of warm, pink brick which looks its best at sunset, or at night when the steeples, massive old bridge and riverside facades are illuminated.

Enclosed within an inner ring of boulevards between **allée de l'Empereur** to the east and the river to the west, the old centre follows the typical *bastide* pattern, with a grid of streets around an arcaded market square, the glorious **place Nationale**, where a daily fresh food market takes place. Between the main shopping streets of pedestrianized **rue de la Résistance** and **rue de la République**, which intersect in the *bastide*'s southern corner, lie a labyrinth of enticing alleys, covered passages and interior courtyards. The greatest delight is simply to wander – the centre is only a ten-minute stroll from end to end – taking in the scattered sights as you go, of which the highlight is the **Musée Ingres**, dedicated to Montauban's most famous son.

Just south of the cathedral, allées Consul Dupuy hosts a busy farmers' **market** on Saturday mornings, while on Wednesday mornings, another market is held in place Lalaque, across the river.

Brief history

Montauban's origins go back to 1144 when Alphonse Jourdain, count of Toulouse, decided to create a **bastide** here as a bulwark against English and French royal power. Indeed, it is generally regarded as the first *bastide*, the model for the medieval new towns found throughout this region (see box, p.244). The city has enjoyed various periods of great prosperity (as one can guess from the proliferation of fine houses), mainly based on trade in silk and other textiles. The first followed the suppression of the Cathar heresy and the final submission of the counts of Toulouse in 1229 and was greatly enhanced by the building of the **Pont-Vieux** in 1335, making it the best crossing

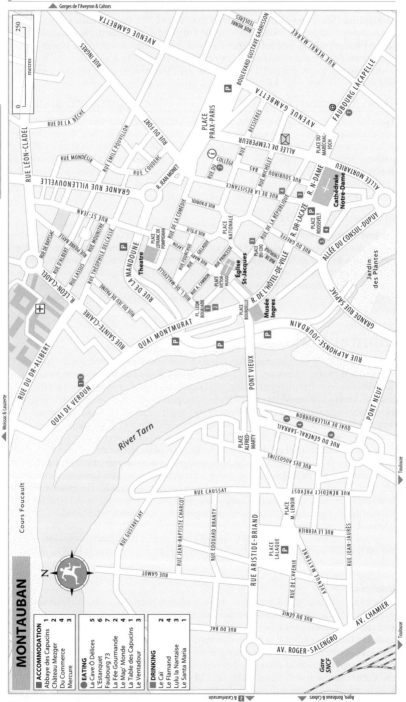

Gorges de l'Aveyron & Cahors

MONTAUBAN

ACCOMMODATION
Abbaye des Capucins	1
Château Mezger	2
Du Commerce	4
Mercure	3

● EATING
La Cave Ô Delices	5
L'Estanquet	6
Faubourg 73	7
La Fée Gourmande	2
Le Map' Monde	4
La Table des Capucins	1
Le Ventadour	3

DRINKING
Le Cai	2
Le Flamand	4
Lulu la Nantaise	3
Le Santa Maria	1

point on the Tarn for miles. The Hundred Years War did its share of damage, as did Montauban's opting for the Protestant cause in the Wars of Religion, but by the time of the Revolution it had become once more one of the richest cities in the southwest.

Place Nationale

The grand **place Nationale** is the epicentre of modern Montauban and the city's main social hub. Rebuilt after a fire in the seventeenth century, it is surrounded on all sides by a double row of arcades beneath two- and three-storeyed townhouses, their uniformity tempered by the square's irregular shape.

6

Église St-Jacques

62 rue de la République • ☎ 04 63 66 42 78

The distinctive octagonal belfry of the **Église St-Jacques**, a couple of minutes' walk west of place Nationale, shows above the southwestern rooftops. First built in the thirteenth century on the pilgrim route to Santiago de Compostela, the church bears the scars of Montauban's troubled history, not only in its mix of architectural styles, but in the holes gouged out of the belfry's fortified base by cannonballs during an unsuccessful siege by twenty thousand Catholic troops – held off by just six thousand locals – in 1621.

Musée Ingres

19 rue de l'Hôtel-de-Ville • July & Aug daily 10am–6pm; Sept & Oct daily 10am–noon & 2–6pm; Nov–June Tues–Sun 10am–noon & 2–6pm • €7 • ☎ 05 63 22 12 91

Overlooking the river south of the Église St-Jacques stands a massive half-palace, half-fortress, begun by the counts of Toulouse, then continued by the Black Prince in 1363. He left it unfinished when the English lost control of the town, and so it remained until 1664 when the bishop of Montauban chose this very prominent spot for his residence. Now the **Musée Ingres**, it houses paintings and more than four thousand drawings left to the city by locally born **Jean-Auguste-Dominique Ingres** (1780–1867). The collection includes several of the supremely realistic, luminous portraits of women which are the artist's trademark. It also contains a substantial collection of works by another native, **Émile-Antoine Bourdelle** (1861–1929), the ubiquitous monumental sculptor and student of Rodin, alongside a hotchpotch of other exhibits, from Gallo-Roman mosaics to fifteenth- and sixteenth-century European fine art. In the early days of World War II, the museum hosted more illustrious visitors when the Louvre dispatched over three thousand works of art to Montauban for safe-keeping prior to the German invasion. When southern France was occupied in 1942, however, they were moved again to more remote locations, including the Château de Montal (see p.193).

Cathédrale Notre-Dame

Rue Notre-Dame • Daily 8am–noon & 3–7pm • €7 • ☎ 05 63 63 10 23

Providing a stark exception to Montauban's red-brick homogeneity is the **Cathédrale Notre-Dame**, a cold, sore-thumb of a building some ten minutes' walk southeast of the Musée Ingres along rue de l'Hôtel-de-Ville. It was erected on the city's highest spot at the end of the seventeenth century as part of the triumphalist campaign to reassert the Catholic faith, following the defeat and harsh repression of the Protestants. Inside the dazzling white Classical facade lies an echoing nave, whose main point of interest is another Ingres painting, *Le Voeu de Louis XIII*, hanging in the north aisle. Specially commissioned for the cathedral, the vast canvas depicts Louis offering France, symbolized by his crown and sword, to a Virgin and Child, and is strongly influenced by Raphael's romantic style.

6

ARRIVAL AND DEPARTURE

MONTAUBAN

By plane The nearest airport is Toulouse-Blagnac (☎ 08 25 38 00 00, ✆ toulouse.aeroport.fr), 40km south of Montauban, straight down the A62 *autoroute*.

By train Montauban's *gare SNCF* lies roughly 1km west of the centre across the Pont-Vieux at the far end of avenue Mayenne. A city bus runs from the train station to the centre (line A), stopping on allée de l'Empereur near place Prax-Paris, on the northeast side of town; tickets can be bought on the bus.

Destinations Agen (up to 20 daily; 35–50min); Brive (2–8 daily; 1hr 50min); Cahors (up to 17 daily; 40min–1hr 20min); Moissac (up to 11 daily 20–30min); Toulouse (every 30min; 25min).

By bus While there are buses from Montauban to Bruniquel, Laguépie, Montricoux and St-Antonin-Noble-Val, these are primarily aimed at schoolchildren to coincide with pickups and dropoffs during term time; as such they're not much use for visitors.

By car The most convenient car park is the underground pay parking on place Prax-Paris or place Roosevelt. Free parking is available along the riverbanks beneath the Pont-Vieux and north of the theatre on rue de la Mandoune.

GETTING AROUND AND INFORMATION

Car rental Near the train station, try Avis, 23 av Mayenne (☎ 05 63 20 45 73); or Europcar, 382 av de Toulouse (☎ 05 63 20 29 00).

Taxis There are taxi stands at the station and the north end of allée de l'Empereur, or contact Taxis Montalbanais (☎ 05 63 66 99 99, ✆ taxis-montauban.com).

Tourist office Rue du Collège (July & Aug Mon–Sat 9am–6.30pm, Sun 10am–12.30pm; Sept–June Mon–Sat 9.30am–12.30pm & 2–6.30pm; ☎ 05 63 63 60 60, ✆ montauban-tourisme.com).

ACCOMMODATION

★ **Abbaye des Capucins** 6–8 quai de Verdun ☎ 05 63 22 00 00, ✆ abbayedescapucins.fr. A large and beautifully renovated hotel in a seventeenth-century monastery with a Michelin-starred restaurant attached, this is the last word in urban luxury. Rooms are spacious and well appointed, and there is a spa, a pool and bike rental (€4). It also owns two excellent restaurants, *La Table des Capucins* (see opposite) and the less formal *Bistro des Capucins*, which serves *menus* from €21. Breakfast €17. Bistro daily 12.30–2.45pm & 7.45–10.45pm. **€120**

★ **Château Mezger** 105 chemin du Bois Vieux de Bernoye, Pignes ☎ 06 77 92 56 96, ✆ chateaumezger.fr. An exquisite *chambre d'hôte* in a lovely county manor house just a 10min drive from Montauban. The three huge rooms each have wooden floors, chandeliers and Egyptian cotton sheets, with views over the ample gardens. There's also a spring-fed swimming pool, a home-made breakfast included and a four-course dinner *menu* available for €36 (advance bookings essential). **€99**

Du Commerce 9 place Roosevelt ☎ 05 63 66 31 32, ✆ hotel-commerce-montauban.com. Charming pops of colour and thoughtful furnishings make good use of the space at this central hotel, making it the best deal for those wanting to be in the thick of it. Breakfast €9. Parking €10–13. Closed mid-Dec to mid-Jan. **€63**

Mercure 12 rue Notre-Dame ☎ 05 63 63 17 23, ✆ mercure.com. Part of the nationwide *Mercure* chain of hotels, this is nevertheless a very good option as it's housed in an attractive eighteenth-century building right in the town centre. It boasts modern, reasonably spacious rooms and a good restaurant (*menus* from €15). Breakfast €14. Restaurant daily noon–2.30pm & 7.30–10pm. **€112**

EATING

Montauban has a surprisingly varied selection of **restaurants**, with options for all budgets. Keep an eye open for the local speciality, **montauriols**, a chocolate-coated cherry preserved in armagnac; you'll find them at pâtisseries all over town.

★ **La Cave Ô Délices** 10 place Roosevelt ☎ 05 63 63 69 69, ✆ cave-o-delices.fr. A local favourite housed in an atmospheric stone cellar and offering lunchtime *formules* at €15 and evening *menus* from €25. Opt for the fish, followed by the divine basil and forest fruits sorbet. Tues–Sat noon–2pm & 7.30–10pm.

L'Estanquet 16 rue General Sarrail ☎ 05 63 66 12 74, ✆ restaurantlestanquet.com. Mismatched furniture and quirky decor set the scene at this hip restaurant on the west bank of the Tarn. Expect well-presented dishes, including casseroles and grills, plus some truly decadent desserts. Mains €13–20. Tues–Sat noon–

2pm & 7.30–10pm.

Faubourg 73 73 Faubourg Lacapelle ☎ 05 63 93 55 54, ✆ faubourg73.fr. Popular place offering tasty, good-value traditional meals and some more modern alternatives, plus a well-rounded wine list. Lunch *menu* €12.50, while in the evenings it's à la carte. Mon–Wed noon–2pm, Thurs–Sat noon–2pm & 7.30–10pm.

★ **La Fée Gourmande** 13 rue du Collége ☎ 05 63 63 89 01, ✆ lafeegourmande.com. With its cutesy decor, home-made delights and beaming proprietress, it's hard not to be swept up in the good vibes at *La Fée Gourmande*. The food is equally enchanting – head here for a healthy lunch of apricot chicken or marinated prawns (mains from €7), or indulge in delicate *macarons*, freshly baked pastries or colourful cupcakes. Tues–Sat noon–3pm.

Le Map' Monde 26 rue du General Sarrail ☎ 05 63 63 72 44. Waving the flag for Brittany, this authentic crêperie is one of the best, with a huge range of sweet crêpes and savoury *galettes*. Try the Vietnamienne, stuffed with caramelized shrimp, sesame and lime, or the Canadienne, oozing with maple syrup and pecans. Mon & Sun 11.30am–2.30pm, Thurs–Sat 11.30am–2.30pm & 7–10.30pm.

La Table des Capucins 6–8 quai de Verdun ☎ 05 63 22 00 00, ⓦ abbayedescapucins.fr. The renowned restaurant attached to *Abbaye des Capucins* (see opposite) is worth a detour even for non-guests. Sample quintessential French specialties like pan-fried frogs' legs or tuck into delicious truffle risotto. *Menus* €21–39. Daily 12.30–2.45pm & 8–10.45pm.

Le Ventadour 23 quai Villebourbon ☎ 05 63 63 34 58, ⓦ le-ventadour.com. Magnificently sited in an old house on the west bank near the Pont-Vieux, this upmarket restaurant serves up dishes like oven-baked sea bream, salmon carpaccio and apricot panna cotta. *Menus* from €15.90. Mon–Fri noon–2pm.

DRINKING AND NIGHTLIFE

Le Caï 8 quai Montmurat ☎ 05 63 91 99 09. With its huge red sign right on the waterfront, it's impossible to miss this hip nightclub, usually teeming with revellers. It's also linked by an underground passageway from nearby sister bar *Le Santa Maria*. Thurs & Fri 7pm–3am, Sat 7pm–5.30am.

Le Flamand 8 rue de la République ☎ 05 63 66 12 20. This lively bar-café is the place to go for a beer – they serve a huge selection, including an impressive number of Belgian brews, both on tap and bottled. There's plenty of choice for hungry drinkers too: the extensive menu offers pizzas (from €8), grills (from €11) and salads (from €6.80) as well as more local fare such as *tartiflette* (potato gratin with lardons and cheese) and

cassoulet. Mon–Sat noon–midnight.

Lulu la Nantaise Place du Coq ☎ 05 63 63 00 99. Busy brasserie-cum-bar, frequented by a large number of locals. With chairs and tables spilling out over the cobbles and non-stop service, this is a great place for afternoon drinks accompanied by tapas (€7–10), but head elsewhere for fine dining. Mon–Sat 8.30am–8pm.

Le Santa Maria 2 place Léon Bourjade ☎ 05 63 91 99 09. The shabby exterior does nothing to deter Montauban's youth from descending on *Le Santa Maria* en-masse come the evening. As well as an ample cocktail menu, they also serve numerous tapas and more substantial Tex Mex meals at about €20, including wine. Tues & Wed 7pm–2am, Thurs & Fri 7pm–3am, Sat 7pm–5.30am.

DIRECTORY

Hospital Centre Hospitalier, rue Léon Cladel, to the north of the old quarter (☎ 05 63 92 82 82).
Police Commissariat de Police, 50 bd Alsace-Lorraine

(☎ 05 63 21 54 00), northeast of the centre.
Post office Allée de l'Empereur.

The Gorges de l'Aveyron and around

In its lower course the Aveyron glides across the dull flood plain surrounding Montauban, offering little reason to stop other than the village of **Montricoux**, with its museum dedicated to a forgotten artist. The scenery becomes more interesting, however, about 30km east of Montauban where the river has sliced a narrow defile through the hills. The entrance to the **Gorges de l'Aveyron** is guarded by the fortress village of **Bruniquel**, its ancient houses assembled higgledy-piggledy on steep cobbled streets, while further east **Penne** perches beneath a crumbling castle. From here on the gorge gets increasingly dramatic as you work your way upriver to **St-Antonin-Noble-Val**, an excellent base for exploring the gorge and surrounding sights. The most compelling of these is the partially ruined **Abbaye de Beaulieu-en-Rouergue**, located 14km northwest, where the Gothic church has been converted into a contemporary art gallery. Beyond St-Antonin, **Laguépie** is less interesting but provides another possible base, from where you can hop south to the beguiling – if very touristy – hilltop town of **Cordes-sur-Ciel**. At Laguépie the Aveyron valley turns abruptly north, and its sides close in again to form a second, increasingly deep, thickly wooded gorge, dominated by the ruins of **Najac**'s mighty fortress. This stands guard over the frontier of the former province of Rouergue, now the Aveyron *département*, and the southern approach to the refreshingly unprettified *bastide* of **Villefranche-de-Rouergue**.

GETTING AROUND   THE GORGES DE L'AVEYRON

By car With bus services sparse and aimed at schoolchildren, you'll need your own transport to get between Montricoux, Bruniquel, Penne, St-Antonin-Noble-Val and Varen.

By train The best way of travelling between Laguépie, Najac and Villefranche is the Toulouse–Brive train line; these trains also stop at Cordes-sur-Ciel, further south.

6

Montricoux

Just before you leave the flat alluvial plains, 25km west of Montauban, **MONTRICOUX** would hardly be worth the stop if it weren't for its intriguing art museum dedicated to **Marcel Lenoir**, a prolific local artist who, like Ingres (see p.273), was born in Montauban in 1872; he died in Montricoux in 1931. Lenoir was much fêted during his early years, when he was at the forefront of Pointillism and Cubism, and he even presaged Art Deco as he searched for new means of expression; but he was also an irascible character and managed to offend so many critics, dealers and galleries that he was eventually cast into oblivion. And there he stays, despite the best efforts of the owner of museum's collection.

Musée Marcel-Lenoir

56 Grand Rue • May–Oct Mon & Wed–Sun 10am–6pm • €5 • ☎ 05 63 67 26 48, ⊕ marcel-lenoir.com

On the west side of Montricoux, the collection at the **Musée Marcel-Lenoir** comprises 140 works spanning Lenoir's whole career. One of the most revealing is the *Kiss of Judas*, in which you see Picasso profiled in blue and Van Gogh cutting off Gauguin's ear, while Judas is portrayed as a well-known art critic of the time.

ACCOMMODATION AND EATING

Aici sèm pla ☎ 05 63 30 98 01, ⊕ aicisempla.com. A delightfully friendly campsite on a farm in Revel, 2km from the village of Vaïssac and 5km southwest of Montricoux. Facilities include a communal BBQ, *boules* court, bike hire and free wi-fi throughout the site, plus mobile homes for rent (€280 weekly). Discounted weekly camping rates available. Closed mid- to late-Dec. **€16**

Chez Terrassier Le Bourg, Vaïssac ☎ 05 63 30 94 60. For comfortable accommodation, head 8km southwest of Montricoux to this pretty, modern place in the middle of Vaïssac; there's a pool, and a restaurant serving *menus* from €24. Breakfast €9.50. Restaurant Mon–Fri noon–1.30pm & 7.30–9pm, Sat & Sun noon–1.30pm. **€57**

Les Gorges de l'Aveyron Le Bugarel ☎ 05 63 24 50 50. As you walk into Montricoux village, you'll pass the entrance to this very swish riverside hotel-restaurant along a lane beside the bridge. It's as good as it looks, with beautifully decorated rooms, a swimming pool, leafy gardens and a restaurant with evening *menus* from €29. Breakfast €13. Restaurant May–Aug daily noon–2pm & 7.30–9pm; Sept–April Wed–Sun noon–2pm & 7.30–9pm. **€100**

Bruniquel

Around 5km east of Montricoux, **BRUNIQUEL** shelters in the lee of its château and has an interesting museum. Once a Protestant stronghold, today it's better known for its striking location, and the drive over from Montricoux is stunning, winding through the hills of the Gorges de l'Aveyron, where fortified villages cling to the rocky crags.

Château de Bruniquel

Daily: March–June & Sept–Oct 10am–6pm; July & Aug 10am–7pm; Nov 10am–5pm • €3.50 • ☎ 05 63 67 24 91

The **Château de Bruniquel** teeters on the edge of a 100m-high cliff at the north side of town. The medieval ruins are actually the remains of two adjacent castles, since the original twelfth-century fortress was divided between rival cousins in 1484. Both are rather knocked about, although there is an impressive carved wooden fireplace in the larger of the two.

Maison des Comtes de Payrol

Place des Monges • April–June & Sept daily 10am–6pm; July & Aug daily 10am–7pm; Oct Sat & Sun 10am–5pm; Nov–Feb by appointment only • €3 • ☎ 05 63 67 26 42

To the west of the castle entrance, and a little more engaging, is the **Maison des Comtes de Payrol**. The thirteenth-century home of a wealthy merchant family, its vaulted cellars and panelled and frescoed rooms now house an unusually good local history **museum**, including an interesting collection of oil lamps and candle holders.

INFORMATION   BRUNIQUEL

6

Tourist office At the entrance to the village (March–June & Sept–Oct Tues–Sat 10am–1pm & 2–6pm; July & Aug daily 10am–7.30pm; Nov–Feb Wed–Sat 10am–1pm & 2–5pm; ☎ 05 63 67 29 84, ⓦ bruniquel.fr). All practical information, including accommodation details, is listed on noticeboards outside.

ACCOMMODATION

Cornelia Promenade de Ravelin-Rue D'Albi ☎ 06 12 48 83 77, ⓦ cornelia-bruniquel.com. The swanky, Dutch-run *Cornelia*, located 200m from the tourist office, has four rooms, including the "Romantique" with a round bed, and the hammock-strewn attic. Meals are available (guests-only, advance booking needed). **€89**

L'Étape du Château Promenade du Ravelin ☎ 05 63 67 25 00, ⓦ etapeduchateau.com. The five double rooms at this upmarket *gîte d'étape* are each decorated in a different colour scheme, plus there's a sauna and spa perfect for a post-sightseeing soak. Meals available for guests by advance booking. Closed mid-Dec to mid-Jan. **€70**

Penne

Six kilometres upriver from Bruniquel lies the even more beautiful ridge-top village of **PENNE**, once a Cathar stronghold, with its ruined castle perched on an impregnable pinnacle. Everything is old and leaning and bulging, but holding together nonetheless, with a harmony that would be impossible to create purposely. There's just one cobbled street leading from an arch under the church belfry and through a second gate – where ancient grain measures are cut into the wall – to a footpath scrambling among the **castle ruins**. There's not much left, although restoration work is being undertaken, and it's an atmospheric spot, the piles of stones overrun with dog-roses, clematis and honeysuckle, with a panorama taking in the village roofs and the wooded country beyond.

EATING   PENNE

La Terrasse 13 rue Peyragude ☎ 05 63 56 35 03, ⓦ www.restaurant-terrasse-tarn.fr. Grills cooked over an open fire are the specialty at this traditional restaurant, but the real star is the location – the terrace offers a spectacular view of Penne's castle and the Aveyron gorges. Mains around €15. July & Aug daily noon–2pm & 7.30–9pm; Sept–June Mon & Thurs–Sun 7.30–9pm.

The Corniche

Beyond Penne the Aveyron gorge becomes deeper and more dramatic. To appreciate it at its best, turn off the main road just after Cazals, 6km from Penne, following signs for the **Corniche**, a single-track road that climbs steeply for a kilometre or so up to the cliff's edge. You'll be rewarded with tremendous views and, a little further on at the village of **Brousses**, a superbly sited **restaurant**, *La Corniche* (see below). Six kilometres later, you drop down to the river again to the west of St-Antonin-Noble-Val.

EATING   THE CORNICHE

La Corniche Brousses ☎ 05 63 68 26 95. Friendly service and tasty country cuisine created from fresh, seasonal ingredients make *La Corniche* a popular choice – reservations are recommended. In summer, take a table on the terrace overlooking the lovely Aveyron valley. *Menus* €30, payment by cash or cheque only. March–Nov Tues, Fri & Sat noon–1.30pm & 7–8.30pm, Sun noon–1.30pm; Jan–March Sat & Sun noon–1.30pm & 7–8.30pm, weekdays by reservation only.

6

St-Antonin-Noble-Val

The finest and most substantial town in the lower stretch of the Aveyron valley is **ST-ANTONIN-NOBLE-VAL**, 16km northeast of Penne. It sits on the river's north bank beneath the beetling white cliffs of the **Roc d'Anglars**, where it developed in the ninth century around an abbey said to house the remains of the evangelizing **St Antonin**. According to legend, his body was carried here in a boat guided by two white eagles from Pamiers, in the Ariège, where the saint met his death. Since then the town has endured all the vicissitudes of this region's history: it sided with the Cathars, then the Protestants and each time was walloped by the alien power of the kings from the north, until it eventually sank into oblivion after the seventeenth century. Yet, in spite of it all, a marvellous heritage of houses endowed by wealthy merchants remains from its medieval glory days, when St-Antonin was an important commercial centre, manufacturing linen and leather goods.

The easiest landmark to head for is the spire of the large but uninteresting Neo-Gothic **church**, towards the town's southeast corner. Along the church's west wall rue du Pont-de-l'Aveyron leads south to the bridge, while rue Guilhelm Peyre curves northeast to **place de la Halle**. This square is St-Antonin at its most picturesque, with its cafés and pint-sized *halle*, and the focus of an important Sunday-morning **market**.

Musée du Vieux St-Antonin

Place de la Halle • July & Aug Mon & Wed–Sat 3–6pm • €1, under-10s free • ☎ 05 63 30 63 47

The finest building in St-Antonin-Noble-Val is the **Maison des Consuls**, whose origins go back to 1125. The facade is pierced with arcades, pairs of colonnaded openings and a contrastingly severe oblong window on the first floor, on one pillar of which Adam and Eve hide their modesty; the old man on the pillar to the left, holding some books and a staff, is Emperor Justinian (483–565), who codified Roman law. The building's most striking feature, however, is the tower with its top-heavy loggia and too-perfect machicolations added by the nineteenth-century architect Viollet-le-Duc – though he did save the building from collapse. It now houses the **Musée du Vieux St-Antonin**, with an uninspiring collection of objects to do with the former life of the place, including various prehistoric finds.

Tourist office In the *mairie* next to the church (March & Oct Mon 2–5.30pm, Tues–Sun 10am–12.30pm & 2–5.30pm; April–June & Sept daily 10am–12.30pm & 2–6pm; July & Aug daily 9.30am–12.30pm & 2–7pm; Nov–Feb Mon & Sat 2–5pm, Tues–Fri 10am–12.30pm & 2–5pm; ☎ 05 63 30 63 47, ☼ tourisme-saint-antonin -noble-val.com).

Outdoor activities St-Antonin is the starting point for canoeing down this lower stretch of the Aveyron. Variation La Plage (☎ 05 63 68 25 25, ☼ variation82.eu) offers canoe rental (from €16/hr for up to two adults and one child), stand-up paddleboarding (from €7/30min) and ATV rides (€15 per half-day), plus rock climbing and pot-holing excursions.

ACCOMMODATION AND EATING

Carré des Gourmets 13 bd des Thermes ☎ 05 63 30 65 49, ☼ carredesgourmets.fr. In an atmospheric spot right on the riverside, this is a good bet for tasty contemporary French cuisine, with *menus* from €20. Mid-Feb to mid-Dec Tues & Sun noon–2pm, Thurs–Sat noon–2pm & 7.30–9pm.

Gorges de l'Aveyron ☎ 05 63 30 69 76, ☼ camping -gorges-aveyron.com. About 1.5km out of town on the Marsac road, this friendly campsite is situated next to the river, overlooked by the cliffs. Facilities include a pool, bar, restaurant and children's play area; they will also lend out BBQs. Closed Oct–April. **€23**

Le Ponget Ponget ☎ 05 63 68 21 13. Just out of town on the Caylus road, you'll find this simple but peaceful and well-kept municipal campsite with great views of the cliffs and river. Closed Sept–May. **€13**

La Résidence 37 rue Droite ☎ 05 63 67 37 56, ☼ laresidence-france.com. Smart Dutch/German-run *chambre d'hôte* on the road leading northwest out of place de la Halle. The five en-suite rooms are large and colourfully decorated – one even has its own roof terrace. **€80**

Les Trois Cantons ☎ 05 63 31 98 57, ☼ 3cantons.fr. Some 6km north up onto the *causse* from St-Antonin, this spacious and well-organized campsite offers three-star facilities including a heated pool, shop and snack bar. Closed mid-Sept to mid-April. **€29.90**

Abbaye de Beaulieu-en-Rouergue

April–June, Sept & Oct Mon & Wed–Sun 10am–12.30pm & 2.30–6pm; July & Aug daily 10am–12.30pm & 2.30–6pm • Free • ☏ 05 63 24 60 00, ⓦ art-beaulieu-rouergue.com

Some 14km northwest of St-Antonin, the beautiful Cistercian **Abbaye de Beaulieu-en-Rouergue** lies deep among wooded hills. The abbey was founded in 1144, though the present buildings date from the thirteenth century, and are remarkably unscathed considering it was sacked and burnt during the Wars of Religion, looted again during the Revolution and then used as a barn until the late 1950s; in 1844 Viollet-le-Duc even wanted to rebuild the whole caboodle in St-Antonin but had to give up through lack of funds. The present owners have now restored the church to create a superb exhibition space for their collection of **contemporary art**; displays change several times a year, in combination with temporary exhibitions. The high, light nave with its clean lines and lack of ornamentation, save for the delicate rose windows and a few sculpted capitals, provides the perfect foil for works by Jean Dubuffet, Simon Hantaï and Henri Michaux, among others.

6

Varen

Upstream from St-Antonin, the Aveyron valley widens out for a while and is spoilt by stone quarries. The only reason to stop is the village of **VAREN**, 16km from St-Antonin on the river's north bank. Its Romanesque **Église St-Pierre** and tiny area of old streets repay a quick wander, but the prime attraction is another excellent though fairly upmarket **restaurant** (see below).

EATING

VAREN

Moulin de Varen ☏ 05 63 65 45 10. An authentic country restaurant housed in an old stone mill, *Moulin de Varen* offers a surprisingly wide menu, paired with a carefully selected wine list. Snag a seat on the garden terrace overlooking the River Aveyron and dig into traditional cuisine (*menus* from €25); don't miss the zesty lemon-vodka sorbet for dessert. Reservations recommended. July & Aug Tues–Sun noon–2pm & 7–9pm; Sept–June Thurs–Sat noon–2pm & 7–9pm, Sun noon–2pm.

Laguépie

LAGUÉPIE, 9km east of Varen, where the cliffs begin to close in again, guards the confluence of the Viaur and Aveyron rivers. The village has nothing in the way of sights, but is pretty enough and provides a useful base, served both by occasional buses from Montauban and by trains on the Toulouse–Brive line. The **church** pinpoints the village centre, occupying a spit of land between the two rivers, while a short stroll southwest is the place du Foirail, where the covered *halle* hosts a fresh produce **market** on Wednesday and Sundays.

ARRIVAL AND INFORMATION

LAGUÉPIE

By train The *gare SNCF* lies 500m northwest on the north bank of the Aveyron. Destinations Cordes-sur-Ciel (4–8 daily; 20min); Figeac (4–8 daily; 1hr); Najac (4–6 daily; 10min); Toulouse (3–8 daily; 1hr 20min); Villefranche-de-Rouergue (4–8 daily; 25min).

Tourist office Place du Foirail (first two weeks in July & last two weeks in Aug Tues–Sat 10am–noon & 2.30–5pm; last two weeks in July Mon–Sat 10am–noon & 3.30–6pm, Sun 10am–12.15pm; Sept–June Fri & Sat 10am–noon & 2.30–5pm; ☏ 05 63 30 20 34, ⓦ laguepie-en-rouergue.fr).

ACCOMMODATION AND EATING

Les Deux Rivières Av de Puech Mignon ☏ 05 63 31 41 41, ⓦ hotel-restaurant-tarn-garonne.fr. Laguépie's one and only hotel is a jovial proposition, with beaming hosts and eight great-value rooms. It's worth opting for half-board: the hotel restaurant offers a good range of French and international dishes, followed by scrumptious desserts. *Menus* from €12 at lunch, €23 in the evening. Breakfast €8. Restaurant June–Aug daily noon–1.45pm

& 7.30–9pm; Sept–May Mon–Thurs noon–1.45pm & 7.30–9pm, Sat 7.30–9pm. **€50**
Les Tilleuls ❶ 05 63 30 22 32, ⓦ camping-les-tilleuls .com. Municipal campsite in a shady spot beside the Viaur

river, roughly 1km to the east of Laguépie. There are chalets available for rent by the week (from €250), plus tennis courts, ping-pong tables, a snack bar, a small swimming pool and children's play areas. Closed Sept–May. **€13.30**

Cordes-sur-Ciel

6

The traveller who, from the terrace of Cordes, watches the summer night knows that he has no need to go further and that, if he so wishes, the beauty of this place, day after day, will lift him from all solitude.   Albert Camus

The spotlight has been shining on **CORDES-SUR-CIEL** since it was honoured with the title of Village Préféré des Français ("France's favourite village") back in 2014, and visitors have long frequented this spectacularly situated fortified town, perched high above the Cérou valley – it's easy to see how it earned its suffix of *sur-ciel* ("in the sky"). Located 15km south of Laguépie on the D922 (and also accessible by train), Cordes is a tourist magnet in July and August, when streets swell with crowds and the growing community of artisans do a roaring trade. Take time to explore away from the main drag and you'll find a tangle of steep cobblestone lanes and impossibly narrow alleyways, where the medieval houses, flower-filled windowboxes and stone arches offer endless inspiration for photographers.

Founded in 1222 by Count Raymond VII of Toulouse, Cordes grew rich on **leatherworking** and in the following century its walls had to be enlarged no fewer than seven times to contain the expanding population. Things took a downturn, however, with the arrival of the plague in the fifteenth century, but Cordes later recovered, and developed a notable **lace industry** in the nineteenth century. However, its real renaissance came in the 1970s, when hippies, including the **craftsmen** and **artisans** whose studios now cram the old town, arrived to put Cordes back on the map, attracted by its beauty and abandon.

Camus' words give some idea of the town's allure, and hard though it may be to achieve such a placid state when the streets are packed during summer days, in the evening or out of season the romance of Cordes returns. It's worth rising early to view the sunrise from the ramparts, and with every other building a medieval mansion, walking the town before the crowds arrive is a delight. Its layout is simple: the old citadelle – known as the **haute cité** – runs along and down the sides of the long and narrow ridge which juts up from the plain, while the modern part consists of a clump of streets at the foot of the old town's eastern tip. The best route to the *haute cité* is the knee-cracking **Grande Rue de l'Horloge** ascending from the tourist office (see opposite), although at busy times it is more pleasant to take one of the picturesque but less crowded side streets. At the town's eastern limit, place de la Bouteillerie hosts a lively **market** each Saturday, selling produce from around the region.

You'll need good shoes and plenty of stamina to scale the steep streets on foot, but if you get tired, you can hop onto a **petit train** (see opposite) which makes frequent trips from outside the tourist office.

Maison de l'Art du Sucre et du Chocolat

33 Grande Rue Raymond VII • Daily: mid-Feb to March & Nov–Dec 10.30am–12.30pm 1.30–6pm; April to mid-July, Sept & Oct 10am–7pm; mid-July to Aug 9am–8pm • €4.90, children €3.90 • ❶ 05 63 56 02 40

Heading straight up the Grande Rue Raymond VII from the tourist office, you'll pass through progressively older gateways towards the heart of the *haute cité*. En route, you'll come across the **Maison de l'Art du Sucre et du Chocolat**, an exhibition of sculptures made entirely out of sugar or chocolate. They have a couple on display in the shop, so it's worth sticking your head round the door even if you don't want to see the full museum.

Musée d'Art Moderne et Contemporain

Grande Rue Raymond VII • Mid-March to mid-Nov Mon & Wed–Sun 10.30am–12.30pm & 2–6pm • €4 • ☎ 05 63 56 14 79

About halfway along Grande Rue Raymond VII, the elegant and symmetrical arcaded face of the fourteenth-century **Maison du Grand Fauconnier** conceals the **Musée d'Art Moderne et Contemporain,** which features works by the figurative painter Yves Brayer, who lived in Cordes from 1940, as well as a French-only audio presentation explaining the town's lace-making tradition and a motley collection of modern art, including minor pieces by Picasso, Miró and Klee.

Grande Rue Raymond VII

Grande Rue Raymond VII holds some of Cordes' most remarkable buildings. Be sure to take in the facade of the **Maison du Grand Veneur** ("House of the Great Hunter"), a wonderful Gothic pile whose otherwise plain stone face is festooned with amusingly sculpted and extremely well-preserved medieval caricatures of beasts and hunters. A few doors down, the former **palace** of Raymond of Toulouse boasts an impressively carved frontage.

Musée Charles Portal

1 rue St Michel • April & May Fri–Sun 2.30–6pm; June–Aug Mon & Wed–Sun 2.30–6.30pm; Sept–Nov Fri–Sun 3–6pm • €2.50 •
☎ 05 63 80 51 72, ⓦ musee-charles-portal.asso-web.com • The official entrance to the museum is off rue St-Michel

At the meeting point of Grande Rue Raymond VII and rue St Michel, close to the **Porte des Ormeaux** ("Gate of the Elms"), is the **Musée Charles Portal.** Inside, the small exhibition rooms house a display on the medieval wells that riddle the town, and which were used in times of siege for water supply or to store grain. If you want to take a closer look, one of the most easily accessible wells lies in the ancient covered market, opposite the Musée d'Art Moderne et Contemporain (see above).

ARRIVAL AND INFORMATION

CORDES-SUR-CIEL

By train Trains stop 5km to the west of Cordes at Vindrac (☎ 05 63 56 05 64), from where it's a pleasant hour-long walk or short taxi ride costing about €5 – taxis are easy to find in July and Aug, otherwise you can call one (☎ 05 63 56 14 80).

Destinations (Cordes-Vindrac) to: Figeac (4–8 daily; 1hr 20min); Laguépie (4–8 daily; 20min); Najac (4–6 daily; 30min); Toulouse (4–8 daily; 1hr); Villefranche-de-Rouergue (4–8 daily; 50min).

By bus Buses from Albi (Mon–Fri 3–5 daily, Sat 1–3 daily; 40min–1hr) stop near the tourist office in the lower town.

By car Parking can be a challenge – in the summer months the area a few metres east of the tourist office soon fills up and cars line the roads leading into town. Don't be tempted to drive into the *haute cité*, better to park at the bottom and walk or take the tourist train (see below).

Tourist office Place Jeanne Ramel-Cals (April–June & Sept–Oct Mon–Sat 10.30am–12.30pm & 2–6pm, Sun 10.30am–12.30pm & 2–5pm; July & Aug Mon–Sat 9.30am–1pm & 2–6.30pm, Sun 10am–1pm & 2–6pm; Nov–March Mon–Fri 10.30am–12.30pm & 2–4pm, Sat 10.30am–12.30pm & 2–5pm; ☎ 05 63 56 00 52, ⓦ cordessurciel.fr).

GETTING AROUND

Le Petit Train Trains run every 10min from place de la Bouteillerie to Porte de la Jane (daily: May to mid-June & Sept 10.30am–12.30pm & 2–4.50pm; mid-June to Aug 9.30am–12.50pm & 2–4.50pm; €3, children €2). In July and Aug 45min tours with commentary are also available, departing hourly on the hour (Mon–Fri & Sun 10am–5pm, Sat 3–5pm; €6.50, children €3.50).

ACCOMMODATION

L'Escuelle des Chevaliers 87 Grande Rue Raymond VII ☎ 05 63 87 14 40, ⓦ micheldemonsegur.free.fr. Housed in a fourteenth-century building and adorned with heraldic tapestries, suits of armour and ancient swords, this medieval-themed *chambre d'hôte* has rooms equipped with four-poster beds and wrought-iron chandeliers, and a restaurant where you can even dress up and dine in medieval costume. Dishes include date-stuffed chicken, roasted chestnuts and suckling pig (*menus* from €20, reservations essential). Restaurant daily noon–2pm & 7.30–9pm; guests only Nov–April. **€68**

Logis Sur Ciel 18 Grande rue Raymond VII ☎ 05 63 56 25 87, ⓦ logissurciel.com. Behind the authentic thirteenth-century façade, this charming *chambre d'hôte*

6

is a maze of stone arches and narrow stairwells. The five rooms are all comfortable and modern, but for the best views, book the top-floor "Estela", which has a huge terrace overlooking the valley and an ingenious pulley system to transport your luggage for you. It's worth sticking around for dinner, too (three-course *menu* €25), which is served in the magnificent Grande Salle. Breakfast €6. Restaurant July & Aug daily 7.30–9pm; hotel closed Nov–March. **€100**

★ **Le Secret du Chat** 16 le Planol ☎ 06 95 48 18 10, ⓦ chambres-cordes-tarn-charme-lesecretduchat.com. Effortlessly walking the line between luxurious and homely, *Le Secret du Chat* is a cut above most other *chambres d'hôtes*. The five rooms each boast a countrified elegance, with original beams, polished wood floors and antique furnishings, jazzed up with patterned bedlinen.

The restaurant is equally impressive, with regional cuisine paired with local Gaillac wines, served in the old cellar. *Menus* from €29, by reservation only. **€120**

Le Vieux Cordes Haute Cité ☎ 05 63 53 79 20, ⓦ hostelleriehvc.com. Original brickwork, spiral staircases and restored wooden beams lend this *hostellerie* a rustic elegance, while the rooms offer big comfy beds, spotless bathrooms and all the mod-cons. Downstairs, the restaurant serves *menus* from €24.50; in summer you can eat in the ancient, cobbled courtyard under a canopy of wisteria. Don't miss out on the desserts, which include perfectly scorched crème brûlée and delicious profiteroles. Breakfast €8.50. Restaurant June–Sept Tues–Sun noon–2pm & 7.30–9pm; Oct–Dec & Feb–May Wed–Sat noon–2pm & 7.30–9pm, Tues 7.30–9pm, Sun noon–2pm. **€98**

EATING

There are numerous options for eating in Cordes. The best **restaurants** are in the town's hotels, but there are plenty of cheaper options around the central place de la Halle and adjacent place de la Bride – some also offer magnificent views over the valley.

Le Cayrols Le Cayrols ☎ 05 63 56 22 46, ⓦ lecayrols .com. For a change of pace from the busy tourist haunts of the *cité*, head up the road to *Le Cayrols*, where dinner is served in a pretty sculpture garden. Choices are limited but dishes like the goat's cheese and vegetable millefeuille and orange-glazed scallops leave a lasting impression. *Formules* start from €20. June–Sept daily noon–2pm & 7.30–9pm.

La Table d'Yvonne 1 Place de la Halle ☎ 05 63 56 92 09. The foie gras made in house by artisan Michel Monteil is the star of the show at this busy restaurant. Most popular is the signature tagliatelle with foie gras (€13), preceded by a complimentary apéritif. You can also buy a range of artisan products at the adjoining boutique. Reservations recommended. Daily noon–2pm & 7.30–9pm.

SHOPPING

There are more than forty **boutiques** in Cordes, selling artisan foods, local wines, art and handicrafts including leather- and metal-work. Many shops are touted as "museums" and the artisans are often happy to discuss their work or perform demonstrations. Pick up the free *Guide des Artistes et Artisans* booklet from the tourist office (see p.281) for a full rundown of outlets. Be aware that most shops don't accept cards, so it's best to carry cash or check before you buy.

La Cave St Michel Place Saint-Michel ☎ 05 63 56 92 07. The place to buy regional wines, apéritifs, whiskies and Eau de Vie, with a huge range available and free wine tasting daily in July & Aug (and rest of the year on request). Wines start from as little as €3. Daily 10am–7.30pm.

Éditions Larroque Place de la Halle ☎ 05 63 56 14 93. Specializing in exquisite hand-bound books, tapestry book covers, calligraphy art and medieval-style books.

Mon–Thurs 9am–5.30pm, Fri 9am–2.30pm, plus July & Aug Sat & Sun 10.30am–6.30pm.

La Fabrique des Petites Mains 3 Grand rue de la Barbacane ☎ 05 63 53 96 94. Showcasing the artistic endeavours of twelve female artists, this boutique is the place to find unique gifts with a feminine touch: think hand-crafted leather purses, jewellery, baby clothes and beautiful origami fairy lights. Daily 10am–7pm.

Najac

At Laguépie (see p.279), the Aveyron valley heads northwards and the river flows through a wooded defile. The most picturesque route along the valley bottom is either the train or the GR36 footpath, while road users should take the D106 and D594 along the western line of hills. Either way, you eventually arrive at a bridge – 15km by road and slightly less on foot – beneath the brooding towers of the semi-ruined **Château de Najac**.

The castle occupies an extraordinary site on the peak of a conical hill isolated in the river's wide meander – a spot chosen in the mid-1200s by **Alphonse de Poitiers**, who wanted to bring the area's Cathar sympathizers to heel. He enlarged the original fortress and laid out a new town to the east in an elongated version of a *bastide* with its arcades and central market square. For a short while Najac prospered as the region's capital, but the site proved too restrictive and by the end of the thirteenth century it had lost out to Villefranche-de-Rouergue (see p.284), leaving the castle to be fought over endlessly in the conflicts that ensued. The Protestants pillaged it in 1572 and the revolutionaries had their turn in 1793, but, in spite of all this, Najac survived.

6

The heart of modern Najac consists of a big, open square lying to the east of the medieval village, where grey-tiled houses tail out westwards in a single street along the narrow spur connecting the valley side to the castle hill.

Château de Najac

Daily: April, May, Sept & Oct 10am–1pm & 3–5.30pm; June 10.30am–1pm & 3–6.30pm; early July 10.30am–1.30pm & 3–6.30pm; end July & Aug 10.30am–7pm; last week in Aug 10.30am–1.30pm & 3–7pm • €5.50 • ☎ 05 65 29 71 65

Entering Najac from the east you come first to the **faubourg**, the elongated market square bordered by houses raised on pillars. It slopes gently downhill towards a cobbled street, overlooked by more ancient houses, which leads past a fountain to the **Château de Najac**. The castle is a model of medieval defensive architecture: its curtain walls reach to over 20m in places, within which five round towers supplement the square twelfth-century turret, and the castle is equipped with unusual multi-storey loopholes for archers. However, the main reason to visit is for the magnificent all-round **view** from the top of the keep, a full 200m above the river.

Église St-Jean

Rue de l'Église • April–Sept daily 10am–noon & 2–6pm; Oct Sun 10am–noon & 2–6pm • Free

Just below Najac's castle, in what was the original medieval village, stands the huge, very solid-looking and austere **Église St-Jean**, which the villagers were forced to build at their own expense in 1258 as a punishment for their conversion to Catharism. In addition to a collection of reliquaries and an extraordinary iron cage for holding candles, the church has one architectural oddity: its windows are solid panels of stone from which the lights have been cut out in trefoil form. Below the church, a surviving Roman road leads downhill to where a thirteenth-century bridge spans the Aveyron.

ARRIVAL AND INFORMATION   NAJAC

By train The *gare SNCF* lies on the north side of the old bridge, 2km by road below the village. Taxis often wait outside the train station, otherwise call ☎ 05 65 81 12 92.
Destinations Cordes-sur-Ciel (4–8 daily; 30min); Figeac (4–8 daily; 50min); Laguépie (4–8 daily; 10min); Toulouse (3–8 daily; 1hr 30min); Villefranche-de-

Rouergue (4–8 daily; 15min).
Tourist office On the south side of the *faubourg* (May–June & Sept Mon–Sat 9.30am–12.30pm & 2–6pm Sun 9.30–12.30pm; July & Aug daily 9.30am–12.30pm & 2–6pm; Oct–April Tues–Sat 10am–12.30pm & 2–5pm; ☎ 05 65 29 72 05, ⊕ tourisme-villefranche-najac.com).

ACCOMMODATION AND EATING

Le Belle Rive ☎ 05 65 29 73 90, ⊕ lebellerive.fr. This charmingly old-fashioned hotel occupies a lovely riverside position near the train station. Rooms are well-sized and comfortable, there's a large pool and the garden offers views of the castle perched high on the hilltop. They also run an excellent restaurant serving good-value regional cooking, with *menus* from €19.50. Breakfast €9. Restaurant April–Sept daily 12.30–2pm & 7.30–9pm; Oct Mon–Sat 12.30–2pm & 7.30–9pm. **€58**

Gîte d'Étape ☎ 05 65 29 73 94, ⊕ aagac.com. Budget accommodation situated at the leisure centre adjacent to the campsite (see p.284). Sparse but clean rooms have 2–6 beds, and there's a communal kitchen and dining area. Closed Oct–April. **€16**

L'Oustal del Barry 2 place Sol del Barry ☎ 05 65 29 74 32, ⊕ oustaldelbarry.com. A taste of the country right in the heart of town, with bright, spacious rooms and a leafy terrace with views of the castle. It's worth opting for

half-board, as the hotel restaurant is renowned for its subtle and inventive cuisine. *Menus* from €21.70; reservations essential. Breakfast €11.50. Restaurant April to mid-Dec daily 12.30–2pm & 7.30–9pm. **€65**
Le Païsserou ☎ 05 65 29 73 96, ⓦ camping-le-paisserou.fr. Najac's four-star riverside campsite, to the southwest of the old bridge, is spacious and very well equipped. Facilities include a restaurant/snack bar and large pool. Closed Oct–April. **€24**
★ **Relais Mont Le Viaur** St André de Najac ☎ 05 65 65

08 08, ⓦ montleviaur.fr. Lovely stone building, some 1km east of Najac, boasting sunny, well-furnished rooms with en-suite bathrooms and air-conditioning. The highlight is its wonderful restaurant – *the* place to eat in the area. They serve beautifully presented food, combining traditional and modern cuisine, with *menus* at €14 for lunch and €21.80 for dinner. All products are market-fresh and reservations are essential. Breakfast €9. Restaurant daily noon–2pm & 7–10pm; hotel and restaurant closed two weeks in Dec. **€64**

Villefranche-de-Rouergue

The second stretch of the Aveyron gorge peters out about 10km north of Najac, but it's worth continuing upstream the same distance again to the laid-back market town of **VILLEFRANCHE-DE-ROUERGUE**, which boasts one of the most atmospheric central squares in the whole region. As its regular form and the die-straight streets indicate, this is a *bastide*, founded in 1252 by the ubiquitous **Alphonse de Poitiers**, as part of the royal policy of extending control over the recalcitrant lands of the south. A prosperous town thanks to its copper-rich mines, Villefranche was also made the seat of the seneschal, the king's representative, in 1369, with the right to mint money. While its wealthy merchants built the ornate houses that grace the cobbled streets to this day, conditions in the surrounding countryside were so desperate that in 1643, more than ten thousand peasants, known as **Croquants** (see p.297), besieged the town for a week. As elsewhere, the rebellion was harshly put down and the leaders strung up in the market square.

The medieval quarter

Villefranche's **medieval quarter** lies on the north bank of the Aveyron, accessed by a modern road-bridge beside its pedestrian fourteenth-century counterpart. From the old bridge, the town's main commercial street, pedestrianized **rue de la République**, runs northwards up a gentle incline into the heart of the *bastide*. It is attractive enough, but no preparation for the central square you come out into, **place Notre-Dame**. The square, too, is built on a slope and is surrounded by unusually tall houses, arcaded at ground-floor level, some of which display elaborate window surrounds. If possible, try to visit on a Thursday morning when local merchants and farmers spread out their produce at the weekly **market**, presided over by the colossal porch and bell tower – nearly 60m high and fortified – of the **Collégiale Notre-Dame**, which dominates the square's east side. The church was started in 1260 but wars and fires intervened and it was not finally completed until 1519. Behind the altar are two fine mid-fifteenth-century stained-glass windows: the one on the left depicts the Creation; that on the right portrays sixteen characters from the Old and New Testaments. Also worth noting are the oak choir stalls alive with a superb array of beasts and demons, as well as scenes from daily life – they took the craftsman, André Sulpice, fifteen years to complete in the late fifteenth century.

Chapelle des Pénitents-Noirs

Boulevard Haute Guyenne • April–June & Oct Tues–Sat 2–6pm; July–Sept daily 10am–noon & 2–6pm • €4 • ☎ 05 65 45 13 18
On boulevard Haute Guyenne, which forms the northern limit of the old town, the seventeenth-century **Chapelle des Pénitents-Noirs** boasts a splendidly Baroque painted ceiling and an enormous gilded retable – resplendent after its extensive renovations.

Chartreuse St-Sauveur

April–June Tues–Sat 2–6pm; July–Sept daily 10am–noon & 2–6pm • €5 • ☎ 05 65 45 13 18 • The site is in the grounds of a hospital about 1km south of town on the main D922 to Najac and Laguépie

Worth the slight detour from central Villefranche, the **Chartreuse St-Sauveur** was completed in the space of ten years from 1450, giving it a singular architectural harmony. The highlight is the second of the two cloisters, a minuscule quadrangle of white, sculpted stone, while the church itself contains more examples of André Sulpice's craftsmanship on the screen and choir stalls.

6

ARRIVAL AND INFORMATION   VILLEFRANCHE-DE-ROUERGUE

By train The *gare SNCF* is located a couple of minutes' walk south across the Aveyron from the old centre.

Destinations Cordes-sur-Ciel (4–8 daily; 50min); Figeac (4–8 daily; 45min); Laguépie (4–8 daily; 25min); Najac (4–8 daily; 15min); Toulouse (3–8 daily; 1hr 40min).

By bus Raynal Voyages (☎ 05 65 23 28 28) run buses to *Cahors*; pick up the timetable, *Les Bus du Lot*, from the tourist office, or book in advance if travelling outside of

school terms. They stop in place de la Liberté and at the *gare routière*, next to the *gare SNCF* on the southern side of the river.

Tourist office Promenade du Giraudet (May, June & Sept Mon–Sat 9am–noon & 2–6pm; July & Aug Mon–Fri 9am–12.30pm & 2–7pm, Sat 9am–noon & 2–6pm, Sun 10am–12.30pm; Oct–April Mon–Fri 9am–noon & 2–5pm, Sat 9am–noon; ☎ 05 65 45 13 18, ⓦ villefranche.com).

ACCOMMODATION

Camping du Rouergue ☎ 05 65 45 16 24, ⓦ camping durouergue.com. Huge but friendly three-star municipal campsite, 1.5km to the south of Villefranche, signed off the D47 to Monteils. Facilities include a pool, table tennis and a summer-only bar. Closed Sept–April. €15

Les Fleurines 17 bd Haute Guyenne ☎ 05 65 45 86 90, ⓦ lesfleurines.com. Ideally situated opposite the Chapelle des Pénitents-Noirs, *Les Fleurines* has a range of great-value rooms. Rooms are smart, well-furnished and

spotless, embellished with some contemporary touches like circular beds and faux-fur scatter cushions. Breakfast €11. €79

Relais de Farrou Rte de Figeac ☎ 05 65 45 18 11, ⓦ relaisdefarrou.com. Smart, ultra-modern hotel about a 20min drive out of town on the Figeac road. Guests have use of a small spa, gym and an outdoor pool, while the hotel also provides bicycles and other activities, and there's a restaurant. Breakfast €11. €89

EATING

L'Assiette Gourmande Place André Lescure ☎ 05 65 45 25 95, ⓦ lassiettegourmande.fr. For traditional French fare and a few surprises, this is a reliable choice, located one block north of the church. The lunchtime *menu* at €15.50 is great value for three courses. Mon & Thurs–Sun noon–1.30pm & 7.30–9pm, Tues noon–1.30pm

★**Côté Saveurs** 5 rue Belle Isle ☎ 05 65 65 83 64, ⓦ cote-saveurs.fr. For a treat that tempts all five senses, head to Villefranche's most impressive restaurant and splash out on the six-course *dégustation menu* (€60). Dishes change seasonally and push the boundaries of gourmet cuisine, while the presentation will have you reaching for your camera. Tues–Sat noon–1.30pm & 7.30–8.30pm.

L'Epicurien 8bis rue Raymond Saint-Gilles ☎ 05 65 45 01 12, ⓦ restaurant-lepicurien-villefranche.fr. Just down the road from the train station, this upmarket restaurant serves creatively presented dishes, including perfectly cooked cod and show-stopping desserts. Evening *menus* from €35. Tues–Sat noon–2.30pm & 7–9.30pm, Sun noon–2.30pm.

La Gabelle 10 rue Belle-Isle ☎ 05 65 45 57 13, ⓦ la gabelle-restaurant-rouergue.com. Well-run restaurant one block south of the church, where you'll find cheerful staff and an extensive menu of pizzas, home-made pastas and grills, as well as some more adventurous options like frogs' legs. Mains from €8. Tues–Sat noon–2pm & 7–10pm.

VINEYARD IN THE LOT REGION

Contexts

287 History

303 Books

305 French

314 Glossary

History

The history of the Dordogne and Lot region is a fascinating illustration of how the political entity that is now a unified France in fact consists of numerous components of entirely distinct historical character. The southwest's vigorously independent cultural identity was forged millennia ago in the artistic endeavours of mysterious but highly gifted cave-dwellers, and hundreds of years ago in the influence of English rule and in the poetry of the troubadours, written in a language now virtually extinct. Even from the fifteenth century onwards, when the region was officially part of metropolitan France, it remained a distant territory, at least a week's travel from Paris, and one where local interests and powerful families held far more sway than the voice of the king. To this political detachment must be added the entirely secluded nature of the life led by the vast majority of the region's population, barely 15 percent of whom lived in towns even as late as 1910. Communicating in myriad local dialects, worshipping the gods of local folklore and working on the land in the same manner as their ancestors had for centuries, the rural poor of the Dordogne and Lot, largely oblivious to the causes – though certainly not the devastating consequences – of the political and religious conflicts going on around them, were only dragged into the familiar historical timeline during the twentieth century.

The beginnings

Primitive flint tools found in the Dordogne indicate human presence dating back at least 400,000 years. However, the region's archeological treasure-trove really gets going with the **Neanderthal** people, who arrived on the scene some 100,000 years ago. Despite their brutish image, evidence now suggests that Neanderthals were surprisingly sophisticated. They developed not only an increasingly elaborate range of stone tools but also complex burial rituals. This didn't, however, equip them to compete with the next wave of immigrants sweeping across Europe between 30,000 and 40,000 years ago, and Neanderthals gradually died out.

Early archeologists named the newcomers **Cro-Magnon** after a rock shelter near Les Eyzies where the first skeletons were identified. Now they are better known as *Homo sapiens sapiens* – in other words, our direct ancestors. While Cro-Magnons developed ever more sophisticated tools, they also began to scratch fertility symbols into the rock, made various pigments and then took the great leap into abstraction that led to drawing, painting and carving. The earliest evidence of **prehistoric art** dates from around 30,000 years ago, but reached its apogee during the **Magdalenian** era

400,000 BC	c.30,000 BC	200 BC	51 BC	c.15 AD
Evidence of human presence in the Dordogne	Cro-Magnons create the earliest cave art near Les Eyzies	Romans begin to colonize southern France	Julius Caesar wins the battle of Uxullodunum (Puy d'Issolud), crushing tribal rule in the area	Administrative centres created at Divona Cadurcorum (Cahors) and Vesunna (Périgueux)

(10,000–17,000 years ago), also named after a shelter in the Dordogne's Vézère valley. It was during this era that Cro-Magnon people covered the walls and ceilings of the region's caves with art of a quality that would not be seen again for several millennia.

Around 10,000 BC the all-important reindeer herds, the Cro-Magnons' one-stop source of meat, fat, skin, bone and sinew, began to move north as the climate grew warmer and wetter. Over the next three thousand years these nomadic hunter-gatherers were gradually replaced by settled **farming and pastoral communities** who left hundreds of **dolmens** (megalithic stone tombs) scattered over the region. This Neolithic era in its turn made way for the great metal-working cultures, culminating in the Iron Age, from around 700 BC. About the same time **Celtic** people began to spread into the region from north and central Europe, establishing trade routes and building towns and hilltop fortresses. They were skilled manufacturers and had their own coinage, but instead of a cohesive entity, they comprised individual or loosely allied clans which were continuously fighting among themselves. It was these disunited tribes that the Roman legions encountered when they arrived in what they called **Gaul** – roughly equivalent to modern France – in the second century BC.

The Roman occupation

At first the **Romans** contented themselves with a colony along the Mediterranean coast, but in 59 BC the threat of a Germanic invasion and various Celtic uprisings prompted **Julius Caesar** to subjugate the entire area. It took him just eight years. By 56 BC he had pacified southwest Gaul and the only real opposition came from a young Arvenian (modern-day Auvergne) chieftain called **Vercingetorix**, who managed to rally a united Gaulish opposition in 52 BC. The Gauls had some initial victories, but in the end were no match for Caesar's disciplined armies. Vercingetorix was taken back to Rome in chains in 52 BC and the following year the Gauls staged their final stand at **Uxellodunum**, under the command of Lucterius, leader of the Cadurci. Caesar himself took command of the siege and eventually cut off their water supply thus forcing the surrender. **Uxellodunum** is generally believed to be at Puy d'Issolud, to the east of Martel (see p.182).

The battle was one of the major turning points in the region's history. In 16 AD Emperor Augustus established the new Gallo-Roman province of **Aquitania**, stretching from Poitiers south to the Pyrenees. Its capital was Burdigala (Bordeaux), and regional administrative centres were set up in Vesunna (Périgueux) and Divona Cadurcorum (Cahors), each with its forum, amphitheatre, law courts and temples. During more than three centuries of peace – the **Pax Romana** – that followed, the Romans built roads, introduced new technologies, traded, planted vineyards and established an urbanized society administered by an educated, Latin-speaking elite. Today, the physical traces of this practically and culturally sophisticated society are most visible in the Roman ruins in Périgueux and Cahors. Just as durable, though, has been the linguistic impact: as well as being the language of the rulers, Latin penetrated rural areas and eventually fused with the local Celtic dialects to form two broad new language groups: the *langue d'Oïl* (where "yes" is *oïl* – later, *oui*), spoken north of the Loire, and the *langue d'Oc*, or *Occitan* (where "yes" is *oc*), to the south.

By the third century AD, Roman authority was starting to crack. Oppressive aristocratic rule and an economic crisis turned the destitute peasantry into gangs of marauding

16 AD	360 AD	507 AD	c.650
Emperor Augustus establishes the Gallo-Roman province of Aquitania	Frankish tribes invade from the north	Clovis, king of the Franks, founds the Merovingian dynasty	St Didier, bishop of Cahors, founds the abbey of St-Pierre at Moissac

brigands, who were particularly rampant in the southwest. But more devastating were the incursions across the Rhine by various restless **Germanic tribes**, starting with the Alemanni and Franks, who pushed down as far as Spain, ravaging farmland and looting towns along the way. In response, urban centres such as Périgueux were hurriedly fortified while the nobles hot-footed it to their country villas, which became increasingly self-sufficient – economically, administratively and militarily.

The crunch came, however, in the fifth century when first the Vandals and then the **Visigoths** stormed through the region as the Roman empire crumbled. For nearly a hundred years the Visigoths ruled a huge territory extending across southern France and into Spain, with its capital at Toulouse.

Christianity and independence

The Visigoths' destructive and mercenary temperament was not conducive to sustained rule, and in 507 AD they were driven out of the region by the **Franks**, a northern tribe who gave their name to modern France. The end of the Visigoths marked the beginning of a long period of relative independence for Aquitaine and the southwest. Although the Frankish king, Clovis, was to found the **Merovingian dynasty** whose power technically extended to this region, he failed to re-establish the same over-arching authority as the Romans had acheived.

The power vacuum had been filled, in part, by representatives of the early Church. **Christianity** had arrived from Rome in the early fourth century and was spreading slowly through France, but the invasion of the Vandals and Visigoths had put its advance on hold. It fell to **bishop Chronope**, active in the region between 506 and 533 AD, to re-establish the faith by a prolific programme of church building, most notably the first cathedral of St-Etienne in Périgueux. Chronope is also thought to have played a role in the creation of the legend of St-Front, after whom Périgueux's modern cathedral is named. Clovis himself had embraced Christianity around 500 AD and thereafter was happy to devolve a great deal of everyday administration to local bishops, such as those at Cahors.

The Merovingian empire began to disintegrate in the late seventh century, leaving the way clear for their chancellors, the Pepin family, to take control. One of their most dynamic scions, **Charles Martel**, defeated the Spanish Moors when they swept up through the southwest as far as Poitiers in 732. His grandson, **Charlemagne**, continued the expansionist policy of the **Carolingian** dynasty – so called for their fondness for the name Charles, or "Carolus" – to create an empire which eventually stretched from the Baltic to the Pyrenees.

Charlemagne and his descendants, however, had no more genuine control over the southwest region than the Merovingians had, preferring, like them, to rule from a distance. In 781 Charlemagne created the quasi-independent **kingdom** of Aquitaine – an area extending from the Loire to the Cévennes and from the Rhône to the Pyrenees. Within the kingdom, the Carolingians delegated administrative power to royally appointed bishops, now joined by a growing number of counts – Quercy and Périgord for example – who had been awarded territory in exchange for their loyalty. In theory, the king retained feudal authority, but in reality the bishops and counts did largely as they pleased.

c.732	781	814	844
Charles Martel defeats the invading Moors and founds the Carolingian dynasty	Charlemagne creates the quasi-independent kingdom of Aquitaine	Death of Charlemagne	Plundering Vikings sail up the Lot, Garonne, Dordogne and Isle rivers

THE WAY OF ST JAMES

According to the Bible, **St James the Apostle** was decapitated in Jerusalem in 44 AD. There is nothing to suggest how his remains came to be buried in northwest Spain, but in 820 it was declared that they had been discovered there, and during the fervent religious revival of the Middle Ages millions of pilgrims began flocking to his supposed tomb in **Santiago de Compostela**. The route took on a life of its own: monasteries, churches and hospitals were founded and villages grew up along the way to cater for the pilgrims wearing their distinctive cockleshell badge.

The pilgrimage faded out during the sixteenth century, partly because of the wars sweeping France and partly because the cathedral canons rather carelessly lost the saint's remains; the relics were allegedly hidden to keep them out of the hands of Sir Francis Drake, who was then sniffing around Galicia, but later no one could remember where they'd put them. By another "miracle" they were rediscovered by archeologists in 1879, declared by the pope to be the genuine article, and the pilgrimage revived, though on a far more modest scale.

In 1998 the whole system of paths and associated buildings was inscribed on the UNESCO World Heritage list. As a result, to walk the **chemin de St-Jacques** (Way of St James) – or at least some of it – has become popular again, partly as a spiritual quest, but also simply as a walking holiday. Three of the four main routes – from Vézelay, Le Puy-en-Velay and Arles – have been waymarked as long-distance footpaths (*grandes randonnées*, or GRs). Of these the GR654 from Vézelay and the GR65 from Le Puy pass through the Dordogne and Lot region; booklets outlining the routes are available in the Topo-guide series (see p.304).

The royal position became weaker still in the ninth century, in part due to a long-drawn-out **battle of succession** following Charlemagne's death in 814, but also thanks to a series of extravagantly destructive raids by the **Vikings**, who sailed their longboats down from Scandinavia. They had been raiding coastal areas for decades, but in 844 they penetrated deep inland along the Garonne, Dordogne, Isle and Lot rivers, plundering towns and churches. Périgueux was razed in 849: the annals of one monastery recount matter-of-factly, "the devastating Normans put fire to Périgueux and, without further ado, got back on their boats."

In the face of these destabilizing invasions the Carolingians were obliged to delegate ever more autonomy to the provincial governors until these eventually grew more powerful than the king. So it was that when **Hugues Capet** succeeded to the French throne in 987, founding a 400-year dynasty that in theory ruled the whole of France, he in practice had authority only over a small area near Paris. Around the turn of the millennium, Aldebert I, one of the counts of Périgord, is supposed to have rebuked a royal demand for payment of feudal dues with the withering question "*Qui vous a fait roi?*" – "Who made you king, then?" By this point, the local aristocratic families were more embroiled in jostling for power with one another than with the king. In the tenth century Périgord was carved up into four **baronies** (Beynac, Mareuil, Bourdeilles and Biron), while Quercy was divided between five powerful families (Turenne, Gourdon, Cardaillac, Castelnau and St-Sulpice). At the same time, the counts of Poitou (based at Poitiers) and Toulouse were fighting for control of what was once again the **Duchy of Aquitaine**. The former emerged victorious, thus creating a vast territory that by the twelfth century reached from the Loire to the Pyrenees. The Poitou counts also ushered in a period of relative peace, rapid economic growth and renewed religious vigour,

849	987	c.990	1122
Vikings raze Périgueux	Hugues Capet crowned king of France and founds the Capetian dynasty	Counts of Poitou take control of Aquitaine and begin construction of the Romanesque churches	Birth of Eleanor of Aquitaine

demonstrated in a wave of church building. To them we owe the lovely Romanesque churches (see box, p.294) seen throughout the region to this day. At least some of this building activity was spurred and financed by the great procession of **pilgrims** passing along the route to Santiago de Compostela in Spain (see box opposite).

English rule

It was the huge kingdom created by the amalgamation of the territories of the counts of Poitou and the dukes of Aquitaine that indirectly allowed the whole of the Dordogne and Lot region to fall into the hands of the **English Crown**. The cause of this catastrophe for the French royal family, the Capetian dynasty, was the strong-willed **Eleanor of Aquitaine** (1122–1204; see box below), who inherited the domains of Aquitaine and Poitou in 1137 at the tender age of 15. Fifteen years later, she ditched her first husband, the French king, to marry **Henry of Anjou**, thereby creating an empire comprising

ELEANOR OF AQUITAINE

The life of **Eleanor of Aquitaine** (1122–1204) is an incredible tale of romance and tragedy, of high farce and low intrigue that rivals any modern-day pot-boiler. As duchess of Aquitaine and countess of Poitou she was already a key figure in twelfth-century Europe. She then married two kings and gave birth to two more, effectively ruled England for a time and died at the grand old age of 82.

In 1137, at the age of just 15, Eleanor inherited the domains of Aquitaine and Poitou. These assets, combined with her intelligence and beauty, gave her a healthy list of suitors, at the head of which was the future King Louis VII of France. They were married in Bordeaux's St-André cathedral, and just a week later, the death of Louis VI made the young couple king and queen of France. The marriage, however, was not a success: it bore no male heirs, and the vivacious Eleanor found her attentions wandering elsewhere. In March 1152, they were divorced.

Just two months later, Eleanor married the handsome, charismatic and extremely ambitious **Henry of Anjou**, who was eleven years her junior, but far closer in temperament. The following year she bore him the all-important heir, and, when Henry II succeeded to the English throne in 1154, Eleanor found herself queen of England.

Although Eleanor spent much of her time in France, she and Henry produced at least eight children. Of these both Richard and John became kings of England, while only two, John and Eleanor, outlived her. In the meantime, since Henry proved reluctant to delegate power, his sons rebelled against him in 1173, supported by both Eleanor and her former husband, Louis VII; the latter hoped to put a more compliant neighbour on the English throne – and was possibly also out for a spot of revenge.

But the rebellion soon collapsed and Henry placed his wife under house arrest. She remained closely guarded until his death in 1189, but her problems had by no means ended. Richard I (the Lionheart), Eleanor's favourite son, was next in line. All went well until he was captured in 1192 while returning from the Third Crusade. The indomitable seventy-year-old waded in as unofficial regent, while also keeping her French possessions under control, for the next two years.

Eleanor withdrew from public life after Richard's release, and even more so after his death in 1199. She retired to the abbey of Fontevraud, in the Loire valley, where she died almost unnoticed in 1204, to be remembered as a popular, shrewd and effective ruler, well able to control her notoriously hot-blooded southern vassals.

1137	c.1140	1152	1154
Eleanor becomes duchess of Aquitaine at the age of 15	The fortified Château de Beynac is constructed at Beynac-et-Cazenac	Henry Plantagenet, Duke of Anjou and Normandy, later Henry II, marries Eleanor of Aquitaine in Poitiers cathedral	Henry Plantagenet succeeds to the English throne and the region comes under English rule, ushering in a golden age of prosperity

Anjou and Normandy in addition to Eleanor's possessions. This in itself was a disastrous blow to the Capetians, but it was compounded in 1154 when Henry succeeded to the English throne (as Henry II). As a result, almost half of France fell under English rule. Much of it would remain so for the next three hundred years.

For the southwest region itself, however, English rule ushered in a period of peace, stability and impressive economic progress. With the major exception of **Richard the Lionheart** (Richard Coeur de Lion), Eleanor's third son, who plundered the area ruthlessly, the **English overlords** proved to be popular. For the most part they ruled from a distance, often preferring to stay put in England, and ensured the loyalty of their southern subjects by granting a large degree of independence to many of Aquitaine's rapidly growing towns and their local lords. Peasants lived under relatively privileged feudal conditions, helped by the fact that local lords were often in competition for their services. An important factor here was the building of dozens of **new towns**, the *bastides*, designed to secure border areas and accommodate the rapidly expanding population. In order to attract peasants to inhabit the new towns and cultivate the surrounding land, feudal lords had to offer enticing terms and considerable freedom.

The region continued to produce wheat and oats, but the real sensation of the era of English rule was the transformation of **wine** production into a lucrative and international industry. Merchants exporting the claret beloved of the English to London and other British ports grew wealthy, and the proceeds filtered through to the whole region. **Urban life**, too, began to take off, with the towns of Périgueux, Bergerac and Sarlat growing to populations of around five thousand each.

As English rule was delivered from across the Channel and therefore somewhat removed, it did not mean any perceptible invasion by the English language. On the contrary, independence from northern France allowed local language and culture to flourish, creating perfect conditions for the high-culture phenomenon of the **troubadours** (see box opposite).

The Cathar crusades

While the English ruled in Aquitaine, an audacious bid for independence from the political and religious dictats of the French Crown was also being made over to the east, by the powerful **counts of Toulouse**. From the mid-twelfth century on, the so-called **Cathars** (also known as Albigensians) had won a great deal of support in the area, which extended as far as the Dordogne valley, by preaching that the material world was created by the Devil and the spiritual world by a benevolent God. They also believed in reincarnation and that the only way to escape the mortal coil was to lead a life of saintly self-denial – all of which completely undermined the role of the clergy. To put an end to such **heresy**, Pope Innocent III unleashed a **crusade** against the Cathars in 1209, starting off with a particularly murderous attack led by **Simon de Montfort** in which the entire population of the Mediterranean town of Béziers, estimated at twenty thousand people, was slaughtered; the papal legate in charge of the assault is famously supposed to have proclaimed, "Kill them all. God will know his own."

A series of crusading armies, composed largely of land-hungry northern nobles, then proceeded to rampage through the region on and off for the next twenty years. This was followed by an equally vicious **inquisition** designed to mop up any remaining Cathars, which culminated in the siege of Montségur, in the eastern foothills of the Pyrenees, in 1244, when two hundred people were burnt alive.

1166	June 11 1183	Mid-12th century
A perfectly preserved body discovered in a cave in the Quercy is declared to be St Amadour. Rocamadour sanctuary is built around it	Henry the Young King dies at Martel, days after ransacking the holy shrines at Rocamadour	Cathars begin to spread through the region

As a result of the Cathar crusades, the French Crown now held sway over the whole of southwestern France, including Toulouse. The new count of Toulouse was **Alphonse de Poitiers**, brother of the future Louis IX, whose lands stretched north through Quercy into Périgord, and west along the Garonne as far as Agen. Like his English neighbours, Alphonse started establishing a rash of *bastides* in order to impose his authority over his new domains.

The Hundred Years War

Though the English had lost their possessions north of the Loire by the mid-thirteenth century, they remained a perpetual thorn in the side of the French kings thanks to their grip on Aquitaine. Skirmishes took place throughout the century, followed by various peace treaties, one of which, in 1259, took Quercy and Périgord back into the English domain. But the spark that ignited the ruinous – and misnamed – **Hundred Years War** (1337–1453) was a Capetian succession crisis. When the last of the line, Charles IV, died without an heir in 1328, the English king, **Edward III**, leapt in to claim the throne of France for himself. It went instead to Charles's cousin, **Philippe de Valois**. Edward acquiesced for a time, but when Philippe began whittling away at English possessions in Aquitaine, Edward renewed his claim and embarked on a war.

The major battles of the war were almost all fought in the northern half of the country, where Edward won an outright victory at **Crécy**, before his son, the **Black Prince**, took the French king, Jean le Bon, prisoner at the Battle of Poitiers in 1356 and established a capital at Bordeaux. The resulting treaty appeared to give the English victory, but the French fought back, banishing the English entirely but for a toehold in Bordeaux. In 1415, though, the tables turned again as Henry V inflicted a crushing

THE LANGUAGE OF LOVE

The **troubadours**, poets and musicians of the twelfth century, were early pioneers of Western Europe's cultural renaissance. Their love poetry, written in **Occitan**, elevated the vernacular of the rural peasantry to the status of high culture and, for the first time since Roman occupation, language was used for something other than essential, practical communication. Troubadour poems focus on courtly love, an idealized, noble emotion which might be romantic, tender, familiar, feudal, patriotic – or, in the best poems, a combination of all these. Thus the Troubadours not only reintroduced art to the region, they also gave it a linguistic and cultural identity – when troubadours talk about their *pays*, they do not mean France as a whole, just the southwest.

The aggressive campaign of unification and standardization waged by the state following the 1789 revolution outlawed the everyday use of the Occitan **language**, causing its gradual disappearance as a native tongue. It continued to inspire poets, however, most notably **Frédéric Mistral**, an early winner of the Nobel Prize for literature, who wrote in Occitan. Today, the language described in 1900 by the visionary politician Jean Jaurès as "a noble language of courtship, poetry and art", is being revived. Basing their strategy on the models for the revival of the Welsh and Irish languages, regional authorities have established a number of Occitan-speaking **schools**, known as *Calandretas*, including one in Périgueux, while local colleges (roughly equivalent to an English secondary school) also offer Occitan as one of their language options. The Toulouse-based newspaper *Dépêche du Midi* prints a regular column in Occitan.

1209	1244	1250
Simon de Montfort leads the first crusade against the Cathars	The siege and surrender of the last Cathar stronghold at Montségur sees 200 people burnt alive	Alphonse de Poitiers, count of Toulouse, begins a massive *bastide*-building programme, including Monflanquin, Cordes, Najac and Ste-Foy-la-Grande

CHURCHES AND CASTLES: THE VIEILLES PIERRES OF PÉRIGORD

In spite of the many conflicts that have ravaged the countryside since the Middle Ages, the Dordogne and Lot region has preserved an impressive wealth of medieval **churches**, at the heart of almost every village in some areas; while the many **castles** (aka **châteaux**) seem to crown the crest of every hill, especially along the golden stretch of the Dordogne valley.

CHURCHES

Few traces now remain of the earliest churches, one exception being in St-Front in Périgueux, where the enthusiastic nineteenth-century restoration conceals traces of the original chapel built by bishop Chronope (see p.289) in the early sixth century. The region's golden age for church-building, however, came in the twelfth and thirteenth centuries, when the style of architecture and sculpture known as **Romanesque** (or sometimes Norman, in England) was dominant. In terms of architecture, these churches are characterized by round arches, sometimes domes (particularly in the Périgord region) and simple, graceful lines, but the highlights are often the sculptures that adorn the key structural points: the tympanum above the main entrance, the capitals at the top of supporting pillars, the keystones in their vaults – these all formed a blank canvas for craftsmen to forge the most beautifully humane and unglorified depictions of saints, prophets and biblical stories. In no other architectural style are religious teachings so organically integrated into the physical structure of the church. The best examples include the churches in Souillac (see p.170) and Beaulieu (see p.188), in the upper reaches of the Dordogne, and the world-famous cloister at Moissac (see p.261) in the Tarn valley, but it's the range and variety of styles, from the Byzantine touches in Périgueux and Souillac to the unembellished purity, almost austerity, of the church at Cadouin (see p.114), which make the region such a goldmine.

Rarer, but of all the more interest for that, are the region's **Gothic** edifices. While in Romanesque architecture the charm lies in the detail, evoking a humble down-to-earth spirituality, in Gothic buildings it's the soaring, awe-inspiring ensemble that appeals, embodying a sense of elevation to a higher realm.

CASTLES

While the Hundred Years War was raging, it was said that "towns were loyal to the king; castles were a law unto themselves." In both the conflict between the French and English and the later religious wars, the region's powerful families sought to strengthen their own positions and independence by fortifying their residences into grand châteaux.

Invariably built on high ground, for strategic reasons, many castles would originally have covered a large area, with entire villages enclosed within their walls. In most cases, they were destroyed or dismantled when captured during various wars, so today it is often just a ruined keep that remains. From a military perspective, two of the most satisfying are those at Beynac (see p.156) and Castelnaud (see p.158), squaring up to each other across the Dordogne river and offering commanding views over the surrounding countryside. For romance, it's hard to beat the rugged keep of Najac (see p.283) rising above the village, shrouded in mist. In more peaceful centuries, the region's aristocracy set about making their residences more comfortable, and places like the Château de Hautefort (see p.73) combined impregnability with stately grandeur, lavish furnishings and extravagant interior design.

In many cases, buildings were designed to serve both a religious purpose and a military one. The churches at Rocamadour (see p.175), St-Amand-de-Coly (see p.150) and Beaumont (see p.112), to name just three, are notable for their imposing, fortified walls and slit windows, revealing them as buildings designed not just for worship, but also to be defended.

June 17 1308	**1332**	**October 25 1415**	**1429**
Construction of the Pont Valentré begins in Cahors	Edward III of England claims the French throne and sparks the Hundred Years War	Henry V of England inflicts a crushing defeat on the French army at Agincourt	Jeanne d'Arc, the maid of Orléans, rallies the French troops

defeat on the French army, against all odds, at the legendary battle of **Agincourt**. Once again, France seemed on the verge of unravelling at the seams, until **Jeanne d'Arc** (Joan of Arc) arrived on the scene. In 1429 she rallied the demoralized French troops, broke the English siege at Orléans and tipped the scales against the invaders. The English were slowly but surely driven back to their southwest heartland until even that was lost at the **Battle of Castillon** in 1453. Within months, the English surrendered Bordeaux, and their centuries-long adventure in France came to an end.

Although Castillon was the only major battle fought in the southwest, the region did not spare itself from **bloodshed**. The region's powerful families, operating from their fortified bases (see box opposite), sought to take advantage of the general chaos by attacking their neighbours and trying to strengthen their own hands. Many nobles swapped sides repeatedly, fighting under English or French colours as it suited them. **Raymond de Montaut**, for example, a powerful baron based in Mussidan, initially swore allegiance to the French Crown, but then fought with the English in the sieges of Bourdeilles (1369) and Limoges (1370). Only when he was captured by the French did he conveniently rediscover his patriotic sentiment and transfer his allegiance back. Most towns and castles were attacked at some point and many changed hands on numerous occasions, either by treaty or force. By the end of the war, farms and villages lay abandoned and roving bands of **brigands** terrorized the countryside, having abandoned all pretence of fighting for one side or the other. The population had been reduced by roughly a half to under twelve million, partly by warfare, but largely through famine and disease; millions died as the bubonic **plague** repeatedly swept through France during the fourteenth and fifteenth centuries.

Gradually the nightmare ended. Though the south now had to kow-tow to the hated northerners – the counts of Périgord were particularly big losers, having their land and privileges confiscated by the Crown – Louis XI proved to be an astute ruler who allowed some of the privileges granted by the English to remain. Trade – particularly in wine – began to revive, towns were rebuilt and land brought back into production.

The Wars of Religion

In the early sixteenth century the ideas, art and architecture of the **Renaissance** began to penetrate France. As elsewhere in Europe, the Renaissance had a profound influence on every aspect of life, engendering a new optimism and spirit of enquiry that appealed in particular to the new class of wealthy merchants. At the same time, increased trade and improved communications, including the invention of the printing press, helped disseminate ideas throughout Europe. Among them came the new **Protestant** message espoused by Martin Luther and John Calvin that the individual was responsible to God alone and not to the Church.

Such ideas gained widespread adherence throughout France, partly feeding on resentment toward a Catholic clergy who were often seen as closely linked to the oppressive feudal regime, but mainly because a handful of powerful families converted and, where the feudal overlord led, his subjects were bound to follow. On the national scale, the most significant families to convert were those of the **Bourbon-d'Albret** royal dynasty. In the southwest, the first Protestant (also known as **Huguenot**) enclaves were at Ste-Foy-la-Grande and Bergerac in the 1540s, followed soon after by Nérac, the fief of the **d'Albret** family (see p.259). As the Protestant faith took hold and Catholics felt

July 17 1453	**February 28 1533**	**August 23 1572**
The crucial battle of Castillon effectively ends the Hundred Years War and with it English rule in southwest France	Michel de Montaigne, influential "Father of the Essay", is born in the Dordogne region	The St Bartholomew's Day massacre sees some 3000 people killed in Paris

increasingly threatened, the sporadic brutal attempts to stamp out Protestantism, such as a massacre in Cahors in 1560, erupted two years later into a series of bitter civil wars. Interspersed with ineffective truces and accords, the **Wars of Religion** lasted for the next thirty years.

On the Catholic side, a powerful lobbying group of traditionalists, organized mainly by the **de Guise** family, led an army against the Huguenots, who were in turn marshalled by **Admiral de Coligny**. The two armies toured northern France, occasionally clashing directly, but more often capturing and converting towns that had taken one side or the other. The duc de Guise was murdered in 1563, an act for which his allies held Coligny responsible. And in 1572, Coligny was among the victims of the war's bloodiest and most notorious date: the **St Bartholomew's Day Massacre**, when some three thousand Protestants, gathered in Paris for the wedding of Protestant **Henri d'Albret** to Marguerite de Valois, the sister of Henry III of France, were slaughtered.

Just as in earlier conflicts, the nationwide dispute was used as a pretext by **powerful families** in the southwest to consolidate their positions. Once again, private armies roamed the region, vying with each other in their savagery, but with only vaguely religious motives. Before his death, Coligny famously complained of Huguenot generals in the southwest who took no interest in the wider struggle and "refused to fight unless they could turn around and see their own chimney". One such general was the impulsive and ingenious **Geoffroi de Vivans**, who even succeeded in briefly capturing the staunchly Catholic towns of Sarlat and Périgueux. One of his most daring exploits, in 1588, involved hiding out in the caves beneath the hilltop town of Domme (see p.162) before scaling the formidable cliffs at dawn and taking the town with only a handful of men.

Some towns were attacked and changed hands repeatedly, either through violence or as a result of various **truces**, by which they were nominally declared either Catholic or Protestant. In reality, the majority of ordinary people, though cruelly affected by the fighting, saw little impact on their **notions of religion**, which remained a hotch-potch of rural paganism and local folklore, with only hints of orthodox Christianity, until several centuries later.

A twist of fate signalled the beginning of the end of the conflicts, when Henri d'Albret – king of Navarre and leader of the Protestant army – became heir to the French throne when Henry III's son died in 1584. Five years later, Henry III himself was dead, leaving a tricky problem, since a Protestant could not be king. After trying to seize the crown by force, Henri d'Albret eventually abjured his faith and became **Henry IV** of France. "Paris is worth a Mass," he is reputed to have said.

Once on the throne, Henry IV set about reconstructing and reconciling his kingdom. Under the visionary **Edict of Nantes** of 1598 the Protestants were accorded freedom of conscience, freedom of worship in specified places, the right to attend the same schools and hold the same offices as Catholics, their own courts and the possession of a number of fortresses, including Montauban, as a guarantee against renewed attack.

The stirrings of discontent

The Dordogne and Lot region had barely drawn breath after the end of the Wars of Religion when a different type of conflict erupted – this time one whose causes the ordinary peasantry could identify with all too easily. The countryside lay in ruins and the

1589	May 1637	1643	July 14 1789
Protestant Henri Bourbon d'Albret abjures his faith and is crowned Henry IV of France	A crushing defeat at Sauvetat-du-Dropt leads to the execution of peasant leaders	Louis XIV, the Sun King, begins his long reign, exerting increasing control over the southwest	Storming of the Bastille in Paris sows the seeds of Revolution

cost of the wars and rebuilding fell squarely on their shoulders. Ruinous taxes, a series of bad harvests, high prices and yet more outbreaks of the plague combined to push them over the edge in the late sixteenth century. There were **peasant rebellions** in Normandy and Brittany, but the worst of the "**Croquants'**" (yokels') uprisings broke out in the southwest. The first major revolt occurred in the winter of 1593, when a number of towns and castles, including Monpazier, Excideuil and Puy-l'Évêque, were attacked. After two years of skirmishes, nobles pulled together an army in 1595 and the rebellion was quickly and savagely put down by the allied forces of the local nobility. The same grievances resurfaced in more uprisings in May 1637, however, no doubt nourished in part by tales of the earlier failed rebellion, passed down by word of mouth from generation to generation. This time, the revolt was altogether more serious. In the face of one tax demand too many, a ten-thousand-strong **peasant army** tried unsuccessfully to seize Périgueux. Instead, they took Bergerac and then marched on Bordeaux. They were stopped, however, at Ste-Foy-la-Grande and the final show-down took place soon after against 3400 royal troops at La Sauvetat-du-Dropt, south of Bergerac, leaving at least a thousand Croquants dead. The leaders were executed, one in Monpazier (see p.246), while the surviving rebels returned to the land.

Thereafter, the long reign of **Louis XIV** (1643–1715) saw the French Crown and Catholic religion begin to reassert control over the southwest. With the exception of the **Frondes** (of 1648–52), when aristocrats joined the lower classes in rebelling against royal taxes and when the army had to be brought in to crush demonstrations in Bordeaux, the state successfully reinstated military and feudal control. At the same time, the bishops of Sarlat and Périgueux set about the "Vendange des Âmes", the **Harvesting of Souls**, an aggressive campaign designed to eradicate strongholds of the Protestant faith. Protestant towns such as Bergerac were seized by the Catholics and Protestant rights were gradually eroded until in 1685 Louis revoked the Edict of Nantes, forbade Protestant worship and set about trying to eliminate the faith completely. Orders were given for the destruction of Protestant churches and of the castles of its most fervent supporters. Thousands of Protestants fled the southwest for the safety of the Netherlands, Germany and England.

At the same time, France began to establish a **colonial empire** in North America, Africa, India and the Caribbean, and, as trade from these places started to grow in the early eighteenth century, so Bordeaux and the other Atlantic ports prospered, in a so-called **golden age.**

Revolution

For the majority of people, however, little had changed. The gap between rich and poor grew ever wider as the clergy and aristocracy clung onto their privileges and the peasants were squeezed for higher taxes. Their general misery was exacerbated by a catastrophic harvest in 1788, followed by a particularly severe winter. Bread prices rocketed and on July 14, 1789, a mob stormed the **Bastille** in Paris, a hated symbol of the oppressive regime. As the **Revolution** spread, similar insurrections occurred throughout the country, accompanied by widespread peasant attacks on landowners' châteaux and the destruction of tax and rent records. In August the new National Assembly abolished the feudal rights and privileges of the nobility and then went on to nationalize Church lands.

1790	**1792**	**1799**	**1808**
Creation of the modern *départements* of Dordogne, Lot and Tarn and Garonne, named after their major rivers	Declaration of the First Republic	Napoleon Bonaparte seizes power, declaring himself emperor in 1804	Napoleon invades Spain, sparking the Peninsular War

In these early stages the general population of the southwest supported the Revolution. However, as the Parisian revolutionaries grew increasingly radical and proposed ever more centralization of power they found themselves in bitter opposition. Towards the end of 1792, as the **First Republic** was being declared, they finally lost out to the extremists and in October the following year **the Terror** was unleashed as mass executions took place throughout France; estimates run to three thousand in Paris and 14,000 in the regions.

Though revolutionary bands wrought a fair amount of havoc in the southwest, looting and burning castles and churches, hacking away at coats of arms and religious statuary, on the whole the region escaped fairly lightly; many aristocrats simply fled and their possessions were sold off at knock-down prices. Among many administrative changes following the Revolution, one of the most significant was the creation of **départements** in 1790 to replace the old provinces. Thus began yet another attempt at national unification, accompanied by efforts to draw the traditionally independent southwest into mainstream France. The campaign continued in the nineteenth century with moves to stamp out Occitan and other regional dialects (see box, p.293).

From Napoleon I to the Third Republic

By the end of 1794, more moderate forces were in charge in Paris. However, continuous infighting left the way open for **Napoleon Bonaparte**, who had made a name for himself as commander of the Revolutionary armies in Italy and Egypt, to seize power in a coup d'état in 1799. Napoleon quickly restored order and continued the process of centralization, replacing the power of local institutions by appointing a *préfet* to each *département* answerable only to the **emperor**, as Napoleon declared himself in 1804. Nevertheless, the Dordogne and Lot *départements* supported the new regime by providing many military leaders – and more lowly troops – for Bonaparte's armies: the most notable examples were Périgueux's Baron Pierre Daumesnil (see box, p.52) and Joachim Murat (1767–1815), the son of a village innkeeper near Cahors, who was proclaimed king of Naples in reward for his numerous military successes. As elsewhere, however, it was the burden of the unceasing **Napoleonic wars** that cost the emperor his support. The economy of Bordeaux in particular and the southwest in general was hard hit when Napoleon banned commerce with Britain, to which Britain responded by blockading French ports in 1807.

Few tears were shed in the region when Napoleon was finally defeated in 1815 at the **Battle of Waterloo**. The subsequent restoration of the **monarchy**, on the other hand, saw opinions divided along predictable lines: the aristocracy and the emerging *bourgeoisie* (the middle classes) rallied to the king, while the working population supported the uprising in 1848 – a shorter and less virulent reprise of the 1789 Revolution – which ended in the declaration of the **Second Republic**. The new government started off well by setting up national workshops to relieve unemployment and extending the vote to all adult males – an unprecedented move for its time. But in elections held later in 1848 the largely conservative vote of the newly enfranchised peasants was sufficient to outweigh the urban, working-class radicals. To everyone's surprise, Louis-Napoléon, nephew of the former emperor, romped home. In spite of his liberal reputation, he restricted the vote again, censored the press and pandered to the Catholic Church. In 1852, following a coup and further street fighting, he had himself proclaimed **Emperor Napoléon III**.

June 17–18 1815	1822	1852		1870
Napoleon is narrowly defeated by Wellington in the Battle of Waterloo	Jean-François Champollion translates the hieroglyphs on the Rosetta Stone	The Garonne Canal is opened	Napoléon III is declared emperor	Cahors-born statesman, Léon Gambetta, crafts the Third Republic

Like his uncle, Napoléon III pursued an expansionist military policy, both in France's colonial empire and in Europe. And also like his uncle, this brought about his downfall. Napoléon III declared war on Prussia in 1870 and was quickly and roundly defeated by the far superior Prussian army. When Napoléon was taken prisoner the politicians in Paris – Cahors' Léon Gambetta among them (see box, p.205) – quickly proclaimed the **Third Republic**. Though it experienced a difficult birth, the Third Republic survived until 1940.

Into the twentieth century

Napoléon was more successful on the economic front, however. From the 1850s on, France experienced rapid **industrial growth**, while foreign trade trebled. The effect on the Dordogne and Lot region, however, was mixed.

The towns along the region's great rivers benefited most from the economic recovery. Although the region had no coal or mineral resources to stimulate large-scale industrialization (beyond metalworking around Fumel), industries were established along the navigable rivers – tanneries, paper mills, textile and glass industries. At the same time, agricultural areas within easy access of the rivers grew wealthy from exporting wheat, wine and tobacco. Many towns were given a facelift, with their ramparts torn down, wide avenues sliced through the cramped medieval quarters and a start made on improving sanitation and water supply. Transport was also modernized, although the **railways** came late to the Dordogne–Paris and Lot and were never very extensive. The region's first railway, the Bordeaux–Paris line, was completed in 1851, while the following year saw the opening of the **Canal latéral** (now the Garonne Canal), linking the Garonne with the Canal du Midi and thus the Mediterranean.

All this created pockets of economic growth, but the **rural areas** in between became increasingly marginalized. Local industries dwindled in the face of competition from cheap manufactured goods and imports, while the railways simply provided the means for people to quit the country for the cities.

But by far the biggest single crisis to hit the area's rural economy in the late nineteenth century was **phylloxera**. The parasite, which attacks the roots of vines, wiped out almost one third of the region's vineyards in the 1870s and 1880s. For a while growers tried all sorts of remedies, from flooding the fields to chemical fumigation, before it was discovered that vines in America, where phylloxera originated, were immune and that by grafting French vines onto American root-stock it was possible to produce resistant plants. The vineyards were slowly re-established, but over a much smaller area. Many farmers turned to alternative crops, such as tobacco around Bergerac and sheep-rearing on the *causse* above Cahors.

The world wars

Such problems paled into insignificance, however, when German troops marched into northern France following the outbreak of **World War I** in 1914. The French government fled south to Bordeaux while thousands of southern men trekked north to lose their lives in the mud and horror of Verdun and the Somme battlefields. By the time the Germans were forced to surrender in 1918, the cost to France was 1.3 million dead,

1870–85	1914	1926	1939
Phylloxera wipes out vast swathes of the region's vine stock	Outbreak of WWI. Thousands of youths from the southwest march north to battle, losing their lives in Flanders fields	The caves of Pech-Merle open to the public	Outbreak of WWII

a quarter of whom were under 25 years of age, and three million wounded. Every town and village in the Dordogne and Lot, as elsewhere in France, has its sad war memorial recording the loss of this generation of young men.

In the aftermath of the war, agricultural and industrial production declined and the birth rate plummeted, although this was offset to some extent in the southwest by an influx of land-hungry refugees from Spain in the late nineteenth century and from Italy in the first decades of the twentieth. The French government lurched from crisis to crisis while events across the border in Germany became increasingly menacing.

In April 1940, eight months after the outbreak of **World War II**, Hitler's western offensive began as he overran Belgium, Denmark and Holland. In June the French government retreated to Bordeaux again and millions of refugees poured south as Paris fell to the Germans. **Maréchal Pétain**, a conservative 84-year-old veteran of World War I, emerged from retirement to sign an armistice with Hitler and head the collaborationist **Vichy government**, based in the spa town of Vichy in the northern foothills of the Massif Central. France was now split in two. The Germans occupied the strategic regions north of the Loire and all along the Atlantic coast, including Bordeaux, while Vichy ostensibly governed the "Free Zone" comprising the majority of southern France. The frontier, with its customs points and guardposts, ran from the Pyrenees north through Langon and Castillon-la-Bataille to just south of Tours, and from there cut east to Geneva. Then, in 1942, German troops moved south to occupy the whole of France until they were driven out by Britain, America and their allies after 1944.

Resistance to the German occupation didn't really get going until 1943 when **General de Gaulle**, exiled leader of the "Free French", sent **Jean Moulin** to unify the disparate and often ideologically opposed Resistance groups. Moulin was soon captured by the Gestapo and tortured to death by Klaus Barbie – the infamous "Butcher of Lyon", who was convicted as recently as 1987 for his war crimes – but the network Moulin established became increasingly effective. Its members provided information to the Allies and blew up train tracks, bridges and factories. They undertook daring raids into enemy-held towns; and the high, empty uplands of the Dordogne and Lot *départements* afforded safe bases for many Resistance fighters. But for every action, the Germans hit back with savage **reprisals**. In May 1944 the SS Das Reich division, based at Montauban, set out to break the local resistance by massacring civilians and torching houses in some twenty towns and villages; the worst atrocities took place in Terrasson-la-Villedieu, Montpezat-de-Quercy, Mussidan and Frayssinet-le-Gélat.

Soon afterwards the Germans were being driven out, but the fighting didn't stop there. In the weeks following **liberation** thousands of **collaborators** were executed or publicly humiliated – women accused of consorting with the enemy had their heads shaved and were sometimes paraded naked through the streets. Not surprisingly, the issue of collaboration left deep scars in rural communities throughout the region, a bitterness which occasionally surfaces to this day in local disputes.

Into the new millennium

The issues that have dominated the last fifty years continue to remain paramount in the Dordogne and Lot. One of the main themes, as in much of rural France, has been that of **depopulation**. On average there are now 25 percent fewer people living on the

1940	September 12 1940	February 1956	1961
Josephine Baker moves to Château Milandes in the Dordogne	The prehistoric cave paintings at Lascaux are discovered by four teenagers	Severe and prolonged frost devastates Cahors vineyards, necessitating a mass replanting	After centuries of mixed produce and livestock, the first market exclusively for truffles is established in Lalbenque

land than at the end of the nineteenth century, rising to thirty percent or more in the worst-hit areas, such as parts of Lot-et-Garonne. Once again this has been partly offset by immigration, in this case by *pieds noirs* – French colonialists forced to flee Algeria after independence in 1962 – many of whom settled on farms in the southwest; and by north Europeans in search of the good life. Agricultural production is in slow decline as the younger generation leave the land, though this has partly been offset by a massive push towards mechanization and the amalgamation of small farms into larger, more efficient holdings – albeit often propped up by subsidies from the European Union.

Agriculture remains the backbone of the region's economy, notably wine production but also poultry, maize, fruit, tobacco, fishing and forestry. Cahors alone has 42 square kilometres planted with AOP (recently changed from the old AOC status) vines. Agen is also known for pharmaceuticals, while other main towns such as Périgueux, Figeac, Montauban, Fumel and Villeneuve-sur-Lot boast modest industrial sectors.

Besides agriculture and industry, **tourism** plays an increasingly important role in the regional economy. In recent years an enormous effort has gone into improving facilities and marketing the region, not just the honeypot attractions of Sarlat, Les Ezyies and the Dordogne valley châteaux, but also in the successful promotion of "green holidays", tempting people away from the Mediterranean and Atlantic coasts to discover all that the countryside has to offer. One of the largest such projects was the reopening of the River Lot and the Garonne Canal to navigation, but at a local level almost every town and village now puts on a programme of summer events to lure visitors.

Across France, however, the economy continues to be hampered by the seemingly perpetual stand-off between advocates of economic reform to liberalize markets and stimulate growth, and uncompromising defenders of the **"French Model"**, with generous social allowances and high job security. Almost every section of society seems to have seen this debate come its way in recent years: from teachers to car manufacturers, employees in all industries have taken action to block any reforms which might erode their privileges. Perhaps most emblematic of the battle lines was the controversy in 2006 surrounding the government's attempt to introduce the **CPE** or "First Employment Contract", aimed at encouraging the employment of young people by making them less costly to hire/employ (with fewer social security benefits and no guarantee that they would be kept on after two years). The intended beneficiaries, however, were less than grateful, and took to the streets in their thousands to protest against the new contract, arguing that it was the first step towards the hire-and-fire culture reviled in left-wing French circles.

In the **2007 presidential election**, it seemed as though momentum was swinging behind the arguments of the economic reformers, as former interior minister **Nicolas Sarkozy**, a member of the centre-right UMP party, was elected president having campaigned for a hard-line "rupture" with the French Model. In power, however, he only fitfully pursued a free-market agenda.

Economic crisis and political swing
The **financial crisis** of 2008–09 hit manufacturing across France badly, and its effect in the Dordogne and Lot region was most strongly felt in the wine industry, with a partial collapse of prices and plummeting export sales. House prices took a nosedive too, sending many estate agents to the wall. In the light of the general discrediting of liberal capitalism,

1971	1992	2004	May 2007	2008
Cahors wine is awarded AOC status	Treaty of Maastricht; the European Union is born	Musée National de la Préhistoire opens in Les Eyzies	Nicolas Sarkozy elected president of France	Financial crisis hits the region, property prices drop and exchange rates fluctuate, forcing many British residents to return to the UK

Sarkozy shrewdly abandoned his rupturist rhetoric in favour of a new-found pride in the traditional French system. This impeccable tactical U-turn left the Socialist opposition lost for words and floundering in the polls: the **2009 European elections** saw Sarkozy's party come out on top with 28 percent of the vote, while across France, including in the southwest region, the Socialists were pushed into third place behind a green alliance – "Europe Ecologie" – led by Daniel Cohn-Bendit, familiar as the youthful leader of the 1968 student uprising. By 2012, however, the power pendulum had swung the other way, with the Socialists once again claiming massive victories in the polls, especially in the southwest. **François Hollande** was elected president, promising to beat the recession by taxing wealthier citizens and larger corporations while separating risky investment-banking enterprises from retail.

As Hollande neared the end of his first term, however, many felt his government had largely failed to deliver on its pledges – and by the middle of 2016, Hollande could only scrape up seventeen percent approval ratings in the polls, making him the most unpopular president in modern French history. **Presidential elections** are due in May 2017, and unless things change radically for the Socialists, it seems likely that the battle for the presidency will be between Marine le Pen of the far-right **Front National** party and the renamed centre-right **Les Républicains** (formerly the UMP); most expect the latter to clinch it, under the hardline **François Fillon**, Nicolas Sarkozy's former prime minister, who knocked both his old boss and former Bordeaux mayor **Alain Juppe** out of the leadership race in late 2016.

Into the future

After an economically rough few years, things had started to look a little brighter by 2015, with tourism in the Dordogne and Lot on the rebound. Then, between January 2015 and July 2016, three Islamic **terrorist strikes** (and a fourth in neighbouring Belgium) hit France. Although the atrocities were geographically remote from the Dordogne and Lot, the impact on tourism was immediate and hoteliers reported significant dips in bookings across the region.

The world's economic woes have also complicated the situation of the thousands of **British residents** in the Dordogne and Lot. Since the 1960s, low property prices, coupled with beautiful scenery and an enviable lifestyle, have attracted Brits, Dutch and other northern Europeans to settle here. However, volatile exchange rates and devalued savings and investments have caused some call the biggest British exodus from France since Dunkirk. The situation was further compounded by the June 2016 **Brexit** vote, which has had its own negative impact in the Dordogne and Lot. The terms of the UK's withdrawal from the EU were yet to be agreed at the time of writing, but the fear is that with the heightened bureaucracy of living in France as a non-EU citizen, alongside the falling value of the pound against the euro and the resultant hike in costs for those reliant on UK-based salaries or pensions, many more expats will be forced to sell up and return to the UK. This departure of British residents could have a significant economic impact upon the numerous villages in the Dordogne and Lot which have been revitalised by the expat community. Despite this uncertainty, the region today retains its strong sense of identity and a deep-burning pride in the land, its produce and its traditions, which will doubtless continue unabated.

May 2012	July 2012	Jan 2015–July 2016	December 2016
François Hollande elected president of France	The Dordogne valley named a UNESCO biosphere reserve	Three terror attacks hit France and tourism is badly affected	The high-tech Lascaux VI complex opens close to the original caves

Books

There are few English-language history books specifically devoted to the
Dordogne and Lot region, and a bit of a dearth of novels, whether in French or
in translation. A few of those that do exist – and are worth recommending –
are detailed below, along with a number of general history books and classic
texts which provide the background to events that have occurred in the region.
The best books in this selection are marked by a ★ symbol.

HISTORY & BIOGRAPHY

Marc Bloch *Strange Defeat*. Moving personal study of the reasons for France's defeat in 1940 and subsequent caving-in to Fascism. Found among the papers of this Sorbonne historian after his death at the hands of the Gestapo in 1942.

Lynn Haney *Naked at the Feast*. A lively warts-and-all biography of the cabaret star Josephine Baker (see box, p.161), which traces the many setbacks and comebacks of her rags-to-riches tale, getting across her amazing charisma and just why France took her to its heart.

Colin Jones *The Cambridge Illustrated History of France*. A political and social history of France from prehistoric times to the mid-1990s, concentrating on issues of regionalism, gender, race and class. Good illustrations and an easy, unacademic writing style.

★ **Don and Petie Kladstrup** *Wine & War*. The role of wine in World War II and the often courageous and ingenious strategies used to prevent the best wines from being plundered by the German army; fascinating reading.

Marion Meade *Eleanor of Aquitaine*. Highly accessible biography of one of the key characters in twelfth-century Europe. The author fleshes out the documented events until they read more like a historical novel.

Ian Ousby *Occupation: The Ordeal of France 1940–1944*. Somewhat revisionist 1997 account looking at how widespread collaboration was and why it took so long for the Resistance to get organized.

★ **Graham Robb** *The Discovery of France*. A fascinating alternative history of France, in which Robb goes in search of the reality of life for the provincial, rural majority ignored by the currents of history, before recounting the way in which the nineteenth century saw this other France gradually discovered and "civilized". Contains some excellent sections on the southwest.

Anne-Marie Walters *Moondrop to Gascony*. An absorbing and spine-tingling account of the real life of a secret agent in World War II; written in the immediate aftermath of the war, it reveals the naked courage of the French Resistance.

★ **Alison Weir** *Eleanor of Aquitaine: By the wrath of God, Queen of England*. A magnificent medieval pot pourri of romantic events that vividly chronicles the extraordinary life of this fascinating woman. Contains some interesting photographs, including one of the effigy on Eleanor's tomb at Fontevrault abbey, the only verifiable image of her still in existence.

★ **Theodore Zeldin** *The French*. Urbane and witty survey of the French world view – chapter titles include "How to be chic" and "How to appreciate a grandmother".

TRAVEL, ART AND LITERATURE

Patricia Atkinson *The Ripening Sun*. The ultimately uplifting tale of an Englishwoman who struggles against all kinds of adversity to establish a well-respected vineyard near Bergerac.

★ **Michael Brown** *Down the Dordogne*. In the late 1980s, Michael Brown fulfilled a long-held ambition to follow the Dordogne from its source in the Massif Central to the Gironde estuary. The story of his journey – on foot, by canoe and bicycle – provides a lyrical introduction to the region.

Elizabeth Chadwick *Daughters of the Grail*. This compelling novel offers an insightful glimpse into the little-known world of the much persecuted Cathars. Set in thirteenth-century southwest France the succession of heroines battle with their beliefs, Catholic prejudice and eventually with the merciless Simon de Montfort.

★ **André Chastel** *French Art*. Authoritative three-volume study by one of France's leading art historians. Discusses individual works of art – from architecture to tapestry, as well as painting – in detail in an attempt to locate the Frenchness of French art. With glossy photographs and serious-minded but readable text.

Angela Clarke *Dark Secrets of the Dordogne*. Easy to read, satirical take on the British expat life in southwest France, but with the added twist of a murder-mystery tale.

★ **Arthur Conan-Doyle** *The White Company*. A far cry from Sherlock Holmes, here Conan-Doyle turns his talents to historical fiction, depicting a Hundred Years War where the English have hearts of gold and all the rest are jolly rotters.

Eugène Le Roy *Jacquou le Croquant*. This novel is one of the most important chronicles of the hardship of rural life in nineteenth-century France. The action takes place in the forest and villages around Montignac, home of the hero Jacquou who leads a vengeful revolt against the tyrannical local feudal lord.

Christian Signol *La Rivière Espérance*. Set in the 1830s, this French novel – which was made into a hugely successful TV film – follows the adventures of a young sailor working the *gabares* that then plied the Dordogne. This nostalgic tale commemorates the end of an era as the railways relentlessly destroy the romanticized river life.

★ **Ruth Silvestre** *A House in the Sunflowers*. There are any number of books about Brits upping sticks and moving to France to renovate a ruin. Most are none-too impressive but this is a cut above the rest. Set in the Lot and Garonne, it's the first in a trilogy that also includes *A Harvest of Sunflowers* and *Reflections of Sunflowers*.

Peter Strafford *Romanesque Churches of France*. This scholarly guide to a handful of France's best churches contains a healthy section on those of the southwest, with several pages devoted to Moissac and Souillac alone. Strafford gives a somewhat dry but detailed account of the architecture and history of the churches featured, and an almost stone-by-stone description of some of the most important sculpture.

GUIDES

Tanja Bulatovic *Living in France Made Simple*. An invaluable guide, packed with ideas and advice on everything from job-hunting, tax and bureaucracy to healthcare.

Cicerone Walking Guides Neat, durable guides, with detailed route descriptions. Titles include *The Way of Saint James; A Walker's Guide* and *The Way of Saint James; A Cyclist's Guide*, both of which follow the route from Le Puy to Santiago (GR65), and *Walking in the Dordogne*.

Peter Knowles *White Water: Massif Central*. Out of print and fairly hard to find but worth tracking down, this guide covers rivers suitable for a spot of gentle family canoeing and canoe touring, including parts of the Dordogne, Lot, Tarn, Vézère, Célé and Aveyron. Packed with good, practical advice.

★ **Joy Law** *Dordogne*. Erudite and accessible thematic guide-cum-history text written by a long-time resident of the *département*, packed with interesting anecdotes and local colour.

Helen Martin *Lot: Travels Through a Limestone Landscape in Southwest France*. It's well worth investing in this updated and expanded edition of Helen Martin's classic book about the Lot if you're going to be spending much time in the *département*. Her passion for the area, which

she has known for more than forty years, comes across loud and clear.

Alain Roussot *Discovering Périgord Prehistory*. Translated into English, this guide provides a solid introduction to the prehistoric caves of the Périgord. It covers the most significant caves in chronological order, while the illustrations give a taste of what's on offer.

Mark Sampson *Essential Questions to Ask When Buying a House in France*. Published in 2014 and, as the name suggests, full of vital advice for those taking the plunge.

Paul Strang *Wines of South-West France*. A bit dated now, but surprisingly still one of the few English-language guides to the region's wines. In addition to the history of viticulture and brief reviews of recommended producers in all the wine-producing areas from Figeac to Bergerac, the book gives a glimpse into local culture and traditions.

Topo-guides The best of the walking guides covering the long-distance paths, Topo-guides are widely available in France and not hard to follow with a working knowledge of French. The series includes guides to the GR65 St-Jacques pilgrimage routes, the *Tour des Gorges de l'Aveyron* (Topo-guide #323), the *Traversée du Périgord* (#321) and, for shorter walks, *Dordogne à Pied* (#D024) and *Lot à Pied* (#D046).

FOOD AND DRINK

Stephanie Alexander *Cooking and Travelling in South-West France*. Inspiring and lavishly illustrated, this is a book for foodies. Alexander is a well-known Australian cookery writer whose deep-rooted passion for this region's food is practically palpable on every page.

Elisabeth Luard *Truffle*. Of all the gourmet treats available in the southwest, a truffle must surely be the ultimate prize. Luard demystifies this unprepossessing but delicious lump of fungus, showing you not only where to buy it, but exactly what to do with it when you get it home.

Orlando Murrin *A Table in the Tarn*. Out of print but worth tracking down, this is a beautifully presented celebration of southern cuisine; the first half of this coffee-table book describes the author's move to a run-down manor and the subsequent transformation to luxury *chambres d'hôtes*.

The second half is a rich hoard of recipes that will have you racing to the kitchen, book in hand.

Jeanne Strang *Goose Fat and Garlic, Country Recipes from South-West France*. A huge store of traditional gastronomy from the old southwest. Strang lived and worked in the area for more than forty years and shares her profound knowledge in this book, which is perhaps a little thin on illustrations but makes up for the lack with recipes that you will find nowhere else.

Paul Strang *Wines of South-West France*. A bit dated now, but surprisingly still one of the few English-language guides to the region's wines. In addition to the history of viticulture and brief reviews of recommended producers in all the wine-producing areas from Figeac to Bergerac, the book gives a glimpse into local culture and traditions.

French

French can be a deceptively familiar language because of the number of words and structures it shares with English. Despite this, it's far from easy, though the bare essentials are not difficult to master and can make all the difference. Even just saying "Bonjour Madame/Monsieur" and then gesticulating will usually get you a smile and helpful service. People working in tourist offices, hotels and so on, almost always speak English, though, and tend to use it when you're struggling to speak French – be grateful, not insulted.

Pronunciation

One easy rule to remember is that consonants at the ends of words are usually silent. *Pas plus tard* (not later) is thus pronounced "pa-plu-tarr". But when the following word begins with a vowel, you run the two together: *les oranges* (the oranges) becomes "layzoronge". Vowels are the hardest sounds to get right. Roughly:

a	as in hat	o	as in hot
e	as in get	ô, au	as in over
é	between get and gate	ou	as in food
è	between get and gut	u	as in a pursed-lip version
eu	like the **u** in hurt		of use
i	as in machine		

More awkward are the combinations *in/im, en/em, an/am, on/om, un/um* at the beginning and end of words, or followed by consonants other than *n* or *m*. Again, roughly:

in/im	like the **an** in anxious	on/om	like the **don** in Doncaster
an/am	like the **don** in		said by someone with
en/em	Doncaster when said with		a heavy cold
	a nasal accent	un/um	like the **u** in understand

Consonants are much as in English, except that: *ch* is always "sh", *h* is silent, *th* is the same as "t", *ll* is often like the "y" in yes, *w* is "v", and *r* is growled.

PHRASEBOOKS AND COURSES

Rough Guide French Phrasebook Mini dictionary-style phrasebook with both English–French and French–English sections, along with cultural tips, a menu reader and downloadable scenarios read by native speakers.

Breakthrough French One of the best teach-yourself courses, with three levels to choose from. Each comes with a book and a CD.

The Complete Merde! The Real French You Were Never Taught at School. More than just a collection of swearwords, this book is a passkey into everyday

French, and a window into French culture.

Oxford Essential French Dictionary Very up-to-date French–English and English–French dictionary, with help on pronunciation and verbs, and links to free online products.

Michel Thomas A fast-paced and effective audio course that promises "No books. No writing. No memorising", with an emphasis on spoken French, rather than conjugating verbs and sentence construction ⓦ michelthomas .com/learn-french.

BASIC WORDS AND PHRASES

French nouns are divided into **masculine** and **feminine**. This causes difficulties with adjectives, whose endings have to change to suit the gender of the nouns they qualify. If you know some grammar, you will know what to do. If not, stick to the masculine form, which is the simplest – it's what we have done in this glossary.

BASICS

hello (morning or afternoon)	bonjour
hello (evening)	bonsoir
goodnight	bonne nuit
goodbye	au revoir
yes	oui
no	non
thank you	merci
please	s'il vous plaît
sorry	pardon/je m'excuse
excuse me	pardon
ok/agreed	d'accord
help!	au secours!
here	ici
there	là
this one	ceci
that one	cela
open	ouvert
closed	fermé
big	grand
small	petit
more	plus
less	moins
a little	un peu
a lot	beaucoup
cheap	bon marché, pas cher
expensive	cher
good	bon
bad	mauvais
hot	chaud
cold	froid
with	avec
without	sans
man	un homme
woman	une femme

NUMBERS

1	un
2	deux
3	trois
4	quatre
5	cinq
6	six
7	sept
8	huit
9	neuf
10	dix
11	onze
12	douze
13	treize
14	quatorze
15	quinze
16	seize
17	dix-sept
18	dix-huit
19	dix-neuf
20	vingt
21	vingt-et-un
22	vingt-deux
30	trente
40	quarante
50	cinquante
60	soixante
70	soixante-dix
75	soixante-quinze
80	quatre-vingts
90	quatre-vingt-dix
95	quatre-vingt-quinze
100	cent
101	cent-et-un
200	deux cents
300	trois cents
500	cinq cents
1000	mille
2000	deux mille
5000	cinq mille
1,000,000	un million

DAYS AND DATES

January	janvier
February	février
March	mars
April	avril
May	mai
June	juin
July	juillet
August	août
September	septembre
October	octobre
November	novembre
December	décembre
Sunday	dimanche
Monday	lundi
Tuesday	mardi
Wednesday	mercredi
Thursday	jeudi
Friday	vendredi

Saturday	samedi
August 1	le premier août
March 2	le deux mars
July 14	le quatorze juillet
November 23	le vingt-trois novembre
2017	deux mille dix-sept

TIME

today	aujourd'hui
yesterday	hier
tomorrow	demain
in the morning	le matin
in the afternoon	l'après-midi
in the evening	le soir
now	maintenant
later	plus tard
at one o'clock	à une heure
at three o'clock	à trois heures
at ten-thirty	à dix heures et demie
at midday	à midi

TALKING TO PEOPLE

When addressing people you should always use *Monsieur* for a man, *Madame* for a woman, *Mademoiselle* for a young woman or girl. Plain *bonjour* by itself is not enough. This isn't as formal as it seems, and it has its uses when you've forgotten someone's name or want to attract someone's attention.

Do you speak English?	Parlez-vous anglais?
How do you say it in French?	Comment ça se dit en français?
What's your name?	Comment vous appelez-vous?
My name is...	Je m'appelle...
I'm	Je suis
...English	...anglais[e]
...Irish	...irlandais[e]
...Scottish	...écossais[e]
...Welsh	...gallois[e]
...American	...américain[e]
...Canadian	...canadien[ne]
...Australian	...australien[ne]
...a New Zealander	...néo-zélandais[e]
I understand	Je comprends
I don't understand	Je ne comprends pas
Can you speak more slowly?	S'il vous plaît, parlez moins vite
How are you?	Comment allez-vous?/ Ça va?
fine, thanks	Très bien, merci
I don't know	Je ne sais pas
Let's go	Allons-y
See you tomorrow	À demain
See you later	À plus tard or À toute à l'heure

See you soon	À bientôt
Leave me alone!	Fichez-moi la paix! (aggressive)
Please help me	Aidez-moi, s'il vous plaît

QUESTIONS AND REQUESTS

The simplest way of asking a question is to start with *s'il vous plaît* (please), then name the thing you want in an interrogative tone of voice. For example:

Where is there a bakery?	S'il vous plaît, la boulangerie?
Which way is it to Cahors?	S'il vous plaît, la route pour Cahors?
Can we have a room for two?	S'il vous plaît, une chambre pour deux?
Can I have a kilo of oranges?	S'il vous plaît, un kilo d'oranges?
where?	Où?
how?	Comment?
how many/how much?	Combien?
when?	Quand?
why?	Pourquoi?
at what time?	À quelle heure?
what is/which is?	Quel est?

GETTING AROUND

bus	autobus/bus/car
bus station	gare routière
bus stop	arrêt de bus
train/taxi/ferry	train/taxi/ferry
boat	bâteau
plane	avion
train station	gare (SNCF)
platform	quai
What time does it leave?	Il part à quelle heure?
What time does it arrive?	Il arrive à quelle heure?
a ticket to...	un billet pour...
single ticket	aller-simple
return ticket	aller-retour
validate your ticket	compostez votre billet
valid for	valable pour
ticket office	vente de billets
how many kilometres?	combien de kilomètres?
how many hours?	combien d'heures?
hitchhiking	autostop
on foot	à pied
Where are you going?	Vous allez où?
I'm going to...	Je vais à...
I want to get off at the road to...	Je voudrais descendre à la route pour...
...near	...près/pas loin
far	loin
left	à gauche
right	à droite

straight on	tout droit
on the other side of	de l'autre côté de
on the corner of	à l'angle de
next to	à côté de
behind	derrière
in front of	devant
before	avant
after	après
under	sous
to cross	traverser
bridge	pont

ACCOMMODATION

a room for one/ two people	une chambre pour une/ deux personne(s)
a twin room	une chambre à deux lits
a double bed	un grand lit
a room with a shower	une chambre avec douche
a room with a bath	une chambre avec salle de bains
for one/two/ three nights	pour une/deux/ trios nuits
Can I see it?	Je peux la voir?
a room on the courtyard	une chambre sur la cour
a room over the street	une chambre sur la rue
first floor	premier étage
second floor	deuxième étage
with a view	avec vue
key	clef
to iron	repasser
do laundry	faire la lessive
sheets	draps
blankets	couvertures
quiet	calme
noisy	bruyant
hot water	eau chaude
cold water	eau froide
Is breakfast included?	Est-ce que le petit déjeuner est compris?
I would like breakfast	Je voudrais prendre le petit déjeuner
I don't want breakfast	Je ne veux pas de petit déjeuner
Can we camp here?	On peut camper ici?
campsite	un camping/terrain de camping
tent	une tente
tent space	un emplacement
youth hostel	auberge de jeunesse

DRIVING

car	voiture
service station	garage
service	service
to park the car	garer la voiture
car park	un parking
no parking	défense de stationner/ stationnement interdit
petrol station	station service
petrol	essence
diesel	gazole/gasoil
(to) fill it up	faire le plein
oil	huile
air line	ligne à air
put air in the tyres	gonfler les pneus
battery	batterie
the battery is dead	la batterie est morte
plugs	bougies
to break down	tomber en panne
gas can	bidon
insurance	assurance
green card	carte verte
traffic lights	feux
red light	feu rouge
green light	feu vert

HEALTH MATTERS

doctor	médecin
dentist	dentiste
I don't feel well	Je ne me sens pas bien
medicines	médicaments
prescription	ordonnance
I feel sick	Je suis malade
I have a headache	J'ai mal à la tête
stomach ache	mal à l'estomac
period	règles
pain	douleur
it hurts	ça fait mal
chemist	pharmacie
hospital	hôpital

OTHER NEEDS

bakery	boulangerie
food shop	alimentation
supermarket	supermarché
to eat	manger
to drink	boire
camping gas	camping gaz
stamps	timbres
bank	banque
money	argent
toilets	toilettes
police	police
telephone	téléphone
cinema	cinéma
theatre	théâtre
to reserve/book	réserver

FOOD AND DISHES

BASIC TERMS

l'addition	bill/check
beurre	butter
bouteille	bottle
chauffé	heated
couteau	knife
cru	raw
cuillère	spoon
cuit	cooked
à emporter	takeaway
formule	lunchtime set menu
fourchette	fork
fumé	smoked
huile	oil
lait	milk
le menu	set menu
moutarde	mustard
oeuf	egg
offert	free
pain	bread
poivre	pepper
salé	salted/savoury
sel	salt
sucre	sugar
sucré	sweet
table	table
tisane	a flower or herb infusion or tea
verre	glass
vinaigre	vinegar

SNACKS AND STARTERS

un sandwich/une baguette	a sandwich
...au jambon	...with ham
...au fromage	...with cheese
...au saucisson	...with sausage
...au poivre	...with pepper
...au pâté (de campagne)	...with pâté (country style)
croque-monsieur	grilled cheese and ham sandwich
croque-madame	grilled cheese and bacon, sausage, chicken or egg sandwich
panini	toasted Italian sandwich
tartine	buttered bread or open sandwich
crudités	raw vegetables with dressings
hors d'oeuvres	combination of charcuterie, crudités, smoked fish and other cold starters

charcuterie	pâté and cold meats
oeufs	eggs
...au plat	...fried
...à la coque	...boiled
...durs	...hard-boiled
...brouillés	...scrambled
...pochés	...poached
omelette	omelette
...nature	...plain
...aux fines herbes	...with herbs
...au fromage	...with cheese
...aux truffes	...with truffles

PASTA (*PÂTES*), PANCAKES (*CRÊPES*) AND FLANS (*TARTES*)

nouilles	noodles
pâtes fraîches	fresh pasta
crêpe au sucre/ aux oeufs	pancake with sugar/ eggs
galette (de sarrasin)	buckwheat pancake
pissaladière	tart of fried onions with anchovies and black olives
tarte flambée	thin pizza-like pastry topped with onion, cream and bacon or other combinations

SOUPS (*SOUPES*)

bisque	shellfish soup
bouillabaisse	Mediterranean fish soup
bouillon	broth or stock
consommé	clear soup
garbure	potato, cabbage and meat soup
miques	dumplings of maize or wheat flour served in a thick soup; or as a large, sliced dumpling in a stew
potage	thick soup, usually vegetable
potée	thick vegetable and meat soup
soupe à l'oignon	onion soup with a chunk of toasted bread and melted cheese topping
tourain, tourin	garlic soup made with duck or goose fat served over bread topped with cheese

FISH (POISSON), SEAFOOD (FRUITS DE MER) AND SHELLFISH (CRUSTACES OR COQUILLAGES)

alose	shad
anchois	anchovies
anguilles	eels
bigourneaux	periwinkles
brandade de morue	puréed, salted cod with oil, milk, garlic and mashed potato
brème	bream
brochet	pike
bulot	whelk
cabillaud	cod
calmar	squid
carrelet	plaice
colin	hake
coques	cockles
coquilles St-Jacques	scallops
crabe	crab
crevettes grises	shrimp
crevettes roses	prawns
daurade	sea bream
écrevisses	freshwater crayfish
éperlan	smelt
escargots	snails
esturgeon	sturgeon
flétan	halibut
gambas	king prawns
hareng	herring
homard	lobster
huîtres	oysters
lamproie	lamprey
langoustines	saltwater crayfish
limande	lemon sole
lotte de mer	monkfish
loup de mer	sea bass
maquereau	mackerel
merlan	whiting
moules (marinière)	mussels (with shallots in white wine sauce)
raie	skate
rascasse	scorpion fish
rouget	red mullet
saumon	salmon
sole	sole
thon	tuna
truite	trout
turbot	turbot

FISH DISHES AND TERMS

aïoli	garlic mayonnaise served with salt cod and other fish
arête	fish bone
beignet	fritter
darne	fillet or steak
la douzaine	a dozen
frit	fried
friture	deep-fried small fish
fumé	smoked
grillé	grilled
hollandaise	butter and vinegar sauce
à la meunière	in a butter, lemon and parsley sauce
mousse/ mousseline	mousse
pané	breaded
quenelles	light dumplings
thermidor	lobster grilled in its shell with cream sauce

MEAT (VIANDE) AND POULTRY (VOLAILLE)

agneau (de pré-salé)	lamb (grazed on salt marshes)
andouille/andouillette	tripe/steak sausage
bifteck	
boeuf	beef
boudin blanc	sausage of white meats
boudin noir	black pudding
caille	quail
canard	duck
caneton	duckling
contrefilet	sirloin roast
dinde, dindon	turkey
entrecôte	rib steak
faux filet	sirloin steak
foie	liver
foie gras	duck/goose liver
gibier	game
gigot (d'agneau)	leg (of lamb)
grenouilles (cuisses de)	frogs (legs)
grillade	grilled meat
hâchis	chopped meat or mince hamburger
langue	tongue
lapin/lapereau	rabbit/young rabbit
lard/lardons	bacon/diced bacon
lièvre	hare
merguez	spicy sausage
mouton	mutton
oie	goose
onglet	cut of beef
os	bone
poitrine	breast
porc	pork
poulet	chicken
ris	sweetbreads
rognons	kidneys (usually lambs')

sanglier	wild boar
steak	steak
tête de veau	calf's head (in jelly)
tournedos	thick slices of fillet
tripes	tripe
tripoux	mutton tripe
veau	veal
venaison	venison
volaille	poultry

MEAT AND POULTRY DISHES AND TERMS

aiguillettes aile	thin, tender pieces of duck wing
au feu de bois	cooked over wood fire
au four	baked
blanquette, daube, estouffade, navarin, ragoût	types of stew
blanquette de veau	veal in cream and mushroom sauce
boeuf bourguignon	beef stew with Burgundy, onions and mushrooms
brochette	kebab
canard de périgourdin	roast duck with prunes, foie gras and truffles
carré	best end of neck, chop or cutlet
choucroute	pickled cabbage with peppercorns, sausages, bacon and salami
civet	game stew
confit	meat preserve
coq au vin	chicken cooked with wine, onions and mushrooms
côte	chop, cutlet or rib
cou	neck
cuisse	thigh or leg
en croûte	in pastry
épaule	shoulder
farci	stuffed
garni	with vegetables
gésier	gizzard
gigot (d'agneau)	leg (of lamb)
grillé	grilled
magret de canard	duck breast
marmite	casserole
médaillon	round piece
noisettes	small, round fillets
pavé	thick slice
poêlé	pan-fried
poule au pot	chicken simmered with vegetables
rôti	roast

sauté	lightly cooked in butter
steak au poivre (vert/rouge)	steak in a black, green or red peppercorn sauce
steak tartare	raw chopped beef, topped with a raw egg yolk
tournedos rossini	beef fillet with foie gras and truffles
viennoise	fried in egg and breadcrumbs

TERMS FOR STEAKS

bleu	almost raw
saignant	rare
à point	medium
bien cuit	well done
très bien cuit	very well done

GARNISHES AND SAUCES

américaine	white wine, cognac and tomato
au porto	in port
béarnaise	sauce of egg yolks, white wine, shallots and vinegar
beurre blanc	sauce of white wine and shallots, with butter
bonne femme	with mushroom, bacon, potato and onions
bordelaise	red wine, shallot and bone-marrow sauce
chasseur	with white wine, mushrooms and shallots
diable	strong mustard seasoning
forestière	with bacon and mushroom
fricassée	rich, creamy sauce
mornay	cheese sauce
périgourdine/périgueux	rich wine sauce, possibly with truffles
provençale	tomatoes, garlic, olive oil and herbs
rouille	a mayonnaise of chillies and garlic
savoyarde	with Gruyère cheese

VEGETABLES (*LÉGUMES*), HERBS (*HERBES*) AND SPICES (*ÉPICES*)

ail	garlic
artichaut	artichoke
asperge	asparagus
avocat	avocado
basilic	basil
betterave	beetroot
câpre	caper

carotte	carrot	parmentier	with potatoes
céleri	celery	pimenté	peppery hot
champignon, cèpe, chanterelle, girolle, morille	types of mushrooms	piquant	spicy
		pistou	ground basil, olive oil, garlic and parmesan
chou (rouge)	(red) cabbage		
choufleur	cauliflower	râpée	grated or shredded
ciboulette	chives	sauté	lightly fried in butter
concombre	cucumber	à la vapeur	steamed
cornichon	gherkin		
échalotes	shallots		
endive	chicory		
épinards	spinach	abricot	apricot
estragon	tarragon	amande	almond
fenouil	fennel	ananas	pineapple
fèves	broad beans	banane	banana
flageolets	white beans	brugnon, nectarine	nectarine
haricots (verts, rouges, beurres)	beans (French, string, kidney, butter)	cacahouète	peanut
		cassis	blackcurrant
lentilles	lentils	cérise	cherry
mange-tout	snow peas	citron	lemon
menthe	mint	citron vert	lime
moutarde	mustard	figue	fig
oignon	onion	fraise (de bois)	strawberry (wild)
persil	parsley	framboise	raspberry
piment	pimento	fruit de la passion	passion fruit
poireau	leek	grenade	pomegranate
pois, petits pois	peas	groseille rouge/blanche	red/white currant
poivron verte/rouge	green/red sweet pepper	kaki	persimmon
pommes de terre	potatoes	mangue	mango
radis	radish	marron	chestnut
riz	rice	melon	melon
salade verte	green salad	melon d'eau	watermelon
tomate	tomato	mirabelle	small yellow plum
truffes	truffles	mûre	blackberry
		myrtille	blueberry
		noisette	hazelnut

FRUIT (*FRUITS*) AND NUTS (*NOIX*)

VEGETABLE DISHES AND TERMS

à l'anglaise/ à l'eau	boiled	noix	nuts, walnuts
beignet	fritter	orange	orange
biologique	organic	pamplemousse	grapefruit
duxelles	fried mushrooms and shallots with cream	pastèque	watermelon
		pêche	peach
farci	stuffed	pistache	pistachio
feuille	leaf	poire	pear
fines herbes	mixture of tarragon, parsley and chives	pomme	apple
		prune	plum
garni	served with vegetables	pruneau	prune
gratiné	browned with cheese or butter	raisin	grape
		reine-claude	greengage
à la grecque	cooked in oil and lemon		
jardinière	with mixed diced vegetables		
mousseline	mashed potato with cream and eggs		

FRUIT DISHES AND TERMS

beignet	fritter or doughnut
compôte	stewed fruit
coulis	sauce of puréed fruit
crème de marrons	chestnut purée

flambé	set aflame in alcohol	pâte	pastry or dough
frappé	iced	petit-suisse	a smooth mixture of
macédoine	fruit salad		cream and curds
		poires belle hélène	pears and ice cream in
			chocolate sauce

DESSERTS (*DESSERTS* OR *ENTREMETS*), PASTRIES (*PÂTISSERIE*) AND RELATED TERMS

		sablé	shortbread biscuit
		savarin	a filled, ring-shaped cake
bavarois	refers to the mould, could	tarte	tart
	be a mousse or custard	tartelette	small tart
bombe	moulded ice-cream	tarte tatin	upside-down apple tart
	dessert	yaourt, yogourt	yogurt
brioche	sweet, high-yeast		
	breakfast roll	**WINE TERMS (*VIN*)**	
charlotte	custard and fruit in lining	barrique	oak barrel for maturing
	of almond fingers		wine
clafoutis	cake-like fruit tart	blanc	white
coupe/boule	a serving of ice cream	cave	wineshop/cellar
crème à l'anglaise	custard	cépage	grape variety
crème Chantilly	vanilla-flavoured		(e.g. Merlot, Pinot noir)
	and sweetened	chais	wine cellars
	whipped cream	corsé	full-bodied
crème fraîche	sour cream	cuvé	vat for fermenting wine
crème pâtissière	thick, eggy pastry-filling	cuvée	a specially blended wine
crêpe	pancake	dégustation	tasting
crêpe suzette	thin pancake with orange	doux/moelleux	sweet
	juice and liqueur	fin	delicate
fromage blanc	cream cheese	fort	strong
gaufre	waffle	léger	light
gênoise	rich sponge cake	millésime	vintage
glace	ice cream	mousseux	sparkling
île flottante/oeufs	soft meringues floating	riche	rich
à la neige	on custard	rosé	rosé
macaron	macaroon	rouge	red
madeleine	small sponge cake	sec	dry
mousse au chocolat	chocolate mousse	vendange	harvest
omelette norvégienne	baked Alaska frozen	vignes	vines
parfait	mousse; sometimes	vignoble	vineyard
	ice cream		

Glossary

GENERAL VOCABULARY AND TERMS

abbaye abbey

abri prehistoric rock shelter

appellation AOP (*appellation d'origine protégée*) wine classification indicating that the wine meets strict requirements regarding its provenance and methods of production

auberge country inn, frequently offering accommodation

auberge de jeunesse youth hostel

autoroute motorway

bastide new town founded in the thirteenth and fourteenth centuries, built on a grid plan around an arcaded market square (see box, p.244)

boules popular French game played with steel balls (see p.34)

cabane, borie *or* **gariotte** dry-stone hut, probably used by shepherds

Capétien Capetian royal dynasty founded by Hugh Capet, which ruled France from 987 to 1328

causse limestone plateau extending from Dordogne *département* south through Lot and into Aveyron

chambre d'hôte bed-and-breakfast accommodation in a private house

chartreuse one-storey building typical of the Bordeaux wine region, slightly raised up and built on top of a half-buried *chai*; also a Carthusian monastery

château castle, mansion, stately home

château fort castle built for a specifically military purpose

collégiale church that shelters a community of priests

colombage traditional building style consisting of a timber frame filled with earth and straw or bricks

commune the basic administrative region, each under a mayor

confiserie confectioner's (shop)

dégustation tasting (wine or food)

département mid-level administrative unit run by a local council – the equivalent of a county in Britain

dolmen Neolithic stone structure, generally held to be a tomb, consisting of two or more upright slabs supporting a horizontal stone

donjon castle keep

église church

falaise cliff

ferme auberge farm licensed to provide meals in which the majority of the produce must come from the farm itself

foire large market held once or twice monthly in some country towns

formule restaurant menu with two courses, usually comprising a choice of starter and main course or main and dessert

fouille archeological excavation

gabare *or* **gabarre** traditional wooden boat used to transport goods on the Dordogne and Lot rivers up until the late nineteenth century

gavage process of force-feeding ducks and geese to make foie gras

gisement deposit, stratified layers of an archeological excavation

gîte self-catering accommodation

gîte d'étape basic accommodation, usually restricted to walkers, pilgrims and cyclists

gouffre limestone chasm or sinkhole

grotte cave

halle(s) covered market (hall)

hôtel hotel, but also an aristocratic townhouse or mansion

lauze small limestone slabs, a traditional roof covering in the Périgord

navette shuttle-bus, for example connecting a town with its airport

Occitan language (and associated culture) formerly spoken throughout most of south and southwest France

pétanque variation of the game of *boules* (see p.34)

pigeonnier dovecote, often built on stilts and used to collect droppings for fertilizer

pisé traditional Périgordin floor made out of small limestone slabs inserted upright into a bed of clay or lime

porte gateway

retable altarpiece

seneschal chief administrator and justice in medieval times, the representative of the king

table d'hôte meals served to residents of a *chambre d'hôte*. Also, a set menu with choices, at a fixed price.

tour tower

version originale (VO) film shown in its original language and subtitled in French

ARCHITECTURAL TERMS

ambulatory passage around the outer edge of the choir of a church

apse semicircular or polygonal termination at the east end of a church

Baroque High Renaissance period of art and architecture, distinguished by extreme ornateness

chevet east end of a church

Classical architectural style incorporating Greek and Roman elements: pillars, domes, colonnades, etc, at its height in France in the seventeenth century and revived in the nineteenth century as Neoclassical

flamboyant very ornate form of Gothic

fresco painting in watercolour on a wall or ceiling while the plaster is still wet

Gallo-Roman period and culture of Roman occupation of Gaul (1st century BC to 4th century AD)

Gothic architectural style prevalent from the twelfth to sixteenth century, characterized by pointed arches and ribbed vaulting

machicolations parapet on a castle, fortified church, gateway, etc, with openings for dropping stones and so forth on attackers

Merovingian dynasty (and art, etc) ruling France and parts of Germany from the sixth to mid-eighth century

narthex entrance hall of church

nave main body of a church

Renaissance architectural and artistic style developed in fifteenth-century Italy and imported to France in the sixteenth century by King Francis I

Romanesque early medieval architecture distinguished by squat, rounded forms and naive sculpture, called *Roman* in French (not to be confused with *Romain* – Roman)

stucco plaster used to embellish ceilings, etc

transept transverse arm of a church, at right angles to the nave

tympanum semicircular panel above the door of a Romanesque church, usually with sculpture

REGIONAL NAMES

Aquitaine Originally a Roman administrative region extending from Poitiers and Limoges south to the Pyrenees. It later became a duchy, which, at its apogee in the twelfth century, covered roughly the same area, though it fluctuated enormously. In the 1960s the name was resurrected with the creation of regional administrative units. Modern Aquitaine is based around Bordeaux and comprises the *départements* of Dordogne, Gironde and Lot-et-Garonne, among others

Gascony The region to the west and south of the River Garonne, named after a Celtic tribe (the Vascons). In the early tenth century it became an independent duchy but was soon subsumed into the duchy of Aquitaine, though still retained its own identity

Guyenne A corruption of the name "Aquitaine" originating during the period of English rule. Prior to the Revolution, the province of Guyenne extended from Gironde to Aveyron. Nowadays, it is occasionally used to refer to an area roughly encompassing Entre-Deux-Mers and St-Émilion, although there is no strict demarcation

Midi-Pyrénées The modern administrative region to the east of Aquitaine, based on Toulouse and incorporating the *départements* of Lot, Tarn-et-Garonne and Aveyron, among others

Périgord The confines of Périgord have changed little since pre-Roman times, when it was the home of the Gaulish tribe, the Petrocori. In the eighth century Périgord became a county, and then a province of France until the name was officially changed to Dordogne when *départements* were created in 1790 (each *département* was named after its principal river). However, Périgord is still used frequently, especially in tourist literature. These days it is often subdivided into Périgord Vert (Green Périgord; the *département's* northern sector); Périgord Blanc (White; the central strip along the Isle valley including Périgueux); Périgord Pourpre (Purple; the southwest corner around Bergerac); and Périgord Noir (Black; the southeast, including Sarlat and the Vézère valley)

Quercy Former province roughly equivalent to the modern *départements* of the Lot and the north part of the Tarn-et-Garonne. The latter is often referred to as Bas-Quercy, while Haut-Quercy comprises the Lot's northern region. Like the Périgord, the Quercy was originally named after its Gaulish settlers, the Cadurci tribe. The name is still in regular use today and the sense of burning pride remains. A native of Cahors is still referred to as a Cadurcien

Small print and index

317 Small print

318 About the author

319 Index

325 Map symbols

Rough Guide credits

Editor: Polly Thomas
Layout: Nikhil Agarwal
Cartography: Ed Wright
Picture editor: Aude Vauconsant
Proofreader: Ruth Reisenberger
Managing editor: Monica Woods
Assistant editor: Payal Sharotri

Production: Jimmy Lao
Cover photo research: Sarah Stewart-Richardson
Editorial assistant: Aimee White
Senior DTP coordinator: Dan May
Programme manager: Gareth Lowe
Publishing director: Georgina Dee

Publishing information

This sixth edition published June 2017 by
Rough Guides Ltd,
80 Strand, London WC2R 0RL
11, Community Centre, Panchsheel Park,
New Delhi 110017, India
Distributed by Penguin Random House
Penguin Books Ltd, 80 Strand, London WC2R 0RL
Penguin Group (USA), 345 Hudson Street, NY 10014, USA
Penguin Group (Australia), 250 Camberwell Road,
Camberwell, Victoria 3124, Australia
Penguin Group (NZ), 67 Apollo Drive, Mairangi Bay,
Auckland 1310, New Zealand
Penguin Group (South Africa), Block D, Rosebank Office
Park, 181 Jan Smuts Avenue, Parktown North, Gauteng,
South Africa 2193
Rough Guides is represented in Canada by DK Canada, 320
Front Street West, Suite 1400, Toronto, Ontario M5V 3B6
Printed in Singapore
© Jan Dodd 2017
Maps © Rough Guides

328pp includes index
A catalogue record for this book is available from the
British Library
ISBN: 978-0-24127-394-4
The publishers and authors have done their best to
ensure the accuracy and currency of all the information in
The Rough Guide to the Dordogne & the Lot, however,
they can accept no responsibility for any loss, injury, or
inconvenience sustained by any traveller as a result of
information or advice contained in the guide.
1 3 5 7 9 8 6 4 2

MIX
Paper from
responsible sources
FSC™ C018179
www.fsc.org

Help us update

We've gone to a lot of effort to ensure that the sixth
edition of **The Rough Guide to the Dordogne &
the Lot** is accurate and up-to-date. However, things
change – places get "discovered", opening hours are
notoriously fickle, restaurants and rooms raise prices
or lower standards. If you feel we've got it wrong or
left something out, we'd like to know, and if you can

remember the address, the price, the hours, the phone
number, so much the better.
    Please send your comments with the subject line
"**Rough Guide the Dordogne & the Lot Update**" to
mail@uk.roughguides.com. We'll credit all contributions
and send a copy of the next edition (or any other Rough
Guide if you prefer) for the very best emails.

A ROUGH GUIDE TO ROUGH GUIDES

Published in 1982, the first Rough Guide – to Greece – was a student scheme that became a
publishing phenomenon. Mark Ellingham, a recent graduate in English from Bristol University,
had been travelling in Greece the previous summer and couldn't find the right guidebook.
With a small group of friends he wrote his own guide, combining a contemporary, journalistic
style with a thoroughly practical approach to travellers' needs.
    The immediate success of the book spawned a series that rapidly covered dozens of
destinations. And, in addition to impecunious backpackers, Rough Guides soon acquired a
much broader readership that relished the guides' wit and inquisitiveness as much as their
enthusiastic, critical approach and value-for-money ethos. These days, Rough Guides include
recommendations from budget to luxury and cover more than 120 destinations around the
globe, from Amsterdam to Zanzibar, all regularly updated by our team of roaming writers.

Browse all our latest guides, read inspirational features and book your trip at **roughguides.com**.

ABOUT THE AUTHOR

Jan Dodd arrived in southwest France by accident in 1992 and has been there ever since, eager to ascertain whether duck fat, red wine and garlic really are the key to longevity. She has co-written several guidebooks, including *The Rough Guide to Japan* and *The Rough Guide to Vietnam*, and updated many more. These days she divides her time between travelling and writing about renewable energy.

Acknowledgements

Stuart Butler: First and foremost I must thank my wife, Heather, and children, Jake and Grace, for their help and patience with this project (and the children's devotion to ice cream testing whenever they accompanied me on my research trips to the Dordogne). Huge thanks also to Micheline Morissonneau of the Dordogne–Périgord Tourist Office for her untiring help; to the staff of the Vieux Logis; and to Jane Parritt of Media Contacts PR.

Zoe Smith: Thanks to Stephanie Gombert at Château de la Treyne for excellent local recommendations; Jane Parritt; Solenne Odon; Sophie Nadin in Martel; Joanne Bond for Agen recommendations; Justine Quetier from the Dordogne Tourist Board; and Natasha Foges, Polly Thomas and Stuart Butler for all their hard work, advice and sharing of ideas.

Readers' updates

Thanks to all the readers who have taken the time to write in with comments and suggestions (and apologies if we've inadvertently omitted or misspelt anyone's name):

Lynn Barclay; Lesley Bradnam; Leeann Hawke; Richard King; Srdjan M. Marjanovic; Sheila Miller; Anne O'Mulloy;

Vivienne Rayner; John Watt.

Photo credits

All photos © Rough Guides, except the following:
(Key: t-top; c-centre; b-bottom; l-left; r-right)

1 Getty Images: Moment Open/Charly Lataste
2 Getty Images: John Burke
4 Corbis: Patrick Escudero (tr); Peet Simard (tl)
5 SuperStock: Photononstop
9 Alamy Stock Photo: Alamy (c). **Corbis:** Peet Simard (b); Photononstop/Lionel Lourdel (t)
11 Alamy Stock Photo: BKWine.com/Per Karlsson (b). **Getty Images:** AgenceImages/Azam (t). **SuperStock:** Photononstop (c)
12 Getty Images: Photographer's Choice RF/Robert George Young
13 Alamy Stock Photo: Les Ladbury (t). **Corbis:** Godong/Julian Kumar (c). **Dreamstime.com:** minnystock (b)
14 Alamy Stock Photo: Hemis (c). **Corbis:** Hemis/Patrick Escudero (b). **Photoshot:** Karl Johaentges (tr). **Robert Harding Picture Library Ltd** (tl)
15 Corbis: Jean-Pierre Lescourret (b); SOPA/Olimpio Fantuz (t). **Getty Images:** Ph. Giraud (c)
16 Alamy Stock Photo: Cro Magnon (c). **Corbis:** Hemis/Jean-Paul Azam (t). **SuperStock:** JD Dallet (b)
17 Alamy Stock Photo: SFL Travel (bl). **Corbis:** Hemis/Jean-Paul Azam (t); Hemis/Sylvain Sonnet (br)
18 Alamy Stock Photo: Hemis (tl); Hemis/SUDRES Jean-Daniel (tr)

42–43 Photoshot: Ian Cook
63 Corbis: Christophe Boisvieux (tl). **Getty Images:** AFP (b)
75 Photoshot: Stuart Black
84–85 Alamy Stock Photo: David Noton Photography
103 Alamy Stock Photo: Andrew Duke (t). **Corbis:** Hemis/Patrick Escudero (b)
119 Corbis: Christophe Boisvieux
139 Alamy Stock Photo: Martin Jenkinson (bl). **Getty Images:** Jmichel Deborde (t)
159 Corbis: Hemis/Francis Cormon
166–167 Getty Images: Photononstop/Lionel Lourdel
169 SES de Padirac: Damien Butaeye
179 Corbis: Robert Harding World Imagery/Ellen Rooney (t)
189 Alamy Stock Photo: imageBROKER (b)
215 Corbis: Hemis/Philippe Body (t); Hemis/Rene Mattes (b)
248–249 Getty Images: hemis.fr/AZAM Jean-Paul
267 SuperStock: Photononstop (b)
286 Robert Harding Picture Library: Philippe Body

Cover: *Church at St-Cirq-Lapopie* **4Corners:** Sime/Francesco Carovillano

Index

Maps are marked in grey

A

accommodation 27–29
Agen 252–258
Agen 254
Aiguillon 243
Airbnb....................................28
airlines 21, 22
Albas 233
Allemans-du-Dropt.................101
Aquarium du Périgord Noir ...140
Aquitaine 315
Aquitaine, Duchy of........289, 290
Argentat.................................191
Arnac-Pompadour.....................80
Assier.....................................226
ATMs 38
Aubeterre-sur-Dronne.............. 64
Autoire..................................194
autoroutes............................. 25
AutoTrain 23
Auvillar 265

B

Baker, Josephine 161
banks......................................38
baronies of Périgord...... 157, 244, 290
bastides.....98, 100, 108, 112, 162, 187, 230, 238, 240, 243, 244, 264, 266, 271, 283, 284, 292
Beaulieu-en-Rouergue, Abbaye de 279
Beaulieu-sur-Dordogne
.... 188–191
Beaumont................................112
bed-and-breakfast 27
beer 31
Belaye 236
Belvès 154
BERGERAC 89–96
Bergerac 90
Bergerac, around 88
accommodation.................................94
airport 93
arrival...93
bars 95
Bergerac, Cyrano de..........................93
bike rental..94

boat trips...94
buses 94
car rental 94
Cloître des Récollets 91
drinking...95
eating..95
festivals..89
halle 93
history 90
hospital...96
Maison des Vins 91
markets...89, 95
Musée du Tabac................................91
Musée du Vin et de la Batellerie ..92
Notre-Dame, Église 93
parking..94
Place de la Myrpe 92
Place Pélissière 93
police..96
post office...96
restaurants...95
Rue de Fontaines 93
shopping...95
St-Jacques, Église 92
tourist office..94
tours...94
trains...93
Bergerac, Cyrano de 93
Beynac, Château de................156
Beynac-et-Cazenac 156
bicycles............................... 26, 33
Biron, Château de....................245
boat rental 27
boat trips 156
boating..........26, 33, 60, 208, 211, 233, 256, 261
Boétie, Étienne de la 123
Bonaguil, Château de.............238
books 303
bories 129
Boschaud, Abbaye de 68
bottled water 32
boules 34
Bourdeilles 60
Bourg-du-Bost 62
Bouriane 230
Bouziès 211
Brantôme 57–59
breakfast 29
Bretenoux................................187
Brexit......................................302
Bridoire, Château de................ 97
BRIVE-LA-GAILLARDE 76–80
Brive-la-Gaillarde 77
accommodation 79
airport 79
arrival..79

buses 79
car rental 79
Chocolaterie Lamy.............................78
Collégiale St-Martin de Brive.......76
Denoix Distillery.................................78
eating..80
Jardins de Colette 78
markets...79
Musée Edmond Michelet...............78
Musée Lalbenche 76
restaurants..80
rugby...76
taxis..79
tourist office...79
trains...79
Brousses 277
Bruniquel 276
buses 24
Buzet-sur-Baïse......................260

C

Cabanes du Breuil 129
Cabrerets 218
Cadouin..................................114
Cadouin, Abbaye de...............114
CAHORS 200–210
Cahors..................................... 203
accommodation 208
arrival..207
bars 210
bike rental..208
boat tours 208
buses 207
Cahors Plage......................................207
canoe rental 208
car rental 207
cathedral..204
Château du Roi 206
cinema 210
clubs...210
drinking..210
eating...209
festivals...202
history 201
hospital...210
Les Jardins Secrets...........................206
Maison du Bourreau 205
Maison de l'Eau 207
markets..202
Mont St-Cyr...207
Musée Henri Martin 206
Musée de la Résistance...................206
nightlife...210
parking..207
Place Jean-Jacques Chapou........205
police..210
Pont Valentré 206

restaurants..............................209
St-Étienne, Cathédrale 204
taxis.......................................207
theatre...................................210
Tour des Pendus....................206
Tour du Pape Jean XXII 206
tourist office..........................208
trains......................................207
wine.......................................209
Cajarc 214
Calès 174
camping 29
Canal de Garonne 26, 256
Caniac-du-Causse....................227
canoe rental..................54, 59, 61,
62, 64, 105, 110, 125, 133, 141,
145, 147, 156, 160, 162, 164,
172, 184, 186, 187, 208, 211,
213, 220, 233, 278
canoeing......................................33
Cap Blanc, Abri du...................137
Cap Cauderoue 260
Capdenac...................................217
car rental.....................................26
carbon offsetting........................21
Carennac...................................185
Carsac-Aillac.............................164
Castelfranc................................233
Castel-Merle 146
Castelnau, Château de.............188
Castelnau-Montratier...............269
Castelnaud, Château de...........158
Castelnaud-la-Chapelle............158
Castillon, Battle of 295
castles.......................................294
Cathars 158, 202, 262, 269,
271, 277, 278, 283, 292
Cathédral St-Front......................51
Causse de Gramat........ 225–228
cave art.....................................121
Cave de Monbazillac 96
cave visits 132, 136
caves
l'Abbaye de Brantôme,
Grottes de 58
Combarelles, Grotte de...........136
Cougnac, Grottes de................229
Cussac, Grotte de....................111
Domme, Grotte de 163
Foissac, Grotte de 217
Font-de-Gaume, Grotte de.......134
Grand Roc, Grotte du..............137
Lacave, Grottes de 173
Lascaux, Grotte de...................149
Maxange, Grottes de...............111
Padirac, Gouffre de..................186
Pech-Merle, Grotte de.............219
Presque, Grottes de.................194
Proumeyssac, Gouffre de 142
Rouffignac, Grotte de..............138
Sorcier, Grotte du....................142

Tourtoirac, Grotte de 74
Villars, Grotte de.......................67
caving 33
Cazals 230
Cazes-Mondenard.....................268
Célé valley 218–220
Cénac 163
Cénevières, Château de 214
chambres d'hôtes 28
Champollion, Jean-François....223
Channel Tunnel 23
Chapelle St Blaise 81
Chapelle St-Martin....................111
Charlemagne 289
châteaux
Assier.....................................226
Beynac....................................156
Biron......................................245
Bonaguil................................238
Bourdeilles...............................60
Bridoire....................................97
Bruniquel................................276
Carennac................................186
Castelnau...............................188
Castelnaud.............................158
Cénevières..............................214
Commarque.............................137
Doyens...................................186
Ducs de Duras.........................102
Duras.....................................102
Excideuil...................................71
Fayrac....................................161
Fénelon..................................165
Gontaut-Biron........................218
Hautefort..................................73
Herm......................................140
Jaubertie..................................97
Jumilhac...................................70
Lanquais.................................107
Losse......................................146
Marqueyssac...........................157
Marthonie.................................67
Milandes.................................161
Monbazillac...............................96
Montaigne...............................106
Montal....................................193
Montfort.................................164
Najac......................................283
Nérac.....................................259
Pompadour................................80
Puyghuilhem.............................67
Puymartin...............................128
Rocamadour...........................177
St-Laurent-les-Tours................192
Tiregand....................................98
Turenne....................................82
children 34
churches 294
Cingle de Montfort 164
Cingle de Trémolat....................109
climate 10
coffee 32
Collonges-la-Rouge 83
Colombier 97

Combarelles, Grotte de 136
Commarque, Château de 137
Cordes-sur-Ciel............ 280–282
Corniche 277
costs 35
Cougnac, Grottes de.................229
Couze-et-St-Front.....................107
Couze valley..............................112
credit cards 38
Creysse 184
crime 35
Cro-Magnon 135, 287
Croquants................140, 284, 297
cycling 26, 33

D

Daumesnil, Baron Pierre ..52, 298
debit cards 38
disabled travellers..................... 40
Domme 162
Domme, Grotte de 163
Dordogne and the Lot........6–7
Dordogne valley,
middle 152–153
Dordogne valley, upper 170
drinks 31
driving 22, 25
Dronne valley.............................. 59
drugs 36
Duras 101
Duravel......................................237

E

Échourgnac................................. 65
Edward I 244, 246
EHIC 37
Eleanor of Aquitaine...... 114, 182,
290
electricity.................................... 36
email... 38
emergencies................................ 36
Espagnac-Ste-Eulalie................220
Espédaillac................................227
Étang de la Jemaye..................... 66
European Health Insurance
Card 37
Eurostar...................................... 22
Eurotunnel.................................. 23
exchange rates 38
Excideuil..................................... 71
Eymet..100

F

faïence 69
Faye 61
Fénelon, Château de 165
Ferme du Parcot.......................66
ferries
    from Ireland 22
    from UK.................................22
festivals 32, 49, 89, 122, 171,
    202, 255
FIGEAC **220–225**
Figeac..**221**
    accommodation............................224
    arrival...224
    bars 225
    bike rental..................................224
    buses 224
    car rental...................................224
    drinking.....................................225
    eating 225
    hospital.....................................225
    Hôtel de la Monnaie 222
    markets......................................222
    Musée Champollion....................223
    Notre-Dame du Puy, Église 223
    parking.......................................224
    Place Carnot..............................222
    Place Champollion......................222
    Place des Écritures....................223
    Place Vival.................................222
    police...225
    restaurants................................225
    St-Sauveur, Église 222
    taxis...224
    tourist office..............................224
    trains..224
Filature de Belvès 155
Fillon, François.....................302
flights
    from Australia.............................22
    from Canada...............................21
    from Ireland 21
    from New Zealand.......................22
    from South Africa.......................22
    from UK.......................................21
    from US.......................................21
foie gras 69
Foissac, Grotte de 217
Font-de-Gaume, Grotte de 135
food..................................5, 29
Forêt du Landais 86
Franks.....................................289
Fronde rebellion 82, 297
Fumel 238

G

Gambetta, Léon 204, 205, 299
Garonne Canal.............................26

gas..25
Gascony 315
Gaulle, General de..................300
gavage 69
gay travellers............................38
gîtes 28
gîtes d'étape 28
Gîtes de France.........................28
glossaries
    architectural terms....................315
    basic words and phrases.....306–308
    food....................................309–313
    regional names..........................315
    wine..313
Gorges de l'Aveyron.... 275–285
Gouffre de Padirac 186
Goujounac 231
Gourdon....................................228
Gluges 184
Gramat.....................................227
Grand-Brassac...........................62
Grand Roc, Grotte du 137
Grézels 236
Guyenne 315

H

Haut-Quercy.............................168
Hautefort 73
Hautefort, Louise de.................71
health......................................36
Henry, the Young King.............182
Henry II of England (Henry
    of Anjou)......111, 175, 182, 290
Henry III.............................90, 296
Henry IV (Henry of Navarre)
    .... 100, 122, 204, 212, 296
Herm, Château de l' 140
hiking.......................................174
history...........................287–302
holidays, public 39
Hollande, François....................302
horseriding 33
hostels 28
hostelling associations 28
hot-air ballooning 156
hotels 27
Hundred Years War 49, 121,
    158, 203, 293

I

Inter-Rail 22
information offices....................40

insurance 37
internet 38
Issigeac 98
itineraries...............................18
itineraries 19

J

Jardins de Colette........................78
Jardins de l'Imaginaire, Les....150
Jardins du Grand Couvent 227
Jardins Panoramiques
    de Limeuil.................................110
Jardins de Sardy....................105
Jardins Suspendus 157
Jaubertie, Château de la 97
Jumilhac-le-Grand 70
Juppe, Alain............................302

K

kayaking 33

L

Abbaye de Brantôme,
    Grottes de l'................................58
La Borie d'Imbert......................178
La Double 65
La Madeleine.............................143
La Roque-Gageac 162
La Roque St-Christophe.........144
La Voie Bleue 54
La Voie Verte........................54, 66
Labyrinthe Préhistorique........141
Lacapelle-Biron 246
Lacave.....................................173
Lalbenque 269
Lalinde....................................108
language 305–313
Lanquais, Château de 107
Lascaux II 149
Laugerie Basse, Abri de...........138
Lauzerte 266
Laguépie 279
Lascaux IV................................148
Lascaux, Grotte de 149
laundry....................................38
lauzes 129
Le Bugue 140–142
Le Buisson-de-Cadouin...........111

Le Conquil..............................145
Le Coux-et-Bigaroque.............154
Le Thot..................................146
Les Eyzies-de-Tayac..... 130–134
Les Jardins de l'Imaginaire.....150
Les Milandes.........................161
Les Pruniers 99
lesbian travellers....................38
LGBT travellers.......................38
L'Hospitalet...........................175
Limeuil.................................109
liqueurs.................................31
Livernon...............................227
Losse, Château de 146
Lot valley 200–201
Loubressac............................195
Louis VII...............................290
Louis VIII..............................121
Louis IX (St Louis) 114, 175,
    188, 238, 269, 293
Louis XIII.....................90, 91, 273
Louis XIV 165, 297
Louis XV 80, 82
Lurçat, Jean..........................192
Luzech.................................232

M

Magdalenian era............. 135, 287
mail......................................38
Mairaux, André......................121
Maison Forte de Reignac........144
Manaurie..............................138
Manoir d'Eyrignac.................128
maps...............................26, 38
Marcilhac.............................219
markets 34, 49, 51, 57, 71, 79,
    89, 95, 122, 171, 202, 255,
    258, 271
Marqueyssac, Château de 157
Martel..................................182
Martignac.............................237
Maxange, Grottes de..............111
meals....................................29
Médici, Catherine de 60, 259
menus.............................28, 29
Meyrals................................153
Meyronne..............................183
Midi-Pyrénées........................315
mineral water.........................32
mobile phones........................40
Moissac........................ 261–264
Moissac................................ 262
Monbazillac............................96
money...................................38

Monflanquin..........................243
Monpazier............................246
Monsempron-Libos 238
Montagrier..............................60
Montaigne, Château de 106
Montaigne, Michel de.... 106, 123
Montal, Château de 193
MONTAUBAN............... 271–275
Montauban............................ 272
    accommodation..........................274
    arrival.......................................274
    bars...275
    buses..274
    car rental...................................274
    cathedral...................................273
    clubs...274
    drinking....................................275
    eating.......................................274
    history.......................................271
    hospital.....................................275
    markets.....................................271
    Musée Ingres..............................273
    nightlife.....................................275
    Notre-Dame, Cathédrale..............273
    parking......................................274
    Place Nationale..........................273
    police..275
    post office..................................275
    restaurants................................274
    St-Jacques, Église........................273
    taxis...274
    tourist office..............................274
    trains...274
Montcabrier...........................238
Montcaret.............................105
Montcuq...............................268
Montferrand-du-Périgord 113
Montfort, Simon de 158, 262,
    292
Monticroux...........................276
Montignac.............................147
Montpezat-de-Quercy...........270
motorail..................................23
Moulin, Jean..........................300
Moulin de Cocussotte..............102
Moulin de Cougnaguet..........174
Moulin de la Rouzique 108
Musée de l'Abri Pataud..........131
Musée Desmoulin 58
Musée National de
    la Préhistoire........................131

N

Najac 282–284
Nérac...................................259
Neuvic....................................65
newspapers 39
Napoléon III 205, 298

Napoléon Bonaparte........80, 223,
    298
National Stud...........................81
Notre-Dame de Bonne-
    Espérance, Abbaye de 65

O

Occitan.................................293
opening hours.........................39

P

package tours..........................23
Padirac, Gouffre de 186
Parc Animalier de Gramat 228
Pécharment.............................98
Pech-Merle, Grotte de.............219
Penne..................................277
Penne-d'Agenais....................239
Périgord Blanc 44, 315
Périgord Noir 118, 315
Périgord Pourpre 86, 315
Périgord Vert 44, 315
PÉRIGUEUX 47–57
Périgueux 48
Périgueux, central 50
Périgueux and the north..... 46
    accommodation..........................54
    airport......................................54
    arrival.......................................54
    bars...56
    buses..54
    canoe hire..................................54
    car rental...................................55
    cathedral...................................51
    cinema......................................56
    drinking....................................56
    eating.......................................55
    festivals.....................................49
    galerie Daumesnil.......................52
    history.......................................47
    hospital.....................................57
    Hôtel d'Abzac de Ladouze...........51
    Hôtel de Saltgourde....................51
    Jardin des Arènes........................53
    La Cité..................................47, 53
    Le Puy-St-Front...........................51
    Maison des Consuls 52
    Maison des Dames de la Foi 51
    Maison Estignard........................52
    Maison Lambert..........................52
    Maison du Pâtissier.....................52
    markets..........................49, 51, 57
    Musée Gallo-Roman Vesunna.......54
    Musée Militaire 51
    Musée du Périgord.......................53
    parking......................................54
    Place de la Clautre.......................51

Place St-Louis 52
police.. 57
Porte Normande 53
post office.. 57
restaurants... 55
Rue de l'Aubergerie....................... 51
Rue du Calvaire............................... 51
Rue Limogeanne.............................. 52
Rue St Roch.. 51
shopping.. 56
St-Étienne de la Cité...................... 53
St-Front, Cathédrale...................... 51
swimming pool................................ 57
theatre 56
Tour Mataguerre 51
Tour de Vésone 54
tourist office..................................... 55
tours... 55
trains.. 54
Vesunna.. 47
Voie Bleue, La 54
Voie Verte, La 54, 66
pétanque 34
petrol 25
Peyrusse-le-Roc.............................. 217
pharmacies 37
phones 39
phylloxera... 299
Piaf, Édith 185
plague.. 295
Plum Village....................................... 99
Poisson, Abri du 138
Poitiers, Alphonse de 100, 240,
    244, 283, 284, 293
Pôle International de la
    Préhistoire 130
police 36
Pompadour, Madame de.......... 80
Pont Valentré................................... 206
Port-de-Gagnac 187
post offices 38
Prayssac.. 234
Préhisto-parc................................... 144
prehistoric art 53, 68, 111, 121,
    130, 131, 132, 135, 146, 148,
    219, 229, 288
prehistoric rock shelters
    Cap Blanc, Abri du 137
    Castel-Merle............................... 146
    Le Conquil.................................. 144
    Laugerie Basse, Abri de 138
    La Madeleine............................. 143
    Pataud, Abri 131
    Poisson, Abri du........................ 138
    La Roque St-Christophe 144
Presque, Grottes de 194
Prieurale d'Arnac, Église............ 81
Proumeyssac, Gouffre de........ 142
pruneaux d'Agen 257
prunes.. 257
public holidays 38
Pujols... 242

Puy-l'Évêque.................................... 236
Puyguilhem, Château de 67
Puymartin, Château de 128

Q

Quercy 198, 315
Quercy Blanc 266–271
Quissac 227

R

racism 36
radio 39
rail passes 22
Rampoux... 230
Resistance, the........... 161, 205, 222
responsible travel....................... 21
restaurants 30
Revolution.. 297
Ribérac.................................... 61–64
Richard the Lionheart... 114, 156,
    182, 239, 265, 290, 292
riding 33
River Lot, south of 252–253
roaming charges.......................... 40
Roc de Cazelle 137
Rocamadour 175–181
Rocamadour................ 176–177
    accommodation.............................. 178
    arrival.. 178
    Basilique St-Sauveur 176
    Borie d'Imbert, La 178
    Cité Religieuse 175
    Chapelle Notre-Dame 176
    Chapelle St-Michel 176
    Château de Rocamadour 177
    eating... 178
    Forêt des Singes 178
    funicular 178
    history 175
    L'Hospitalet................................... 178
    lift... 178
    Petit Train, Le 178
    parking.. 178
    restaurants.................................... 178
    Rocher des Algies 177
    tourist information 178
    trains.. 178
rock climbing 33
Roman occupation 288
Romanesque churches............ 61, 294
Rosetta Stone................................. 223
Rostand, Edmund 93
Rouffignac...................................... 138
Rouffignac, Grotte de.............. 138
rugby.. 34

S

safety... 35
saffron.. 216
St-Amand-de-Coly 150
St-Antonin-Noble-Val............... 278
St-Avit-Sénieur 113
St-Céré 191–193
St-Cirq-Lapopie........... 212–214
St-Cyprien....................................... 152
St-Denis-près-Martel................. 182
St-Eutrope, Église 101
St Front 47, 108
St-Front, Cathédral..................... 51
St-Geniès 128
St-Jacques, Église....................... 64
St-James, Way of 290
Saint-Jean, Église Souterraine ...64
St-Jean-de-Côle........................... 66
St-Laurent-les-Tours,
    Château de 192
St-Léon-sur-Vézère.................... 145
St Louis (Louis IX) 114, 145,
    175, 188, 238, 269, 293
St-Martial-Viveyrol..................... 62
St Médard....................................... 231
St-Michel-de-Montaigne 106
St-Nicholas-de-la-Grave........... 264
St-Pierre de Brantôme, Abbaye
    57
Ste-Foy-la-Grande 104
Ste-Marie, Église 171
Ste-Nathalène............................... 128
Salviac.. 230
Santiago de Compostela 290
Sarkozy, Nicolas 301, 302
SARLAT-LA-CANÉDA.... 121–127
Sarlat-la-Canéda 123
Sarlat and the Périgord Noir
    .. 120
    accommodation.............................. 125
    arrival.. 125
    Ascenseur Panoramique 124
    bike rental..................................... 125
    buses.. 125
    car rental 125
    cathedral....................................... 124
    eating.. 127
    festivals... 122
    Gorodka... 124
    history 121
    hospital.. 127
    Hôtel de Maleville........................ 122
    Lanterne des Morts...................... 124
    Maison de la Boétie...................... 122
    Manoir de Gisson.......................... 124
    markets.. 122
    parking.. 125
    Passage des Enfeus...................... 124
    Place de la Liberté........................ 122

police......................................127
post office............................127
Présidial..............................124
restaurants.........................127
St-Sacerdos, Cathédrale.......124
shopping...............................127
taxis...125
tourist office.......................125
tours...125
trains.......................................125
Saut de la Mounine...............217
self-catering accommodation...28
service charges.......................30
shopping.....................................34
Siorac-en-Périgord.................154
Siorac-de-Ribérac....................62
smoking......................................40
SNCF..24
soft drinks.................................31
Sorcier, Grotte du..................142
Souillac.......................... 170–174
South of the River Lot
.....................................252–253
spirits...31
sports..32
stamps...38
student discounts......................35
studying in France.....................41
swimming.....................................34

T

taxes...35
Tayac...132
tea...32
telephones...............................39
telephone codes........................39
temperature................................10
Terrasson-la-Villedieu............150
Thénac...99
Thiviers......................................68
time...40
tipping...30
Tiregand, Château de................98

tolls, motorway.......................25
Toulouse, counts of........244, 266,
  271, 280, 290, 292
tour operators..........................23
tourist offices...........................40
Tourtoirac, Abbaye de..............74
Tourtoirac, Grotte de.................74
trains
  Eurostar..................................22
  fares....................................22, 24
  from UK...................................22
  in the Dordogne & Lot..................24
  tickets.............................22, 23, 24
train passes................................22
travel agents.............................23
travel insurance.........................37
Trémolat....................................109
troubadours.....................292, 293
truffles.................................72, 73
Turenne..82
Turenne, viscounts of.......82, 83,
  182, 191
Tursac.......................................143

U

Uxellodunum...............................288

V

Vaissac.......................................276
Varen...279
VAT..35
vegetarians.................................30
Vers..211
Vesunna................................47, 54
Vézère valley................ 129–151
Vézère valley............. 131–132
Vikings.......................................290
Villa Gallo Romaine de
  Montcaret................................105

Village du Bournat...................140
Villars, Grotte de.........................67
Villefranche-de-Rouergue......284
Villeneuve-sur-Lot....... 240–242
Villeneuve-sur-Lot............. 241
Viollet-le-Duc...................278, 279
visas...36
Voie Bleue, La..............................54
Voie Verte, La........................54, 66

W

walnuts......................................160
walking..32
Wars of Religion.........49, 90, 121,
  204, 222, 246, 295
water...32
weather......................................10
wi-fi..38
wine producers
  Ancienne Cure, Domaine de l'......97
  Côtes d'Olt...........................209
  Haut-Pécharmant, Domaine du ...92
  Jaubertie, Château de la................97
  Lagrézette, Château..........209
  Monbazillac Château de...........92, 96
  Tiregand, Château de.................98
  Les Vignerons de Buzet................260
wines
  Bergerac..........................90, 92
  Cahors...................................209
  Duras.............................101, 102
  general....................................31
  Monbazillac.....................92, 96
  Pécharmant.....................92, 98
World War I..............................299
World War II..............................300
working in France......................41

Y

youth hostels................................28

Map symbols

The symbols below are used on maps throughout the book

✈	Airport	∴	Ruins/rock shelter	🗼	Lighthouse	—	Wall
★	Bus/taxi	⚓	Church/chapel	⊤	Gardens	····	Tourist train
P	Parking	⌂	Abbey	⌢	Mountain range	▬	Church
@	Internet café/access	🏠	Windmill	⌣	Bridge	▨	Building
⊠	Post office	♀	Fortress	●–●	Cable car	▢	Park/national park
ⓘ	Tourist office	♜	Château	⊠—⊠	Gate	⊞	Cemetery
⊞	Hospital	🏰	Tower	⊞⊞	Steps	····	River
⬥	Place of interest	🐘	Wildlife park	═══	Pedestrianized street	– –	Ferry route
⌂	Cave	🔱	Viewpoint				

Listings key

- ◼ Accommodation
- ● Eating
- ◼ Drinking/ nightlife
- ● Shopping